I0058643

Mastering Linux Security and Hardening

Third Edition

A practical guide to protecting your Linux system
from cyber attacks

Donald A. Tevault

<packt>

BIRMINGHAM—MUMBAI

Mastering Linux Security and Hardening
Third Edition

Copyright © 2023 Packt Publishing

All rights reserved. No part of this book may be reproduced, stored in a retrieval system, or transmitted in any form or by any means, without the prior written permission of the publisher, except in the case of brief quotations embedded in critical articles or reviews.

Every effort has been made in the preparation of this book to ensure the accuracy of the information presented. However, the information contained in this book is sold without warranty, either express or implied. Neither the author, nor Packt Publishing or its dealers and distributors, will be held liable for any damages caused or alleged to have been caused directly or indirectly by this book.

Packt Publishing has endeavored to provide trademark information about all of the companies and products mentioned in this book by the appropriate use of capitals. However, Packt Publishing cannot guarantee the accuracy of this information.

Senior Publishing Product Manager: Aaron Tanna

Acquisition Editor – Peer Reviews: Gaurav Gavas

Project Editor: Rianna Rodrigues

Content Development Editor: Liam Draper

Copy Editor: SafisE diting

Technical Editor: Karan Sonawane

Proofreader: SafisE diting

Indexer: Manju Arasan

Presentation Designer: Ganesh Bhadwalkar

Developer Relations Marketing Executive: Meghal Patel

First published: January 2018

Second edition: February 2020

Third edition: February 2023

Production reference: 1210223

Published by Packt Publishing Ltd.
Livery Place
35 Livery Street
Birmingham
B3 2PB, UK.

ISBN 978-1-83702-357-8

www.packt.com

Contributors

About the author

Donald A. Tevault – you can call him Donnie – got involved with Linux way back in 2006 and has been working with it ever since. He holds the Linux Professional Institute Level 3 Security certification and the GIAC Incident Handler certification. Donnie is a professional Linux trainer, and thanks to the magic of the Internet, has taught Linux classes all over the world from the comfort of his living room. He has also been a Linux security researcher for an IoT security company.

I'd like to thank the good folk at Packt Publishing for making the publishing of this book such a smooth process. I'd also like to thank my cats for graciously allowing me to use their names in the demos, and Mike, my intrepid technical reviewer, for his suggestions that made the book better than it would have been.

About the reviewer

Michael Ernstoff is a Unix and Linux infrastructure and security specialist with over 25 years of experience. An independent consultant for over 20 years, Michael has worked for many well-known blue-chip companies, mainly in the banking and finance industries.

With extensive knowledge of host-based security, security hardening, and identity and access management. Michael has developed and implemented solutions for Security and Regulatory Compliance.

He is a keen amateur musician and has four children.

Join our book community

Join our community's Discord space for discussions with the author and other readers:

https://packt.link/CyberSec

Table of Contents

Chapter 2: Securing Administrative User Accounts 31

Chapter 3: Securing Normal User Accounts 57

Chapter 5: Securing Your Server with a Firewall — Part 2   131

Chapter 6: Encryption Technologies   167

Chapter 7: SSH Hardening   223

Section II: Mastering File and Directory Access Control (DAC)   277

Chapter 8: Mastering Discretionary Access Control   279

Preface

Who this book is for

This book is aimed at Linux administrators in general, whether or not they specialize in Linux security. The techniques that we present can be used on either Linux servers or on Linux workstations.

We assume that our target audience has had some hands-on experience with the Linux command line and has basic knowledge of the Linux essentials.

What this book covers

Chapter 1, Running Linux in a Virtual Environment, gives an overview of the IT security landscape, and will inform the reader why learning Linux security would be a good career move. We'll also show how to set up a virtual lab environment for the hands-on labs.

Chapter 2, Securing Administrative User Accounts, covers the dangers of always using the root user account, and introduces the benefits of using sudo instead.

Chapter 3, Securing Normal User Accounts, covers how to lock down normal user accounts, and ensure that the users use good-quality passwords.

Chapter 4, Securing Your Server with a Firewall – Part 1, involves working with the various types of firewall utilities.

Chapter 5, Securing Your Server with a Firewall – Part 2, continues the discussion about working with the various types of firewall utilities.

Chapter 6, Encryption Technologies, makes sure that important information—both at rest and in transit—are safeguarded with proper encryption.

Chapter 7, SSH Hardening, covers how to safeguard data in transit. The default Secure Shell configuration is anything but secure, and could lead to a security breach if left as is. This chapter shows how to fix that.

Chapter 8, Mastering Discretionary Access Control, covers how to set ownership and permissions on files and directories. We'll also cover what SUID and SGID can do for us, and the security implications of using them. We'll wrap things up by covering extended file attributes.

Chapter 9, Access Control Lists and Shared Directory Management, explains that normal Linux file and directory permissions settings aren't very granular. With Access Control Lists, we can allow only a certain person to access a file, or we can allow multiple people to access a file with different permissions for each person. We're also going to put what we've learned together in order to manage a shared directory for a group.

Chapter 10, Implementing Mandatory Access Control with SELinux and AppArmor, talks about SELinux, which is a Mandatory Access Control technology that is included with Red Hat-type Linux distributions. We'll give a brief introduction here on how to use SELinux to prevent intruders from compromising a system. We'll also give a brief introduction to AppArmor, which is another Mandatory Access Control technology that is included with Ubuntu and SUSE-type Linux distributions.

Chapter 11, Kernel Hardening and Process Isolation, covers how to tweak the Linux kernel to make it even more secure against certain types of attacks. It also covers some process isolation techniques to help prevent attackers from exploiting a Linux system.

Chapter 12, Scanning, Auditing, and Hardening, talks about how viruses that are a big problem for Windows users aren't yet a huge problem for Linux users. If your organization has Windows clients that access Linux file servers, then this section is for you. You can use auditd to audit accesses to files, directories, or system calls on a Linux system. It won't prevent security breaches, but it will let you know if some unauthorized person is trying to access a sensitive resource. SCAP, the Security Content Application Protocol, is a compliance framework that's promulgated by the National Institute of Standards and Technology. OpenSCAP, the open source implementation, can be used to apply a hardening policy to a Linux computer.

Chapter 13, Logging and Log Security, gives you the basics about ryslog and journald, the two most prevalent logging systems that come with Linux-based operating systems. We'll show you a cool way to make log reviews easier, and how to set up a secure central log server. We'll do all of this just with the packages that come in your normal Linux distribution's repositories.

Chapter 14, Vulnerability Scanning and Intrusion Detection, explains how to scan our systems to see if we've missed anything in our security configurations. We'll also take a quick look at an intrusion detection system.

Chapter 15, Prevent Unwanted Programs from Running, explains how to use fapolicyd and partition mounting options to prevent untrusted programs from running on your system.

Chapter 16, Security Tips and Tricks for the Busy Bee, explains that since you're dealing with security, we know that you're a busy bee. This chapter introduces you to some quick tips and tricks to help make the job easier.

To get the most out of this book
- A working knowledge of basic Linux commands and how to navigate through the Linux filesystem.
- A basic knowledge about tools such as less and grep.

- Familiarity with command-line editing tools, such as vim or nano.
- A basic knowledge of how to control systemd services with systemctl commands.

For hardware, you don't need anything fancy. All you need is a machine that's capable of running 64-bit virtual machines. So, you can use any host machine that runs with almost any modern CPU from either Intel or AMD. (There are a couple of exceptions, though. First, some Intel Core i3 and Core i5 CPUs lack the required hardware acceleration to run virtual machines. Also, AlmaLinux 9, which we'll be using, won't run on the first generation of x86_64 CPUs. So, if you have an x86_64 machine that was made prior to 2010, AlmaLinux 9 won't run on it.) For memory, I'd recommend using a host machine with at least 8 GB.

You can run any of the three major desktop operating systems on your machine, because the virtualization software that we'll be using comes in flavors for Windows, macOS, and Linux.

Download the example code files

The code bundle for the book is hosted on GitHub at https://github.com/PacktPublishing/ Mastering-Linux-Security-and-Hardening-3E. We also have other code bundles from our rich catalog of books and videos available at https://github.com/PacktPublishing/. Check them out!

Download the color images

We also provide a PDF file that has color images of the screenshots/diagrams used in this book. You can download it here: https://packt.link/wcaG3

Conventions used

There are a number of text conventions used throughout this book.

CodeInText: Indicates code words in text, database table names, folder names, filenames, file extensions, pathnames, dummy URLs, user input, and Twitter handles. For example: "open Firefox and navigate to https://localhost:9392"

A block of code is set as follows:

```
HTTP TRACK method is active, suggesting the host is vulnerable to XST
Cookie wordpress_test_cookie created without the httponly flag
```

Any command-line input or output is written as follows:

```
sudo apt update
sudo apt install podman
```

Bold: Indicates a new term, an important word, or words that you see on the screen. For instance, words in menus or dialog boxes appear in the text like this. For example: "Set one to **Bridged** mode and leave the other in **NAT** mode."

Warnings or important notes appear like this.

Tips and tricks appear like this.

Get in touch

Feedback from our readers is always welcome.

General feedback: Email feedback@packtpub.com and mention the book's title in the subject of your message. If you have questions about any aspect of this book, please email us at questions@packtpub.com.

Errata: Although we have taken every care to ensure the accuracy of our content, mistakes do happen. If you have found a mistake in this book, we would be grateful if you reported this to us. Please visit http://www.packtpub.com/submit-errata, click **Submit Errata**, and fill in the form.

Piracy: If you come across any illegal copies of our works in any form on the internet, we would be grateful if you would provide us with the location address or website name. Please contact us at copyright@packtpub.com with a link to the material.

If you are interested in becoming an author: If there is a topic that you have expertise in and you are interested in either writing or contributing to a book, please visit http://authors.packtpub.com.

Share your thoughts

Once you've read *Mastering Linux Security and Hardening, Third Edition*, we'd love to hear your thoughts! Scan the QR code below to go straight to the Amazon review page for this book and share your feedback.

https://packt.link/r/1837630518

Your review is important to us and the tech community and will help us make sure we're delivering excellent quality content.

Download a free PDF copy of this book

Thanks for purchasing this book!

Do you like to read on the go but are unable to carry your print books everywhere?

Is your eBook purchase not compatible with the device of your choice?

Don't worry, now with every Packt book you get a DRM-free PDF version of that book at no cost.

Read anywhere, any place, on any device. Search, copy, and paste code from your favorite technical books directly into your application.

The perks don't stop there, you can get exclusive access to discounts, newsletters, and great free content in your inbox daily

Follow these simple steps to get the benefits:

1. Scan the QR code or visit the link below

https://packt.link/free-ebook/9781837630516

2. Submit your proof of purchase
3. That's it! We'll send your free PDF and other benefits to your email directly

Section 1

Setting up a Secure Linux System

In this section, we will set up a practice lab with Ubuntu, CentOS, and AlmaLinux virtual machines. Windows users will learn how to remotely access Linux machines from Windows.

This section contains the following chapters:

1

Running Linux in a Virtual Environment

So, you may be asking yourself: *Why do I need to study Linux security? Isn't Linux already secure? After all, it's not Windows.* But the fact is, there are many reasons.

It's true that Linux has certain advantages over Windows when it comes to security. These include the following:

- Unlike Windows, Linux was designed from the ground up as a multiuser operating system. So, user security tends to be a bit better on a Linux system.
- Linux offers a better separation between administrative users and unprivileged users. This makes it a bit harder for intruders, and it also makes it a bit harder for a user to accidentally infect a Linux machine with something nasty.
- Linux is much more resistant to viruses and malware infections than Windows is. Certain Linux distributions come with built-in mechanisms, such as SELinux in Red Hat and its free-of-charge clones, and AppArmor in Ubuntu and SUSE, that help prevent intruders from taking control of a system.
- Linux is free and open source software. This allows anyone who has the skill to audit Linux code to hunt for bugs or backdoors.

But even with those advantages, Linux is just like everything else that's been created by mankind. That is, it isn't perfect.

Here are the topics that we'll cover in this chapter:

- Looking at the threat landscape
- Why every Linux administrator needs to learn about Linux security
- A bit about the threat landscape, with some examples of how attackers have, at times, been able to breach Linux systems
- Resources for keeping up with IT security news

- Differences between physical, virtual, and cloud setups
- Setting up Ubuntu Server and Red Hat-type virtual machines with VirtualBox, and installing the **Extra Packages for Enterprise Linux (EPEL)** repository in the Red Hat-type virtual machines
- Creating virtual machine snapshots
- Installing Cygwin on a Windows host so that Windows users can connect to a virtual machine from their Windows hosts
- Using the Windows 10/11 Bash shell to access Linux systems
- How to keep your Linux systems updated

Let's begin by talking about threats.

Looking at the threat landscape

If you've kept up with IT technology news over the past few years, you'll likely have seen at least a few articles about how attackers have compromised Linux servers. For example, while it's true that Linux isn't really susceptible to virus infections, there have been several cases where attackers have planted other types of malware on Linux servers. Here are some examples:

- **Botnet malware:** This causes a server to join a botnet that is controlled by a remote attacker. One of the more famous cases involved joining Linux servers to a botnet that launched **denial-of-service (DoS)** attacks against other networks.
- **Ransomware:** This is designed to encrypt user data until the server owner pays a ransom fee. But even after paying the fee, there's no guarantee that the data can be recovered.
- **Cryptocoin mining software:** This causes the CPUs of the server on which it's planted to work extra hard and consume more energy. Cryptocoins that get mined go to the accounts of the attackers who planted the software.

And, of course, there have been plenty of breaches that don't involve malware, such as where attackers have found a way to steal user credentials, credit card data, or other sensitive information.

> Some security breaches come about because of plain carelessness. Here's an example of where a careless Adobe administrator placed the company's private security key on a public security blog: https://arstechnica.com/information-technology/2017/09/in-spectacular-fail-adobe-security-team-posts-private-pgp-key-on-blog/.

Now, let's talk a bit more about security breaches.

Why do security breaches happen?

Regardless of whether you're running Linux, Windows, or whatever else, the reasons for security breaches are usually the same. They could be security bugs in the operating system or security bugs in an application that's running on that operating system. Often, a bug-related security breach could have been prevented had the administrators applied security updates in a timely manner.

Another big issue is poorly configured servers. A standard, out-of-the-box configuration of a Linux server is actually quite insecure and can cause a whole ton of problems. One cause of poorly configured servers is simply the lack of properly trained personnel to securely administer Linux servers. (Of course, that's great news for the readers of this book, because—trust me—there's no lack of well-paying IT security jobs.)

And now, in addition to Linux on servers and desktops, we have Linux on devices that are part of the **Internet of Things** (IoT). There have been many security problems with these devices, in large part because people just don't know how to configure them securely.

As we journey through this book, we'll see how to do business the right way, to make our servers as secure as possible. One thing we can do is to keep up with security-related news.

Keeping up with security news

If you're in the IT business, even if you're not a security administrator, you'll want to keep up with the latest security news. In the age of the Internet, that's easy to do.

First, there are quite a few websites that specialize in network security news. Examples include *Packet Storm Security* and *The Hacker News.* Regular tech news sites and Linux news websites, such as *Ars Technica*, *Fudzilla*, *The Register*, *ZDNet*, and *LXer*, also carry reports about network security breaches. And, if you'd rather watch videos than read, you'll find plenty of good YouTube channels, such as *BeginLinux Guru.*

Finally, regardless of which Linux distro you're using, be sure to keep up with the news and current documentation for your Linux distro. Distro maintainers should have a way of letting you know if a security problem crops up in their products.

Here are some links to some good security-related websites:

- **Packet Storm Security**: `https://packetstormsecurity.com/`
- **The Hacker News**: `https://thehackernews.com/`

Here are some links to more generalized tech websites:

- **Ars Technica**: `https://arstechnica.com/`
- **Fudzilla**: `https://www.fudzilla.com/`
- **The Register**: `https://www.theregister.co.uk/`
- **ZDNet**: `https://www.zdnet.com/`

You can check out some general Linux learning resources as well as Linux news sites:

- **LXer**: `http://lxer.com/`
- **BeginLinux Guru on YouTube**: `https://www.youtube.com/channel/UC88eard_2sz89an6unm1beA`

  (Full disclosure: I am the world-famous BeginLinux Guru.)

One thing to always remember as you go through this book is that the only operating system you'll ever see that's totally 100% secure will be installed on a computer that never gets turned on.

Differences between physical, virtual, and cloud setups

So you can do the hands-on labs, I'll introduce you to the concept of virtual machines. This is just a way of running one operating system within another operating system. So, it doesn't matter whether you're running Windows, macOS, or Linux on your host machine. In any case, you can run a Linux virtual machine that you can use for practice, and that you won't have to worry about if it gets trashed.

Oracle's VirtualBox, which is what we'll be using, is great for what we'll be doing. In an enterprise setting, you'll find other forms of virtualization software that are better suited for use in data centers. In the past, server hardware could only handle doing one thing at a time, which meant that you had to have one server running DNS, another running DHCP, and so on. Nowadays, we have servers with gobs of memory, gobs of drive space, and CPUs with as many as 96 cores each. So, it's now cheaper and more convenient to install multiple virtual machines on each server, with each virtual machine doing its own specific job. This also means that you not only have to worry about security on the physical server that hosts these virtual machines but you also need to worry about the security of each virtual machine. An added problem is that you need to ensure that the virtual machines remain properly isolated from each other, especially ones that contain sensitive data.

And then, there's the cloud. Many different outfits provide cloud services, where a person or a company can spin up an instance of either Windows or their choice of a Linux distro. When setting up a Linux distro on a cloud service, there are things that you'll have to do right away to enhance security. (That's something that we'll cover in *Chapter 7, SSH Hardening*.) And realize that when you set up a server on a cloud service, you'll always have more concerns about proper security, because it will have an interface that connects to the wild and woolly Internet. (Your on-premises servers, except for ones that are meant to serve the public, are usually isolated from the Internet.)

With our introductory material out of the way, let's get to the real meat of the matter, starting with an introduction to our virtualization software.

Introducing VirtualBox and Cygwin

Whenever I write or teach, I try very hard not to provide students with a cure for insomnia. Throughout this book, you'll see a bit of theory whenever it's necessary, but I mainly like to provide good, practical information. There will also be plenty of step-by-step hands-on labs and an occasional bit of humor.

The best way to do the labs is to use Linux virtual machines. Most of what we'll do can apply to any Linux distro, but we will also do some things that are specific to either **Red Hat Enterprise Linux** **(RHEL)** or Ubuntu Linux. (RHEL is the most popular for enterprise use, while Ubuntu is the most popular for cloud deployments.) SUSE is the third big enterprise Linux distro. We won't be doing too much with SUSE, but on occasion, I'll point out some of its little quirks.

> Red Hat is a billion-dollar company, so there's no doubt about where they stand in the Linux market. But since Ubuntu Server is free of charge, we can't judge its popularity strictly on the basis of its parent company's worth. The reality is that Ubuntu Server is the most widely used Linux distribution for deploying cloud-based applications.
>
> See here for details: `http://www.zdnet.com/article/ubuntu-linux-continues-to-dominate-openstack-and-other-clouds/`.

Since Red Hat is a fee-based product, we'll substitute CentOS 7, AlmaLinux8, and AlmaLinux9, which are built from Red Hat source code and are free of charge. (We're using all three of these distros because there are some differences between them, and all of them will be supported for quite some time to come.) CentOS and AlmaLinux offer various download images. You'll want to download the DVD images, because they contain necessary things that are missing from the minimal images. Specifically, download these image files:

- **CentOS 7**: CentOS-7-x86_64-DVD-2009.iso
- **AlmaLinux 8**: AlmaLinux-8-latest-x86_64-dvd.iso
- **AlmaLinux 9**: AlmaLinux-9-latest-x86_64-dvd.iso

For Ubuntu, we'll concentrate on version 22.04, since it's the newest **Long Term Support** (**LTS**) version. (We'll also take an occasional look at Ubuntu 20.04, since it's still supported and there are a few differences between it and 22.04.) A new LTS version of Ubuntu comes out in April of every even-numbered year, and non-LTS versions come out in April of every odd-numbered year and every October. For production use, you'll mainly want to stick with the LTS versions, because the non-LTS versions can sometimes be a bit problematic.

There are several different virtualization platforms that you can use, but my own preferred choice is VirtualBox.

VirtualBox is available for Windows, Linux, and Mac hosts, and is free of charge for all of them. (It's also available for Solaris hosts, but I doubt that many of you will be running that.) It has features that you have to pay for on other platforms, such as the ability to create snapshots of virtual machines.

Some of the labs that we'll be doing will require you to simulate creating a connection from your host machine to a remote Linux server. If your host machine is either a Linux or a Mac machine, you'll just be able to open the terminal and use the built-in **Secure Shell** (**SSH**) tools. If your host machine is running Windows, you'll need to install some sort of Bash shell, such as Cygwin, or just use the Bash shell that's built into Windows 10/11 Pro.

Installing a virtual machine in VirtualBox

For those of you who've never used VirtualBox, here's a quick guide to get you going:

1. Download and install VirtualBox and the VirtualBox Extension Pack. You can get them from `https://www.virtualbox.org/`.

2. Download the installation `.iso` files for Ubuntu Server 22.04, CentOS 7, AlmaLinux8, and AlmaLinux9. You can get them from `https://ubuntu.com/`, `https://almalinux.org/`, and `https://www.centos.org/`.

3. Start VirtualBox and click the **New** icon at the top of the screen. Fill out the information where requested. Increase the virtual drive size to 20 GB, but leave everything else as the default settings, as shown here:

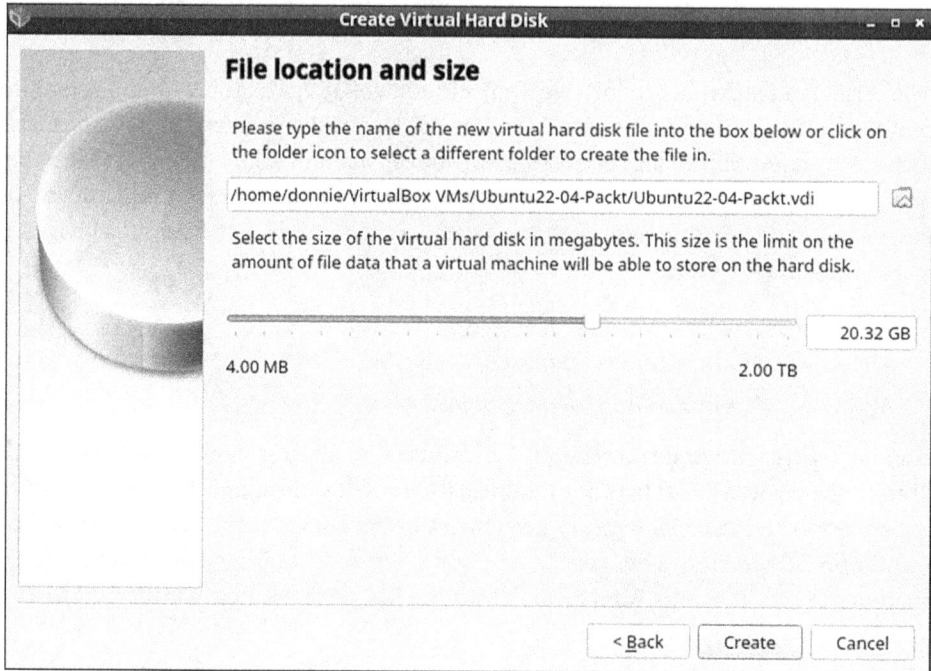

Figure 1.1:Create the virtual drive

4. Start the new virtual machine. Click on the folder icon that's beside the **Location** dialog box and navigate to the directory where you stored the `.iso` files that you downloaded. Choose either the Ubuntu ISO file, the CentOS ISO file, or one of the AlmaLinux ISO files, as shown in the following screenshot. (If the ISO file doesn't show up in the list, click the **Add** button in the top-left corner to add it.)

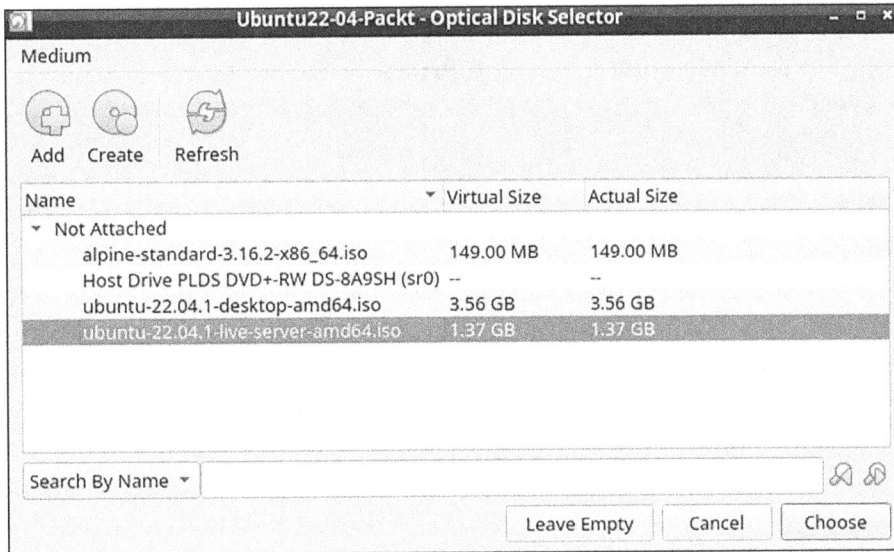

Figure 1.2: Choose the .iso file

5. Click the **Start** button on the dialog box to start installing the operating system. Note that for Ubuntu Server, you won't be installing a desktop interface. For the CentOS 7 and AlmaLinux virtual machines, choose to install a Server without a graphical interface. (Later on, we'll go through at least one exercise that will require a desktop interface for an AlmaLinux machine. You can create a virtual machine with a graphical interface at that time.)

6. When installing Ubuntu, choose **Try or Install Ubuntu Server** when you get to this screen:

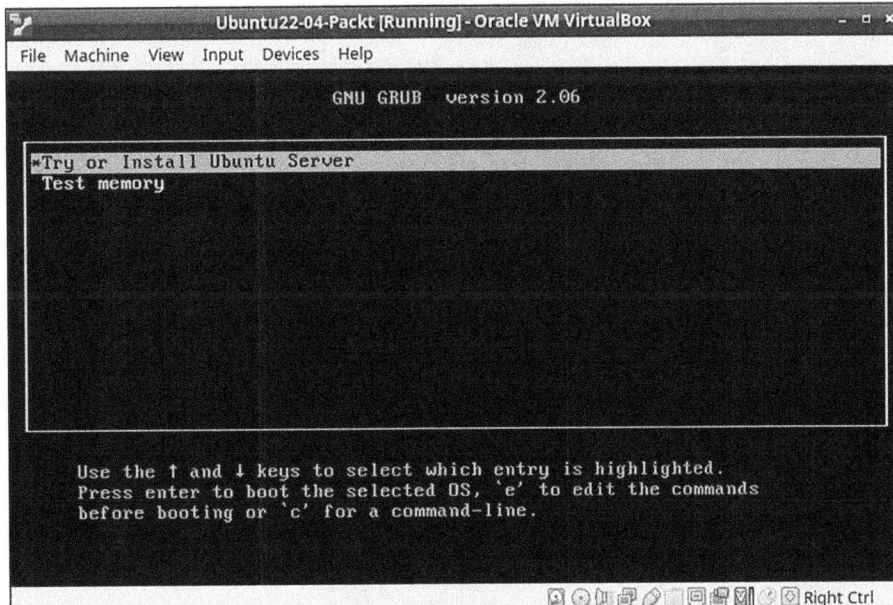

Figure 1.3: Installing Ubuntu

7. Repeat the procedure for the other Linux distros.

8. Update the Ubuntu virtual machine with these two commands:

```
sudo apt update
sudo apt dist-upgrade
```

9. Hold off on updating the CentOS and AlmaLinux virtual machines because we'll do that in the next exercise.

10. For Ubuntu, choose to install the OpenSSH Server on the **SSH setup** screen.

> When installing Ubuntu, you'll be asked to create a normal user account and password for yourself. It won't ask you to create a root user password, but will instead automatically add you to the sudo group so that you'll have admin privileges.
>
> When you get to the user account creation screen of the CentOS or AlmaLinux installer, be sure to check the **Make this user administrator** box for your own user account, since it isn't checked by default. It will offer you the chance to create a password for the root user, but that's entirely optional. (In fact, I never do.)

The user account creation screen of the AlmaLinux 9 installer—which looks the same as the one on CentOS 7 and AlmaLinux 8—is shown here:

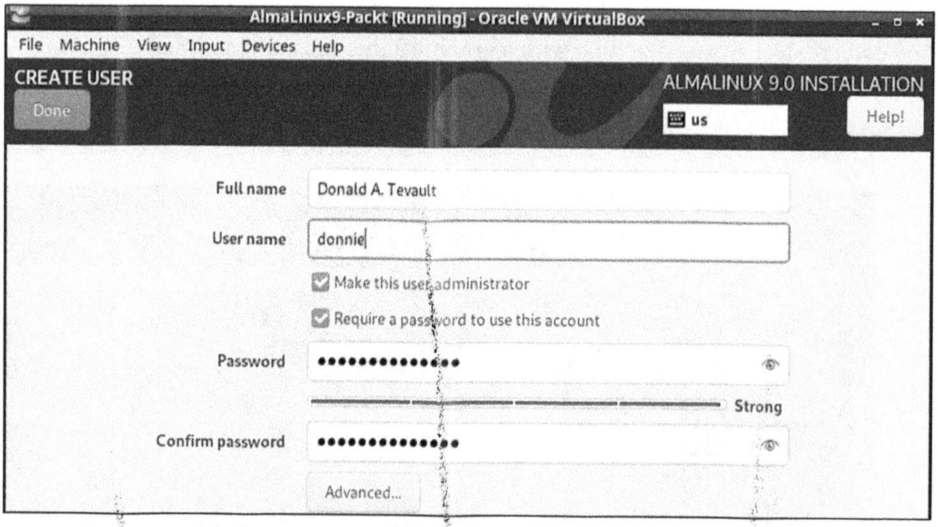

Figure 1.4: User creation for AlmaLinux

Important:

RHEL 9.1 and all of its clones were released a few months after I wrote the first draft of this chapter. You might already have noticed that there's a bug in the 9.1 installer that wasn't in the 9.0 installer. That is, the option to create a normal user account isn't visible on the installer screen. I mean, it's there, but you can't see it and can't scroll down to it. To bring it up, just keep hitting the *Tab* key until you've highlighted the option to create the root user password. Then, hit the *Tab* key once more, and then hit the *Enter* key. (Of course, there's always the chance that the problem will get fixed by the time you read this.)

For Ubuntu 22.04, you'll see just one self-explanatory screen to set up your real name, a username, and a password. The Ubuntu installer will automatically add your user account to the sudo group, which will give you full administrator privileges.

Here's the user account creation screen for Ubuntu 22.04:

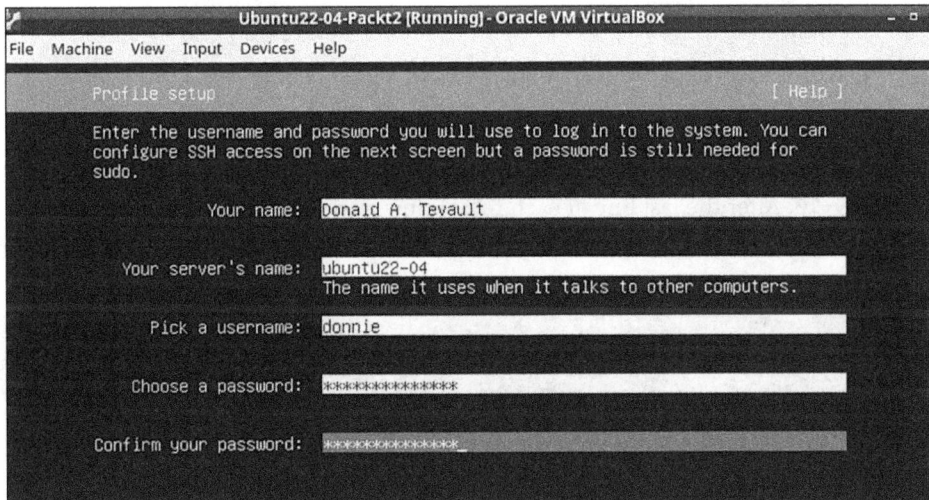

Figure 1.5: Ubuntu user creation

Now, let's change gears and move on to CentOS 7.

Installing the EPEL repository on the CentOS 7 virtual machine

While the Ubuntu package repositories have pretty much everything that you need for this course, the CentOS and AlmaLinux package repositories are—shall we say—lacking. To have the packages that you'll need for the CentOS and AlmaLinux hands-on labs, you'll need to install the EPEL repository. (The EPEL project is run by the Fedora team.) When you install third-party repositories on Red Hat 7 and CentOS 7 systems, you'll also need to install a priorities package and edit the .repo files to set the proper priorities for each repository. This will prevent packages from the third-party repository from overwriting official Red Hat and CentOS packages if they just happen to have the same name. The following steps will help you install the required packages and edit the .repo files:

1. The two packages that you'll need to install EPEL are in the normal CentOS 7 repositories. To install them, just run this command:

```
sudo yum install yum-plugin-priorities epel-release
```

2. When the installation completes, navigate to the /etc/yum.repos.d directory, and open the CentOS-Base.repo file in your favorite text editor. After the last line of the base, updates, and extras sections, add the line priority=1. After the last line of the centosplus section, add the line priority=2. Save the file and close the editor. Each of the sections that you've edited should look something like this, except with the appropriate name and priority number:

```
[base]
name=CentOS-$releasever - Base
mirrorlist=http://mirrorlist.centos.org/?
release=$releasever&arch=$basearch&repo=os&infra=$infra
#baseurl=http://mirror.centos.org/centos/
$releasever/os/$basearch/
gpgcheck=1
gpgkey=file:///etc/pki/rpm-gpg/RPM-GPG-KEY-CentOS-7
priority=1
```

3. Open the epel.repo file for editing. After the last line of the epel section, add the line priority=10. After the last line of each remaining section, add the line priority=11.

4. Update the system and then create a list of the installed and available packages by running the following commands:

```
sudo yum upgrade
sudo yum list > yum_list.txt
```

Now, let's move on to AlmaLinux.

Installing the EPEL repository on the AlmaLinux 8/9 virtual machines

To install the EPEL repository on AlmaLinux, all you have to do is run this command:

```
sudo dnf install epel-release
```

There's no priorities package as there is on CentOS 7 and earlier, so we won't have to worry about configuring the repository priorities.

When the package installation is complete, update the system and create a list of available software packages with these two commands:

```
sudo dnf upgrade
sudo dnf list > dnf_list.txt
```

Next, let's configure our network.

Configuring a network for VirtualBox virtual machines

Some of our training scenarios will require you to simulate creating a connection to a remote server. You would do this by using your host machine to connect to a virtual machine. When you first create a virtual machine on VirtualBox, the networking is set to **NAT** mode. In order to connect to the virtual machine from the host, you'll need to set the virtual machine's network adapter to **Bridged Adapter** mode. Here's how you can do this:

1. Shut down any virtual machines that you've already created.
2. On the VirtualBox Manager screen, open the **Settings** dialog for a virtual machine.
3. Click the **Network** menu item. Change the **Attached to** setting from **NAT** to **Bridged Adapter**, and change the **Promiscuous Mode** setting to **Allow All**, as shown in this screenshot:

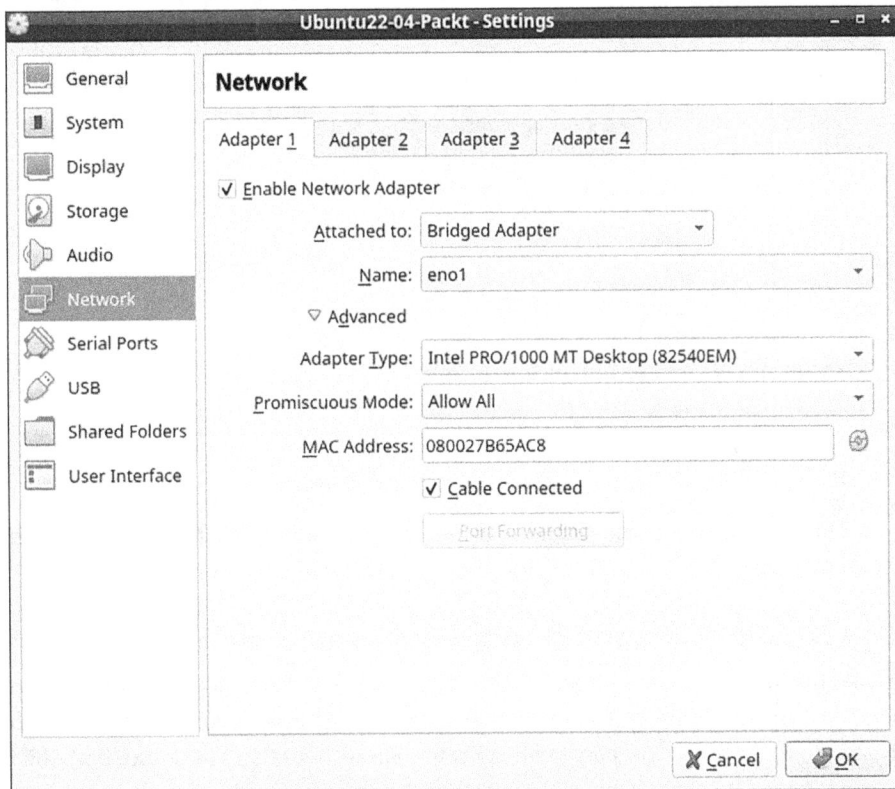

Figure 1.6: Configuring the network

4. Restart the virtual machine and set it to use a static IP address.

> **Tip**
>
> If you assign static IP addresses from the high end of your subnet range, it will be easier to prevent conflicts with low-number IP addresses that get handed out from your internet gateway.

Creating a virtual machine snapshot with VirtualBox

One of the beautiful things about working with virtual machines is that you can create a snapshot and roll back to it if you mess something up. With VirtualBox, that's easy to do, by following these steps:

1. From the **Machine** menu of the VirtualBox Manager screen, select **Tools/Snapshots**.

2. Further right on the screen, click on the **Take** icon to bring up the **Snapshot** dialog box. Either fill in the desired **Snapshot Name** or accept the default name. Optionally, you can create a description, as you see in this screenshot:

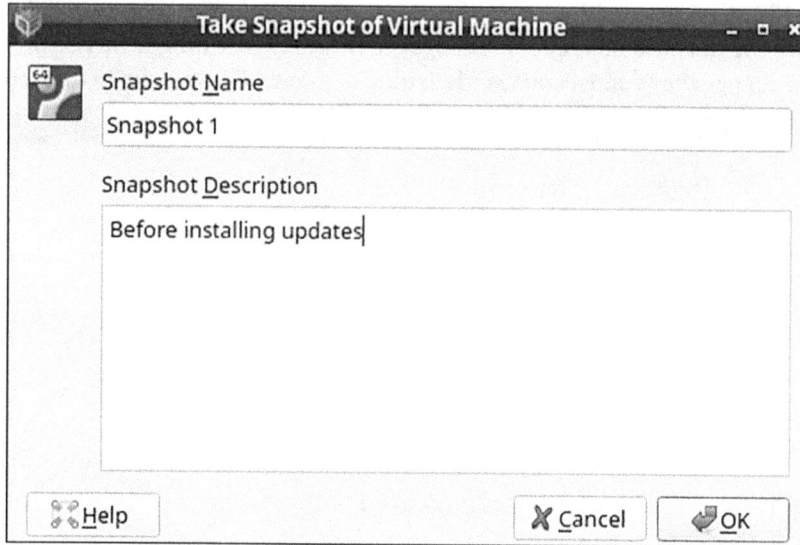

Figure 1.7: Taking a snapshot

After you've made changes to the virtual machine, you can roll back to the snapshot by shutting down the virtual machine, then highlighting the snapshot name, and clicking on the **Restore** button.

Using Cygwin to connect to your virtual machines

If your host machine is either a Linux or Mac machine, you'll simply open the host's terminal and use the tools that are already there to connect to the virtual machine. Windows 10 and Windows 11, even in the base Home Edition, now come with a **Secure Shell** client that's built into both the normal **Command Prompt** and **PowerShell**, and you can use that if you desire. But if you'd prefer to use something that comes closer to the actual Linux experience, you might consider Cygwin.

Cygwin, a project of the Red Hat company, is a free open source Bash shell that's built for Windows. It's free of charge and easy to install.

Installing Cygwin on your Windows host

Here's a quick how-to to get you going with Cygwin:

1. In your host machine's browser, download the appropriate `setup*.exe` file for your version of Windows from `http://www.cygwin.com/`.

2. Double-click on the setup icon to begin the installation. For the most part, just accept the defaults until you get to the package selection screen. (The one exception will be the screen where you select a download mirror.)

3. At the top of the package selection screen, select **Category** from the **View** menu.

4. Expand the **Net** category, as shown in the following screenshot:

⊟ Net ✪ Default				
	✪ Skip	n/a	n/a	1.071k	aria2: Download utility for HTTP/HTTPS. FTP. Bit Torrent and Metalink
	✪ Skip	n/a	n/a	24k	autossh: Automatically restart SSH sessions and tunnels

Figure 1.8: Installing Cygwin packages

5. Scroll down until you see the openssh package. Under the **New** column, click on **Skip** (this causes a version number to appear in place of **Skip**), as you see in this screenshot:

✪ Skip	n/a	n/a	1.89k	openldap-server: Lightweight Directory Access Protocol suite (server)
✪ Skip	n/a	n/a	750k	openssh: The OpenSSH server and client programs
✪ Skip	n/a	n/a	570k	openssl: A general purpose cryptography toolkit with TLS implementation
✪ Skip	n/a	n/a	7.693k	openssl-devel: A general purpose cryptography toolkit with TLS implementation (development)

Figure 1.9: Select the OpenSSH package

⟳ Skip	n/a	n/a	1.898k	openldap-server: Lightweight Directory Access Protocol suite (server)
✪ 7.5p 1-1	⊠	☐	750k	openssh: The OpenSSH server and client programs
✪ Skip	n/a	n/a	570k	openssl: A general purpose crytography toolkit with TLS implementation
✪ Skip	n/a	n/a	4.693k	openssl-devel: Ageneral purpose cryptography toolkit with TLS implementation (development)

6. After you have selected the proper package, your screen should look like this:

✪ Skip	n/a	n/a	1.898k	openldap-server: Lightweight Directory Access Protocol suite (server)
✪ Skip	n/a	n/a	750k	openssh: The OpenSSH server and client programs
✪ Skip	n/a	n/a	570k	openssl: A general purpose cryptography toolkit with TLS implementation
✪ Skip	n/a	n/a	4,693k	openssl-devel: A general purpose cryptography toolkit with TLS impletation (development)

Figure 1.10: After selecting the OpenSSH package

7. In the bottom right-hand corner, click **Next**. If a **Resolving Dependencies** screen pops up, click **Next** on it as well.

8. Keep the setup file that you downloaded, because you'll use it later to either install more software packages or to update Cygwin. (When you open Cygwin, any updated packages will show up on the **Pending** view on the **View** menu.)

9. Once you open Cygwin from the Windows **Start** menu, you can resize it as you desire, and use either the *Ctrl + +* or *Ctrl + -* key combinations to resize the font.

Next, we'll look at the Windows 10/11 Bash shell.

Using the Windows 10 SSH client to interface with Linux virtual machines

If you're using Windows 10, you already have an SSH client built into your operating system.

So, let's see how to do this:

1. To get to it, you can open the traditional **Command Prompt** from the **Windows System** menu, like so:

Figure 1.11: Windows 10 Command Prompt

2. Then, just type in the SSH commands the same as you would from a Mac or Linux machine, like this:

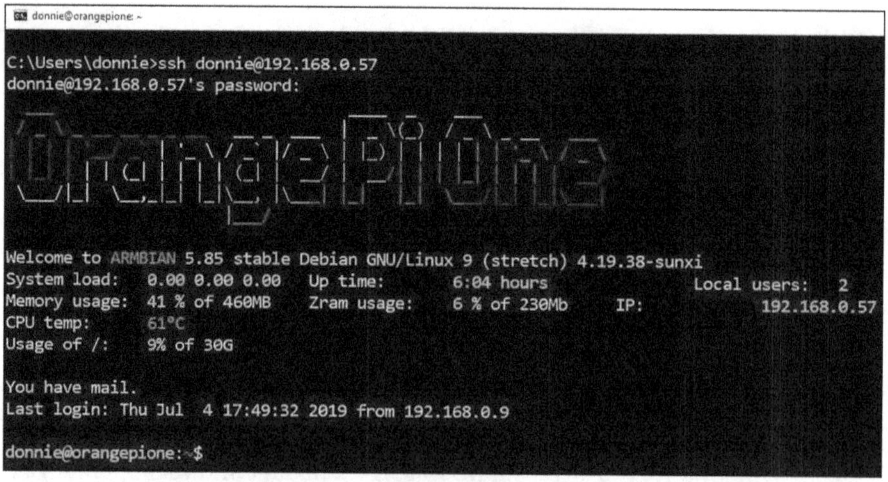

Figure 1.12: SSH remote from Windows Command Prompt

3.   A better option is to use **Windows PowerShell** instead of the normal **Command Prompt.** Get
      to it as you see here:

Figure 1.13: PowerShell command prompt

4.   As before, let's use it to log in to my Orange Pi device, as you see here:

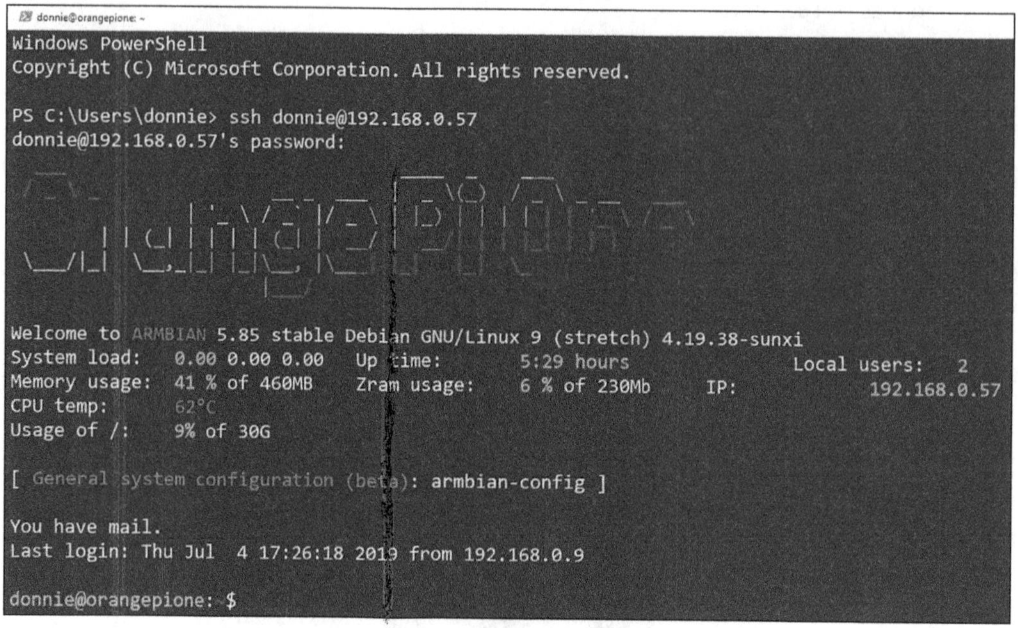

Figure 1.14: Remote login from PowerShell

If you have the choice, go with **PowerShell** instead of **Command Prompt**. **PowerShell** is a bit closer to the Linux Bash shell experience, and you'll be much happier with it.

Using the Windows 11 SSH client to interface with Linux virtual machines

You'll work with Windows 11 the same way, except that the menu entries for the **Command Prompt** and **PowerShell** are in different places. The **Command Prompt** now has its own **Terminal** item on the main menu, and **PowerShell** is now under the **Windows Tools** submenu. Windows 11 also has a third option, which is a built-in Ubuntu virtual machine. You'll see an icon for that in the bottom taskbar.

Cygwin versus the Windows shell

Both Cygwin and the SSH client that's built into Windows 10/11 have their pros and cons. In favor of Cygwin, you can install a variety of packages to customize it pretty much any way you want. Also, Cygwin stores the SSH known_hosts and keys files in the .ssh directory of the user's home directory, which is where you'd expect to find them if you're used to working with Linux. If you use the SSH client that's built into Windows, you'll have to search for these files in other locations.

In favor of the Windows 10/11 built-in SSH client, there's the fact that it's already there. Also, it's much easier to use if you need to access your normal Windows folders because Cygwin traps you in its own sandboxed directory structure.

Keeping the Linux systems updated

Spend some time perusing the **Common Vulnerabilities and Exposures** database, and you'll soon see why it's so important to keep your systems updated. Yes, indeed, you'll even find that there have been security flaws with our beloved Linux, as you can see here:

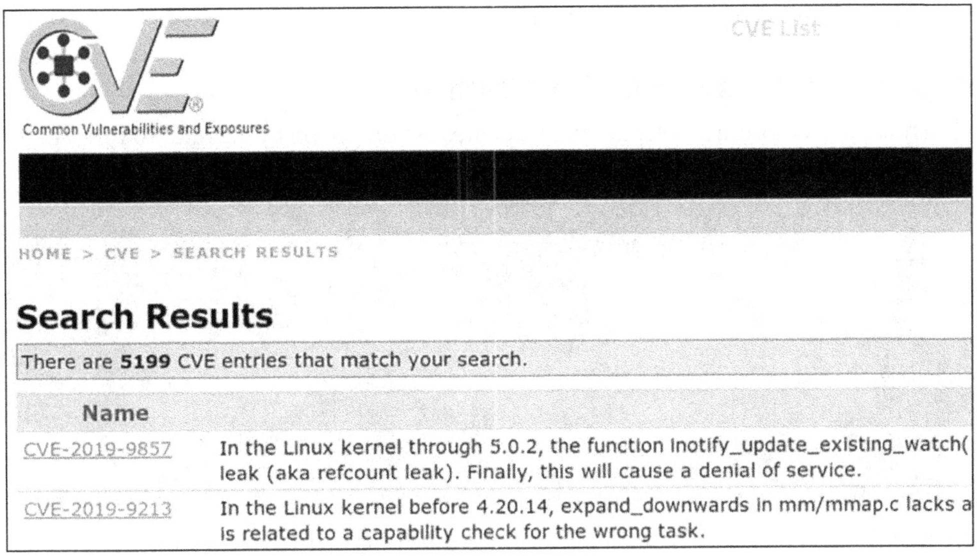

Figure 1.15: Common Vulnerabilities and Exposures

Updating a Linux system only requires one or two simple commands, and it's generally faster and less painful than updating a Windows system.

> You can find the **Common Vulnerabilities and Exposures** database here:
>
> `https://cve.mitre.org/`
>
> All of you conscientious, dedicated Linux administrators will definitely want to become familiar with this site.

Next, let's look at updating the Debian-based systems, which include Ubuntu.

Updating Debian-based systems

Let's take a look at how to update Debian-based systems:

1. On Debian and its many children, including Ubuntu, run two commands, as shown here:

```
sudo apt update
sudo apt dist-upgrade
```

2. Occasionally, you'll also need to remove some old packages that are no longer needed. How will you know? Easy. When you log in to the system, a message will appear on the command line. To remove these old packages, just run this command:

```
sudo apt auto-remove
```

Next, we will configure auto updates for Ubuntu.

Configuring auto updates for Ubuntu

When you first install Ubuntu 22.04, automatic updates are turned on by default. To verify that, you'll first check the status of the unattended-upgrades service, like so:

```
donnie@ubuntu2204-packt:~$ systemctl status unattended-upgrades
• unattended-upgrades.service - Unattended Upgrades Shutdown
     Loaded: loaded (/lib/systemd/system/unattended-upgrades.service; enabled;
vendor preset: enabled)
     Active: active (running) since Sat 2022-10-08 19:25:54 UTC; 52min ago
 .  .  .

 .  .  .
donnie@ubuntu2204-packt:~$
```

Then, look in the /etc/apt/apt.conf.d/20auto-upgrades file. If auto-updating is enabled, you'll see this:

```
APT::Periodic::Update-Package-Lists "1";
APT::Periodic::Unattended-Upgrade "1";
```

I must confess, though, that I have mixed feelings about this. I mean, it's nice that the security updates get installed without me having to do anything, but a lot of those updates require that the system be rebooted before they can take effect. By default, Ubuntu systems don't automatically reboot after an update is installed. If you keep it that way, you'll see a message about it when you log into the system. But if you prefer, you can set Ubuntu to automatically reboot after it automatically updates itself. Here's how to do it:

1. Go into the /etc/apt/apt.conf.d directory and open the 50unattended-upgrades file in your favorite text editor. In the vicinity of line *67*, you'll see a line that says:

```
//Unattended-Upgrade::Automatic-Reboot "false";
```

2. Uncomment the line by removing the leading slashes, and change false to true, like so:

```
Unattended-Upgrade::Automatic-Reboot "true";
```

3. With this new configuration, Ubuntu will now reboot itself immediately after the automatic update process has completed. If you'd rather have the machine reboot at a specific time, scroll down to about line *103*, where you'll see this:

```
//Unattended-Upgrade::Automatic-Reboot-Time "02:00";
```

4. Since this line is commented out with its pair of leading slashes, it currently has no effect. To have the machine reboot at 2:00 A.M., just uncomment this line. To have it reboot at, say, 10:00 P.M., uncomment the line and change the time to 22:00, like so:

```
Unattended-Upgrade::Automatic-Reboot-Time "22:00";
```

> Of course, there's that old, basic precept that thou shalt not install system updates on a production system without first testing them on a test system. Any operating system vendor can occasionally supply you with problematic updates, and that has included Ubuntu. (I know what you're saying: *Preach it, Donnie.*) Ubuntu's automatic update feature is in direct opposition to that basic precept. If automatic updates have been enabled, disabling them is quite easy, if you choose to do so.

5. To disable automatic updates, just go into the /etc/apt/apt.conf.d directory and open the 20auto-upgrades file in your favorite text editor. Here's what you'll see:

```
APT::Periodic::Update-Package-Lists "1";
APT::Periodic::Unattended-Upgrade "1";
```

6. Change the parameter for that second line to 0, so that the file will now look like this:

```
APT::Periodic::Update-Package-Lists "1";
APT::Periodic::Unattended-Upgrade "0";
```

> Now, the system will still check for updates and show a message on the login screen when any are available, but it won't automatically install them. And of course, it should go without saying that you need to check your systems on a regular basis to see if updates are available. If you do prefer to leave automatic updates enabled, be sure to either enable automatic rebooting or to log in to the system at least a couple of times a week to see if it needs to be rebooted.

7. If you want to see if there are any security-related updates available, but don't want to see any non-security updates, use the unattended-upgrade command, like so:

```
sudo unattended-upgrade --dry-run -d
```

8. To manually install the security-related updates without installing non-security updates, just run:

```
sudo unattended-upgrade -d
```

If you're running some form of desktop Ubuntu on a workstation that gets shut down after every use, you can enable the automatic updates if you like, but there's no need to enable automatic reboots.

Also, if you're running a non-Ubuntu flavor of Debian, which would include Raspbian for the Raspberry Pi, you can give it the same functionality as Ubuntu by installing the `unattended-upgrades` package. Just run this command:

```
sudo apt install unattended-upgrades
```

You can also use the apt command to install only the security updates, but it would require piping the apt output into a convoluted set of text filters in order to mask the non-security updates. Using the `unattended-upgrade` command is much easier.

I said before that we should always test updates on a test system before we install them on a production system, and that certainly does hold true for corporate servers. But what do we do when we have a whole bunch of IoT devices that we need to keep updated, especially if these devices are all over the place out in the field and in consumer devices?

In the wonderful world of IoT, the ARM CPU versions of Ubuntu, Raspbian, and Debian are the most popular Linux distros for use on the various Pi devices, including the ubiquitous Raspberry Pi. If you have lots of IoT devices in the field and in consumer devices, you might not have direct control over them once they've been deployed or sold. They still need to be kept updated, so setting up unattended updates with automatic rebooting would certainly be advantageous. But keep in mind that in the world of IoT, we have to be concerned about safety as well as security. So, for example, if you have devices that are set up as some sort of critical, safety-related industrial controller, then you most likely don't want the device to automatically reboot after doing automatic updates. But if you're a television vendor who installs Linux on smart televisions, then definitely set them up to automatically update and to automatically reboot themselves after an update.

Next, let's look at updating the RHEL 7 systems.

Updating Red Hat 7-based systems

With Red Hat-based systems, which include CentOS and Oracle Linux, there's no automatic update mechanism that you can set up during installation. So, with the default configuration, you'll need to perform updates yourself:

1. To update a Red Hat 7-based system, just run this one command:

    ```
    sudo yum upgrade
    ```

2. Sometimes, you might just want to see if there are any security-related updates that are ready to be installed. Do that by running this command:

    ```
    sudo yum updateinfo list updates security
    ```

3. If any security updates are available, you'll see them at the end of the command output. On the system that I just tested, there was only one security update available, which looks like this:

```
FEDORA-EPEL-2019-d661b588d2 Low/Sec. nagios-common-4.4.3-1.el7.x86_64
updateinfo list done
```

4. If the only thing you want to install is the security updates, run this command:

```
sudo yum upgrade --security
```

5. Now, let's say that you need a CentOS system to automatically update itself. You're in luck because there's a package for that. Install and enable it, and start it by running these two commands:

```
sudo yum install yum-cron
sudo systemctl enable --now yum-cron
```

6. To configure it, go into the /etc/yum directory, and edit the yum-cron.conf file. At the top of the file, you'll see this:

```
[commands]
# What kind of update to use:
# default = yum upgrade
# security = yum --security upgrade
# security-severity:Critical = yum --sec-severity=Critical upgrade
# minimal = yum --bugfix update-minimal
# minimal-security = yum --security update-minimal
# minimal-security-severity:Critical = --sec-severity=Critical update-
minimal
update_cmd = default
```

This lists the various types of upgrades we can do. The last line shows that we're set to update everything.

7. Let's say that you only want security updates to get applied automatically. Just change the last line to the following:

```
update_cmd = security
```

8. On lines *15* and *20*, you'll see this:

```
download_updates = yes
apply_updates = no
```

9. This indicates that by default, yum-cron is only set to automatically download updates, but not to install them.

10. If you want the updates to get automatically installed, change the apply_updates parameter to yes.

> Note that unlike Ubuntu, there's no setting to make the system automatically
> reboot itself after an update.

11. Finally, let's look at the mail settings for yum-cron, which you'll find on lines *48* through *57* of
    the yum-cron.conf file, as shown here:

```
[email]
# The address to send email messages from.
# NOTE: 'localhost' will be replaced with the value of system_name.
email_from = root@localhost

# List of addresses to send messages to.
email_to = root

# Name of the host to connect to to send email messages.
email_host = localhost
```

As you can see, the email_to = line is set to send messages to the root user account. If you
want to receive messages on your own account, just change it here.

12. To see the messages, you'll need to install a mail reader program, if one isn't already installed.
    (It hasn't been installed if you chose **Minimal installation** when you installed the operating
    system.) Your best bet is to install mutt, like so:

```
sudo yum install mutt
```

13. When you open mutt and look at a message, you'll see something like this:

```
File  Edit  Tabs  Help
 Exit    :PrevPg  <Space>:NextPg  v:View Attachm.    d:Del  r:Reply   j:Next ?:Help
Date: Sun,  7 Jul 2019 16:40:24 -0400 (EDT)
From: Anacron <root@git1.xyzwidgets.com>
To: root@git1.xyzwidgets.com
Subject: Anacron job 'cron.daily' on git1.xyzwidgets.com

/etc/cron.daily/0yum-daily.cron:

The following updates will be downloaded on git1.xyzwidgets.com:
================================================================================
 Package                   Arch    Version                      Repository
                                                                          Size
================================================================================
Installing:
 kernel                    x86_64  3.10.0-957.21.3.el7          updates   48 M
Updating:
 NetworkManager            x86_64  1:1.12.0-10.el7_6            updates  1.7 M
 NetworkManager-libnm      x86_64  1:1.12.0-10.el7_6            updates  1.4 M
 NetworkManager-ppp        x86_64  1:1.12.0-10.el7_6            updates  165 k
 NetworkManager-team       x86_64  1:1.12.0-10.el7_6            updates  159 k
 NetworkManager-tui        x86_64  1:1.12.0-10.el7_6            updates  239 k
 augeas-libs               x86_64  1.4.0-6.el7_6.1              updates  355 k
 bind-libs                 x86_64  32:9.9.4-74.el7_6.1          updates  1.0 M
 bind-libs-lite            x86_64  32:9.9.4-74.el7_6.1          updates  741 k
 bind-license              noarch  32:9.9.4-74.el7_6.1          updates   87 k
 1/1: Anacron               Anacron job 'cron.daily' on git1.xyzwidg  (8%)
```

Figure 1.16: Mutt mail client

14. As with all operating systems, certain updates will require that the system be restarted. And how do you know when the system needs to be restarted? With the needs-restarting command, of course. First, though, you need to make sure that needs-restarting is installed on your system. Do that with this command:

```
sudo yum install yum-utils
```

Once the package is installed, there are three ways to use needs-restarting. If you just run the command without any option switches, you'll see the services that need to be restarted and the packages that require you to reboot the machine. You can also use the -s or -r options, as shown here:

Command	Explanation
sudo needs-restarting	This shows the services that need to be restarted, and the reasons why the system might need to be rebooted.
sudo needs-restarting -s	This only shows the services that need to be restarted.
sudo needs-restarting -r	This only shows the reasons why the system needs to be rebooted.

Next, we will be updating Red Hat 8/9-based systems.

Updating Red Hat 8/9-based systems

The old yum utility has been around for practically forever, and it's been a good, hard-working utility. But it does have its occasional quirks, and at times it can be excruciatingly slow. But, not to worry. Our heroes at Red Hat have finally done something about that, by replacing yum with dnf. So, when you work with your AlmaLinux 8/9 virtual machines, you'll use dnf instead of yum. Let's see how to do this:

1. For the most part, you use dnf the same way that you'd use yum, with the same arguments and options. For example, to do a system upgrade, just do:

    ```
    sudo dnf upgrade
    ```

2. The main functional difference between yum and dnf is that dnf has a different automatic update mechanism. Instead of installing the yum-cron package, you'll now install the dnf-automatic package, like so:

    ```
    sudo dnf install dnf-automatic
    ```

3. In the /etc/dnf directory, you'll see the automatic.conf file, which you'll configure the same way as you did the yum-cron.conf file for CentOS 7. Instead of working as a cron job, as the old yum-cron did, dnf-automatic works with a systemd timer. When you first install dnf-automatic, the timer is disabled. Enable it and start it by running this command:

    ```
    sudo systemctl enable --now dnf-automatic.timer
    ```

4. Verify that it's running with this command:

    ```
    sudo systemctl status dnf-automatic.timer
    ```

5. If it started successfully, you should see something like this when you check the status:

    ```
    [donnie@redhat-8 ~]$ sudo systemctl status dnf-automatic.timer
     dnf-automatic.timer - dnf-automatic timer
       Loaded: loaded (/usr/lib/systemd/system/dnf-automatic.timer; enabled;
    vendor preset: disabled)
       Active: active (waiting) since Sun 2019-07-07 19:17:14 EDT; 13s ago
      Trigger: Sun 2019-07-07 19:54:49 EDT; 37min left

    Jul 07 19:17:14 redhat-8 systemd[1]: Started dnf-automatic timer.
    [donnie@redhat-8 ~]$
    ```

> To determine if a system needs to be restarted, just install the yum-utils package and run the needs-restarting command, the same as you did for CentOS 7. (For some reason, the Red Hat developers never bothered to change the package name to dnf-utils.)
>
> For more details about dnf-automatic, just type:
>
> ```
> man dnf-automatic
> ```

And that's all there is to it.

> Automatic updating sounds like a good thing, right? Well, it is in some circumstances. On my own personal Linux workstations, I always like to turn it off. That's because it drives me crazy whenever I want to install a package, and the machine tells me that I have to wait until the update process finishes. In an enterprise, it might also be desirable to disable automatic updates in some cases, so that administrators can have more control over the update process.

There are special considerations about doing updates in an enterprise environment. Let's look at them next.

Managing updates in an enterprise

When you first install any Linux distro, it will be configured to access its own package repositories. This allows the user to install software packages and updates directly from these normal distro repositories. This is great for home or small business use, but not so great for the enterprise.

In an enterprise setting, there are two additional considerations:

- You want to restrict what packages the end users are allowed to install.
- You always want to test updates on a separate test network before allowing them to be installed on a production network.

For these reasons, enterprises will often set up their own repository servers that only have approved packages and approved updates. All other machines on the network will be configured to pull their packages and updates from them, rather than from the normal distro repository. (We won't go into how to set up on-premises repository servers here, because that topic is better suited for a Linux administration book.)

> Ubuntu has always been one of the more innovative Linux distros, but it's also had more than its fair share of quality-control problems. In its early days, there was at least one Ubuntu update that completely broke the operating system, requiring the user to re-install the operating system. So, yeah, in any mission-critical environment, test those updates before putting them into production.

I think that that's about it for our introductory chapter. Let's wrap things up in a summary, shall we?

Summary

We've made a good start with our journey into Linux security and hardening. In this chapter, we looked at why it's just as important to know about securing and hardening Linux systems as it is to know how to secure and harden Windows systems. We provided a few examples of how a poorly configured Linux system can be compromised, and we mentioned that learning about Linux security could be good for your career. We then looked at some special considerations for setting up Linux servers either as virtual machines or on a cloud service.

After that, we looked at how to set up a virtualized lab environment using VirtualBox, Cygwin, and the Windows 10/11 shell. We wrapped things up with a quick look at how to keep your Linux systems updated.

In the next chapter, we'll look at locking down user accounts, and ensuring that the wrong people never get administrative privileges. I'll see you there.

Questions

1. Because Linux is more securely designed than Windows, we never have to worry about Linux security.

    a. True
    b. False

2. Which of the following is true about Linux on IoT devices?

    a. There are too many of them.
    b. They're taking over the world.
    c. Too many of them are configured insecurely.
    d. They're so securely configured that they'll put security practitioners out of their jobs.

3. Which of the following is true about automatic operating system updates in an enterprise?

    a. You should always leave them enabled.
    b. They violate the basic precept of testing updates on a test network before installing them on a production network.
    c. Unlike with manual updates, you never have to reboot a system after automatic updates.
    d. For IoT devices, it isn't useful to enable automatic updates.

Further reading

Here are some handy resources for your viewing pleasure:

*   **Linux Security:** https://linuxsecurity.com/
*   **The official VirtualBox website:** https://www.virtualbox.org/
*   **The official CentOS page:** https://www.centos.org/
*   **RHEL documentation (this also works for CentOS and AlmaLinux):** https://access.redhat.com/documentation/en-us/red_hat_enterprise_linux/9
*   *Enabling automatic updates in RHEL 7 and CentOS 7*: https://linuxaria.com/howto/enabling-automatic-updates-in-centos-7-and-rhel-7
*   **Managing and Monitoring Security Updates for RHEL 8:** https://access.redhat.com/documentation/en-us/red_hat_enterprise_linux/8/html/managing_and_monitoring_security_updates/index

Answers

1. b
2. c
3. b

Join our book community

Join our community's Discord space for discussions with the author and other readers:

```
https://packt.link/CyberSec
```

2

Securing Administrative User Accounts

Managing users is one of the more challenging aspects of IT administration. You need to make sure that users can always access their stuff and that they can perform the required tasks to do their jobs. You also need to ensure that users' stuff is always secure from unauthorized users and that users can't perform any tasks that don't fit their job description. It's a tall order, but we aim to show that it's doable. In this chapter, we'll look at how to lock down user accounts and user credentials to protect them from attackers and snoopers. We'll also look at how to prevent users from having any more privileges than they have to have in order to perform their jobs.

The specific topics covered in this chapter are as follows:

- The dangers of logging in as the root user
- The advantages of using sudo
- Setting up sudo privileges for full administrative users and for users with only certain delegated privileges
- Advanced tips and tricks to use sudo

The dangers of logging in as the root user

A huge advantage that Unix and Linux operating systems have over Windows is that Unix and Linux do a much better job of keeping privileged administrative accounts separated from normal user accounts. Indeed, one reason that older versions of Windows were so susceptible to security issues, such as drive-by virus infections, was the common practice of setting up user accounts with administrative privileges, without having the protection of the **User Access Control** (**UAC**) that's in newer versions of Windows. (Even with UAC, Windows systems still do get infected, just not quite as often.) With Unix and Linux, it's a lot harder to infect a properly configured system.

You probably already know that the all-powerful administrator account on a Unix or Linux system is the root account. If you're logged in as the root user, you can do anything you want to do to that system. So you may think, "Yeah, that's handy, so that's what I'll do." However, always logging in as the root user can present a whole load of security problems. Logging in as the root user can do the following:

- Make it easier for you to accidentally perform an action that causes damage to the system
- Make it easier for someone else to perform an action that causes damage to the system

So if you always log on as the root user, or even if you just make the root user account readily accessible, you could say that you're doing a big part of attackers' and intruders' work for them. Also, imagine if you were the head Linux administrator at a large corporation, and the only way to allow users to perform admin tasks was to give them all the root password. What would happen if one of those users were to leave the company? You wouldn't want that person to still have the ability to log in to the systems, so you'd have to change the password and distribute the new one to all of the other users. And what if you just want users to have admin privileges only for certain tasks, instead of having full root privileges?

What we need is a mechanism that allows users to perform administrative tasks without incurring the risk of having them always log on as the root user, and that would also allow users to have only the admin privileges they really need to perform a certain job. In Linux and Unix, we have that mechanism in the form of the sudo utility.

The advantages of using sudo

Used properly, the sudo utility can greatly enhance the security of your systems, and it can make an administrator's job much easier. With sudo, you can do the following:

- Assign certain users full administrative privileges, while assigning other users only the privileges they need to perform tasks that are directly related to their respective jobs.
- Allow users to perform administrative tasks by entering their own normal user passwords so that you don't have to distribute the root password to everybody and their brother.
- Make it harder for intruders to break into your systems. If you implement sudo and disable the root user account, would-be intruders won't know which account to attack because they won't know which one has admin privileges.
- Create sudo policies that you can deploy across an entire enterprise network, even if that network has a mix of Unix, BSD, and Linux machines.
- Improve your auditing capabilities because you'll be able to see what users are doing with their admin privileges.

With regard to that last bullet point, consider the following snippet from the secure log of my CentOS 7 virtual machine:

```
Sep 29 20:44:33 localhost sudo: donnie : TTY=pts/0 ; PWD=/home/donnie ;
USER=root ; COMMAND=/bin/su -
Sep 29 20:44:34 localhost su: pam_unix(su-l:session): session opened for
user root by donnie(uid=0)
```

```
Sep 29 20:50:39 localhost su: pam_unix(su-l:session): session closed for
user root
```

You can see that I used su - to log in to the root command prompt and that I then logged back out. While I was logged in, I did several things that require root privileges, but none of that got recorded. What did get recorded though is something that I did with sudo. That is, because the root account is disabled on this machine, I used my sudo privilege to get su - to work for me. Let's look at another snippet to show a bit more detail about how this works:

```
Sep 29 20:50:45 localhost sudo: donnie : TTY=pts/0 ; PWD=/home/donnie ;
USER=root ; COMMAND=/bin/less /var/log/secure
Sep 29 20:55:30 localhost sudo: donnie : TTY=pts/0 ; PWD=/home/donnie ;
USER=root ; COMMAND=/sbin/fdisk -l
Sep 29 20:55:40 localhost sudo: donnie : TTY=pts/0 ; PWD=/home/donnie ;
USER=root ; COMMAND=/bin/yum upgrade
Sep 29 20:59:35 localhost sudo: donnie : TTY=tty1 ; PWD=/home/donnie ;
USER=root ; COMMAND=/bin/systemctl status sshd
Sep 29 21:01:11 localhost sudo: donnie : TTY=tty1 ; PWD=/home/donnie ;
USER=root ; COMMAND=/bin/less /var/log/secure
```

This time, I used my sudo privilege to open a log file, to view my hard drive configuration, to perform a system update, to check the status of the Secure Shell daemon, and to once again view a log file. So, if you were the security administrator at my company, you'd be able to see whether or not I'm abusing my sudo power.

Now, you're asking, "What's to prevent a person from just doing a sudo su - to prevent his or her misdeeds from being detected?" That's easy. Just don't give people the power to go to the root command prompt.

Setting up sudo privileges for full administrative users

Before we look at how to limit what users can do, let's first look at how to allow a user to do everything, including logging in to the root command prompt. There are a couple of methods for doing that.

Adding users to a predefined admin group

The first method, which is the simplest, is to add users to a predefined administrators group and then, if it hasn't already been done, to configure the sudo policy to allow that group to do its job. It's simple enough to do except that different Linux distro families use different admin groups.

On Unix, BSD, and most Linux systems, you would add users to the wheel group. (Members of the Red Hat family, including CentOS and AlmaLinux, fall into this category.) When I do the groups command on any of my RHEL-type machines, I get this:

```
[donnie@localhost ~]$ groups
donnie wheel
[donnie@localhost ~]$
```

This shows that I'm a member of the wheel group. By doing sudo visudo, I'll open the sudo policy file. Scrolling down, we'll see the line that gives the wheel group its awesome power:

```
## Allows people in group wheel to run all commands
%wheel ALL=(ALL) ALL
```

The percent sign indicates that we're working with a group. The three appearances of ALL mean that members of that group can perform ALL commands, as ALL users, on ALL machines in the network on which this policy is deployed. The only slight catch is that group members will be prompted to enter their own normal user account passwords in order to perform a sudo task. Scroll down a bit more and you'll see this:

```
## Same thing without a password
# %wheel ALL=(ALL) NOPASSWD: ALL
```

If we were to comment out the %wheel line in the former snippet and remove the comment symbol from in front of the %wheel line in this snippet, then members of the wheel group would be able to perform all of their sudo tasks without ever having to enter any password. That's something that I really don't recommend, even for home use. In a business setting, allowing people to have password-less sudo privileges is a definite no-no.

To add an existing user to the wheel group, use usermod with the -G option. You might also want to use the -a option, in order to prevent removing the user from other groups to which he or she belongs. For our example, let's add Maggie:

```
sudo usermod -a -G wheel maggie
```

You can also add a user account to the wheel group as you create it. Let's do that now for Frank:

```
sudo useradd -G wheel frank
```

Tip

Note that, with my usage of useradd, I'm assuming that we're working with a member of the Red Hat family, which comes with predefined default settings to create user accounts. For non-Red Hat-type distros that use the wheel group, you'd need to either reconfigure the default settings or use extra option switches in order to create the user's home directory and to assign the correct shell. Your command would then look something like this:

```
sudo useradd -G wheel -m -d /home/frank -s /bin/bash frank
```

For members of the Debian family, including Ubuntu, the procedure is the same, except that you would use the sudo group instead of the wheel group. (This kind of figures, considering that the Debian folk have pretty much always marched to the beat of a different drum.)

> **Tip**
>
> One way in which this technique would come in handy is whenever you need to create a virtual private server on a cloud service, such as Rackspace, DigitalOcean, or Vultr. When you log in to one of those services and initially create your virtual machine, the cloud service will have you log in to that virtual machine as the root user. (This even happens with Ubuntu, even though the root user account is disabled whenever you do a local installation of Ubuntu.)
>
> The first thing that you'll want to do in this scenario is to create a normal user account for yourself and give it full sudo privileges. Then, log out of the root account and log back in with your normal user account. You'll then want to disable the root account with this command:
>
> ```
> sudo passwd -l root
> ```
>
> You'll also want to do some additional configuration to lock down Secure Shell access, but we'll cover that in *Chapter 7, SSH Hardening*.

Creating an entry in the sudo policy file

Okay, adding users to either the wheel group or the sudo group works great if you're either just working with a single machine or if you're deploying a sudo policy across a network that uses just one of these two admin groups. But what if you want to deploy a sudo policy across a network with a mixed group of both Red Hat and Ubuntu machines? Or what if you don't want to go around to each machine to add users to an admin group? Then, just create an entry in the sudo policy file. You can either create an entry for an individual user or create a user alias. If you do sudo visudo on either your CentOS or one of your AlmaLinux virtual machines, you'll see a commented-out example of a user alias:

```
# User_Alias ADMINS = jsmith, mikem
```

You can uncomment this line and add your own set of usernames, or you can just add a line with your own user alias. To give members of the user alias full sudo power, add another line that would look like this:

```
ADMINS ALL=(ALL) ALL
```

It's also possible to add a visudo entry for just a single user, and you might need to do that under very special circumstances. Here's an example:

```
frank ALL=(ALL) ALL
```

But for ease of management, it's best to go with either a user group or a user alias.

> **Tip**
>
> The sudo policy file is the /etc/sudoers file. I always hesitate to tell students that because, every once in a while, I have a student try to edit it in a regular text editor. That doesn't work though, so please don't try it. Always edit sudoers with the sudo visudo command.

Setting up sudo for users with only certain delegated privileges

A basic tenet of IT security philosophy is to give network users enough privileges so that they can get their jobs done, but no privileges beyond that. So, you'll want as few people as possible to have full sudo privileges. (If you have the root user account enabled, you'll want even fewer people to know the root password.) You'll also want a way to delegate privileges to people according to what their specific jobs are. Backup admins will need to be able to perform backup tasks, help desk personnel will need to perform user management tasks, and so on. With sudo, you can delegate these privileges and disallow users from doing any other administrative jobs that don't fit their job description.

The best way to explain this is to have you open visudo on any of the RHEL-type virtual machines. CentOS 7, AlmaLinux 8, and AlmaLinux 9 all work well for this. So, go ahead and start up one of them and enter:

```
sudo visudo
```

Unlike Ubuntu, the RHEL-type distros have a fully commented and well-documented sudoers file. I've already shown you the line that creates the ADMIN user alias, and you can create other user aliases for other purposes. You can, for example, create a BACKUPADMINS user alias for backup administrators, a WEBADMINS user alias for web server administrators, or whatever else you desire. So, you could add a line that looks something like this:

```
User_Alias SOFTWAREADMINS = vicky, cleopatra
```

That's good, except that Vicky and Cleopatra still can't do anything. You'll need to assign some duties to the user alias.

If you look at the example user alias mentioned later, you'll see a list of example command aliases. One of these examples just happens to be SOFTWARE, which contains the commands that an admin would need in order to either install or remove software or to update the system. It's commented out, as are all of the other example command aliases, so you'll need to remove the hash symbol from the beginning of the line before you can use it:

```
Cmnd_Alias SOFTWARE = /bin/rpm, /usr/bin/up2date, /usr/bin/yum
```

Now, it's just a simple matter of assigning the SOFTWARE command alias to the SOFTWAREADMINS user alias:

```
SOFTWAREADMINS ALL=(ALL) SOFTWARE
```

Vicky and Cleopatra, both members of the SOFTWAREADMINS user alias, can now run the rpm, up2date, and yum commands with root privileges, on all servers on which this policy is installed.

All but one of these predefined command aliases are ready to use after you uncomment them and assign them to either a user, group, or user alias. The one exception is the SERVICES command alias:

```
Cmnd_Alias SERVICES = /sbin/service, /sbin/chkconfig, /usr/bin/systemctl start,
/usr/bin/systemctl stop, /usr/bin/systemctl reload, /usr/bin/systemctl restart,
/usr/bin/systemctl status, /usr/bin/systemctl enable, /usr/bin/systemctl
disable
```

The problem with this SERVICES alias is that it also lists the different subcommands for the systemctl command. The way sudo works is that if a command is listed by itself, then the assigned user can use that command with any subcommands, options, or arguments. So, in the SOFTWARE example, members of the SOFTWARE user alias can run a command such as this:

```
sudo yum upgrade
```

But when a command is listed in the command alias with a subcommand, option, or argument, that's all anyone who's assigned to the command alias can run. With the SERVICES command alias in its current configuration, the systemctl commands just won't work. To see why, let's set Charlie and Lionel up in the SERVICESADMINS user alias and then uncomment the SERVICES command alias, as we did earlier:

```
User_Alias SERVICESADMINS = charlie, lionel
SERVICESADMINS ALL=(ALL) SERVICES
```

Now, watch what happens when Lionel tries to check the status of the Secure Shell service:

```
[lionel@centos-7 ~]$ sudo systemctl status sshd
[sudo] password for lionel:
Sorry, user lionel is not allowed to execute '/bin/systemctl status sshd' as
root on centos-7.xyzwidgets.com.
[lionel@centos-7 ~]$
```

Okay, so Lionel can run sudo systemctl status, which is pretty much useless, but he can't do anything meaningful, such as specifying the service that he wants to check. That's a bit of a problem. There are two ways to fix this, but there's only one way that you want to use. You could just eliminate all of the systemctl subcommands and make the SERVICES alias look like this:

```
Cmnd_Alias SERVICES = /sbin/service, /sbin/chkconfig, /usr/bin/systemctl
```

But if you do that, Lionel and Charlie will also be able to shut down or reboot the system, edit the services files, or change the machine from one systemd target to another. That's probably not what you want. Because the systemctl command covers a lot of different functions, you have to be careful not to allow delegated users to access too many of those functions. A better solution would be to add a wildcard to each of the systemctl subcommands:

```
Cmnd_Alias SERVICES = /sbin/service, /sbin/chkconfig, /usr/bin/systemctl start
*, /usr/bin/systemctl stop *, /usr/bin/systemctl reload *, /usr/bin/systemctl
```

```
restart *, /usr/bin/systemctl status *, /usr/bin/systemctl enable *, /usr/bin/
systemctl disable *
```

Now, Lionel and Charlie can perform any of the `systemctl` functions that are listed in this command alias, for any service:

```
[lionel@centos-7 ~]$ sudo systemctl status sshd
[sudo] password for lionel:
● sshd.service - OpenSSH server daemon
    Loaded: loaded (/usr/lib/systemd/system/sshd.service; enabled; vendor
preset: enabled)
   Active: active (running) since Sat 2017-09-30 18:11:22 EDT; 23min ago
     Docs: man:sshd(8)
              man:sshd_config(5)
 Main PID: 13567 (sshd)
    CGroup: /system.slice/sshd.service
              └─13567 /usr/sbin/sshd -D
 Sep 30 18:11:22 centos-7.xyzwidgets.com systemd[1]: Starting OpenSSH server
daemon...
 Sep 30 18:11:22 centos-7.xyzwidgets.com sshd[13567]: Server listening on
0.0.0.0 port 22.
 Sep 30 18:11:22 centos-7.xyzwidgets.com sshd[13567]: Server listening on ::
port 22.
 Sep 30 18:11:22 centos-7.xyzwidgets.com systemd[1]: Started OpenSSH server
daemon.
 [lionel@centos-7 ~]$
```

Keep in mind that you're not limited to using user aliases and command aliases. You can also assign privileges to either a Linux group or an individual user. You can also assign individual commands to a user alias, Linux group, or individual user. Here's an example:

```
katelyn ALL=(ALL) STORAGE
gunther ALL=(ALL) /sbin/fdisk -l
%backup_admins ALL=(ALL) BACKUP
```

Katelyn can now do all of the commands in the STORAGE command alias, whereas Gunther can only use `fdisk` to look at the partition tables. The members of the `backup_admins` Linux group can do commands in the BACKUP command alias.

The last thing we'll look at in this topic is the host aliases examples that you see preceding the user alias example:

```
# Host_Alias FILESERVERS = fs1, fs2
# Host_Alias MAILSERVERS = smtp, smtp2
```

Each host alias consists of a list of server hostnames. This is what allows you to create one sudoers file on one machine and deploy it across the network. For example, you could create a WEBSERVERS host alias, a WEBADMINS user alias, and a WEBCOMMANDS command alias with the appropriate commands. Your configuration would look something like this:

```
Host_Alias WEBSERVERS = webserver1, webserver2
User_Alias WEBADMINS = junior, kayla
Cmnd_Alias WEBCOMMANDS = /usr/bin/systemctl status httpd, /usr/bin/systemctl
start httpd, /usr/bin/systemctl stop httpd, /usr/bin/systemctl restart httpd

WEBADMINS WEBSERVERS=(ALL) WEBCOMMANDS
```

Now, when a user types a command into a server on the network, sudo will first look at the hostname of that server. If the user is authorized to perform that command on that server, then sudo allows it. Otherwise, sudo denies it. In a small to medium-sized business, it would probably work just fine to manually copy the master sudoers file to all the servers on the network. But in a large enterprise, you'll want to streamline and automate the process. For this, you could use something like Puppet, Chef, or Ansible. (These three technologies are beyond the scope of this book, but you'll find plenty of books and video courses about all three of them on the Packt website.)

All of these techniques will work on your Ubuntu VM as well as on the CentOS VM. The only catch is that Ubuntu doesn't come with any predefined command aliases, so you'll have to type them in yourself.

Anyway, I know that you're tired of reading, so let's do some work.

Hands-on lab for assigning limited sudo privileges

In this lab, you'll create some users and assign them different levels of privileges. To simplify things, let's use the AlmaLinux 9 virtual machine:

1. Log in to the AlmaLinux virtual machine and create user accounts for Lionel, Katelyn, and Maggie:

```
sudo useradd lionel
sudo useradd katelyn
sudo useradd Maggie
sudo passwd lionel
sudo passwd katelyn
sudo passwd Maggie
```

2. Open visudo:

```
sudo visudo
```

Find the STORAGE command alias and remove the comment symbol from in front of it.

3. Add the following lines to the end of the file, using tabs to separate the columns:

```
lionel ALL=(ALL) ALL
katelyn ALL=(ALL) /usr/bin/systemctl status sshd
maggie ALL=(ALL) STORAGE
```

Save the file and exit `visudo`.

4. To save time, we'll use `su` to log in to the different user accounts. That way, you won't need to log out of your own account to perform these steps. First, log in to Lionel's account and verify that he has full `sudo` privileges by running several root-level commands:

```
su - lionel
sudo su -
exit
sudo systemctl status sshd
sudo fdisk -l
exit
```

5. This time, log in as Katelyn and try to run some root-level commands. Don't be too disappointed if they don't all work, though:

```
su - katelyn
sudo su -
sudo systemctl status sshd
sudo systemctl restart sshd
sudo fdisk -l
exit
```

6. Finally, log in as Maggie, and run the same set of commands that you ran for Katelyn.

7. Keep in mind that, although we only had three individual users for this lab, you could just as easily have handled more users by setting them up in user aliases or Linux groups.

Since `sudo` is such a great security tool, you would think that everyone would use it, right? Sadly, that's not the case. Pretty much any time you look at either a Linux tutorial website or a Linux tutorial YouTube channel, you'll see the person who's doing the demo logged in at the root user command prompt. In some cases, I've seen the person remotely logged in as the root user on a cloud-based virtual machine. Now, if logging in as the root user is already a bad idea, then logging in across the Internet as the root user is an even worse idea. In any case, seeing everybody do these tutorial demos from the root user's shell drives me absolutely crazy.

Having said all this, there are some things that don't work with `sudo`. Bash shell internal commands such as `cd` don't work with it, and using `echo` to inject kernel values into the `/proc` filesystem also doesn't work with it. For tasks such as these, a person would have to go to the root command prompt. Still, though, make sure that only users who absolutely have to use the root user command prompt have access to it.

Next, let's look at some more advanced sudo usage.

Advanced tips and tricks for using sudo

Now that we've looked at the basics of setting up a good sudo configuration, we're confronted with a bit of a paradox. That is, even though sudo is a security tool, certain things that you can do with it can make your system even more insecure than it was. Let's see how to avoid that.

The sudo timer

By default, the sudo timer is set for 5 minutes. This means that once a user performs one sudo command and enters a password, he or she can perform another sudo command within 5 minutes without having to enter the password again. Although this is obviously handy, it can also be problematic if users were to walk away from their desks with a command terminal still open.

If the 5-minute timer hasn't yet expired, someone else could come along and perform some root-level task. If your security needs require it, you can easily disable this timer by adding a line to the Defaults section of the sudoers file. This way, users will have to enter their passwords every time they run a sudo command. You can make this a global setting for all users, or you can just set it for certain individual users.

Let's also say that you're sitting in your nice, cozy cubicle, logged in to a remote Linux server that still has the 5-minute timer enabled. If you need to leave your desk for a moment, your best action would be to log out of the server first. Short of that, you could just reset the sudo timer by running this command:

```
sudo -k
```

This is one of the few sudo actions you can do without entering a password. But the next time you do a sudo command, you will have to enter your password, even if it has been less than 5 minutes since you entered your password previously.

View your sudo privileges

Are you unsure of what sudo privileges you possess? Not to worry, you have a way to find out. Just run this command:

```
sudo -l
```

When I do this for myself, I first see some of the environmental variables for my account, and then I see that I have full sudo privileges:

```
donnie@packtpub1:~$ sudo -l
 [sudo] password for donnie:
 Matching Defaults entries for donnie on packtpub1:
 env_reset, mail_badpass, secure_path=/usr/local/sbin\:/usr/local/bin\:/usr/
 sbin\:/usr/bin\:/sbin\:/bin\:/snap/bin
```

```
User donnie may run the following commands on packtpub1:
(ALL : ALL) ALL
donnie@packtpub1:~$
```

When Frank, my formerly feral flamepoint Siamese cat, does this for his account, he sees that he can only do the `fdisk -l` command:

```
frank@packtpub1:~$ sudo -l
[sudo] password for frank:
Matching Defaults entries for frank on packtpub1:
env_reset, mail_badpass, secure_path=/usr/local/sbin\:/usr/local/bin\:/usr/
sbin\:/usr/bin\:/sbin\:/bin\:/snap/bin

User frank may run the following commands on packtpub1:
(ALL) /sbin fdisk -l
frank@packtpub1:~$
```

But since he's a cat, he doesn't complain. Instead, he'll just try to do something sneaky, as we'll see in just a bit.

Hands-on lab for disabling the sudo timer

For this lab, you'll disable the `sudo` timer on your AlmaLinux VM:

1. Log in to the same AlmaLinux virtual machine that you used for the previous lab. We'll be using the user accounts that you've already created.

2. At your own user account command prompt, enter the following commands:

```
sudo fdisk -l
sudo systemctl status sshd
sudo iptables -L
```

You'll see that you only needed to enter the password once to do all three commands

3. At your own user account command prompt, run the following:

```
sudo fdisk -l
sudo -k
sudo fdisk -l
```

Note how the `sudo -k` command resets your timer, so you'll have to enter your password again. Open `visudo` with the following command:

```
sudo visudo
```

In the `Defaults` specification section of the file, add the following line:

```
Defaults timestamp_timeout = 0
```

Save the file and exit `visudo`.

4. Perform the commands that you performed in *step 2*. This time, you should see that you have to enter a password every time.

5. Open `visudo` and modify the line that you added so that it looks like this:

```
Defaults:lionel timestamp_timeout = 0
```

Save the file and exit `visudo`.

6. From your own account shell, repeat the commands that you performed in *step 2*. Then, log in as Lionel and perform the commands again.

7. View your own `sudo` privileges by running the following:

```
sudo -l
```

Note that this procedure also works for Ubuntu.

Preventing users from having root shell access

Let's say that you want to set up a user with limited `sudo` privileges, and you decide to do so by adding a line like this:

```
maggie ALL=(ALL) /bin/bash, /bin/zsh
```

I'm sorry to say that you haven't limited Maggie's access at all. You have effectively given her full `sudo` privileges with both the Bash shell and the ZSH shell. So, don't add lines like this to your `sudoers` because it will get you into trouble.

Preventing users from using shell escapes

Certain programs, especially text editors and pagers, have a handy shell escape feature. This allows a user to run a shell command without having to exit the program first. For example, from the command mode of the Vi and Vim editors, someone could run the `ls` command by running `:!ls`. Executing the command would look like this:

```
# useradd defaults file
GROUP=100
HOME=/home
INACTIVE=-1
EXPIRE=
SHELL=/bin/bash
SKEL=/etc/skel
CREATE_MAIL_SPOOL=yes
```

```
~
~
:!ls
```

The output would look like this:

```
[donnie@localhost default]$ sudo vim useradd
 [sudo] password for donnie:
 grub nss useradd
 Press ENTER or type command to continue
 grub nss useradd
 Press ENTER or type command to continue
```

That was a harmless command, as you can see. But, the user could just as easily have executed a command that requires root privileges, or even have used the :shell command to go to the root user's shell.

Now, imagine that you want Frank to be able to edit the sshd_config file and only that file. You might be tempted to add a line to your sudo configuration that would look like this:

```
frank ALL=(ALL) /bin/vim /etc/ssh/sshd_config
```

This looks like it would work, right? Well, it doesn't, because once Frank has opened the sshd_config file with his sudo privilege, he can then use Vim's shell escape feature to perform other root-level commands, which includes being able to edit other configuration files, create new users, manipulate system services, or install malware. Let's see how this works.

Here, we see that Frank has used his sudo power to open the sshd_config file in the Vim editor. At the bottom of the screen, he'll type the :shell command:

```
. . .
. . .
# Authentication:

#LoginGraceTime 2m
:shell
```

Now, watch what happens when Frank hits the *Enter* key:

```
[frank@localhost ~]$ sudo vim /etc/ssh/sshd_config
[sudo] password for frank:

[root@localhost frank]#
```

Yikes! That is not good. By assigning Frank the sudo power to edit a single system configuration file, we've effectively given Frank full root privileges on the system.

You can fix this problem by having Frank use sudoedit instead of vim. Let's change the sudoers rule to reflect that:

```
frank ALL=(ALL) sudoedit /etc/ssh/sshd_config
```

sudoedit doesn't allow users to escape to a shell with root privileges, so you can safely allow Frank to use it. With this new configuration, Frank can no longer open the sshd_config file in Vim:

```
[frank@localhost ~]$ sudo vim /etc/ssh/sshd_config
[sudo] password for frank:
Sorry, user frank is not allowed to execute '/bin/vim /etc/ssh/sshd_config' as
root on localhost.localdomain.
[frank@localhost ~]$
```

However, he can open it with sudoedit:

```
[frank@localhost ~]$ sudoedit /etc/ssh/sshd_config
[sudo] password for frank:
sudoedit: /etc/ssh/sshd_config unchanged
[frank@localhost ~]$
```

We see that Frank decided not to actually make any edits, but that's okay. Let's have him open the file again, and try to escape to a root shell. First, he'll type in the :shell command, as he did before:

```
. . .

. . .
# Authentication:

#LoginGraceTime 2m
:shell
```

Watch what happens this time when he hits the *Enter* key:

```
[frank@localhost ~]$ sudoedit /etc/ssh/sshd_config

[frank@localhost ~]$
```

He can still escape to a shell, but it's his own non-privileged shell instead of the root user's shell.

Other programs that have a shell escape feature include the following:

- emacs
- less
- view
- more

So, how do we deal with these? That's easy. We'll use the NOEXEC: option when we set up our sudoers rules. For example, let's say that we want to grant Vicky the power to view files that are only readable by the root user. We could set up a rule that looks like this:

```
vicky ALL=(ALL) /usr/bin/less
```

She now decides to view the system log file:

```
[vicky@localhost ~]$ cd /var/log
[vicky@localhost log]$ sudo less messages
```

To open a shell from within less, Vicky will type !bash instead of :shell:

```
. . .

. . .
Jan 15 13:02:23 localhost NetworkManager[902]: <info>  [1673805743.2807]
settings: Loaded settings plugin: keyfile (internal)
Jan 15 13:02:23 localhost systemd[1]: Starting Network Manager Script
Dispatcher Service...
Jan 15 13:02:23 localhost NetworkManager[902]: <info>  [1673805743.3039]
settings: Loaded settings plugin: ifcfg-rh ("/usr/lib64/
NetworkManager/1.40.0-1.el9/libnm-settings-plugin-ifcfg-rh.so
!bash
```

Once again, watch what happens when she hits the *Enter* key:

```
. . .

. . .
!done  (press RETURN)
[root@localhost log]#
```

Obviously, that's not what we want to happen. Let's fix that by adding the NOEXEC: option to the sudoers rule:

```
vicky ALL=(ALL) NOEXEC: /usr/bin/less
```

This prevents Vicky from escaping to even her own shell:

```
. . .

. . .
!done  (press RETURN)
```

That looks much better, and we have achieved coolness.

Preventing users from using other dangerous programs

Some programs that don't have shell escapes can still be dangerous if you give users unrestricted privileges to use them. These include the following:

- cat
- cut
- awk
- sed

If you must give someone sudo privileges to use one of these programs, it's best to limit their use to only specific files. And that brings us to our next tip.

Limiting the user's actions with commands

Let's say that you create a sudo rule so that Sylvester can use the systemctl command:

```
sylvester ALL=(ALL) /usr/bin/systemctl
```

This allows Sylvester to have full use of the systemctl features. He can control daemons, edit service files, shut down or reboot, and carry out every other function that systemctl does. That's probably not what you want. It would be better to specify what systemctl functions Sylvester is allowed to do. Let's say that you want him to be able to control just the Secure Shell service. You can make the line look like this:

```
sylvester ALL=(ALL) /usr/bin/systemctl * sshd
```

Sylvester can now do everything he needs to do with the Secure Shell service, but he can't shut down or reboot the system, edit other service files, or change systemd targets. But what if you want Sylvester to do only certain specific actions with the Secure Shell service? Then you'll have to omit the wildcard and specify all of the actions that you want Sylvester to do:

```
sylvester ALL=(ALL) /usr/bin/systemctl status sshd, /usr/bin/systemctl restart
sshd
```

Now, Sylvester can only restart the Secure Shell service or check its status.

> **Tip**
>
> When writing sudo policies, you'll want to be aware of the differences between the different Linux and Unix distributions on your network. For example, on Red Hat-type systems, the systemctl binary file is located in the /usr/bin directory. On Debian/Ubuntu systems, it's located in the /bin directory. If you have to roll out a sudoers file to a large enterprise network with mixed operating systems, you can use host aliases to ensure that servers will only allow the execution of commands that are appropriate for their operating systems.
>
> Also, be aware that some system services have different names on different Linux distributions. On Red Hat-type systems, the Secure Shell service is sshd. On Debian/Ubuntu systems, it's just plain ssh.

Letting users run as other users

In the following line, (ALL) means that Sylvester can run the systemctl commands as any user:

```
sylvester ALL=(ALL) /usr/bin/systemctl status sshd, /usr/bin/systemctl restart
sshd
```

This effectively gives Sylvester root privileges for these commands because the root user is definitely any user. You could, if desired, change that (ALL) to (root) in order to specify that Sylvester can only run these commands as the root user:

```
sylvester ALL=(root) /usr/bin/systemctl status sshd, /usr/bin/systemctl restart
sshd
```

Okay, there's probably not much point in that because nothing changes. Sylvester had root privileges for these systemctl commands before, and he still has them now. But there are more practical uses for this feature. Let's say that Vicky is a database admin, and you want her to run as the database user:

```
vicky ALL=(database) /usr/local/sbin/some_database_script.sh
```

Vicky could then run the command as the database user by entering the following command:

```
sudo -u database some_database_script.sh
```

This is one of those features that you might not use that often, but keep it in mind anyway. You never know when it might come in handy.

Preventing abuse via a user's shell scripts

So, what if a user has written a shell script that requires sudo privileges? To answer that, let's have Frank create the frank_script.sh shell script that looks like this:

```
#!/bin/bash

echo "This script belongs to Frank the Cat."
```

Okay, he wouldn't need sudo privileges for that, but let's pretend that he does. After he sets the executable permission and runs it with sudo, the output will look like this:

```
frank@packtpub1:~$ sudo ./frank_script.sh
[sudo] password for frank:
Sorry, user frank is not allowed to execute './frank_script.sh' as root on
packtpub1.tds.
frank@packtpub1:~$
```

Naturally frustrated, Frank requested that I create a sudo rule so that he can run the script. So, I open visudo and add this rule for Frank:

```
frank ALL=(ALL) /home/frank/frank_script.sh
```

Now, when Frank runs the script with sudo, it works:

```
frank@packtpub1:~$ sudo ./frank_script.sh
[sudo] password for frank:
This script belongs to Frank the Cat.
frank@packtpub1:~$
```

But since this file is in Frank's own home directory and he is its owner, he can edit it any way he wants. So, being the sneaky type, he adds the sudo -i line to the end of the script so that it now looks like this:

```
#!/bin/bash

echo "This script belongs to Frank the Cat."
sudo -i
```

Be prepared for a shock as you watch what happens next:

```
frank@packtpub1:~$ sudo ./frank_script.sh
This script belongs to Frank the Cat.
root@packtpub1:~#
```

As you can see, Frank is now logged in as the root user.

What sudo -i does is to log a person in to the root user's shell, the same way that sudo su - does. If Frank were to do sudo -i from his own command prompt, it would fail because he doesn't have the privilege to do that. But he does have the sudo privilege to run his own shell script. By leaving the shell script in his own home directory, Frank can put root-level commands into it. By running the script with sudo, the root-level commands in the script will execute with root-level privileges.

To remedy this, I'll use my awesome powers of sudo to move Frank's script to the /usr/local/sbin/ directory and change the ownership to the root user so that Frank won't be able to edit it. And of course, before I do that, I'll make sure to delete that sudo -i line from it:

```
donnie@packtpub1:~$ sudo -i
root@packtpub1:~# cd /home/frank
root@packtpub1:/home/frank# mv frank_script.sh /usr/local/sbin
root@packtpub1:/home/frank# chown root: /usr/local/sbin/frank_script.sh
root@packtpub1:/home/frank# exit
logout
donnie@packtpub1:~$
```

Finally, I'll open visudo and change his rule to reflect the new location of the script. The new rule looks like this:

```
frank ALL=(ALL) /usr/local/sbin/frank_script.sh
```

Frank can still run the script, but he can't edit it:

```
frank@packtpub1:~$ sudo frank_script.sh
This script belongs to Frank the Cat.
frank@packtpub1:~$
```

Detecting and deleting default user accounts

One challenge of dealing with **Internet of Things (IoT)** devices is that you don't do a normal operating system installation on them as you would when setting up a normal server. Instead, you download an image that has the operating system pre-installed and burn that image to a microSD card. The installed operating system is set up with a default user account, and many times, that user is set up with full sudo privileges and isn't required to enter a sudo password. Let's take, for example, the RaspEX Linux distribution for the Raspberry Pi. (RaspEX is built from Ubuntu source code.) On the documentation page of the RaspEX download site, we see that the default user is raspex, and the default password for that user is also *raspex*. We also see that the default password for the root user is *root*:

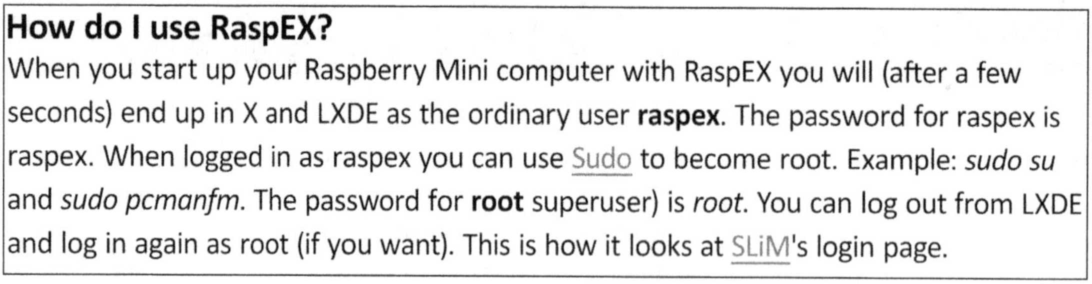

How do I use RaspEX?

When you start up your Raspberry Mini computer with RaspEX you will (after a few seconds) end up in X and LXDE as the ordinary user **raspex**. The password for raspex is raspex. When logged in as raspex you can use Sudo to become root. Example: *sudo su* and *sudo pcmanfm*. The password for **root** superuser) is *root*. You can log out from LXDE and log in again as root (if you want). This is how it looks at SLiM's login page.

Figure 2.1: The default username and password

So, the default credentials are out there for all the world to see. Obviously, the first thing you want to do when setting up an IoT device is to set up your own user account, give it a good password, and give it sudo privileges. Then get rid of that default account, because leaving it in place, especially if you leave the default password, is just asking for trouble.

But let's dig deeper. Look in the /etc/password file on RaspEX, and you'll see the default user there:

```
raspex:x:1000:1000:,,,:/home/raspex:/bin/bash
```

Then, look in the /etc/sudoers file, and you'll see this line, which allows the raspex user to do all sudo commands without having to enter a password:

```
raspex ALL=(ALL) NOPASSWD: ALL
```

Another thing to watch out for is that some Linux distributions for IoT devices have this rule in a separate file in the /etc/sudoers.d directory, instead of in the main sudoers file. Either way, you'll want to delete this rule, as well as the default user account, when you set up your IoT device. And of course, you'll also want to change the root user password, and then lock the root user account.

All right, let's take a quick look at some new features that have been recently added to sudo.

New sudo features

I mentioned before that one of the beautiful things about sudo is that it allows you to see what users are doing with their sudo privileges. Beginning with sudo version 1.9.0, the sudo logging experience has been greatly enhanced. You can now save sudo log messages in JSON format, which allows sudo to log much more information than it normally would, in a format that's easier to parse. Beginning with sudo version 1.9.4, you can also have sudo send its log messages to a central log server, making it more difficult for bad actors to delete mention of their dirty deeds from the system log files.

Unfortunately, space constraints don't allow me to do a full write-up about these new features here. That's okay, though. Over at `https://opensource.com/`, Mr. Peter Czanik has written a great article that explains them very well. So, I'll just refer you to him:

> *5 new sudo features sysadmins need to know in 2022*– `https://opensource.com/article/22/2/new-sudo-features-2022`

I should also mention that in order to know which new sudo features your Linux distro supports, you'll need to know which version of sudo that it includes. Find out by doing:

```
sudo --version
```

Next, let's look at some SUSE quirkiness.

Special sudo considerations for SUSE and OpenSUSE

If you've ever worked with any kind of SUSE machine, you may have been puzzled by the fact that it asks for the root user's password, rather than your own password, when you perform a sudo command. That's because SUSE has a whole different way of doing business with sudo.

When you install a SUSE distro, you'll see a user creation screen that looks similar to the one that you've seen on the RHEL-type distros.

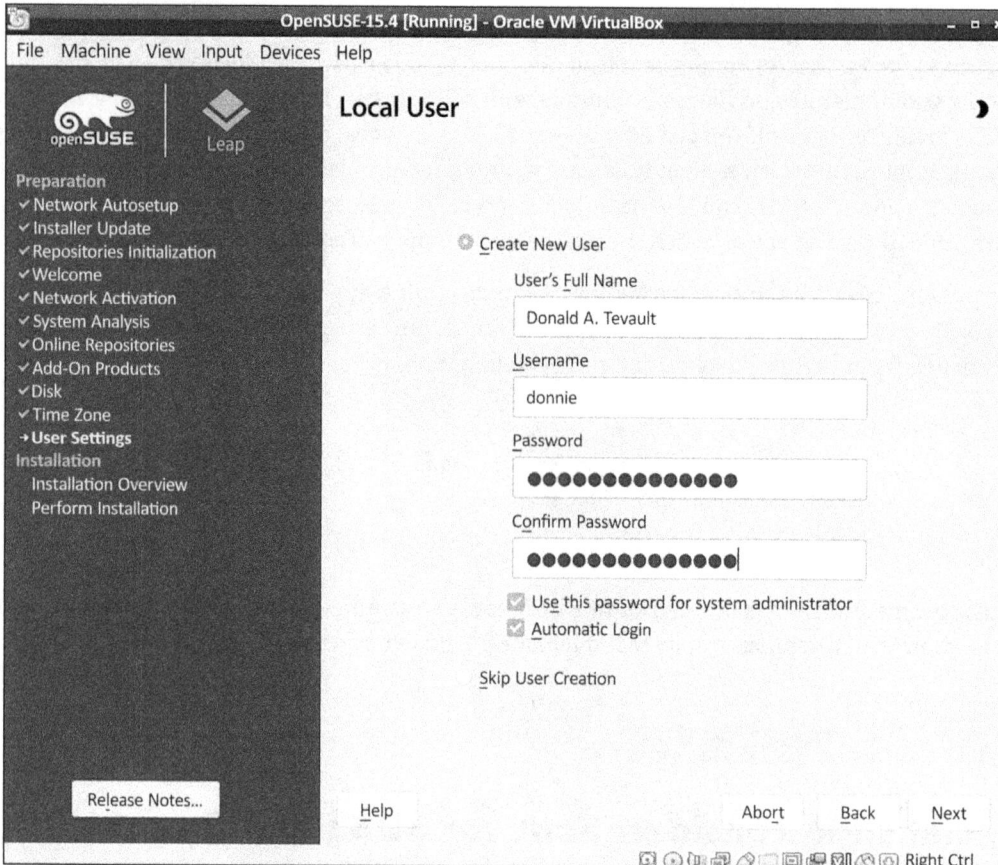

Figure 2.2: The OpenSUSE installer

However, when you check the **Use this password for system administrator** box, it doesn't add your user account to the wheel group as the RHEL-type distros do. Instead, it automatically assigns the same password that you created for yourself to the root user account. So, you and the root user will both have the same password.

When you do sudo visudo on a SUSE machine, you'll see these two lines that you don't see on any other Linux distro:

```
Defaults targetpw    # ask for the password of the target user i.e. root
ALL    ALL=(ALL) ALL   # WARNING! Only use this together with 'Defaults
targetpw'!
```

This means that any user who has the root user password can perform all sudo commands. To be fair though, the comments that precede these two lines inform us that this is only for the initial system setup, and that we should reconfigure sudo in the normal way before putting the machine into production use. To do that, first add your own user account to the wheel group, like so:

```
donnie@localhost:~> sudo usermod -a -G wheel donnie
[sudo] password for root:
donnie@localhost:~>
```

Cause the group membership to take effect by logging out of the system and then logging back in. Use the groups command to verify wheel group membership, like so:

```
donnie@localhost:~> groups
users wheel
donnie@localhost:~>
```

Next, do sudo visudo, and comment out the two lines that we looked at before. They should now look like this:

```
#Defaults targetpw    # ask for the password of the target user i.e. root
#ALL    ALL=(ALL) ALL   # WARNING! Only use this together with 'Defaults
targetpw'!
```

(Or, better yet, just delete the lines.)

Scroll down in the file until you see this line:

```
# %wheel ALL=(ALL:ALL) ALL
```

Remove the preceding comment symbol to make the line look like this:

```
%wheel ALL=(ALL:ALL) ALL
```

Save the file and exit visudo. Now, when you do a sudo command, you'll be asked to enter your own password instead of the root user's password:

```
donnie@localhost:~> sudo fdisk -l
[sudo] password for donnie:
. . .
. . .
```

Of course, the root user account is still enabled, so let's disable it, like so:

```
donnie@localhost:~> sudo passwd -l root
passwd: password expiry information changed.
donnie@localhost:~>
```

All righty, that pretty much covers the sudo topic. Let's wrap up and move on.

Summary

We covered a lot of ground in this chapter, and hopefully, you found some suggestions that you can actually use. We started out by showing you the dangers of always logging in as the root user and how you should use sudo instead. In addition to showing you the basics of sudo usage, we also looked at some good sudo tips and tricks.

In the next chapter, we'll look at some best practices for securing the accounts of normal users. I'll see you there.

Questions

1. What is the best way to grant administrative privileges to users?

    a. Give every administrative user the root user password.

    b. Add each administrative user to either the sudo group or the wheel group.

    c. Create sudo rules that only allow administrative users to do tasks that are directly related to their jobs.

    d. Add each administrative user to the sudoers file and grant them full administrative privileges.

2. Which of the following is true?

    a. When users log in as the root user, all the actions that they perform will be recorded in the auth.log or the secure log file.

    b. When users use sudo, all the actions that they perform will be recorded in the messages or the syslog file.

    c. When users log in as the root user, all the actions that they perform will be recorded in the messages or the syslog file.

    d. When users use sudo, all the actions that they perform will be recorded in the auth. log or the secure log file.

3. Which of the following methods would you use to create sudo rules for other users?

    a. Open the /etc/sudoers file in your favorite text editor.

    b. Open the /etc/sudoers file with visudo.

    c. Add a sudoers file to each user's home directory.

    d. Open the /var/spool/sudoers file with visudo.

4. Which one of the following represents best security practice?

    a. Always give the root user password to all users who need to perform administrative tasks.

    b. Always give full sudo privileges to all users who need to perform administrative tasks.

    c. Always just give specific, limited sudo privileges to all users who need to perform administrative tasks.

    d. Always edit the sudoers file in a normal text editor, such as nano, vim, or emacs.

5. Which of the following statements is true?

    a. sudo can only be used on Linux.

    b. sudo can be used on Linux, Unix, and BSD operating systems.

    c. When a user performs a task using sudo, the task does not get recorded in a security log.

    d. When using sudo, users must enter the root user password.

6. You want specific users to edit a specific system configuration file, but you don't want them to use a shell escape that would allow them to perform other administrative tasks. Which two of the following could you do?

   a. In the sudoers file, specify that the users can only use vim to open a specific configuration file.

   b. In the sudoers file, specify that the users can use sudoedit to edit a specific configuration file.

   c. In the sudoers file, specify the no shell escape option for these users.

   d. In the sudoers file, place these users into a group that does not have shell escape privileges.

Further reading

- Linux Privilege Escalation exploiting sudo rights: https://medium.com/schkn/linux-privilege-escalation-using-text-editors-and-files-part-1-a8373396708d
- sudo Main Page: https://www.sudo.ws/
- Granting sudo access: https://www.golinuxhub.com/2013/12/how-to-give-permission-to-user-to-run.html

Answers

1. c
2. d
3. b
4. c
5. b
6. b

Join our book community

Join our community's Discord space for discussions with the author and other readers:

https://packt.link/CyberSec

3

Securing Normal User Accounts

Managing users is one of the more challenging aspects of IT administration. You need to make sure that users can always access their stuff and that they can perform the required tasks to do their jobs. You also need to ensure that users' stuff is always secure from unauthorized users. In this chapter, we'll look at how to lock down user accounts and user credentials to protect them from attackers and snoopers. We'll wrap up by taking a brief look at a few centralized user management systems:

- Locking down users' home directories
- Enforcing strong password criteria
- Setting and enforcing password and account expiration
- Preventing brute-force password attacks
- Locking user accounts
- Setting up security banners
- Detecting compromised passwords
- Understanding central user management systems

Locking down users' home directories the Red Hat way

This is another area where different Linux distro families do business differently from each other. As we shall see, each distro family comes with different default security settings for users' home directories. A security administrator who oversees a mixed environment of different Linux distros will need to take this into account.

Traditionally, Red Hat Enterprise Linux and all of its offspring, such as CentOS and AlmaLinux, have had better out-of-the-box security than any other family of Linux distros. This makes it quicker and easier to harden Red Hat-type systems because much of the work has already been done. One thing that's already been done for us is locking down users' home directories:

```
[donnie@localhost home]$ sudo useradd charlie
[sudo] password for donnie:
[donnie@localhost home]$
```

```
[donnie@localhost home]$ ls -l
total 0
drwx------. 2 charlie charlie 59 Oct 1 15:25 charlie
drwx------. 2 donnie donnie 79 Sep 27 00:24 donnie
drwx------. 2 frank frank 59 Oct 1 15:25 frank
[donnie@localhost home]$
```

By default, the `useradd` utility on Red Hat-type systems creates user home directories with a permissions setting of `700`. This means that only the user who owns the home directory can access it. All other normal users are locked out. We can see why by looking at the `/etc/login.defs` file. On your CentOS 7 VM, scroll down toward the bottom of the file, and you'll see this:

```
CREATE_HOME yes
UMASK 077
```

In the `login.defs` file of a RHEL 8 or RHEL 9-type distro, such as AlmaLinux, you'll see that the `UMASK` is set for wide-open permissions, which seems a bit strange. Here's what that looks like:

```
UMASK              022
```

But a few lines below that, you'll see a brand-new directive that we never had before, which looks like this:

```
HOME_MODE          0700
```

So even though the `UMASK` is wide-open, new user home directories still get properly locked down.

The `login.defs` file is one of two files where the default settings for `useradd` are configured. Either the `UMASK` line or the `HOME_MODE` line is what determines the permissions values on home directories as they get created. Red Hat-type distros have them configured to remove all permissions from the group and others. Either the `HOME_MODE` line or the `UMASK` line is in the `login.defs` file for all Linux distros, but until recently, Red Hat-type distros have been the only ones that have had them set to such a restrictive value by default. Most non-Red Hat distros usually have a `UMASK` value of `022`, which creates home directories with a permissions value of `755`. This allows everybody to enter everybody else's home directories and access each others' files.

Locking down users' home directories the Debian/ Ubuntu way

Debian and its offspring, such as Ubuntu, have two user creation utilities:

- `useradd`
- `adduser`

Let's look at both of them.

useradd on Debian/Ubuntu

The useradd utility is there, but Debian and Ubuntu don't come with handy preconfigured defaults as the Red Hat-type distros do. If you were to just do sudo useradd frank on a Debian/Ubuntu machine, Frank would have no home directory and would be assigned the wrong default shell. So, to create a user account with useradd on a Debian or Ubuntu system, the command will look something like this:

```
sudo useradd -m -d /home/frank -s /bin/bash frank
```

Here's a breakdown of what all this means:

- **-m** creates the home directory.
- **-d** specifies the home directory.
- **-s** specifies Frank's default shell. (Without the -s, Debian/Ubuntu would assign to Frank the /bin/sh shell.)

When you look at the home directories on either a Debian machine or an Ubuntu 20.04 machine, you'll see that they're wide open, with execute and read privileges for everybody:

```
donnie@packt:/home$ ls -l
total 8
drwxr-xr-x 3 donnie donnie 4096 Oct 2 00:23 donnie
drwxr-xr-x 2 frank frank 4096 Oct 1 23:58 frank
donnie@packt:/home$
```

As you can see, Frank and I can get into each other's stuff. (And no, I don't want Frank getting into my stuff.) Each user could change the permissions on his or her own directory, but how many of your users would know how to do that? So, let's fix that ourselves:

```
cd /home
sudo chmod 700 *
```

Let's see what we have now:

```
donnie@packt:/home$ ls -l
total 8
drwx------ 3 donnie donnie 4096 Oct 2 00:23 donnie
drwx------ 2 frank frank 4096 Oct 1 23:58 frank
donnie@packt:/home$
```

That looks much better.

To change the default permissions setting for home directories, open /etc/login.defs for editing. Look for this line:

```
UMASK 022
```

Change it to this:

```
UMASK 077
```

Now, new users' home directories will get locked down on creation, just as they do with Red Hat and its offspring.

On Ubuntu 22.04, things are different. Ubuntu developers have finally realized that users' home directories should be locked down by default. So, the HOME_MODE setting in an Ubuntu 22.04 login.defs file now looks like this:

```
HOME_MODE          0750
```

This includes access permissions for a user's own personal group, but that's okay. It still effectively means that only the respective owners of the various home directories can get into them.

adduser on Debian/Ubuntu

The adduser utility is an interactive way to create user accounts and passwords with a single command, which is unique to the Debian family of Linux distros. Most of the default settings that are missing from the Debian implementation of useradd are already set for adduser. On Debian and Ubuntu 20.04, it creates user home directories with the wide-open 755 permissions value. Fortunately, that's easy to change. (We'll see how in just a bit.) On Ubuntu 22.04, it creates properly locked-down home directories with the restrictive 750 permissions value. You'll see that setting in the /etc/adduser.conf file, in the vicinity of line 56:

```
DIR_MODE=750
```

As I mentioned before, that will be set to a 755 value in Ubuntu 20.04. Just change that value to 750 to lock down the new home directories.

Although adduser is handy for just casual creation of user accounts, it doesn't offer the flexibility of useradd and it isn't suitable for use in shell scripting. One thing that adduser can do that useradd can't is to automatically encrypt a user's home directory as you create the account. To make it work, you'll first have to install the ecryptfs-utils package. So, to create an account with an encrypted home directory for Cleopatra, you do the following:

```
donnie@ubuntu-steemnode:~$ sudo apt install ecryptfs-utils

donnie@ubuntu-steemnode:~$ sudo adduser --encrypt-home cleopatra
 [sudo] password for donnie:
 Adding user 'cleopatra' ...
 Adding new group 'cleopatra' (1004) ...
 Adding new user 'cleopatra' (1004) with group 'cleopatra' ...
 Creating home directory '/home/cleopatra' ...
 Setting up encryption ...
 ************************************************************************
 YOU SHOULD RECORD YOUR MOUNT PASSPHRASE AND STORE IT IN A SAFE LOCATION.
```

```
    ecryptfs-unwrap-passphrase ~/.ecryptfs/wrapped-passphrase
    THIS WILL BE REQUIRED IF YOU NEED TO RECOVER YOUR DATA AT A LATER TIME.
    ********************************************************************
Done configuring.
 Copying files from '/etc/skel' ...
 Enter new UNIX password:
 Retype new UNIX password:
 passwd: password updated successfully
 Changing the user information for cleopatra
 Enter the new value, or press ENTER for the default
  Full Name []: Cleopatra Tabby Cat
  Room Number []: 1
  Work Phone []: 555-5556
  Home Phone []: 555-5555
  Other []:
 Is the information correct? [Y/n] Y
 donnie@ubuntu-steemnode:~$
The first time that Cleopatra logs in, she'll need to run the ecryptfs-unwrap-
passphrase command that's mentioned in the preceding output. She'll then want
to write her passphrase down and store it in a safe place:
 cleopatra@ubuntu-steemnode:~$ ecryptfs-unwrap-passphrase
 Passphrase:
 d2a6cf0c3e7e46fd856286c74ab7a412
 cleopatra@ubuntu-steemnode:~$
```

We'll look at the whole encryption thing in more detail when we get to the encryption chapter.

Hands-on lab for creating an encrypted home directory with adduser

For this lab, we'll be working with the adduser utility on an Ubuntu 22.04 VM:

1. Install the ecryptfs-utils package:

    ```
    sudo apt install ecryptfs-utils
    ```

2. Create a user account with an encrypted home directory for Cleopatra and then view the results:

    ```
    sudo adduser --encrypt-home cleopatra
    ls -l /home
    ```

3. Log in as Cleopatra and run the ecryptfs-unwrap-passphrase command:

    ```
    su - cleopatra
    ecryptfs-unwrap-passphrase
    exit
    ```

Note that some of the information that adduser asks for is optional, and you can just hit the *Enter* key for those items.

Enforcing strong password criteria

You wouldn't think that a benign-sounding topic such as strong password criteria would be so controversial, but it is. The conventional wisdom that you've undoubtedly heard for your entire computer career says:

- Make passwords of a certain minimum length.
- Make passwords that consist of a combination of uppercase letters, lowercase letters, numbers, and special characters.
- Ensure that passwords don't contain any words that are found in the dictionary or that are based on the users' own personal data.
- Force users to change their passwords on a regular basis.

But using your favorite search engine, you'll see that different experts disagree on the details of these criteria. For example, you'll see disagreements about whether passwords should be changed every 30, 60, or 90 days, disagreements about whether all four types of characters need to be in a password, and even disagreements on what the minimum length of a password should be.

The most interesting controversy of all comes from—of all places—the guy who invented the preceding criteria to begin with. He now says that it's all bunk and regrets having come up with it. He now says that we should be using passphrases that are long, yet easy to remember. He also says that they should be changed only if they've been breached.

Bill Burr, the former National Institutes of Standards and Technology (NIST) engineer who created the strong password criteria that I outlined earlier, shares his thoughts about why he now disavows his own work. Refer to `https://www.pcmag.com/news/355496/you-might-not-need-complex-alphanumeric-passwords-after-all`.

And, since the original edition of this book was published, NIST has come to agree with Bill Burr. They have now changed their password implementation criteria to match Mr. Burr's recommendations. You can read about that at:

`https://www.riskcontrolstrategies.com/2018/01/08/new-nist-guidelines-wrong/`.

However, having said all that, there is the reality that many organizations are still wedded to the idea of using complex passwords that regularly expire, and you'll have to abide by their rules if you can't convince them otherwise. And besides, if you are using traditional passwords, you do want them to be strong enough to resist any sort of password attack. So now, we'll take a look at the mechanics of enforcing strong password criteria on a Linux system.

I have to confess that I had never before thought to try creating a passphrase to use in place of a password on a Linux system. So, I just tried it on my CentOS virtual machine to see if it would work.

I created an account for Maggie, my black-and-white tuxedo kitty. For her password, I entered the passphrase I like other kitty cats. You may think, "Oh, that's terrible. This doesn't meet any complexity criteria, and it uses dictionary words. How is that secure?" But the fact that it's a phrase with distinct words separated by blank spaces does make it secure and very difficult to brute-force.

Now, in real life, I would never create a passphrase that expresses my love for cats because it's not hard to find out that I really do love cats. Rather, I would choose a passphrase about some more obscure part of my life that nobody but me knows about. In any case, there are two advantages of passphrases over passwords. They're more difficult to crack than traditional passwords, yet they're easier for users to remember. For extra security though, don't create passphrases about a fact of your life that everybody knows about.

Installing and configuring pwquality

We'll be using the pwquality module for the **Pluggable Authentication Module (PAM)**. This is a newer technology that has replaced the old cracklib module. On any Red Hat 7 or newer type of system, and on SUSE and OpenSUSE, pwquality is installed by default, even if you do a minimal installation. If you cd into the /etc/pam.d/ directory, you can do a grep operation to check that the PAM configuration files are already set up. retry=3 means that a user will only have three tries to get the password right when logging in to the system:

```
[donnie@localhost pam.d]$ grep 'pwquality' *
password-auth:password requisite pam_pwquality.so try_first_pass
local_users_only retry=3 authtok_type=
password-auth-ac:password requisite pam_pwquality.so try_first_pass
local_users_only retry=3 authtok_type=
system-auth:password requisite pam_pwquality.so try_first_pass
local_users_only retry=3 authtok_type=
system-auth-ac:password requisite pam_pwquality.so try_first_pass
local_users_only retry=3 authtok_type=
[donnie@localhost pam.d]$
```

On Debian and Ubuntu, you'll need to install pwquality yourself, like this:

```
sudo apt install libpam-pwquality
```

The rest of the procedure is the same for all of our operating systems and consists of just editing the /etc/security/pwquality.conf file. When you open this file in your text editor, you'll see that everything is commented out, which means that no password complexity criteria are in effect. You'll also see that it's very well documented because every setting has its own explanatory comment.

You can set password complexity criteria however you want just by uncommenting the appropriate lines and setting the appropriate values. Let's take a look at just one setting:

```
# Minimum acceptable size for the new password (plus one if
# credits are not disabled which is the default). (See pam_cracklib manual.)
# Cannot be set to lower value than 6.
# minlen = 8
```

The minimum length setting works on a credit system. This means that for every different type of character class in the password, the minimum required password length will be reduced by one character. For example, let's set `minlen` to a value of 19 and try to assign Katelyn the password of `turkeylips`:

```
minlen = 19


[donnie@localhost ~]$ sudo passwd katelyn
 Changing password for user katelyn.
 New password:
 BAD PASSWORD: The password is shorter than 18 characters
 Retype new password:
 [donnie@localhost ~]$
```

Because the lowercase characters in `turkeylips` count as credit for one type of character class, we're only required to have 18 characters instead of 19. If we try this again with `TurkeyLips`, we'll get:

```
[donnie@localhost ~]$ sudo passwd katelyn
 Changing password for user katelyn.
 New password:
 BAD PASSWORD: The password is shorter than 17 characters
 Retype new password:
 [donnie@localhost ~]$
```

This time, the uppercase `T` and uppercase `L` count as a second character class, so we only need to have 17 characters in the password.

Just below the `minlen` line, you'll see the credit lines. Let's say that you don't want lowercase letters to count toward your credits. You would find this line:

```
# lcredit = 1
```

Uncomment it, and change the 1 to a 0:

```
lcredit = 0
```

Then, try assigning Katelyn `turkeylips` as a password:

```
[donnie@localhost ~]$ sudo passwd katelyn
 Changing password for user katelyn.
 New password:
```

```
BAD PASSWORD: The password is shorter than 19 characters
Retype new password:
[donnie@localhost ~]$
```

This time, the pwquality really does want 19 characters. If we set a credit value to something higher than 1, we would get credit for multiple characters of the same class type up to that value.

We can also set the credit values to negative numbers in order to require a certain number of characters types in a password. For example, we could have this:

```
dcredit = -3
```

This would require at least three digits in a password. However, it's a really bad idea to use this feature, because someone who's doing a password attack would soon find the patterns that you require, which would help the attacker to direct the attack more precisely. If you need to require that a password has multiple character types, it would be better to use the minclass parameter:

```
# minclass = 3
```

It's already set to a value of 3, which would require characters from three different classes. To use this value, all you have to do is to remove the comment symbol.

The rest of the parameters in pwquality.conf work pretty much the same way, and each one has a well-written comment to explain what it does.

> If you use your sudo privilege to set someone else's password, the system will complain if you create a password that doesn't meet the complexity criteria, but it will let you do it. If a normal user were to try to change his or her own password without sudo privileges, the system would not allow a password that doesn't meet the complexity criteria.

Hands-on lab for setting password complexity criteria

For this lab, you can use either a CentOS, AlmaLinux, or Ubuntu virtual machine, as desired. The only difference is that you won't perform *Step 1* for either CentOS or AlmaLinux:

1. For Ubuntu only, install the libpam-pwquality package:

    ```
    sudo apt install libpam-pwquality
    ```

2. Open the /etc/security/pwquality.conf file in your preferred text editor. Remove the comment symbol from in front of the minlen line and change the value to 19. It should now look like this:

    ```
    minlen = 19
    ```

3. Save the file and exit the editor.

4. Create a user account for Goldie and attempt to assign her the passwords turkeylips, TurkeyLips, and Turkey93Lips. Note the change in each warning message.

5. In the `pwquality.conf` file, comment out the `minlen` line. Uncomment the `minclass` line and the `maxclassrepeat` line. Change the `maxclassrepeat` value to 5. The lines should now look like this:

```
minclass = 3
maxclassrepeat = 5
```

6. Save the file and exit the text editor.

7. Try assigning various passwords that don't meet the complexity criteria that you've set to Goldie's account and view the results.

> • In the `/etc/login.defs` file on your CentOS 7 machine, you'll see the line `PASS_MIN_LEN 5`.
> • Supposedly, this is to set the minimum password length, but in reality, `pwquality` overrides it. So, you could set this value to anything at all, and it would have no effect. (Note that the `PASS_MIN_LEN` parameter is no longer supported on RHEL 8/9-type distros.)

Setting and enforcing password and account expiration

Something you never want is to have unused user accounts remain active. There have been incidents where an administrator set up user accounts for temporary usage, such as for a conference, and then just forgot about them after the accounts were no longer needed.

Another example would be if your company were to hire contract workers whose contract expires on a specific date. Allowing those accounts to remain active and accessible after the temporary employees leave the company would be a huge security problem. In cases like these, you want a way to ensure that temporary user accounts aren't forgotten about when they're no longer needed. If your employer subscribes to the conventional wisdom that users should change their passwords on a regular basis, then you'll also want to ensure that it gets done.

Password expiration data and account expiration data are two different things. They can be set either separately or together. When someone's password expires, he or she can change it, and everything will be all good. If somebody's account expires, only someone with the proper admin privileges can unlock it.

To get started, take a look at the expiry data for your own account. Note that you won't need `sudo` privileges to look at your own data, but you will still need to specify your own username:

```
donnie@packt:~$ chage -l donnie
 [sudo] password for donnie:
 Last password change : Oct 03, 2017
 Password expires : never
 Password inactive : never
 Account expires : never
 Minimum number of days between password change : 0
```

```
Maximum number of days between password change : 99999
Number of days of warning before password expires : 7
donnie@packt:~$
```

You can see here that no expiration data have been set. Everything here is set according to the out-of-the-box system default values. Other than the obvious items, here's a breakdown of what you see:

- **Password inactive**: If this was set to a positive number, I would have that many days to change an expired password before the system would lock out my account.
- **Minimum number of days between password change**: Because this is set to 0, I can change my password as often as I like. If it was set to a positive number, I would have to wait that number of days after changing my password before I could change it again.
- **Maximum number of days between password change**: This is set to the default value of 99999, meaning that my password will never expire.
- **Number of days of warning before password expires**: The default value is 7, but that's rather meaningless when the password is set to never expire.

> With the chage utility, you can either set password and account expiration data for other users or use the -l option to view expiration data. Any unprivileged user can use chage -l without sudo to view his or her own data. To either set data or view someone else's data, you need sudo. We'll take a closer look at chage a bit later.

Before we look at how to change expiration data, let's first look at where the default settings are stored. We'll first look at the /etc/login.defs file. Here are the three relevant lines:

```
PASS_MAX_DAYS 99999
PASS_MIN_DAYS 0
PASS_WARN_AGE 7
```

You can edit these values to fit your organization's needs. For example, changing PASS_MAX_DAYS to a value of 30 would cause all new user passwords from that point on to have 30-day expiration data. (By the way, setting the default password expiry data in login.defs works for all of the Linux distros that we're using.)

Configuring default expiry data for useradd for Red Hat-type systems only

The /etc/default/useradd file has the rest of the default settings. In this case, we'll look at the one from the AlmaLinux 9 machine:

> Ubuntu also has the useradd configuration file, but it doesn't work. No matter how you configure it, the Ubuntu version of useradd just won't read it. So, the write-up about this file only applies to Red Hat-type systems.

```
# useradd defaults file
GROUP=100
HOME=/home
INACTIVE=-1
EXPIRE=
SHELL=/bin/bash
SKEL=/etc/skel
CREATE_MAIL_SPOOL=yes
```

The EXPIRE= line sets the default expiration date for new user accounts. By default, there is no default expiration date. INACTIVE=-1 means that user accounts won't be automatically locked out after the users' passwords expire. If we set this to a positive number, then any new users will have that many days to change an expired password before the account gets locked. To change the defaults in the useradd file, you can either hand-edit the file or use useradd -D with the appropriate option switch for the item that you want to change. For example, to set a default expiration date of December 31, 2025, the command would be as follows:

```
sudo useradd -D -e 2025-12-31
```

To see the new configuration, you can either open the useradd file or just do sudo useradd -D:

```
[donnie@localhost ~]$ sudo useradd -D
 GROUP=100
 HOME=/home
 INACTIVE=-1
 EXPIRE=2023-12-31
 SHELL=/bin/bash
 SKEL=/etc/skel
 CREATE_MAIL_SPOOL=yes
[donnie@localhost ~]$
```

You've now set it so that any new user accounts that get created will have the same expiration date. You can do the same thing with either the INACTIVE setting or the SHELL setting:

```
sudo useradd -D -f 5
sudo useradd -D -s /bin/zsh

[donnie@localhost ~]$ sudo useradd -D
GROUP=100
HOME=/home
INACTIVE=5
EXPIRE=2019-12-31
SHELL=/bin/zsh
SKEL=/etc/skel
CREATE_MAIL_SPOOL=yes
[donnie@localhost ~]$
```

Now, any new user accounts that get created will have the Zsh shell set as the default shell and will have to have expired passwords changed within five days to prevent the account from being automatically locked out.

> useradd doesn't do any safety checks to ensure that the default shell that you've assigned is installed on the system. In our case, Zsh isn't installed, but useradd will still allow you to create accounts with Zsh as the default shell.

So, just how useful is this useradd configuration feature in real life? Probably not that much, unless you need to create a whole bunch of user accounts at once with the same settings. Even so, a savvy admin would just automate the process with a shell script, rather than messing around with this configuration file.

Setting expiry data on a per-account basis with useradd and usermod

You might find it useful to set the default password expiry data in login.defs, but you probably won't find it too useful to configure the useradd configuration file. Really, what are the chances that you'll want to create all user accounts with the same account expiration date? Setting password expiry data in login.defs is more useful because you'll just be saying that you want new passwords to expire within a certain number of days, rather than to have them all expire on a specific date.

Most likely, you'll want to set account expiry data on a per-account basis, depending on whether you know that the accounts will no longer be needed as of a specific date. There are three ways that you can do this:

- Use useradd with the appropriate option switches to set expiry data as you create the accounts. (If you need to create a whole bunch of accounts at once with the same expiry data, you can automate the process with a shell script.)
- Use usermod to modify expiry data on existing accounts. (The beautiful thing about usermod is that it uses the same option switches as useradd.)
- Use chage to modify expiry data on existing accounts. (This one uses a whole different set of option switches.)

You can use useradd and usermod to set account expiry data, but not to set password expiry data. The only two option switches that affect account expiry data are as follows:

- -e: Use this to set an expiration date for the account, in the form YYYY-MM-DD.
- -f: Use this to set the number of days after the user's password expires that you want for his or her account to get locked out.

Let's say that you want to create an account for Charlie that will expire at the end of 2025. On a Red Hat-type machine, you could enter this:

```
sudo useradd -e 2025-12-31 charlie
```

On a non-Red Hat-type machine, you'd have to add the option switches that create the home directory and assign the correct default shell:

```
sudo useradd -m -d /home/charlie -s /bin/bash -e 2025-12-31 charlie
```

Use `chage -l` to verify what you've entered:

```
donnie@ubuntu-steemnode:~$ sudo chage -l charlie
Last password change : Oct 06, 2017
Password expires : never
Password inactive : never
Account expires : Dec 31, 2025
Minimum number of days between password change : 0
Maximum number of days between password change : 99999
Number of days of warning before password expires : 7
donnie@ubuntu-steemnode:~$
```

Now, let's say that Charlie's contract has been extended, and you need to change his account expiration to the end of January 2026. You'll use `usermod` the same way on any Linux distro:

```
sudo usermod -e 2026-01-31 charlie
```

Again, verify that everything is correct with `chage -l`:

```
donnie@ubuntu-steemnode:~$ sudo chage -l charlie
Last password change : Oct 06, 2017
Password expires : never
Password inactive : never
Account expires : Jan 31, 2026
Minimum number of days between password change : 0
Maximum number of days between password change : 99999
Number of days of warning before password expires : 7
donnie@ubuntu-steemnode:~$
```

Optionally, you can set the number of days before an account with an expired password will get locked out:

```
sudo usermod -f 5 charlie
```

But if you were to do that now, you wouldn't see any difference in the `chage -l` output because we still haven't set expiration data for Charlie's password.

Setting expiry data on a per-account basis with chage

You will only use `chage` to modify existing accounts, and you will use it for setting either an account expiration or a password expiration. Here are the relevant option switches:

Option	Explanation
-d	If you use the -d 0 option on someone's account, you'll force the user to change his or her password on their next login.
-E	This is equivalent to the lowercase -e for useradd or usermod. It sets the expiration date for the user account.
-I	This is equivalent to -f for useradd or usermod. It sets the number of days before an account with an expired password will be locked out.
-m	This sets the minimum number of days between password changes. In other words, if Charlie changes his password today, the -m 5 option will force him to wait five days before he can change his password again.
-M	This sets the maximum number of days before a password expires. (Be aware, though, that if Charlie last set his password 89 days ago, using a -m 90 option on his account will cause his password to expire tomorrow, not 90 days from now.)
-W	This will set the number of warning days for passwords that are about to expire.

You can set just one of these data items at a time or you can set them all at once. In fact, to avoid frustrating you with a different demo for each individual item, let's set them all at once, except for -d 0, and then we'll see what we've got:

```
donnie@ubuntu-steemnode:~$ sudo chage -E 2026-02-28 -I 4 -m 3 -M 90 -W 4
charlie

donnie@ubuntu-steemnode:~$ sudo chage -l charlie
 Last password change : Oct 06, 2019
 Password expires : Jan 04, 2026
 Password inactive : Jan 08, 2026
 Account expires : Feb 28, 2026
 Minimum number of days between password change : 3
 Maximum number of days between password change : 90
 Number of days of warning before password expires : 4
donnie@ubuntu-steemnode:~$
```

All the expiration data have now been set.

For our final example, let's say that you've just created a new account for Samson, and you want to force him to change his password the first time he logs in. There are two ways to do that. Either way, you would do it after you've set his password initially, using one of these two commands:

```
sudo chage -d 0 samson
  or
sudo passwd -e samson
```

```
donnie@ubuntu-steemnode:~$ sudo chage -l samson
Last password change : password must be changed
Password expires : password must be changed
Password inactive : password must be changed
Account expires : never
Minimum number of days between password change : 0
Maximum number of days between password change : 99999
Number of days of warning before password expires : 7
donnie@ubuntu-steemnode:~$
```

Next, we will go through a hands-on lab.

Hands-on lab for setting account and password expiry data

In this lab, you'll create a couple of new user accounts, set expiration data, and view the results. You can do this lab on any of your virtual machines. The only difference will be with the useradd commands:

1. On your CentOS or AlmaLinux VM, create a user account for Samson with the expiration date of June 30, 2025, and view the results:

```
sudo useradd -e 2025-06-30 samson
sudo chage -l samson
```

2. For Ubuntu, run these commands:

```
sudo useradd -m -d /home/samson -s /bin/bash -e 2025-06-30 samson
sudo chage -l samson
```

3. Use usermod to change Samson's account expiration date to July 31, 2025:

```
sudo usermod -e 2025-07-31 samson
sudo chage -l samson
```

4. Assign a password to Samson's account, then force him to change his password on his first login. Log in as Samson, change his password, then log in to your own account:

```
sudo passwd samson
sudo passwd -e samson
sudo chage -l samson
su - samson
exit
```

5. Use chage to set a five-day waiting period for changing passwords, a password expiration period of 90 days, an inactivity period of two days, and a warning period of five days:

```
sudo chage -m 5 -M 90 -I 2 -W 5 samson
sudo chage -l samson
```

6. Keep this account because you'll be using it for the lab in the next section.

Next, let's see how to prevent brute-force attacks.

Preventing brute-force password attacks

Amazingly enough, this is another topic that engenders a bit of controversy. I mean, nobody denies the wisdom of automatically locking out user accounts that are under attack. The controversial part concerns the number of failed login attempts that we should allow before locking the account.

Back in the stone age of computing, so long ago that I still had a full head of hair, the early Unix operating systems only allowed users to create a password with a maximum of eight lowercase letters. So in those days, it was possible for early man to brute-force someone else's password just by sitting down at the keyboard and typing in random passwords. That's when the philosophy started of having user accounts get locked out after only three failed login attempts. Nowadays, with strong passwords, or better yet, a strong passphrase, setting a lockout value of three failed login attempts will do three things:

- It will unnecessarily frustrate users.
- It will cause extra work for help desk personnel.
- If an account really is under attack, it will lock the account before you've had a chance to gather information about the attacker.

Setting the lockout value to something more realistic, such as 100 failed login attempts, will still provide good security, while still giving you enough time to gather information about the attackers. Just as importantly, you won't cause undue frustration to users and help desk personnel.

Anyway, regardless of how many failed login attempts your employer allows you to allow, you'll still need to know how to set it all up. On RHEL 7-type systems and Ubuntu 18.04, you'll do this by configuring the pam_tally2 PAM. On RHEL 8/9-type systems and Ubuntu 20.04/22.04, you'll instead configure the pam_faillock PAM module. Let's dig in and see how it's done.

Configuring the pam_tally2 PAM module on CentOS 7

To make this magic work, we'll rely on our good friend, PAM. The pam_tally2 module comes already installed on CentOS 7, but it isn't configured. We'll begin by editing the /etc/pam.d/login file. Figuring out how to configure it is easy because there's an example at the bottom of the pam_tally2 man page:

```
EXAMPLES
 Add the following line to /etc/pam.d/login to lock the account after
4 failed logins. Root account will be locked as well. The accounts will be
automatically unlocked after 20 minutes. The module does not have to be
called in the account phase because the login calls pam_setcred(3)
correctly.
 auth required pam_securetty.so
 auth required pam_tally2.so deny=4 even_deny_root
unlock_time=1200
 auth required pam_env.so
 auth required pam_unix.so
```

```
auth required pam_nologin.so
account required pam_unix.so
password required pam_unix.so
session required pam_limits.so
session required pam_unix.so
session required pam_lastlog.so nowtmp
session optional pam_mail.so standard
```

> If you're working with a text-mode server, you'll only need to configure the `/etc/pam.d/login` file. But if you're working with a machine that's running a graphical desktop environment, you'll also need to configure the `/etc/pam.d/password.auth` and `/etc/pam.d/system.auth` files. You'll see how to do that when you get to the hands-on lab.

In the second line of the example, we see that `pam_tally2` is set with the following parameters:

- **deny=4:** This means that the user account under attack will get locked out after only four failed login attempts.
- **even_deny_root:** This means that even the root user account will get locked if it's under attack.
- **unlock_time=1200:** The account will get automatically unlocked after 1,200 seconds, or 20 minutes.

Now, if you look at the actual `login` file on your virtual machine, you'll see that it doesn't look exactly like this example `login` file that's on the man page. That's okay, we'll still make it work.

Once you've configured the `login` file and have had a failed login, you'll see a new file created in the `/var/log` directory. You'll view information from that file with the `pam_tally2` utility. You can also use `pam_tally2` to manually unlock a locked account if you don't want to wait for the timeout period:

```
donnie@centos7:~$ sudo pam_tally2
Login Failures Latest failure From
charlie 5 10/07/17 16:38:19
donnie@centos7:~$ sudo pam_tally2 --user=charlie --reset
Login Failures Latest failure From
charlie 5 10/07/17 16:38:19
donnie@centos7:~$ sudo pam_tally2
donnie@centos7:~$
```

Note that, after I did the reset on Charlie's account, I received no output from doing another query.

Hands-on lab for configuring pam_tally2 on CentOS 7

Configuring `pam_tally2` is super easy because it only requires adding one line to the `/etc/pam.d/login`, `/etc/pam.d/password.auth`, and `/etc/pam.d/system.auth` files. To make things even easier, you can just copy and paste that line from the example on the `pam_tally2` man page. In spite of what I said earlier about bumping the number of failed logins up to 100, we'll keep that number at 4 for now, because I know that you don't want to have to do 100 failed logins in order to demo this:

1. On the CentOS 7 virtual machine, open the `/etc/pam.d/login` file for editing. Look for the line that invokes the `pam_securetty` module. (That should be around line 2.) Beneath that line, insert this line:

```
auth required pam_tally2.so deny=4 even_deny_root unlock_time=1200
```

2. Save the file and exit the editor.

3. Place the same line at the top of the `/etc/pam.d/password.auth` and `/etc/pam.d/system.auth` files, just above the first `auth required` line. (The comment at the top of these files says to not hand-edit them because running `authconfig` will destroy the edits. Unfortunately, you have to hand edit them, because `authconfig` won't configure this for you.)

4. For this step, you'll need to log out of your own account because `pam_tally2` doesn't work with `su`. So log out and, while purposely using the wrong password, attempt to log in to the `samson` account that you created in the previous lab. Keep doing that until you see a message saying that the account is locked. Note that when the `deny` value is set to 4, it will actually take five failed login attempts to lock Samson out.

5. Log back in to your own user account. Run this command and note the output:

```
sudo pam_tally2
```

6. For this step, you'll simulate that you're a help desk worker, and Samson has just called to request that you unlock his account. After verifying that you really are talking to the real Samson, enter the following two commands:

```
sudo pam_tally2 --user=samson --reset
sudo pam_tally2
```

7. Now that you've seen how this works, open the `/etc/pam.d/login` file for editing. Change the `deny=` parameter from 4 to 100 and save the file. (This will make your configuration a bit more realistic in terms of modern security philosophy.)

Next, let's look at configuring `pam_faillock` on our AlmaLinux machines.

Configuring pam_faillock on AlmaLinux 8/9

The `pam_faillock` module is already installed on any RHEL 8 or RHEL 9-type of Linux distro. Since the basic concepts of `pam_faillock` are pretty much the same as they are for `pam_tally2`, we'll dispense with the preliminary explanations and jump right to the hands-on procedure.

Hands-on lab for configuring pam_faillock on AlmaLinux 8 or AlmaLinux 9

Although you can enable and configure `pam_faillock` by hand-editing the PAM configuration files, the RHEL distros provide an easier method, which is called **authselect**. (Note that this procedure works exactly the same for either a text-mode or GUI-type machine.)

1. On either an AlmaLinux 8 or AlmaLinux 9 VM, view the available authselect profiles by doing:

    ```
    [donnie@localhost ~]$ sudo authselect list
    - minimal      Local users only for minimal installations
    - sssd         Enable SSSD for system authentication (also for local users
    only)
    - winbind      Enable winbind for system authentication
    [donnie@localhost ~]$
    ```

2. For now, at least, we're only dealing with local users. So, we'll use the `minimal` profile. View the features of this profile like this:

    ```
    [donnie@localhost ~]$ sudo authselect list-features minimal

    . . .

    . . .

    with-faillock

    . . .

    . . .

    [donnie@localhost ~]$
    ```

3. Note that there are a lot of included features, but we're only interested in the `with-faillock` feature.

4. Enable the minimal profile, like this:

    ```
    sudo authselect select minimal --force
    ```

5. After enabling a profile, we can now enable the `pam_faillock` module, like this:

    ```
    sudo authselect enable-feature with-faillock
    ```

6. In the `/etc/security/` directory, open the `faillock.conf` file in your favorite text editor. Look for these four lines:

    ```
    # silent
    # deny = 3
    # unlock_time = 600
    # even_deny_root
    ```

7. Remove the preceding comment symbols from all four lines, and save the file.

8. Create a user account for Vicky by doing:

    ```
    sudo useradd vicky
    sudo passwd vicky
    ```

9. Open another terminal, and have Vicky deliberately make three failed login attempts. View the results in your own terminal, like this:

```
[donnie@localhost ~]$ sudo faillock
donnie:
When                    Type   Source
Valid
vicky:
When                    Type   Source
Valid
2022-10-12 15:54:35 RHOST 192.168.0.16
V
2022-10-12 15:54:42 RHOST 192.168.0.16
V
2022-10-12 15:54:46 RHOST 192.168.0.16
V
[donnie@localhost ~]$
```

10. Then, before the timer expires, have Vicky try to log in again with her own correct password.

11. After the 10-minute timer expires, have Vicky try to log in with the correct password.

12. Have the user log out. Then, have the user again deliberately make three failed login attempts. This time, reset the user's account before the timer expires, like this:

```
sudo faillock --reset --user vicky
```

That's it for this lab.

Doing this on Ubuntu is a bit different, so let's now look at that.

Configuring pam_faillock on Ubuntu 20.04 and Ubuntu 22.04

Sadly, the `authselect` utility isn't available for Ubuntu, so we'll just have to hand-edit the PAM configuration files. Here's the procedure.

Hands-on lab for configuring pam_faillock on Ubuntu 20.04 and Ubuntu 22.04

1. Open the `/etc/pam.d/common-auth` file in your favorite text editor. At the top of the file, insert these two lines:

```
auth        required                    pam_faillock.so preauth silent

auth        required                    pam_faillock.so authfail
```

2. Open the `/etc/pam.d/common-account` file in your text editor. At the bottom of the file, add this line:

```
account     required                    pam_faillock.so
```

3. Configure the `/etc/security/faillock.conf` file the same way that I showed you in Step 5 of the preceding lab for AlmaLinux.

4. Test the setup as outlined in Steps 6 through 8 of the preceding AlmaLinux lab.

5. And that's all there is to it. Next, let's look at how to manually lock a user's account.

Locking user accounts

Okay, you've just seen how to have Linux automatically lock user accounts that are under attack. There will also be times when you'll want manually lock out user accounts. Let's look at a few examples:

- When a user goes on vacation and you want to ensure that nobody monkeys around with that user's account while he or she is gone
- When a user is under investigation for questionable activities
- When a user leaves the company

With regard to the last point, you may be asking yourself, *Why can't we just delete the accounts of people who are no longer working here?* And, you certainly can, easily enough. However, before you do so, you'll need to check with your local laws to make sure that you don't get yourself into deep trouble. Here in the United States, for example, we have the **Sarbanes-Oxley** law, which restricts what files publicly traded companies can delete from their computers. If you were to delete a user account, along with that user's home directory and mail spool, you just might be running afoul of Sarbanes-Oxley or whatever you may have as the equivalent law in your own home country.

Anyway, there are two utilities that you can use to temporarily lock a user account:

- **usermod**
- **passwd**

> In apparent contradiction to what I just said, at some point, you will need to remove inactive user accounts. That's because malicious actors can use an inactive account to perform their dirty deeds, especially if that inactive account had any sort of administrative privileges. But when you do remove the accounts, make sure that you do so in accordance with local laws and with company policy. In fact, your best bet is to ensure that your organization has written guidelines for removing inactive user accounts in its change management procedures.

Using usermod to lock a user account

Let's say that Katelyn has gone on maternity leave and will be gone for several weeks. We can lock her account by doing:

```
sudo usermod -L katelyn
```

When you look at Katelyn's entry in the `/etc/shadow` file, you'll now see an exclamation point in front of her password hash, like this:

```
katelyn:!$6$uA5ecH1A$MZ6q5U.cyY2SRSJezV000AudP.
ckXXndBNsXUdMI1vPO8aFmlLXcbGV25K5HSSaCv4RlDilwzlXq/hKvXRkpB/:17446:0:99999:7:::
```

This exclamation point prevents the system from reading her password hash, which effectively locks her out of the system.

To unlock her account, just do this:

```
sudo usermod -U katelyn
```

You'll see that the exclamation point has been removed so that she can now log in to her account.

Using passwd to lock user accounts

You could also lock Katelyn's account like this:

```
sudo passwd -l katelyn
```

This does the same job as usermod -L, but in a slightly different manner. For one thing, passwd -l will give you some feedback about what's going on, whereas usermod -L gives you no feedback at all. On Ubuntu, the feedback looks like this:

```
donnie@ubuntu-steemnode:~$ sudo passwd -l katelyn
 passwd: password expiry information changed.
donnie@ubuntu-steemnode:~$
```

On CentOS or AlmaLinux, the feedback looks like this:

```
[donnie@localhost ~]$ sudo passwd -l katelyn
 Locking password for user katelyn.
 passwd: Success
[donnie@localhost ~]$
```

Also, on a CentOS or AlmaLinux machine, you'll see that passwd -l places two exclamation points in front of the password hash, instead of just one. Either way, the effect is the same.

To unlock Katelyn's account, just do this:

```
sudo passwd -u katelyn
```

> In versions of Red Hat or CentOS prior to version 7, usermod -U would remove only one of the exclamation points that passwd -l places in front of the shadow file password hash, thereby leaving the account still locked. No big deal, though, because running usermod -U again would remove the second exclamation point.
>
> Ever since the introduction of the RHEL 7-type distros, this has been fixed. The passwd -l command still places two exclamation points in the shadow file, but usermod -U now removes both of them. (That's a shame, really, because it ruined a perfectly good demo that I liked to do for my students.)

Locking the root user account

The cloud is big business nowadays, and it's now quite common to rent a virtual private server from companies such as Rackspace, DigitalOcean, or Microsoft Azure. These can serve a variety of purposes:

- You can run your own website, where you install your own server software instead of letting a hosting service do it.
- You can set up a web-based app for other people to access.
- Recently, I saw a YouTube demo on a crypto-mining channel that showed how to set up a Proof of Stake master node on a rented virtual private server.

One thing that most of these cloud services have in common is that when you first set up your account and the provider sets up a virtual machine for you, they'll have you log in to the root user account. (It even happens with Ubuntu, even though the root account is disabled on a local installation of Ubuntu.)

I know that there are some folks who just keep logging in to the root account of these cloud-based servers and think nothing of it, but that's really a horrible idea. There are botnets, such as the Hail Mary botnet, that continuously scan the Internet for servers that have their Secure Shell port exposed to the Internet. When the botnets find one, they'll do a brute-force password attack against the root user account of that server. And yes, the botnets sometimes are successful at breaking in, especially if the root account is set with a weak password.

So, the first thing that you want to do when you set up a cloud-based server is to create a normal user account for yourself and set it up with full sudo privileges. Then, log out of the root user account, log in to your new account, and do this:

```
sudo passwd -l root
```

I mean, really, why take the chance of getting your root account compromised?

Setting up security banners

Something that you really, really don't want is to have a login banner that says something to the effect of *Welcome to our network*. I say that because, quite a few years ago, I attended a mentored SANS course on incident handling. Our instructor told us a story about how a company took a suspected network intruder to court, only to get the case thrown out. The reason? The alleged intruder said, "Well, I saw the message that said *Welcome to the network*, so I thought that I really was welcome there." Yeah, supposedly, that was enough to get the case thrown out.

A few years later, I related that story to the students in one of my Linux admin classes. One student said, "That makes no sense. We all have welcome mats at our front doors, but that doesn't mean that burglars are welcome to come in." I have to confess that he had a good point, and I now have to wonder about the veracity of the story.

At any rate, just to be on the safe side, you do want to set up login messages that make it clear that only authorized users are allowed to access the system.

Using the motd file

The /etc/motd file will present a message banner to anyone who logs in to a system through Secure Shell. On your CentOS or AlmaLinux machine, an empty motd file is already there. On your Ubuntu machine, the motd file isn't there, but it's a simple matter to create one. Either way, open the file in your text editor and create your message. Save the file and test it by remotely logging in through Secure Shell. You should see something like this:

```
maggie@192.168.0.100's password:
Last login: Sat Oct 7 20:51:09 2017
Warning: Authorized Users Only!
All others will be prosecuted.
[maggie@localhost ~]$
```

motd stands for **Message of the Day.**

Ubuntu comes with a dynamic MOTD system that displays messages from Ubuntu's parent company and messages about the operating system. When you create a new motd file in the /etc directory, whatever message you put in it will show up at the end of the dynamic output, like so:

```
Welcome to Ubuntu 22.04.1 LTS (GNU/Linux 5.15.0-48-generic x86_64)

 * Documentation:  https://help.ubuntu.com
 * Management:     https://landscape.canonical.com
 * Support:        https://ubuntu.com/advantage

  System information as of Thu Oct 13 06:20:54 PM UTC 2022

  System load:  0.0            Processes:               103
  Usage of /:   47.8% of 9.75GB  Users logged in:         1
  Memory usage: 12%            IPv4 address for enp0s3: 192.168.0.11
  Swap usage:   0%

39 updates can be applied immediately.
To see these additional updates run: apt list --upgradable

Warning!!! Authorized users only!
Last login: Thu Oct 13 17:14:52 2022 from 192.168.0.16
```

The Warning!!! Authorized users only! line is what I placed into the /etc/motd file.

Using the issue file

The issue file, also found in the /etc directory, shows a message on the local terminal, just above the login prompt. A default issue file will just contain macro code that shows information about the machine. Here's an example from an Ubuntu machine:

```
Ubuntu 22.04.1 LTS \n \l
```

On a Red Hat-type machine, it would look like this:

```
\S
Kernel \r on an \m
```

On an Ubuntu machine, the banner would look something like this:

```
Ubuntu 18.04 LTS packtpub1 tty1

Hint: Num Lock on

packtpub1 login: _
```

Figure 3.1 -- The issue file banner

On a Red Hat-type machine, it would look something like this:

```
CentOS Linux 7 (Core)
Kernel 3.10.0-693.2.2 e17.x86_64 on an x86_64

localhost login: _
```

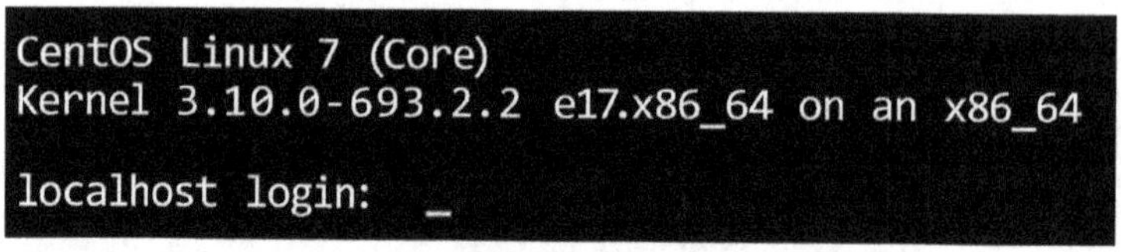

Figure 3.2 -- A default CentOS issue file banner

You could put a security message in the issue file, and it would show up after a reboot:

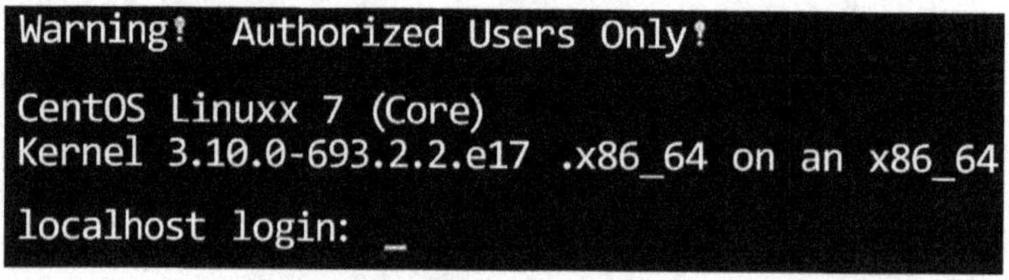

```
Warning!  Authorized Users Only!

CentOS Linuxx 7 (Core)
Kernel 3.10.0-693.2.2.e17 .x86_64 on an x86_64

localhost login: _
```

Figure 3.3 -- A modified CentOS issue file banner

In reality, is there really any point in placing a security message in the issue file? If your servers are properly locked away in a server room with controlled access, then probably not. For desktop machines that are out in the open, this would be more useful.

Using the issue.net file

Just don't. It's for `telnet` logins, and anyone who has `telnet` enabled on their servers is seriously screwing up. However, for some strange reason, the `issue.net` file still hangs around in the `/etc` directory.

Detecting compromised passwords

Yes, dear hearts, the bad guys do have extensive dictionaries of passwords that either are commonly used or have been compromised. One of the most effective ways of brute-forcing passwords is to use these dictionaries to perform a dictionary attack. This is when the password-cracking tool reads passwords from a specified dictionary and tries each one until either the list has been exhausted or the attack is successful. So, how do you know if your password is on one of those lists? Easy. Just use one of the online services that will check your password for you. One popular site is *Have I Been Pwned?*, which you can see here:

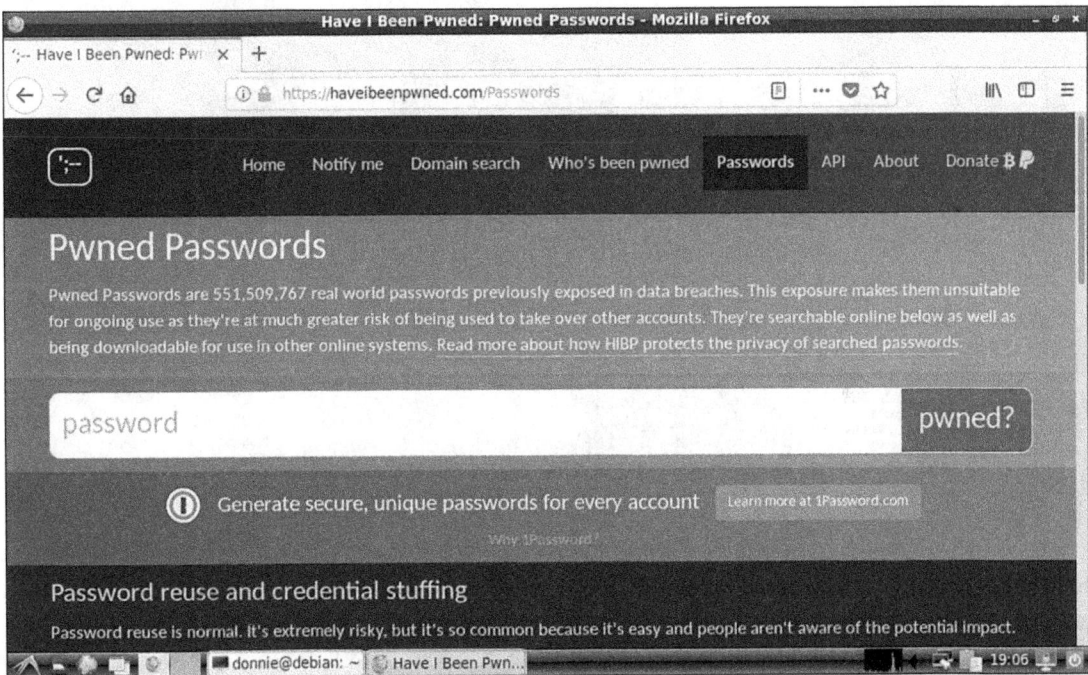

Figure 3.4 -- The Have I Been Pwned site

You can get to *Have I Been Pwned?* here:

`https://haveibeenpwned.com`

All you really have to do is to type in your password, and the service will show if it's on any lists of compromised passwords. But think about it. Do you really want to send your production password to somebody's website? Yeah, I thought not. Instead, let's just send a hash value of the password. Better yet, let's just send enough of the hash to allow the site to find the password in its database, but not so much that they can figure out what your exact password is. We'll do that by using the *Have I Been Pwned?* **Application Programming Interface** (**API**).

To demonstrate the basic principle, let's use `curl`, along with the API, to see a list of password hashes that have `21BD1` as part of their values. (You can do this on any of your virtual machines. I'll just do it on the Fedora workstation that I'm currently using to type this.) Just run this:

```
curl https://api.pwnedpasswords.com/range/21BD1
```

You're going to get a lot of output like this, so I'll just show the first few lines:

```
[donnie@fedora-teaching ~]$ curl https://api.pwnedpasswords.com/range/21BD1
0018A45C4D1DEF81644B54AB7F969B88D65:1
00D4F6E8FA6EECAD2A3AA415EEC418D38EC:2
011053FD0102E94D6AE2F8B83D76FAF94F6:1
012A7CA357541F0AC487871FEEC1891C49C:2
0136E006E24E7D152139815FB0FC6A50B15:3
01A85766CD276B17DE6DA022AA3CADAC3CE:3
024067E46835A540D6454DF5D1764F6AA63:3
02551CADE5DDB7F0819C22BFBAAC6705182:1
025B243055753383B479EF34B44B562701D:2
02A56D549B5929D7CD58EEFA97BFA3DDDB3:8
02F1C470B30D5DDFF9E914B90D35AB7A38F:3
03052B53A891BDEA802D11691B9748C12DC:6
. . .
. . .
```

Let's pipe this into `wc -1`, a handy counting utility, to see how many matching results we've found:

```
[donnie@fedora-teaching ~]$ curl https://api.pwnedpasswords.com/range/21BD1 |
wc -1
% Total % Received % Xferd Average Speed Time Time Time Current
Dload Upload Total Spent Left Speed
100 20592 0 20592 0 0 197k 0 --:--:-- --:--:-- --:--:-- 199k
526
[donnie@fedora-teaching ~]$
```

According to this, we've found 526 matches. But that's not very useful, so let's fancy things up just a bit. We'll do that by creating the `pwnedpasswords.sh` shell script, which looks like this:

```
#!/bin/bash
candidate_password=$1
```

```
echo "Candidate password: $candidate_password"
full_hash=$(echo -n $candidate_password | sha1sum | awk '{print substr($1, 0,
32)}')
prefix=$(echo $full_hash | awk '{print substr($1, 0, 5)}')
suffix=$(echo $full_hash | awk '{print substr($1, 6, 26)}')
if curl https://api.pwnedpasswords.com/range/$prefix | grep -i $suffix;
 then echo "Candidate password is compromised";
 else echo "Candidate password is OK for use";
fi
```

Okay, I can't try to turn you into a shell scripting guru at the moment, but here's a simplified explanation:

- **candidate_password=$1:** This requires you to enter the password that you want to check when you invoke the script.
- **full_hash= , prefix=, suffix=:** These lines calculate the SHA1 hash value of the password, and then extract just the portions of the hash that we want to send to the password-checking service.
- **if curl:** We wrap up with an `if..then..else` structure that sends the selected portions of the password hash to the checking service, and then tells us whether or not the password has been compromised.

After saving the file, add the executable privilege for the user, like so:

```
chmod u+x pwnedpasswords.sh
```

Now, let's see if TurkeyLips, my all-time favorite password, has been compromised:

```
[donnie@fedora-teaching ~]$ ./pwnedpasswords.sh TurkeyLips
Candidate password: TurkeyLips
% Total % Received % Xferd Average Speed Time Time Time Current
Dload Upload Total Spent Left Speed
0 0 0 0 0 0 0 0 --:--:-- --:--:-- --:--:--
09FDEDF4CA44D6B432645D6C1D3A8D4A16BD:2
100 21483 0 21483 0 0 107k 0 --:--:-- --:--:-- --:--:-- 107k
Candidate password is compromised
[donnie@fedora-teaching ~]$
```

Yeah, it's been compromised, all right. So, I reckon that I don't want to use that for a production password.

Now, let's try it again, except with a random two-digit number tacked on at the end:

```
[donnie@fedora-teaching ~]$ ./pwnedpasswords.sh TurkeyLips98
Candidate password: TurkeyLips98
% Total % Received % Xferd Average Speed Time Time Time Current
Dload Upload Total Spent Left Speed
100 20790 0 20790 0 0 110k 0 --:--:-- --:--:-- --:--:-- 110k
```

```
Candidate password is OK for use
[donnie@fedora-teaching ~]$
```

Well, it says that this one is okay. Still, though, you probably don't want to use such a simple permutation of a password that's known to have been compromised.

> I'd like to take credit for the shell script that I've presented here, but I can't. That was a creation of my buddy, Leo Dorrendorf of the former VDOO Internet of Things security company, which has since been acquired by JFrog. (I've reproduced the script here with his kind permission.)
>
> If you're interested in security solutions for your Internet of Things devices, you can check them out here:
>
> https://jfrog.com/security-and-compliance/?vr=1/
>
> Full disclosure: the VDOO/JFrog company has been one of my clients.

Now, having said all of this, I still need to remind you that a passphrase is still better than a password. Not only is a passphrase harder to crack, it's also much less likely to be on anyone's list of compromised credentials.

Hands-on lab for detecting compromised passwords

In this lab, you'll use the pwnedpasswords API in order to check your own passwords:

1. Use curl to see how many passwords there are with the 21BD1 string in their password hashes:

```
curl https://api.pwnedpasswords.com/range/21BD1
```

2. In the home directory of any of your Linux virtual machines, create the pwnpassword.sh script with the following content:

```
#!/bin/bash
candidate_password=$1
echo "Candidate password: $candidate_password"

full_hash=$(echo -n $candidate_password | sha1sum | awk '{print
substr($1, 0, 32)}')
prefix=$(echo $full_hash | awk '{print substr($1, 0, 5)}')
suffix=$(echo $full_hash | awk '{print substr($1, 6, 26)}')

if curl https://api.pwnedpasswords.com/range/$prefix | grep -i $suffix;
        then echo "Candidate password is compromised";
        else echo "Candidate password is OK for use";
fi
```

3. Add the executable permission to the script:

```
chmod u+x pwnedpasswords.sh
```

4. Run the script, specifying TurkeyLips as a password:

```
./pwnedpasswords.sh TurkeyLips
```

5. Repeat *Step 4* as many times as you like, using a different password each time.

The user management techniques that we've looked at so far work great on a small number of computers. But what if you're working in a large enterprise? We'll look at that next.

Understanding centralized user management

In an enterprise setting, you'll often have hundreds or thousands of users and computers that you need to manage. So, logging in to each network server or each user's workstation to perform the procedures that we've just outlined would be quite unworkable. (But do bear in mind that you still need those skills.) What we need is a way to manage computers and users from one central location. Space doesn't permit me to give the complete details about the various methods for doing this. So for now, we'll just have to settle for a high-level overview.

Microsoft Active Directory

I'm not exactly a huge fan of either Windows or Microsoft. But when it comes to Active Directory, I'll have to give credit where it's due. It's a pretty slick product that vastly simplifies the management of very large enterprise networks. And yes, it is possible to add Unix/Linux computers and their users to an Active Directory domain.

I've been keeping a dark secret, and I hope that you won't hate me for it. Before I got into Linux, I obtained my MCSE certification for Windows Server 2003. Mostly, my clients work with nothing but Linux computers, but I occasionally do need to use my MCSE skills. Several years ago, a former client needed me to set up a Linux-based Nagios server as part of a Windows Server 2008 domain so that its users would be authenticated by Active Directory. It took me a while to get it figured out, but I finally did, and my client was happy.

Unless you wear many hats, as I sometimes have to do, you—as a Linux administrator—probably won't need to learn how to use Active Directory. Most likely, you'll just tell the Windows Server administrators what you need, and let them take care of it.

I know, you've been chomping at the bit to see what we can do with a Linux server. So, here goes.

Samba on Linux

Samba is a Unix/Linux daemon that can serve three purposes:

* Its primary purpose is to share directories from a Unix/Linux server with Windows workstations. The directories show up in Windows File Explorer as if they were being shared from other Windows machines.

- It can also be set up as a network print server.
- It can also be set up as a Windows domain controller.

You can install Samba version 3 on a Linux server, and set it up to act as an old-style Windows NT domain controller. It's a rather complex procedure, and it takes a while. Once it's done, you can join both Linux and Windows machines to the domain and use the normal Windows user management utilities to manage users and groups.

One of the Linux community's Holy Grails was to figure out how to emulate Active Directory on a Linux server. That became something of a reality just a few years ago, with the introduction of Samba version 4. But setting it up is a very complex procedure, and isn't something that you'll likely enjoy doing. So, perhaps we should keep searching for something even better.

FreeIPA/Identity Management on RHEL-type distros

Several years ago, the Red Hat company introduced FreeIPA as a set of packages for Fedora. Why Fedora? It's because they wanted to give it a thorough test on Fedora before making it available for actual production networks. It's now available for RHEL 7 through RHEL 9 and all of their offspring, including CentOS and AlmaLinux. This is what IPA stands for:

- Identity
- Policy
- Audit

It's something of an answer to Microsoft's Active Directory, but it still isn't a complete one. It does some cool stuff, but it's still very much a work in progress. The coolest part about it is how simple it is to install and set up. All it really takes is installing the packages from the normal repositories, opening the proper firewall ports, and then running a setup script. Then, you're all set to start adding users and computers to the new domain via FreeIPA's web interface. Here, I'm adding Cleopatra, my gray-and-white tabby kitty:

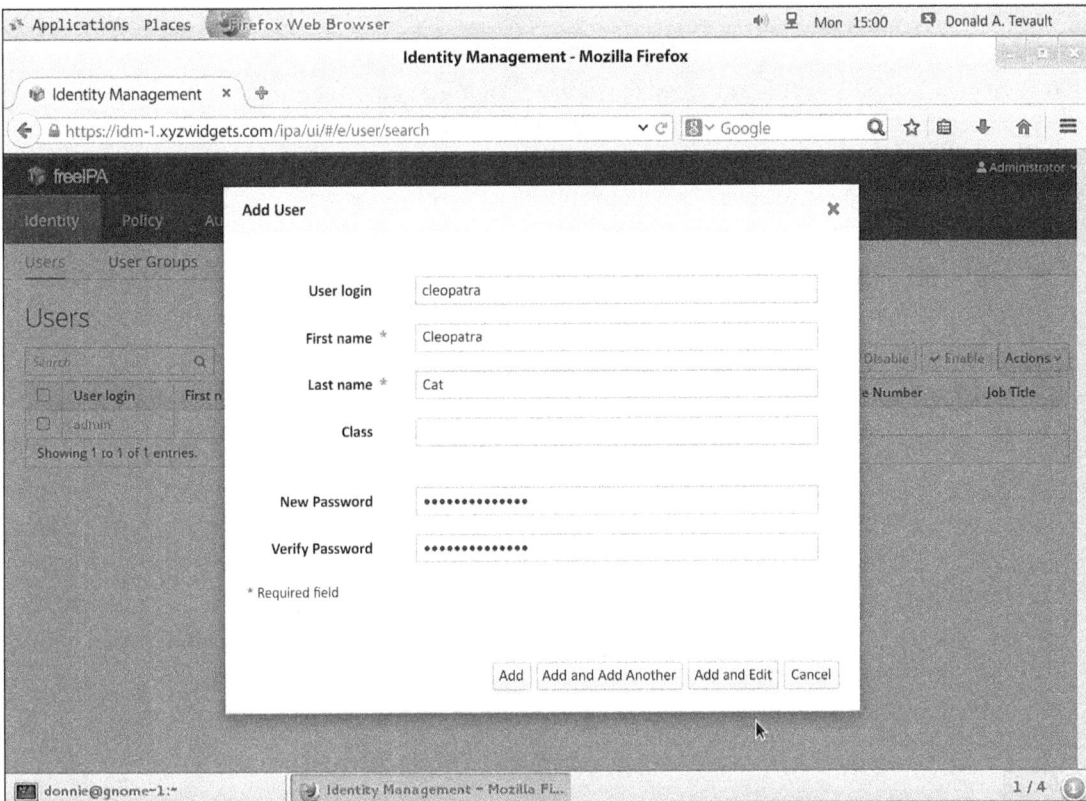

Figure 3.5 -- Adding a user via FreeIPA

Although you can add Windows machines to a FreeIPA domain, it's not recommended. But starting with RHEL/CentOS 7.1, you can use FreeIPA to create cross-domain trusts with an Active Directory domain.

> The official name of this program is FreeIPA. But for some strange reason, the Red Hat folk refuse to mention that name in their documentation. They always just refer to it as either Identity Management or IdM.

That's pretty much it for the user management topic. Let's summarize, and then move on to the next chapter.

Summary

In this chapter, we looked at how to lock down users' home directories, how to enforce strong password policies, and how to enforce account and password expiration policies. Then, we talked about a way to prevent brute-force password attacks, how to manually lock out user accounts, how to set up security banners, and how to check for compromised passwords. We wrapped things up with a brief overview of central user management systems.

In the next chapter, we'll look at how to work with various firewall utilities. I'll see you there.

Questions

1. In which file would you configure complex password criteria?

2. When using the `useradd` utility on a RHEL 7-type machine, what should the UMASK setting be in the `/etc/login.defs` file?

3. When using the `adduser` utility on an Ubuntu 20.04 machine, how would you configure the `/etc/adduser.conf` file so that new users' home directories will prevent other users from accessing them?

4. What change did the National Institute for Standards and Technology recently make to its recommended password policy?

5. Which three of the following utilities can you use to set user account expiry data?

    a. Useradd

    b. Adduser

    c. Usermod

    d. chage

6. Why might you want to lock out the user account of a former employee, rather than delete it?

    a. It's easier to lock an account than it is to delete it.

    b. It takes too long to delete an account.

    c. It's not possible to delete a user account.

    d. Deleting a user account, along with the users' files and mail spool, might get you into trouble with the law.

7. You've just created a user account for Samson, and you now want to force him to change his password the first time he logs in. Which two of the following commands will do that?

    a. `sudo chage -d 0 samson`

    b. `sudo passwd -d 0 samson`

    c. `sudo chage -e samson`

    d. `sudo passwd -e samson`

8. Which one of the following is an advantage that the adduser utility has over the traditional useradd utility?

    a. adduser can be used in shell scripts.

    b. adduser is available for all Linux distributions.

    c. adduser has an option that allows you to encrypt a user's home directory as you create the user account.

    d. adduser is also available for Unix and BSD.

9. In the newest Linux distributions, what is the name of the PAM module that you can use to enforce strong passwords?

    a. cracklib

    b. passwords

    c. Secure

    d. pwquality

Further reading

- You might not need complex, alphanumeric passwords after all: https://www.pcmag.com/news/355496/you-might-not-need-complex-alphanumeric-passwords-after-all

- The new NIST Guidelines-We had it all wrong before: https://www.riskcontrolstrategies.com/2018/01/08/new-nist-guidelines-wrong/

- Linux user management: https://www.youtube.com/playlist?list=PL6IQ3nFZzWfpy2gISpCppFk3UQVGf_x7G

- The FreeIPA Project home page: https://www.freeipa.org/page/Main_Page

- RHEL 9 Documentation (Scroll down to the Identity Management section):

- https://access.redhat.com/documentation/en-us/red_hat_enterprise_linux/9

- RHEL 8 Documentation (Scroll down to the Identity Management section): https://access.redhat.com/documentation/en-us/red_hat_enterprise_linux/8/

- RHEL 7 Documentation (Scroll down to the Identity Management section): https://access.redhat.com/documentation/en-us/red_hat_enterprise_linux/7/

- pam_faillock: Lock user account after X failed attempts: https://www.golinuxcloud.com/pam-faillock-lock-user-account-linux/

Answers

1. /etc/security/pwquality.conf

2. 077

3. Change the DIR_MODE= value to DIR_MODE=750

4. They abandoned their old philosophy about password complexity and password expirations.

5. a, c, and d

6. d
7. a and d
8. c
9. d

Join our book community

Join our community's Discord space for discussions with the author and other readers:

`https://packt.link/CyberSec`

4

Securing Your Server with a Firewall — Part 1

Security is one of those things that's best done in layers. Security-in-depth, we call it. So, on any given corporate network, you will find a firewall appliance separating the Internet from the **demilitarized zone (DMZ)**, where your Internet-facing servers are kept. You will also find a firewall appliance between the DMZ and the internal LAN, and firewall software installed on each individual server and client. We want to make it as tough as possible for intruders to reach their final destinations within our networks.

Interestingly, though, of all the major Linux distros, only the SUSE distros and the Red Hat-type distros come with a firewall already set up and enabled. Newer versions of Ubuntu come with a pre-configured firewall, but you need to activate it by running a couple of simple commands.

Since the focus of this book is on hardening our Linux servers, we'll focus this chapter on that last level of defense: the firewalls on our servers and clients. We'll cover both of the command-line netfilter interfaces, which are **iptables** and **nftables**.

In this chapter, we'll cover the following topics:

- An overview of the Linux firewall
- An overview of iptables
- An overview of nftables

In the next chapter, we'll cover **ufw** and **firewalld**, which are handy frontends for iptables and nftables.

Technical requirements

The code files for this chapter are available here: https://github.com/PacktPublishing/Mastering-Linux-Security-and-Hardening-3E.

An overview of the Linux firewall

In a typical business setting, especially in larger enterprises, you may encounter various types of firewalls in various places that can provide various types of functionality. Here are some examples:

- Edge devices that separate the Internet from an internal network translate routable public IP addresses to non-routable private IP addresses. They can also provide various types of access control to keep out unauthorized people. By also providing various types of packet inspection services, they can help prevent attacks on the internal network, keep out malware, and prevent the leakage of sensitive information from the internal network to the Internet.

- Large enterprise networks are normally divided into subnetworks, or *subnets*, with each corporate department having a subnet to call its own. Best practice dictates separating the subnets with firewalls. This helps ensure that only authorized personnel can access any given subnet.

- And, of course, you also have firewalls running on the individual servers and workstations. By providing a form of access control, they can help prevent an intruder who has compromised one machine from performing a lateral movement to another machine on the network. They can be also configured to prevent certain types of port scanning and **denial-of-service** (**DoS**) attacks.

For the first two items in the preceding list, you will likely see dedicated firewall appliances and teams of firewall administrators taking care of them. The third item in the list is where you, the Linux professional, come into the picture. In this chapter and the next, we'll look at the firewall technologies that come packaged with your Linux server and Linux workstation distros.

The name of the Linux firewall is **netfilter**. This netfilter code is compiled into the Linux kernel and is what performs the actual packet filtering. There's no way for human users to directly interface with netfilter, which means that we need some sort of helper program to interface with netfilter for us. There have been three helper programs, which are:

- **ipchains**: This was the first one and was part of the Linux kernel up through kernel version 2.4. It's now ancient history, so we won't say any more about it.

- **iptables**: This replaced ipchains in Linux kernel version 2.6. It's still used in a lot of Linux distros but is rapidly disappearing.

- **nftables**: This is the new kid on the block and is rapidly replacing iptables. As we'll see later, it has a lot of advantages over the older iptables.

All three of these helper programs do two things for us:

- They provide a command-line interface for human users.
- They take the commands that human users input and inject them into netfilter.

To make things even more interesting, we also have helper programs for our helper programs. The **Uncomplicated Firewall** (**ufw**) was created by Ubuntu developers and is a frontend for either iptables or nftables. Ubuntu comes with ufw already installed, and you can install ufw yourself on Debian and other Debian-type distros. On the Red Hat side, we have firewalld, which is also a frontend for either iptables or nftables. Note that firewalld is installed and active by default on all Red Hat-type distros, as well as the SUSE distros.

It's available as an option for Ubuntu and Debian. Both ufw and firewalld can vastly simplify the process of setting up a proper firewall. Still, though, it's sometimes helpful to know how to work with either bare iptables or bare nftables. So, let's begin by looking at iptables.

An overview of iptables

As I've mentioned, iptables is one of two command-line utilities that we can currently use to directly manage netfilter. It was originally introduced as a feature of Linux kernel version 2.6, so it's been around for a long time. With iptables, you do have a few advantages:

- It's been around long enough that most Linux admins already know how to use it.
- It's easy to use iptables commands in shell scripts to create your own custom firewall configuration.
- It has great flexibility in that you can use it to set up a simple port filter, a router, or a virtual private network.
- It still comes pre-installed on some Linux distros, although it's rapidly getting replaced by nftables.
- It's very well documented and has free-of-charge, book-length tutorials available on the Internet.

However, as you might know, there are also a few disadvantages:

- IPv4 and IPv6 each require their own special implementation of iptables. So, if your organization still needs to run IPv4 while in the process of migrating to IPv6, you'll have to configure two firewalls on each server and run a separate daemon for each. (One for IPv4; the other for IPv6.)
- If you need to do MAC bridging, that requires **ebtables**, which is the third component of iptables, with its own unique syntax.
- **arptables**, the fourth component of iptables, also requires its own daemon and syntax.
- Whenever you add a rule to a running iptables firewall, the entire iptables ruleset has to be reloaded, which can have an impact on performance.

Until recently, just plain iptables was the default firewall manager on every Linux distro. It still is on some distros, but Red Hat Enterprise Linux 7 and all of its offspring now use the new firewalld as an easier-to-use frontend for configuring iptables rules. Ubuntu comes with **Uncomplicated Firewall** (ufw), which is also an easy-to-use frontend for iptables on all Ubuntu versions up through 20.04.

In this chapter, we'll discuss setting up iptables firewall rules for both IPv4 and IPv6.

Mastering the basics of iptables

iptables consists of five tables of rules, each with its own distinct purpose:

- **Filter table:** For basic protection of our servers and clients, this might be the only table that we use.
- **Network Address Translation (NAT) table:** NAT is used to connect the public Internet to private networks.
- **Mangle table:** This is used to alter network packets as they go through the firewall.

- **Raw table:** This is for packets that don't require connection tracking.
- **Security table:** The security table is only used for systems that have SELinux installed.

Since we're currently only interested in basic host protection, we will only look at the filter table for the time being. (In a few moments, I'll show you a couple of fancy tricks that we can do with the mangle table.) Each table consists of chains of rules, and the filter table consists of the INPUT, FORWARD, and OUTPUT chains. Let's look at this on an Ubuntu 20.04 virtual machine.

> Ubuntu 20.04 LTS comes with iptables, and Ubuntu 22.04 comes with nftables. However, even if you're running Ubuntu 22.04 or newer, you'll still want to learn how to work with iptables commands. The first reason is that Ubuntu 22.04 includes a cool feature that automatically translates iptables commands to nftables commands. This allows you to use any iptables scripts that you might already have without worrying about converting them to nftables format. The second reason is that once we start talking about Ubuntu's **Uncomplicated Firewall** (**ufw**), you'll see that you still need to know iptables commands in order to configure it, regardless of which Ubuntu version that you're using.

First, we'll look at our current configuration by using the sudo `iptables -L` command:

```
donnie@ubuntu:~$ sudo iptables -L
[sudo] password for donnie:
Chain INPUT (policy ACCEPT)
target prot opt source destination
Chain FORWARD (policy ACCEPT)
target prot opt source destination
Chain OUTPUT (policy ACCEPT)
target prot opt source destination
donnie@ubuntu:~$
```

Remember that we said that you need a separate component of iptables to deal with IPv6. Here, we'll use the sudo `ip6tables -L` command:

```
donnie@ubuntu:~$ sudo ip6tables -L
Chain INPUT (policy ACCEPT)
target prot opt source destination
Chain FORWARD (policy ACCEPT)
target prot opt source destination
Chain OUTPUT (policy ACCEPT)
target prot opt source destination
donnie@ubuntu:~$
```

In both cases, you can see that there are no rules and that the machine is wide open. (Understand that Ubuntu actually does come with a pre-configured Uncomplicated Firewall and you'll also see some output that is specific to it, but we'll ignore that for the time-being so that we can work directly with iptables.) We'll start by creating a rule that will allow us to pass incoming packets from servers that our host has requested a connection to:

```
sudo iptables -A INPUT -m conntrack --ctstate ESTABLISHED,RELATED -j ACCEPT
```

Here's the breakdown of this command:

- **-A INPUT:** `-A` places a rule at the end of the specified chain, which in this case is the `INPUT` chain. We would have used `-I` had we wanted to place the rule at the beginning of the chain.
- **-m:** This calls in an iptables module. In this case, we're calling in the `conntrack` module to track connection states. This module allows `iptables` to determine whether our client has made a connection to another machine, for example.
- **--ctstate:** The `ctstate`, or connection state, portion of our rule is looking for two things. First, it's looking for a connection that the client established with a server. Then, it looks for the related connection that's coming back from the server in order to allow it to connect to the client. So, if a user was to use a web browser to connect to a website, this rule would allow packets from the web server to pass through the firewall to get to the user's browser.
- **-j:** This stands for jump. Rules jump to a specific target, which in this case is `ACCEPT`. (Please don't ask me who came up with this terminology.) So, this rule will accept packets that have been returned from the server to which the client has requested a connection.

Our new ruleset looks like this:

```
donnie@ubuntu:~$ sudo iptables -L
Chain INPUT (policy ACCEPT)
target prot opt source destination
ACCEPT all -- anywhere anywhere ctstate RELATED,ESTABLISHED
Chain FORWARD (policy ACCEPT)
target prot opt source destination
Chain OUTPUT (policy ACCEPT)
target prot opt source destination
donnie@ubuntu:~$
```

Next, we'll open up port 22 so that we can connect through Secure Shell:

```
sudo iptables -A INPUT -p tcp --dport ssh -j ACCEPT
```

Here's the breakdown:

- **-A INPUT:** As before, we want to place this rule at the end of the `INPUT` chain with `-A`.
- **-p tcp:** `-p` indicates the protocol that this rule affects. This rule affects the TCP protocol, of which Secure Shell is a part.
- **--dport ssh:** When an option name consists of more than one letter, we need to precede it with two dashes, instead of just one. The `--dport` option specifies the destination port on which we want this rule to operate. (Note that we could have also listed this portion of the rule as `--dport 22` since 22 is the number of the SSH port.)
- **-j ACCEPT:** If we put this all together with `-j ACCEPT`, then we have a rule that allows other machines to connect to this one through Secure Shell.

Now, let's say that we want this machine to be a DNS server. For that, we need to open port 53 for both the TCP and UDP protocols:

```
sudo iptables -A INPUT -p tcp --dport 53 -j ACCEPT
sudo iptables -A INPUT -p udp --dport 53 -j ACCEPT
```

Finally, we have an almost complete, usable ruleset for our INPUT chain:

```
donnie@ubuntu:~$ sudo iptables -L
Chain INPUT (policy ACCEPT)
target prot opt source destination
ACCEPT all -- anywhere anywhere ctstate
RELATED,ESTABLISHED
ACCEPT tcp -- anywhere anywhere tcp dpt:ssh
DROP all -- anywhere anywhere
Chain FORWARD (policy ACCEPT)
target prot opt source destination
Chain OUTPUT (policy ACCEPT)
target prot opt source destination
donnie@ubuntu:~$
```

However, this is only *almost* complete, because there's still one little thing that we forgot. That is, we need to allow traffic for the loopback interface. This is okay because it gives us a good chance to see how to insert a rule where we want it if we don't want it at the end. In this case, we'll insert the rule at INPUT 1, which is the first position of the INPUT chain:

```
sudo iptables -I INPUT 1 -i lo -j ACCEPT
```

> Tip: Before you inserted the ACCEPT rule for the lo interface, you may have noticed that sudo commands were taking a long time to complete and that you were getting sudo: unable to resolve host. . .Resource temporarily unavailable messages. That's because sudo needs to know the machine's hostname so that it can know which rules are allowed to run on a particular machine. It uses the loopback interface to help resolve the hostname. If the lo interface is blocked, it takes longer for sudo to resolve the hostname.

Our ruleset now looks like this:

```
donnie@ubuntu:~$ sudo iptables -L
Chain INPUT (policy ACCEPT)
target     prot opt source              destination
ACCEPT     all  --  anywhere            anywhere
ACCEPT     all  --  anywhere            anywhere            ctstate
RELATED,ESTABLISHED
ACCEPT     tcp  --  anywhere            anywhere            tcp dpt:ssh
ACCEPT     tcp  --  anywhere            anywhere            tcp dpt:domain
```

```
ACCEPT     udp  --  anywhere              anywhere              udp dpt:domain


Chain FORWARD (policy ACCEPT)
target     prot opt source               destination
Chain OUTPUT (policy ACCEPT)
target     prot opt source               destination
donnie@ubuntu:~$
```

Note how port 53 is listed as the domain port. To see port numbers instead of port names, we can use the -n switch:

```
donnie@ubuntu3:~$ sudo iptables -L -n
Chain INPUT (policy ACCEPT)
target     prot opt source               destination
ACCEPT     all  --  0.0.0.0/0            0.0.0.0/0
ACCEPT     all  --  0.0.0.0/0            0.0.0.0/0            ctstate
RELATED,ESTABLISHED
ACCEPT     tcp  --  0.0.0.0/0            0.0.0.0/0            tcp dpt:22
ACCEPT     tcp  --  0.0.0.0/0            0.0.0.0/0            tcp dpt:53
ACCEPT     udp  --  0.0.0.0/0            0.0.0.0/0            udp dpt:53


Chain FORWARD (policy ACCEPT)
target     prot opt source               destination


Chain OUTPUT (policy ACCEPT)
target     prot opt source               destination
donnie@ubuntu3:~$
```

Now, as things currently stand, we're still allowing *everything* to get through, because we still haven't created a rule that blocks what we haven't specifically allowed. Before we do that, though, let's look at a few more things that we might want to allow.

Blocking ICMP with iptables

The conventional wisdom that you may have heard for most of your career is that we need to block all the packets from the **Internet Control Message Protocol (ICMP)**. The idea you may have been told is to make your server invisible to hackers by blocking ping packets. Of course, there are some vulnerabilities that are associated with ICMP, such as the following:

- By using a botnet, a hacker could inundate your server with ping packets from multiple sources at once, exhausting your server's ability to cope.
- Certain vulnerabilities that are associated with the ICMP protocol can allow a hacker to either gain administrative privileges on your system, redirect your traffic to a malicious server, or crash your operating system.

By using some simple hacking tools, someone could embed sensitive data in the data field of an ICMP packet in order to secretly exfiltrate it from your organization.

However, while blocking certain types of ICMP packets is good, blocking all ICMP packets is bad. The harsh reality is that certain types of ICMP messages are necessary for the proper functionality of the network. Since the *drop all that's not allowed* rule that we'll eventually create also blocks ICMP packets, we'll need to create some rules that allow the types of ICMP messages that we have to have. So, here goes:

```
sudo iptables -A INPUT -m conntrack -p icmp --icmp-type 3 --ctstate
NEW,ESTABLISHED,RELATED -j ACCEPT

sudo iptables -A INPUT -m conntrack -p icmp --icmp-type 11 --ctstate
NEW,ESTABLISHED,RELATED -j ACCEPT

sudo iptables -A INPUT -m conntrack -p icmp --icmp-type 12 --ctstate
NEW,ESTABLISHED,RELATED -j ACCEPT
```

Here's the breakdown:

- **-m conntrack**: As before, we're using the conntrack module to allow packets that are in a certain state. This time, though, instead of just allowing packets from a host to which our server has been connected (ESTABLISHED, RELATED), we're also allowing NEW packets that other hosts are sending to our server.
- **-p icmp**: This refers to the ICMP protocol.
- **--icmp-type**: There are quite a few types of ICMP messages, which we'll outline next.

Here are the three types of ICMP messages that we want to allow:

- **type 3**: These are the "destination unreachable" messages. Not only can they tell your server that it can't reach a certain host, but they can also tell it why. For example, if the server has sent out a packet that's too large for a network switch to handle, the switch will send back an ICMP message that tells the server to fragment that large packet. Without ICMP, the server would have connectivity problems every time it tries to send out a large packet that needs to be broken up into fragments.
- **type 11**: Time-exceeded messages let your server know that a packet that it has sent out has either exceeded its **Time-to-Live** (**TTL**) value before it could reach its destination, or that a fragmented packet couldn't be reassembled before the TTL expiration date.
- **type 12**: Parameter problem messages indicate that the server had sent a packet with a bad IP header. In other words, the IP header is either missing an option flag or it's of an invalid length.

Three common message types are conspicuously absent from our list:

- **type 0** and **type 8**: These are the infamous ping packets. Actually, type 8 is the echo request packet that you would send out to ping a host, while type 0 is the echo reply that the host would return to let you know that it's alive. Of course, allowing ping packets to get through could be a big help when troubleshooting network problems. If that scenario ever comes up, you could just add a couple of iptables rules to temporarily allow pings.

- **type 5**: Now, we have the infamous redirect messages. Allowing these could be handy if you have a router that can suggest more efficient paths for the server to use, but hackers can also use them to redirect you to someplace that you don't want to go. So, just block them.

There are lots more ICMP message types than I've shown here, but these are the only ones that we need to worry about for now.

When we use `sudo iptables -L`, we'll see our new ruleset, as things currently stand:

```
Chain INPUT (policy ACCEPT)
target     prot opt source               destination
ACCEPT     all  --  anywhere             anywhere
ACCEPT     all  --  anywhere             anywhere             ctstate
RELATED,ESTABLISHED
ACCEPT     tcp  --  anywhere             anywhere             tcp dpt:ssh
ACCEPT     tcp  --  anywhere             anywhere             tcp dpt:domain
ACCEPT     udp  --  anywhere             anywhere             udp dpt:domain
ACCEPT     icmp --  anywhere             anywhere             ctstate
NEW,RELATED,ESTABLISHED icmp destination-unreachable
ACCEPT     icmp --  anywhere             anywhere             ctstate
NEW,RELATED,ESTABLISHED icmp source-quench
ACCEPT     icmp --  anywhere             anywhere             ctstate
NEW,RELATED,ESTABLISHED icmp time-exceeded
ACCEPT     icmp --  anywhere             anywhere             ctstate
NEW,RELATED,ESTABLISHED icmp parameter-problem
Chain FORWARD (policy ACCEPT)
target     prot opt source               destination
Chain OUTPUT (policy ACCEPT)
target     prot opt source               destination
```

Looks good, eh? Well, not really. We haven't blocked anything with this ruleset yet. So, let's take care of that.

Blocking everything that isn't allowed with iptables

To start blocking stuff that we don't want, we have to do one of two things. We can set a default DROP or REJECT policy for the INPUT chain, or we can leave the policy set to ACCEPT and create a DROP or REJECT rule at the end of the INPUT chain. Which one you choose is really a matter of preference. (Of course, before you choose one over the other, you might want to check your organization's policy manual to see if your employer has a preference.)

The difference between DROP and REJECT is that DROP blocks packets without sending any message back to the sender. REJECT blocks packets, and then sends a message back to the sender about why the packets were blocked. For our present purposes, let's say that we just want to DROP packets that we don't want to get through.

> Tip: There are times when DROP is better, and times when REJECT is better. Use DROP if it's important to make your host invisible. (Although, even that isn't that effective, because there are other ways to discover hosts.) If you need your hosts to inform other hosts about why they can't make a connection, then use REJECT. The big advantage of REJECT is that it will let connecting hosts know that their packets are being blocked so that they will know to immediately quit trying to make a connection. With DROP, the host that's trying to make the connection will just keep trying to make the connection until it times out.

To create a DROP rule at the end of the INPUT chain, use this command:

```
donnie@ubuntu:~$ sudo iptables -A INPUT -j DROP
donnie@ubuntu:~$
```

To set a default DROP policy instead, we can use this command:

```
donnie@ubuntu:~$ sudo iptables -P INPUT DROP
donnie@ubuntu:~$
```

The big advantage of setting up a default DROP or REJECT policy is that it makes it easier to add new ACCEPT rules if need be. This is because if we decide to keep the default ACCEPT policy and create a DROP or REJECT rule instead, that rule has to be at the bottom of the list.

Since iptables rules are processed in order, from top to bottom, any ACCEPT rules that come after that DROP or REJECT rule would have no effect. You would need to insert any new ACCEPT rules above that final DROP or REJECT rule, which is just a tiny bit less convenient than just being able to append them to the end of the list. For now, in order to illustrate my next point, I've just left the default ACCEPT policy and added the DROP rule.

When we look at our new ruleset, we'll see something that's rather strange:

```
donnie@ubuntu:~$ sudo iptables -L
Chain INPUT (policy ACCEPT)
target     prot opt source              destination
ACCEPT     all  --  anywhere            anywhere
ACCEPT     all  --  anywhere            anywhere             ctstate
RELATED,ESTABLISHED

. . .

. . .
ACCEPT     icmp --  anywhere            anywhere             ctstate
NEW,RELATED,ESTABLISHED icmp parameter-problem
DROP       all  --  anywhere            anywhere

Chain FORWARD (policy ACCEPT)
target     prot opt source              destination
. . .

. . .
```

The first rule and the last rule of the INPUT chain look the same, except that one is a DROP and the other is an ACCEPT. Let's look at it again with the -v (verbose) option:

```
donnie@ubuntu:~$ sudo iptables -L -v
Chain INPUT (policy ACCEPT 0 packets, 0 bytes)
 pkts bytes target prot opt in out source destination
   67 4828 ACCEPT all -- lo any anywhere anywhere
  828 52354 ACCEPT all -- any any anywhere anywhere ctstate RELATED,ESTABLISHED
. . .

. . .
    0 0 ACCEPT icmp -- any any anywhere anywhere ctstate
NEW,RELATED,ESTABLISHED icmp parameter-problem
  251 40768 DROP all -- any any anywhere anywhere

Chain FORWARD (policy ACCEPT 0 packets, 0 bytes)
 pkts bytes target prot opt in out source destination
. . .
. . .
```

Now, we can see that lo, for loopback, shows up under the in column of the first rule, and that any shows up under the in column of the last rule. We can also see that the -v switch shows the number of packets and bytes that have been counted by each rule. So, in the preceding example, we can see that the ctstate RELATED,ESTABLISHED rule has accepted 828 packets and 52,354 bytes. The DROP all rule has blocked 251 packets and 40,763 bytes.

This all looks great, except that if we were to reboot the machine right now, the rules would disappear. The final thing that we need to do is make them permanent. There are several ways to do this, but the simplest way to do this on an Ubuntu machine is to install the iptables-persistent package:

```
sudo apt install iptables-persistent
```

During the installation process, you'll be presented with two screens that ask you whether you want to save the current set of iptables rules. The first screen will be for IPv4 rules, while the second will be for IPv6 rules:

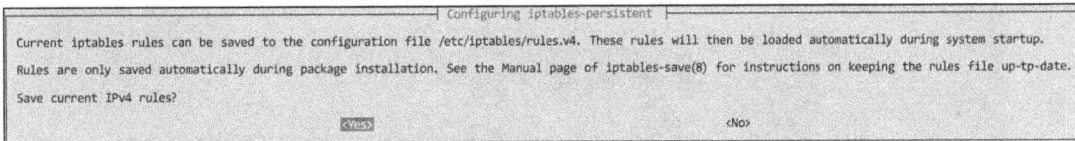

```
┤ Configuring iptables-persistent ├
Current iptables rules can be saved to the configuration file /etc/iptables/rules.v4. These rules will then be loaded automatically during system startup.
Rules are only saved automatically during package installation. See the Manual page of iptables-save(8) for instructions on keeping the rules file up-tp-date.
Save current IPv4 rules?
                              <Yes>                                        <No>
```

Figure 4.1 -- Configuring iptables-persistent on Ubuntu

You'll now see two new rules files in the /etc/iptables/ directory:

```
donnie@ubuntu:~$ ls -l /etc/iptables*
total 8
-rw-r--r-- 1 root root 336 Oct 10 10:29 rules.v4
```

```
-rw-r--r-- 1 root root 183 Oct 10 10:29 rules.v6
donnie@ubuntu:~$
```

If you were to reboot the machine now, you'd see that your iptables rules are still there and in effect. The only slight problem with `iptables-persistent` is that it won't save any subsequent changes that you make to the rules. That's okay, though. I'll show you how to deal with that in just a bit.

Hands-on lab for basic iptables usage

You'll complete this lab on your Ubuntu 20.04 virtual machine. Follow these steps to get started:

1. Shut down your Ubuntu virtual machine and create a snapshot. After you boot it back up, look at your iptables rules, or lack thereof, by using this command:

    ```
    sudo iptables -L
    ```

2. With a default Ubuntu setup, the Uncomplicated Firewall (ufw) service is already running, albeit with an unactivated firewall configuration. We want to disable it to work directly with iptables. Do that now with this command:

    ```
    sudo systemctl disable --now ufw
    ```

3. Create the rules that you need for a basic firewall, allowing for Secure Shell access, DNS queries and zone transfers, and the proper types of ICMP. Deny everything else:

    ```
    sudo iptables -A INPUT -m conntrack   --ctstate ESTABLISHED,RELATED   -j
    ACCEPT

    sudo iptables -A INPUT -p tcp --dport ssh -j ACCEPT
    sudo iptables -A INPUT -p tcp --dport 53 -j ACCEPT
    sudo iptables -A INPUT -p udp --dport 53 -j ACCEPT
    sudo iptables -A INPUT -m conntrack -p icmp --icmp-type 3 --ctstate
    NEW,ESTABLISHED,RELATED -j ACCEPT

    sudo iptables -A INPUT -m conntrack -p icmp --icmp-type 11 --ctstate
    NEW,ESTABLISHED,RELATED -j ACCEPT

    sudo iptables -A INPUT -m conntrack -p icmp --icmp-type 12 --ctstate
    NEW,ESTABLISHED,RELATED -j ACCEPT

    sudo iptables -A INPUT -j DROP
    ```

4. Use this command to view the results:

    ```
    sudo iptables -L
    ```

5. Oops – it looks like you forgot about that loopback interface. Add a rule for it at the top of the list:

    ```
    sudo iptables -I INPUT 1 -i lo -j ACCEPT
    ```

6. View the results by using the following two commands. Note the difference between the output of each:

```
sudo iptables -L
sudo iptables -L -v
```

7. Install the `iptables-persistent` package and choose to save the IPv4 and IPv6 rules when prompted:

```
sudo apt install iptables-persistent
```

8. Reboot the virtual machine and verify that your rules are still active.

9. Keep this virtual machine; you'll be adding more to it in the next hands-on lab.

That's the end of this lab—congratulations!

Blocking invalid packets with iptables

If you've been in the IT business for any length of time, you're most likely familiar with the good old TCP three-way handshake. If you're not, no worries. Here's the simplified explanation.

Let's say that you're sitting at your workstation, and you pull up Firefox to visit a website. To access that website, your workstation and the web server have to set up the connection. Here's what happens:

- Your workstation sends a packet with only the SYN flag set to the web server. This is your workstation's way of saying, "Hello, Mr. Server. I'd like to make a connection with you."
- After receiving your workstation's SYN packet, the web server sends back a packet with the SYN and ACK flags set. With this, the server is saying, "Yeah, bro. I'm here, and I'm willing to connect with you."
- Upon receipt of the SYN-ACK packet, the workstation sends back a packet with only the ACK flag set. With this, the workstation is saying, "Cool deal, dude. I'm glad to connect with you."
- Upon receipt of the ACK packet, the server sets up the connection with the workstation so that they can exchange information.

This sequence works the same way for setting up any kind of TCP connection. This includes connections that involve Secure Shell, telnet, and various mail server protocols, among other things.

However, clever people can use a variety of tools to craft TCP packets with some very weird combinations of flags. With these so-called *invalid* packets, a few things could happen:

- The invalid packets could be used to elicit responses from the target machine in order to find out what operating system it's running, what services are running on it, and which versions of the services are running.
- The invalid packets could be used to trigger certain sorts of security vulnerabilities on the target machine.
- Some of these invalid packets require more processing power than what normal packets require, which could make them useful for performing Denial-of-Service (DoS) attacks.

Now, in truth, the DROP all rule at the end of the filter table's INPUT chain will block some of these invalid packets. However, there are some things that this rule might miss. And even if we could count on it to block all the invalid stuff, this still isn't the most efficient way of doing things. By depending on this DROP all rule, we're allowing these invalid packets to travel through the entire INPUT chain, looking for a rule that will let them through. When no ALLOW rule is found for them, they'll finally get blocked by the DROP all rule, which is the last rule in the chain. So, what if we could find a more efficient solution?

Ideally, we'd like to block these invalid packets before they travel through the entire INPUT chain. We could do that with a PREROUTING chain, but the filter table doesn't have a PREROUTING chain. Therefore, we need to use the PREROUTING chain of the mangle table instead. Let's start by adding these two rules:

```
donnie@ubuntu:~$ sudo iptables -t mangle -A PREROUTING -m conntrack --ctstate
INVALID -j DROP

donnie@ubuntu:~$ sudo iptables -t mangle -A PREROUTING -p tcp ! --syn -m
conntrack --ctstate NEW -j DROP
donnie@ubuntu:~$
```

The first of these rules will block most of what we would consider *invalid*. However, there are still some things that it misses. Due to this, we added the second rule, which blocks all NEW packets that are not SYN packets. Now, let's see what we have:

```
donnie@ubuntu:~$ sudo iptables -L
Chain INPUT (policy ACCEPT)
target       prot opt source              destination
ACCEPT       all  --  anywhere            anywhere
ACCEPT       all  --  anywhere            anywhere            ctstate
RELATED,ESTABLISHED
ACCEPT       tcp  --  anywhere            anywhere            tcp dpt:ssh
DROP         all  --  anywhere            anywhere


Chain FORWARD (policy ACCEPT)
target       prot opt source              destination


Chain OUTPUT (policy ACCEPT)
target       prot opt source              destination
donnie@ubuntu:~$
```

Hmm…

We can't see our new rules, can we? That's because, by default, iptables -L only shows rules for the filter table. We need to see what we've just placed in the mangle table, so let's do this, instead:

```
donnie@ubuntu:~$ sudo iptables -t mangle -L
Chain PREROUTING (policy ACCEPT)
```

```
    target      prot opt source               destination
    DROP        all  --  anywhere             anywhere              ctstate INVALID
    DROP        tcp  --  anywhere             anywhere              tcp
    flags:!FIN,SYN,RST,ACK/SYN ctstate NEW


    Chain INPUT (policy ACCEPT)
    target      prot opt source               destination
    Chain FORWARD (policy ACCEPT)
    target      prot opt source               destination
    Chain OUTPUT (policy ACCEPT)
    target      prot opt source               destination
    Chain POSTROUTING (policy ACCEPT)
    target      prot opt source               destination
    donnie@ubuntu:~$
```

Here, we used the `-t mangle` option to indicate that we want to see the configuration for the mangle table. Something rather curious that you may have noticed is how iptables renders the rule that was created by the `sudo iptables -t mangle -A PREROUTING -p tcp ! --syn -m conntrack --ctstate NEW -j DROP` command. For some reason, it renders like this:

```
    DROP   tcp  --  anywhere   anywhere   tcp flags:!FIN,SYN,RST,ACK/SYN ctstate NEW
```

It looks strange, but don't let that throw you. It still means that it's blocking NEW packets that aren't SYN packets.

Previously, I mentioned that the `iptables-persistent` package won't save subsequent changes to your iptables rules. So, as things stand now, the mangle table rules that we just added will disappear once I reboot this virtual machine. To make these changes permanent, I'll use the `iptables-save` command to save a new file in my own home directory. Then, I'll copy the file over to the `/etc/iptables` directory, replacing the original one:

```
    donnie@ubuntu:~$ sudo iptables-save > rules.v4
    [sudo] password for donnie:
    donnie@ubuntu:~$ sudo cp rules.v4 /etc/iptables/
    donnie@ubuntu:~$
```

To test this, we'll use a handy utility called Nmap. It's a free utility that you can install on your Windows, Mac, or Linux workstation. Or, if you don't want to install it on your host machine, you can install it on one of your Linux virtual machines. It's in the normal repositories of Debian/Ubuntu, RHEL/CentOS 7, and RHEL/AlmaLinux 8. So, just install the Nmap package with the appropriate install command for your distro. If you want to install Nmap on your Windows or Mac host machine, you'll need to download it from the Nmap website.

You can download Nmap from the official website, which can be found here: `https://nmap.org/download.html`.

With our new mangle table rules in place, let's perform an XMAS scan of our Ubuntu machine. I have Nmap installed here on the Fedora workstation that I'm currently using, so I'll just use this for now. I can do this like so:

```
[donnie@fedora-teaching ~]$ sudo nmap -sX 192.168.0.15
[sudo] password for donnie:
Starting Nmap 7.70 ( https://nmap.org ) at 2019-07-26 21:20 EDT
Nmap scan report for 192.168.0.15
Host is up (0.00052s latency).
All 1000 scanned ports on 192.168.0.15 are open|filtered
MAC Address: 08:00:27:A4:95:1A (Oracle VirtualBox virtual NIC)

Nmap done: 1 IP address (1 host up) scanned in 21.41 seconds
[donnie@fedora-teaching ~]$
```

By default, Nmap only scans the most commonly used 1,000 ports. The XMAS scan sends invalid packets that consist of the FIN, PSH, and URG flags. The fact that all 1,000 scanned ports show as open|filtered means that the scan was blocked, and that Nmap can't determine the true state of the ports. (In reality, port 22 is open.) We can view the result to see which rule did the blocking. (To simplify things a bit, I'll only show the output for the PREROUTING chain since it's the only mangle table chain that's doing anything):

```
donnie@ubuntu:~$ sudo iptables -t mangle -L -v
 Chain PREROUTING (policy ACCEPT 2898 packets, 434K bytes)
  pkts bytes target     prot opt in     out     source
destination

  2000 80000 DROP  all  --  any    any    anywhere             anywhere
ctstate INVALID

   0     0 DROP      tcp  --  any    any    anywhere             anywhere
tcp flags:!FIN,SYN,RST,ACK/SYN ctstate NEW

 . . .

 . . .

 donnie@ubuntu:~$
```

Here, you can see that the first rule—the INVALID rule — blocked 2,000 packets and 80,000 bytes. Now, let's zero out the counter so that we can do another scan:

```
donnie@ubuntu:~$ sudo iptables -t mangle -Z
donnie@ubuntu:~$ sudo iptables -t mangle -L -v
Chain PREROUTING (policy ACCEPT 22 packets, 2296 bytes)
 pkts bytes target prot opt in out source destination
```

```
 0 0 DROP all -- any any anywhere anywhere ctstate INVALID
 0 0 DROP tcp -- any any anywhere anywhere tcp flags:!FIN,SYN,RST,ACK/SYN
ctstate NEW


 . . .

 . . .
 donnie@ubuntu:~$
```

This time, let's do a Window scan, which bombards the target machine with ACK packets:

```
[donnie@fedora-teaching ~]$ sudo nmap -sW 192.168.0.15
 Starting Nmap 7.70 ( https://nmap.org ) at 2019-07-26 21:39 EDT
 Nmap scan report for 192.168.0.15
 Host is up (0.00049s latency).
 All 1000 scanned ports on 192.168.0.15 are filtered
 MAC Address: 08:00:27:A4:95:1A (Oracle VirtualBox virtual NIC)

 Nmap done: 1 IP address (1 host up) scanned in 21.44 seconds
 [donnie@fedora-teaching ~]$
```

As before, the scan was blocked, as indicated by the message that all 1,000 scanned ports have been filtered. Now, let's view what we have on the target Ubuntu machine:

```
 donnie@ubuntu:~$ sudo iptables -t mangle -L -v
 Chain PREROUTING (policy ACCEPT 45 packets, 6398 bytes)
  pkts bytes target     prot opt in      out     source
destination

    0     0 DROP     all -- any    any    anywhere        anywhere
ctstate INVALID

  2000 80000 DROP       tcp -- any    any    anywhere        anywhere
tcp flags:!FIN,SYN,RST,ACK/SYN ctstate NEW

 . . .

 . . .
 donnie@ubuntu:~$
```

This time, we can see that our invalid packets got past the first rule, but were blocked by the second rule.

Now, just for fun, let's clear out the mangle table rules and do our scans again. We'll use the -D option to delete the two rules from the mangle table:

```
 donnie@ubuntu:~$ sudo iptables -t mangle -D PREROUTING 1
 donnie@ubuntu:~$ sudo iptables -t mangle -D PREROUTING 1
 donnie@ubuntu:~$
```

When you delete a rule, you have to specify the rule number, just like you do when you insert a rule. Here, I specified rule 1 twice, because deleting the first rule moved the second rule up to first place. Now, let's verify that the rules are gone:

```
donnie@ubuntu:~$ sudo iptables -t mangle -L
Chain PREROUTING (policy ACCEPT)
target prot opt source destination


. . .

. . .
donnie@ubuntu:~$
```

Yes, they are. Cool. Now, let's see what we get when we perform another XMAS scan:

```
[donnie@fedora-teaching ~]$ sudo nmap -sX 192.168.0.15
[sudo] password for donnie:
Starting Nmap 7.70 ( https://nmap.org ) at 2019-07-26 21:48 EDT
Nmap scan report for 192.168.0.15
Host is up (0.00043s latency).
All 1000 scanned ports on 192.168.0.15 are open|filtered
MAC Address: 08:00:27:A4:95:1A (Oracle VirtualBox virtual NIC)

Nmap done: 1 IP address (1 host up) scanned in 21.41 seconds
[donnie@fedora-teaching ~]$
```

Even without the mangle table rules, it shows that my scan is still blocked. What's up with that? This is happening because I still have the DROP all rule at the end of the INPUT table. Let's disable that and see what we get with another scan.

First, I need to see what the rule number is:

```
donnie@ubuntu:~$ sudo iptables -L
 Chain INPUT (policy ACCEPT)
 target      prot opt source              destination
 ACCEPT      all  --  anywhere            anywhere
 ACCEPT      all  --  anywhere            anywhere              ctstate
RELATED,ESTABLISHED
 ACCEPT      tcp  --  anywhere            anywhere              tcp dpt:ssh
 DROP        all  --  anywhere            anywhere

 Chain FORWARD (policy ACCEPT)
 target      prot opt source              destination

 Chain OUTPUT (policy ACCEPT)
 target      prot opt source              destination
donnie@ubuntu:~$
```

Counting down, I can see that it's rule number 4, so I'll delete it:

```
donnie@ubuntu:~$ sudo iptables -D INPUT 4
donnie@ubuntu:~$donnie@ubuntu:~$ sudo iptables -L
Chain INPUT (policy ACCEPT)
target     prot opt source               destination
ACCEPT     all  --  anywhere             anywhere
ACCEPT     all  --  anywhere             anywhere            ctstate
RELATED,ESTABLISHED
ACCEPT     tcp  --  anywhere             anywhere            tcp dpt:ssh


Chain FORWARD (policy ACCEPT)
target     prot opt source               destination


Chain OUTPUT (policy ACCEPT)
target     prot opt source               destination
donnie@ubuntu:~$
```

Now, for the XMAS scan:

```
[donnie@fedora-teaching ~]$ sudo nmap -sX 192.168.0.15
Starting Nmap 7.70 ( https://nmap.org ) at 2019-07-26 21:49 EDT
Nmap scan report for 192.168.0.15
Host is up (0.00047s latency).
Not shown: 999 closed ports
PORT STATE SERVICE
22/tcp open|filtered ssh
MAC Address: 08:00:27:A4:95:1A (Oracle VirtualBox virtual NIC)


Nmap done: 1 IP address (1 host up) scanned in 98.76 seconds
[donnie@fedora-teaching ~]$
```

This time, the scan shows that 999 ports are closed and that port 22, the SSH port, is either open or filtered. This shows that the scan is no longer being blocked by anything.

Restoring the deleted rules

When I used the iptables -D commands, I only deleted the rules from the runtime configuration, not from the rules.v4 configuration file. To restore the rules that I deleted, I can either reboot the machine or restart the netfilter-persistent service. The latter choice is quicker, so I'll activate it like this:

```
donnie@ubuntu:~$ sudo systemctl restart netfilter-persistent
[sudo] password for donnie:
donnie@ubuntu:~$
```

The `iptables -L` and `iptables -t mangle -L` commands will show that all the rules are now back in effect.

Hands-on lab for blocking invalid IPv4 packets

For this lab, you'll use the same virtual machine that you used for the previous lab. You won't replace any of the rules that you already have. Rather, you'll just add a couple. Let's get started:

1. Look at the rules for the filter and the mangle tables. (Note that the `-v` option shows you statistics about packets that were blocked by the DROP and REJECT rules.) Then, zero out the blocked packets counter:

```
sudo iptables -L -v
sudo iptables -t mangle -L -v
sudo iptables -Z
sudo iptables -t mangle -Z
```

2. From either your host machine or another virtual machine, perform the NULL and Windows Nmap scans against the virtual machine:

```
sudo nmap -sN ip_address_of_your_VM
sudo nmap -sW ip_address_of_your_VM
```

3. Repeat *Step 1*. You should see a large jump in the number of packets that were blocked by the final DROP rule in the INPUT chain of the filter table:

```
sudo iptables -L -v
sudo iptables -t mangle -L -v
```

4. Make the firewall work more efficiently by using the PREROUTING chain of the mangle table to drop invalid packets, such as those that are produced by the two Nmap scans that we just performed. Add the two required rules with the following two commands:

```
sudo iptables -t mangle -A PREROUTING -m conntrack --ctstate INVALID -j
DROP

sudo iptables -t mangle -A PREROUTING -p tcp ! --syn -m conntrack
--ctstate NEW -j DROP
```

5. Save the new configuration to your own home directory. Then, copy the file to its proper location and zero out the blocked packet counters:

```
sudo iptables-save > rules.v4
sudo cp rules.v4 /etc/iptables
sudo iptables -Z
sudo iptables -t mangle -Z
```

6. Perform only the NULL scan against the virtual machine:

```
sudo nmap -sN ip_address_of_your_VM
```

7. Look at the `iptables` ruleset and observe which rule was triggered by the `Nmap` scan:

```
sudo iptables -L -v
sudo iptables -t mangle -L -v
```

8. This time, perform just the Windows scan against the virtual machine:

```
sudo nmap -sW ip_address_of_your_VM
```

9. Observe which rule was triggered by this scan:

```
sudo iptables -L -v
sudo iptables -t mangle -L -v
```

That's the end of this lab—congratulations!

Protecting IPv6

I know, you're used to having all networking based on IPv4, with its nice, short, easy-to-use IP address-es. However, that can't last forever, considering that the world is now out of new IPv4 addresses. IPv6 offers a much larger address space that will last for a long time to come. Some organizations, especially wireless carriers, are either in the process of switching over to IPv6 or have already switched to it.

So far, all we've covered is how to set up an IPv4 firewall with iptables. But remember what we said before. With iptables, you need one daemon and one set of rules for the IPv4 network, and another daemon and set of rules for IPv6. This means that when using iptables to set up a firewall, protecting IPv6 means doing everything twice. Most Linux distros come with IPv6 networking enabled by default, so you either need to protect it with a firewall or disable it. Otherwise, your IPv6 address will still be open for attack since the IPv4 firewall that you've just configured won't protect it. This is true even if your server or device is facing the IPv4 Internet because there are ways to tunnel IPv6 packets through an IPv4 network. Fortunately, the commands for setting up an IPv6 firewall are mostly the same as what we've just covered. The biggest difference is that instead of using the `iptables` command, you'll use the `ip6tables` command. Let's start with our basic setup, just like what we did for IPv4:

```
donnie@ubuntu3:~$ sudo ip6tables -A INPUT -i lo -j ACCEPT
donnie@ubuntu3:~$ sudo ip6tables -A INPUT -m conntrack --ctstate
ESTABLISHED,RELATED -j ACCEPT

donnie@ubuntu3:~$ sudo ip6tables -A INPUT -p tcp --dport ssh -j ACCEPT
donnie@ubuntu3:~$ sudo ip6tables -A INPUT -p tcp --dport 53 -j ACCEPT
donnie@ubuntu3:~$ sudo ip6tables -A INPUT -p udp --dport 53 -j ACCEPT
```

The other big difference between IPv4 and IPv6 is that with IPv6, you must allow more types of ICMP messages than you need to for IPv4. This is due to the following reasons:

- With IPv6, new types of ICMP messages have replaced the **Address Resolution Protocol (ARP)**.
- With IPv6, dynamic IP address assignments are normally done by exchanging ICMP discovery messages with other hosts, rather than by DHCP.

- With IPv6, echo requests and echo replies, the infamous ping packets, are required when you need to tunnel IPv6 packets through an IPv4 network.

And of course, we still need the same types of ICMP messages that we need for IPv4. So, let's start with those:

```
donnie@ubuntu3:~$ sudo ip6tables -A INPUT -p icmpv6 --icmpv6-type 1 -j ACCEPT
[sudo] password for donnie:
donnie@ubuntu3:~$ sudo ip6tables -A INPUT -p icmpv6 --icmpv6-type 2 -j ACCEPT
donnie@ubuntu3:~$ sudo ip6tables -A INPUT -p icmpv6 --icmpv6-type 3 -j ACCEPT
donnie@ubuntu3:~$ sudo ip6tables -A INPUT -p icmpv6 --icmpv6-type 4 -j ACCEPT
donnie@ubuntu3:~$
```

These message types are as follows, in order of appearance:

- Destination unreachable
- Packet too big
- Time exceeded
- Parameter problem with the packet header

Next, we'll enable echo requests (type 128) and echo responses (type 129) so that IPv6 over IPv4 tunneling will work:

```
donnie@ubuntu3:~$ sudo ip6tables -A INPUT -p icmpv6 --icmpv6-type 128 -j ACCEPT
donnie@ubuntu3:~$ sudo ip6tables -A INPUT -p icmpv6 --icmpv6-type 129 -j ACCEPT
donnie@ubuntu3:~$
```

The Teredo protocol is one of a few different ways to tunnel IPv6 packets across an IPv4 network. This protocol is what requires echo requests and echo replies, the infamous ping packets, to be allowed through a firewall. However, if you search through your distro repositories for a Teredo package, you won't find it. That's because the Linux implementation of the Teredo protocol is called miredo. So, when installing the Teredo protocol on a Linux machine, you'll need to install the `miredo` and `miredo-server` packages.

The next four ICMP message types that we need are for the Link-local Multicast Receiver Notification messages:

```
donnie@ubuntu3:~$ sudo ip6tables -A INPUT --protocol icmpv6 --icmpv6-type 130
donnie@ubuntu3:~$ sudo ip6tables -A INPUT --protocol icmpv6 --icmpv6-type 131
donnie@ubuntu3:~$ sudo ip6tables -A INPUT --protocol icmpv6 --icmpv6-type 132
donnie@ubuntu3:~$ sudo ip6tables -A INPUT --protocol icmpv6 --icmpv6-type 143
donnie@ubuntu3:~$
```

These are as follows, in order of appearance:

- Listener query
- Listener report

- Listener done
- Listener report v2

Next up are our neighbor and router discovery message types:

```
donnie@ubuntu3:~$ sudo ip6tables -A INPUT -p icmpv6 --icmpv6-type 134 -j ACCEPT
donnie@ubuntu3:~$ sudo ip6tables -A INPUT -p icmpv6 --icmpv6-type 135 -j ACCEPT
donnie@ubuntu3:~$ sudo ip6tables -A INPUT -p icmpv6 --icmpv6-type 136 -j ACCEPT
donnie@ubuntu3:~$ sudo ip6tables -A INPUT -p icmpv6 --icmpv6-type 141 -j ACCEPT
donnie@ubuntu3:~$ sudo ip6tables -A INPUT -p icmpv6 --icmpv6-type 142 -j ACCEPT
donnie@ubuntu3:~$
```

These are as follows, in order of appearance:

- Router solicitation
- Router advertisement
- Neighbor solicitation
- Neighbor advertisement
- Inverse neighbor discovery solicitation
- Inverse neighbor discovery advertisement

Space doesn't permit me to go into the details of these message types. So, for now, let's just say that they're required in order for IPv6 hosts to dynamically assign themselves an IPv6 address.

For times when you're using security certificates to authenticate the routers that are attached to your network, you'll also need to allow **Secure Neighbor Discovery (SEND)** messages:

```
donnie@ubuntu3:~$ sudo ip6tables -A INPUT -p icmpv6 --icmpv6-type 148 -j ACCEPT
donnie@ubuntu3:~$ sudo ip6tables -A INPUT -p icmpv6 --icmpv6-type 149 -j ACCEPT
donnie@ubuntu3:~$
```

Are your fingers tired yet? If so, have no fear. This next group of ICMP rules is the last one. This time, we need to allow Multicast Router Discovery messages:

```
donnie@ubuntu3:~$ sudo ip6tables -A INPUT -p icmpv6 --icmpv6-type 151 -j ACCEPT
donnie@ubuntu3:~$ sudo ip6tables -A INPUT -p icmpv6 --icmpv6-type 152 -j ACCEPT
donnie@ubuntu3:~$ sudo ip6tables -A INPUT -p icmpv6 --icmpv6-type 153 -j ACCEPT
donnie@ubuntu3:~$
```

Finally, we'll add our `DROP` rule to block everything else:

```
donnie@ubuntu3:~$ sudo ip6tables -A INPUT -j DROP
donnie@ubuntu3:~$
```

I know you're thinking, "Wow, that's a lot of hoops to jump through just to set up a basic firewall." And yeah, you're right, especially when you also need to configure rules for IPv6. Soon, I'll show you what the Ubuntu folk came up with to make things simpler.

> You can get the whole scoop on how to use iptables on Ubuntu here: `https://help.`
> `ubuntu.com/community/IptablesHowTo`.

Hands-on lab for ip6tables

For this lab, you'll use the same Ubuntu virtual machine that you used in the previous iptables labs. You'll leave the IPv4 firewall setup that's already there as-is and create a new firewall for IPv6. Let's get started:

1. View your IPv6 rules, or lack thereof, with this command:

```
sudo ip6tables -L
```

2. Create the IPv6 firewall. Due to formatting constraints, I can't list the entire code block of commands here. You can find the respective commands in this chapter's directory, in the code file that you can download from the Packt Publishing website.

3. View the new ruleset by using the following command:

```
sudo ip6tables -L
```

4. Next, set up the mangle table rules for blocking invalid packets:

```
sudo ip6tables -t mangle -A PREROUTING -m conntrack --ctstate INVALID -j
DROP

sudo ip6tables -t mangle -A PREROUTING -p tcp ! --syn -m conntrack
--ctstate NEW -j DROP
```

5. Save the new ruleset to a file in your own home directory, and then transfer the rules file to the proper location:

```
sudo ip6tables-save > rules.v6
sudo cp rules.v6 /etc/iptables/
```

6. Obtain the IPv6 address of the virtual machine with this command:

```
ip a
```

7. On the machine on which you installed Nmap, perform a Windows scan of the virtual machine's IPv6 address. The command will look like this, except with your own IP address:

```
sudo nmap -6 -sW fe80::a00:27ff:fe9f:d923
```

8. On the virtual machine, observe which rule was triggered with this command:

```
sudo ip6tables -t mangle -L -v
```

You should see non-zero numbers for the packet counters for one of the rules.

1. On the machine on which you installed Nmap, perform an XMAS scan of the virtual machine's IPv6 address. The command will look like this, except with your own IP address:

```
sudo nmap -6 -sX fe80::a00:27ff:fe9f:d923
```

2. As before, on the virtual machine, observe which rule was triggered by this scan:

```
sudo ip6tables -t mangle -L -v
```

3. Shut down the virtual machine, and restore it from the snapshot that you created at the beginning of the *Hands-on lab for basic iptables usage* section.

That's the end of this lab – congratulations!

So far, you've seen the good, the bad, and the ugly of iptables. It's very flexible, and there's a lot of power in the iptables commands. If you're clever at shell scripting, you can create some rather complex shell scripts that you can use to deploy firewalls on machines all across your network.

On the other hand, getting everything right can be quite complex, especially if you need to consider that your machines have to run both IPv4 and IPv6, and that everything you do for IPv4 has to be done again for IPv6. (If you're a masochist, you might actually enjoy it.)

nftables – a more universal type of firewall system

Now, let's turn our attention to nftables, the new kid on the block. So, what does nftables bring to the table? (Yes, the pun was intended.):

- You can forget about needing separate daemons and utilities for all of the different networking components. The functionality of iptables, ip6tables, ebtables, and arptables is now all combined in one neat package. The nft utility is now the only firewall utility that you'll need.
- With nftables, you can create multi-dimensional trees to display your rulesets. This makes troubleshooting vastly easier because it's now easier to trace a packet all the way through all of the rules.
- With iptables, you have the filter, NAT, mangle, and security tables installed by default, whether or not you use each one.
- With nftables, you only create the tables that you intend to use, resulting in enhanced performance.
- Unlike iptables, you can specify multiple actions in one rule, instead of having to create multiple rules for each action.
- Unlike iptables, new rules get added atomically. (That's a fancy way of saying that there's no longer a need to reload the entire ruleset in order to just add one rule.)
- nftables has its own built-in scripting engine, allowing you to write scripts that are more efficient and more human-readable.
- If you already have lots of iptables scripts that you still need to use, you can install a set of utilities that will help you convert them into the nftables format. (That is unless you're running Ubuntu 22.04, which can automatically translate iptables commands for you.)

Although nftables was created by Red Hat, Ubuntu was the first enterprise-grade Linux distro to offer it as an option, beginning with Ubuntu 16.04. It's now the default option for Ubuntu 22.04, SUSE, OpenSUSE, and the RHEL 8/9-type distros. Let's begin by looking at some basic nftables concepts.

Learning about nftables tables and chains

If you're used to iptables, you might recognize some of the nftables terminology. The only problem is that some of the terms are used in different ways, with different meanings. Let's go over some examples so that you'll know what I'm talking about:

- **Tables:** Tables in nftables refer to a particular protocol family. The table types are ip, ip6, inet, arp, bridge, and netdev.
- **Chains:** Chains in nftables roughly equate to tables in iptables. For example, in nftables, you could have filter, route, or NAT chains.

Getting started with nftables

Let's start with a clean snapshot of our Ubuntu 22.04 virtual machine since it comes with nftables already installed.

> Tip: You can use Ubuntu 20.04 if you really want to, but you'll first have to install nftables by doing:
>
> ```
> sudo apt install nftables
> ```

Now, let's take a look at the list of installed tables:

```
sudo nft list tables
```

You didn't see any tables, did you? So, let's load some up.

Configuring nftables on Ubuntu

On the Ubuntu virtual machine that we'll be using, the default nftables.conf file is nothing more than a meaningless placeholder. The file you need, which you'll copy over to replace the default nftables.conf file, is elsewhere. Let's check it out.

First, we'll go into the directory where the sample configurations are stored and list the sample configuration files:

```
cd /usr/share/doc/nftables/examples/
ls -l
```

You should see something similar to this:

```
donnie@ubuntu2204-packt:/usr/share/doc/nftables/examples$ ls -l
total 124
-rw-r--r-- 1 root root  1016 Mar 23  2022 all-in-one.nft
-rw-r--r-- 1 root root   129 Mar 23  2022 arp-filter.nft
```

```
 .   .   .
 .   .   .
-rwxr-xr-x 1 root root    817 Mar 23  2022 workstation.nft
donnie@ubuntu2204-packt:/usr/share/doc/nftables/examples$
```

If you view the contents of the workstation.nft file, you'll see that it's the one we need.

Next, we'll copy the workstation file over to the /etc directory, changing its name to nftables.conf. (Note that this will overwrite the old nftables.conf file, which is what we want.):

```
sudo cp workstation.nft /etc/nftables.conf
```

Here's a breakdown of what you'll see in the /etc/nftables.conf file that you'll be using:

- **#!/usr/sbin/nft -f:** Although you can create normal Bash shell scripts with nftables commands, it's better to use the built-in scripting engine that's included with nftables. That way, we can make our scripts more human-readable, and we don't have to type nft in front of everything we want to execute.
- **flush ruleset:** We want to start with a clean slate, so we'll flush out any rules that may have already been loaded.
- **table inet filter:** This creates an inet family filter, which works for both IPv4 and IPv6. The name of this table is filter, but it could just as well have been something a bit more descriptive.
- **chain input:** Within the first pair of curly brackets, we have a chain called input. (Again, the name could have been something more descriptive.)
- **type filter hook input priority 0;:** Within the next pair of curly brackets, we define our chain and list the rules. This chain is defined as a filter type. hook input indicates that this chain is meant to process incoming packets. Because this chain has both a hook and a priority, it will accept packets directly from the network stack.

Finally, we have the standard rules for a very basic host firewall, starting with the **Input Interface (iif)** rule, which allows the loopback interface to accept packets.

Next is the standard connection tracking (ct) rule, which accepts traffic that's in response to a connection request from this host.

Then, there's a commented-out rule to accept Secure Shell and both secure and nonsecure web traffic. ct state new indicates that the firewall will allow other hosts to initiate connections to our server on these ports.

The meta nfproto ipv6 rule accepts neighbor discovery packets, allowing IPv6 functionality.

The counter drop rule at the end silently blocks all other traffic and counts both the number of packets and the number of bytes that it blocks. (This is an example of how you can have one nftables rule perform multiple different actions.)

If all you need on your Ubuntu server is a basic, no-frills firewall, your best bet is to just edit this `/etc/nftables.conf` file so that it suits your own needs. For starters, let's set this up to match the setup that we created for the iptables section. In other words, let's say that this is a DNS server, and we need to allow connections to port 22 and port 53. Remove the comment symbol from in front of the `tcp dport` line, get rid of ports 80 and 443, and add port 53. The line should now look like this:

```
tcp dport { 22, 53 } ct state new accept
```

Note how you can use one nftables rule to open multiple ports.

DNS also uses port 53/udp, so let's add a line for it:

```
udp dport 53 ct state new accept
```

When you're only opening one port, you don't need to enclose that port number within curly brackets. When opening multiple ports, just include the comma-separated list within curly brackets, with a blank space after each comma, before the first element, and after the last element.

Load the configuration file and view the results:

```
donnie@ubuntu2204-packt:/etc$ sudo systemctl reload nftables
donnie@ubuntu2204-packt:/etc$ sudo nft list ruleset
table inet filter {
    chain input {
        type filter hook input priority 0; policy accept;
        iif "lo" accept
        ct state established,related accept
        tcp dport { ssh, domain } ct state new accept
        udp dport domain ct state new accept
        icmpv6 type { nd-router-advert, nd-neighbor-solicit, nd-neighbor-advert
} accept
        counter packets 1 bytes 32 drop
    }
}
donnie@ubuntu2204-packt:/etc$
```

The `counter drop` rule is another example of how an nftables rule can do multiple things. In this case, the rule drops and counts unwanted packets. So far, the rule has blocked one packet and 32 bytes. To demonstrate how this works, let's say that we want to make a log entry when packets are dropped. Just add the `log` keyword to the `drop` rule, like so:

```
counter log drop
```

To make these messages easier to find, add a tag to each log message, like this:

```
counter log prefix "Dropped packet: " drop
```

Now, when you need to peruse the `/var/log/kern.log` file to see how many dropped packets you've had, just search for the `Dropped` packet text string.

Now, let's say that we want to block certain IP addresses from reaching the Secure Shell port of this machine. To do this, we can edit the file, placing a `drop` rule above the rule that opens port 22. The relevant section of the file will look like this:

```
tcp dport 22 ip saddr { 192.168.0.7, 192.168.0.10 } log prefix "Blocked SSH
packets: " drop


tcp dport { 22, 53 } ct state new accept
```

After we reload the file, we'll be blocking SSH access from two different IPv4 addresses. Any attempts to log in from either of those two addresses will create a `/var/log/kern.log` message with the `Blocked SSH packets` tag. Note that we've placed the `drop` rule ahead of the `accept` rule because if the `accept` rule gets read first, the `drop` rule won't have an effect.

Next, we need to allow the desired types of ICMP packets, like so:

```
ct state new,related,established icmp type { destination-unreachable, time-
exceeded, parameter-problem } accept

ct state established,related,new icmpv6 type { destination-unreachable, time-
exceeded, parameter-problem } accept
```

In this case, you need separate rules for ICMPv4 and ICMPv6.

Finally, we'll block invalid packets by adding a new prerouting chain to the filter table, like so:

```
chain prerouting {
            type filter hook prerouting priority 0;

            ct state invalid counter log prefix "Invalid Packets:  " drop

            tcp flags & (fin|syn|rst|ack) != syn ct state new counter log
drop
        }
```

Now, we can save the file and close the text editor.

> Due to formatting constraints, I can't show the entire completed file here. To see the whole file, download the code file from the Packt website, and look in the `Chapter 4` directory. The example file you seek is the `nftables_example_1.conf` file.

Now, let's load up the new rules:

```
sudo systemctl reload nftables
```

Another really cool thing to note is how we've mixed IPv4 (ip) rules with IPv6 (ip6) rules in the same configuration file. Also, unless we specify otherwise, all the rules that we create will apply to both IPv4 and IPv6. That's the beauty of using an inet-type table. For simplicity and flexibility, you'll want to use inet tables as much as possible, rather than separate tables for IPv4 and IPv6.

Most of the time, when all you need is just a simple host firewall, your best bet would be to just use this `nftables.conf` file as your starting point, and edit the file to suit your own needs. However, there's also a command-line component that you may find useful.

Using nft commands

My preferred method of working with nftables is to just start with a template and hand-edit it to my liking, as we did in the previous section. But for those who'd rather do everything from the command line, there's the nft utility.

> Tip: Even if you know that you'll always create firewalls by hand-editing `nftables.conf`, there are still a couple of practical reasons to know about the nft utility.
>
> Let's say that you've observed an attack in progress, and you need to stop it quickly without bringing down the system. With an `nft` command, you can create a custom rule on the fly that will block the attack. Creating nftables rules on the fly also allows you to test the firewall as you configure it, before making any permanent changes.
>
> And, if you decide to take a Linux security certification exam, you might see questions about `nft` commands. (I happen to know.)

There are two ways to use the `nft` utility. For one, you could just do everything directly from the Bash shell, prefacing every action you want to perform with `nft`, followed by the `nft` subcommands. The other way is to use `nft` in interactive mode. For our present purposes, we'll just go with the Bash shell.

First, let's delete our previous configuration and create an inet table since we want something that works for both IPv4 and IPv6. We'll want to give it a somewhat descriptive name, so let's call it ubuntu_filter:

```
sudo nft delete table inet filter
sudo nft list tables
sudo nft add table inet ubuntu_filter
sudo nft list tables
```

Next, we'll add an input filter chain to the table that we just created (note that since we're doing this from the Bash shell, we need to escape the semicolon with a backslash):

```
sudo nft add chain inet ubuntu_filter input { type filter hook input priority
0\; policy drop\; }
```

We could have given it a more descriptive name, but for now, input works. Within the pair of curly brackets, we're setting the parameters for this chain.

Each nftables protocol family has its own set of hooks, which define how the packets will be processed. For now, we're only concerned with the ip/ip6/inet families, which have the following hooks:

- Prerouting
- Input
- Forward
- Output
- Postrouting

Of these, we're only concerned with the input and output hooks, which apply to filter-type chains. By specifying a hook and a priority for our input chain, we're saying that we want this chain to be a base chain that will accept packets directly from the network stack. You will also see that certain parameters must be terminated by a semicolon, which in turn would need to be escaped with a backslash if you're running the commands from the Bash shell. Finally, we're specifying a default policy of drop. If we had not specified drop as the default policy, then the policy would have been accept by default.

> Tip: Every nft command that you enter takes effect immediately. So, if you're doing this remotely, you'll drop your Secure Shell connection as soon as you create a filter chain with a default drop policy.
>
> Some people like to create chains with a default accept policy and then add a drop rule as the final rule. Other people like to create chains with a default drop policy and then leave off the drop rule at the end. Be sure to check your local procedures to see what your organization prefers.

Verify that the chain has been added. You should see something like this:

```
donnie@ubuntu2004-packt:~$ sudo nft list table inet ubuntu_filter
[sudo] password for donnie:
table inet filter {
        chain input {
                type filter hook input priority 0; policy drop;
        }
}
donnie@ubuntu2004-packt:~$
```

That's great, but we still need some rules. Let's start with a connection tracking rule and a rule to open the Secure Shell port. Then, we'll verify that they were added:

```
sudo nft add rule inet ubuntu_filter input ct state established accept
sudo nft add rule inet ubuntu_filter input tcp dport 22 ct state new accept
sudo nft list table inet ubuntu_filter
table inet ubuntu_filter {
    chain input {
```

```
            type filter hook input priority 0; policy drop;
            ct state established accept
            tcp dport ssh ct state new accept
        }
    }
```

Okay, that looks good. You now have a basic, working firewall that allows Secure Shell connections. Well, except that just as we did in the iptables section of this chapter, we forgot to create a rule to allow the loopback adapter to accept packets. Since we want this rule to be at the top of the rules list, we'll use `insert` instead of `add`:

```
sudo nft insert rule inet ubuntu_filter input iif lo accept

sudo nft list table inet ubuntu_filter
 table inet ubuntu_filter {
     chain input {
            type filter hook input priority 0; policy drop;
            iif lo accept
            ct state established accept
            tcp dport ssh ct state new accept
        }
    }
```

Now, we're all set. But what if we want to insert a rule at a specific location? For that, you'll need to use list with the `-a` option to see the rule handles:

```
sudo nft list table inet ubuntu_filter -a
 table inet ubuntu_filter {
     chain input {
            type filter hook input priority 0; policy drop;
            iif lo accept # handle 4
            ct state established accept # handle 2
            tcp dport ssh ct state new accept # handle 3
        }
    }
```

As you can see, there's no real rhyme or reason for the way the handles are numbered. Let's say that we want to insert the rule about blocking certain IP addresses from accessing the Secure Shell port. We can see that the SSH accept rule is handle 3, so we'll need to insert our drop rule before it. This command will look like this:

```
sudo nft insert rule inet ubuntu_filter input position 3 tcp dport 22 ip saddr
{ 192.168.0.7, 192.168.0.10 } drop
```

```
sudo nft list table inet ubuntu_filter -a
 table inet ubuntu_filter {
        chain input {
                type filter hook input priority 0; policy drop;
                iif lo accept # handle 4
                ct state established accept # handle 2
                tcp dport ssh ip saddr { 192.168.0.10, 192.168.0.7} drop #
handle 6
                tcp dport ssh ct state new accept # handle 3
        }
 }
```

So, to place the rule before the rule with the `handle 3` label, we have to insert it at position 3. The new rule that we just inserted has the label `handle 6`. To delete a rule, we have to specify the rule's handle number:

```
sudo nft delete rule inet ubuntu_filter input handle 6

sudo nft list table inet ubuntu_filter -a
 table inet ubuntu_filter {
        chain input {
                type filter hook input priority 0; policy drop;
                iif lo accept # handle 4
                ct state established accept # handle 2
                tcp dport ssh ct state new accept # handle 3
        }
 }
```

As is the case with iptables, everything you do from the command line will disappear once you reboot the machine. To make it permanent, let's redirect the output of the `list` subcommand to the `nftables.conf` configuration file (of course, we'll want to have made a backup copy of the already-existing file, in case we want to revert back to it):

```
sudo sh -c "nft list table inet ubuntu_filter > /etc/nftables.conf"
```

Due to a quirk in the Bash shell, we can't just redirect output to a file in the /etc/ directory in the normal manner, even when we use `sudo`. That's why I had to add the `sh -c` command, with the `nft list` command surrounded by double quotes. Also, note that the file has to be named `nftables.conf` because that's what the nftables systemd service looks for. Now, when we look at the file, we'll see that there are a couple of things that are missing:

```
table inet ubuntu_filter {
    chain input {
        type filter hook input priority 0; policy drop;
        iif lo accept
```

```
            ct state established accept
            tcp dport ssh ct state new accept
    }
}
```

Those of you who are sharp-eyed will see that we're missing the `flush` rule and the shebang line to specify the shell that we want to interpret this script. Let's add them:

```
#!/usr/sbin/nft -f
flush ruleset
table inet ubuntu_filter {
    chain input {
        type filter hook input priority 0; policy drop;
        iif lo accept
        ct state established accept
        tcp dport ssh ct state new accept
    }
}
```

Much better. Let's test this by loading the new configuration and observing the `list` output:

```
sudo systemctl reload nftables

sudo nft list table inet ubuntu_filter
 table inet ubuntu_filter {
        chain input {
                type filter hook input priority 0; policy drop;
                iif lo accept
                ct state established accept
                tcp dport ssh ct state new accept
        }
}
```

That's all there is to creating your own simple host firewall. Of course, running commands from the command line, rather than just creating a script file in your text editor, does make for a lot more typing. However, it does allow you to test your rules on the fly as you create them. And creating your configuration in this manner, and then redirecting the `list` output to your new configuration file, relieves you of the burden of having to keep track of all of those curly brackets as you try to hand-edit the file.

It's also possible to take all of the `nft` commands that we just created and place them into a regular, old-fashioned Bash shell script. Trust me, though, you really don't want to do that. Just use the nft-native scripting format, as we've done here, and you'll have a script that performs better and is much more human-readable.

Hands-on lab for nftables on Ubuntu

For this lab, you'll need a clean snapshot of your Ubuntu 22.04 virtual machine. Let's get started.

Restore your Ubuntu virtual machine to a clean snapshot to clear out any firewall configurations that you created previously. (Or, if you prefer, start with a new virtual machine.) Disable ufw and verify that no firewall rules are present:

```
sudo systemctl disable --now ufw
sudo iptables -L
```

You should see no rules listed for nftables.

Copy the workstation.nft template over to the /etc/ directory and rename it nftables.conf:

```
sudo cp /usr/share/doc/nftables/examples/syntax/workstation /etc/nftables.conf
```

Edit the /etc/nftables.conf file to create your new configuration. (Note that due to formatting constraints, I have to break this into three different code blocks.) Make the top portion of the file look like this:

```
#!/usr/sbin/nft -f flush ruleset
table inet filter {
    chain prerouting {
        type filter hook prerouting priority 0;
        ct state invalid counter log prefix "Invalid Packets:   " drop
        tcp flags & (fin|syn|rst|ack) != syn ct state new counter log prefix
"Invalid Packets 2: " drop
    }
```

Make the second portion of the file look like this:

```
chain input {
    type filter hook input priority 0;
    # accept any localhost traffic
    iif lo accept
    # accept traffic originated from us
    ct state established,related accept
        # activate the following line to accept common local services
        tcp dport 22 ip saddr { 192.168.0.7, 192.168.0.10 } log prefix "Blocked
SSH packets: " drop
        tcp dport { 22, 53 } ct state new accept
        udp dport 53 ct state new accept
        ct state new,related,established icmp type { destination-unreachable,
time-exceeded, parameter-problem } accept
```

Make the final portion of the file look like this:

```
        ct state new,related,established icmpv6 type { destination-unreachable,
time-exceeded, parameter-problem } accept
        # accept neighbour discovery otherwise Ipv6 connectivity breaks.
        ip6 nexthdr icmpv6 icmpv6 type { nd-neighbor-solicit,  nd-router-
advert, nd-neighbor-advert } accept

# count and drop any other traffic
    counter log prefix "Dropped packet: " drop
    }
}
```

Save the file and reload `nftables`:

```
        sudo systemctl reload nftables
```

View the results:

```
sudo nft list tables
sudo nft list tables
sudo nft list table inet filter
sudo nft list ruleset
```

From either your host computer or from another virtual machine, do a Windows scan against the Ubuntu virtual machine:

```
sudo nmap -sW ip_address_of_UbuntuVM
```

Look at the packet counters to see which blocking rule was triggered. (Hint: It's in the prerouting chain.):

```
sudo nft list ruleset
```

This time, do a null scan of the virtual machine:

```
sudo nmap -sN ip_address_of_UbuntuVM
```

Finally, look at which rule was triggered this time. (Hint: It's the other one in the prerouting chain.):

```
sudo nft list ruleset
```

In the `/var/log/kern.log` file, search for the `Invalid Packets` text string to view the messages about the dropped invalid packets.

That's the end of this lab – congratulations!

In this section, we looked at the ins and outs of nftables, and we looked at ways to configure it to help prevent certain types of attacks. In the next chapter, we'll look at the helper programs for our helper programs.

Summary

In this chapter, we looked at both of the helper programs that directly interface with the netfilter firewall. First, we looked at our trusty old friend, iptables. We saw that even though it's been around forever and still works, it does have some shortcomings. Then, we worked with nftables and saw that it has certain advantages over the old iptables.

In the space that's been allotted for this chapter, I've only been able to present the essentials that you need in order to set up basic host protection. However, this should be enough to get you started.

In the next chapter, we'll look at ufw and firewalld, which are helper programs for the two helper programs that we discussed in this chapter. I'll see you there.

Questions

1. Which of the following statements is true?

    1. iptables is the easiest firewall system to work with.
    2. With iptables, any rule that you create applies to both IPv4 and IPv6.
    3. With iptables, you have to create IPv6 rules separately from IPv4 rules.
    4. With nftables, you have to create IPv6 rules separately from IPv4 rules.

2. What is the official name of the Linux firewall?

    a. iptables
    b. ufw
    c. Nftables
    d. netfilter

3. Which of the following statements about nftables is false?

    a. With nftables, rules are added atomically.
    b. With nftables, a table refers to a particular protocol family.
    c. With nftables, ports and their associated rules are bundled into zones.
    d. With nftables, you can write scripts in either normal Bash shell scripting, or with the scripting engine that's built into nftables.

4. Which iptables command would show you how many packets have been dropped by a particular rule?

5. Which nftables command would you use to see how many packets have been dropped by a particular rule?

6. In iptables, which of the following targets would cause packets to be blocked without sending a notification back to the source?

    a. STOP
    b. DROP
    c. REJECT
    d. BLOCK

7. Which of the following six choices are tables in iptables?

    a. Netfilter

    b. Filter

    c. Mangle

    d. Security

    e. ip6table

    f. NAT

8. Which firewall system loads its rules atomically?

Further reading

-   25 iptables netfilter firewall examples: `https://www.cyberciti.biz/tips/linux-iptables-examples.html`

-   Linux IPv6 how-to: `http://tldp.org/HOWTO/html_single/Linux+IPv6-HOWTO/`

-   Recommendations for Filtering ICMPv6 Messages in Firewalls: `https://www.ietf.org/rfc/rfc4890.txt`

-   nftables wiki: `https://wiki.nftables.org/wiki-nftables/index.php/Main_Page`

-   nftables examples: `https://wiki.gentoo.org/wiki/Nftables/Examples`

Answers

1. c

2. d

3. c

4. `sudo iptables -L -v`

5. `sudo nft list ruleset`

6. b

7. b, c, d, and f

8. `nftables`

Join our book community

Join our community's Discord space for discussions with the author and other readers:

`https://packt.link/CyberSec`

5

Securing Your Server with a Firewall — Part 2

In *Chapter 4, Securing Your Server with a Firewall - Part 1*, we covered iptables and nftables, which are management utilities that directly interface with netfilter. Although it's helpful to be familiar with iptables and nftables commands in order to create advanced firewall configurations, having to use these commands all the time can become a bit unwieldy for performing normal day-to-day operations. In this chapter, we'll look at ufw and firewalld, which are helper utilities that can simplify the process of working with either iptables or nftables.

First, we'll look at the Uncomplicated Firewall, or ufw. We'll look at its structure, its commands, and its configuration. Then, we'll do the same for firewalld. In both cases, you'll get plenty of hands-on practice.

We will cover the following topics in this chapter:

- **ufw** for Ubuntu systems
- **firewalld** for Red Hat systems

One thing you'll notice is that dealing with either ufw or firewalld is somewhat simpler than dealing directly with either iptables or nftables. So, you might be wondering why the chapter with the more complicated stuff comes before this one. Well, it's just that ufw and firewalld are not stand-alone programs. Instead, they both use either iptables or nftables as their backend. Older versions of Linux come with iptables, so running either a ufw command or a firewalld command, as applicable, would cause iptables to run its own corresponding command in the background. The same thing is true of newer Linux versions that come with nftables. So, in order to get the most out of your experience with ufw and firewalld, you'll need to have a good understanding of iptables and nftables. So, with that out of the way, let's get started.

Technical requirements

The code files for this chapter are available here: https://github.com/PacktPublishing/Mastering-Linux-Security-and-Hardening-3E.

The Uncomplicated Firewall for Ubuntu systems

The Uncomplicated Firewall (ufw) is already installed on Ubuntu 20.04 and Ubuntu 22.04. It still uses the iptables backend on Ubuntu 20.04, and the nftables backend on Ubuntu 22.04. For normal operations, it offers a vastly simplified set of commands. Perform just one simple command to open the desired ports and another simple command to activate it, and you have a good, basic firewall. Whenever you perform a ufw command, it will automatically configure both the IPv4 and the IPv6 rules. This alone is a huge time-saver, and much of what we've had to configure by hand with either iptables or nftables is already there by default. Although our two versions of Ubuntu use different backends, ufw configuration is identical for both of them.

> ufw is also available for Debian and other Debian-based distros, but it might not be installed. If that's the case, install it by issuing the sudo apt install ufw command.

Configuring ufw

On both Ubuntu 20.04 and Ubuntu 22.04, the ufw service is already enabled by default, but the firewall itself isn't activated. In other words, the system's service is running, but it isn't enforcing any firewall rules yet. (I'll show you how to activate it in just a bit, after we go over how to open the ports that you need to open.) Check the ufw status with these two commands:

```
systemctl status ufw
sudo ufw status
```

The systemctl command should show you that the service is enabled, and the ufw command should show you that the firewall is inactive.

The first thing we want to do is open port 22 to allow connections to the machine via Secure Shell, like so:

```
sudo ufw allow 22/tcp
```

Okay, that looks good. Let's now activate the firewall, like this:

```
sudo ufw enable
```

By using sudo iptables -L on Ubuntu 20.04, you'll see that the new Secure Shell rule shows up in the ufw-user-input chain:

```
Chain ufw-user-input (1 references)
  target prot opt source destination
  ACCEPT tcp -- anywhere anywhere tcp dpt:ssh
```

On Ubuntu 22.04, use the `sudo nft list ruleset` command to see the new rule in the `ufw-user-input` chain:

```
chain ufw-user-input {
    eta l4proto tcp tcp dport 22 counter packets 0 bytes 0 accept
}
```

You'll also see that the total output of both of these commands is quite lengthy because so much of what we had to do with bare `iptables` or `nftables` has already been done for us with `ufw`. In fact, there's even more here than what we did with `iptables` and `nftables`. For example, with `ufw`, we already have rate-limiting rules that help protect us against **Denial-of-Service** (**DoS**) attacks, and we also have rules that record log messages about packets that have been blocked. It's almost the no fuss, no muss way of setting up a firewall. (I'll get to that *almost* part in a bit.)

In the preceding `sudo ufw allow 22/tcp` command, we had to specify the TCP protocol because TCP is all we need for Secure Shell. We can also open a port for both TCP and UDP just by not specifying a protocol. For example, if you're setting up a DNS server, you'll want to have port 53 open for both protocols. (You'll see the entries for port 53 listed as domain ports). On either version of Ubuntu, do:

```
sudo ufw allow 53
```

On Ubuntu 20.04, view the results by doing:

```
sudo iptables -L
. . .

. . .
Chain ufw-user-input (1 references)
target prot opt source destination
ACCEPT tcp -- anywhere anywhere tcp dpt:ssh
ACCEPT tcp -- anywhere anywhere tcp dpt:domain
ACCEPT udp -- anywhere anywhere udp dpt:domain
```

On Ubuntu 22.04, view the results by doing:

```
sudo nft list ruleset
chain ufw-user-input {
        meta l4proto tcp tcp dport 22 counter packets 0 bytes 0 accept
        meta l4proto tcp tcp dport 53 counter packets 0 bytes 0 accept
        meta l4proto udp udp dport 53 counter packets 0 bytes 0 accept
    }
```

If you do `sudo ip6tables -L` on the 20.04 machine, you'll see that a rule for IPv6 was also added for both of the two preceding examples. And, again, you'll see that most of what we had to do with the `ip6tables` commands has already been taken care of. (It's especially nice that we don't have to mess around with setting up all of those pesky ICMP rules.) On the 22.04 machine, the `sudo nft list ruleset` command that you did previously will show the IPv6 configuration in the `ufw6-user-input` stanza.

To see just a quick summary of your firewall configuration, use the `status` option. The output should look something like this:

```
donnie@ubuntu-ufw:~$ sudo ufw status
Status: active

To                        Action       From
--                        ------       ----
22/tcp                    LIMIT        Anywhere
53                        LIMIT        Anywhere
22/tcp (v6)               LIMIT        Anywhere (v6)
53 (v6)                   LIMIT        Anywhere (v6)

donnie@ubuntu-ufw:~$
```

Next, we will look at the `ufw` configuration files.

Working with the ufw configuration files

You can find the `ufw` firewall rules in the `/etc/ufw/` directory. As you see, the rules are stored in several different files:

```
donnie@ubuntu-ufw:/etc/ufw$ ls -l
total 48
-rw-r----- 1 root root  915 Aug  7 15:23 after6.rules
-rw-r----- 1 root root 1126 Jul 31 14:31 after.init
-rw-r----- 1 root root 1004 Aug  7 15:23 after.rules
drwxr-xr-x 3 root root 4096 Aug  7 16:45 applications.d
-rw-r----- 1 root root 6700 Mar 25 17:14 before6.rules
-rw-r----- 1 root root 1130 Jul 31 14:31 before.init
-rw-r----- 1 root root 3467 Aug 11 11:36 before.rules
-rw-r--r-- 1 root root 1391 Aug 15  2017 sysctl.conf
-rw-r--r-- 1 root root  313 Aug 11 11:37 ufw.conf
-rw-r----- 1 root root 3014 Aug 11 11:37 user6.rules
-rw-r----- 1 root root 3012 Aug 11 11:37 user.rules
donnie@ubuntu-ufw:/etc/ufw$
```

At the bottom of the list, you'll see the `user6.rules` and `user.rules` files. You can't hand-edit either of these two files. You'll be able to save the files after you've made the edits, but when you use `sudo ufw reload` to load the new changes, you'll see that your edits have been deleted. Let's look into the `user.rules` file to see what we can see there.

As you'll soon see, all of the files for both Ubuntu 20.04 and 22.04 contain firewall rules that are in the `iptables` format, even though 22.04 uses `nftables` as its backend. That's because Ubuntu 22.04 can automatically translate `iptables` rules into `nftables` rules. So, the files for both 20.04 and 22.04 are identical, which makes things very easy for us.

At the top of the file, you'll see the definition for the `iptables` filter table, as well as the list of its associated chains:

```
*filter
:ufw-user-input - [0:0]
:ufw-user-output - [0:0]
:ufw-user-forward - [0:0]

. . .

. . .
```

Next, in the `### RULES ###` section, we have the list of rules that we created with the `ufw` command. Here's what our rules for opening the DNS ports look like:

```
### tuple ### allow any 53 0.0.0.0/0 any 0.0.0.0/0 in
-A ufw-user-input -p tcp --dport 53 -j ACCEPT
-A ufw-user-input -p udp --dport 53 -j ACCEPT
```

As you see, `ufw` uses `iptables` syntax for its configuration files, even on Ubuntu 22.04.

Below the `### RULES ###` section, we see the rules for logging messages about any packets that the firewall has blocked:

```
### LOGGING ###
-A ufw-after-logging-input -j LOG --log-prefix "[UFW BLOCK] " -m limit --limit
3/min --limit-burst 10

-A ufw-after-logging-forward -j LOG --log-prefix "[UFW BLOCK] " -m limit
--limit 3/min --limit-burst 10

-I ufw-logging-deny -m conntrack --ctstate INVALID -j RETURN -m limit --limit
3/min --limit-burst 10

-A ufw-logging-deny -j LOG --log-prefix "[UFW BLOCK] " -m limit --limit 3/min
--limit-burst 10

-A ufw-logging-allow -j LOG --log-prefix "[UFW ALLOW] " -m limit --limit 3/min
--limit-burst 10

### END LOGGING ###
```

These messages get sent to the /var/log/kern.log file. So that we don't overwhelm the logging system when lots of packets are getting blocked, we'll only send three messages per minute to the log file, with a burst rate of 10 messages per minute. Most of these rules will insert a [UFW BLOCK] tag into the log message, which makes it easy for us to find them. The last rule creates messages with a [UFW ALLOW] tag, and curiously enough, the INVALID rule doesn't insert any kind of tag.

Lastly, we have the rate-limiting rules, which allow only three connections per user per minute:

```
### RATE LIMITING ###
-A ufw-user-limit -m limit --limit 3/minute -j LOG --log-prefix "[UFW LIMIT
BLOCK] "

-A ufw-user-limit -j REJECT
-A ufw-user-limit-accept -j ACCEPT
### END RATE LIMITING ###
```

Any packets that exceed that limit will be recorded in the /var/log/kern.log file with the [UFW LIMIT BLOCK] tag.

The /etc/ufw user6.rules file looks pretty much the same, except that it's for IPv6 rules. Any time you create or delete a rule with the ufw command, it will modify both the user.rules file and the user6.rules file.

To store rules that will run before the rules in the user.rules and user6.rules files, we have the before.rules file and the before6.rules file. To store rules that will run after the rules in the user. rules and user6.rules files, we have – you guessed it – the after.rules file and the after6.rules file. If you need to add custom rules that you can't add with the ufw command, just hand-edit one of these pairs of files. (We'll get to that in a moment.)

If you look at the before and after files, you'll see where so much has already been taken care of for us. This is all the stuff that we had to do by hand with either iptables/ip6tables or nftables.

However, as you might know, there is one slight caveat to all this ufw goodness. You can perform simple tasks with the ufw utility, but anything more complex requires you to hand-edit a file. (This is what I meant when I said that ufw is *almost* no fuss, no muss.)

> To see more examples of what you can do with the ufw command, view its man page by doing:
>
> ```
> man ufw
> ```

For example, in the before files, you'll see that one of the rules for blocking invalid packets has already been implemented. Here's the code snippet from the before.rules file, which you'll find near the top of the file:

```
# drop INVALID packets (logs these in loglevel medium and higher)
-A ufw-before-input -m conntrack --ctstate INVALID -j ufw-logging-deny
-A ufw-before-input -m conntrack --ctstate INVALID -j DROP
```

The second of these two rules actually drops the invalid packets, and the first rule logs them. But as we've already seen in the *An overview of iptables* section of *Chapter 4, Securing Your Server with a Firewall – Part 1*, this one particular DROP rule doesn't block all of the invalid packets. And, for performance reasons, we'd rather have this rule in the mangle table instead of in the filter table where it is now. To fix that, we'll edit both of the before files. Open the /etc/ufw/before.rules file in your favorite text editor and look for the following pair of lines at the very bottom of the file:

```
# don't delete the 'COMMIT' line or these rules won't be processed
COMMIT
```

Just below the COMMIT line, add the following code snippet to create the mangle table rules:

```
# Mangle table added by Donnie
*mangle
:PREROUTING ACCEPT [0:0]
-A PREROUTING -m conntrack --ctstate INVALID -j DROP
-A PREROUTING -p tcp -m tcp ! --tcp-flags FIN,SYN,RST,ACK SYN -m conntrack
--ctstate NEW -j DROP
COMMIT
```

Now, we'll repeat this process for the /etc/ufw/before6.rules file. Then, we'll reload the rules by doing:

```
sudo ufw reload
```

By using the iptables -L and ip6tables -L commands on Ubuntu 20.04 or the nft list ruleset command on Ubuntu 22.04, you'll see the new rules show up in the mangle table, just where we want them to be.

Hands-on lab for basic ufw usage

You'll need to complete this lab on a clean snapshot of either an Ubuntu 20.04 or an Ubuntu 22.04 virtual machine. Let's get started:

1. Shut down your Ubuntu virtual machine and restore the snapshot to get rid of all of the iptables or nftables stuff that you just did. (Or, if you prefer, just start with a fresh virtual machine.)

2. When you've restarted the virtual machine, verify that the iptables rules are now gone. On Ubuntu 20.04 do:

```
sudo iptables -L
```

On Ubuntu 22.04, do:

```
sudo nft list ruleset
```

3. View the status of ufw. Open port 22/TCP and then enable ufw. Then, view the results:

```
sudo ufw status
sudo ufw allow 22/tcp
sudo ufw enable
sudo ufw status
```

On Ubuntu 20.04, do:

```
sudo iptables -L
sudo ip6tables -L
```

On Ubuntu 22.04, do:

```
sudo nft list ruleset
```

4. This time, open port 53 for both TCP and UDP:

```
sudo ufw allow 53
sudo ufw status
```

On Ubuntu 20.04, do:

```
sudo iptables -L
sudo ip6tables -L
```

On Ubuntu 22.04, do:

```
sudo nft list ruleset
```

5. cd into the /etc/ufw/ directory. Familiarize yourself with the contents of the files that are there.

```
Open the /etc/ufw/before.rules file in your favorite text editor. At
the bottom of the file, below the COMMIT line, add the following code
snippet:


# Mangle table added by Donnie
*mangle
:PREROUTING ACCEPT [0:0]
-A PREROUTING -m conntrack --ctstate INVALID -j DROP

-A PREROUTING -p tcp -m tcp ! --tcp-flags FIN,SYN,RST,ACK SYN -m
conntrack --ctstate NEW -j DROP

COMMIT
```

(Note that the second PREROUTING command wraps around on the printed page.)

6. Repeat *step 6* for the `/etc/ufw/before6.rules` file.

7. Reload the firewall with this command:

```
sudo ufw reload
```

8. On Ubuntu 20.04, observe the rules by doing:

```
sudo iptables -L
sudo iptables -t mangle -L
sudo ip6tables -L
sudo ip6tables -t mangle -L
```

On Ubuntu 22.04, observe the rules by doing:

```
sudo nft list ruleset
```

9. Take a quick look at the `ufw` status:

```
sudo ufw status
```

That's the end of the lab – congratulations!

I think you'll agree that `ufw` is pretty cool technology. Its commands for doing basic things are easier to remember than the equivalent `iptables` or `nftables` commands, and it takes care of both IPv4 and IPv6 with just a single command. On either of our Ubuntu versions, you can still do some fancy stuff just by hand-editing the `ufw` configuration files. But, `ufw` isn't the only cool firewall manager that's available. In the next section, we'll take a look at what the Red Hat folk have given us.

firewalld for Red Hat systems

For our next act, we turn our attention to **firewalld**, which is the default firewall manager on Red Hat Enterprise Linux 7 through 9 and all of their offspring.

As we just saw with `ufw` on Ubuntu, `firewalld` can be a frontend for either `iptables` or `nftables`. On RHEL/CentOS 7, `firewalld` uses the `iptables` engine as its backend. On the RHEL 8- and 9-type distros, `firewalld` uses `nftables` as its backend. Either way, you can't create rules with normal `iptables` or `nftables` commands while `firewalld` is enabled because `firewalld` stores the rules in an incompatible format.

> Until very recently, `firewalld` was only available for the newer RHEL versions and their offspring. Now, however, `firewalld` is also available in the Ubuntu repositories. So, if you want to run `firewalld` on Ubuntu, you finally have that choice. Also, the combination of `firewalld` and `nftables` now comes already installed and activated on the SUSE distros.

If you're running Red Hat, CentOS, or AlmaLinux on a desktop machine, you'll see that there is a GUI frontend for `firewalld` in the applications menu. On a text-mode server, though, all you have is the `firewalld` commands. For some reason, the Red Hat folk haven't created an `ncurses`-type program for text-mode servers as they did for `iptables` configuration on older versions of Red Hat.

A big advantage of `firewalld` is the fact that it's dynamically managed. That means that you can change the firewall configuration without restarting the firewall service, and without interrupting any existing connections to your server.

Before we look at the differences between the RHEL 7/CentOS 7 and the RHEL/AlmaLinux 8 and 9 versions of `firewalld`, let's look at the stuff that's the same for both.

Verifying the status of firewalld

For this section, you can use a CentOS 7, AlmaLinux 8, or AlmaLinux 9 virtual machine. Let's start by verifying the status of `firewalld`. There are two ways to do this. The first way is to use the `--state` option of `firewall-cmd`:

```
[donnie@localhost ~]$ sudo firewall-cmd --state
running
[donnie@localhost ~]$
```

Alternatively, if we want a more detailed status, we can just check the daemon, the same as we would for any other daemon on a `systemd` machine:

```
[donnie@localhost ~]$ sudo systemctl status firewalld
  firewalld.service - firewalld - dynamic firewall daemon
   Loaded: loaded (/usr/lib/systemd/system/firewalld.service; enabled;
vendor preset: enabled)
   Active: active (running) since Fri 2017-10-13 13:42:54 EDT; 1h 56min ago
   Docs: man:firewalld(1)
   Main PID: 631 (firewalld)
   CGroup: /system.slice/firewalld.service
   └─631 /usr/bin/python -Es /usr/sbin/firewalld --nofork --nopid
. . .
  Oct 13 15:19:41 localhost.localdomain firewalld[631]: WARNING: reject-
  route: INVALID_ICMPTYPE: No supported ICMP type., ignoring for run-time.
  [donnie@localhost ~]$
```

Next, let's have a look at `firewalld` zones.

Working with firewalld zones

`firewalld` is a rather unique animal in that it comes with several pre-configured zones and services. If you look in the `/usr/lib/firewalld/zones/` directory of any of your CentOS or AlmaLinux machines, you'll see the zones files, all in `.xml` format:

```
[donnie@localhost ~]$ cd /usr/lib/firewalld/zones
[donnie@localhost zones]$ ls
block.xml dmz.xml drop.xml external.xml home.xml internal.xml public.xml
trusted.xml work.xml
[donnie@localhost zones]$
```

Each zone file specifies which ports are to be open and which ones are to be blocked for various given scenarios. Zones can also contain rules for ICMP messages, forwarded ports, masquerading information, and rich language rules. For example, the .xml file for the public zone, which is set as the default, looks like this:

```
<?xml version="1.0" encoding="utf-8"?>
<zone>
 <short>Public</short>
 <description>For use in public areas. You do not trust the other
computers on networks to not harm your computer. Only selected incoming
connections are accepted.</description>
 <service name="ssh"/>
 <service name="dhcpv6-client"/>
</zone>
```

In the service name lines, you see that the only open ports are for Secure Shell access and for DHCPv6 discovery. If you look at the home.xml file, you'll see that it also opens the ports for Multicast DNS, as well as the ports that allow this machine to access shared directories from either Samba servers or Windows servers:

```
<?xml version="1.0" encoding="utf-8"?>
<zone>
 <short>Home</short>
 <description>For use in home areas. You mostly trust the other computers
on networks to not harm your computer. Only selected incoming connections
are accepted.</description>
 <service name="ssh"/>
 <service name="mdns"/>
 <service name="samba-client"/>
 <service name="dhcpv6-client"/>
</zone>
```

The firewall-cmd utility is what you would use to configure firewalld. You can use it to view the list of zone files on your system, without having to cd into the zone file directory:

```
[donnie@localhost ~]$ sudo firewall-cmd --get-zones
[sudo] password for donnie:
block dmz drop external home internal public trusted work
[donnie@localhost ~]$
```

A quick way to see how each zone is configured is to use the `--list-all-zones` option:

```
[donnie@localhost ~]$ sudo firewall-cmd --list-all-zones
 block
  target: %%REJECT%%
  icmp-block-inversion: no
  interfaces:
  sources:
  services:
  ports:
  protocols:
  masquerade: no
  forward-ports:
. . .
. . .
```

Of course, this is only a portion of the output because the listing for all zones is more than we can display here. It's more likely that you'll only want to see information about one particular zone:

```
[donnie@localhost ~]$ sudo firewall-cmd --info-zone=internal
 internal
  target: default
  icmp-block-inversion: no
  interfaces:
  sources:
  services: ssh mdns samba-client dhcpv6-client
  ports:
  protocols:
  masquerade: no
  forward-ports:
 source-ports:
  icmp-blocks:
  rich rules:
[donnie@localhost ~]$
```

So, the `internal` zone allows the `ssh`, `mdns`, `samba-client`, and `dhcpv6-client` services. This is handy for setting up client machines on your internal LAN.

Any given server or client will have one or more installed network interface adapters. Each adapter in a machine can be assigned one, and only one, `firewalld` zone. To see the default zone, do this:

```
[donnie@localhost ~]$ sudo firewall-cmd --get-default-zone
 public
[donnie@localhost ~]$
```

This is great, except that it doesn't tell you anything about which network interface is associated with this zone. To see that information, do this:

```
[donnie@localhost ~]$ sudo firewall-cmd --get-active-zones
 public
  interfaces: enp0s3
[donnie@localhost ~]$
```

When you install Red Hat, CentOS, or AlmaLinux for the first time, the firewall will already be active with the public zone as the default. Now, let's say that you're setting up your server in the DMZ and you want to make sure that its firewall is locked down for that. You can change the default zone to the dmz zone. Let's take a look at the dmz.xml file to see what that does for us:

```
<?xml version="1.0" encoding="utf-8"?>
<zone>
 <short>DMZ</short>
 <description>For computers in your demilitarized zone that are publicly-
accessible with limited access to your internal network. Only selected
incoming connections are accepted.</description>
 <service name="ssh"/>
</zone>
```

So, the only thing that the DMZ allows through is Secure Shell. Okay; that's good enough for now, so let's set the dmz zone as the default:

```
[donnie@localhost ~]$ sudo firewall-cmd --set-default-zone=dmz
 [sudo] password for donnie:
 success
[donnie@localhost ~]$
```

Let's verify it:

```
[donnie@localhost ~]$ sudo firewall-cmd --get-default-zone
 dmz
[donnie@localhost ~]$
```

And we're all good. However, an Internet-facing server in the DMZ probably needs to allow more than just SSH connections. This is where we'll use the firewalld services. But before we look at that, let's consider one more important point.

> You don't need to use the --permanent option when setting the default zone. In fact, you'll get an error message if you do.

You never want to modify the files in the /usr/lib/firewalld/ directory. Whenever you modify the firewalld configuration, you'll see the modified files show up in the /etc/firewalld/ directory. So far, all we've modified is the default zone. So, we'll see the following files in /etc/firewalld/:

```
[donnie@localhost ~]$ sudo ls -l /etc/firewalld
total 12
-rw-------. 1 root root 2003 Oct 11 17:37 firewalld.conf
-rw-r--r--. 1 root root 2006 Aug 4 17:14 firewalld.conf.old
. . .
```

We can do a diff on those two files to see the difference between them:

```
[donnie@localhost ~]$ sudo diff /etc/firewalld/firewalld.conf /etc/firewalld/
firewalld.conf.old
6c6
< DefaultZone=dmz
---
> DefaultZone=public
[donnie@localhost ~]$
```

So, the newer of the two files shows that the dmz zone is now the default.

> To find out more about firewalld zones, enter the man firewalld.zones command.

Adding services to a firewalld zone

Each service file contains a list of ports that need to be opened for a particular service. Optionally, the service files may contain one or more destination addresses, or call in any needed modules, such as for connection tracking. For some services, all you need to do is open just one port. Other services, such as the Samba service, require that multiple ports be opened. Either way, it's sometimes handier to remember the service name that goes with each service rather than the port numbers.

The services files are in the /usr/lib/firewalld/services/ directory. You can look at them by using the firewall-cmd command, just as you could with the list of zones:

```
[donnie@localhost ~]$ sudo firewall-cmd --get-services
 RH-Satellite-6 amanda-client amanda-k5-client bacula bacula-client bitcoin
bitcoin-rpc bitcoin-testnet bitcoin-testnet-rpc ceph ceph-mon cfengine condor-
collector ctdb dhcp dhcpv6 dhcpv6-client dns docker-registry dropbox-lansync
elasticsearch freeipa-ldap freeipa-ldaps freeipa-replication freeipa-trust
ftp ganglia-client ganglia-master high-availability http https imap imaps ipp
ipp-client ipsec iscsi-target kadmin kerberos kibana klogin kpasswd kshell
ldap ldaps libvirt libvirt-tls managesieve mdns mosh mountd ms-wbt mssql
```

```
mysql nfs nrpe ntp openvpn ovirt-imageio ovirt-storageconsole ovirt-vmconsole
pmcd pmproxy pmwebapi pmwebapis pop3 pop3s postgresql privoxy proxy-dhcp ptp
pulseaudio puppetmaster quassel radius rpc-bind rsh rsyncd samba samba-client
sane sip sips smtp smtp-submission smtps snmp snmptrap spideroak-lansync
squid ssh synergy syslog syslog-tls telnet tftp tftp-client tinc tor-socks
transmission-client vdsm vnc-server wbem-https xmpp-bosh xmpp-client xmpp-local
xmpp-server
[donnie@localhost ~]$
```

Before we add any more services, let's check which ones are already enabled:

```
[donnie@localhost ~]$ sudo firewall-cmd --list-services
[sudo] password for donnie:
ssh dhcpv6-client
[donnie@localhost ~]$
```

Here, `ssh` and `dhcpv6-client` are all we have.

The `dropbox-lansync` service would be very handy for us Dropbox users. Let's see which ports this opens:

```
[donnie@localhost ~]$ sudo firewall-cmd --info-service=dropbox-lansync
 [sudo] password for donnie:
 dropbox-lansync
   ports: 17500/udp 17500/tcp
   protocols:
   source-ports:
   modules:
   destination:
[donnie@localhost ~]$
```

It looks like Dropbox uses port 17500 on UDP and TCP.

Now, let's say that we have our web server set up in the DMZ, with the dmz zone set as its default:

```
[donnie@localhost ~]$ sudo firewall-cmd --info-zone=dmz
 dmz (active)
   target: default
   icmp-block-inversion: no
   interfaces: enp0s3
   sources:
   services: ssh
   ports:
   protocols:
   masquerade: no
   forward-ports:
```

```
   source-ports:
   icmp-blocks:
   rich rules:
[donnie@localhost ~]$
```

As we saw previously, the Secure Shell port is the only one that's open. Let's fix that so that users can actually access our website:

```
[donnie@localhost ~]$ sudo firewall-cmd --add-service=http
 success
[donnie@localhost ~]$
```

When we look at the information for the dmz zone once more, we'll see the following:

```
[donnie@localhost ~]$ sudo firewall-cmd --info-zone=dmz
 dmz (active)
   target: default
   icmp-block-inversion: no
   interfaces: enp0s3
   sources:
   services: ssh http
   ports:
   protocols:
   masquerade: no
   forward-ports:
   source-ports:
   icmp-blocks:
   rich rules:
[donnie@localhost ~]$
```

Here, we see that the http service is now allowed through. But look what happens when we add the --permanent option to this info command:

```
[donnie@localhost ~]$ sudo firewall-cmd --permanent --info-zone=dmz
 dmz
   target: default
   icmp-block-inversion: no
   interfaces:
   sources:
   services: ssh
   ports:
   protocols:
   masquerade: no
   forward-ports:
```

```
     source-ports:
     icmp-blocks:
     rich rules:
 [donnie@localhost ~]$
```

Oops! The http service isn't here. What's going on?

For pretty much every command-line alteration of either zones or services, you need to add the --permanent option to make the change persistent across reboots. But without the --permanent option, the change takes effect immediately. With the --permanent option, you'll have to reload the firewall configuration for the change to take effect. To demonstrate this, I'm going to reboot the virtual machine to get rid of the http service.

Okay, I've rebooted, and the http service is now gone:

```
[donnie@localhost ~]$ sudo firewall-cmd --info-zone=dmz
 dmz (active)
   target: default
   icmp-block-inversion: no
   interfaces: enp0s3
   sources:
   services: ssh
   ports:
   protocols:
   masquerade: no
   forward-ports:
   source-ports:
   icmp-blocks:
   rich rules:
 [donnie@localhost ~]$
```

This time, I'll add two services with just one command and specify that the change will be permanent:

```
[donnie@localhost ~]$ sudo firewall-cmd --permanent --add-service={http,https}
 [sudo] password for donnie:
 success
 [donnie@localhost ~]$
```

You can add as many services as you need to with a single command, but you have to separate them with commas and enclose the whole list within a pair of curly brackets. Also, unlike what we just saw with nftables, we can't have blank spaces within the curly brackets. Let's look at the results:

```
[donnie@localhost ~]$ sudo firewall-cmd --info-zone=dmz
 dmz (active)
   target: default
   icmp-block-inversion: no
```

```
    interfaces: enp0s3
    sources:
    services: ssh
    ports:
    protocols:
    masquerade: no
    forward-ports:
    source-ports:
    icmp-blocks:
    rich rules:
[donnie@localhost ~]$
```

Since we decided to make this configuration permanent, it hasn't taken effect yet. However, if we add the `--permanent` option to the `--info-zone` command, we'll see that the configuration files have indeed been changed:

```
[donnie@localhost ~]$ sudo firewall-cmd --permanent --info-zone=dmz
    dmz
      target: default
      icmp-block-inversion: no
      interfaces:
      sources:
      services: ssh http https
      ports:
      protocols:
      masquerade: no
      forward-ports:
      source-ports:
      icmp-blocks:
      rich rules:
[donnie@localhost ~]$
```

Now, we need to reload the configuration so that it will take effect:

```
[donnie@localhost ~]$ sudo firewall-cmd --reload
    success
[donnie@localhost ~]$
```

Now, if you run the `sudo firewall-cmd --info-zone=dmz` command again, you'll see that the new configuration is in effect.

To remove a service from a zone, just replace `--add-service` with `--remove-service`.

Note that we never specified which zone we're working with in any of these service commands. That's because if we don't specify a zone, `firewalld` just assumes that we're working with the default zone. If you want to add a service to something other than the default zone, just add the `--zone=` option to your commands.

Adding ports to a firewalld zone

Having the service files is handy, except that not every service that you'll need to run has its own predefined service file. Let's say that you've installed Webmin on your server, which requires port 10000/ tcp to be open. A quick grep operation will show that port 10000 isn't in any of our predefined services:

```
donnie@localhost services]$ pwd
 /usr/lib/firewalld/services
[donnie@localhost services]$ grep '10000' *
[donnie@localhost services]$
```

So, let's just add that port to our default zone, which is still the dmz zone:

```
donnie@localhost ~]$ sudo firewall-cmd --add-port=10000/tcp
 [sudo] password for donnie:
 success
[donnie@localhost ~]$
```

Again, this isn't permanent, because we didn't include the `--permanent` option. Let's do this again and reload:

```
[donnie@localhost ~]$ sudo firewall-cmd --permanent --add-port=10000/tcp
 success
[donnie@localhost ~]$ sudo firewall-cmd --reload
 success
[donnie@localhost ~]$
```

You can also add multiple ports at once by enclosing the comma-separated list within a pair of curly brackets, just as we did with the services. (I purposely left out the `--permanent` option. You'll see why in a moment):

```
[donnie@localhost ~]$ sudo firewall-cmd --add-port={636/tcp,637/tcp,638/udp}
 success
[donnie@localhost ~]$
```

And of course, you can remove ports from a zone by substituting `--remove-port` for `--add-port`.

If you don't want to type `--permanent` every time you create a new permanent rule, just leave it out. Then, when you're done creating rules, make them all permanent at once by typing:

```
sudo firewall-cmd --runtime-to-permanent
```

Now's, let's turn our attention to controlling ICMP.

Blocking ICMP

Let's take another look at the status of the default public zone:

```
[donnie@localhost ~]$ sudo firewall-cmd --info-zone=public
public (active)
  target: default
  icmp-block-inversion: no
  interfaces: enp0s3
  sources:
  services: ssh dhcpv6-client
  ports: 53/tcp 53/udp
  protocols:
  masquerade: no
  forward-ports:
  source-ports:
  icmp-blocks:
  rich rules:
[donnie@localhost ~]$
```

Toward the bottom, we see the `icmp-block` line, with nothing beside it. This means that our public zone allows all ICMP packets to come through. This isn't ideal, of course, because there are certain types of ICMP packets that we want to block. Before we block anything, let's look at all of the ICMP types that are available to us:

```
[donnie@localhost ~]$ sudo firewall-cmd --get-icmptypes
[sudo] password for donnie:
address-unreachable bad-header communication-prohibited destination-unreachable
echo-reply echo-request fragmentation-needed host-precedence-violation host-
prohibited host-redirect host-unknown host-unreachable ip-header-bad neighbour-
advertisement neighbour-solicitation network-prohibited network-redirect
network-unknown network-unreachable no-route packet-too-big parameter-problem
port-unreachable precedence-cutoff protocol-unreachable redirect required-
option-missing router-advertisement router-solicitation source-quench source-
route-failed time-exceeded timestamp-reply timestamp-request tos-host-redirect
tos-host-unreachable tos-network-redirect tos-network-unreachable ttl-zero-
during-reassembly ttl-zero-during-transit unknown-header-type unknown-option
[donnie@localhost ~]$
```

As we did with zones and services, we can view information about the different ICMP types. In this example, we'll look at one ICMPv4 type and one ICMPv6 type:

```
[donnie@localhost ~]$ sudo firewall-cmd --info-icmptype=network-
redirectnetwork-redirect  destination: ipv4
```

```
[donnie@localhost ~]$ sudo firewall-cmd --info-icmptype=neighbour-
advertisementneighbour-advertisement
destination: ipv6

[donnie@localhost ~]$
```

We've already seen that we're not blocking any ICMP packets. We can also see if we're blocking any specific ICMP packets:

```
[donnie@localhost ~]$ sudo firewall-cmd --query-icmp-block=host-redirect
no
[donnie@localhost ~]$
```

We've already established that redirects can be a bad thing since they can be exploited. So, let's block host-redirect packets:

```
[donnie@localhost ~]$ sudo firewall-cmd --add-icmp-block=host-redirect
success
[donnie@localhost ~]$ sudo firewall-cmd --query-icmp-block=host-redirect
yes
[donnie@localhost ~]$
```

Now, let's check the status:

```
[donnie@localhost ~]$ sudo firewall-cmd --info-zone=public
public (active)
  target: default
  icmp-block-inversion: no
  interfaces: enp0s3
  sources:
  services: ssh dhcpv6-client
  ports: 53/tcp 53/udp
  protocols:
  masquerade: no
  forward-ports:
  source-ports:
  icmp-blocks: host-redirect
  rich rules:
[donnie@localhost ~]$
```

Cool – it worked. Now, let's see if we can block two ICMP types with just one command:

```
[donnie@localhost ~]$ sudo firewall-cmd --add-icmp-block={host-
redirect,network-redirect}
success
[donnie@localhost ~]$
```

As before, we'll check the status:

```
[donnie@localhost ~]$ sudo firewall-cmd --info-zone=public
public (active)
  target: default
  icmp-block-inversion: no
  interfaces: enp0s3
  sources:
  services: cockpit dhcpv6-client ssh
  ports:
  protocols:
  masquerade: no
  forward-ports:
  source-ports:
  icmp-blocks: host-redirect network-redirect
  rich rules:
[donnie@localhost ~]$
```

This also worked, which means that we have achieved coolness. However, since we didn't include
--permanent with these commands, these ICMP types will only be blocked until we reboot the computer. So, let's make them permanent:

```
[donnie@localhost ~]$ sudo firewall-cmd --runtime-to-permanent
success
[donnie@localhost ~]$
```

And with this, we've achieved even more coolness. (Of course, all of my cats already think that I'm pretty cool.)

Using panic mode

You've just seen evidence that bad people are trying to break into your system. What do you do? Well, one option is to activate panic mode, which cuts off all network communications.

> I can just see this now in the Saturday morning cartoons when some cartoon character yells, *Panic mode, activate!*

To activate panic mode, use this command:

```
[donnie@localhost ~]$ sudo firewall-cmd --panic-on
[sudo] password for donnie:
success
[donnie@localhost ~]$
```

Of course, your access will be cut off if you're logged in remotely, and you'll have to go to the local terminal to get back in. To turn `panic` mode off, use this command:

```
[donnie@localhost ~]$ sudo firewall-cmd --panic-off
[sudo] password for donnie:
success
[donnie@localhost ~]$
```

If you're logged in remotely, there's no need to check the status of `panic` mode. If it's on, you're not accessing the machine. But if you're sitting at the local console, you might want to check it. Just do:

```
[donnie@localhost ~]$ sudo firewall-cmd --query-panic
[sudo] password for donnie:
no
[donnie@localhost ~]$
```

That's all there is to `panic` mode.

Logging dropped packets

Here's another time-saver that you're sure to like. If you want to create log entries whenever packets get blocked, just use the `--set-log-denied` option. Before we do that, let's see if it's already enabled:

```
[donnie@localhost ~]$ sudo firewall-cmd --get-log-denied
[sudo] password for donnie:
off
[donnie@localhost ~]$
```

It's not, so let's turn it on and check the status again:

```
[donnie@localhost ~]$ sudo firewall-cmd --set-log-denied=all
success
[donnie@localhost ~]$ sudo firewall-cmd --get-log-denied
all
[donnie@localhost ~]$
```

We've set it up to log all denied packets. However, you might not always want that. Your other choices are `unicast`, `broadcast`, and `multicast`.

So, for example, if all you want is to log blocked packets that are going to multicast addresses, do this:

```
[donnie@localhost ~]$ sudo firewall-cmd --set-log-denied=multicast
[sudo] password for donnie:
success
[donnie@localhost ~]$ sudo firewall-cmd --get-log-denied
multicast
[donnie@localhost ~]$
```

So far, we've just set the runtime configuration, which will disappear once we reboot the machine. To make this permanent, we can use any of the methods that we've already used. For now, let's just do this:

```
[donnie@localhost ~]$ sudo firewall-cmd --runtime-to-permanent
success
[donnie@localhost ~]$
```

Unlike what we saw with the Debian/Ubuntu distros, there's no separate kern.log file for our packet-denied messages. Instead, the RHEL-type distros log the packet-denied messages in the /var/log/messages file, which is the main log file in the RHEL world. Several different message tags are already defined, which will make it easier to audit the logs for dropped packets. For example, here's a message that tells us about blocked broadcast packets:

```
Aug 20 14:57:21 localhost kernel: FINAL_REJECT: IN=enp0s3 OUT= MAC=ff:ff:ff:f
f:ff:ff:00:1f:29:02:0d:5f:08:00 SRC=192.168.0.225 DST=255.255.255.255 LEN=140
TOS=0x00 PREC=0x00
 TTL=64 ID=62867 DF PROTO=UDP SPT=21327 DPT=21327 LEN=120
```

The tag is FINAL_REJECT, which tells us that this message was created by the catch-all, final REJECT rule that's at the end of our input chain. The DST=255.255.255.255 part tells us that this was a broadcast message.

Here's another example, where I did an Nmap NULL scan against this machine:

```
sudo nmap -sN 192.168.0.8

Aug 20 15:06:15 localhost kernel: STATE_INVALID_DROP: IN=enp0s3 OUT= MAC=08:00
:27:10:66:1c:00:1f:29:02:0d:5f:08:00 SRC=192.168.0.225 DST=192.168.0.8 LEN=40
TOS=0x00 PREC=0x00 TTL=42 ID=27451 PROTO=TCP SPT=46294 DPT=23 WINDOW=1024
RES=0x00 URGP=0
```

In this case, I triggered the rule that blocks INVALID packets, as indicated by the STATE_INVALID_DROP tag.

So, now you're saying, *But wait*. These two rules that we just tested aren't anywhere to be found in the firewalld configuration files that we've looked at so far. What gives? And you're right. The location of these default, pre-configured rules is something that the Red Hat folk apparently want to keep hidden from us. However, in the following sections that are specific to RHEL/CentOS 7 and RHEL/AlmaLinux 8 and 9, we'll spoil their fun, because I can show you where these rules are.

Using firewalld rich language rules

What we've looked at so far might be all you'll ever need for general use scenarios, but for more granular control, you'll want to know about **rich language rules**. (Yes, that really is what they're called.)

Compared to `iptables` rules, rich language rules are a bit less cryptic and are closer to plain English. So, if you're new to the business of writing firewall rules, you might find rich language a bit easier to learn. On the other hand, if you're already used to writing `iptables` rules, you might find some elements of the rich language a bit quirky. Let's look at one example:

```
sudo firewall-cmd --permanent --add-rich-rule='rule family="ipv4" source
address="200.192.0.0/24" service name="http" drop'
```

Here, we're adding a rich rule that blocks website access from an entire geographic block of IPv4 addresses. Note that the entire rule is surrounded by a pair of single quotes, and the assigned value for each parameter is surrounded by a pair of double quotes. With this rule, we're saying that we're working with IPv4 and that we want to silently block the `http` port from accepting packets from the `200.192.0.0/24` network. I used the `--permanent` option here, because the rich-rule commands don't work correctly if I don't use it. Let's see what our zone looks like with this new rule:

```
[donnie@localhost ~]$ sudo firewall-cmd --permanent --info-zone=dmz
  dmz (active)
  target: default
  icmp-block-inversion: no
  interfaces: enp0s3
  sources:
  services: ssh http https
  ports: 10000/tcp 636/tcp 637/tcp 638/udp
. . .
. . .
  rich rules:
  rule family="ipv4" source address="200.192.0.0/24" service name="http"
  drop
[donnie@localhost ~]$
```

The rich rule shows up at the bottom.

You could just as easily write a rule for IPv6 by replacing `family="ipv4"` with `family="ipv6"` and supplying the appropriate IPv6 address range.

Some rules are generic and apply to either IPv4 or IPv6. Let's say that we want to log messages about **Network Time Protocol (NTP)** packets for both IPv4 and IPv6 and that we want to log no more than one message per minute. The command to create that rule would look like this:

```
sudo firewall-cmd --add-rich-rule='rule service name="ntp" audit limit
value="1/m" accept'
```

There is, of course, a lot more to `firewalld` rich language rules than we can present here. But for now, you know the basics. For more information, consult the man page:

```
man firewalld.richlanguage
```

> If you go to the official documentation page for Red Hat Enterprise Linux 8, you'll see no mention of rich rules. However, I've just tested them on a RHEL 8-type machine and a RHEL 9-type machine, and they work fine.
>
> To read about rich rules, you'll need to go to the documentation page for Red Hat Enterprise Linux 7. What's there also applies to RHEL 8/9. But even there, there's not much detail. To find out more, see the man page on either RHEL/CentOS 7, RHEL/AlmaLinux 8, or RHEL/AlmaLinux 9.

To make the rule permanent, just use any of the methods that we've already discussed. When you do, the rule will show up in the `.xml` file for the default zone. In my case, the default zone is still set to public. So, let's look in the `/etc/firewalld/zones/public.xml` file:

```xml
<?xml version="1.0" encoding="utf-8"?>
<zone>
  <short>Public</short>
  <description>For use in public areas. You do not trust the other computers
on networks to not harm your computer. Only selected incoming connections are
accepted.</description>
  <service name="ssh"/>
  <service name="dhcpv6-client"/>
  <service name="cockpit"/>
  <rule family="ipv4">
    <source address="192.168.0.225"/>
    <service name="http"/>
    <drop/>
  </rule>
</zone>
```

Our rich rule shows up in the `rule family` block at the bottom of the file.

Now that we've covered what's common between the RHEL/CentOS 7 and the RHEL/CentOS/AlmaLinux 8/9 versions of `firewalld`, let's look at what's particular to each different version.

Looking at iptables rules in RHEL/CentOS 7 firewalld

RHEL 7 and its offspring use the `iptables` engine as the `firewalld` backend. You can't create rules with the normal `iptables` commands as long as `firewalld` is enabled. However, every time you create a rule with a `firewall-cmd` command, the `iptables` backend creates the appropriate `iptables` rule and inserts it into its proper place. You can view the active rules with `iptables -L`. Here's the first part of a very long output:

```
[donnie@localhost ~]$ sudo iptables -L
Chain INPUT (policy ACCEPT)
target      prot opt source              destination
ACCEPT      all  --  anywhere        anywhere            ctstate
RELATED,ESTABLISHED
ACCEPT      all  --  anywhere        anywhere
INPUT_direct      all  --  anywhere        anywhere
INPUT_ZONES_SOURCE all  --  anywhere        anywhere
INPUT_ZONES   all  --  anywhere        anywhere
DROP        all  --  anywhere        anywhere            ctstate INVALID
REJECT      all  --  anywhere        anywhere
reject-with icmp-host-prohibited
```

As was the case with ufw on Ubuntu, a lot has already been configured for us. At the top, in the INPUT chain, we see that the connection state rule and the rule to block invalid packets are already there. The default policy for the chain is ACCEPT, but the final rule of the chain is set to REJECT what isn't specifically allowed. In between these, we see rules that direct other packets to other chains for processing. Now, let's look at the next portion:

```
Chain IN_public_allow (1 references)
target      prot opt source              destination
ACCEPT      tcp  --  anywhere        anywhere            tcp dpt:ssh
ctstate NEW
ACCEPT      tcp  --  anywhere        anywhere            tcp dpt:domain
ctstate NEW
ACCEPT      udp  --  anywhere        anywhere            udp dpt:domain
ctstate NEW

Chain IN_public_deny (1 references)
target      prot opt source              destination
REJECT      icmp --  anywhere        anywhere
icmp host-redirect reject-with icmp-host-prohibited
```

Toward the bottom of the very long output, we see the IN_public_allow chain, which contains the rules that we created for opening firewall ports. Just below that is the IN_public_deny chain, which contains the REJECT rule for blocking unwanted ICMP types. In both the INPUT chain and the IN_public_deny chain, the REJECT rules return an ICMP message to inform the sender that the packets were blocked.

Now, keep in mind that there's a lot of this IPTABLES -L output that we haven't shown. So, look at it for yourself to see what's there. When you do, you may ask yourself, *Where are these default rules stored?* *Why am I not seeing them in the* /etc/firewalld/ *directory?*

To answer that question, I had to do some rather extensive investigation. For some truly bizarre reason, the Red Hat folk have left this completely undocumented. I finally found the answer in the `/usr/lib/python2.7/site-packages/firewall/core/` directory. Here, there's a set of Python scripts that set up the initial default firewall:

```
[donnie@localhost core]$ ls
base.py fw_config.pyc fw_helper.pyo fw_ipset.py fw_policies.pyc fw_service.
pyo fw_zone.py icmp.pyc ipset.pyc logger.pyo rich.py base.pyc fw_config.pyo
fw_icmptype.py fw_ipset.pyc fw_policies.pyo fw_test.py fw_zone.pyc icmp.pyo
ipset.pyo modules.py rich.pyc base.pyo fw_direct.py fw_icmptype.pyc fw_ipset.
pyo fw.py fw_test.pyc fw_zone.pyo __init__.py ipXtables.py modules.pyc rich.
pyo ebtables.py fw_direct.pyc fw_icmptype.pyo fw_nm.py fw.pyc fw_test.pyo
helper.py __init__.pyc ipXtables.pyc modules.pyo watcher.py ebtables.pyc fw_
direct.pyo fw_ifcfg.py fw_nm.pyc fw.pyo fw_transaction.py helper.pyc __init__.
pyo ipXtables.pyo prog.py watcher.pyc ebtables.pyo fw_helper.py fw_ifcfg.pyc
fw_nm.pyo fw_service.py fw_transaction.pyc helper.pyo io logger.py prog.pyc
watcher.pyo fw_config.py fw_helper.pyc fw_ifcfg.pyo fw_policies.py fw_service.
pyc fw_transaction.pyo icmp.py ipset.py logger.pyc prog.pyo
[donnie@localhost core]$
```

The script that does most of the work is the `ipXtables.py` script. If you look inside it, you'll see that its list of `iptables` commands matches up with the `iptables -L` output.

Creating direct rules in RHEL/CentOS 7 firewalld

As we've seen, any time we do anything with the normal `firewall-cmd` commands on RHEL/CentOS 7, `firewalld` automatically translates those commands into `iptables` rules and inserts them into the proper place. (Or, it deletes the rules, if you've issued some sort of delete command.) However, there are some things that we can't do with the normal `firewalld-cmd` commands. For example, we can't use normal `firewall-cmd` commands to place rules in a specific `iptables` chain or table. To do things like that, we need to use direct configuration commands.

The `firewalld.direct` man page and the documentation on the Red Hat site both warn you to only use direct configuration as an absolute last resort when nothing else will work. That's because, unlike the normal `firewall-cmd` commands, the direct commands won't automatically place your new rules into the proper places so that everything works correctly. With the direct commands, you can break the whole firewall by placing a rule in the wrong spot.

In the example output of the previous section, in the default ruleset, you saw that there's a rule in the filter table's INPUT chain that blocks invalid packets. In the *Blocking invalid packets with iptables* section of *Chapter 4*, *Securing Your Server with a Firewall – Part 1*, you saw that this rule misses certain types of invalid packets. So, we'd like to add a second rule to block what the first rule misses. We'd also like to place these rules into the PREROUTING chain of the mangle table in order to enhance firewall performance. To do this, we need to create a couple of direct rules. (This isn't hard if you're familiar with normal `iptables` syntax.) So, let's get to it.

First, let's verify that we don't have any effective direct rules, like so:

```
sudo firewall-cmd --direct --get-rules ipv4 mangle PREROUTING
sudo firewall-cmd --direct --get-rules ipv6 mangle PREROUTING
```

You should get no output for either command. Now, let's add our two new rules, for both IPv4 and IPv6, with the following four commands:

```
sudo firewall-cmd --direct --add-rule ipv4 mangle PREROUTING 0 -m conntrack
--ctstate INVALID -j DROP

sudo firewall-cmd --direct --add-rule ipv4 mangle PREROUTING 1 -p tcp ! --syn
-m conntrack --ctstate NEW -j DROP

sudo firewall-cmd --direct --add-rule ipv6 mangle PREROUTING 0 -m conntrack
--ctstate INVALID -j DROP

sudo firewall-cmd --direct --add-rule ipv6 mangle PREROUTING 1 -p tcp ! --syn
-m conntrack --ctstate NEW -j DROP
```

The direct command syntax is very similar to that of normal iptables commands. So, I won't repeat the explanations that I've already presented in the iptables section. However, I do want to point out the 0 and the 1 that come after PREROUTING in each of the commands. Those represent the priority of the rule. The lower the number, the higher the priority, and the higher up the rule is in the chain. So, the rules with the 0 priority are the first rules in their respective chains, while the rules with the 1 priority are the second rules in their respective chains. If you give the same priority to each rule you create, there's no guarantee that the order will remain the same upon each reboot. So, be sure to assign a different priority to each rule.

Now, let's verify that our rules are in effect:

```
[donnie@localhost ~]$ sudo firewall-cmd --direct --get-rules ipv4 mangle
PREROUTING
0 -m conntrack --ctstate INVALID -j DROP

1 -p tcp '!' --syn -m conntrack --ctstate NEW -j DROP
[donnie@localhost ~]$ sudo firewall-cmd --direct --get-rules ipv6 mangle
PREROUTING
0 -m conntrack --ctstate INVALID -j DROP

1 -p tcp '!' --syn -m conntrack --ctstate NEW -j DROP
[donnie@localhost ~]$
```

We see that they are. When you use the `iptables -t mangle -L` command and the `ip6tables -t mangle -L` command, you'll see that the rules show up in the `PREROUTING_direct` chain. (I'm only showing the output once since it's the same for both commands.):

```
. . .

. . .

Chain PREROUTING_direct (1 references)
target prot opt source destination
DROP all -- anywhere anywhere ctstate INVALID
DROP tcp -- anywhere anywhere tcp flags:!FIN,SYN,RST,ACK/SYN ctstate NEW

. . .

. . .
```

To show that it works, we can perform some Nmap scans against the virtual machine, just like how I showed you in the *Blocking invalid packets with iptables* section of *Chapter 4, Securing Your Server With A Firewall – Part 1*. (Don't fret if you don't remember how to do it. You'll see the procedure in the upcoming hands-on lab.) Then, we can use `sudo iptables -t mangle -L -v` and `sudo ip6tables -t mangle -L -v` to see the packets and bytes that these two rules blocked.

We didn't use the `--permanent` option with these commands, so they're not permanent yet. Let's make them permanent now:

```
[donnie@localhost ~]$ sudo firewall-cmd --runtime-to-permanent
[sudo] password for donnie:
success
[donnie@localhost ~]$
Now, let's take a look in the /etc/firewalld/ directory. Here, you'll see a
direct.xml file that wasn't there before:
[donnie@localhost ~]$ sudo ls -l /etc/firewalld
total 20
-rw-r--r--. 1 root root  532 Aug 26 13:17 direct.xml

. . .

. . .

[donnie@localhost ~]$
```

Look inside the file; you'll see the new rules:

```
<?xml version="1.0" encoding="utf-8"?>
<direct>
  <rule priority="0" table="mangle" ipv="ipv4" chain="PREROUTING">-m conntrack
--ctstate INVALID -j DROP</rule>


  <rule priority="1" table="mangle" ipv="ipv4" chain="PREROUTING">-p tcp '!'
--syn -m conntrack --ctstate NEW -j DROP</rule>
```

```
    <rule priority="0" table="mangle" ipv="ipv6" chain="PREROUTING">-m conntrack
--ctstate INVALID -j DROP</rule>

    <rule priority="1" table="mangle" ipv="ipv6" chain="PREROUTING">-p tcp '!'
--syn -m conntrack --ctstate NEW -j DROP</rule>

</direct>
```

The official Red Hat 7 documentation page does cover direct rules, but only briefly. For more detailed information, see the `firewalld.direct` man page.

Looking at nftables rules in RHEL/AlmaLinux 8 and 9 firewalld

RHEL 8/9 and their offspring use `nftables` as the default `firewalld` backend. Every time you create a rule with a `firewall-cmd` command, the appropriate `nftables` rule is created and inserted into its proper place. To look at the ruleset that's currently in effect, we'll use the same `nft` command that we used with `nftables` on Ubuntu:

```
[donnie@localhost ~]$ sudo nft list ruleset
. . .
. . .
table ip firewalld {
    chain nat_PREROUTING {
        type nat hook prerouting priority -90; policy accept;
        jump nat_PREROUTING_ZONES_SOURCE
        jump nat_PREROUTING_ZONES
    }

    chain nat_PREROUTING_ZONES_SOURCE {
    }
. . .
. . .
[donnie@localhost ~]$
```

Again, we see a very lengthy list of default, pre-configured firewall rules. (To see the whole list, run the command for yourself.) You'll find these default rules in the `/usr/lib/python3.6/site-packages/firewall/core/nftables.py` script on RHEL 8-type machines, and in the `/usr/lib/python3.9/site-packages/firewall/core/nftables.py` script on RHEL 9-type machines. This script runs every time you boot up the machine.

Creating direct rules in RHEL/AlmaLinux firewalld

Okay, here's where things get downright weird. Even though the direct rule commands create `iptables` rules and the RHEL 8/9 distros use `nftables` for the `firewalld` backend, you can still create direct rules.

Just create and verify them the same way that you did in the *Creating direct rules in RHEL/CentOS 7* firewalld section. Apparently, firewalld allows these iptables rules to peacefully coexist with the nftables rules. However, if you need to do this on a production system, be sure to thoroughly test your setup before putting it into production.

There's nothing about this in the Red Hat 8/9 documentation, but there is the firewalld.direct man page if you want to find out more.

Hands-on lab for firewalld commands

By completing this lab, you'll get some practice with basic firewalld commands:

1. Log into your CentOS 7 virtual machine or either of the AlmaLinux virtual machines and run the following commands. Observe the output after each one:

    ```
    sudo firewall-cmd --get-zones
    sudo firewall-cmd --get-default-zone
    sudo firewall-cmd --get-active-zones
    ```

2. Briefly view the man pages that deal with firewalld.zones:

    ```
    man firewalld.zones
    man firewalld.zone
    ```

    (Yes, there are two of them. One explains the zone configuration files, while the other explains the zones themselves.)

3. Look at the configuration information for all of the available zones:

    ```
    sudo firewall-cmd --list-all-zones
    ```

4. Look at the list of predefined services. Then, look at the information about the dropbox-lansync service:

    ```
    sudo firewall-cmd --get-services
    sudo firewall-cmd --info-service=dropbox-lansync
    ```

5. Set the default zone to dmz. Look at the information concerning the zone, add the http and https services, and then look at the zone information again:

    ```
    sudo firewall-cmd --set-default-zone=dmz
    sudo firewall-cmd --permanent --add-service={http,https}
    sudo firewall-cmd --info-zone=dmz
    sudo firewall-cmd --permanent --info-zone=dmz
    ```

6. Reload the firewall configuration and look at the zone information again. Also, look at the list of services that are being allowed:

```
sudo firewall-cmd --reload
sudo firewall-cmd --info-zone=dmz
sudo firewall-cmd --list-services
```

7. Permanently open port 10000/tcp and view the results:

```
sudo firewall-cmd --permanent --add-port=10000/tcp
sudo firewall-cmd --list-ports
sudo firewall-cmd --reload
sudo firewall-cmd --list-ports
sudo firewall-cmd --info-zone=dmz
```

8. Remove the port that you just added:

```
sudo firewall-cmd --permanent --remove-port=10000/tcp
sudo firewall-cmd --reload
sudo firewall-cmd --list-ports
sudo firewall-cmd --info-zone=dmz
```

9. Add a rich language rule to block a geographic range of IPv4 addresses:

```
sudo firewall-cmd --permanent --add-rich-rule='rule family="ipv4" source
address="200.192.0.0/24" service name="http" drop'
```

10. Block the host-redirect and network-redirect ICMP types:

```
sudo firewall-cmd --permanent --add-icmp-block={host-redirect,network-
redirect}
```

11. Add the directive to log all dropped packets:

```
sudo firewall-cmd --set-log-denied=all
```

12. View both the runtime and permanent configurations and note the differences between them:

```
sudo firewall-cmd --info-zone=dmz
sudo firewall-cmd --info-zone=dmz --permanent
```

13. Make the runtime configuration permanent and verify that it took effect:

```
sudo firewall-cmd --runtime-to-permanent
sudo firewall-cmd --info-zone=dmz --permanent
```

14. On CentOS 7, view the complete list of effective firewall rules by doing:

```
sudo iptables -L
```

15. On AlmaLinux 8 or 9, view the complete list of effective firewall rules by doing:

```
sudo nft list ruleset
```

16. Create the `direct` rules in order to block invalid packets from the mangle table's `PREROUTING` chain:

```
sudo firewall-cmd --direct --add-rule ipv4 mangle PREROUTING 0 -m
conntrack --ctstate INVALID -j DROP

sudo firewall-cmd --direct --add-rule ipv4 mangle PREROUTING 1 -p tcp !
--syn -m conntrack --ctstate NEW -j DROP

sudo firewall-cmd --direct --add-rule ipv6 mangle PREROUTING 0 -m
conntrack --ctstate INVALID -j DROP

sudo firewall-cmd --direct --add-rule ipv6 mangle PREROUTING 1 -p tcp !
--syn -m conntrack --ctstate NEW -j DROP
```

17. Verify that the rules took effect and make them permanent:

```
sudo firewall-cmd --direct --get-rules ipv4 mangle PREROUTING
sudo firewall-cmd --direct --get-rules ipv6 mangle PREROUTING
sudo firewall-cmd --runtime-to-permanent
```

18. View the contents of the `direct.xml` file that you've just created:

```
sudo less /etc/firewalld/direct.xml
```

19. Perform XMAS Nmap scans for both IPv4 and IPv6 against the virtual machine. Then, observe which rule was triggered by the scan:

```
sudo nmap -sX ipv4_address_of_Test-VM
sudo nmap -6 -sX ipv6_address_of_Test-VM
sudo iptables -t mangle -L -v
sudo ip6tables -t mangle -L -v
```

20. Repeat *step 19*, but this time with a Windows scan:

```
sudo nmap -sW ipv4_address_of_Test-VM
sudo nmap -6 -sW ipv6_address_of_Test-VM
sudo iptables -t mangle -L -v
sudo ip6tables -t mangle -L -v
```

21. View the list of main pages for `firewalld`:

```
apropos firewall
```

That's the end of the lab – congratulations!

Summary

In this chapter, we looked at two helper utilities that can simplify using either `iptables` or `nftables`. We started with `ufw`, which is available for the Debian and Ubuntu families. Then, we looked at `firewalld`, which used to be specific to Red Hat-type distros, but is now also available in Ubuntu repositories and comes already installed and activated on the SUSE distros.

In the space that I've been allotted, I've presented the basics of using these technologies to set up single-host protection. I've also presented some details about the innards of `firewalld` that you won't find documented anywhere else, including in the official Red Hat documentation.

In the next chapter, we'll look at the various encryption technologies that can help keep your data private. I'll see you there.

Questions

1. What is the major difference between `firewalld` on RHEL 7-type distros and `firewalld` on RHEL 8/9-type distros?

2. In which of the following formats does `firewalld` store its rules?

    a. `.txt`

    b. `.config`

    c. `.html`

    d. `.xml`

3. Which of the following commands would you use to list all of the `firewalld` zones on your system?

    a. `sudo firewalld --get-zones`

    b. `sudo firewall-cmd --list-zones`

    c. `sudo firewall-cmd --get-zones`

    d. `sudo firewalld --list-zones`

4. With `ufw`, everything you'll ever need to do can be done with the `ufw` utility.

    a. True

    b. False

5. Your system is set up with `firewalld` and you need to open port `10000/tcp`. Which of the following commands would you use?

    a. `sudo firewall-cmd --add-port=10000/tcp`

    b. `sudo firewall-cmd --add-port=10000`

    c. `sudo firewalld --add-port=10000`

    d. `sudo firewalld --add-port=10000/tcp`

6. Which of the following `ufw` commands would you use to open the default Secure Shell port?

    a.   `sudo ufw allow 22`

    b.   `sudo ufw permit 22`

    c.   `sudo ufw allow 22/tcp`

    d.   `sudo ufw permit 22/tcp`

Further reading

- Rate-limiting with `ufw`: `https://45squared.com/rate-limiting-with-ufw/`
- `firewalld` documentation for RHEL 7: `https://access.redhat.com/documentation/en-us/red_hat_enterprise_linux/7/html/security_guide/sec-using_firewalls`
- `firewalld` documentation for RHEL 8: `https://access.redhat.com/documentation/en-us/red_hat_enterprise_linux/8/html/securing_networks/using-and-configuring-firewalld_securing-networks`
- The `firewalld` home page: `https://firewalld.org/`
- UFW Community Help Wiki: `https://help.ubuntu.com/community/UFW`
- How to set up a Linux firewall with UFW on Ubuntu 18.04: `https://linuxize.com/post/how-to-setup-a-firewall-with-ufw-on-ubuntu-18-04/`

Answers

1. RHEL 7 distros use `iptables` as the `firewalld` backend, and RHEL 8/9 distros use `nftables` as the `firewalld` backend.

2. d

3. c

4. b

5. a

6. c

Join our book community

Join our community's Discord space for discussions with the author and other readers:

`https://packt.link/CyberSec`

6

Encryption Technologies

You may work for a super-secret government agency, or you may be just a regular Joe or Jane citizen. Either way, you still have sensitive data that you need to protect from prying eyes. Business secrets, government secrets, personal secrets—it doesn't matter. It all needs protection. Locking down users' home directories with restrictive permissions settings, as we saw in *Chapter 3, Securing Normal User Accounts*, is only part of the puzzle; we also need encryption. This encryption will provide three things for us:

- **Confidentiality:** This ensures that only people who are authorized to see the data can see it.
- **Integrity:** This ensures that the original data haven't been altered by unauthorized people.
- **Availability:** This ensures that sensitive data are always available, and can't be deleted by unauthorized people.

The two general types of data encryption that we'll look at in this chapter are meant to protect data at rest and data in transit. We'll begin with using file, partition, and directory encryption to protect data at rest. We'll wrap up with a look at using OpenSSL to protect data in transit.

In this chapter, we'll cover the following topics:

- **GNU Privacy Guard (GPG)**
- Encrypting partitions with **Linux Unified Key Setup (LUKS)**
- Encrypting directories with eCryptfs
- Using VeraCrypt for the cross-platform sharing of encrypted containers
- OpenSSL and the Public Key Infrastructure
- Commercial certificate authorities
- Creating keys, certificate requests, and certificates
- Creating an on-premises certificate authority
- Adding a certificate authority to an operating system
- OpenSSL and the Apache webserver
- Setting up mutual authentication

If you're ready to get cryptic, let's get started.

GNU Privacy Guard (GPG)

We'll begin with **GNU Privacy Guard** (GPG). This is a free open source implementation of Phil Zimmermann's Pretty Good Privacy, which he created back in 1991. You can use either one of them to either encrypt or cryptographically sign files or messages. In this section, we'll focus strictly on GPG.

There are some advantages of using GPG:

- It uses strong, hard-to-crack encryption algorithms.
- It uses the private/public key scheme, which eliminates the need to transfer a password to a message or file recipient in a secure manner. Instead, just send along your public key, which is useless to anyone other than the intended recipient.
- You can use GPG to just encrypt your own files for your own use, the same as you'd use any other encryption utility.
- It can be used to encrypt email messages, allowing you to have true end-to-end encryption for sensitive emails.
- There are a few GUI-type frontends available to make it somewhat easier to use.

But, as you might know, there are also some disadvantages:

- Using public keys instead of passwords is great when you work directly only with people who you implicitly trust. But for anything beyond that, such as distributing a public key to the general population so that everyone can verify your signed messages, you're dependent upon a web-of-trust model that can be very hard to set up.
- For the end-to-end encryption of email, the recipients of your email must also have GPG set up on their systems and know how to use it. That might work in a corporate environment, but lots of luck getting your friends to set that up. (I've never once succeeded in getting someone else to set up email encryption.)
- If you use a standalone email client, such as Mozilla Thunderbird, you can install a plugin that will encrypt and decrypt messages automatically. But every time a new Thunderbird update is released, the plugin breaks, and it always takes a while before a new working version gets released.
- Even if you could get other people to set up their email clients with GPG, it's still not the perfect privacy solution. That's because the email **metadata**—the email addresses of the sender and the recipient—can't be encrypted. So, hackers, advertisers, or government agencies can still see who you're exchanging email messages with, and use that information to build a profile that tells them a lot about your activities, your beliefs, and what kind of a person you are. If you really need complete privacy, your best bet is to go with a private messenger solution, such as the **Session** messenger. (That however, is beyond the scope of this book.)

Even with its numerous weaknesses, GPG is still one of the best ways to share encrypted files and emails. GPG comes preinstalled on most Linux distros. So, you can use any of your *newer* virtual machines for these demos. (I say *newer*, because the procedure will differ slightly on older distros, such as CentOS 7.)

Hands-on lab – creating your GPG keys

1. On a text-mode AlmaLinux machine, the first thing you need to do is to install the `pinentry` package. Do that with:

```
sudo dnf install pinentry
```

(Note that you won't have to do this with either a GUI-mode AlmaLinux machine or with Ubuntu Server.)

2. Next, create your pair of GPG keys:

```
gpg --full-generate-key
```

3. Note that since you're setting this up for yourself, you don't need `sudo` privileges.

The first thing that this command does is to create a populated `.gnupg` directory in your home directory:

```
gpg: /home/donnie/.gnupg/trustdb.gpg: trustdb created
gpg: key 56B59F39019107DF marked as ultimately trusted
gpg: directory '/home/donnie/.gnupg/openpgp-revocs.d' created
gpg: revocation certificate stored as '/home/donnie/.gnupg/openpgp-
revocs.d/BD057E0E01E664424E8B812E56B59F39019107DF.rev'
public and secret key created and signed.
```

4. You'll then be asked to select which kinds of keys you want. We'll just go with the default RSA and RSA. RSA keys are stronger and harder to crack than the older DSA keys. Elgamal keys are good, but they may not be supported by older versions of GPG:

```
Please select what kind of key you want:
  (1) RSA and RSA (default)
  (2) DSA and Elgamal
  (3) DSA (sign only)
  (4) RSA (sign only)
 (14) Existing key from card
Your selection?
```

5. For decent encryption, you'll want to go with a key of at least 3,072 bits, because anything smaller is now considered vulnerable. (This is according to the newest guidance from the U.S. National Institute of Standards and Technology, or NIST.) That's now the default on our newest Linux distros, so you're already good there. On older distros, such as CentOS 7, the default is only 2,048 bits, so you'll need to change it.

6. Next, select how long you want the keys to remain valid before they automatically expire. For our purposes, we'll go with the default key does not expire:

```
Please specify how long the key should be valid.
  0 = key does not expire
```

```
<n> = key expires in n days
<n>w = key expires in n weeks
<n>m = key expires in n months
<n>y = key expires in n years
Key is valid for? (0)
```

7. Provide your personal information:

```
GnuPG needs to construct a user ID to identify your key.
Real name: Donald A. Tevault
Email address: donniet@something.net
Comment: No comment
You selected this USER-ID:
  "Donald A. Tevault (No comment) <donniet@something.net>"
Change (N)ame, (C)omment, (E)mail or (O)kay/(Q)uit?
Create a passphrase for your private key:
You need a Passphrase to protect your secret key.
```

8. We need to generate a lot of random bytes. It is a good idea to perform some other action (type on the keyboard, move the mouse, utilize the disks) during the prime generation; this gives the random number generator a better chance to gain enough entropy.

9. On older Linux distros, this could take a while, even when you're doing all of the recommended things to create entropy. On newer Linux distros, the random number generator works more efficiently, so you can disregard the notice about how the key generation could take a long time. Here's what you'll see when the process has finished:

```
gpg: /home/donnie/.gnupg/trustdb.gpg: trustdb created
gpg: key 19CAEC5B marked as ultimately trusted
public and secret key created and signed.
gpg: checking the trustdb
gpg: 3 marginal(s) needed, 1 complete(s) needed, PGP trust model
gpg: depth: 0 valid: 1 signed: 0 trust: 0-, 0q, 0n, 0m, 0f, 1u
pub 2048R/19CAEC5B 2017-10-26
  Key fingerprint = 8DE5 8894 2E37 08C4 5B26 9164 C77C 6944 19CA EC5B
uid Donald A. Tevault (No comment) <donniet@something.net>
sub 2048R/37582F29 2017-10-26
```

10. Verify that the keys did get created:

```
[donnie@localhost ~]$ gpg --list-keys
/home/donnie/.gnupg/pubring.gpg
--------------------------------
pub 2048R/19CAEC5B 2017-10-26
uid Donald A. Tevault (No comment) <donniet@something.net>
```

```
    sub 2048R/37582F29 2017-10-26
    [donnie@localhost ~]$
```

11. While you're at it, take a look at the files that you created:

```
[donnie@localhost ~]$ ls -l .gnupg/
total 12
drwx------. 2 donnie donnie   58 Oct 26 14:53 openpgp-revocs.d
drwx------. 2 donnie donnie  110 Oct 26 14:53 private-keys-v1.d
-rw-r--r--. 1 donnie donnie 1970 Oct 26 14:53 pubring.kbx
-rw-------. 1 donnie donnie   32 Oct 26 14:43 pubring.kbx~
-rw-------. 1 donnie donnie 1280 Oct 26 15:51 trustdb.gpg
[donnie@localhost ~]$
```

These files are your public and private keyrings, a revocation database, and a trusted users database.

Hands-on lab — symmetrically encrypting your own files

You may find GPG useful for encrypting your own files, even when you never plan to share them with anyone else. For this, you'll use symmetric encryption, which involves using your own private key for encryption. Before you try this, you'll need to generate your keys, as I outlined in the previous section:

> Symmetric key encryption is, well, just that, symmetric. It's symmetric in the sense that the key that you would use to encrypt a file is the same key that you would use to decrypt the file. That's great for if you're just encrypting files for your own use. But if you need to share an encrypted file with someone else, you'll need to figure out a secure way to give that person the password. I mean, it's not like you'd want to just send the password in a plain-text email.

1. In addition to your own user account, you'll also need a user account for Maggie. On AlmaLinux, create her account like this:

```
sudo useradd maggie
sudo passwd maggie
```

For Ubuntu, create Maggie's account like this:

```
sudo adduser maggie
```

2. Let's encrypt a super-secret file that we just can't allow to fall into the wrong hands:

```
[donnie@localhost ~]$ gpg -c secret_squirrel_stuff.txt
[donnie@localhost ~]$
```

Note that the -c option indicates that I chose to use symmetric encryption with a passphrase for the file. The passphrase that you enter will be for the file, not for your private key.

3. Look at your new set of files. One slight flaw with this is that GPG makes an encrypted copy of the file, but it also leaves the original unencrypted file intact:

```
[donnie@localhost ~]$ ls -l
 total 1748
 -rw-rw-r--. 1 donnie donnie 37 Oct 26 14:22 secret_squirrel_stuff.txt
 -rw-rw-r--. 1 donnie donnie 94 Oct 26 14:22
 secret_squirrel_stuff.txt.gpg
[donnie@localhost ~]$
```

4. Let's get rid of that unencrypted file with shred. We'll use the -u option to delete the file, and the -z option to overwrite the deleted file with zeros:

```
[donnie@localhost ~]$ shred -u -z secret_squirrel_stuff.txt
[donnie@localhost ~]$
```

It doesn't look like anything happened, because shred doesn't give you any output. But ls -l will prove that the file is gone.

5. Now, if I were to look at the encrypted file with less secret_squirrel_stuff.txt.gpg, I would be able to see its contents after being asked to enter my private key passphrase. Try this for yourself:

```
less secret_squirrel_stuff.txt.gpg


Shhh!!!! This file is super-secret.
secret_squirrel_stuff.txt.gpg (END)
```

6. As long as my private key remains loaded into my keyring, I'll be able to view my encrypted file again without having to reenter the passphrase. Now, just to prove to you that the file really is encrypted, I'll create a shared directory, and move the file there for others to access. Again, go ahead and give it a try:

```
sudo mkdir /shared
sudo chown donnie: /shared
sudo chmod 755 /shared
mv secret_squirrel_stuff.txt.gpg /shared
```

When I go into that directory to view the file with less, I can still see its contents without having to reenter my passphrase.

7. But now, let's see what happens when Maggie tries to view the file. Use su - maggie to switch to her account, and have her try:

```
su - maggie
cd /shared
```

```
[maggie@localhost shared]$ less secret_squirrel_stuff.txt.gpg
"secret_squirrel_stuff.txt.gpg" may be a binary file. See it anyway?
```

And when she hits the *Y* key to see it anyway, she gets this:

```
<8C>^M^D^C^C^B<BD>2=<D3>ψ<93><CE><C9>MOOy<B6>^O<A2><AD>}
Rg9<94><EB><C4>^W^E

<A6><8D><B9><B8><D3>(<98><C4>æF^_8Q2b<B8>C<B5><DB>^]<F1><CD>#<90>H<EB><90><
 C5>^S%X [<E9><EF><C7>
  ^@y+<FC><F2><BA><U+058C>H'+<D4>v<84>Y<98>G<D7>-
secret_squirrel_stuff.txt.gpg (END)
```

Poor Maggie really wants to see my file, but all she can see is encrypted gibberish.

What I've just demonstrated is another advantage of GPG. After entering your private key passphrase once, you can view any of your encrypted files without having to manually decrypt them, and without having to reenter your passphrase. With other symmetric file encryption tools, such as bcrypt, you wouldn't be able to view your files without manually decrypting them first.

8. But let's now say that you no longer need to have this file encrypted, and you want to decrypt it in order to let other people see it. Exit Maggie's account by typing exit. Then, just use gpg with the -d option:

```
[maggie@localhost shared]$ exit

[donnie@localhost shared]$ gpg -o secret_squirrel_stuff.txt -d secret_
squirrel_stuff.txt.gpg

gpg: AES256.CFB encrypted data
gpg: encrypted with 1 passphrase
Shhh!!!! This file is super-secret.
[donnie@localhost shared]$
```

This works differently from how it worked on older Linux distros. On our newer distros, we now have to use the -o option along with the filename of the decrypted file that we want to create. Also, note that the -o option has to come before the -d option, or else you'll get an error message.

Hands-on lab — encrypting files with public keys

In this lab, you'll learn about how to encrypt and share a file with GPG public key encryption:

1. To begin, create a user account for Frank, as you did for Maggie in the previous lab.

2. Create a key set for both yourself and for Frank, as I've already shown you. Next, extract your own public keys into an ASCII text file:

```
cd .gnupg
gpg --export -a -o donnie_public-key.txt
```

Log in as Frank, and repeat this command for him.

3.   Normally, the participants in this would send their keys to each other either through an email attachment or by placing the keys in a shared directory. In this case, you and Frank will receive each other's public key files and place them into your respective .gnupg directories. Once that's done, import each other's keys:

```
donnie@ubuntu:~/.gnupg$ gpg --import frank_public-key.txt
gpg: key 4CFC6990: public key "Frank Siamese (I am a cat.) <frank@any.
net>" imported
gpg: Total number processed: 1
gpg: imported: 1 (RSA: 1)
donnie@ubuntu:~/.gnupg$


frank@ubuntu:~/.gnupg$ gpg --import donnie_public-key.txt
gpg: key 9FD7014B: public key "Donald A. Tevault <donniet@something.net>"
imported
gpg: Total number processed: 1
gpg:                  imported: 1  (RSA: 1)
frank@ubuntu:~/.gnupg$
```

4.   Now for the good stuff. Create a super-secret message for Frank, asymmetrically encrypt it (-e), and sign it (-s). Signing the message is the verification that the message really is from you, rather than from an impostor:

```
donnie@ubuntu:~$ gpg -s -e secret_stuff_for_frank.txt

. . .

. . .

It is NOT certain that the key belongs to the person named
in the user ID.  If you *really* know what you are doing,
you may answer the next question with yes.


Use this key anyway? (y/N) y


Current recipients:
2048R/CD8104F7 2017-10-27 "Frank Siamese (I am a cat.) <frank@any.net>"


Enter the user ID.  End with an empty line:
donnie@ubuntu:~$
```

So, the first thing you have to do is to enter the passphrase for your private key. Where it says to enter the user ID, enter frank, since he's the intended recipient of your message. But look at the line after that, where it says There is no assurance this key belongs to the named user. That's because you still haven't trusted Frank's public key. We'll get to that in a bit. The last line of the output again says to enter a user ID so that we can designate multiple recipients. But Frank is the only one you care about right now, so just hit the *Enter* key to break out of the routine. This results in a .gpg version of your message to Frank:

```
donnie@ubuntu:~$ ls -l
total 8
. . .
-rw-rw-r-- 1 donnie donnie 143 Oct 27 18:37 secret_stuff_for_frank.txt
-rw-rw-r-- 1 donnie donnie 790 Oct 27 18:39 secret_stuff_for_frank.txt.
gpg
donnie@ubuntu:~$
```

5. The final step on your end is to send Frank his encrypted message file by whatever means available.

6. When Frank receives his message, he'll use the -d option to view it:

```
frank@ubuntu:~$ gpg -d secret_stuff_for_frank.txt.gpg
. . .
. . .
gpg: gpg-agent is not available in this session
gpg: encrypted with 2048-bit RSA key, ID CD8104F7, created 2017-10-27
      "Frank Siamese (I am a cat.) <frank@any.net>"
This is TOP SECRET stuff that only Frank can see!!!!!
If anyone else see it, it's the end of the world as we know it.
(With apologies to REM.)
gpg: Signature made Fri 27 Oct 2017 06:39:15 PM EDT using RSA key ID
9FD7014B
gpg: Good signature from "Donald A. Tevault <donniet@something.net>"
gpg: WARNING: This key is not certified with a trusted signature!
gpg:           There is no indication that the signature belongs to the
owner.
Primary key fingerprint: DB0B 31B8 876D 9B2C 7F12  9FC3 886F 3357 9FD7
014B
frank@ubuntu:~$
```

7. Frank enters the passphrase for his private key, and he sees the message. At the bottom, he sees the warning about how your public key isn't trusted, and that `There is no indication that the signature belongs to the owner`. Let's say that you and Frank know each other personally, and he knows for a fact that the public key really is yours. He then adds your public key to the trusted list:

```
frank@ubuntu:~$ cd .gnupg
frank@ubuntu:~/.gnupg$ gpg --edit-key donnie
gpg (GnuPG) 1.4.20; Copyright (C) 2015 Free Software Foundation, Inc.
This is free software: you are free to change and redistribute it.
There is NO WARRANTY, to the extent permitted by law.
gpg: checking the trustdb
gpg: 3 marginal(s) needed, 1 complete(s) needed, PGP trust model
gpg: depth: 0 valid:   2 signed:   0 trust: 0-, 0q, 0n, 0m, 0f, 2u
pub   2048R/9FD7014B  created: 2017-10-27  expires: never       usage: SC
                      trust: ultimate      validity: ultimate
sub   2048R/9625E7E9  created: 2017-10-27  expires: never       usage: E
[ultimate] (1). Donald A. Tevault <donniet@something.net>
gpg>
```

8. The last line of this output is the command prompt for the gpg shell. Frank is concerned with trust, so he'll enter the `trust` command:

```
gpg> trust
pub   2048R/9FD7014B  created: 2017-10-27  expires: never       usage: SC
                      trust: unknown       validity: unknown
sub   2048R/9625E7E9  created: 2017-10-27  expires: never       usage: E
[ unknown] (1). Donald A. Tevault <donniet@something.net>
Please decide how far you trust this user to correctly verify other
users' keys
(by looking at passports, checking fingerprints from different sources,
etc.)
  1 = I don't know or won't say
  2 = I do NOT trust
  3 = I trust marginally
  4 = I trust fully
  5 = I trust ultimately
  m = back to the main menu
Your decision? 5
Do you really want to set this key to ultimate trust? (y/N) y
```

9. Frank has known you for quite a while, and he knows for a fact that you're the one who sent the key. So, he chooses option 5 for ultimate trust. Once Frank logs out and logs back in, that trust will take effect:

```
frank@ubuntu:~$ gpg -d secret_stuff_for_frank.txt.gpg

You need a passphrase to unlock the secret key for
user: "Frank Siamese (I am a cat.) <frank@any.net>"
2048-bit RSA key, ID CD8104F7, created 2017-10-27 (main key ID 4CFC6990)

gpg: gpg-agent is not available in this session
gpg: encrypted with 2048-bit RSA key, ID CD8104F7, created 2017-10-27
      "Frank Siamese (I am a cat.) <frank@any.net>"
This is TOP SECRET stuff that only Frank can see!!!!!
If anyone else see it, it's the end of the world as we know it.
(With apologies to REM.)
gpg: Signature made Fri 27 Oct 2017 06:39:15 PM EDT using RSA key ID
9FD7014B
gpg: Good signature from "Donald A. Tevault <donniet@something.net>"
frank@ubuntu:~$
```

10. With no more warning messages, this looks much better. At your end, do the same thing with Frank's public key.

> As you can see in the screen output in *step 8*, you can assign the marginal, full, or ultimate trust level to someone else's public key. Space doesn't permit me to provide a full explanation of the trust levels, but you can read a rather colorful explanation here: PGP Web of Trust: Core Concepts Behind Trusted Communication—https://www.linux.com/tutorials/pgp-web-trust-core-concepts-behind-trusted-communication/.

What's so very cool about this is that even though the whole world may have your public key, it's useless to anyone who isn't a designated recipient of your message.

Now, let's look at how to sign a file *without* encrypting it.

Hands-on lab – signing a file without encryption

If a file isn't secret but you still need to ensure authenticity and integrity, you can just sign it without encrypting it:

1. Create an unencrypted message for Frank and then sign it:

```
donnie@ubuntu:~$ gpg -s not_secret_for_frank.txt

You need a passphrase to unlock the secret key for
user: "Donald A. Tevault <donniet@something.net>"
2048-bit RSA key, ID 9FD7014B, created 2017-10-27

gpg: gpg-agent is not available in this session
```

```
donnie@ubuntu:~$ ls -l
. . .
-rw-rw-r-- 1 donnie donnie  40 Oct 27 19:30 not_secret_for_frank.txt
-rw-rw-r-- 1 donnie donnie 381 Oct 27 19:31 not_secret_for_frank.txt.gpg
```

Just as before, this creates a `.gpg` version of the file.

2. Send the message to Frank.
3. Log in as Frank. Have him try to open it with `less`:

```
frank@ubuntu:~$ less not_secret_for_frank.txt.gpg
```

On older Linux distros, you'll see a lot of gibberish because of the signature, but you'll also see the plain-text message. On newer Linux distros, you'll only see the plain-text message, without the gibberish.

4. Have Frank use gpg with the `--verify` option to verify that the signature really does belong to you:

```
frank@ubuntu:~$ gpg --verify not_secret_for_frank.txt.gpg
gpg: Signature made Fri 27 Oct 2017 07:31:12 PM EDT using RSA key ID
9FD7014B
gpg: Good signature from "Donald A. Tevault <donniet@something.net>"
frank@ubuntu:~$
```

This wraps it up for our discussion of encrypting individual files. Let's now take a look at encrypting block devices and directories.

Encrypting partitions with Linux Unified Key Setup (LUKS)

Being able to encrypt individual files can be handy, especially if you want to share sensitive files with other users. But, other types of encryption are also available:

*   **Block encryption:** We can use this for either whole-disk encryption or to encrypt individual partitions.
*   **File-level encryption:** We'd use this to encrypt individual directories without having to encrypt the underlying partitions.

- **Containerized encryption:** Using third-party software that doesn't come with any Linux distribution, we can create encrypted, cross-platform containers that can be opened on either Linux, macOS, or Windows machines.

Linux Unified Key Setup (LUKS) falls into the first category. It's built into pretty much every Linux distribution, and directions for use are the same for each. LUKS is now the default encryption mechanism for pretty much all of the newest Linux distros.

> You might be wondering if there's any performance impact with all of this disk encryption business. Well, with today's fast CPUs, not really. I run Fedora with full-disk encryption on a low-spec, Core i5 laptop, and other than having to enter the disk-encryption password when I first boot up, I don't even notice that encryption is taking place.

Okay, let's look at encrypting a disk while installing the operating system.

Disk encryption during operating system installation

When you install most any Linux-based operating system, you have the option of encrypting the drive during the installation. Just click the **Encryption** option on the drive setup screen:

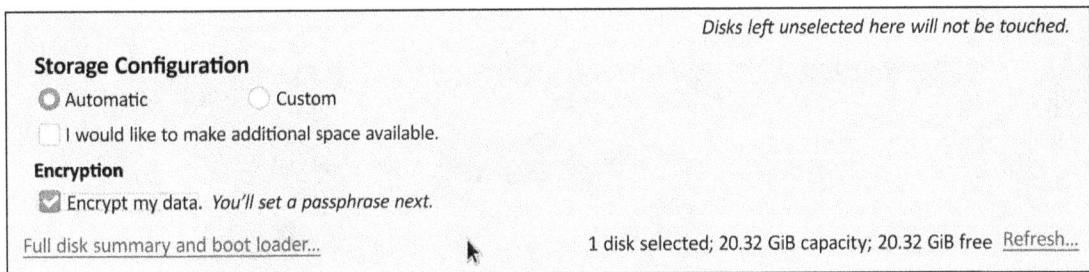

Figure 6.1: Encrypt the disk during installation

Other than that, I just let the installer create the default partitioning scheme. On this AlmaLinux 9 machine, that means that the / filesystem and the swap partition will both be encrypted logical volumes. (I'll cover that in a moment.)

Before the installation can continue, I have to create a passphrase to mount the encrypted disk:

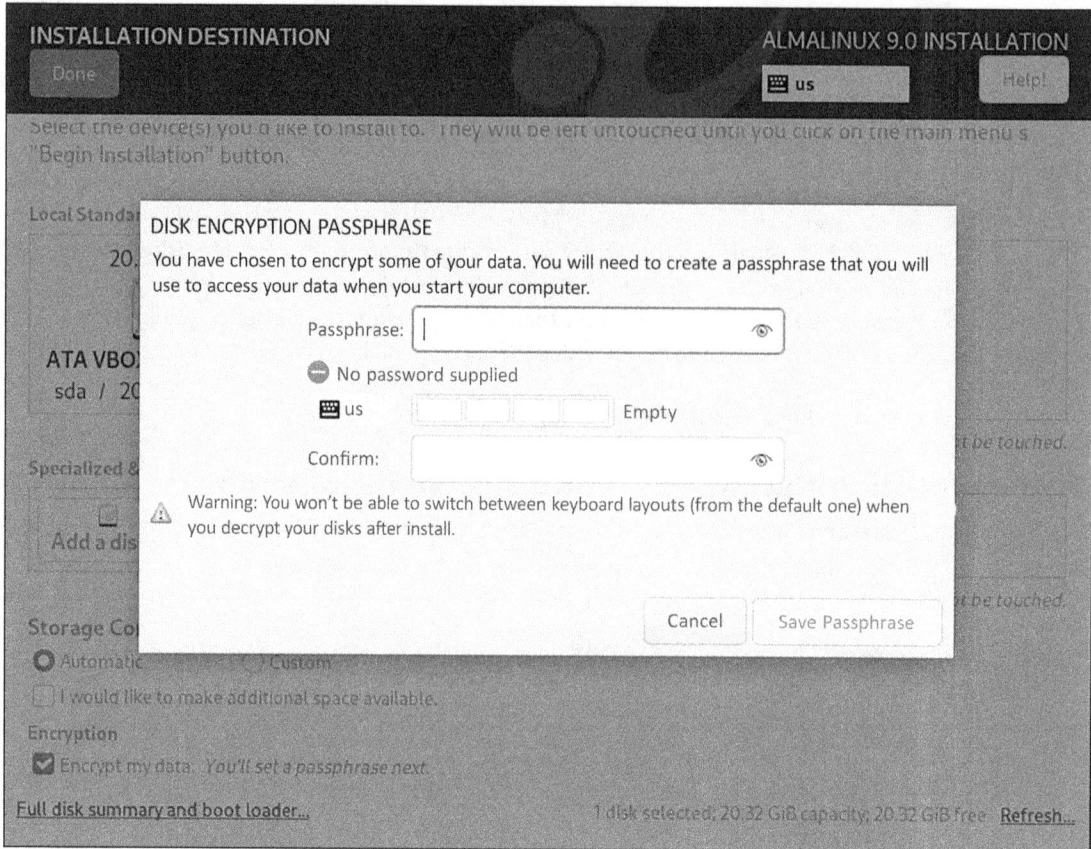

Figure 6.2: Create encryption passphrase

Now, whenever I reboot the system, I need to enter this passphrase:

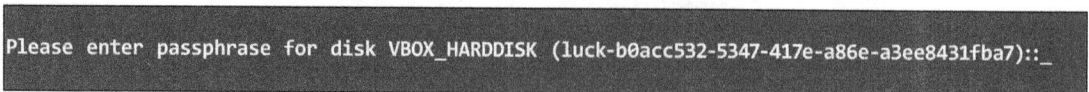

Figure 6.3: Enter the encryption passphrase

Rather than actually encrypting a normal disk partition, the installer will set up encrypted **logical volumes**. Once the machine is up and running, I can look at the list of logical volumes. Here, I see both the / logical volume and the swap logical volume:

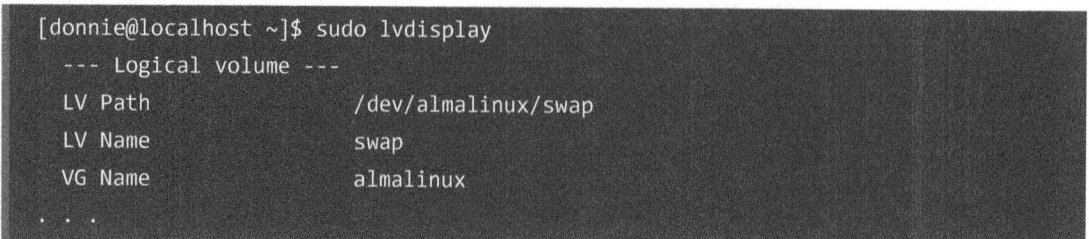

```
[donnie@localhost ~]$ sudo lvdisplay
   --- Logical volume ---
   LV Path                /dev/almalinux/swap
   LV Name                swap
   VG Name                almalinux
. . .
```

```
. . .

   --- Logical volume ---
  LV Path                   /dev/almalinux/root
  LV Name                   root
  VG Name                   almalinux

. . .

. . .

[donnie@localhost ~]$
```

Now, let's look at the list of **physical volumes**. Actually, there's only one physical volume in the list, and it's listed as a luks physical volume:

```
[donnie@localhost ~]$ sudo pvdisplay
  --- Physical volume ---
  PV Name                   /dev/mapper/luks-b0acc532-5347-417e-a86e-a3ee8431fba7
  VG Name                   almalinux
  PV Size                   <19.30 GiB / not usable 2.00 MiB
  Allocatable               yes (but full)
  PE Size                   4.00 MiB
  Total PE                  4940
  Free PE                   0
  Allocated PE              4940
  PV UUID                   mRI75u-aVJI-uRjC-GY1O-ih7N-T3co-vssRRX

[donnie@localhost ~]$
```

In the /etc/ directory, you'll find the crypttab file, which contains an entry for this physical volume:

```
[donnie@localhost ~]$ sudo cat /etc/crypttab
luks-b0acc532-5347-417e-a86e-a3ee8431fba7 UUID=b0acc532-5347-417e-a86e-
a3ee8431fba7 none discard
[donnie@localhost ~]$
```

This shows that the underlying physical volume is encrypted, which means that both the / and the swap logical volumes are also encrypted. That's a good thing because leaving the swap space unencrypted—a common mistake when setting up disk encryption manually—can lead to data leakage. (We'll talk more about this crypttab file in just a bit.)

Hands-on lab — adding an encrypted partition with LUKS

There may be times when you'll need to either add another encrypted drive to an existing machine or encrypt a portable device, such as a USB memory stick. This procedure works for both scenarios. Also, the procedure is the same for all of the Linux distros that we're using, so it doesn't matter which virtual machine you use. Follow these steps to add an encrypted partition:

1. Shut down your virtual machine and add a second virtual drive:

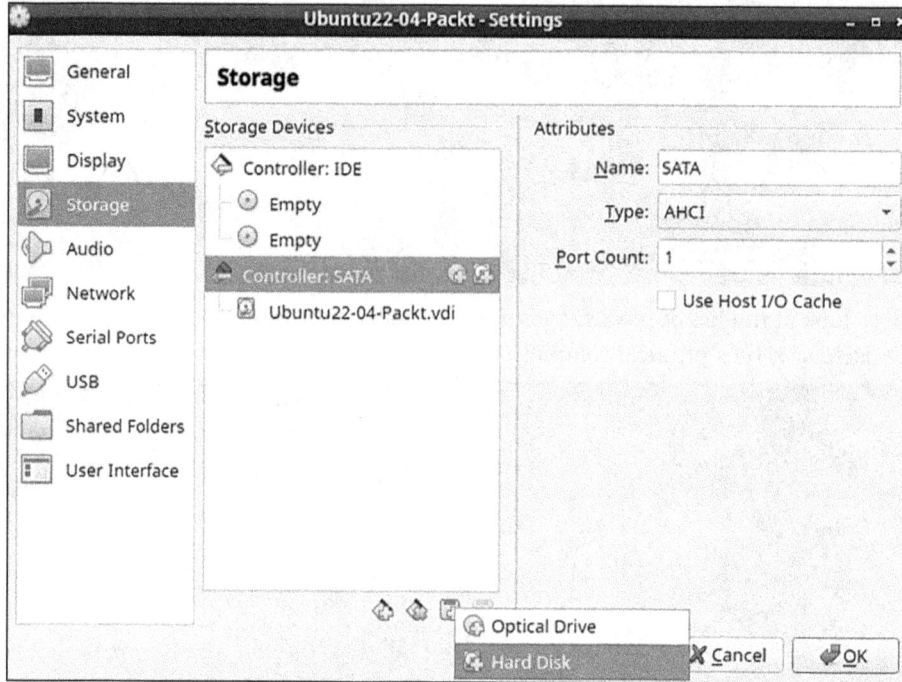

Figure 6.4: Add a new drive

2. Bump the size up to 20 GB:

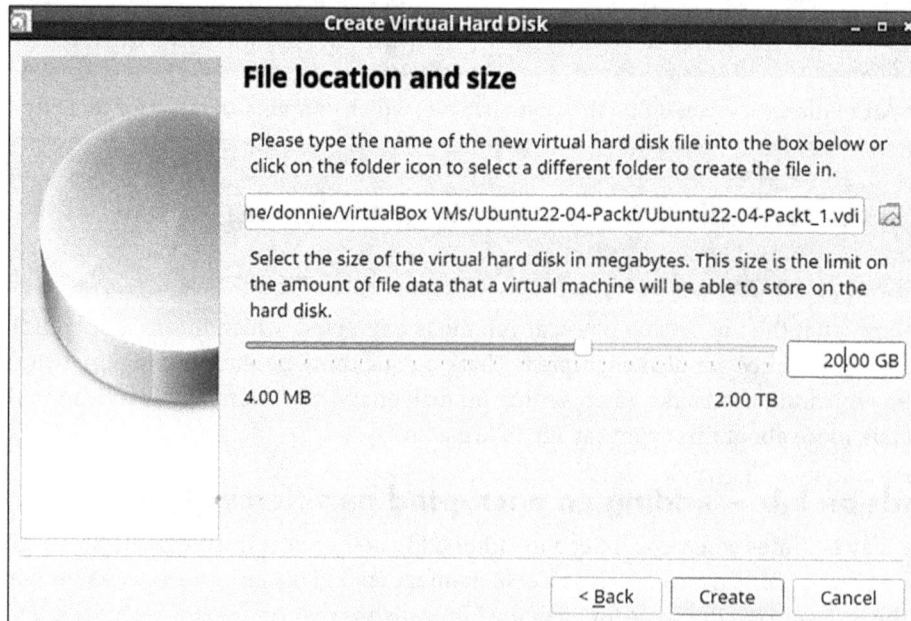

Figure 6.5: Set the size of the new drive

3. After rebooting the machine, you'll now have a /dev/sdb drive to play with. We can see that here:

```
donnie@ubuntu2204-packt:~$ ls -l /dev/sd*
brw-rw---- 1 root disk 8,  0 Oct 27 19:33 /dev/sda
brw-rw---- 1 root disk 8,  1 Oct 27 19:33 /dev/sda1
brw-rw---- 1 root disk 8,  2 Oct 27 19:33 /dev/sda2
brw-rw---- 1 root disk 8,  3 Oct 27 19:33 /dev/sda3
brw-rw---- 1 root disk 8, 16 Oct 27 19:33 /dev/sdb
donnie@ubuntu2204-packt:~$
```

4. Open the drive in gdisk. Use the entire drive for the partition, and leave the partition type set at the default type 8300:

```
sudo gdisk /dev/sdb
```

5. View the details about your new /dev/sdb1 partition:

```
donnie@ubuntu2204-packt:~$ sudo gdisk -l /dev/sdb
GPT fdisk (gdisk) version 1.0.8
Partition table scan:
  MBR: protective
  BSD: not present
  APM: not present
  GPT: present
. . .
. . .
Number  Start (sector)    End (sector)  Size       Code  Name
   1            2048         41943006    20.0 GiB   8300  Linux filesystem
donnie@ubuntu2204-packt:~$
```

6. Next, use cryptsetup to convert the partition to LUKS format. In this command, the -v signifies verbose mode, and the -y signifies that you'll have to enter your passphrase twice in order to properly verify it. Note that when it says to type yes all in uppercase, it really does mean to type it in uppercase:

```
donnie@ubuntu2204-packt:~$ sudo cryptsetup -v -y luksFormat /dev/sdb1

WARNING!
========
This will overwrite data on /dev/sdb1 irrevocably.

Are you sure? (Type 'yes' in capital letters): YES
Enter passphrase for /dev/sdb1:
Verify passphrase:
Key slot 0 created.
```

```
Command successful.
donnie@ubuntu2204-packt:~
```

7. Look at the information about your new encrypted partition:

```
donnie@ubuntu2204-packt:~$ sudo cryptsetup luksDump /dev/sdb1
LUKS header information
Version:          2
Epoch:            3
Metadata area:    16384 [bytes]
Keyslots area:    16744448 [bytes]
UUID:             e38e087a-205c-4aeb-81d5-03f03b8e8020
Label:            (no label)
Subsystem:        (no subsystem)
Flags:            (no flags)
. . .

. . .
```

There's a lot more to the output than I can show here, but you get the idea.

8. Map the partition to a device name. You can name the device pretty much whatever you want. For now, just name this one `secrets`. I know, it's a corny name. In real life, you won't want to make it so obvious where you're storing your secrets:

```
donnie@ubuntu2204-packt:~$ sudo cryptsetup luksOpen /dev/sdb1 secrets
Enter passphrase for /dev/sdb1:
donnie@ubuntu2204-packt:~$
```

9. Look in the `/dev/mapper/` directory. You'll see your new `secrets` device listed as a symbolic link to some sort of `dm` device. (In this case, it's `dm-1`.):

```
donnie@ubuntu2204-packt:~$ cd /dev/mapper
donnie@ubuntu2204-packt:/dev/mapper$ ls -l secrets
lrwxrwxrwx 1 root root 7 Oct 27 19:50 secrets -> ../dm-1
donnie@ubuntu2204-packt:/dev/mapper$
```

10. Use `dmsetup` to look at the information about your new device:

```
donnie@ubuntu2204-packt:~$ sudo dmsetup info secrets
Name:             secrets
State:            ACTIVE
Read Ahead:       256
Tables present:   LIVE
Open count:       0
Event number:     0
Major, minor:     253, 1
```

```
Number of targets: 1
UUID: CRYPT-LUKS2-e38e087a205c4aeb81d503f03b8e8020-secrets


donnie@ubuntu2204-packt:~$
```

11. Format the partition in the usual manner. You can use any filesystem that's supported by your Linux distro. On a production server, that will generally mean either XFS or EXT4. Just for fun, let's go with XFS:

```
donnie@ubuntu2204-packt:~$ sudo mkfs.xfs /dev/mapper/secrets

meta-data=/dev/mapper/secrets   isize=512     agcount=4, agsize=1309631
blks
         =                      sectsz=512    attr=2, projid32bit=1
         =                      crc=1         finobt=1, sparse=1,
rmapbt=0
         =                      reflink=1     bigtime=0 inobtcount=0
data     =                      bsize=4096    blocks=5238523, imaxpct=25
         =                      sunit=0       swidth=0 blks
naming   =version 2             bsize=4096    ascii-ci=0, ftype=1
log      =internal log          bsize=4096    blocks=2560, version=2
         =                      sectsz=512    sunit=0 blks, lazy-count=1
realtime =none                  extsz=4096    blocks=0, rtextents=0
donnie@ubuntu2204-packt:~$
```

12. Create a mount point and mount the encrypted partition:

```
donnie@ubuntu2204-packt:~$ sudo mkdir /secrets
donnie@ubuntu2204-packt:~$ sudo mount /dev/mapper/secrets /secrets/
donnie@ubuntu2204-packt:~$
```

13. Use the mount command to verify that the partition is mounted properly:

```
donnie@ubuntu2204-packt:~$ mount | grep 'secrets'
/dev/mapper/secrets on /secrets type xfs
(rw,relatime,attr2,inode64,logbufs=8,logbsize=32k,noquota)
donnie@ubuntu2204-packt:~$
```

Configuring the LUKS partition to mount automatically

The only missing piece of the puzzle is to configure the system to automatically mount the LUKS partition upon boot-up. To do that, configure two different files:

- /etc/crypttab
- /etc/fstab

If you encrypted the sda drive while installing the operating system, you'll already have a crypttab file that contains information about that drive. It would look something like this:

```
luks-b0acc532-5347-417e-a86e-a3ee8431fba7 UUID=b0acc532-5347-417e-a86e-
a3ee8431fba7 none discard
```

The first two fields describe the name and location of the encrypted partition. The third field is for the encryption passphrase. If it's set to none, as it is here, then the passphrase will have to be manually entered upon boot-up.

In the fstab file, we have the entry that actually mounts the partition:

```
/dev/mapper/almalinux-root /              xfs      defaults,x-systemd.device-
timeout=0 0 0
UUID=28218289-34cb-4c57-9755-379c65d580af /boot         xfs        defaults        0
0
/dev/mapper/almalinux-swap none          swap     defaults,x-systemd.device-
timeout=0 0 0
```

Well, there are actually two entries in this case, because we have two logical volumes, / and swap, on top of the encrypted physical volume. The UUID line is the /boot/ partition, which is the only part of the drive that isn't encrypted. Now, let's add our new encrypted partition so that it will mount automatically, as well.

Hands-on lab — configuring the LUKS partition to mount automatically

In this lab, you'll set up the encrypted partition that you created in the previous lab to automatically mount when you reboot the machine:

> This is where it would be extremely helpful to remotely log in to your virtual machine from your desktop host machine. By using a GUI-type terminal, be it Terminal from a Linux or macOS machine or Cygwin from a Windows machine, you'll have the ability to perform copy-and-paste operations, which you won't have if you work directly from the virtual machine terminal. (Trust me, you don't want to be typing in those long UUIDs.)

1. The first step is to obtain the UUID of the encrypted partition:

```
donnie@ubuntu2204-packt:~$ sudo cryptsetup luksUUID /dev/sdb1
e38e087a-205c-4aeb-81d5-03f03b8e8020
donnie@ubuntu2204-packt:~$
```

2. Copy that UUID and paste it into the /etc/crypttab file. (If a cryptab file isn't already there, just create a new one.) Also, note that you'll paste the UUID in twice. The first time, you'll prepend it with luks-, and the second time you'll append it with UUID=:

```
luks-e38e087a-205c-4aeb-81d5-03f03b8e8020 UUID=e38e087a-205c-4aeb-81d5-
03f03b8e8020 none
```

3. Edit the `/etc/fstab` file, adding the last line in the file for your new encrypted partition. Note that you again have to use `luks-`, followed by the UUID number:

```
/dev/mapper/luks-e38e087a-205c-4aeb-81d5-03f03b8e8020 /secrets xfs
defaults 0 0
```

> When editing the `fstab` file for adding normal, unencrypted partitions, I always like to do `sudo mount -a` to check the `fstab` file for typos. That won't work with LUKS partitions though, because `mount` won't recognize the partition until the system reads in the `crypttab` file, and that won't happen until I reboot the machine. So, just be extra careful with editing `fstab` when adding LUKS partitions.

4. Now for the moment of truth. Reboot the machine to see if everything works. Use the `mount` command to verify that your endeavors have been successful:

```
donnie@ubuntu2204-packt:~$ mount | grep 'secrets'
/dev/mapper/luks-e38e087a-205c-4aeb-81d5-03f03b8e8020 on /secrets type
xfs (rw,relatime,attr2,inode64,logbufs=8,logbsize=32k,noquota)
donnie@ubuntu2204-packt:~$
```

5. End of lab.

> **Tip :**
>
> Although it's possible to include passwords or keys in the `/etc/crypttab` file, my own preference is to not do so. If you must do so, be sure that the passwords or keys are stored on an encrypted / partition, for which you'll always have to enter a password upon boot-up. You can read more about that here: *Store the passphrase of encrypted disk in /etc/crypttab encrypted*: `https://askubuntu.com/questions/181518/store-the-passphrase-of-encrypted-disk-in-etc-crypttab-encrypted`

Now that we've seen LUKS, let's move on to eCryptfs.

Encrypting directories with eCryptfs

Encrypting entire partitions is cool, but you might, at times, just need to use file-level encryption to encrypt an individual directory. For that, we can use eCryptfs. We'll need to use our Ubuntu machines for this, because Red Hat and its offspring no longer include eCryptfs. (It was in Red Hat 6 and CentOS 6, but it's no longer even available for installation in any newer versions.)

> Tip
>
> It's possible to use eCryptfs on a LUKS-encrypted disk. But, it's not at all necessary, and I really don't recommend it.

Hands-on lab — encrypting a home directory for a new user account

In *Chapter 3, Securing Normal User Accounts*, I showed you how Ubuntu allows you to encrypt a user's home directory as you create his or her user account. To review, let's see the command for creating Goldie's account:

1. If it hasn't already been done, install the `ecryptfs-utils` package:

    ```
    sudo apt install ecryptfs-utils
    ```

2. On an Ubuntu VM, create Goldie's account with an encrypted directory:

    ```
    sudo adduser --encrypt-home goldie
    ```

    Have Goldie log in. Have her unwrap her mount passphrase, write it down, and store it in a secure place. She'll need it if she ever needs to recover a corrupted directory:

    ```
    ecryptfs-unwrap-passphrase .ecryptfs/wrapped-passphrase
    ```

When you use `adduser --encrypt-home`, home directories for new users will automatically be set to a restrictive permissions value that will keep everyone out except for the owner of the directory. This happens even on Ubuntu 20.04 when you leave the `adduser.conf` file set with its default settings.

Creating a private directory within an existing home directory

Let's say that you have users on your Ubuntu servers who, for whatever strange reason, don't want to encrypt their entire home directories, and want to keep the 755 permissions settings on their home directories so that other people can access their files. But they also want a private directory that nobody but them can access.

Instead of encrypting an entire home directory, any user can create an encrypted private directory within his or her own home directory. Let's check it out:

1. If it hasn't already been done, install the `ecryptfs-utils` package:

    ```
    sudo apt install ecryptfs-utils
    ```

    To create this private directory, use the interactive `ecryptfs-setup-private` utility. If you have admin privileges, you can do this for other users. Users without admin privileges can do it for themselves. For our demo, let's say that Charlie, my big Siamese/Gray Tabby guy, needs his own encrypted private space. (Who knew that cats had secrets, right?)

    Create Charlie's account in the normal manner, *without* the encrypted home directory option.

2. Then, log in as Charlie and have him create his own private directory:

    ```
    charlie@ubuntu2:~$ ecryptfs-setup-private
    Enter your login passphrase [charlie]:
    Enter your mount passphrase [leave blank to generate one]:
    Enter your mount passphrase (again):
    ```

```
********************************************************************
YOU SHOULD RECORD YOUR MOUNT PASSPHRASE AND STORE IT IN A SAFE LOCATION.
  ecryptfs-unwrap-passphrase ~/.ecryptfs/wrapped-passphrase
THIS WILL BE REQUIRED IF YOU NEED TO RECOVER YOUR DATA AT A LATER TIME.
********************************************************************
. . .

. . .
charlie@ubuntu2:~$
```

For the login passphrase, Charlie enters his normal password or passphrase for logging in to his user account. He could have let the system generate its own mount passphrase, but he decided to enter his own. Since he did enter his own mount passphrase, he didn't need to do the `ecryptfs-unwrap-passphrase` command to find out what the passphrase is. But, just to show how that command works, let's say that Charlie entered `TurkeyLips` as his mount passphrase:

```
charlie@ubuntu2:~$ ecryptfs-unwrap-passphrase .ecryptfs/wrapped-
passphrase
Passphrase:
TurkeyLips
charlie@ubuntu2:~$
```

Yes, it's a horribly weak passphrase, but for our demo purposes, it works.

Have Charlie log out, and then log back in. After this, he can start using his new private directory. Also, you can see that he has three new hidden directories within his home directory. All three of these new directories are only accessible by Charlie, even if he set his top-level home directory so that it's open to everybody:

```
charlie@ubuntu2:~$ ls -la
total 40
drwxr-xr-x 6 charlie charlie 4096 Oct 30 17:00 .
drwxr-xr-x 4 root    root    4096 Oct 30 16:38 ..
-rw-------  1 charlie charlie  270 Oct 30 17:00 .bash_history
-rw-r--r--  1 charlie charlie  220 Aug 31 2015 .bash_logout
-rw-r--r--  1 charlie charlie 3771 Aug 31 2015 .bashrc
drwx------  2 charlie charlie 4096 Oct 30 16:39 .cache
drwx------  2 charlie charlie 4096 Oct 30 16:57 .ecryptfs
drwx------  2 charlie charlie 4096 Oct 30 16:57 Private
drwx------  2 charlie charlie 4096 Oct 30 16:57 .Private
-rw-r--r--  1 charlie charlie  655 May 16 08:49 .profile
charlie@ubuntu2:~$
```

3. Run the `grep 'ecryptfs' *` command in the `/etc/pam.d` directory. You'll see that PAM is configured to automatically mount users' encrypted directories whenever they log in to the system:

```
donnie@ubuntu2:/etc/pam.d$ grep 'ecryptfs' *
common-auth:auth       optional     pam_ecryptfs.so unwrap
common-password:password     optional     pam_ecryptfs.so
common-session:session     optional     pam_ecryptfs.so unwrap
common-session-noninteractive:session     optional     pam_ecryptfs.so
unwrap
donnie@ubuntu2:/etc/pam.d$
```

4. End of lab.

All righty, then. We now know how to encrypt users' home directories. Now, let's find out how to encrypt other directories.

Hands-on lab – encrypting other directories with eCryptfs

Encrypting other directories is a simple matter of mounting them with the `ecryptfs` filesystem:

1. Create a `secrets2` directory in the top level of the filesystem:

```
donnie@ubuntu2204-packt:~$ sudo mkdir /secrets2
[sudo] password for donnie:
donnie@ubuntu2204-packt:~$
```

2. Use `mount` with the `-t ecryptfs` option to encrypt the directory. Note that you'll list the directory name twice, because then it will be used as its own mount point. From the menu, choose 1 to enter your desired passphrase, and choose the encryption algorithm and the key length:

```
donnie@ubuntu2204-packt:~$ sudo mount -t ecryptfs /secrets2/ /secrets2/
Select key type to use for newly created files:
 1) passphrase
 2) tspi
Selection: 1
Passphrase:
Select cipher:
 1) aes: blocksize = 16; min keysize = 16; max keysize = 32
 2) blowfish: blocksize = 8; min keysize = 16; max keysize = 56
 3) des3_ede: blocksize = 8; min keysize = 24; max keysize = 24
 4) twofish: blocksize = 16; min keysize = 16; max keysize = 32
 5) cast6: blocksize = 16; min keysize = 16; max keysize = 32
 6) cast5: blocksize = 8; min keysize = 5; max keysize = 16
Selection [aes]:
```

Go with the default of aes, and 16 bytes for the key.

3. Go with the default of no for `plaintext passthrough`, and with yes for filename encryption:

```
Enable plaintext passthrough (y/n) [n]:
Enable filename encryption (y/n) [n]: y
```

4. Go with the default `Filename Encryption Key` and verify the mounting options:

```
Filename Encryption Key (FNEK) Signature [e339e1ebf3d58c36]:
Attempting to mount with the following options:
  ecryptfs_unlink_sigs
  ecryptfs_fnek_sig=e339e1ebf3d58c36
  ecryptfs_key_bytes=16
  ecryptfs_cipher=aes
  ecryptfs_sig=e339e1ebf3d58c36
```

5. This warning only comes up when you mount the directory for the first time. For the final two questions, type yes in order to prevent that warning from coming up again:

```
WARNING: Based on the contents of [/root/.ecryptfs/sig-cache.txt],
it looks like you have never mounted with this key
before. This could mean that you have typed your
passphrase wrong.

Would you like to proceed with the mount (yes/no)? : yes
Would you like to append sig [e339e1ebf3d58c36] to
[/root/.ecryptfs/sig-cache.txt]
in order to avoid this warning in the future (yes/no)? : yes
Successfully appended new sig to user sig cache file
Mounted eCryptfs
```

6. Just for fun, create a file within your new encrypted `secrets2` directory, and then unmount the directory. Then, try to do a directory listing:

```
cd /secrets2
sudo vim secret_stuff.txt
cd
sudo umount /secrets2

donnie@ubuntu2204-packt:~$ ls -l /secrets2/
total 12
-rw-rw-r-- 1 donnie donnie 12288 Oct 28 19:04 ECRYPTFS_FNEK_ENCRYPTED.
FXbXCS5fwxKABUQtEPlumGPaN-RGvqd13yybkpTr1eCVWVHdr-lrmi1X9Vu-mLM-A-
VeqIdN6KNZGcs-
donnie@ubuntu2204-packt:~$
```

By choosing to encrypt filenames, nobody can even tell what files you have when the directory is unmounted. When you're ready to access your encrypted files again, just remount the directory the same as you did before.

Encrypting the swap partition with eCryptfs

If you're just encrypting individual directories with eCryptfs instead of using LUKS whole-disk encryption, you'll need to encrypt your swap partition in order to prevent accidental data leakage. Fixing that problem requires just one simple command:

```
donnie@ubuntu:~$ sudo ecryptfs-setup-swap

WARNING:
An encrypted swap is required to help ensure that encrypted files are not
leaked to disk in an unencrypted format.
HOWEVER, THE SWAP ENCRYPTION CONFIGURATION PRODUCED BY THIS PROGRAM WILL BREAK
HIBERNATE/RESUME ON THIS SYSTEM!
NOTE: Your suspend/resume capabilities will not be affected.

Do you want to proceed with encrypting your swap? [y/N]: y

INFO: Setting up swap: [/dev/sda5]
WARNING: Commented out your unencrypted swap from /etc/fstab
swapon: stat of /dev/mapper/cryptswap1 failed: No such file or directory
donnie@ubuntu:~$
```

Don't mind the warning about the missing /dev/mapper/cryptswap1 file. It will get created the next time you reboot the machine.

Using VeraCrypt for cross-platform sharing of encrypted containers

Once upon a time, there was TrueCrypt, a cross-platform program that allowed the sharing of encrypted containers across different operating systems. But the project was always shrouded in mystery because its developers would never reveal their identities. And then, right out of the blue, the developers released a cryptic message about how TrueCrypt was no longer secure, and shut down the project.

VeraCrypt is the successor to TrueCrypt, and it allows the sharing of encrypted containers across Linux, Windows, macOS, and FreeBSD machines. Although LUKS and eCryptfs are good, VeraCrypt offers more flexibility in certain ways:

- As mentioned, VeraCrypt offers cross-platform sharing, whereas LUKS and eCryptfs don't.
- VeraCrypt allows you to encrypt either whole partitions or whole storage devices, or to create virtual encrypted disks.

- Not only can you create encrypted volumes with VeraCrypt, you can also hide them, giving you plausible deniability.

- VeraCrypt comes in both command-line and GUI variants, so it's appropriate for either server use or for the casual desktop user.

- Like LUKS and eCryptfs, VeraCrypt is free open source software, which means that it's free to use, and that the source code can be audited for either bugs or backdoors.

Hands-on lab — getting and installing VeraCrypt

Follow these steps to install VeraCrypt:

1. Download VeraCrypt from here: `https://www.veracrypt.fr/en/Downloads.html`

2. The Linux version of VeraCrypt comes two ways. First, there's a `.tar.bz2` file, which contains a set of universal installer scripts that should work on any Linux distribution. Once you extract the `.tar.bz2` archive file, you'll see three scripts for GUI installation and two for console-mode installation. There are scripts for both 32-bit and 64-bit versions of Linux:

```
donnie@donnie-VirtualBox:~$ tar xjvf veracrypt-1.25.9-setup.tar.bz2
veracrypt-1.25.9-setup-console-x64
veracrypt-1.25.9-setup-console-x86
veracrypt-1.25.9-setup-gtk3-console-x64
veracrypt-1.25.9-setup-gtk3-gui-x64
veracrypt-1.25.9-setup-gui-x64
veracrypt-1.25.9-setup-gui-x86
donnie@donnie-VirtualBox:~$
```

3. The executable permission is already set, so all you have to do to install is this:

```
donnie@donnie-VirtualBox:~$ ./veracrypt-1.25.9-setup-gui-x64
```

4. You'll need `sudo` privileges, but the installer will prompt you for your `sudo` password. After reading and agreeing to a rather lengthy license agreement, the installation only takes a few seconds.

5. **Optional step:** Recently, the VeraCrypt developers added a second way to install VeraCrypt on Linux. On their Downloads page, you'll now see that there are `.deb` and `.rpm` package files for various versions of Debian, Ubuntu, OpenSUSE, and Red Hat/CentOS/Fedora. For Debian/Ubuntu systems, install the package by doing:

```
sudo dpkg -i veracrypt-packageversion.deb
```

6. For Red Hat/CentOS/Fedora and OpenSUSE, do

```
sudo rpm -Uvh veracrypt-packageversion.rpm
```

7. Note though that there's still nothing here for the newer Red Hat 9-type distros, but I found that the CentOS 8 package does work on AlmaLinux 9.

8. End of lab.

More recently, the VeraCrypt developers have also begun supplying `.deb` and `.rpm` installer packages for specific Linux distros. For Debian-/Ubuntu-type systems, use `sudo dpkg -i` to install the `.deb` file. On RHEL/CentOS/AlmaLinux/SUSE systems, use `sudo rpm -Uvh` to install the `.rpm` file. Note that you might receive an error message telling you to install other packages as dependencies. Also, note that there's no `.rpm` package for the RHEL/AlmaLinux 9 distros. Not to worry though, because I've just verified that the CentOS 8 package works just fine on AlmaLinux 9.

Hands-on lab – creating and mounting a VeraCrypt volume in console mode

I haven't been able to find any documentation for the console-mode variant of VeraCrypt, but you can see a list of the available commands just by typing `veracrypt`. For this demo, you'll create a 2 GB encrypted directory. But you can just as easily create an encrypted directory elsewhere, such as on a USB memory stick:

1. To create a new encrypted volume, type the following:

```
veracrypt -c
```

2. This will take you into an easy-to-use interactive utility. For the most part, you'll be fine just accepting the default options:

```
donnie@ubuntu:~$ veracrypt -c
Volume type:
 1) Normal
 2) Hidden
Select [1]:
Enter volume path: /home/donnie/good_stuff
Enter volume size (sizeK/size[M]/sizeG): 2G
Encryption Algorithm:
 1) AES
 2) Serpent
 . . .
 . . .
Select [1]:
 . . .
 . . .
```

3. For the filesystem, the default option of `FAT` gives you the best cross-platform compatibility between Linux, macOS, and Windows:

```
Filesystem:
 1) None
 2) FAT
```

```
   3) Linux Ext2
   4) Linux Ext3
   5) Linux Ext4
   6) NTFS
   7) exFAT
Select [2]:
```

4. Select your password and a **PIM** (short for **Personal Iterations Multiplier**). For my PIM, I entered 8891. (High PIM values give better security, but they will also cause the volume to take longer to mount.) Then, type at least 320 random characters in order to generate the encryption key (this is where it would be handy to have my cats walking across my keyboard.):

```
Enter password:
Re-enter password:

Enter PIM: 8891

Enter keyfile path [none]:

Please type at least 320 randomly chosen characters and then press Enter:
```

5. After you hit the *Enter* key, be patient, because the final generation of your encrypted volume will take a few moments. Here, you see that my 2 GB good_stuff container has been successfully created:

```
donnie@ubuntu:~$ ls -l good_stuff
-rw------- 1 donnie donnie 2147483648 Nov  1 17:02 good_stuff
donnie@ubuntu:~$
```

6. Mount this container in order to use it. Begin by creating a mount point directory:

```
donnie@ubuntu:~$ mkdir good_stuff_dir
donnie@ubuntu:~$
```

7. Use the veracrypt utility to mount your container on this mount point:

```
donnie@ubuntu:~$ veracrypt good_stuff good_stuff_dir
Enter password for /home/donnie/good_stuff:
Enter PIM for /home/donnie/good_stuff: 8891
Enter keyfile [none]:
Protect hidden volume (if any)? (y=Yes/n=No) [No]:
Enter your user password or administrator password:
donnie@ubuntu:~$
```

8. To see what VeraCrypt volumes you have mounted, use `veracrypt -l`:

```
donnie@ubuntu:~$ veracrypt -l
1: /home/donnie/secret_stuff /dev/mapper/veracrypt1 /home/donnie/secret_
stuff_dir
2: /home/donnie/good_stuff /dev/mapper/veracrypt2 /home/donnie/good_
stuff_dir
donnie@ubuntu:~$
```

9. End of lab. That's all there is to it.

Using VeraCrypt in GUI mode

Desktop users of any of the supported operating systems can install the GUI variant of VeraCrypt. Be aware, though, that you can't install both the console-mode variant and the GUI variant on the same machine, because one will overwrite the other. Here's what that looks like:

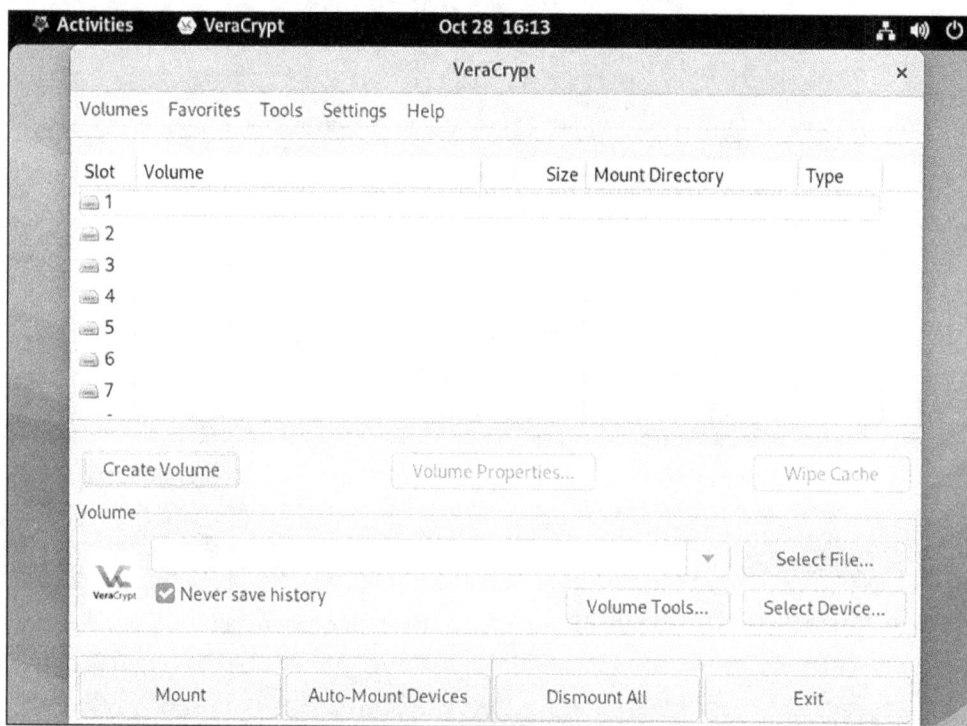

Figure 6.6: VeraCrypt control panel

Since the main focus of this book is server security, I won't go into the details of the GUI version here. But it's fairly self-explanatory, and you can view the full VeraCrypt documentation on their website.

You can get VeraCrypt from here: `https://www.veracrypt.fr/en/Home.html`.

OpenSSL and the Public Key Infrastructure

With OpenSSL, we can encrypt information on the fly as it goes across the network. There's no need to manually encrypt our data before we send them across the network because OpenSSL encryption happens automatically. This is important because online commerce and banking couldn't exist without it.

The **Secure Sockets Layer** (SSL) is the original in-transit encryption protocol. Ironically, even though we're using the OpenSSL suite of programs and libraries, we no longer want to use SSL. Instead, we now want to use the **Transport Layer Security** (TLS) protocol. SSL is full of legacy code and a lot of vulnerabilities that go along with that legacy code. TLS is newer, and is much more secure. But, even when working with TLS, we can still use the OpenSSL suite.

One reason that the older SSL protocol is so bad is because of past government regulations, especially here in the U.S., that prohibited the use of strong encryption. For the first few years of the public Internet, U.S. website operators couldn't legally implement encryption keys that were longer than a measly 40 bits. Even back then, a 40-bit key didn't provide a whole lot of security. But the U.S. government considered strong encryption as a type of munition, and tried to control it so that the governments of other countries couldn't use it. Meanwhile, an Australian outfit named Fortify started producing a strong encryption plugin that people could install in their Netscape web browsers. This plugin allowed the use of 128-bit encryption, and my geek buddies and I all eagerly installed it on our own machines. Looking back, I'm not sure that it did a lot of good, because website operators in the U.S. were still prohibited from using strong encryption keys on their webservers.

Amazingly, the Fortify outfit still has their website up. You can still download the Fortify plugin, even though it's now completely useless. Here's a screenshot of the Fortify website:

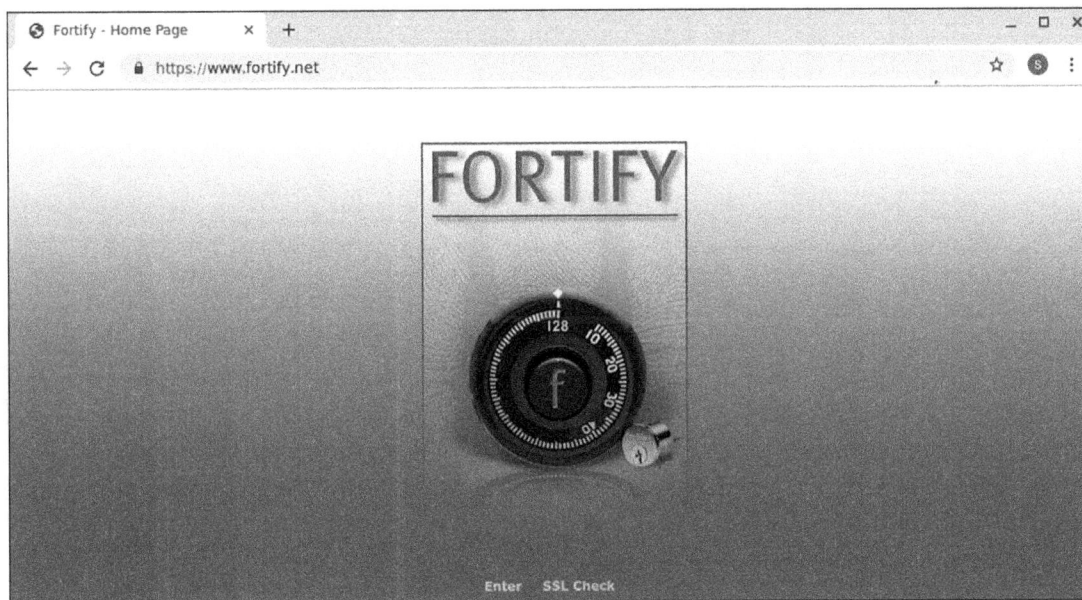

Figure 6.7: The Fortify.net website

An encrypted SSL/TLS session uses both symmetric and asymmetric mechanisms. For acceptable performance, it uses symmetric encryption to encrypt the data in transit. But symmetric encryption requires a private key to be exchanged between the two communication partners. To do that, SSL/TLS first negotiates an asymmetric session using the same public key exchange mechanism that we looked at in the GPG section.

Once that asymmetric session is set up, the two communication partners can safely exchange the private key that they'll use for the symmetric session.

Commercial certificate authorities

To make this magic work, you need to install a security certificate onto your webserver. The certificate serves two purposes:

- It contains the public key that's needed to set up an asymmetric key-exchange session.
- Optionally, it can verify the identity of, or authenticate, your website. So, for example, users can theoretically be sure that they're connected to their real bank, instead of to Joe Hacker's Bank of Crooks and Criminals that's disguised as their bank.

When you shop for a certificate, you'll find quite a few vendors, which are all referred to as **certificate authorities**, or **CAs**. Most CAs, including vendors such as Thawte, Symantec, GoDaddy, and Let's Encrypt, among others, offer several different grades of certificates. To help explain the differences between the grades of certificates, here's a screenshot from the GoDaddy site:

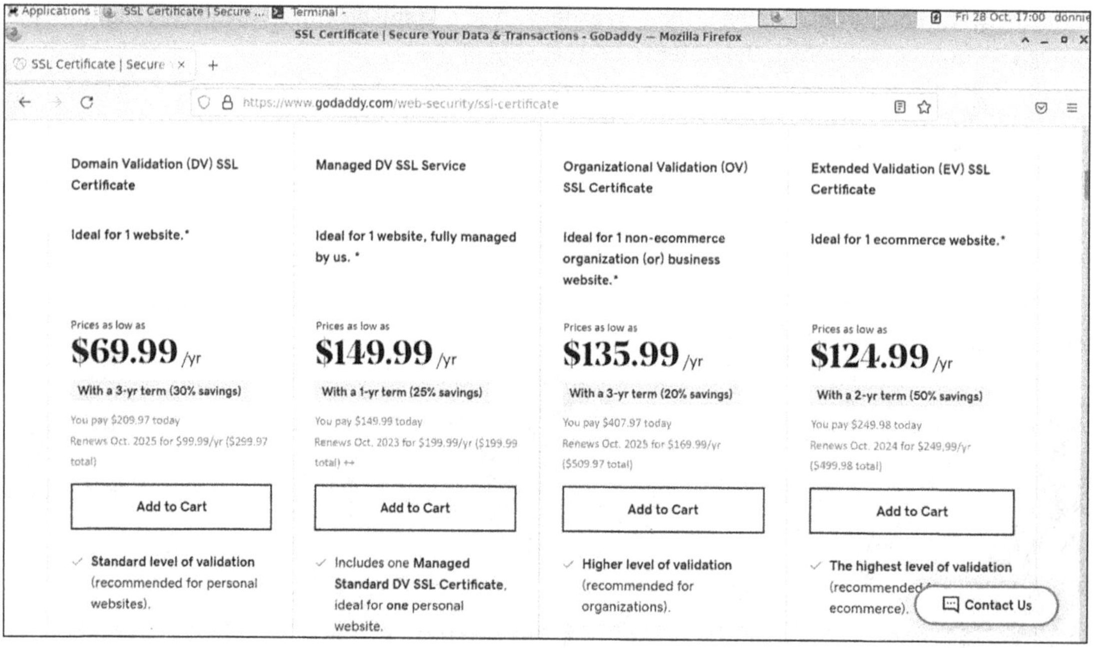

Figure 6.8: Certificate pricing

At the left-hand side of the list, at the cheapest price, is the **standard Domain Verification (DV)** offering. Vendors advertise this type of certificate for use where all you really care about is encryption. Identity verification is limited to domain verification, which means that yeah, records for your site have been found on a publicly accessible DNS server.

At the right, we see the **premium Extended Verification (EV)** offering. This is the top-of-the-line, highest-grade certificate that certificate vendors offer. With this extended verification grade of certificate, you have to jump through some hoops to prove that you are who you really are and that your website and your business are both legit. It used to be that both Firefox and Chrome would show a green High-Assurance bar in the URL of any site with an EV certificate, but they no longer do, for reasons that I'll explain in a moment.

So, just how good is this **Premium SSL EV** certificate with rigorous identity testing? Well, not quite as good as I thought. Two days after I wrote this explanation about the different types of certificates for the previous edition of this book, I received the latest edition of the *Bulletproof TLS Newsletter* from Feisty Duck Publishing. The big news was that Google and Mozilla decided to remove the green high assurance bar from future editions of Chrome and Firefox. Their reasons were as follows:

- The green high assurance bar was meant to help users avoid phishing attacks. But for that to be useful, users had to notice that the high assurance bar was even there. Studies have shown that most people didn't even notice it.
- Ian Carrol, a security researcher, questioned the value of extended validation certificates. As an experiment, he was able to register a bogus certificate for Stripe, Inc., which is a legitimate company. The certificate vendor finally did notice their mistake and revoked the certificate, but it's something that shouldn't have happened in the first place.
- On top of everything else, it was also possible to register extended validation certificates with incorrect information. This indicated that the verification process isn't quite as thorough as the certificate vendors would have us believe.

But in spite of these occasional problems, I still believe that extended validation certificates are useful. When I access my bank account, I like to believe that extra identity verification is never a bad thing.

Something else that's rather curious is that certificate vendors still market their certificates as SSL certificates. Don't be fooled, though. As long as the website owners configure their servers correctly, they'll be using the more secure TLS protocol, rather than SSL.

Let's Encrypt is a fairly new organization that has the goal of ensuring that all websites everywhere are set up with encryption. It's a worthy goal, but it has also introduced a new problem. Here's what the Let's Encrypt website looks like:

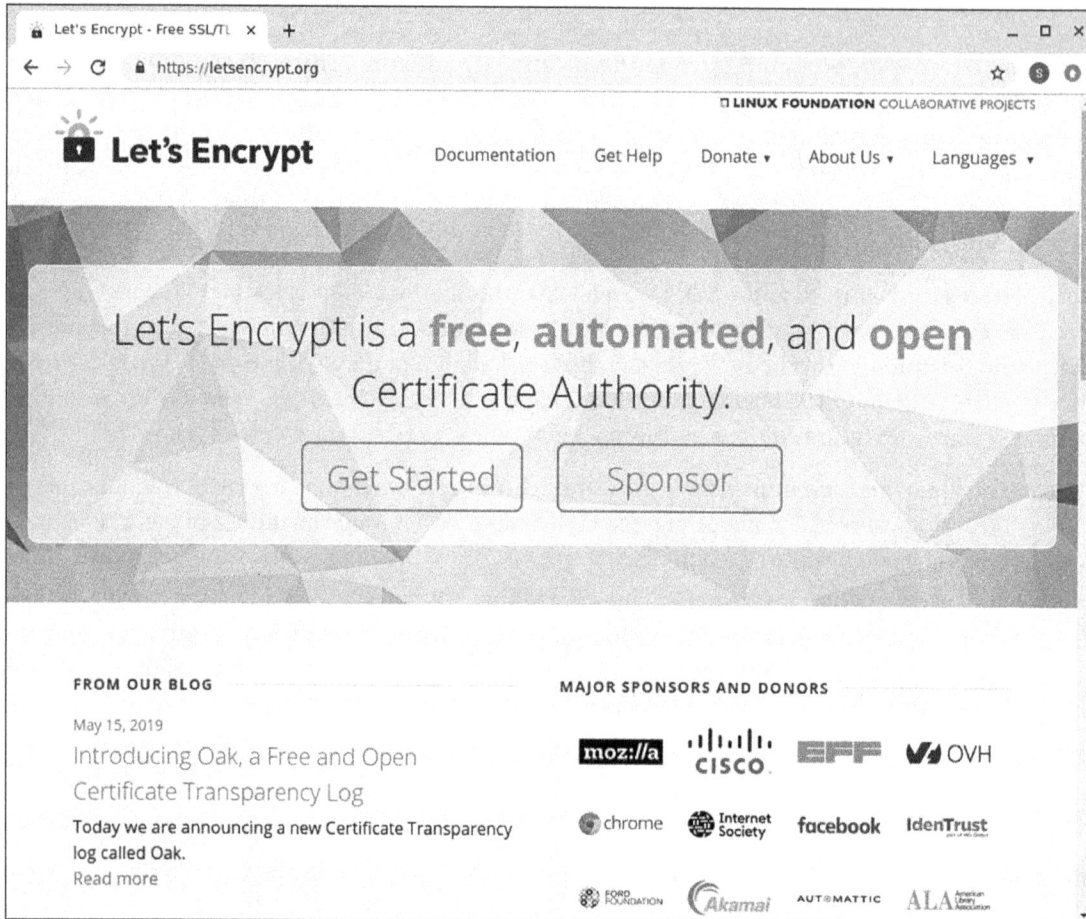

Figure 6.9: Let's Encrypt home page

To obtain a certificate from one of the traditional vendors, you have to use the OpenSSL utility to create your keys and a certificate request. Then, you'll submit the certificate request, proof of identity if applicable, and your payment to the certificate authority. Depending upon which grade of certificate you purchase, you'll have to wait anywhere from one to several days before you get the certificate.

Unlike the traditional certificate vendors, Let's Encrypt is totally free of charge, and you don't have to jump through hoops to get the certificate. Instead, you configure your webserver to automatically obtain a new Let's Encrypt certificate each time you set up a new website. If Let's Encrypt sees that your new site has a valid record on a publicly accessible DNS server, it will automatically create and install the certificate on your server. Other than having to configure your webserver to use Let's Encrypt, it's no fuss, no muss.

The problem with Let's Encrypt is that it's even easier to abuse than the extended validation certificates. Shortly after Let's Encrypt began operation, criminals began setting up domains that appeared to be subdomains of legitimate business websites. So, people see that the website is encrypted and that the domain name seems to be legit, and they merrily enter their credentials without giving things a second thought. Let's Encrypt is handy and useful for legitimate purposes, but be aware of its downside, too.

> Tip
>
> Before you choose a certificate vendor, do some research. Sometimes, even the big-name vendors have problems. A few years ago, Google removed Symantec from Chrome's list of trusted certificate authorities because Symantec had allegedly violated industry best practices several times. That's rather ironic, considering that Symantec has had a long history of being a trusted vendor of security products.

Now that we've covered the basics of SSL/TLS encryption, let's see how to implement it with the OpenSSL suite.

Creating keys, certificate signing requests, and certificates

The good news is that, regardless of which *newer* Linux distribution we're on, this procedure is the same. (I say *newer*, because the newest versions of Ubuntu and RHEL/AlmaLinux use OpenSSL version 3. Some of the Version 3 commands are different from what you'll see on the older versions.) The not-so-good news is that OpenSSL can be a bit tricky to learn because it has loads of sub-commands, each with its own set of options and arguments. Bear with me, and I'll break it down the best I can.

Creating a self-signed certificate with an RSA key

A self-signed certificate is useful when all you need is encryption, or for testing purposes. There's no identity verification involved with self-signed certificates, so you never want to use them on servers that your users need to trust. Let's say that I need to test my new website setup before putting it into production, and I don't want to do my testing with a for-real key and certificate. I'll create the key and the self-signed certificate with one single command:

```
openssl req -newkey rsa:2048 -nodes -keyout donnie-domain.key-x509 -days 365
-out donnie-domain.crt
```

Here's the breakdown:

- **openssl:** I'm using OpenSSL with just my normal user privileges. For now, I'm doing everything in my own home directory, so there's no need for root or sudo privileges.
- **req:** This is the sub-command for managing **certificate signing requests** (CSRs). When creating self-signed certificates, OpenSSL will create a temporary CSR.
- **-newkey rsa:2048:** I'm creating an RSA keypair that's 2,048 bits in length. I'd actually like to use something a bit longer, but that might impact server performance when setting up the TLS handshake. (Again, this is preceded by only a single dash.)

- **-nodes**: This means that I'm not encrypting the private key that I'm about to create. If I were to encrypt the private key, I would have to enter the private key passphrase every time I restart the webserver.
- **-keyout donnie-domain.key-x509**: I'm creating the private key with the name `donnie-domain.key-x509`. The `x509` part indicates that this will be used for a self-signed certificate.
- **-days 365**: The certificate will expire in one year.
- **-out donnie-domain.crt**: Finally, I'm creating the `donnie-domain.crt` certificate.

When you run this command, you'll be prompted to enter information about your business and your server. (We'll look at that in just a moment.) After creating this key and certificate, I'll need to move them to their proper locations and configure my webserver to find them. (We'll also touch on that in a bit.)

Encrypting the private key is an optional step, which I didn't do. If I were to encrypt the private key, I would have to enter the passphrase every time that I restart the webserver. That could be problematic if there are any webserver admins who don't have the passphrase. And, even though this sounds counter-intuitive, encrypting the private key that's on the webserver doesn't really help that much with security. Any malicious person who can get physical access to the webserver can use memory forensics tools to get the private key from system memory, even if the key is encrypted. But if you plan to make a backup of the key to store elsewhere, definitely encrypt that copy. So now, let's make an encrypted backup copy of my private key that I can safely store somewhere other than on the webserver:

```
[donnie@localhost ~]$ openssl rsa -aes256 -in donnie-domain.key-x509 -out
donnie-domain-encrypted.key-x509

writing RSA key
Enter PEM pass phrase:
Verifying - Enter PEM pass phrase:
[donnie@localhost ~]$
```

There are two things to look at here:

- `rsa -aes256` means that I'm using the AES256 encryption algorithm to encrypt an RSA key.
- To ensure that I made a copy instead of overwriting the original unencrypted key, I specified `donnie-domain-encrypted.key-x509` as the name for the copy.

Creating a self-signed certificate with an Elliptic Curve key

RSA keys were okay in their day, but they do have their disadvantages. (I'll cover this more in just a bit.) **Elliptic Curve (EC)** keys are superior in pretty much every way. So, let's now create a self-signed certificate with an EC key, instead of with an RSA key, like so:

```
openssl req -new -x509 -nodes -newkey ec:<(openssl ecparam -name secp384r1)
-keyout cert.key.x509 -out cert.crt -days 3650
```

The only part of this that's different is the `ec:<(openssl ecparam -name secp384r1)` part. It looks strange, but it's really quite logical. When creating an EC key, you have to specify a parameter with the `ecparam` command. You'll normally see this as two separate `openssl` commands, but it's handier to combine the two commands together as one command within another command. The inner `openssl` command is feeding its output back to the outer `openssl` command via the input redirection symbol (`<`). The `-name secp384r1` part means that we're creating a 384-bit EC key with the `secp384` named curve algorithm.

Creating an RSA key and a Certificate Signing Request

Normally, we won't use a self-signed certificate for anything that's meant for the general public to interface with. Instead, we want to obtain a certificate from a commercial CA because we want users to know that they're connecting to a server for which the identity of its owners has been verified. To obtain a certificate from a trusted CA, you'll first need to create a key and a **Certificate Signing Request** (**CSR**). Let's do that now:

```
openssl req --out CSR.csr -new -newkey rsa:2048 -nodes -keyout server-
  privatekey.key
```

Here's the breakdown:

- **openssl**: I'm using OpenSSL with just my normal user privileges. For now, I'm doing everything in my own home directory, so there's no need for root or sudo privileges.
- **req**: This is the sub-command for managing CSRs.
- **--out CSR.csr**: The `--out` means that I'm creating something. In this case, I'm creating the CSR with the name `CSR.csr`. All CSRs will have the `.csr` filename extension.
- **-new**: This is a new request. (And yes, this is preceded by a single dash, unlike the out in the previous line that's preceded by two dashes.)
- **-newkey rsa:2048**: I'm creating an RSA key pair that's 2,048 bits in length. I'd actually like to use something a bit longer, but that will impact server performance when setting up the TLS handshake. (Again, this is preceded by only a single dash.)
- **-nodes**: This means that I'm not encrypting the private key that I'm about to create. If I were to encrypt the private key, I would have to enter the private key passphrase every time I restart the webserver.
- **-keyout server-privatekey.key**: Finally, I'm creating the private key with the name `server-privatekey.key`. Since this key isn't for a self-signed certificate, I didn't put the `-x509` at the end of the key's filename.

Let's now look at a snippet from the command output:

```
[donnie@localhost ~]$ openssl req --out CSR.csr -new -newkey rsa:2048 -nodes
-keyout server-privatekey.key
Generating a RSA private key
. . .
. . .
```

```
Country Name (2 letter code) [XX]:US
State or Province Name (full name) []:GA
Locality Name (eg, city) [Default City]:Saint Marys
Organization Name (eg, company) [Default Company Ltd]:Tevault Enterprises
Organizational Unit Name (eg, section) []:Education
Common Name (eg, your name or your server's hostname) []:www.
tevaultenterprises.com
Email Address []:any@any.net
Please enter the following 'extra' attributes
to be sent with your certificate request
A challenge password []:TurkeyLips
An optional company name []:
```

So, I've entered my information about my company location, name, and website name. Note the bottom where it asks me for a **challenge password**. This password doesn't encrypt either the key or the certificate. Rather, it's just a shared secret between the certificate authority and me that's embedded into the certificate. I'll need to keep it in a safe place in case I ever need to reinstall the certificate. (And, for goodness' sake, when you do this for real, pick a better password than TurkeyLips.)

As before, I didn't encrypt the private key. But if you need to make a backup copy, just follow the procedure that you saw in the previous section.

To obtain a certificate from a commercial CA, go to their website and follow their directions. When you receive your certificate, install it in the proper place in your webserver and configure the webserver to find it.

Creating an EC key and a CSR

Up until a few years ago, you would have wanted to use RSA keys on your webservers. They don't have the security weaknesses that certain other key types have, and they're widely supported by pretty much every web browser. But RSA keys do have two weaknesses:

- Even at the standard 2,048-bit length, they require more computational power than other key types. Increasing the key length for better security could degrade webserver performance.
- RSA doesn't offer **Perfect Forward Secrecy** (**PFS**). In other words, if someone were to capture a session key that's produced by the RSA algorithm, they would be able to decrypt material from the past. If the same person were to capture a session key that was produced by a PFS algorithm, they would only be able to decrypt the current communication stream.

Using the new-fangled EC algorithms instead of the creaky old RSA solves both of these problems. But if you pick up a book from even a couple of years ago, you'll see that it recommends using RSA keys for backward compatibility with older web browsers. That's partly because certain operating systems, along with their associated proprietary web browsers, lingered on for far longer than they should have. (*I'm looking at you, Windows XP.*) Now though, as I sit here writing this in October 2022, I think it's safe to start ignoring the needs of anyone who refuses to move on from these antiquated platforms. I mean, Windows XP and Windows 7 both reached end-of-life several years ago. So, let's get with the times, people.

Unlike what we just saw with the RSA keys, we can't create the EC private key and the CSR all with one simple command. With EC, we need to do this in two separate steps.

First, I'll create the private key:

```
openssl genpkey -algorithm EC -out eckey.pem -pkeyopt ec_paramgen_curve:P-384
-pkeyopt ec_param_enc:named_curve
```

Here's the breakdown:

- **genpkey -algorithm EC**: The genpkey command is a fairly recent addition to OpenSSL and is now the recommended way to create private keys. Here, I'm telling it to create a key with the EC algorithm.
- **-out eckey.pem**: I'm creating the eckey.pem key, which is in the **Privacy Enhanced Mail** (**PEM**) format. The RSA keys that I created in the previous section were also PEM keys, but I used the .key filename extension on them. You can use either the .key or the .pem filename extension, and they'll both work. But if you use the .pem extension, everyone who looks at them can tell at a glance that they are PEM keys.
- **-pkeyopt ec_paramgen_curve:P-384**: This tells OpenSSL to create an EC key that's 384 bits in length. A beautiful thing about EC is that its shorter-length keys provide the same encryption strength as the longer RSA keys. In this case, we have a 384-bit key that's actually stronger than a 2,048-bit RSA key. And, it requires less computational power. (I call that a total win!)
- **-pkeyopt ec_param_enc:named_curve**: This is the encoding method that I'm using for the EC parameters. It has to be set to either named_curve or explicit.

Now, I'll create a CSR and sign it with my new private key, like so:

```
[donnie@localhost ~]$ openssl req -new -key eckey.pem -out eckey.csr
. . .
. . .
[donnie@localhost ~]$
```

The output that I didn't include is the same as what you saw in the RSA key section.

The final steps are the same as before. Choose a CA and let them tell you how to submit the CSR. When they issue the certificate, install it on your webserver.

Creating an on-premises CA

Buying a certificate from a commercial CA is good when you're dealing with the general public on a website that they need to trust. But for an organization's own internal use, it's not always necessary or feasible to buy commercial certificates. Let's say that your organization has a group of developers who need their own client certificates to access the development server. Buying a commercial certificate for each developer would be costly, and it would require the development server to have a publicly accessible domain name so that the commercial CA can do domain verification. Even going with the free-of-charge Let's Encrypt certificates isn't a good option, because that would also require that the development server have a publicly accessible domain name.

Option 2 is to go with self-signed certificates. But that won't work because client authentication doesn't work with self-signed certificates. That leaves Option 3, setting up a private, on-premises CA.

If you search around on the web, you'll find lots of guides for setting up your own private CA. But almost all of them are woefully outdated, and most of them are for setting up a CA with OpenSSL. There's nothing wrong with using OpenSSL for a CA, except that setting it up is a rather convoluted, multi-stage process. Then, when you finally do have it set up, you have to use complex commands from the command line in order to do anything. What we want is something a bit more user-friendly for both you and your users.

Hands-on lab — setting up a Dogtag CA

Dogtag PKI is much simpler to set up, and it has a nice web interface that OpenSSL doesn't have. It's available in the normal repositories of Debian/Ubuntu and RHEL/AlmaLinux, but under different package names. In the Debian/Ubuntu repositories, the package name is dogtag-pki. In the RHEL/AlmaLinux repositories, the name is pki-ca. (For some reason that I don't understand, you'll never see Red Hat folk use the "Dogtag" name.)

Before we install the Dogtag packages, we need to do a couple of simple chores:

- Set a **Fully Qualified Domain Name (FQDN)** on the server.
- Either create a record in a local DNS server for the Dogtag server, or create an entry for it in its own /etc/hosts file.

You can do this on either your AlmaLinux 9 or your Ubuntu 22.04 VM, and I'll give directions for both. To access the Dogtag dashboard, we'll use a second Linux VM with a desktop environment installed. With all this out of the way, let's get started:

1. On your server virtual machine, set an FQDN, substituting your own for the one that I'm using:

    ```
    sudo hostnamectl set-hostname donnie-ca.local
    ```

2. Edit the /etc/hosts file to add a line like the following:

    ```
    192.168.0.53 donnie-ca.local
    ```

3. Use your virtual machine's own IP address and FQDN.

4. Next, increase the number of file descriptors that your system can have open at one time. (Otherwise, you'll get a warning message when you run the Directory Server installer.) Do that by editing the /etc/security/limits.conf file. At the end of the file, add these two lines:

    ```
    root          hard    nofile        4096
    root          soft    nofile        4096
    ```

5. Reboot the machine so that the new hostname and file descriptor limits can take effect.

6. Dogtag stores its certificate and user information in an LDAP database. In this step, we'll install the LDAP server package, along with the Dogtag package. For AlmaLinux 9, do this:

    ```
    sudo dnf install 389-ds-base pki-ca
    ```

7. For Ubuntu 22.04, do this:

```
sudo apt install 389-ds-base dogtag-pki
```

8. Next, create an LDAP **Directory Server (DS)** instance by first creating an `instance.inf` file in the root user's home directory:

```
sudo vim /root/instance.inf
```

9. Make its contents look something like this, using your own `suffix` and `root_password`:

```
# /root/instance.inf
[general]
config_version = 2

[slapd]
root_password = TurkeyLips

[backend-userroot]
sample_entries = yes
suffix = dc=donnie-ca,dc=local
```

10. (Yes, I know that it's bad practice to put passwords into plain-text configuration files. That's okay, though. We'll take care of that in just a bit.)

11. We can now use this `instance.inf` file, along with the `dscreate` utility, to create the Directory Server instance:

```
sudo dscreate from-file /root/instance.inf
```

12. Finally, it's time to create the CA:

```
sudo pkispawn
```

Accept all the defaults until you get to the very end. When it asks **Begin Installation?**, type Yes. When you get to the Directory Server part, enter the password that you used to create the DS instance in the previous step. Note that you'll be offered the choice to access the LDAP DS instance via a secure port. But since we're setting up LDAP and Dogtag on the same machine, this isn't necessary.

13. Ensure that the Dogtag service will automatically start by enabling the `pki-tomcatd.target`. Do that with:

```
sudo systemctl enable pki-tomcatd.target
sudo shutdown -r now
```

14. After everything is set up, you'll no longer need the `instance.inf` file that holds your password in plain-text. Get rid of it by doing:

```
sudo shred -u -z /root/instance.inf
```

15. You'll access the Dogtag web interface via port 8443/tcp. On the AlmaLinux machine, open that port like this:

```
sudo firewall-cmd --permanent --add-port=8443/tcp
sudo firewall-cmd --reload
```

16. On the Ubuntu machine, assuming that you're using the Uncomplicated Firewall, open the port like this:

```
sudo ufw allow 8443/tcp
```

17. On another Linux virtual machine that has a desktop interface, edit the /etc/hosts file to add the same line that you added to the server hosts file in *step 2*. Then, open the Firefox web browser on that machine and navigate to the Dogtag dashboard. In keeping with the example in this scenario, the URL would look like this:

```
https://donnie-ca.local:8443
```

You'll receive a warning about the certificate being invalid because it's self-signed. That's normal, because every CA has to start with a self-signed certificate, and you haven't yet imported this certificate into your trust store. Temporarily add the exception and continue. (In other words, clear the checkmark from the **Add permanently** box. You'll see why in the next lab.) Click through the links until you reach this screen:

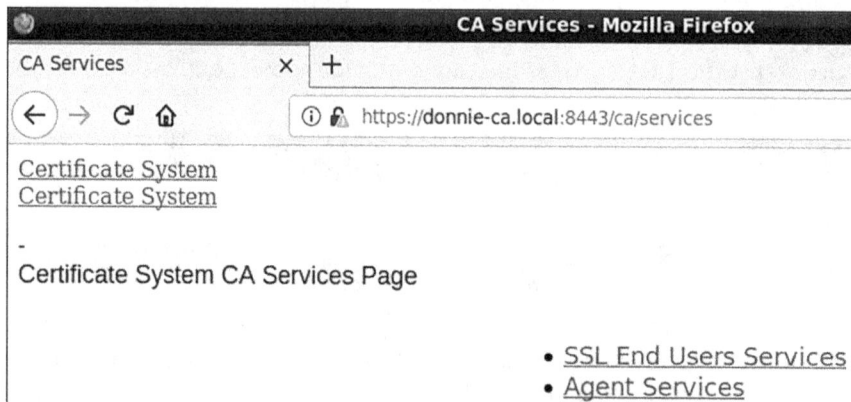

Figure 6.10: Local certificate server

1. Click the **SSL End Users Services** link. This is where end users can request various types of certificates. Click the back button to return to the previous screen. This time, click on the **Agent Services** link. You won't be able to go there because it requires you to install a certificate into your web browser for authentication.

2. The certificate that you need to install is in the /root/.dogtag/pki-tomcat/ directory of your Dogtag VM. Copy this file to the VM on which you're using Firefox to access the Dogtag dashboard. Do the following:

```
sudo su -
cd /root/.dogtag/pki-tomcat
scp ca_admin_cert.p12 donnie@192.168.0.14:
exit
```

Of course, substitute your own username and IP address. Note that the file will automatically land in your own home directory, and that its ownership will change from root to your own username.

On the VM with Firefox, import the certificate into Firefox. From the Firefox menu, choose **Settings**, then **Privacy and Security**. At the very bottom of the screen, click on **View Certificates**. Click the **Your Certificates** tab at the top and the **Import** button at the bottom. Navigate to your home directory and choose the certificate that you just sent over from the Dogtag server VM. Once the import operation is complete, you should see the **PKI Administrator** certificate in the list of imported certificates:

Figure 6.11: Local certificate manager

3. Now try to access the **Agent Services** page. You'll be allowed access once you confirm that you want to use the certificate that you just imported.

4. End of lab.

When a user needs to request a certificate for their own use, they'll use openssl to create a key and a CSR, as I've already shown you earlier in this chapter. They'll then go to the **SSL End User Services** page and paste the contents of their CSR into the box for the certificate that they're requesting. An administrator will then go to the Agent Services page to approve the request and issue the certificate. (To help familiarize yourself with Dogtag, I encourage you to click around on the web interface, exploring all the options.)

Adding a CA to an operating system

Most of the major web browsers, such as Firefox, Chrome, and Chromium, come with their own pre-defined database of trusted CAs and their associated certificates. When you create a private CA, you'll need to import the CA certificate into your browser's trust store. Otherwise, your users will keep receiving messages about how the sites that they're viewing are using untrusted certificates. Indeed, that's the case with our Dogtag server. Any user who accesses it to request a certificate will receive a warning about how the CA is using a non-trusted certificate. We'll fix that by exporting the CA certificate from the Dogtag server and importing it into all of your users' browsers. Let's dig in, shall we?

Hands-on lab — exporting and importing the Dogtag CA certificate

The Dogtag web portal doesn't have an option for this, so we'll have to use the command line:

1. In your home directory of the Dogtag server, create the `password.txt` file. On the first line of the file, insert the password for the server's certificate. (It's the password that you set when you ran the `pkispawn` command.)

2. Extract the server key and certificate like so:

    ```
    sudo pki-server ca-cert-chain-export --pkcs12-file pki-server.p12
    --pkcs12-password-file password.txt
    ```

3. Run an `ls -l` command to verify that the `pki-server.p12` file was created.

4. The problem with the p12 file is that it contains both the server's private key and its certificate. But to add a certificate to the CA section of your browser's trusted store, you have to have just the certificate without the key. Extract the certificate like so:

    ```
    openssl pkcs12 -info -in pki-server.p12 -out pki-server.crt -nokeys
    ```

5. Transfer this new `pki-server.crt` file to a machine with a graphical desktop. In Firefox, open **Settings/Privacy & Security**. Click the **View Certificates** button at the bottom. Click the **Authorities** tab and import the new certificate. Select **Trust this CA to identify websites** and **Trust this CA to identify email users**:

Figure 6.12: Local certificate manager

6. Close Firefox and then open it again to ensure that the certificate takes effect. Navigate to the Dogtag portal. This time, you shouldn't receive any warning messages about using an untrusted certificate.

7. End of lab.

Importing the CA into Windows

With either Firefox or Chrome, you'll import the CA certificate directly into the browser's trust store, regardless of which operating system you're running. But if you're stuck running one of Microsoft's own proprietary browsers on that off-brand operating system that's known as Windows, then you'll need to import the certificate into the Windows trust store instead of into the browser. Fortunately, that's incredibly easy to do. After you copy the certificate to the Windows machine, just open up Windows File Explorer and double-click on the certificate file. Then, click the **Install Certificate** button on the pop-up dialog box. If your organization is running an Active Directory domain, just ask one of the AD administrators to import it into Active Directory for you.

OpenSSL and the Apache webserver

A default installation of any webserver isn't all that secure, so you'll need to harden it up a bit. One way to do that is by disabling the weaker SSL/TLS encryption algorithms. The general principles apply to all webservers, but for our examples, we'll just look at Apache. (The topic of webserver hardening is quite extensive. For the present, I'll confine the discussion to hardening the SSL/TLS configuration.) You can use either Ubuntu 22.04 or AlmaLinux 9 for this section, but the package names and configuration files are different between the two distros. The configurations also differ between CentOS 7 and AlmaLinux 9, so we'll look at them as well. But, before I can explain the configuration options, I need to say a word or two about the history of the SSL/TLS protocol.

In the 1990s, engineers at Netscape invented the SSL protocol. Version 1 never saw the light of day, so the first released version was **SSL version 2 (SSLv2)**. SSLv2 had its share of weaknesses, many of which were addressed in SSLv3. At the insistence of Microsoft, the next version was renamed **Transport Layer Security (TLS) version 1 (TLSv1)**. (I have no idea why Microsoft objected to the SSL name.) The current version is TLSv1.3, which is finally now supported by most Linux distros. By default, Apache still supports some of the older protocols. Our goal is to disable those older protocols. Only a couple of years ago, that would have meant disabling SSLv2 and SSLv3 and leaving TLSv1 through TLSv1.2, due to questionable browser support for anything newer. Now, though, I think it's safe to disable support for anything older than TLSv1.3. When I wrote the Second Edition of this book back in 2019, Apple Safari was the only major browser that didn't support TLSv1.3. Fortunately, even Apple is now on board with the newest TLS.

Hardening Apache SSL/TLS on Ubuntu

For this demo, we'll use two Ubuntu 22.04 virtual machines. We'll install Apache on the first one and sslscan on the second one. (This sslscan package isn't available in the AlmaLinux repository.):

1. To install Apache on your Ubuntu machine, just do the following:

    ```
    sudo apt install apache2
    ```

    This also installs the mod_ssl package, which contains the libraries and configuration files for SSL/TLS implementation.

    And, of course, if you have a firewall enabled, be sure that port 443/tcp is open.

2. The Apache service is already enabled and running, so you don't have to mess with that. But you do need to enable the default SSL site and the SSL module with these three commands:

    ```
    sudo a2ensite default-ssl.conf
    sudo a2enmod ssl
    sudo systemctl restart apache2
    ```

3. Before we look at the SSL/TLS configuration, let's set up a scanner machine to externally test our configuration. On the second Ubuntu VM, install the sslscan package:

    ```
    sudo apt install sslscan
    ```

On the scanner machine, scan the Ubuntu machine on which you installed Apache, substituting the IP address of your own machine:

```
sslscan 192.168.0.3
```

Note the algorithms and the protocol versions that are supported. You should see that SSLv2, SSLv3, TLSv1.0, and TLSv1.1 are all disabled. TLSv1.2 and TLSv1.3 are the only ones that are enabled.

4. On the Ubuntu VM with Apache, edit the /etc/apache2/mods-enabled/ssl.conf file. Look for the line that says this:

```
SSLProtocol all -SSLv3
```

Change it to this:

```
SSLProtocol all -SSLv3 -TLSv1.2
```

5. Restart the Apache daemon to make this change take effect:

```
sudo systemctl restart apache2
```

6. Scan this machine again, and note the output. You should see that the older TLSv1.2 protocol has also now been disabled. So, congratulations! You've just made a quick and easy security upgrade to your webserver.

7. End of lab.

Now, let's take a look at RHEL 9/AlmaLinux 9.

Hardening Apache SSL/TLS on RHEL 9/AlmaLinux 9

For this demo, you'll install Apache and mod_ssl on an AlmaLinux 9 VM. (Unlike on Ubuntu, you have to install these as two separate packages.) Use the same scanner VM that you used in the previous lab. A new feature of the RHEL 8/9 distros is that you can now set system-wide crypto policies for most of your services and applications that require cryptography. We'll take a quick look at it here, and again in *Chapter 7, SSH Hardening*:

1. Before doing anything, shut down your AlmaLinux 9 VM and create a snapshot from the VirtualBox console. That's because in just a bit, you'll need to go back to a clean snapshot in order to test the crypto policies feature.

2. On your AlmaLinux 9 VM, install Apache and mod_ssl, and start the service:

```
sudo dnf install httpd mod_ssl
sudo systemctl enable --now httpd
```

3. Open port 443 on the firewall:

```
sudo firewall-cmd --permanent --add-service=https
sudo firewall-cmd --reload
```

4. From the scanner VM, scan the Apache VM, substituting your own IP address:

```
sslscan 192.168.0.160
```

As you just saw on the Ubuntu server, nothing older than TLSv1.2 is supported.

5. Next, on the Apache VM, view the status of the system-wide crypto configuration:

```
sudo update-crypto-policies --show
```

You should see DEFAULT as the output. With DEFAULT, you get TLSv1.2 as the minimum protocol version along with the goodness of TLSv1.3. But you'll also see some TLSv1.2 algorithms that we can do without.

6. Shut down the Apache VM. Go to the VirtualBox console and restore the snapshot that you created in Step 1, in order to get rid of the Apache installation. Then, restart the virtual machine and set the crypto policy to FUTURE, like this:

```
sudo update-crypto-policies --set FUTURE
```

> I had a good reason for having you create and restore the snapshot before setting FUTURE mode. It's just that if you install Apache before setting FUTURE mode, you'll no longer be able to start Apache. So, if you want to run your Apache webserver with FUTURE mode, you'll need to set FUTURE mode first, then install Apache.

Reboot the Apache VM so that the FUTURE mode will take effect. Verify that FUTURE mode has taken effect by doing:

```
sudo update-crypto-policies --show
```

7. Install the mod_ssl and Apache packages, and start Apache as you did in Step 2.
8. Scan the webserver VM as you did in Step 4. You'll see that TLSv1.2 is still enabled, but with a much smaller list of enabled algorithms.
9. End of lab.

There are two other crypto policy modes besides the two that I've shown here. LEGACY mode enables some really old algorithms that we don't want to use unless it's absolutely necessary to support older clients. But, as I keep saying, anyone who's using a client that's that old needs to upgrade.

> **Important**
>
> At the time of this writing, the certificate for the EPEL repository is not compatible with FUTURE mode. You can still use EPEL, but you'll need to go back to DEFAULT mode if you ever need to install or update any EPEL packages. Then, you can go back to FUTURE mode. (Of course, this might change by the time you read this.)

There's also the FIPS mode, which you might need to use if you're doing business with the U.S. government. Even though the update-crypto-policies utility appears to work with FIPS mode, Red Hat recommends against doing that. Instead, they recommend setting FIPS mode as you install the operating system. We'll look at that next.

Setting FIPS mode on RHEL 9/AlmaLinux 9

FIPS stands for **Federal Information Processing Standards**, and is a set of cybersecurity requirements for people and companies who want to do business with the United States government. Setting your server to run in FIPS mode involves more than just disabling some weak encryption algorithms. It also involves installing a set of modules that help harden other aspects of the operating system.

Even though the update-crypto-policies utility has an option for setting FIPS mode, you'll never use it. To set FIPS mode on a machine on which the operating system has already been installed, you'd instead use the sudo fips-mode-setup --enable command. But, Red Hat recommends against doing that. Instead, they recommend setting FIPS mode as you install the operating system. Their concern is that setting FIPS mode after installing the operating system might leave behind encryption keys that were created with non-FIPS algorithms. Fortunately, that's easy. All you have to do is interrupt the installer's boot process and make a quick edit to the kernel configuration. Here's how to do it as you create a new AlmaLinux VM:

1. Create a new AlmaLinux VM and boot up the AlmaLinux installer. Hit the *Up* arrow key to highlight the **Install AlmaLinux** option. Instead of hitting the *Enter* key to continue, hit the *Tab* key to bring up the kernel options. Here's what you should see:

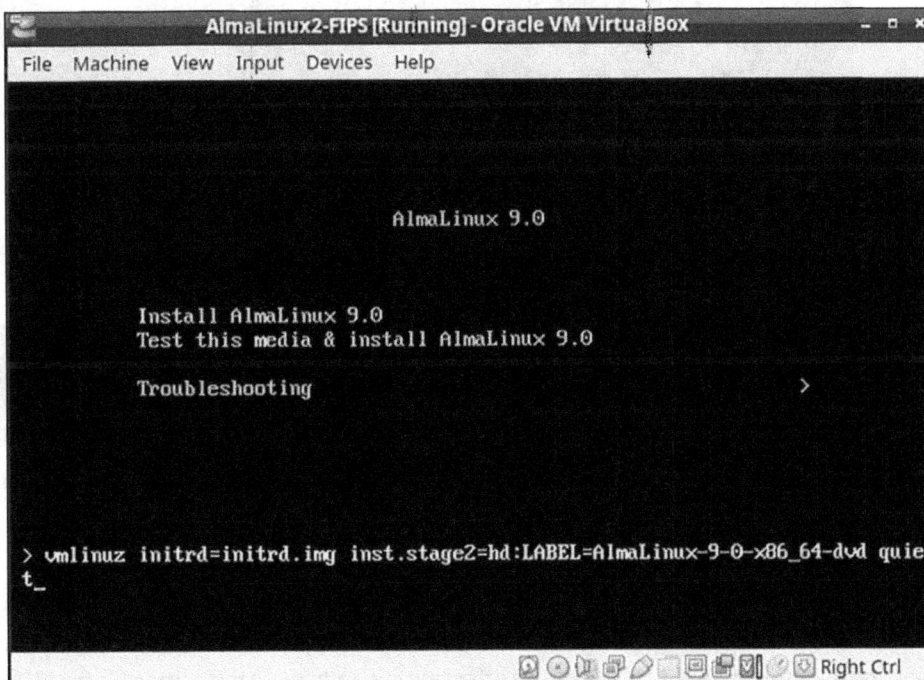

Figure 6.13: The AlmaLinux installer screen

2. At the bottom of the screen, add `fips=1` to the end of the kernel option line. It should now look like this:

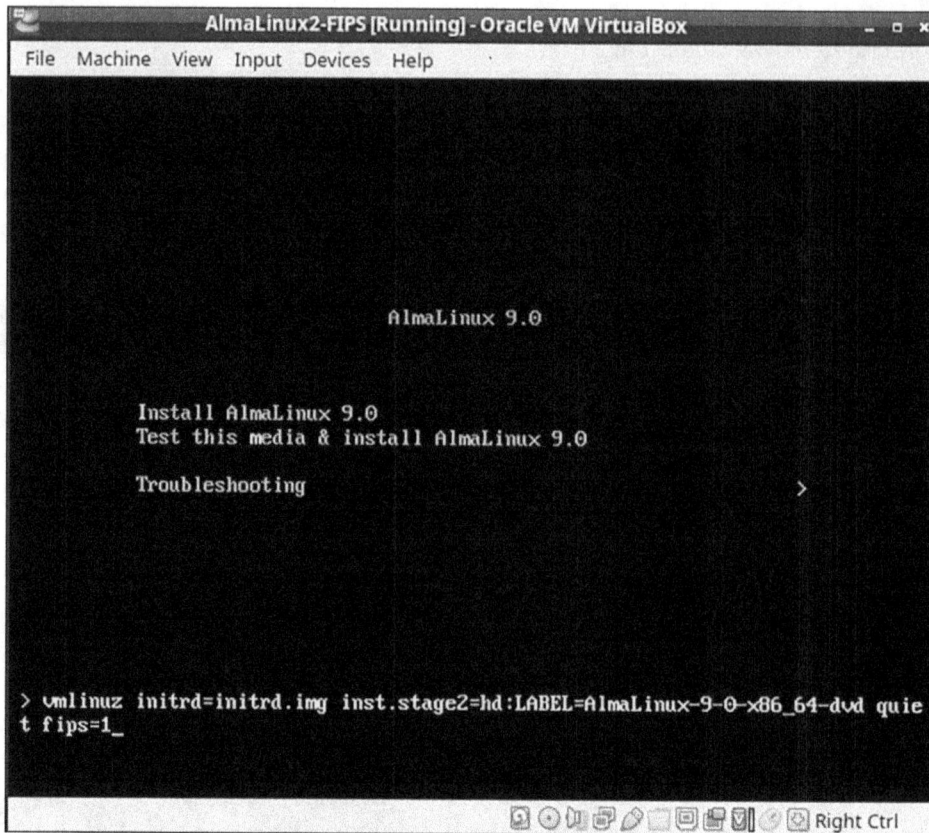

Figure 6.14: Add the FIPS parameter

3. Hit the *Enter* key and continue installation as you normally would.

4. Once the installation is complete and the VM has rebooted, check the status of `FIPS` mode, like this:

```
[donnie@localhost ~]$ fips-mode-setup --check
FIPS mode is enabled.
[donnie@localhost ~]$
```

5. Finally, install `mod_ssl` and Apache. Open the the firewall port and scan the VM with `sslscan`, as you did in the previous exercise.

6. End of lab.

There are a couple of caveats that you should know about when setting `FIPS` mode on any RHEL 9-type distro. One is that the current version of the FIPS standard is version 140-3. However, at the time of this writing in October 2022, RHEL 9 and its offspring still only meet the standards for FIPS 140-2. The Red Hat documentation gives no insight into when that might change.

The other caveat is that whenever a new point upgrade comes out for RHEL-type operating systems, just doing a normal sudo `dnf upgrade` command will automatically upgrade you to the new version. In this case, I started doing this write-up with AlmaLinux 9.0, and later upgraded to AlmaLinux 9.1. I found out by accident that upgrading a FIPS mode machine to a new point release will break the machine, causing it to no longer boot. That's because the FIPS modules refused to load with the new 9.1 kernel. (This is a prime example of why you need to always test system updates before you deploy them on a production system.) As far as I can see, there's no mention of this in the official Red Hat documentation.

> If you're wondering why I'm not covering FIPS mode on Ubuntu, it's just that it's not possible to set FIPS mode on the free-of-charge version of Ubuntu. If you want to run Ubuntu in FIPS mode, you'll have to purchase a support contract.

Now, let's take a quick look at the legacy CentOS 7.

Hardening Apache SSL/TLS on RHEL 7/CentOS 7

Okay, I did say that we'd look at doing this on a CentOS 7 machine. But, I'll make it brief.

You'll install Apache and mod_ssl on CentOS 7 the same way that you did on AlmaLinux 9, except that you'll use the yum command instead of the dnf command. As with AlmaLinux, you'll need to enable and start Apache with systemctl, but you won't need to enable the ssl site or the ssl module. And, of course, make sure that port 443 is open on the firewall.

When you do an sslscan of a CentOS 7 machine, you'll see a very long list of supported algorithms, from TLSv1 through TLSv1.2. Even with TLSv1.2, you'll see a few really bad things, like this:

```
Accepted  TLSv1.2  112 bits  ECDHE-RSA-DES-CBC3-SHA     Curve P-256 DHE 256
Accepted  TLSv1.2  112 bits  EDH-RSA-DES-CBC3-SHA       DHE 2048 bits
Accepted  TLSv1.2  112 bits  DES-CBC3-SHA
```

The DES and SHA in these lines indicate that we're supporting the use of the antiquated **Data Encryption Standard** (DES) and version 1 of the **Secure Hash Algorithm** (SHA). That is not good. Get rid of them by editing the /etc/httpd/conf.d/ssl.conf file. Look for these two lines:

```
SSLProtocol all -SSLv2 -SSLv3
SSLCipherSuite HIGH:3DES:!aNULL:!MD5:!SEED:!IDEA
```

Change them to this:

```
SSLProtocol all -SSLv2 -SSLv3 -TLSv1 -TLSv1.1
SSLCipherSuite HIGH:!3DES:!aNULL:!MD5:!SEED:!IDEA:!SHA
```

Reload Apache with this command:

```
sudo systemctl reload httpd
```

Scan the machine again, and you'll see a lot fewer supported algorithms. (And by the way, one advantage of the new TLSv1.3 is that it completely gets rid of these legacy algorithms.)

Next, let's look at how users can identify themselves to a server.

Setting up mutual authentication

When you access your bank's secure website, your web browser requires that the webserver authenticate itself to the browser. In other words, the browser demands to see the server's certificate for the website so that it can verify if it's valid. This way, you have some assurance that you're logging in to the bank's real, genuine website instead of a counterfeit site. You then have to authenticate yourself to the webserver, but you'll normally do that with a username and password.

If a webserver is set up to allow it, users can instead authenticate themselves with a certificate. This way, there's no password for the bad guys to either steal or crack. You already saw how this is done when you imported Dogtag's `ca_admin_cert.p12` certificate into your web browser. This certificate gave you the awesome power to access Dogtag's administrator page. Your normal end users won't have this certificate, so all they can access is just the end-user page where they can request certificates.

The major webservers—Apache, Nginx, `lighttpd`, and some others—support mutual authentication. Space doesn't permit me to go into the details of setting this up on a server, but the documentation for whichever server you use will cover it.

Next, let's get back to the future!

Introducing quantum-resistant encryption algorithms

You've likely heard of quantum computers, which have nothing to do with the old *Quantum Leap* show on television. This new type of computer is still in the experimental stage, and likely will remain there for some time to come. Still, there's a lot of hype about what they'll be like when they finally are ready for production use. Supposedly, they'll be way more powerful than the current generation of computers, and they'll supposedly be able to easily crack even the strongest of the current encryption algorithms. Indeed, that's a rather scary prediction. (Perhaps it's fitting that I'm typing this on Halloween, the scariest day of the year.)

Even though there's some skepticism about whether this dire prediction will come true, or whether production-grade quantum computers will even see the light of day, the U.S. federal government is taking this seriously. Here's the list of quantum-resistant algorithms that the **National Institute of Standards and Technology (NIST)** currently recommends:

- **CRYSTALS-Kyber:** This one is for general encryption. Cloudflare, Amazon, and IBM already use it.
- **CRYSTALS-Dilithium:** This is for encrypted digital signatures. NIST recommends this one as the primary signature algorithm.
- **FALCON:** This is also a signature algorithm. NIST recommends it for whenever you need a signature that's smaller than what CRYSTALS-Dilithium can provide.

- **SPHINCS+:** This is the third signature algorithm, which is slower and larger than the first two. It uses a different approach than what the first two use, which is why NIST recommends it as a backup, in case the first two get hacked.

So, how do we know that a particular encryption algorithm is resistant to quantum computer hacking if viable quantum computers don't yet exist? Well, I wish that I could tell you, but I can't. At any rate, you might not have to worry too much about this just yet, but it's still worthwhile to learn.

Okay, let's wrap this baby up and move on to the next chapter.

Summary

As always, we've covered a lot of ground in this chapter. We began by using GPG to encrypt, sign, and share encrypted files. We then looked at various methods of encrypting drives, partitions, directories, and shareable containers. After that, we looked at how to use OpenSSL to create keys, CSRs, and certificates. But since we don't want to use self-signed certificates all the time and commercial certificates aren't always necessary, we looked at how to set up a private CA with Dogtag. We then looked at simple ways to harden the TLS configuration on the Apache webserver, and we touched on the subject of mutual authentication. Finally, we saw an introduction to quantum-resistant encryption algorithms.

Along the way, we had plenty of hands-on labs. That's good, because after all, idle hands are the devil's workshop, and we certainly don't want any of that.

In the next chapter, we'll look at ways to harden Secure Shell. I'll see you there.

Questions

1. Which of the following is not an advantage of GPG?

    a. It uses strong, hard-to-crack algorithms.

    b. It works well for sharing secrets with people you don't know.

    c. Its public/private key scheme eliminates the need to share passwords.

    d. You can use it to encrypt files that you don't intend to share, for your own personal use.

2. You need to send an encrypted message to Frank. What must you do before you can encrypt his message with GPG so that you don't have to share a password?

    a. Nothing. Just encrypt the message with your own private key.

    b. Import Frank's private key into your keyring and send Frank your private key.

    c. Import Frank's public key into your keyring and send Frank your public key.

    d. Just import Frank's public key into your keyring.

    e. Just import Frank's private key into your keyring.

3. Which of the following would be the proper choice for whole-disk encryption on a Linux system?

    a. BitLocker

    b. VeraCrypt

      c.   eCryptfs

      d.   LUKS

4. If you use eCryptfs to encrypt users' home directories and you're not using whole-disk encryption, what other action must you take in order to prevent leakage of sensitive data?

      a.   None.

      b.   Ensure that users use strong private keys.

      c.   Encrypt the swap partition.

      d.   You must use eCryptfs in whole-disk mode.

5. In which of the following scenarios would you use VeraCrypt?

      a.   Whenever you want to implement whole-disk encryption.

      b.   Whenever you just want to encrypt users' home directories.

      c.   Whenever you'd prefer to use a proprietary, closed-source encryption system.

      d.   Whenever you need to create encrypted containers that you can share with Windows, macOS, and BSD users.

6. You need to ensure that your web browser trusts certificates from the Dogtag CA. How do you do it?

      a.   You use `pki-server` to export the CA certificate and key, and then use `openssl pkcs12` to extract just the certificate. Then, import the certificate into your browser.

      b.   You import the `ca_admin.cert` certificate into your browser.

      c.   You import the `ca_admin_cert.p12` certificate into your browser.

      d.   You import the `snakeoil.pem` certificate into your browser.

Further reading

Explanations about TLS and OpenSSL:

- *OpenSSL Tutorial: How Do SSL Certificate, Private keys, and CSRs Work?*: `https://phoenixnap.com/kb/openssl-tutorial-ssl-certificates-private-keys-csrs`

- Transport Layer Security version 1.3 in Red Hat 8: `https://www.redhat.com/en/blog/transport-layer-security-version-13-red-hat-enterprise-linux-8`

- The OpenSSL website: `https://www.openssl.org/`

- Feisty Duck Publishing, who offer books, training, and newsletters about OpenSSL: `https://www.feistyduck.com/`

Problems with EV certificates:

- Chrome browser moving EV UI to Page Info: `https://chromium.googlesource.com/chromium/src/+/HEAD/docs/security/ev-to-page-info.md`

- Extended validation is broken: `https://www.cyberscoop.com/easy-fake-extended-validation-certificates-research-shows/`

- EV certificates issued with "Default City" as the location: https://groups.google.com/forum/#!topic/mozilla.dev.security.policy/1oReSOPCNy0
- EV certificates issued with erroneous information: https://twitter.com/Scott_Helme/status/1163546360328740864

Problems with free Let's Encrypt certificates:

- *Cyber criminals abusing free Let's Encrypt certificates*: https://www.infoworld.com/article/3019926/cyber-criminals-abusing-free-lets-encrypt-certificates.html

Dogtag CA:

- How to increase the number of file descriptors in Linux: https://www.tecmint.com/increase-set-open-file-limits-in-linux/
- Dogtag PKI Wiki: https://www.dogtagpki.org/wiki/PKI_Main_Page
- Import CA into Linux and Windows: https://thomas-leister.de/en/how-to-import-ca-root-certificate/
- Red Hat (Dogtag) certificate authority documentation: https://access.redhat.com/documentation/en-us/red_hat_certificate_system/9/

RHEL 9/AlmaLinux 9:

- Setting system-wide cryptographic policies: https://access.redhat.com/documentation/en-us/red_hat_enterprise_linux/9/html/security_hardening/using-the-system-wide-cryptographic-policies_security-hardening

FIPS:

- FIPS home page: https://www.nist.gov/itl/fips-general-information
- Installing Red Hat in FIPS mode: https://access.redhat.com/documentation/en-us/red_hat_enterprise_linux/9/html/security_hardening/assembly_installing-the-system-in-fips-mode_security-hardening

Quantum-resistant encryption:

- NIST announces quantum-resistant algorithms: https://www.nist.gov/news-events/news/2022/07/nist-announces-first-four-quantum-resistant-cryptographic-algorithms
- Some people are skeptical about quantum-computing: https://www.fudzilla.com/news/55434-quantum-computing-is-neither-dead-or-alive

Answers

1. b
2. c
3. d
4. c
5. d
6. a

Join our book community

Join our community's Discord space for discussions with the author and other readers:

`https://packt.link/CyberSec`

7

SSH Hardening

The **Secure Shell (SSH)** suite is one of those must-have tools for Linux administrators. It allows you to take care of Linux servers from the comfort of your cubicle, or even from the comfort of your own home. Either way, it's a lot better than having to don your parka and jump through security hoops to enter a cold server room. The *secure* in Secure Shell means that everything that you either type or transfer gets encrypted. That eliminates the possibility of someone obtaining sensitive data by plugging a sniffer into your network.

By this stage in your Linux career, you should already know how to use Secure Shell, or SSH, to do remote logins and remote file transfers. What you may not know is that the default configuration of SSH is actually quite insecure. In this chapter, we'll look at how to harden the default configuration in various ways. We'll look at how to use encryption algorithms that are stronger than the default, how to set up passwordless authentication, and how to set up a jail for users of the **Secure File Transfer Protocol (SFTP)**. As a bonus, we'll look at how to scan SSH servers to find vulnerable configurations and how to share a remote directory via **Secure Shell Filesystem (SSHFS)**.

In this chapter, we'll cover the following topics:

- Ensuring that SSH protocol 1 is disabled
- Creating and managing keys for passwordless logins
- Disabling root user login
- Disabling username/password logins
- Enabling two-factor authentication
- Configuring Secure Shell with strong encryption algorithms
- Setting system-wide encryption policies on RHEL 8/9 and AlmaLinux 8/9
- Configuring more detailed logging
- Configuring access control with whitelists and TCP Wrappers
- Configuring automatic logouts and security banners
- Configuring other miscellaneous security settings
- Setting up different configurations for different users and groups

- Setting up different configurations for different hosts
- Setting up a chroot environment for SFTP users
- Sharing a directory with SSHFS
- Remotely connecting from Windows desktops

So, if you're ready, let's get started.

Ensuring that SSH protocol 1 is disabled

In the two previous editions of this book, I told you about how version 1 of the SSH protocol is severely flawed, and how you should always ensure that it's not enabled in the /etc/ssh/sshd_config file. Nowadays, you don't have to worry about that, because SSH protocol 1 is now gone, and is nothing but a thing of the past. So, yee-haw! It's time to celebrate.

Creating and managing keys for passwordless logins

The Secure Shell suite is a great set of tools for communication with remote servers. You can use the ssh component to remotely log in to the command line of a remote machine, and you can use either scp or sftp to securely transfer files. The default way to use any of these SSH components is to use the username of a person's normal Linux user account. So, logging into a remote machine from the terminal of my openSUSE workstation would look something like this:

```
donnie@linux-0ro8:~> ssh donnie@192.168.0.8
donnie@192.168.0.8's password:
```

While it's true that the username and password go across the network in an encrypted format, making it hard for malicious actors to intercept them, it's still not the most secure way of doing business. The problem is that attackers have access to automated tools that can perform brute-force password attacks against an SSH server. Botnets, such as the *Hail Mary Cloud*, perform continuous scans across the Internet to find Internet-facing servers with SSH enabled.

If a botnet finds that the servers allow SSH access via a username and password, it will launch a brute-force password attack. Sadly, such attacks have been successful quite a few times, especially when the server operators allow the root user to log in via SSH.

> This older article provides more details about the Hail Mary Cloud botnet: http://futurismic.com/2009/11/16/the-hail-mary-cloud-slow-but-steady-brute-force-password-guessing-botnet/.

In the next section, we'll look at two ways to help prevent these types of attacks:

- Enabling SSH logins through an exchange of public keys
- Disabling the root user login through SSH

Now, let's create some keys.

Creating a user's SSH key set

Each user has the ability to create his or her own set of private and public keys. It doesn't matter whether the user's client machine is running Linux, macOS, Cygwin on Windows, or Bash Shell for Windows. In all cases, the procedure is exactly the same.

There are several different types of keys that you can create, and 3,072-bit RSA keys are normally the default. Until very recently, 2,048-bit RSA keys were considered strong enough for the foreseeable future. But now, the most recent guidance from the US **National Institute of Standards and Technology (NIST)** says to use either an RSA key of at least 3,072 bits or an **Elliptic Curve Digital Signature Algorithm (ECDSA)** key of at least 384 bits. (You'll sometimes see these **ECDSA** keys referred to as *P-384*.) Their reasoning is that they want to get us ready for quantum computing, which will be so powerful that it will render any weaker encryption algorithms obsolete. Of course, quantum computing isn't practical yet, and so far, it seems to be one of those things that's always just ten years off in the future, regardless of what year it is. But even if we discount the whole quantum thing, we still have to acknowledge that even our current, non-quantum computers keep getting more and more powerful. So, it's still not a bad idea to start going with stronger encryption standards.

> To see the NIST list of recommended encryption algorithms and the recommended key lengths, go to `https://cryptome.org/2016/01/CNSA-Suite-and-Quantum-Computing-FAQ.pdf`.

For these next few demos, let's switch over to an Ubuntu 22.04 client. To create a 3,072-bit RSA key pair, just do this:

```
donnie@ubuntu2204-packt:~$ ssh-keygen
```

We didn't have to use any option switches because the command will already create a 3,072-bit RSA pair by default. When prompted for the location and name of the keys, I'll just hit the *Enter* key to accept the defaults. You could just leave the private key with a blank passphrase, but that's not a recommended practice. That's because if you get up and leave your workstation while it's running, someone could come along and easily access your private keys, which would allow them to access the servers that you administer.

Note that if you choose an alternative name for your key files, you'll need to type in the entire path to make things work properly. For example, in my case, I could specify the path for `donnie_rsa` keys as `/home/donnie/.ssh/donnie_rsa`. Also, note that in order to add a key to your session keyring, you'll need to just accept the default key filenames, because the `ssh-add` utility that we'll be using won't read key files with non-default filenames. (I'll explain more about the session keyring and `ssh-add` in just a bit.)

You'll see your new keys in the `.ssh` directory:

```
donnie@ubuntu2204-packt:~$ ls -l .ssh
total 16
-rw------- 1 donnie donnie    0 Oct  6 22:09 authorized_keys
```

```
-rw-------  1 donnie donnie 2655 Nov  1 19:49 id_rsa
-rw-r--r--  1 donnie donnie  577 Nov  1 19:49 id_rsa.pub
-rw-------  1 donnie donnie  978 Oct 26 20:41 known_hosts
-rw-r--r--  1 donnie donnie  142 Oct 26 20:41 known_hosts.old
donnie@ubuntu2204-packt:~$
```

The id_rsa key is the private key, with read and write permissions only for me. The id_rsa.pub public key has to be world-readable. For ECDSA keys, the default length is 256 bits. If you choose to use ECDSA instead of RSA, do the following to create a strong 384-bit key:

```
donnie@ubuntu2204-packt:~$ ssh-keygen -t ecdsa -b 384
```

Either way, when you look in the .ssh directory, you'll see that the ECDSA keys are named differently from the RSA keys:

```
donnie@ubuntu2204-packt:~$ ls -l .ssh/id*
-rw-------  1 donnie donnie  667 Nov  1 19:55 .ssh/id_ecdsa
-rw-r--r--  1 donnie donnie  229 Nov  1 19:55 .ssh/id_ecdsa.pub
-rw-------  1 donnie donnie 2655 Nov  1 19:49 .ssh/id_rsa
-rw-r--r--  1 donnie donnie  577 Nov  1 19:49 .ssh/id_rsa.pub
donnie@ubuntu2204-packt:~$
```

The beauty of elliptic curve algorithms is that their seemingly short key lengths are just as secure as RSA keys with longer key lengths. And, even the largest ECDSA keys require less computing power than RSA keys. The maximum key length you can have with ECDSA is 521 bits. (Yes, you read that correctly. It's 521 bits, not 524 bits.) So, you may be thinking, *Why don't we just go for the gusto with 521-bit keys?* Well, it's mainly because 521-bit keys aren't recommended by NIST. There's some fear that they may be subject to **padding attacks,** which could allow the bad guys to break your encryption and steal your data. (If you're really curious about how padding attacks work, I'll provide a reference in the *Further reading* section.)

If you take a gander at the man page for ssh-keygen, you'll see that you can also create an Ed25519 type of key, which you'll sometimes see referred to as curve25519. This one isn't included in the NIST list of recommended algorithms and also isn't allowed by the **Federal Information Processing Standard (FIPS)** regulations, but there are a couple of reasons why some people like to use it.

RSA and DSA can leak private key data when creating signatures if the random number generator of the operating system is flawed. Ed25519 doesn't require a random number generator when creating signatures, so it's immune to this problem. Also, Ed25519 is coded in a way that makes it much less vulnerable to side-channel attacks. (A side-channel attack is when someone tries to exploit weaknesses in the underlying operating system, rather than in the encryption algorithm.)

The second reason why some folk like Ed25519 is precisely because it's *not* on the NIST list. These are the folk who, rightly or wrongly, don't trust the recommendations of government agencies.

Quite a few years ago, in the early part of this century, there was a bit of a scandal that involved the **Dual Elliptic Curve Deterministic Random Bit Generator (Dual_EC_DRBG)**. This was a random number generator that was meant for use in elliptic curve cryptography. The problem was that, early on, independent researchers found that it had the capability to have *back doors* inserted by anyone who knew about this capability. And, it just so happened that the only people who were supposed to know about this capability were the folk who work at the US **National Security Agency (NSA)**. At the NSA's insistence, NIST included `Dual_EC_DRBG` in their NIST list of recommended algorithms, and it stayed there until they finally removed it in April 2014. You can get more details about this at the following links:

```
https://www.pcworld.com/article/2454380/overreliance-on-the-nsa-led-to-
weak-crypto-standard-nist-advisers-find.html
```

```
http://www.math.columbia.edu/~woit/wordpress/?p=7045
```

You can read the details about `Ed25519` here: `https://ed25519.cr.yp.to/`.

There's only one key size for `Ed25519`, which is 256 bits. So, to create a `curve25519` key, just do this:

```
donnie@ubuntu2204-packt:~$ ssh-keygen -t ed25519
```

Here are the keys that I've created:

```
donnie@ubuntu2204-packt:~$ ls -l .ssh/*25519*
-rw------- 1 donnie donnie 464 Nov  1 20:35 .ssh/id_ed25519
-rw-r--r-- 1 donnie donnie 105 Nov  1 20:35 .ssh/id_ed25519.pub
donnie@ubuntu2204-packt:~$
```

There are, however, some potential downsides to `Ed25519`:

- First, it isn't supported by older SSH clients. However, if everyone on your team is using current operating systems that use current SSH clients, this shouldn't be a problem.
- The second is that it only supports one certain set key length, which is the equivalent of either 256-bit elliptic curve algorithms or 3,000-bit RSA algorithms. So, it might not be quite as future-proof as the other algorithms that we've covered.
- Lastly, you can't use it if your organization is required to remain compliant with either NIST recommendations or FIPS requirements.

Okay, there is one other type of key that we haven't covered. That's the old-fashioned `DSA` key, which `ssh-keygen` will still create if you tell it to. But, don't do it. The `DSA` algorithm is old, creaky, and very insecure by modern standards. So, when it comes to `DSA`, just say *No*.

Transferring the public key to the remote server

Transferring my public key to a remote server allows the server to readily identify both me and my client machine. Before I can transfer the public key to the remote server, I need to add the private key to my session keyring. This requires two commands. (One command invokes ssh-agent, while the other actually adds the private key to the keyring):

```
donnie@ubuntu2204-packt:~$ exec /usr/bin/ssh-agent $SHELL
donnie@ubuntu2204-packt:~$ ssh-add
Enter passphrase for /home/donnie/.ssh/id_rsa:
Identity added: /home/donnie/.ssh/id_rsa (donnie@ubuntu2204-packt)
Identity added: /home/donnie/.ssh/id_ecdsa (donnie@ubuntu2204-packt)
Identity added: /home/donnie/.ssh/id_ed25519 (donnie@ubuntu2204-packt)
donnie@ubuntu2204-packt:~$
```

Finally, I can transfer my public key(s) to my AlmaLinux 9 server, which is at address 192.168.0.17:

```
donnie@ubuntu2204-packt:~$ ssh-copy-id donnie@192.168.0.17
The authenticity of host '192.168.0.17 (192.168.0.17)' can't be established.
ED25519 key fingerprint is SHA256:GkpFwJdpWRQ5GawgFEz9bgDSny//E1I5aLGkjU9DWWY.
This key is not known by any other names
Are you sure you want to continue connecting (yes/no/[fingerprint])? yes
/usr/bin/ssh-copy-id: INFO: attempting to log in with the new key(s), to filter
out any that are already installed
/usr/bin/ssh-copy-id: INFO: 3 key(s) remain to be installed -- if you are
prompted now it is to install the new keys
donnie@192.168.0.17's password:
Number of key(s) added: 3
Now try logging into the machine, with:   "ssh 'donnie@192.168.0.17'"
and check to make sure that only the key(s) you wanted were added.
donnie@ubuntu2204-packt:~$
```

Normally, you would only create one pair of keys of whichever type you choose. As you can see here, I've created three key pairs, one pair of each type. All three private keys were added to my session keyring, and all three public keys were transferred to the remote server.

The next time that I log in, I'll use the key exchange, and I won't have to enter a password:

```
donnie@ubuntu2204-packt:~$ ssh donnie@192.168.0.17
Last login: Tue Nov  1 16:52:27 2022
[donnie@donnie-ca ~]$
```

As I mentioned previously, you would normally only create one key pair on your local workstation. However, there are exceptions to this rule. Some administrators prefer to use a different key pair for each server that they administer, rather than using the same key pair for all servers. This way, if the private key for one machine gets compromised, it won't necessarily mean that the whole network gets compromised. A handy way to do this is to create keys with filenames that match the hostnames of the respective servers. Then, you can use the -i option to specify which key pair that you want to use. (Note that if you create keys with custom filenames, you won't be able to add them to the keyring, which means that you'll need to type the password of your private key every time you need to use it. I'll explain more about that in just a bit.)

In this example, I only have one server, but I have multiple keys of multiple types for it, all with the default filenames. Let's say that I prefer to use the Ed25519 keys:

```
donnie@ubuntu2204-packt:~$ ssh -i ~/.ssh/id_ed25519 donnie@192.168.0.17
Last login: Tue Nov  1 16:56:43 2022 from 192.168.0.14
[donnie@donnie-ca ~]$
```

So, now you're wondering, *How is that secure if I can log in without entering my password?* The answer is that once you close the client machine's terminal window that you used for logging in, the private key will be removed from your session keyring. When you open a new terminal and try to log in to the remote server, you'll see this:

```
donnie@ubuntu2204-packt:~$ ssh donnie@192.168.0.17
Enter passphrase for key '/home/donnie/.ssh/id_rsa':
Last login: Tue Nov  1 16:58:22 2022 from 192.168.0.14
[donnie@donnie-ca ~]$
```

Now, every time I log in to this server, I'll need to enter the passphrase for my private key until I add it back to the session keyring with the two commands that I showed you in the preceding section.

This all sounds good, but you might know that there is a bit of a caveat. That is, this procedure only works if you create keys with their default filenames. If you create keys with custom filenames, such as server1_id_rsa, for example, the ssh-add utility will refuse to read them, and there's no option switch that will make it read them. So, you won't be able to add these custom keys to your session keyring, which means that you won't be able to transfer them to the target server with ssh-copy-id. You can still use keys with custom filenames, but you'll need to use another means of transferring the public keys to the target server. For example, let's say that you've created a pair of keys that you've named ubuntu1_id_rsa that you want to use to log in to an Ubuntu server. After you've created the key, you can use normal scp to transfer it, like so:

```
[donnie@localhost ~]$ cd .ssh
[donnie@localhost .ssh]$ scp ubuntu1_id_rsa.pub donnie@192.168.0.5:
donnie@192.168.0.5's password:
ubuntu1_id_rsa.pub                          100%  582   229.1KB/s   00:00
[donnie@localhost .ssh]$
```

Next, I'll go over to the ubuntu1 machine, and copy the contents of this public key file to the authorized_keys file, like so:

```
donnie@ubuntu1:~$ ls -l
total 4
-rw------- 1 donnie donnie 582 Jan  8 20:10 ubuntu1_id_rsa.pub
donnie@ubuntu1:~$ cat ubuntu1_id_rsa.pub > .ssh/authorized_keys
donnie@ubuntu1:~$
```

By using the single > operator in this command, I created a whole new authorized_keys file. If you already have an authorized_keys file that you want to keep, use the >> operator instead so that the contents of your public key file will be appended to the end of the existing authorized_keys file. Also, be aware that since you can't add keys with custom filenames to your session keyring, you won't be able to do passwordless logins. Instead, you'll just be prompted for the private key password every time.

Hands-on lab — creating and transferring SSH keys

In this lab, you'll use one **virtual machine** (**VM**) as your client, and one VM as the server. Alternatively, if you're using a Windows host machine, you can use Cygwin, PowerShell, or the built-in Windows Bash shell for the client. (Be aware, though, that PowerShell and the Windows Bash shell store the key files in alternate locations.) If you're on either a Mac or a Linux host machine, you can use the host machine's native command-line terminal as the client. In any case, the procedure will be the same.

For the server VM, use either Ubuntu 22.04 or CentOS 7.

> This procedure does work the same on AlmaLinux 8 and 9. However, we'll be using this same VM for the next few labs, and AlmaLinux has some special considerations that we'll look at later.

Let's get started:

1. On the client machine, create a pair of 384-bit elliptic curve keys. Accept the default filename and location and create a passphrase:

    ```
    ssh-keygen -t ecdsa -b 384
    ```

2. Observe the keys, taking note of the permissions settings:

    ```
    ls -l ./ssh
    ```

3. Add your private key to your session keyring. Enter your passphrase when prompted:

    ```
    exec /usr/bin/ssh-agent $SHELL
    ssh-add
    ```

4. Transfer the public key to the server VM. When prompted, enter the password for your user account on the server VM. (Substitute your own username and IP address in the following command.):

```
ssh-copy-id donnie@192.168.0.7
```

5. Log in to the server VM as you normally would:

```
ssh donnie@192.168.0.7
```

6. Observe the authorized_keys file that was created on the server VM:

```
ls -l .ssh
cat .ssh/authorized_keys
```

7. Log out of the server VM and close the terminal window on the client. Open another terminal window and try to log in to the server again. This time, you should be prompted to enter the passphrase for your private key.

8. Log back out of the server VM and add your private key back to the session keyring of your client. Enter the passphrase for your private key when prompted:

```
exec /usr/bin/ssh-agent $SHELL
ssh-add
```

9. As long as you keep this terminal window open on your client, you'll be able to log in to the server VM as many times as you want without having to enter a password. However, when you close the terminal window, your private key will be removed from your session keyring.

10. Keep your server VM, because we'll do more with it in a bit.

You've reached the end of the lab – congratulations!

What we've done here is good, but it's still not quite enough. One flaw is that if you go to another client machine, you'll still be able to use the normal username/password authentication to log in. That's okay. We'll fix that in a few moments.

Disabling root user login

A few years ago, there was a somewhat celebrated case where malicious actors had managed to plant malware on quite a few Linux servers somewhere in southeast Asia. There were three reasons that the bad guys found this so easy to do:

*   The Internet-facing servers involved were set up to use username/password authentication for SSH.
*   The root user was allowed to log in through SSH.
*   User passwords, including the root user's password, were incredibly weak.

All this meant that it was easy for the Hail Mary botnet to brute-force its way in.

Different distros have different default settings for root user login. In the /etc/ssh/sshd_config file of your CentOS 7 or AlmaLinux 8 machine, you'll see this line:

```
#PermitRootLogin yes
```

Unlike what you have in most configuration files, the commented-out lines in `sshd_config` define the default settings for the Secure Shell daemon. So, this line indicates that the root user is indeed allowed to log in through SSH. To change that, I'll remove the comment symbol and change the setting to no:

```
PermitRootLogin no
```

To make the new setting take effect, I'll reload the SSH daemon, which is named `sshd` on CentOS and AlmaLinux, and is named `ssh` on Ubuntu:

```
sudo systemctl reload sshd
```

On the Ubuntu machine, the default setting looks a bit different:

```
PermitRootLogin prohibit-password
```

This means that the root user is allowed to log in, but only via a public key exchange. This is probably secure enough if you really need to allow the root user to log in. But in most cases, you'll want to force admin users to log in with their normal user accounts and use `sudo` for their admin needs. So, in most cases, you still want to change this setting to `no`.

On your AlmaLinux 9 machine, you'll see that it also has `PermitRootLogin` set to `prohibit-password` by default.

> Be aware that if you deploy a Linux instance on a cloud service, such as Rackspace or Vultr, the service owners will have you log in to the VM with the root user account. The first thing you'll want to do is create your own normal user account, log back in with that account, disable the root user account, and disable the root user login in `sshd_config`. Microsoft Azure is one exception to this rule because it automatically creates a non-privileged user account for you.

You'll be able to practice this in just a few moments, in the next section.

Disabling username/password logins

This is something that you'll only want to do after you've set up the key exchange with your clients. Otherwise, clients will be locked out of doing remote logins.

Hands-on lab – Disabling root login and password authentication

For this lab, use the same server VM that you used for the previous lab. Let's get started:

1. On either an Ubuntu, CentOS, or AlmaLinux 8 server VM, look for this line in the `sshd_config` file:

    ```
    #PasswordAuthentication yes
    ```

2. Remove the comment symbol, change the parameter value to no, and reload the SSH daemon. The line should now look like this:

    ```
    PasswordAuthentication no
    ```

3. Now, when the botnets scan your system, they'll see that doing a brute-force password attack would be useless. They'll then just go away and leave you alone.

4. Look for either of these two lines, depending on whether the server is an Ubuntu or a CentOS 7/AlmaLinux VM:

```
#PermitRootLogin yes
#PermitRootLogin prohibit-password
```

Uncomment the line and change it to the following:

```
PermitRootLogin no
```

5. Reload the SSH daemon so that it will read in the new changes. On Ubuntu, do this:

```
sudo systemctl reload ssh
```

6. On CentOS/AlmaLinux, do this:

```
sudo systemctl reload sshd
```

7. Attempt to log in to the server VM from the client that you used in the previous lab.

8. Attempt to log in to the server VM from another client on which you haven't created a key pair. (You shouldn't be able to.)

9. As before, keep the server VM, because we'll do more with it in a bit.

You've reached the end of the lab – congratulations!

Now that we've covered how to create a private/public key pair on the client side and how to transfer the public key to the server, let's talk about setting up two-factor authentication.

Enabling two-factor authentication

Two-factor authentication can provide an extra layer of protection. If you own a smart phone, you can set this up with **Google Authenticator**, which will present you with a **one-time password** for logging in at the local terminal, invoking a sudo command, or logging in remotely via SSH. Before we get started though, there are a few caveats that you need to understand:

- To make this work on a Linux machine, you'll need to install a PAM module that isn't supplied by Google. It's in the repositories for some, but not all, Linux distros. (Of course, you could download the source code from the GitHub repository and compile it yourself, but that's beyond the scope of this book.)

- The creator of this PAM module has created some semblance of documentation, but it's not very useful. If you search for documentation, you'll find some blog posts with procedures that are worse than useless, because they *will* break your system if you follow them.

- You can set up your machine to require Google Authenticator for either global usage, or for just logging in via SSH. (Global usage means that an Authenticator code will be needed for logging in at the local terminal, using sudo, *and* logging in remotely via SSH.)

- If you're dealing with multiple users, each user will need to set up Google Authenticator for his or her own user account with his or her own smart phone.

Now, with that out of the way, let's set up our Ubuntu 22.04 server with Google Authenticator for local logins and sudo:

> Note that this PAM module is in the normal Ubuntu repository and in the EPEL repository for RHEL 8-type distros. It's not available at all for RHEL 9-type distros.

Hands-on lab — Setting up two-factor authentication on Ubuntu 22.04

For this lab, start with a fresh Ubuntu 22.04 VM that's not set up for public key authentication. (That will save a lot of confusion when going through this procedure):

1. Install Google Authenticator on your smart phone. (It's in the normal app stores for both Android and iPhone.)

2. On your Ubuntu VM, install the `libpam-google-authenticator` package, like this:

```
sudo apt install libpam-google-authenticator
```

3. For this step, if you haven't already, use SSH to remotely log in to the Ubuntu VM from the GUI-type terminal of your host machine. (That's because you might need to resize things to make the next step work.) Now, from this GUI-type terminal, run the `google-authenticator` app, like so:

```
google-authenticator
```

A big QR code will now show up on your screen. If the whole code graphic isn't visible, use your GUI terminal controls to zoom out until the whole graphic is visible.

Bring up the Google Authenticator app on your smart phone, and touch the + sign in the lower right-hand corner of the screen. Choose the **Scan a QR code** option, and then take a picture of your QR code.

On your smart phone, note that a new entry for your Ubuntu VM has been added to the list. On the Ubuntu VM, enter the verification code that shows up with that entry.

The next thing you'll see on the Ubuntu terminal is your emergency scratch codes. Copy them down and store them in a safe location. (If you lose your mobile phone, you'll use these scratch codes to log in.)

4. Next, you'll be asked a series of questions. Just enter y for everything.

In this step, you'll set up two-factor authentication for logging in at the local terminal and for using sudo. Open the `/etc/pam.d/common-auth` file in your favorite text editor. Add the `auth required pam_google_authenticator.so` line as the first parameter. The top portion of the file should now look something like this:

```
# /etc/pam.d/common-auth - authentication settings common to all services
#
# This file is included from other service-specific PAM config files,
. . .

. . .
auth required pam_google_authenticator.so

# here are the per-package modules (the "Primary" block)
. . .

. . .
```

> Certain blog posts that you'll find tell you to add this line to the *end* of the file. Be aware that if you do that, you *will* get locked out of your machine, and you'll need to perform an emergency procedure to get back in to fix it. Any time you edit a PAM file, it's vitally important that you place the directives in the proper order. (In case you're wondering, I'll show you the emergency procedure in *Chapter 16, Security Tips and Tricks for the Busy Bee*.)

At the local terminal of the Ubuntu VM, log out and then log back in. When prompted, enter the verification code from your smart phone app. Perform a command that requires sudo privileges. You should see something like this:

```
donnie@ubuntu2204-packt:~$ sudo nft list ruleset
Verification code:
[sudo] password for donnie:
. . .

. . .
Enter the verification code at the prompt.
```

> Note that you won't be required to enter a verification code again until the sudo timer times out.

From either your host machine or another VM, remotely log in to the Ubuntu VM via SSH. You should still be able to do that because we haven't yet configured the /etc/ssh/sshd_config file. Open the sshd_config file in your text editor, and change the KbdInteractiveAuthentication no line to KbdInteractiveAuthentication yes.

5. Reload the Secure Shell configuration:

```
sudo systemctl reload ssh
```

Try logging in again from either your host machine or another VM. This time, you should be prompted to enter your verification code.

6. Now, let's say that your organization needs two-factor authentication for remote SSH logins, but doesn't need it for either local logins or sudo operations. Let's change the configuration so that only remote users will need to enter a code. Open the /etc/pam.d/common-auth file in your text editor, and remove the line that you inserted in *step 9*.

7. Open the /etc/pam.d/sshd file in your text editor, and add that line just under the @include common-auth line at the top of the file. The top portion of the file should now look like this:

```
PAM configuration for the Secure Shell service
    # Standard Un*x authentication.
@include common-auth
auth required pam_google_authenticator.so
```

8. You should now be able to log in to the local terminal and perform sudo actions without having to enter a verification code. Instead, you should only have to enter a verification code when logging in remotely.

9. End of lab.

Next, let's look at using Google Authenticator together with key exchange on our Ubuntu machine.

Hands-on lab – Using Google Authenticator with key exchange on Ubuntu

For this lab, use the same Ubuntu VM that you used for the previous lab:

1. On either your host machine or another VM, create a pair of keys and transfer them to the Ubuntu VM, as you did in the *Creating and transferring SSH keys* lab. This time, you should be prompted to enter a verification code when you execute the ssh-copy-id command.

2. On the Ubuntu VM, open the /etc/ssh/sshd_config file in your text editor. This time, instead of changing the #PasswordAuthentication yes line, add this line below the KbdInteractiveAuthentication yes line:

```
AuthenticationMethods publickey keyboard-interactive:pam
```

3. After reloading the SSH configuration, you'll see that you'll be able to remotely log in by using key exchange if you're logging in from a machine that has that set up. If you're logging in from a machine that doesn't have key exchange set up, you'll still be able to log in with a password and a verification code. So, we don't have true two-factor authentication just yet.

4. To require both key-based authentication and Google Authenticator verification, change the above line to look like this:

```
AuthenticationMethods publickey,keyboard-interactive:pam
```

5. After reloading the SSH configuration, you'll only be allowed to log in from machines for which you've set up key exchange. You now effectively have three-factor authentication because you'll still be prompted to enter your normal login password.

6. To disable the password login so that you'll only be using key exchange and a verification code, open the /etc/pam.d/sshd file in your text editor. At the very top of the file, find the @include common-auth line and change it to #@include common-auth.

7. Verify that the key exchange works by trying to log in from a VM on which you haven't performed the key exchange setup. (You shouldn't be allowed to.)

8. That's it. End of lab.

Now, let's see what we can do with AlmaLinux 8.

Hands-on lab — Setting up two-factor authentication on AlmaLinux 8

For this lab, I assume that you've already installed the Google Authenticator app on your smart phone.

The Authenticator PAM module isn't in any of the repositories for the RHEL 9 distros, but it is in the EPEL repository for the RHEL 8 distros. (That might change by the time you read this, so it won't hurt to check if you want to try this on AlmaLinux 9.) So, fire up a fresh AlmaLinux 8 VM, and let's get started:

1. Install the PAM module like this:

```
sudo dnf install epel-release
sudo dnf install google-authenticator qrencode-libs
```

2. Note that you need the qrencode-libs package in order to produce a QR code.

3. From the GUI terminal of your host machine, use SSH to remotely log in to the AlmaLinux 8 VM. This will allow you to resize the QR code image so that you can take a picture of it with your smart phone. Then, run the google-authenticator:

```
google-authenticator -s ~/.ssh/google_authenticator
```

4. This time, we're creating the google_authenticator file within the .ssh directory because AlmaLinux is set up to use SELinux. When you try to log in remotely with Authenticator enabled, the SSH daemon will try to write to the google_authenticator file. SELinux prevents SSH from writing to files that are outside of the .ssh directory. (We'll talk more about SELinux in *Chapter 10, Implementing Mandatory Access Control with SELinux and AppArmor*.)

5. Follow through on the Authenticator setup, the same as you did in *steps 4* through *8* of the *Setting up two-factor authentication on Ubuntu 22.04* lab.

6. Open the /etc/pam.d/sshd file in your text editor. Add this line to the very bottom of the file:

```
auth required pam_google_authenticator.so secret=/home/${USER}/.ssh/
google_authenticator
```

(Note that the line wraps around on the printed page.)

7. Open the /etc/ssh/sshd_config file in your text editor. Find the line that says #ChallengeResponseAuthentication no and change it to ChallengeResponseAuthentication yes.

8. Reload or restart the sshd service:

```
sudo systemctl reload sshd
```

9. Set the proper SELinux security context on the google_authenticator file that you created:

```
cd
sudo restorecon .ssh/google_authenticator
```

10. Log out of the remote session, and try logging back in. This time, you should be prompted to enter a verification code.

Next, let's set AlmaLinux up for using key exchange.

Hand-on lab — Using Google Authenticator with key exchange on AlmaLinux 8

This will mostly be the same as it was for Ubuntu, with only a few differences:

1. Transfer the public key from your host machine to the AlmaLinux 8 machine as you did in the *Creating and transferring SSH keys* lab.

2. In the /etc/ssh/sshd_config file, change the #PasswordAuthentication yes line to PasswordAuthentication no, and reload the SSH configuration. Now, you'll only be using key exchange to log in, which will completely bypass the Authenticator. Let's fix things so that you'll be using both.

3. In the /etc/ssh/sshd_config file, add the following line just beneath the PasswordAuthentication no line:

```
AuthenticationMethods publickey,password publickey,keyboard-interactive
```

4. After reloading the SSH configuration, you'll have three-factor authentication, because you'll need to enter both your password and a verification code along with the key exchange.

5. If desired, you can easily disable the password prompt and just use the key exchange and verification code. In the /etc/pam.d/sshd file, find the auth substack password-auth line at the top of the file, and change it to #auth substack password-auth.

6. That's all there is to Google Authenticator.

In the next section, let's make sure that we're only using the strongest encryption algorithms.

Configuring Secure Shell with strong encryption algorithms

As I mentioned previously, the current set of NIST recommendations, the **Commercial National Security Algorithm Suite (CNSA Suite)**, involves using stronger algorithms and longer keys than what we needed to use previously. I'll summarize the new recommendations here in this table:

Algorithm	Usage
RSA, 3,072 bits or larger	Key establishment and digital signatures
Diffie-Hellman (DH), 3,072 bits or larger	Key establishment
ECDH with NIST P-384	Key establishment
ECDSA with NIST P-384	Digital signatures

| SHA-384 | Integrity |
| Advanced Encryption Standard (AES-256) | Confidentiality |

In other publications, you might see that NIST Suite B is the recommended standard for encryption algorithms. Suite B is an older standard that has been replaced by the CNSA Suite.

Another cryptographic standard that you might have to work with is the **Federal Information Processing Standard (FIPS)**, which is also promulgated by the US government. The current version is FIPS 140-3, which gained final approval on September 22, 2019.

Understanding SSH encryption algorithms

SSH works with a combination of symmetric and asymmetric cryptography, similar to how **Transport Layer Security (TLS)** works. The SSH client starts the process by using the public key method to set up an asymmetric session with an SSH server. Once this session has been set up, the two machines can agree on and exchange a secret code, which they'll use to set up a symmetric session. (As we saw previously with TLS in *Chapter 6, Encryption Technologies*, we want to use symmetric cryptography for performance reasons, but we need an asymmetric session to perform the secret key exchange.) To perform this magic, we need four classes of encryption algorithms, which we'll configure on the server side. These are:

- **Ciphers:** These are the symmetric algorithms that encrypt the data that the client and server exchange with each other.
- **HostKeyAlgorithms:** This is the list of host key types that the server can use.
- **KexAlgorithms:** These are the algorithms that the server can use to perform the symmetric key exchange.
- **MAC:** Message Authentication Codes are hashing algorithms that cryptographically sign the encrypted data in transit. This ensures data integrity and will let you know if someone has tampered with your data.

The best way to get a feel for this is to look at the `sshd_config` man page, like this:

```
man sshd_conf
```

I could use any VM to demo this. For now, though, I'm going with CentOS 7, unless I state otherwise. (The lists of default and available algorithms will be different for different Linux distros and versions.) Also, note that to demo this, we want to look at the `sshd_config` man page to see the lists of algorithms that are **available** and **enabled**. The **enabled** list is in the man pages for CentOS 7 and AlmaLinux 8, but not in the man page for AlmaLinux 9.

First, let's look at the list of supported ciphers. Scroll down the man page until you see them:

```
3des-cbc
aes128-cbc
aes192-cbc
aes256-cbc
aes128-ctr
```

```
aes192-ctr
aes256-ctr
aes128-gcm@openssh.com
aes256-gcm@openssh.com
arcfour
arcfour128
arcfour256
blowfish-cbc
cast128-cbc
chacha20-poly1305@openssh.com
```

However, not all of these supported ciphers are enabled. Just below this list, we can see the list of ciphers that are enabled by default:

```
chacha20-poly1305@openssh.com,
aes128-ctr,aes192-ctr,aes256-ctr,
aes128-gcm@openssh.com,aes256-gcm@openssh.com,
aes128-cbc,aes192-cbc,aes256-cbc,
blowfish-cbc,cast128-cbc,3des-cbc
```

Next, in alphabetical order, are the **HostKeyAlgorithms**. The list on CentOS 7 looks like this:

```
ecdsa-sha2-nistp256-cert-v01@openssh.com,
ecdsa-sha2-nistp384-cert-v01@openssh.com,
ecdsa-sha2-nistp521-cert-v01@openssh.com,
ssh-ed25519-cert-v01@openssh.com,
ssh-rsa-cert-v01@openssh.com,
ssh-dss-cert-v01@openssh.com,
ecdsa-sha2-nistp256,ecdsa-sha2-nistp384,ecdsa-sha2-nistp521,
ssh-ed25519,ssh-rsa,ssh-dss
```

Next, scroll down to the **KexAlgorithms** (short for **Key Exchange Algorithms**) section. You'll see a list of supported algorithms, which looks like this:

```
curve25519-sha256
curve25519-sha256@libssh.org
diffie-hellman-group1-sha1
diffie-hellman-group14-sha1
diffie-hellman-group-exchange-sha1
diffie-hellman-group-exchange-sha256
ecdh-sha2-nistp256
ecdh-sha2-nistp384
ecdh-sha2-nistp521
```

Be aware that this list can vary from one distro to the next. For example, RHEL 8/AlmaLinux 8 supports three additional algorithms that are newer and stronger. Its list looks like this:

```
curve25519-sha256
curve25519-sha256@libssh.org
diffie-hellman-group1-sha1
diffie-hellman-group14-sha1
diffie-hellman-group14-sha256
diffie-hellman-group16-sha512
diffie-hellman-group18-sha512
diffie-hellman-group-exchange-sha1
diffie-hellman-group-exchange-sha256
ecdh-sha2-nistp256
ecdh-sha2-nistp384
ecdh-sha2-nistp521
```

You'll see the same list on an AlmaLinux 9 machine, except that the `sntrup761x25519-sha512@openssh.com` algorithm has been added.

Next, you'll see the list of algorithms that are enabled by default:

```
curve25519-sha256,curve25519-sha256@libssh.org,
ecdh-sha2-nistp256,ecdh-sha2-nistp384,ecdh-sha2-nistp521,
diffie-hellman-group-exchange-sha256,
diffie-hellman-group14-sha1,
diffie-hellman-group1-sha1
```

This list can also vary from one Linux distro to another. (In this case, though, there's no difference between CentOS 7 and AlmaLinux 8.)

Finally, we have the MAC algorithms. The default list of enabled algorithms looks like this on CentOS 7:

```
umac-64-etm@openssh.com,umac-128-etm@openssh.com,
hmac-sha2-256-etm@openssh.com,hmac-sha2-512-etm@openssh.com,
hmac-sha1-etm@openssh.com,
umac-64@openssh.com,umac-128@openssh.com,
hmac-sha2-256,hmac-sha2-512,hmac-sha1,
hmac-sha1-etm@openssh.com
```

To see the list of algorithms that your particular system supports, either look at the `sshd_config` man page for that machine or perform the following `ssh -Q` commands:

```
ssh -Q cipher
ssh -Q key
ssh -Q kex
ssh -Q mac
```

When you look in the /etc/ssh/sshd_config file, you won't see any lines that configure any of these algorithms. That's because the default list of algorithms is hard-coded into the SSH daemon. The only time you'll configure any of these is if you want to either enable an algorithm that isn't enabled or disable one that is. Before we do that, let's scan our system to see what is enabled and see if the scanner can make any recommendations.

Scanning for enabled SSH algorithms

We have two good ways to scan an SSH server. If your server is accessible via the Internet, you can go to the SSHCheck site at https://sshcheck.com/.

Then, just type in either the IP address or hostname of your server. If you've changed the port from the default port 22, enter the port number as well. When the scan completes, you'll see the list of enabled algorithms, along with recommendations on which ones to either enable or disable.

If the machine that you want to scan isn't accessible from the Internet, or even if it is, you can use a local scanning tool. In the previous edition of this book, we used the **ssh_scan** tool. Sadly, this tool is no longer supported, and it doesn't work on newer Linux distros that come with OpenSSL version 3. So instead, let's try this with the Nmap scripting engine.

Hands-on lab — Scanning with Nmap

For this lab, you can use any of your VMs. Let's get started:

1. First, install the nmap package from your normal distro repository. On Ubuntu, do:

    ```
    sudo apt update
    sudo apt install nmap
    ```

2. On CentOS 7, do this:

    ```
    sudo yum install nmap
    ```

3. On AlmaLinux 8 or 9, do this:

    ```
    sudo dnf install nmap
    ```

4. Use nmap with the ssh2-enum-algos.nse script to scan the server VM that you created and configured in the previous labs. Substitute your own IP address for the one I'm using here. Note that even if you haven't created a key pair on the scanner machine, the scan still works against machines that have had username/password authentication disabled. (But, of course, you won't be able to log in from the scanner machine):

    ```
    nmap --script=ssh2-enum-algos.nse 192.168.0.14
    ```

5. Note that if you're scanning a machine with an enabled firewall, you might get an error message about how the scan has been blocked. If that happens, try adding the -Pn switch, so that the command will look like this:

    ```
    nmap -Pn --script=ssh2-enum-algos.nse 192.168.0.14
    ```

6. Repeat the scan, but this time, save the output to a normal text file, like so:

```
nmap --script=ssh2-enum-algos.nse 192.168.0.14 -oN ubuntuscan.txt
```

7. Open the text file in a normal text editor or pager. You'll see a complete list of all of the algorithms that are enabled. Compare your results with the standards that are applicable to your circumstances, such as NIST's CNSA standard, to be sure you enable or disable the right things.

8. On either your host machine or a VM with a desktop interface, visit the Shodan website at https://www.shodan.io. Type ssh into the search window and observe the list of Internet-facing SSH servers that comes up. Click on different IP addresses until you find an SSH server that's *not* running on the default port 22. Observe the list of enabled algorithms for that device.

9. Scan the device, using the -p switch to scan the different ports, like so:

```
nmap -p 2222 --script=ssh2-enum-algos.nse 192.168.0.14
```

10. Note that in addition to the list of enabled algorithms that you saw on Shodan, you now have a list of weak ones that the owner of this device needs to disable.

11. Keep both this scanner and this server VM handy because we'll use them again after we disable some algorithms.

You've reached the end of the lab – congratulations!

Okay, let's disable some of the creaky, old, and weak stuff.

Disabling weak SSH encryption algorithms

As I said before, we want to compare our scan results against the NIST recommendations and configure things accordingly. Understand, though, that the list of available algorithms differs from one Linux distro to the next. To make things less confusing, I'll present two hands-on procedures in this section. One is for Ubuntu 22.04, while the other is for CentOS 7. AlmaLinux 8 and 9 have their own unique way of doing business, so I'm saving that for the next section.

Hands-on lab – disabling weak SSH encryption algorithms – Ubuntu 22.04

For this lab, you'll need the VM that you've been using as a scanner, and another Ubuntu 22.04 VM to scan and configure. Let's get started:

1. If you haven't done so already, scan the Ubuntu 22.04 VM and save the output to a file:

```
nmap --script=ssh2-enum-algos.nse 192.168.0.14 -oN ubuntuscan.txt
```

2. Count the number of lines in the file by doing:

```
wc -l ubuntuscan.txt
```

3. On the target Ubuntu 22.04 VM, open the /etc/ssh/sshd_config file in your preferred text editor. Toward the top of the file, find these two lines:

```
# Ciphers and keying
#RekeyLimit default none
```

4. Beneath those two lines, insert these three lines:

```
Ciphers -aes128-ctr,aes192-ctr,aes128-gcm@openssh.com


KexAlgorithms ecdh-sha2-nistp384


MACs -hmac-sha1-etm@openssh.com,hmac-sha1,umac-64-etm@openssh.
com,umac-64@openssh.com,umac-128-etm@openssh.com,umac-128@openssh.
com,hmac-sha2-256-etm@openssh.com,hmac-sha2-256
```

5. In the `Ciphers` and `MACs` lines, you see a comma-separated list of algorithms that were disabled by the preceding - sign. (You only need one - to disable all the algorithms in the list.) In the `KexAlgorithms` line, there's no - sign. This means that the algorithm that's listed on that line is the only one that is enabled.

6. Save the file and restart the SSH daemon. Verify that it started correctly:

```
sudo systemctl restart ssh
sudo systemctl status ssh
```

7. Scan the Ubuntu 22.04 VM again, saving the output to a different file:

```
nmap --script=ssh2-enum-algos.nse 192.168.0.14 -oN ubuntuscan_modified.
txt
```

8. Count the number of lines in the new file:

```
wc -l ubuntuscan_modified.txt
```

9. On the scanner VM, use `diff` to compare the two files. You should see fewer algorithms than you saw previously:

```
diff -y ubuntuscan.txt ubuntuscan_modified.txt
```

> The sharp-eyed among you will notice that we left one cipher that isn't on the NIST CNSA list. `chacha20-poly1305@openssh.com` is a lightweight algorithm that's good for use with low-powered, hand-held devices. It's a good, strong algorithm that can replace the venerable **Advanced Encryption Standard** (**AES**) algorithm, but with higher performance. However, if you have to remain 100% compliant with the NIST CNSA standard, then you might have to disable it.

You've reached the end of the lab – congratulations!

Next, let's work with CentOS 7.

Hands-on lab – disabling weak SSH encryption algorithms – CentOS 7

You'll notice two things when you start working with CentOS 7:

- **More algorithms enabled**: A default SSH configuration on CentOS 7 has a lot more enabled algorithms than what Ubuntu 22.04 has. This includes some really ancient stuff that you really don't want to see anymore. I'm talking about things such as Blowfish and 3DES, which should have been retired years ago.
- **A different configuration technique**: On CentOS, placing a - sign in front of a list of algorithms that you want to disable doesn't work. Instead, you'll need to list all of the algorithms that you want to enable.

For this lab, you'll need a CentOS 7 VM and the same scanner VM that you've been using. With that in mind, let's get to work:

1. Scan the CentOS 7 VM and save the output to a file. Note that due to the CentOS 7 firewall, you'll need to add the -Pn option:

```
nmap -Pn --script=ssh2-enum-algos.nse 192.168.0.12 -oN centos7scan.txt
```

2. Count the number of lines in the output file:

```
wc -l centos7scan.txt
```

3. On the target CentOS 7 VM, open the /etc/ssh/sshd_config file in your preferred text editor. Toward the top of the file, find these two lines:

```
# Ciphers and keying
#RekeyLimit default none
```

4. Beneath those two lines, insert these three lines:

```
Ciphers aes256-gcm@openssh.com,aes256-ctr,chacha20-poly1305@openssh.com

KexAlgorithms ecdh-sha2-nistp384

MACs hmac-sha2-256-etm@openssh.com,hmac-sha2-256
```

5. As I mentioned previously, with CentOS, using - to disable algorithms doesn't work. Instead, we have to list all of the algorithms that we do want to enable.

6. Save the file and reload the SSH daemon. Verify that it started correctly:

```
sudo systemctl reload sshd
sudo systemctl status sshd
```

7. Scan the CentOS 7 VM again, saving the output to a different file:

```
nmap -Pn --script=ssh2-enum-algos.nse 192.168.0.12 -oN centos7scan_
modified.txt
```

8. Count the number of lines in the new output file:

```
wc -l centos7scan_modified.txt
```

9. On the scanner VM, use `diff` to compare the two files. You should see fewer algorithms than you saw previously:

```
diff -y centos7scan.txt centos7scan_modified.txt
```

> As before, I left the `chacha20-poly1305@openssh.com` algorithm enabled. If you have to remain 100% compliant with the NIST CNSA standard, then you might have to disable it.

You've reached the end of the lab – congratulations!

Next, let's look at a handy new feature that comes with the RHEL 8 and 9 families.

Setting system-wide encryption policies on RHEL 8/9 and AlmaLinux 8/9

In *Chapter 6, Encryption Technologies*, we briefly looked at how to set system-wide encryption policies on AlmaLinux 8 and 9. With this cool feature, you no longer have to configure crypto policies for each individual daemon. Instead, you just run a couple of simple commands, and the policy is instantly changed for multiple daemons. To see which daemons are covered, look in the `/etc/crypto-policies/back-ends/` directory. Here's a partial view of what's there:

```
[donnie@localhost back-ends]$ ls -l
total 0
. . .
. . .
lrwxrwxrwx. 1 root root 46 Sep 24 18:17 openssh.config -> /usr/share/crypto-
policies/DEFAULT/openssh.txt

lrwxrwxrwx. 1 root root 52 Sep 24 18:17 opensshserver.config -> /usr/share/
crypto-policies/DEFAULT/opensshserver.txt

lrwxrwxrwx. 1 root root 49 Sep 24 18:17 opensslcnf.config -> /usr/share/crypto-
policies/DEFAULT/opensslcnf.txt

lrwxrwxrwx. 1 root root 46 Sep 24 18:17 openssl.config -> /usr/share/crypto-
policies/DEFAULT/openssl.txt
[donnie@localhost back-ends]$
```

As you see, this directory contains symbolic links to text files that contain directives about which algorithms to either enable or disable for the `DEFAULT` configuration. One level up, in the `/etc/crypto-policies/` directory, there's the `config` file. Open it, and you'll see that this is where the system-wide configuration is set:

```
DEFAULT
```

Scanning this VM with its DEFAULT configuration shows that quite a few older algorithms are still enabled. To get rid of them, we can change to either FUTURE mode orto FIPS mode.

> At the time of this writing, the EPEL repository uses a security certificate that's not compatible with FUTURE mode. This will prevent you from updating or installing any software packages from the EPEL repository. If you need to set up your machine with both FUTURE mode and the EPEL repository, be aware that you'll need to set the machine back to DEFAULT mode before you can either fully update your system or install packages from EPEL. (Of course, this problem could be fixed by the time you read this.)

To show you how this works, let's get our hands dirty with another lab.

Hands-on lab — setting encryption policies on AlmaLinux 9

Start with a fresh AlmaLinux 9 VM and the scanner VM that you've been using. Now, follow these steps:

1. On an AlmaLinux 9 VM, use the update-crypto-policies utility to verify that it's running in DEFAULT mode:

```
sudo update-crypto-policies --show
```

2. Scan the AlmaLinux 9 VM in its DEFAULT configuration and save the output to a file:

```
nmap -Pn --script=ssh2-enum-algos.nse 192.168.0.17 -oN alma9_default.txt
```

3. On the AlmaLinux 9 VM, set the system-wide crypto policy to FUTURE:

```
sudo update-crypto-policies --set FUTURE
```

4. In the /etc/ssh/ directory, remove the current host machine keys:

```
sudo rm /etc/ssh/*key*
```

5. (Don't worry. New keys will get created when you reboot the machine.)

6. Reboot the VM:

```
sudo shutdown -r now
```

7. On the scanner VM, open the ~/.ssh/known_hosts file in your text editor. Delete the entry that was previously made for the AlmaLinux VM and save the file. (We have to do this because the public key fingerprint on the AlmaLinux VM will have changed because of the new policy.)

8. Scan the AlmaLinux VM again, saving the output to a different file:

```
nmap -Pn --script=ssh2-enum-algos.nse 192.168.0.17 -oN alma9_future.txt
```

9. Compare the two output files. You should now see fewer enabled algorithms than you did previously:

```
diff -y alma9_default.txt alma9_future.txt
```

10. Look at the files in the /etc/crypto-policies/back-ends/ directory:

```
ls -l /etc/crypto-policies/back-ends/
```

11. You'll now see that the symbolic links point to files in the FUTURE directories.

12. Look at the host keys in the /etc/ssh/ directory, and see if they differ from what you had before:

```
ls -l /etc/ssh/*key*
```

13. Scan the AlmaLinux 9 VM that you set up in FIPS mode for the lab in *Chapter 6, Encryption Technologies*. Compare the results with the DEFAULT and FUTURE mode scans.

14. End of lab.

> If FUTURE mode hasn't disabled enough algorithms for you, you can always just create your own custom policy. See the details here:
>
> https://access.redhat.com/documentation/en-us/red_hat_enterprise_linux/9/
> html/security_hardening/using-the-system-wide-cryptographic-policies_
> security-hardening#customizing-system-wide-cryptographic-policies-with-
> subpolicies_using-the-system-wide-cryptographic-policies

You now know how to configure SSH to use only the most modern, most secure algorithms. Next, let's look at logging.

Configuring more detailed logging

In its default configuration, SSH already creates log entries whenever someone logs in via SSH, SCP, or SFTP. On Debian/Ubuntu systems, the entry is made in the /var/log/auth.log file. On Red Hat/CentOS/AlmaLinux systems, the entry is made in the /var/log/secure file. Either way, the log entry looks something like this:

```
Oct  1 15:03:23 donnie-ca sshd[1141]: Accepted password for donnie from
192.168.0.225 port 54422 ssh2

Oct  1 15:03:24 donnie-ca sshd[1141]: pam_unix(sshd:session): session opened
for user donnie by (uid=0)
```

Open the sshd_config man page and scroll down to the LogLevel item. There, you'll see the various settings that provide different levels of detail for logging SSH messages. The levels are as follows:

- QUIET
- FATAL
- ERROR
- INFO
- VERBOSE
- DEBUG or DEBUG1

- DEBUG2
- DEBUG3

Normally, the only two of these we would care about are INFO and VERBOSE. INFO is the default setting, while VERBOSE is the only other one that we would use under normal circumstances. The various DEBUG levels might come in handy for troubleshooting, but the man page warns us that using DEBUG in production settings would violate users' privacy.

Let's go ahead and get our hands dirty, just to get a feel for what gets logged with the various levels.

Hands-on lab — configuring more verbose SSH logging

For this lab, use the same VM that you've been using for the previous labs. That way, you'll get a better picture of what a complete sshd_config file should look like when it's fully locked down. Remotely log in to the target VM via SSH and follow these steps:

1. Open the main log file and scroll down to where you see the entry that was made due to your login and observe what it says. For Ubuntu, do:

```
sudo less /var/log/auth.log
```

2. For CentOS or AlmaLinux, do:

```
sudo less /var/log/secure
```

3. As I mentioned previously, you never want to run a production machine with the SSH log level set to any of the DEBUG levels. But, just so you can see what it does log, set your machine to DEBUG now. Open the /etc/ssh/sshd_config file in your favorite text editor. Find the line that says the following:

```
#LogLevel INFO
```

4. Change it to the following:

```
LogLevel DEBUG3
```

5. After saving the file, reload SSH. On Ubuntu, do:

```
sudo systemctl reload ssh
```

6. On CentOS or AlmaLinux, do this:

```
sudo systemctl reload sshd
```

7. Log out of the SSH session, and then log back in. View the system log file to see the new entries from this new login.

8. Open the /etc/ssh/sshd_config file for editing. Change the LogLevel DEBUG3 line to the following:

```
LogLevel VERBOSE
```

9. After saving the file, reload or restart the SSH daemon. Log out of the SSH session, log back in, and look at the entries in the system log file.

> The main benefit of VERBOSE mode is that it will log the fingerprints of any key that was used to log in. This can be a big help with key management.

You've reached the end of the lab – congratulations!

So, you've just seen how to get more information about SSH logins in your system logs. Next, let's talk a bit about access control.

Configuring access control with whitelists and TCP Wrappers

We've already locked things down pretty well just by requiring that clients authenticate via key exchange, rather than by username and password. When we prohibit password authentication, the bad guys can do brute-force password attacks against us until the cows come home, and it won't do them any good. (Although, in truth, they'll just give up as soon as they find that password authentication has been disabled.) For an extra measure of security, we can also set up a couple of access control mechanisms that will allow only certain users, groups, or client machines to log in to an SSH server. These two mechanisms are:

*   Whitelists within the sshd_config file
*   TCP Wrappers, via the /etc/hosts.allow and /etc/hosts.deny files

Okay, you're now saying, *But what about firewalls? Isn't that a third mechanism that we can use?* And yeah, you're right. But, we already covered firewalls in *Chapter 4, Securing Your Server with a Firewall – Part 1*, and *Chapter 5, Securing Your Server with a Firewall – Part 2*, so I won't repeat any of that here. You can also place access control directives in your systemd unit files for SSH. For our present discussion though, I'd rather avoid the complexities of explaining how to edit a systemd unit file. At any rate, these are the ways of controlling access to your SSH server. You can use all of them together if you really want to, or you can just use one of them at a time. (It really depends on just how paranoid you are.)

> There are two competing philosophies about how to do access control. With blacklists, you specifically prohibit access by certain people or machines. That's difficult to do because the list could get very long, and you still won't block everybody that you need to block. The preferred and easier method is to use whitelists, which specifically allow access to certain people or machines.

First, let's look at creating whitelists within sshd_config with a hands-on lab.

Configuring whitelists within sshd_config

The four access control directives that you can set within sshd_config are as follows:

- **DenyUsers**
- **AllowUsers**
- **DenyGroups**
- **AllowGroups**

For each directive, you can specify more than one username or group name, separating them with a blank space. Also, these four directives are processed in the order that I've listed them here. In other words, if a user is listed with both the DenyUsers and the AllowUsers directives, DenyUsers takes precedence. If a user is listed with DenyUsers and is a member of a group that's listed with AllowGroups, DenyUsers again takes precedence. To demonstrate this, let's do a lab.

Hands-on lab — configuring whitelists within sshd_config

This lab will work on any of your VMs. Follow these steps:

1. On the VM that you wish to configure, create user accounts for Frank, Charlie, and Maggie. On Ubuntu, do it like this:

   ```
   sudo adduser frank
   ```

2. On CentOS or AlmaLinux, do it like this:

   ```
   sudo useradd frank
   sudo passwd frank
   ```

3. Create the webadmins group and add Frank to it:

   ```
   sudo groupadd webadmins
   sudo usermod -a -G webadmins frank
   ```

4. From either your host machine or from another VM, have the three users log in. Then, log them back out.

5. Open the /etc/ssh/sshd_config file in your favorite text editor. At the bottom of the file, add an AllowUsers line with your own username, like so:

   ```
   AllowUsers donnie
   ```

6. Then, restart or reload the SSH service and verify that it has started correctly:

   For Ubuntu:

   ```
   sudo systemctl restart ssh
   sudo systemctl status ssh
   ```

For CentOS:

```
sudo systemctl restart sshd
sudo systemctl status sshd
```

7. Repeat *step 3*. This time, these three kitties shouldn't be able to log in. Open the /etc/ssh/ sshd_config file in your text editor. This time, add an AllowGroups line to the bottom of the file for the webadmins group, like so:

```
AllowGroups webadmins
```

8. Restart the SSH service and verify that it started properly.

9. From either your host machine or another VM, have Frank try to log in. You'll see that even though he's a member of the webadmins group, he'll still be denied. That's because the AllowUsers line with your own username takes precedence.

10. Open sshd_config in your text editor and remove the AllowUsers line that you inserted in *step 4*. Restart the SSH service and verify that it started properly.

11. Try to log in to your own account, and then try to log in to the accounts of all the other users. You should now see that Frank is the only one who is allowed to log in. The only way that any of the other users can now log in to the VM is from the VM's local console.

12. Log in to your own account at the VM's local console. Delete the AllowGroups line from sshd_ config and restart the SSH service.

You've reached the end of the lab – congratulations!

You've just seen how to configure a whitelist at the daemon level using the SSH daemon's own configuration file. Next, we'll look at configuring whitelists at the network level.

Configuring whitelists with TCP Wrappers

It's a strange name, but a simple concept. TCP Wrappers – singular, not plural – listens to incoming network connections and either allows or denies connection requests. Whitelists and blacklists are configured in the /etc/hosts.allow file and the /etc/hosts.deny file. Both of these files work together. If you create a whitelist in hosts.allow without adding anything to hosts.deny, nothing will be blocked. That's because TCP Wrappers consults hosts.allow first, and if it finds a whitelisted item there, it will just skip over looking in hosts.deny. If a connection request comes in for something that isn't whitelisted, TCP Wrappers will consult hosts.allow, find that there's nothing there for the source of this connection request, and then will consult hosts.deny. If nothing is in hosts.deny, the connection request will still go through. So, after you configure hosts.allow, you have to also configure hosts.deny in order to block anything.

You'll want to note that the Red Hat folk have stripped TCP Wrappers from RHEL 8/9 and their offspring. So, if you decide to practice with the techniques that I present here, you can do so with either your Ubuntu or CentOS 7 VMs, but not on your AlmaLinux 8/9 VMs. (The Red Hat folk now recommend doing access control via `firewalld`, rather than TCP Wrappers.)

You can read about it here: `https://access.redhat.com/solutions/3906701`.

(You'll need a Red Hat account to read the whole article. If you don't need to pay for Red Hat support, you can open a free-of-charge developers' account.)

Now, here's something that's extremely important. Always, *always*, configure `hosts.allow` before you configure `hosts.deny`. That's because as soon as you save either one of these files, the new configuration immediately takes effect. So, if you configure the blocking rule in `hosts.deny` while logged in remotely, your SSH connection will break just as soon as you save the file. The only way to get back in will be to enter the server room and reconfigure things from the local console. Your best bet is to get used to the idea of always configuring `hosts.allow` first, even when you're working from the local console. That way, you'll always be sure. (Amazingly, though, there are other TCP Wrappers tutorials out there that tell you to configure `hosts.deny` first. What *are* these guys thinking?)

You can do some rather fancy tricks with TCP Wrappers, but for now, I just want to keep things simple. So, let's look at some of the most used configurations.

To whitelist a single IP address, place a line like this into the `/etc/hosts.allow` file:

```
SSHD: 192.168.0.225
```

Then, place this line into the `/etc/hosts.deny` file:

```
SSHD: ALL
```

Now, if you try to log in from anywhere else besides the IP address that's listed in `hosts.allow`, you will be denied access.

You can also list either multiple IP addresses or multiple network addresses in `hosts.allow`. For details on how to do this, see the `hosts.allow` man page.

As I mentioned previously, you can do some fancy things with TCP Wrappers. But, now that the Red Hat folk have deprecated it, you should probably get used to the idea of either setting up firewall rules or configuring the `sshd_config` file. On the other hand, TCP Wrappers could come in handy whenever you need to configure an access control rule very quickly, provided that you're on a machine that supports it.

Configuring automatic logouts and security banners

Best security practice dictates that people log out of their computers before they walk away from their desks. This is especially important when an administrator uses his or her cubicle computer to remotely log in to a sensitive server. By default, SSH allows a person to remain logged in forever without complaining. However, you can set it up to automatically log out idle users. We'll look at two quick methods for doing that.

Configuring automatic logout for both local and remote users

This first method will automatically log out idle users who are logged in either at the local console or remotely via SSH. Go into the `/etc/profile.d/` directory and create the `autologout.sh` file with the following contents:

```
TMOUT=100
readonly TMOUT
export TMOUT
```

This sets a timeout value of `100` seconds. (`TMOUT` is a Linux environmental variable that sets timeout values.)

Set the executable permission for everybody:

```
sudo chmod +x autologout.sh
```

Log out and then log back in. Then, let the VM sit idle. After 100 seconds, you should see that the VM is back at the login prompt. Note, though, that if any users are already logged in at the time you create this file, the new configuration won't take effect for them until they log out and then log back in.

Configuring automatic logout in sshd_config

The second method only logs out users who are logged in remotely via SSH. Instead of creating the `/etc/profile.d/autologout.sh` file, look for these two lines in the `/etc/ssh/sshd_config` file:

```
#ClientAliveInterval 0
#ClientAliveCountMax 3
```

Change them to the following:

```
ClientAliveInterval 100
ClientAliveCountMax 0
```

Then, restart or reload the SSH service to make the change take effect.

> I've used 100 seconds for the timeout value in both of these examples. However, you can set the timeout value to suit your own needs.

You now know how to automatically log out your users. Now, let's look at setting up security banners.

Creating a pre-login security banner

In *Chapter 3, Securing Normal User Accounts*, I showed you how to create a security message that shows up *after* a user has logged in. You do this by inserting a message into the `/etc/motd` file. But, when you think about it, wouldn't it be better for people to see a security banner *before* they log in? You can do that with `sshd_config`.

First, let's create the `/etc/ssh/sshd-banner` file, with the following contents:

```
Warning!!  Authorized users only.  All others will be prosecuted.
```

In the `/etc/ssh/sshd_config` file, look for this line:

```
#Banner none
```

Change it to this:

```
Banner /etc/ssh/sshd-banner
```

As always, restart or reload the SSH service. Now, whoever logs in remotely will see something like this:

```
[donnie@fedora-teaching ~]$ ssh donnie@192.168.0.3
Warning!!  Authorized users only.  All others will be prosecuted.
donnie@192.168.0.3's password:
Welcome to Ubuntu 18.04.3 LTS (GNU/Linux 4.15.0-64-generic x86_64)
. . .
. . .
```

So, will this banner keep your system safe and secure from the bad guys? No, but it could be useful if you ever have to take a case to court. Sometimes, it's important to show a judge and jury that the intruders knew that they were going where they don't belong.

Now that you know how to set up security banners and automatic logouts, let's look at a few miscellaneous settings that don't fit neatly into any one category.

Configuring other miscellaneous security settings

Our SSH configuration is a lot more secure than it used to be, but we can still make it better. Here are a few little tricks that you might not have seen elsewhere.

Disabling X11 forwarding

When you SSH into a server in the normal manner, as we've been doing, you can only run text-mode programs. If you try to remotely run any GUI-based program, such as Firefox, you'll get an error message. But, when you open the `sshd_config` file of pretty much any Linux distro, you'll see this line:

```
X11Forwarding yes
```

This means that with the right option switch, you can remotely run GUI-based programs. Assuming that you're logging into a machine that has a graphical desktop environment installed, you can use either the -Y or the -X option when logging in, like so:

```
ssh -X donnie@192.168.0.12
```

or

```
ssh -Y donnie@192.168.0.12
```

The problem here is that the X11 protocol, which powers graphical desktop environments on most Linux and Unix systems, has a few security weaknesses that make it somewhat dangerous to use remotely. The bad guys have ways of using it to compromise an entire system. Your best bet is to disable it by changing the X11Forwarding line to look like this:

```
X11Forwarding no
```

As usual, restart or reload the SSH service to make it read in the new configuration.

Now that you know about X11 forwarding, let's dig some tunnels.

Disabling SSH tunneling

SSH tunneling, or as it's sometimes called, SSH port forwarding, is a handy way to protect non-secure protocols. For example, by tunneling normal HTTP through an SSH tunnel, you can access a non-secure website in a secure fashion. Here's what that looks like:

```
sudo ssh -L 80:localhost:80 donnie@192.168.0.12
```

I had to use sudo here because all network ports below port 1024 are **privileged ports**. If I were to change the web server configuration to listen on a non-privileged high-number port, I wouldn't need sudo.

Now, to connect to this site in a secure manner, I can just open the web browser on my local machine and type in the following URL:

```
http://localhost
```

Yeah, it seems strange to access a remote machine by typing in localhost, but that's the designator I used when I logged in with SSH. I could have used another name, but localhost is the name you traditionally see in SSH tutorials, so I'm following suit here. Now, as soon as I log out of the SSH session, my connection to the web server will break.

Even though this sounds like a good idea, it actually creates a security problem. Let's say that your corporate firewalls are set up to prevent people from going home and remotely logging into their company workstations. That's a good thing, right? Now, let's say that the company firewall has to allow outbound SSH connections. A user could create an SSH tunnel from his or her company workstation to a computer at another location, and then go to that location and create a reverse tunnel back to the company workstation. So, if it isn't possible to block outgoing SSH traffic at the firewall, then your best bet is to disable SSH tunneling. In your sshd_config file, ensure that you have lines that look like this:

```
AllowTcpForwarding no
AllowStreamLocalForwarding no
GatewayPorts no
PermitTunnel no
```

Restart or reload the SSH service, as always. Now, port tunneling will be disabled.

Now that you know how to disable SSH tunneling, let's talk about changing the default port.

Changing the default SSH port

By default, SSH listens on port 22/TCP. If you've been around for a while, you've surely seen plenty of documentation about how important it is to use some other port in order to make it harder for the bad guys to find your SSH server. But, I must say, this notion is a bit controversial.

In the first place, if you enable key authentication and disable password authentication, then changing the port has limited value. When a scanner bot finds your server and sees that password authentication is disabled, it will just go away and won't bother you anymore. In the second place, if you were to change the port, the bad guys' scanning tools can still find it. If you don't believe me, just go to Shodan. io and search for ssh. In this example, someone thought they were smart by changing to port 2211:

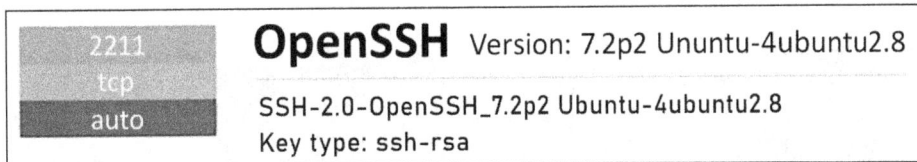

2211	**OpenSSH** Version: 7.2p2 Ununtu-4ubuntu2.8
tcp	
auto	SSH-2.0-OpenSSH_7.2p2 Ubuntu-4ubuntu2.8
	Key type: ssh-rsa

Figure 7.1: An OpenSSH port on Shodan

Yeah, smarty-pants. That didn't hide things so well, now, did it?

On the other hand, security expert Daniel Miessler says that it's still useful to change the port, in case someone tries to leverage a zero-day exploit against SSH. He recently published the results of an informal experiment that he did, in which he set up a public server that listens for SSH connections to both port 22 and port 24, and observed the number of connection attempts to each port. He said that over a single weekend, there were 18,000 connection attempts to port 22 and only five to port 24. But, although he doesn't explicitly say, it appears that he left password authentication enabled. To have truly scientifically accurate results, he needs to conduct the same study with password authentication disabled. He also needs to conduct the study on separate servers that have SSH enabled for either port 22 or port 24, instead of having both ports enabled on a single machine. My hunch is that when the scanner bots found that port 22 was open, they didn't bother to scan for any other open SSH ports.

You can read about his experiment here: `https://danielmiessler.com/study/security-by-obscurity/`.

Anyway, if you do want to change ports, just uncomment the `#Port 22` line in `sshd_config`, and change the port number to whatever you want.

Next, let's talk about key management.

Managing SSH keys

Earlier, I showed you how to create a pair of keys on your local workstation, and then transfer the public key to a remote server. This allows you to disable username/password authentication on the server, making it much harder for the bad guys to break in. The only problem with this that we didn't address is that the public key goes into an `authorized_keys` file that's in the user's own home directory. So, the user can manually add extra keys to the file, which would allow the user to log in from other locations besides the one that's been authorized. And there's also the problem of having `authorized_keys` files all over the place, in every user's home directory. That makes it a bit hard to keep track of everyone's keys.

One way to handle this is to move everyone's `authorized_keys` file to one central location. Let's take Vicky, my 15-and-a-half-year old solid gray kitty. The administrator created an account on the server that she needs to access and allowed her to create and transfer her key to it before disabling password authentication. So, Vicky now has her `authorized_keys` file in her home directory on that server, as we see here:

```
vicky@ubuntu-nftables:~$ cd .ssh
vicky@ubuntu-nftables:~/.ssh$ ls -l
total 4
-rw------- 1 vicky vicky 233 Oct  3 18:24 authorized_keys
vicky@ubuntu-nftables:~/.ssh$
```

Vicky owns the file, and she has both read and write permissions on it. So, even though she can't transfer other keys to it the normal way once the administrator has disabled password authentication, she can still transfer key files manually, and manually edit the `authorized_keys` file to include them. To thwart her efforts, our intrepid administrator will create a directory within the `/etc/ssh/` directory to hold everyone's `authorized_keys` files, like so:

```
sudo mkdir /etc/ssh/authorized-keys
```

Our intrepid administrator's full admin privileges allow him to log in to the root user's shell, which allows him to go into the directories of all other users:

```
donnie@ubuntu-nftables:~$ sudo su -
[sudo] password for donnie:
root@ubuntu-nftables:~# cd /home/vicky/.ssh
root@ubuntu-nftables:/home/vicky/.ssh# ls -l
total 4
-rw------- 1 vicky vicky 233 Oct 3 18:24 authorized_keys
root@ubuntu-nftables:/home/vicky/.ssh#
```

The next step is to move Vicky's authorized_keys file to the new location, changing its name to vicky, like so:

```
root@ubuntu-nftables:/home/vicky/.ssh# mv authorized_keys /etc/ssh/authorized-
keys/vicky

root@ubuntu-nftables:/home/vicky/.ssh# exit
donnie@ubuntu-nftables:~$
```

Now, we have a bit of a conundrum. As you see here, the file still belongs to Vicky, and she has both read and write privileges. So, she can still edit the file without any administrator privileges. Removing the write privilege won't work, because since the file belongs to her, she could just add the write privilege back. Changing ownership to the root user is part of the answer, but that will prevent Vicky from being able to read the file, which will prevent her from logging in. To see the whole solution, let's see what I've already done with my own authorized_keys file:

```
donnie@ubuntu-nftables:~$ cd /etc/ssh/authorized-keys/
donnie@ubuntu-nftables:/etc/ssh/authorized-keys$ ls -l
total 8
-rw------- 1 vicky vicky 233 Oct 3 18:24 vicky
-rw-r-----+ 1 root root 406 Oct 3 16:24 donnie
donnie@ubuntu-nftables:/etc/ssh/authorized-keys$
```

The eagle-eyed among you have surely noticed what's going on with the donnie file. You see that I changed ownership to the root user and then added an access control list, as indicated by the + sign. Let's do the same for Vicky:

```
donnie@ubuntu-nftables:/etc/ssh/authorized-keys$ sudo chown root: vicky

donnie@ubuntu-nftables:/etc/ssh/authorized-keys$ sudo setfacl -m u:vicky:r
vicky

donnie@ubuntu-nftables:/etc/ssh/authorized-keys$
```

Looking at the permissions settings, we see that vicky has read access to the vicky file:

```
donnie@ubuntu-nftables:/etc/ssh/authorized-keys$ ls -l
total 8
-rw-r-----+ 1 root root 406 Oct 3 16:24 donnie
-rw-r-----+ 1 root root 233 Oct 3 18:53 vicky
donnie@ubuntu-nftables:/etc/ssh/authorized-keys$
```

While we're at it, let's look at her access control list:

```
donnie@ubuntu-nftables:/etc/ssh/authorized-keys$ getfacl vicky
# file: vicky
```

```
# owner: root
# group: root
user::rw-
user:vicky:r--
group::---
mask::r--
other::---
donnie@ubuntu-nftables:/etc/ssh/authorized-keys$
```

Vicky can now read the file so that she can log in, but she can't change it.

The final step is to reconfigure the `sshd_config` file, and then restart or reload the SSH service. Open the file in your text editor and look for this line:

```
#AuthorizedKeysFile     .ssh/authorized_keys .ssh/authorized_keys2
```

Change it to this:

```
AuthorizedKeysFile      /etc/ssh/authorized-keys/%u
```

The `%u` at the end of the line is a mini-macro that tells the SSH service to look for a keys file that has the same name as the user who's logging in. Now, even if users were to manually create their own `authorized_keys` files in their own home directories, the SSH service would just ignore them. Another benefit is that having the keys all in one place makes it a bit easier for an administrator to revoke someone's access, should the need arise.

Be aware that there's a lot more to managing SSH keys than what I've been able to present here. One problem is that while there are a few different free open source software solutions for managing public keys, there aren't any for managing private keys. A large corporation could have thousands or perhaps even millions of private and public keys in different places. Those keys never expire, so they'll be around forever unless they get deleted. If the wrong people get hold of a private key, your whole network could become compromised. As much as I hate to say it, your best bet for managing SSH keys is to go with a commercial solution, such as ones from SSH.com and CyberArk.

> Check out the key management solutions from SSH.com here: `https://www.ssh.com/academy/iam/ssh-key-management`.
>
> Head here for CyberArk's key management solutions: `https://www.cyberark.com/resources/blog/ssh-keys-the-powerful-unprotected-privileged-credentials`.
>
> Full disclosure: I have no connection with either SSH.com or CyberArk, and receive no payment for telling you about them.

You've learned several cool tricks here for beefing up your server security. Now, let's look at how to create different configurations for different users and groups.

Setting different configurations for different users and groups

On the server side, you can use the `Match User` or `Match Group` directive to set up custom configurations for certain users or groups. To see how it's done, look at the example at the very bottom of the /etc/ssh/sshd_config file. There, you'll see the following:

```
# Match User anoncvs
# X11Forwarding no
# AllowTcpForwarding no
# PermitTTY no
# ForceCommand cvs server
```

Of course, this has no effect since it's commented out, but that's okay. Here's what we see for user anoncvs:

- He can't do **X11 forwarding**.
- He can't do **TCP forwarding**.
- He won't have the use of a command terminal.

As soon as he logs in, he'll be starting the **Concurrent Versioning Service (CVS)** server. By not having use of the terminal, anoncvs can start the CVS server, but can't do anything else.

You can set up different configurations for as many users as you need to. Anything that you put in the custom configurations will override the global settings. To set up a custom configuration for a group, just replace `Match User` with `Match Group`, and supply a group name instead of a user name.

Creating different configurations for different hosts

For a change of pace, let's look at the client's end now. This time, we'll look at a handy trick to help ease the pain of logging into different servers that require different keys or SSH options. This also allows you to access servers via easy-to-remember names, rather than having to remember multiple server IP addresses. All you have to do is go into the `.ssh` directory in your own home directory and create a config file. To demonstrate this, let's create a configuration that allows us to easily access server1. In the `~/.ssh/config` file, we can add a stanza that looks something like this:

```
Host server1
  Hostname 192.168.0.8
  User donnie
  IdentityFile ~/.ssh/server1_id_rsa
  IdentitiesOnly yes
  ForwardX11 yes
  Cipher aes256-gcm@openssh.com
```

Here's the breakdown:

- **Host:** This is the common name that you can use in your login command.
- **Hostname:** For this, use either the IP address or hostname of the server. (If you use the hostname, it will either have to be registered in DNS or have an entry in your local `/etc/hosts` file.)
- **User:** You'll log in as this user.
- **IdentityFile:** This specifies the key that goes with this server. You can use a key with a custom filename if you desire, as long as you don't mind typing in the private key password every time you need to access this server. (As a reminder, that's because `ssh-add` won't add keys with custom filenames to your session keyring.)
- **IdentitiesOnly yes:** If you happen to have more than one key loaded into your session keyring, this forces your client to only use the key that's specified here.
- **ForwardX11 yes:** We want this client to use *X11* forwarding. (Of course, this will only be effective if the server has been configured to allow it.)
- **Cipher aes256-gcm@openssh.com:** We want to use this algorithm, and *only* this algorithm, to perform our encryption.

To create custom configurations for other hosts, just add a stanza for each one to this file. Then, to log in to a server that's listed in this `config` file, just invoke the `ssh` command with the desired `Host` designation. For example, to log in to Donnie's account on `server1`, as you see configured above, just do this:

```
[donnie@localhost ~]$ ssh server1
```

There's a lot more we can do with custom configurations, and I'll leave some references for you in the *Further reading* section.

Next, let's talk about SFTP, where we'll make good use of the `Match Group` directive that we just looked at.

Setting up a chroot environment for SFTP users

Secure File Transfer Protocol (SFTP) is a great tool for performing secure file transfers. There is a command-line client, but users will most likely use a graphical client, such as FileZilla. With a default SSH setup, anyone who has a user account on a Linux machine can log in through either SSH or SFTP and can navigate through the server's entire filesystem. What we really want for SFTP users is to prevent them from logging into a command prompt via SSH, and to confine them to their own designated directories.

> One good use for this trick would be to set up SFTP configurations for website creators. Instead of allowing these users to transfer files to and from their own home directories, just allow them to transfer files to and from the website content directories, instead.

Creating a group and configuring the sshd_config file

With the exception of the slight difference in user creation commands, this procedure works the same on any of your VMs.

1. We'll begin by creating an sftpusers group:

    ```
    sudo groupadd sftpusers
    ```

2. Create the user accounts and add them to the sftpusers group. We'll do both operations in one step. On your CentOS or AlmaLinux machine, the commands for creating Max's account would look like this:

    ```
    sudo useradd -G sftpusers max
    sudo passwd max
    ```

3. On your Ubuntu machine, it would look like this:

    ```
    sudo useradd -m -d /home/max -s /bin/bash -G sftpusers max
    ```

4. Open the /etc/ssh/sshd_config file in your favorite text editor. Find the line that says this:

    ```
    subsystem sftp /usr/lib/openssh/sftp-server
    ```

5. Change it to this:

    ```
    subsystem sftp internal-sftp
    ```

6. This setting allows you to disable normal SSH login for certain users.

7. At the bottom of the sshd_config file, add a Match Group stanza:

    ```
    Match Group sftpusers
            ChrootDirectory /home
            AllowTCPForwarding no
            AllowAgentForwarding no
            X11Forwarding no
            ForceCommand internal-sftp
    ```

8. An important consideration here is that the ChrootDirectory has to be owned by the root user, and it can't be writable by anyone other than the root user. When Max logs in, he'll be in the /home/ directory, and will then have to cd into his own directory. This also means that you want all your users' home directories to have the restrictive 700 permissions setting in order to keep everyone out of everyone else's stuff.

9. Save the file and restart the SSH daemon. Then, try to log on as Max through normal SSH, just to see what happens:

    ```
    donnie@linux-0ro8:~> ssh max@192.168.0.8
    max@192.168.0.8's password:
    This service allows sftp connections only.
    Connection to 192.168.0.8 closed.
    donnie@linux-0ro8:~>
    ```

Okay, so he can't do that. Now, let's have Max try to log in through SFTP and verify that he is in the /home/ directory:

```
donnie@linux-0ro8:~> sftp max@192.168.0.8
max@192.168.0.8's password:
Connected to 192.168.0.8.
drwx------    7 1000     1000         4096 Nov  4 22:53 donnie
drwx------    5 1001     1001         4096 Oct 27 23:34 frank
drwx------    3 1003     1004         4096 Nov  4 22:43 katelyn
drwx------    2 1002     1003         4096 Nov  4 22:37 max
sftp>
Now, let's see him try to cd out of the /home/ directory:
sftp> cd /etc
Couldn't stat remote file: No such file or directory
sftp>
```

So, our chroot jail does indeed work.

Hands-on lab — Setting up a chroot directory for the sftpusers group

For this lab, you can use either the CentOS VM or the Ubuntu VM. You'll add a group, then configure the `sshd_config` file to allow group members to only be able to log in via SFTP, and then confine them to their own directories. For the simulated client machine, you can use the terminal of your macOS or Linux desktop machine, or any of the available Bash shells from your Windows machine. Let's get started:

1. Create the `sftpusers` group:

   ```
   sudo groupadd sftpusers
   ```

2. Create a user account for Max and add him to the `sftpusers` group. On CentOS or AlmaLinux, do this:

   ```
   sudo useradd -G sftpusers max
   sudo passwd max
   ```

   On Ubuntu, do this:

   ```
   sudo useradd -m -d /home/max -s /bin/bash -G sftpusers max
   ```

3. For Ubuntu, ensure that the users' home directories are all set with read, write, and execute permissions for only the directory's user. If that's not the case, do this:

   ```
   sudo chmod 700 /home/*
   ```

4. Open the `/etc/ssh/sshd_config` file in your preferred text editor. Find the line that says the following:

   ```
   subsystem sftp /usr/lib/openssh/sftp-server
   ```

5. Change it to the following:

```
subsystem sftp internal-sftp
```

6. At the end of the `sshd_config` file, add this stanza:

```
Match Group sftpusers
        ChrootDirectory /home
        AllowTCPForwarding no
        AllowAgentForwarding no
        X11Forwarding no
        ForceCommand internal-sftp
```

7. Reload the SSH configuration. On CentOS or AlmaLinux, do this:

```
sudo systemctl reload sshd
```

8. On Ubuntu, do this:

```
sudo systemctl reload ssh
```

9. Have Max try to log in through normal SSH to see what happens:

```
ssh max@IP_Address_of_your_vm
```

10. Now, have Max log in through SFTP. Once he's in, have him try to `cd` out of the `/home/` directory:

```
sftp max@IP_Address_of_your_vm
```

You've reached the end of the lab – congratulations!

Now that you know how to securely configure SFTP, let's look at how to securely share a directory.

Sharing a directory with SSHFS

There are several ways to share a directory across a network. In enterprise settings, you'll find the **Network Filesystem** (**NFS**), **Samba**, and various distributed filesystems. **SSHFS** isn't used in enterprises quite as much, but it can still come in handy. The beauty of it is that all of its network traffic is encrypted by default, unlike with NFS or Samba. And, other than installing the SSHFS client program and creating a local mount-point directory, it doesn't require any configuration beyond what you've already done. It's especially handy for accessing a directory on a cloud-based **Virtual Private Server** (**VPS**) because it allows you to just create files in the shared directory rather than using `scp` or `sftp` commands to transfer the files. So, if you're ready, let's jump in.

Hands-on lab — Sharing a directory with SSHFS

For this lab, we'll use two VMs. For the server, you can use any of your VMs. The same is true of the client, except that each distro has the SSHFS client in a different repository. Here's what I'm talking about:

- The client is in the normal Ubuntu repositories, so you don't have to do anything special to get it.

- For CentOS 7 and AlmaLinux 9, you'll need to install the `epel-release` package with the normal `yum install` or `dnf install` command.
- AlmaLinux 8 has the SSHFS client in its own PowerTools repository, which isn't enabled by default. To enable it, open the `/etc/yum.repos.d/almalinux-powertools.repo` file in your favorite text editor. In the `[powertools]` section, find the line that says `enabled=0`, and change it to `enabled=1`.

Now that we have all that straight, let's get started:

1. Boot up one VM for a server. (That's all you need to do for the server end.)
2. On the other VM that you'll use as a client, create a mount-point directory within your own home directory, like so:

```
mkdir remote
```

3. On the client VM, install the SSHFS client. On Ubuntu, do this:

```
sudo apt install sshfs
```

On CentOS 7, do this:

```
sudo yum install fuse-sshfs
```

On AlmaLinux 8 or 9, do this:

```
sudo dnf install fuse-sshfs
```

4. From the client machine, mount your own home directory that's on the server:

```
sshfs donnie@192.168.0.10: /home/donnie/remote
```

> Note that if you don't specify a directory to share, the default is to share the home directory of the user who is logging in.

5. Verify that the directory was mounted properly with the `mount` command. You should see your new shared mount at the bottom of the output:

```
donnie@ubuntu-nftables:~$ mount
. . .
. . .
donnie@192.168.0.10: on /home/donnie/remote type fuse.sshfs
(rw,nosuid,nodev,relatime,user_id=1000,group_id=1004)
```

6. `cd` into the `remote` directory and create some files. Verify that they actually do show up on the server.

7. At the local console of the server VM, create some files in your own home directory. Verify that they show up in the `remote/` directory of your client VM.

You've reached the end of the lab – congratulations!

With this lab, I just showed you how to mount your own home directory from a remote server. You can also mount other server directories by specifying them in the `sshfs` command. For example, let's say that I want to mount the `/maggie_files/` directory, with the `~/remote3/` directory as my local mount point. (I chose that name because Maggie cat is sitting here in front of me where my keyboard should be.) Just do it like this:

```
sshfs donnie@192.168.0.53:/maggie_files /home/donnie/remote3
```

You can also make the remote directory automatically mount every time you boot your client machine by adding an entry to the `/etc/fstab` file. But, that's generally not a good idea. If the server isn't available when you boot the client machine, it could cause the boot process to hang up.

Okay, so you've seen how to use SSHFS to create an encrypted connection with a shared remote directory. Let's now log in to the server from a Windows desktop machine.

Remotely connecting from Windows desktops

I know, all of us Penguinistas would like to use Linux, and nothing but Linux. But, in an enterprise environment, things just don't always work that way. There, you'll most likely have to administer your Linux servers from a Windows 10/11 desktop machine that's sitting on your cubicle desk. In *Chapter 1*, *Running Linux in a Virtual Environment*, I showed you how to use either Cygwin or the new Windows 10/11 shell to remotely connect to your Linux VMs. You can also use these techniques to connect to actual Linux servers.

But, some shops require that admins use a terminal program, rather than a full-blown Bash shell such as Cygwin. Normally, these shops will require that you use **PuTTY** on your Windows machine.

> PuTTY is a free program that you can download from here: `https://www.chiark.greenend.org.uk/~sgtatham/putty/latest.html`

Installation is simple. Just double-click the installer file and follow through the installer screens:

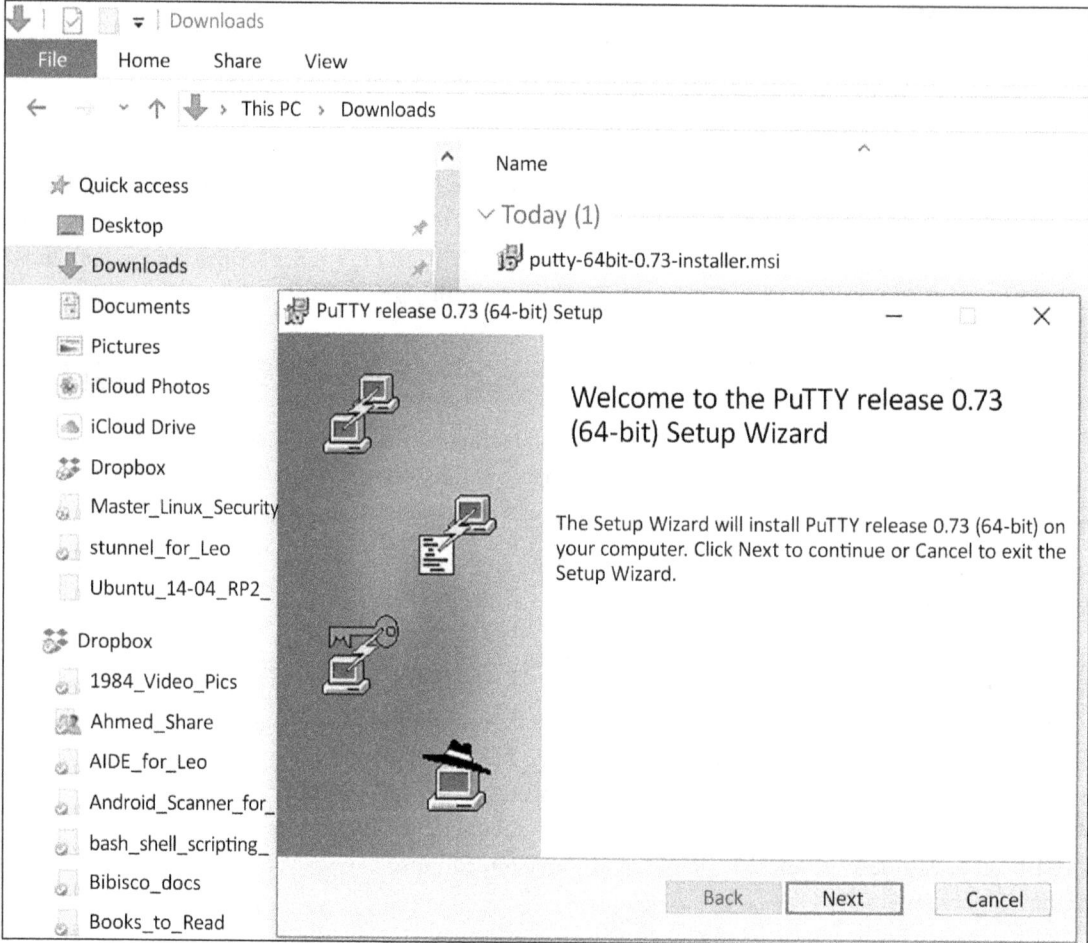

Figure 7.2: The PuTTY setup wizard

You can open the PuTTY user manual from your Windows 10/11 **Start** menu:

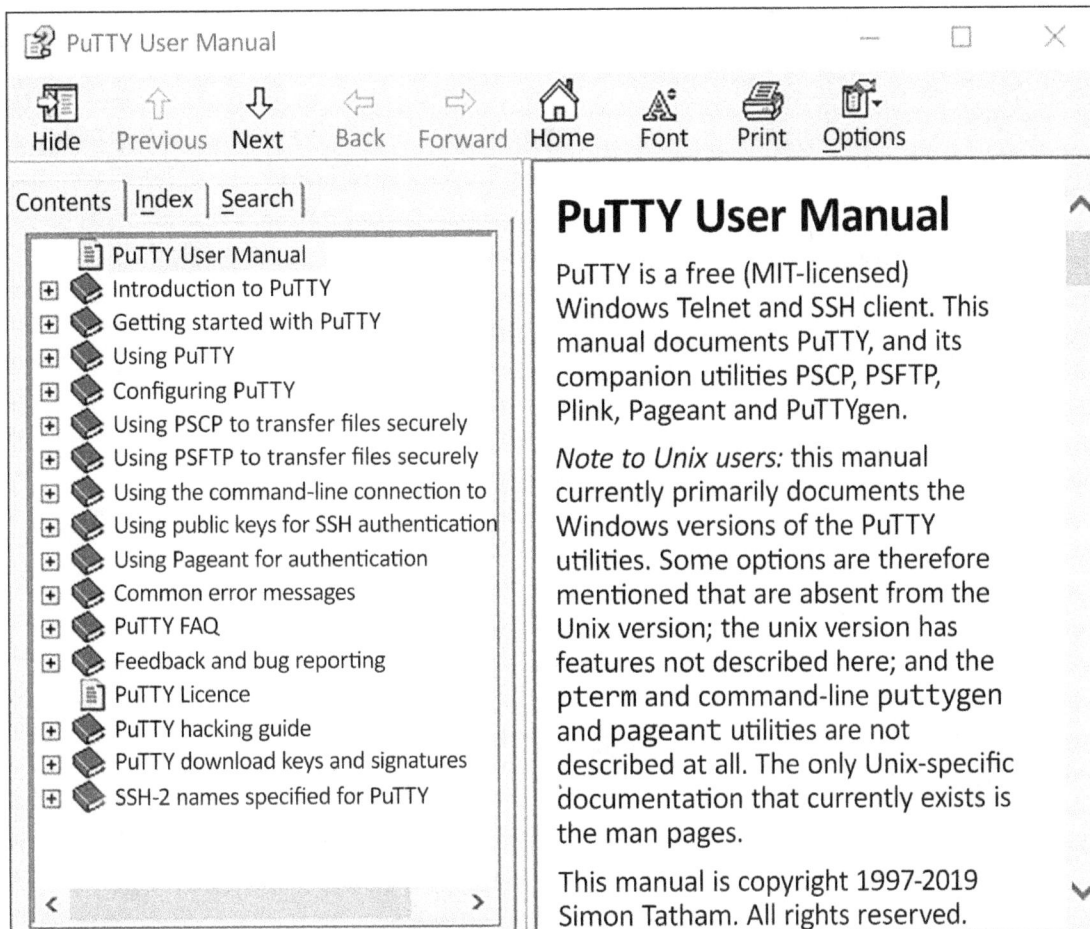

PuTTY User Manual — □ ✕

| Hide | Previous | **Next** | Back | Forward | Home | Font | Print | Options |

Contents | Index | Search |

- PuTTY User Manual
- ⊞ Introduction to PuTTY
- ⊞ Getting started with PuTTY
- ⊞ Using PuTTY
- ⊞ Configuring PuTTY
- ⊞ Using PSCP to transfer files securely
- ⊞ Using PSFTP to transfer files securely
- ⊞ Using the command-line connection to
- ⊞ Using public keys for SSH authentication
- ⊞ Using Pageant for authentication
- ⊞ Common error messages
- ⊞ PuTTY FAQ
- ⊞ Feedback and bug reporting
- PuTTY Licence
- ⊞ PuTTY hacking guide
- ⊞ PuTTY download keys and signatures
- ⊞ SSH-2 names specified for PuTTY

PuTTY User Manual

PuTTY is a free (MIT-licensed) Windows Telnet and SSH client. This manual documents PuTTY, and its companion utilities PSCP, PSFTP, Plink, Pageant and PuTTYgen.

Note to Unix users: this manual currently primarily documents the Windows versions of the PuTTY utilities. Some options are therefore mentioned that are absent from the Unix version; the unix version has features not described here; and the `pterm` and command-line `puttygen` and `pageant` utilities are not described at all. The only Unix-specific documentation that currently exists is the man pages.

This manual is copyright 1997-2019 Simon Tatham. All rights reserved.

Figure 7.3: The PuTTY user manual

Connecting to a remote Linux machine is easy. Just enter the machine's IP address and click on **Open**:

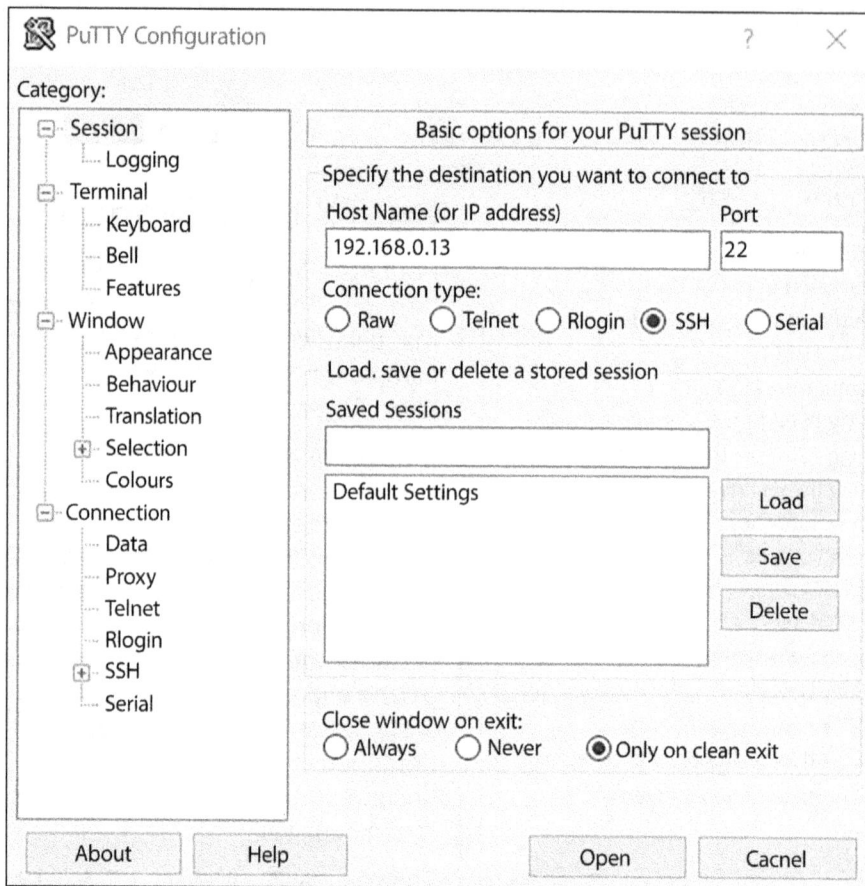

Figure 7.4: Creating the connection

Note that this also gives you the option to save your sessions. So, if you have to administer multiple servers, you can open PuTTY and just click on the name of the server that you want to connect to, and then click on **Open**:

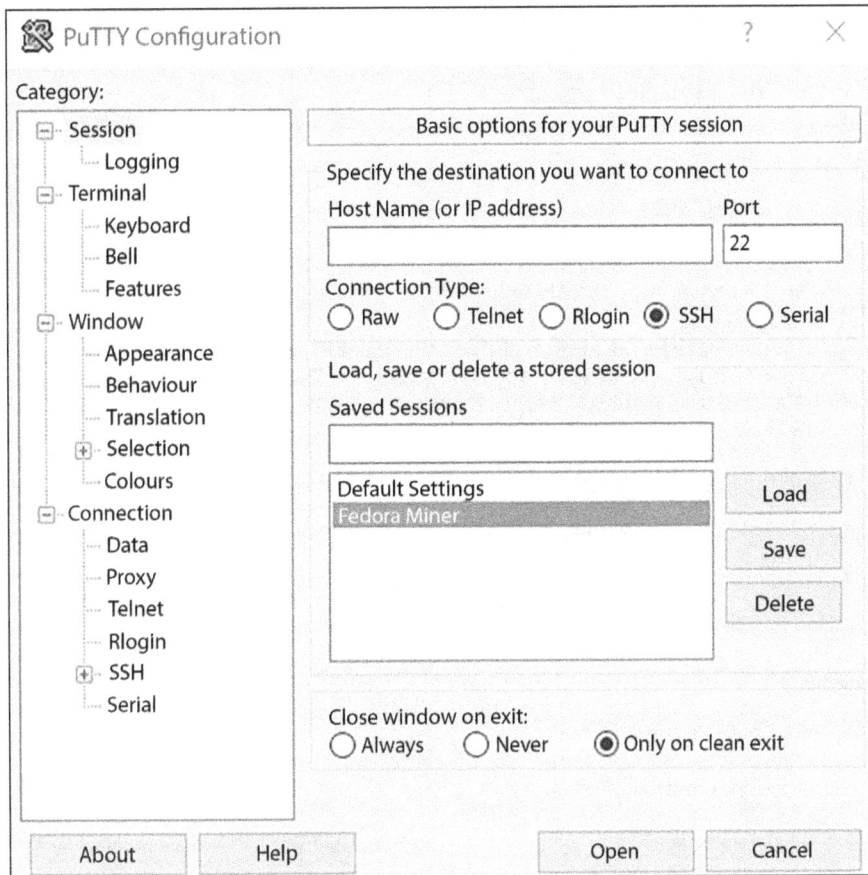

Figure 7.5: Saving the session

As you can see, this is a lot handier than having to manually type in the ssh command every time you need to log in to a server, and it prevents you from having to remember a whole list of IP addresses for multiple servers. (But of course, you can accomplish the same thing with either Cygwin or a Windows 10 shell by creating a login shell script for each Linux machine that you need to administer.)

Either way, you'll end up at the remote machine's Bash shell:

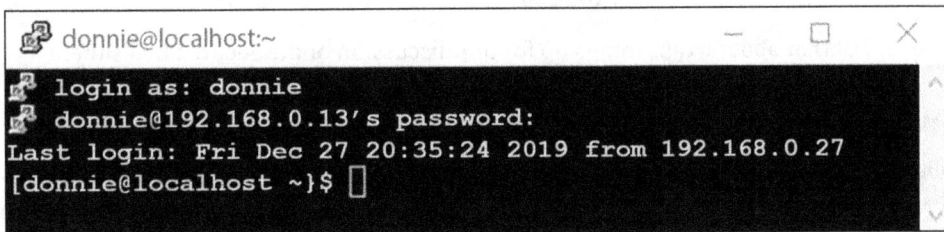

Figure 7.6: Logging into the PuTTY session

To set up key-exchange authentication, use `PuTTYgen` to create the key pair. The only slight catch is that you'll have to transfer the public key to the server by manually copying and pasting the key into the server's `authorized_keys` file:

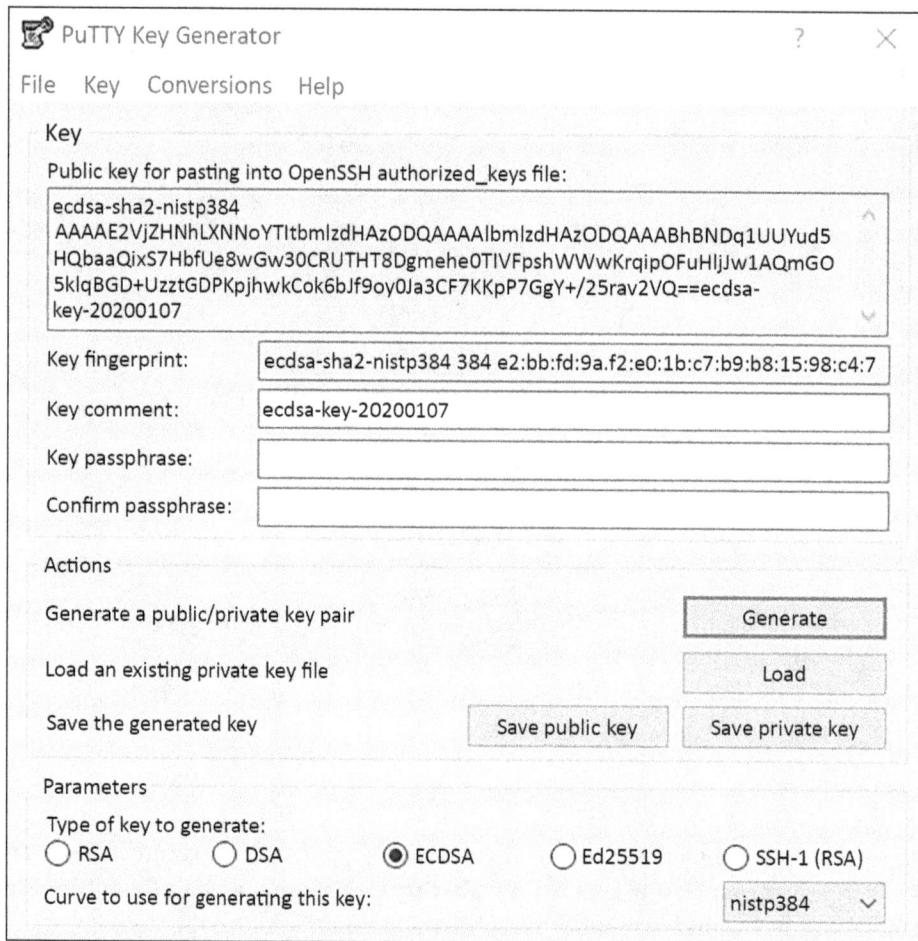

Figure 7.7: Setting up key exchange

I've given you the basics about PuTTY. You can read the PuTTY manual to get the nitty-gritty details.

Okay, I think that that about wraps things up for our discussion of the Secure Shell suite.

Summary

In this chapter, we've seen that a default configuration of Secure Shell isn't as secure as we'd like it to be, and we've seen what to do about it. We've looked at how to set up key-based authentication and two-factor authentication, and we've looked at lots of different options that can lock down the SSH server. We also looked at how to disable weak encryption algorithms, and at how the new system-wide crypto policies on RHEL 8/CentOS 8 and RHEL 9/AlmaLinux 9 make doing that really easy.

Along the way, we looked at setting up access controls, and at creating different configurations for different users, groups, and hosts. After demoing how to confine SFTP users to their own home directories, we used SSHFS to share a remote directory. We wrapped up this chapter by presenting a handy way to log in to our Linux servers from a Windows desktop machine.

Conspicuous by their absence are a couple of technologies that you may have seen recommended elsewhere. Port knocking and Fail2Ban are two popular technologies that can help control access to an SSH server. However, they're only needed if you allow password-based authentication to your SSH server. If you set up key-based authentication, as I've shown you here, you won't need the added complexity of those other solutions.

In the next chapter, we'll take an in-depth look at the subject of discretionary access control. I'll see you there.

Questions

1. Which of the following statements is true?

   a. Secure Shell is completely secure in its default configuration.

   b. It's safe to allow the root user to use Secure Shell to log in across the Internet.

   c. Secure Shell is insecure in its default configuration.

   d. The most secure way to use Secure Shell is to log in with a username and password.

2. Which three of the following things would you do to conform with the best security practices for Secure Shell?

   a. Make sure that all users are using strong passwords to log in via Secure Shell.

   b. Have all users create a public/private key pair, and transfer their public keys to the server to which they want to log in.

   c. Disable the ability to log in via username/password.

   d. Ensure that the root user is using a strong password.

   e. Disable the root user's ability to log in.

3. Which one of the following lines in the `sshd_config` file will cause botnets to not scan your system for login vulnerabilities?

   a. `PasswordAuthentication no`

   b. `PasswordAuthentication yes`

   c. `PermitRootLogin yes`

   d. `PermitRootLogin no`

4. How would you confine a user of SFTP to his or her own specified directory?

   a. Ensure that proper ownership and permissions are set on that user's directory.

   b. In the `sshd_config` file, disable that user's ability to log in via normal SSH and define a chroot directory for that user.

    c.   Define the user's limitations with TCP Wrappers.

    d.   Use whole-disk encryption on the server so that SFTP users will only be able to access their own directories.

5. Which two of the following commands would you use to add your private SSH key to your session keyring?

    a.   `ssh-copy-id`

    b.   `exec /usr/bin/ssh-agent`

    c.   `exec /usr/bin/ssh-agent $SHELL`

    d.   `ssh-agent`

    e.   `ssh-agent $SHELL`

    f.   `ssh-add`

6. Which of the following is *not* on NIST's list of recommended algorithms?

    a.   `RSA`

    b.   `ECDSA`

    c.   `Ed25519`

7. Which of the following is the correct directive for creating a custom configuration for Katelyn?

    a.   `User Match katelyn`

    b.   `Match katelyn`

    c.   `Match Account katelyn`

    d.   `Match User katelyn`

8. Which of the following crypto policies provides the strongest encryption on RHEL 8/9-type distros?

    a.   `LEGACY`

    b.   `FIPS`

    c.   `DEFAULT`

    d.   `FUTURE`

9. Which of the following standards defines NIST's current recommendations for encryption algorithms?

    a.   FIPS 140-2

    b.   FIPS 140-3

    c.   CNSA

    d.   Suite B

Further reading

- How to set up SSH keys on Debian 10 Buster: `https://devconnected.com/how-to-set-up-ssh-keys-on-debian-10-buster/`
- How to configure the OpenSSH server: `https://www.ssh.com/academy/ssh/sshd_config`
- Setting up passwordless SSH: `https://www.redhat.com/sysadmin/passwordless-ssh`
- OpenSSH best practices for Unix, Linux, and BSD: `https://www.cyberciti.biz/tips/linux-unix-bsd-openssh-server-best-practices.html`
- Different SSH configurations for different hosts: `https://www.putorius.net/how-to-save-per-user-per-host-ssh-client-settings.html`
- SSH Query at Shodan: `https://www.shodan.io/search?query=ssh`
- Mozilla OpenSSH Security Guide: `https://infosec.mozilla.org/guidelines/openssh`
- Execute commands on a remote system over SSH: `https://www.2daygeek.com/execute-run-linux-commands-remote-system-over-ssh/`
- CNSA Suite and quantum cryptography: `https://cryptome.org/2016/01/CNSA-Suite-and-Quantum-Computing-FAQ.pdf`
- FIPS 140-3: `https://csrc.nist.gov/projects/fips-140-3-transition-effort`
- ChaCha20 and Poly1305: `https://tools.ietf.org/html/rfc7539`
- System-wide cryptographic policies on Red Hat Enterprise Linux 8: `https://access.redhat.com/documentation/en-us/red_hat_enterprise_linux/8/html/security_hardening/using-the-system-wide-cryptographic-policies_security-hardening#system-wide-crypto-policies_using-the-system-wide-cryptographic-policies`
- How to log out inactive users in Linux: `https://www.ostechnix.com/auto-logout-inactive-users-period-time-linux/`
- Configure host-specific SSH settings: `https://www.putorius.net/how-to-save-per-user-per-host-ssh-client-settings.html`
- How to use SSHFS to mount remote directories over SSH: `https://linuxize.com/post/how-to-use-sshfs-to-mount-remote-directories-over-ssh/`
- Padding oracle attacks: `https://resources.infosecinstitute.com/topic/padding-oracle-attack-2/`
- How to use an SSH config file: `https://linuxhandbook.com/ssh-config-file/`
- Using the SSH config file: `https://linuxize.com/post/using-the-ssh-config-file`

Answers

1. c
2. b, c, e
3. a
4. b
5. c, f

6. c
7. d
8. d
9. c

Join our book community

Join our community's Discord space for discussions with the author and other readers:

```
https://packt.link/CyberSec
```

Section 2

Mastering File and Directory Access Control (DAC)

This section will talk about protecting sensitive files and directories by setting proper permissions and ownership, and by using Extended Attributes (xattr). You will also see how to avoid security-related problems with Set User ID (SUID) and Set Group ID (SGID).

The section contains the following chapters:

8

Mastering Discretionary Access Control

Discretionary Access Control (DAC) really just means that each user has the ability to control who can get into their stuff. If I wanted to open my home directory so that every other user on the system can get into it, I could do that. Having done so, I could then control who can access each specific file. In the next chapter, we'll use our DAC skills to manage shared directories, where members of a group might need different levels of access to the files within.

At this point in your Linux career, you likely know the basics of controlling access by setting file and directory permissions. In this chapter, we'll review the basics, and then we'll look at some more advanced concepts.

In this chapter, we'll cover the following topics:

- Using chown to change the ownership of files and directories
- Using chmod to set permissions on files and directories
- What the **Set User ID (SUID)** and the **Set Group ID (SGID)** settings can do for us on regular files
- The security implications of having the SUID and SGID permissions set on files that don't need them
- How to use extended file attributes to protect sensitive files
- Securing system configuration files

Using chown to change ownership of files and directories

Controlling access to files and directories really just boils down to ensuring that the proper users can access their own files and directories, and that each file and directory has permissions set in such a way that only authorized users can access them. The chown utility covers the first part of this equation.

One unique thing about chown is that you must have sudo privileges to use it, even if you're working with your own files in your own directory. You can use it to change the user of a file or directory, the group that's associated with a file or directory, or both at the same time.

First, let's say that you own the perm_demo.txt file and that you want to change both the user and group association to that of another user. In this case, I'll change the file ownership from me to maggie:

```
[donnie@localhost ~]$ ls -l perm_demo.txt
-rw-rw-r--. 1 donnie donnie 0 Nov  5 20:02 perm_demo.txt

[donnie@localhost ~]$ sudo chown maggie:maggie perm_demo.txt

[donnie@localhost ~]$ ls -l perm_demo.txt
-rw-rw-r--. 1 maggie maggie 0 Nov  5 20:02 perm_demo.txt
[donnie@localhost ~]$
```

The first maggie in maggie:maggie is the user to whom you want to grant ownership. The second maggie, after the colon, represents the group that you want the file to be associated with. Since I was changing both the user and the group to maggie, I could have left off the second maggie, with the first maggie followed by a colon, and I would have achieved the same result:

```
sudo chown maggie: perm_demo.txt
```

To just change the group association without changing the user, just list the group name, preceded by a colon:

```
[donnie@localhost ~]$ sudo chown :accounting perm_demo.txt

[donnie@localhost ~]$ ls -l perm_demo.txt
-rw-rw-r--. 1 maggie accounting 0 Nov  5 20:02 perm_demo.txt
[donnie@localhost ~]$
```

Finally, to just change the user without changing the group, list the username without the trailing colon:

```
[donnie@localhost ~]$ sudo chown donnie perm_demo.txt

[donnie@localhost ~]$ ls -l perm_demo.txt
-rw-rw-r--. 1 donnie accounting 0 Nov  5 20:02 perm_demo.txt
[donnie@localhost ~]$
```

These commands work the same way on a directory as they do on a file. However, if you also want to change the ownership and/or the group association of the contents of a directory, while also making the change on the directory itself, use the -R option, which stands for *recursive*. In this case, I just want to change the group for the perm_demo_dir directory to accounting. Let's see what we have to begin with:

```
[donnie@localhost ~]$ ls -ld perm_demo_dir
drwxrwxr-x. 2 donnie donnie 74 Nov  5 20:17 perm_demo_dir

[donnie@localhost ~]$ ls -l perm_demo_dir
total 0
```

```
-rw-rw-r--. 1 donnie donnie 0 Nov  5 20:17 file1.txt
-rw-rw-r--. 1 donnie donnie 0 Nov  5 20:17 file2.txt
-rw-rw-r--. 1 donnie donnie 0 Nov  5 20:17 file3.txt
-rw-rw-r--. 1 donnie donnie 0 Nov  5 20:17 file4.txt
```

Now, let's run the command and look at the results:

```
[donnie@localhost ~]$ sudo chown -R :accounting perm_demo_dir

[donnie@localhost ~]$ ls -ld perm_demo_dir
drwxrwxr-x. 2 donnie accounting 74 Nov  5 20:17 perm_demo_dir

[donnie@localhost ~]$ ls -l perm_demo_dir
total 0
-rw-rw-r--. 1 donnie accounting 0 Nov  5 20:17 file1.txt
-rw-rw-r--. 1 donnie accounting 0 Nov  5 20:17 file2.txt
-rw-rw-r--. 1 donnie accounting 0 Nov  5 20:17 file3.txt
-rw-rw-r--. 1 donnie accounting 0 Nov  5 20:17 file4.txt
[donnie@localhost ~]$
```

That's all there is to chown. Next, let's change some permissions.

Using chmod to set permissions on files and directories

On Unix and Linux systems, you would use the chmod utility to set permissions values on files and directories. You can set permissions for the user of the file or directory, the group that's associated with the file or directory, and more. The three basic permissions are as follows:

- **r**: This indicates a read permission.
- **w**: This indicates a write permission.
- **x**: This is the executable permission. You can apply it to any type of program file, or to directories. If you apply an executable permission to a directory, authorized people will be able to cd into it.

If you perform ls -l on a file, you'll see something like this:

```
-rw-rw-r--. 1 donnie donnie    804692 Oct 28 18:44 yum_list.txt
```

The first character of this line indicates the type of file. In this case, we can see a dash, which indicates a regular file. (A regular file is pretty much every type of file that a normal user would be able to access in his or her daily routine.) The next three characters, rw-, indicate that the file has read and write permissions for the user, which is the person who owns the file. Then, we can see the rw- permissions for the group and the r-- permissions for others. A program file would also have the executable permissions set:

```
-rwxr-xr-x. 1 root root      62288 Nov 20  2015 xargs
```

Here, we can see that the xargs program file has executable permissions set for everybody.

There are two ways that you can use chmod to change permissions settings:

- The symbolic method
- The numerical method

We'll cover these methods next.

Setting permissions with the symbolic method

Whenever you create a file as a normal user, by default, it will have read/write permissions for the user, and read permission for the group and for others. That's because the default umask setting of 022 causes files to be created without write permissions for the group or others. You can see what the umask setting is like this:

```
[donnie@donnie-ca ~]$ umask
0022
[donnie@donnie-ca ~]$
```

The actual umask setting is just 022, even though it shows up here as 0022. That extra leading 0 just indicates that this number is in octal format.

Regular files will always get created without executable permissions regardless of the umask, which is why when you create a script or a program, you'll always need to set the executable permissions yourself. Here's how to do it with the symbolic method:

```
chmod u+x donnie_script.sh
chmod g+x donnie_script.sh
chmod o+x donnie_script.sh
chmod u+x,g+x donnie_script.sh
chmod a+x donnie_script.sh
```

The first three commands add the executable permission for the user, the group, and others. The fourth command adds executable permissions for both the user and the group, while the last command adds executable permissions for everybody (a for all). You can also remove the executable permissions by replacing + with -. Finally, you can also add or remove the read or write permissions, as appropriate.

While this method can be handy at times, it also has a bit of a flaw. That is, it can only add permissions to what's already there, or remove permissions from what's already there. If you need to ensure that all of the permissions for a particular file get set to a certain value, the symbolic method can get a bit unwieldy. And for shell scripting, forget about it. In a shell script, you'd need to add all kinds of extra code just to determine which permissions have already been set. The numerical method can vastly simplify things for us.

Setting permissions with the numerical method

With the numerical method, you'll use an octal value to represent the permissions settings on a file or directory. For the r, w, and x permissions, you assign the numerical values 4, 2, and 1, respectively.

You would do this for the user, group, and others positions, and then add them all up to get the permissions value for the file or directory:

User	Group	Others
rwx	rwx	rwx
421	421	421
7	7	7

So, if you have all the permissions set for everybody, the file or directory will have a value of 777. If I were to create a shell script file, by default, it would have the standard 664 permissions, meaning read and write for the user and group, and read-only for others:

```
-rw-rw-r--. 1 donnie donnie 0 Nov  6 19:18 donnie_script.sh
```

> If you create a file with root privileges, either with sudo or from the root user command prompt, you'll see that the default permissions setting is the more restrictive 644.

Let's say that I want to make this script executable, but I want to be the only person in the whole world who can do anything with it. To do this, I could do the following:

```
[donnie@localhost ~]$ chmod 700 donnie_script.sh

[donnie@localhost ~]$ ls -l donnie_script.sh
-rwx------. 1 donnie donnie 0 Nov  6 19:18 donnie_script.sh
[donnie@localhost ~]$
```

With this one simple command, I've removed all permissions from the group and from others, and set the executable permission for myself. This is the sort of thing that makes the numerical method so handy for writing shell scripts.

Once you've been working with the numerical method for a while, looking at a file and figuring out its numerical permissions value will become second nature. In the meantime, you can use stat with the -c %a option to show you the values. This can be done like so:

```
[donnie@localhost ~]$ stat -c %a yum_list.txt
664
[donnie@localhost ~]$

[donnie@localhost ~]$ stat -c %a donnie_script.sh
700
[donnie@localhost ~]$
```

```
[donnie@localhost ~]$ stat -c %a /etc/fstab
644
[donnie@localhost ~]$
```

If you want to view the numerical permissions of all the files at once, do this:

```
[donnie@donnie-ca ~]$ stat -c '%n %a ' *
dropbear 755
internal.txt 664
password.txt 664
pki-server.crt 664
pki-server.p12 644
yum_list.txt 664
[donnie@donnie-ca ~]$
```

Here, you can see the wildcard (*) at the end of the command, indicating that you want to view the settings for all the files. %n indicates that you want to view the filenames, along with the permissions settings. Since we're using two -c options, we have to enclose both of the options within a pair of single quotes. The only slight catch here is that this output doesn't show which of these items are files, and which are directories. However, since directories require executable permissions so that people can cd into them, we can guess that dropbear is probably a directory. To be sure though, just use ls -1, like so:

```
[donnie@donnie-ca ~]$ ls -l
total 2180
drwxr-xr-x. 1 donnie donnie  277144 Apr 22  2018 dropbear
-rw-rw-r--. 1 donnie donnie      13 Sep 19 13:32 internal.txt
-rw-rw-r--. 1 donnie donnie      11 Sep 19 13:42 password.txt
-rw-rw-r--. 1 donnie donnie    1708 Sep 19 14:41 pki-server.crt
-rw-r--r--. 1 root   root      1320 Sep 20 21:08 pki-server.p12
-rw-rw-r--. 1 donnie donnie 1933891 Sep 19 18:04 yum_list.txt
[donnie@donnie-ca ~]$
```

Now, let's move on to a couple of very special permissions settings.

Using SUID and SGID on regular files

When a regular file has its SUID permission set, whoever accesses the file will have the same privileges as the user of the file.

To demo this, let's say that Maggie, a regular, unprivileged user, wants to change her own password. Since it's her own password, she would just use the one-word passwd command, without using sudo:

```
[maggie@localhost ~]$ passwd
Changing password for user maggie.
Changing password for maggie.
(current) UNIX password:
```

```
New password:
Retype new password:
passwd: all authentication tokens updated successfully.
[maggie@localhost ~]$
```

To change a password, a person has to make changes to the /etc/shadow file. On my CentOS and AlmaLinux machines, the shadow file's permissions look like this:

```
[donnie@localhost etc]$ ls -l shadow
----------. 1 root root 840 Nov  6 19:37 shadow
[donnie@localhost etc]$
```

On an Ubuntu machine, they look like this:

```
donnie@ubuntu:/etc$ ls -l shadow
-rw-r----- 1 root shadow 1316 Nov  4 18:38 shadow
donnie@ubuntu:/etc$
```

Either way, the permissions settings don't allow Maggie to directly modify the shadow file. However, by changing her password, she is able to modify the shadow file. So, what's going on? To answer this, let's go into the /usr/bin/ directory and look at the permissions settings for the passwd executable file:

```
[donnie@localhost etc]$ cd /usr/bin

[donnie@localhost bin]$ ls -l passwd
-rwsr-xr-x. 1 root root 27832 Jun 10 2014 passwd
[donnie@localhost bin]$
```

For the user permissions, you will see rws instead of rwx. The s indicates that this file has the SUID permission set. Since the file belongs to the root user, anyone who accesses this file has the same privileges as the root user. The fact that we see a lowercase s means that the file also has the executable permission set for the root user. Since the root user is allowed to modify the shadow file, whoever uses this passwd utility to change his or her own password can also modify the shadow file.

A file with the SGID permission set has an s in the executable position for the group:

```
[donnie@localhost bin]$ ls -l write
-rwxr-sr-x. 1 root tty 19536 Aug  4 07:18 write
[donnie@localhost bin]$
```

The write utility, which is associated with the tty group, allows users to send messages to other users via their command-line consoles. Having tty group privileges allows users to do this.

The security implications of the SUID and SGID permissions

As useful as it may be to have SUID or SGID permissions on your executable files, we should consider it as just a necessary evil. While having SUID or SGID set on certain operating system files is essential for the operation of your Linux system, it becomes a security risk when users set SUID or SGID on other files.

The problem is that, if intruders find an executable file that belongs to the root user and has the SUID bit set, they can use that to exploit the system. Before they leave, they might leave behind their own root-owned file with an SUID set, which will allow them to easily gain entry to the system the next time they encounter it. If the intruder's SUID file isn't found, the intruder will still have access, even if the original problem has been fixed.

The numerical value for SUID is 4000, and for SGID, it's 2000. To set SUID on a file, you'd just add 4000 to whichever permissions value that you would set otherwise. For example, if you have a file with a permissions value of 755, you'd set SUID by changing the permissions value to 4755. (This would give you read/write/execute access for the user, read/execute for the group, and read/execute for others, with the SUID bit added on.)

Finding spurious SUID or SGID files

One quick security trick is to run the `find` command to take inventory of the SUID and SGID files on your system. You can also save the output to a text file so that you can verify whether anything has been added since you ran the command. Your command will look something like this:

```
sudo find / -type f \( -perm -4000 -o -perm -2000 \) > suid_sgid_files.txt
```

Here's the breakdown:

- `/`: We're searching through the entire filesystem. Since some directories are only accessible to someone with root privileges, we need to use `sudo`.
- `-type f`: This means that we're searching for regular files, which includes executable program files and shell scripts.
- `-perm 4000`: We're searching for files with the 4000, or SUID, permission bit set.
- `-o`: The or operator.
- `-perm 2000`: We're searching for files with the 2000, or SGID, permission bit set.
- `>`: Here, we're redirecting the output into the `suid_sgid_files.txt` text file with the `>` operator.

Note that the two `-perm` items need to be combined into a term that's enclosed in a pair of parentheses. To prevent the Bash shell from interpreting the parenthesis characters incorrectly, we need to escape each one with a backslash. We also need to place a blank space between the first parenthesis character and the first `-perm`, and another between 2000 and the last backslash. Also, the and operator between `-type f` and the `-perm` term is understood to be there, even without inserting `-a`. The text file that you'll create should look something like this:

```
/usr/bin/chfn
/usr/bin/chsh
/usr/bin/chage
/usr/bin/gpasswd
/usr/bin/newgrp
/usr/bin/mount
/usr/bin/su
/usr/bin/umount
```

```
/usr/bin/sudo

. . .

. . .

/usr/lib64/dbus-1/dbus-daemon-launch-helper
```

Optionally, if you want to see details about which files are SUID and which are SGID, you can add the -ls option:

```
sudo find / -type f \( -perm -4000 -o -perm -2000 \) -ls > suid_sgid_files.txt
```

Okay, you're now saying, *Hey, Donnie, this is just too much to type*. And, I hear you. Fortunately, there's a shorthand equivalent of this. Since 4000 + 2000 = 6000, we can create a single expression that will match either the SUID (4000) or the SGID (2000) value, like this:

```
sudo find / -type f -perm /6000 -ls > suid_sgid_files.txt
```

The /6000 in this command means that we're looking for either the 4000 or the 2000 value. For our purposes, these are the only two addends that can combine to make 6000.

> In some older references, you might see +6000 instead of /6000. Using the + sign for this has been deprecated, and no longer works.

Now, let's say that Maggie, for whatever reason, decides to set the SUID bit on a shell script file in her home directory:

```
[maggie@localhost ~]$ chmod 4755 bad_script.sh

[maggie@localhost ~]$ ls -l
total 0
-rwsr-xr-x. 1 maggie maggie 0 Nov  7 13:06 bad_script.sh
[maggie@localhost ~]$
```

Run the find command again, saving the output to a different text file. Then, perform a diff operation on the two files to see what changed:

```
[donnie@localhost ~]$ diff suid_sgid_files.txt suid_sgid_files2.txt
17a18
> /home/maggie/bad_script.sh
[donnie@localhost ~]$
```

The only difference is the addition of Maggie's shell script file.

Hands-on lab — searching for SUID and SGID files

You can perform this lab on either of your virtual machines. You'll save the output of the find command to a text file. Let's get started:

1. Search through the entire filesystem for all the files that have either SUID or SGID set before saving the output to a text file:

```
sudo find / -type f -perm /6000 -ls > suid_sgid_files.txt
```

2. Log into any other user account that you have on the system and create a dummy shell script file. Then, set the SUID permission on that file and log back out and back into your own user account:

```
su - desired_user_account
touch some_shell_script.sh
chmod 4755 some_shell_script.sh
ls -l some_shell_script.sh
exit
```

3. Run the `find` command again, saving the output to a different text file:

```
sudo find / -type f -perm /6000 -ls > suid_sgid_files_2.txt
```

4. View the difference between the two files:

```
diff suid_sgid_files.txt suid_sgid_files_2.txt
```

That's the end of the lab – congratulations!

Preventing SUID and SGID usage on a partition

As we mentioned previously, you don't want users to assign SUID and SGID to files that they create, because of the security risk that it presents. You can prevent SUID and SGID usage on a partition by mounting it with the nosuid option. So, the /etc/fstab file entry for the luks partition that I created in the previous chapter would look like this:

```
/dev/mapper/luks-6cbdce17-48d4-41a1-8f8e-793c0fa7c389 /secrets    xfs   nosuid  0
0
```

Different Linux distributions have different ways of setting up default partition schemes during an operating system's installation. Mostly, the default way of doing business is to have all the directories, except for the /boot/ directory, under the / partition. If you were to set up a custom partition scheme instead, you could have the /home/ directory in its own partition, where you could set the nosuid option. Keep in mind that you don't want to set nosuid for the / partition; otherwise, you'll have an operating system that doesn't function properly.

Using extended file attributes to protect sensitive files

Extended file attributes are another tool that can help you protect sensitive files. They won't keep intruders from accessing your files, but they can help you prevent sensitive files from being altered or deleted. There are quite a few extended attributes, but we only need to look at the ones that deal with file security.

First, let's use the `lsattr` command to see which extended attributes we already have set. On a CentOS or AlmaLinux machine, your output would look something like this:

```
[donnie@localhost ~]$ lsattr
--------------- ./yum_list.txt
--------------- ./perm_demo.txt
--------------- ./perm_demo_dir
--------------- ./donnie_script.sh
--------------- ./suid_sgid_files.txt
--------------- ./suid_sgid_files2.txt
[donnie@localhost ~]$
```

So far, I don't have any extended attributes set on any of my files.

On an Ubuntu machine, the output would look more like this:

```
donnie@ubuntu:~$ lsattr
-------------e-- ./file2.txt
-------------e-- ./secret_stuff_dir
-------------e-- ./secret_stuff_for_frank.txt.gpg
-------------e-- ./good_stuff
-------------e-- ./secret_stuff
-------------e-- ./not_secret_for_frank.txt.gpg
-------------e-- ./file4.txt
-------------e-- ./good_stuff_dir
donnie@ubuntu:~$
```

We won't worry about the e attribute because that only means that the partition is formatted with the ext4 filesystem. CentOS and AlmaLinux don't have that attribute set because their partitions are formatted with the **XFS** filesystem.

The two attributes that we'll look at in this section are as follows:

- a: You can append text to the end of a file that has this attribute, but you can't overwrite it. Only someone with proper sudo privileges can set or delete this attribute.
- i: This makes a file immutable, and only someone with proper sudo privileges can set or delete it. Files with this attribute can't be deleted or changed in any way. It's also not possible to create hard links to files that have this attribute.

To set or delete attributes, you need to use the chattr command. You can set more than one attribute on a file, but only when it makes sense. For example, you wouldn't set both the a and i attributes on the same file because the i will override the a.

Let's start by creating the perm_demo.txt file, which contains the following text:

```
This is Donnie's sensitive file that he doesn't want to have overwritten.
```

Now, let's go ahead and set the attributes.

Setting the a attribute

Now, I'll set the a attribute:

```
[donnie@localhost ~]$ sudo chattr +a perm_demo.txt
[sudo] password for donnie:
[donnie@localhost ~]$
```

You use + to add an attribute and - to delete it. Also, it doesn't matter that the file belongs to me and is in my own home directory. I still need sudo privileges to add or delete this attribute.

Now, let's see what happens when I try to overwrite this file:

```
[donnie@localhost ~]$ echo "I want to overwrite this file." > perm_demo.txt
-bash: perm_demo.txt: Operation not permitted

[donnie@localhost ~]$ sudo echo "I want to overwrite this file." > perm_demo.
txt
-bash: perm_demo.txt: Operation not permitted
[donnie@localhost ~]$
```

With or without sudo privileges, I can't overwrite it. So, how about if I try to append something to it?

```
[donnie@localhost ~]$ echo "I want to append this to the end of the file." >>
perm_demo.txt

[donnie@localhost ~]$
```

There's no error message this time. Let's see what's in the file:

```
This is Donnie's sensitive file that he doesn't want to have overwritten.
I want to append this to the end of the file.
```

In addition to not being able to overwrite the file, I'm also unable to delete it:

```
[donnie@localhost ~]$ rm perm_demo.txt
rm: cannot remove 'perm_demo.txt': Operation not permitted

[donnie@localhost ~]$ sudo rm perm_demo.txt
[sudo] password for donnie:
rm: cannot remove 'perm_demo.txt': Operation not permitted
[donnie@localhost ~]$
```

So, the a works. However, I've decided that I no longer want this attribute to be set, so I'll remove it:

```
[donnie@localhost ~]$ sudo chattr -a perm_demo.txt
[donnie@localhost ~]$ lsattr perm_demo.txt
```

```
---------------- perm_demo.txt
[donnie@localhost ~]$
```

Setting the i attribute

When a file has the i attribute set, the only thing you can do with it is view its contents. You can't change it, move it, delete it, rename it, or create hard links to it. Let's test this with the perm_demo.txt file:

```
[donnie@localhost ~]$ sudo chattr +i perm_demo.txt
[donnie@localhost ~]$ lsattr perm_demo.txt
----i---------- perm_demo.txt
[donnie@localhost ~]$
```

Now for the fun part:

```
[donnie@localhost ~]$ sudo echo "I want to overwrite this file." > perm_demo.
txt
-bash: perm_demo.txt: Permission denied
[donnie@localhost ~]$ echo "I want to append this to the end of the file." >>
perm_demo.txt
-bash: perm_demo.txt: Permission denied
[donnie@localhost ~]$ sudo echo "I want to append this to the end of the file."
>> perm_demo.txt
-bash: perm_demo.txt: Permission denied
[donnie@localhost ~]$ rm -f perm_demo.txt
rm: cannot remove 'perm_demo.txt': Operation not permitted
[donnie@localhost ~]$ sudo rm -f perm_demo.txt
rm: cannot remove 'perm_demo.txt': Operation not permitted
[donnie@localhost ~]$ sudo rm -f perm_demo.txt
```

There are a few more commands that I could try, but you get the idea. To remove the i attribute, do this:

```
[donnie@localhost ~]$ sudo chattr -i perm_demo.txt
[donnie@localhost ~]$ lsattr perm_demo.txt
---------------- perm_demo.txt
[donnie@localhost ~]$
```

Hands-on lab — setting security-related extended file attributes

For this lab, you'll need to create a perm_demo.txt file with some text of your choice. You'll set the i and a attributes and view the results. Let's get started:

1. Using your preferred text editor, create the perm_demo.txt file with a line of text.
2. View the extended attributes of the file:

```
lsattr perm_demo.txt
```

3. Add the a attribute:

```
sudo chattr +a perm_demo.txt
lsattr perm_demo.txt
```

4. Try to overwrite and delete the file:

```
echo "I want to overwrite this file." > perm_demo.txt
sudo echo "I want to overwrite this file." > perm_demo.txt
rm perm_demo.txt
sudo rm perm_demo.txt
```

5. Now, append something to the file:

```
echo "I want to append this line to the end of the file." >> perm_demo.
txt
```

6. Remove the a attribute and add the i attribute:

```
sudo chattr -a perm_demo.txt
lsattr perm_demo.txt
sudo chattr +i perm_demo.txt
lsattr perm_demo.txt
```

7. Repeat *Step 4*.

8. Additionally, try to change the filename and create a hard link to the file:

```
mv perm_demo.txt some_file.txt
sudo mv perm_demo.txt some_file.txt
ln ~/perm_demo.txt ~/some_file.txt
sudo ln ~/perm_demo.txt ~/some_file.txt
```

9. Now, try to create a symbolic link to the file:

```
ln -s ~/perm_demo.txt ~/some_file.txt
```

> Note that the i attribute won't let you create hard links to a file, but it will let you create symbolic links.

That's the end of the lab – congratulations!

Securing system configuration files

If you look at the configuration files for any given Linux distro, you'll see that most of them belong to either the root user or to a specified system user. You'll also see that most of these files have read and write privileges for their respective owners, and read privileges for everyone else. This means that everybody and his brother can read most Linux system configuration files. Take, for example, this Apache web server configuration file:

```
[donnie@donnie-ca ~]$ cd /etc/httpd/conf
[donnie@donnie-ca conf]$ pwd
/etc/httpd/conf
[donnie@donnie-ca conf]$ ls -l httpd.conf
-rw-r--r--. 1 root root 11753 Aug  6 09:44 httpd.conf
[donnie@donnie-ca conf]$
```

With that r in the "others" position, everybody who logs in, regardless of their privilege level, can view the Apache configuration.

So, is this a big deal? It really depends upon your circumstances. Some configuration files, especially ones for certain PHP-based **Content Management Systems** (CMSs) on a web server, can contain plain text passwords that the CMS must be able to access. In these cases, it's quite obvious that you need to restrict access to these configuration files. But what about other configuration files that don't contain sensitive passwords?

For servers that only a chosen few administrators can access, this isn't such a big deal. But what about servers that normal, non-administrative users can access remotely via Secure Shell? If they don't have any sudo privileges, they can't edit any configuration files, but they can view them to see how your server has been configured. If they see how things are configured, would that help them in their efforts to compromise the system, should they choose to do so?

I have to confess, this is something that I hadn't thought much about until recently, when I became a Linux consultant for a company that specializes in the security of **Internet of Things** (IoT) devices. With IoT devices, you have a bit more to worry about than you do with normal servers. Normal servers are protected with a high degree of physical security, while IoT devices often have little to no physical security. You could go your entire IT career without actually seeing a server, unless you're one of the few who have been authorized to enter the inner sanctum of the server room. Conversely, IoT devices are generally out in the open.

The IoT security company that I work with has a set of guidelines that help harden IoT devices against compromise and attack. One of them is to ensure that all the configuration files on the devices are set with the 600 permissions setting. This would mean that only the owner of the files – generally either the root user or a system account – can read them. However, there are a lot of configuration files, and you need an easy way to change the settings. You can do that with our trusty friend, the find utility. Here's how you can do this:

```
sudo find / -iname '*.conf' -exec chmod 600 {} \;
```

Here's the breakdown:

- `sudo find / -iname '*.conf'`: This does exactly what you would expect it to do. It performs a case-insensitive (`-iname`) search throughout the entire root filesystem (`/`) for all the files with the `.conf` filename extension. Other filename extensions you might look for include `.ini` and `.cfg`. Also, because `find` is inherently recursive, you don't have to provide an option switch to get it to search through all the lower-level directories.

- `-exec`: This is what performs the magic. It automatically executes the following command on each file that `find` finds, without prompting the user. If you'd rather answer *yes* or *no* for each file that `find` finds, use -ok instead of -exec.

- `chmod 600 {} \;`: `chmod 600` is the command that we want to perform. As `find` finds each file, its filename is placed within the pair of curly brackets (`{}`). Every `-exec` clause has to end with a semicolon. To prevent the Bash shell from interpreting the semicolon incorrectly, we have to escape it with a backslash.

If you decide to do this, test things thoroughly to ensure that you haven't broken anything. Most things work just fine with their configuration files set to a 600 permissions setting, but some don't. I've just performed this command on one of my virtual machines. Let's see what happens when I try to ping an Internet site:

```
[donnie@donnie-ca ~]$ ping www.civicsandpolitics.com
ping: www.civicsandpolitics.com: Name or service not known
[donnie@donnie-ca ~]$
```

This looks bad, but the explanation is simple. It's just that in order to have Internet access, the machine has to be able to find a DNS server. DNS server information can be found in the `/etc/resolv.conf` file, from which I've just removed read permissions for others. Without the read permissions for others, only someone with root user privileges can access the Internet. So, unless you want to restrict Internet access to users with root or `sudo` privileges, you'll need to change the `resolv.conf` permission setting back to 644:

```
[donnie@donnie-ca etc]$ ls -l resolv.conf
-rw-------. 1 root root 66 Sep 23 14:22 resolv.conf

[donnie@donnie-ca etc]$ sudo chmod 644 resolv.conf
[donnie@donnie-ca etc]$
```

Okay, let's try this again:

```
[donnie@donnie-ca etc]$ ping www.civicsandpolitics.com
PING www.civicsandpolitics.com (64.71.34.94) 56(84) bytes of data.
64 bytes from 64.71.34.94: icmp_seq=1 ttl=51 time=52.1 ms
64 bytes from 64.71.34.94: icmp_seq=2 ttl=51 time=51.8 ms
64 bytes from 64.71.34.94: icmp_seq=3 ttl=51 time=51.2 ms
^C
--- www.civicsandpolitics.com ping statistics ---
```

```
3 packets transmitted, 3 received, 0% packet loss, time 2002ms
rtt min/avg/max/mdev = 51.256/51.751/52.176/0.421 ms
[donnie@donnie-ca etc]$
```

That looks much better. Now, let's reboot the machine. When you do, you'll get this output:

```
donnie-ca login: donnie
Password:
Last login: Wed Jan 11 16:23:49 on tty1
/usr/bin/sed: can't read /etc/locale.conf: Permission denied
[donnie@donnie-ca ~]$
```

Figure 8.1: Wrong permission setting on the locale.conf file

So, I also need to set the /etc/locale.conf file back to the 644 permission setting for the machine to boot properly. As I mentioned previously, be sure to test everything if you choose to set more restrictive permissions on your configuration files.

As I've already stated, you might not always find it necessary to change the permissions of your configuration files from their default settings. But if you ever do find it necessary, you now know how to do it.

> You definitely want to make friends with the find utility. It's useful both on the command line and within shell scripts, and it's extremely flexible. The man page for it is very well-written, and you can learn just about everything you need to know about find from it. To see it, just use the man find command.
>
> Once you get used to find, you'll never want to use any of those fancy GUI-type search utilities again.

Okay, I think that this wraps things up for this chapter.

Summary

In this chapter, we reviewed the basics of setting ownership and permissions for files and directories. Then, we covered what SUID and SGID can do for us when they're used properly, as well as the risk of setting them on our own executable files. After looking at the two extended file attributes that deal with file security, we wrapped things up with a handy, time-saving trick for removing world-readable permissions from your system configuration files.

In the next chapter, we'll extend what we've learned here to more advanced file and directory access techniques. I'll see you there.

Questions

1. Which of the following partition mount options would prevent setting the SUID and SGID permissions on files?

    a. nosgid
    b. noexec

    c.   nosuid

    d.   nouser

2.   Which of the following represents a file with read and write permissions for the user and the group, and read-only permissions for others?

    a.   775

    b.   554

    c.   660

    d.   664

3.   You want to change the ownership and group association of the `somefile.txt` file to Maggie. Which of the following commands would do that?

    a.   `sudo chown maggie somefile.txt`

    b.   `sudo chown :maggie somefile.txt`

    c.   `sudo chown maggie: somefile.txt`

    d.   `sudo chown :maggie: somefile.txt`

4.   Which of the following is the numerical value for the SGID permission?

    a.   6000

    b.   2000

    c.   4000

    d.   1000

5.   Which command would you use to view the extended attributes of a file?

    a.   `lsattr`

    b.   `ls -a`

    c.   `ls -l`

    d.   `chattr`

6.   Which of the following commands would search through the entire filesystem for regular files that have either the SUID or SGID permission set?

    a.   `sudo find / -type f -perm \6000`

    b.   `sudo find / \( -perm -4000 -o -perm -2000 \)`

    c.   `sudo find / -type f -perm -6000`

    d.   `sudo find / -type r -perm \6000`

7.   Which of the following statements is true?

    a.   Using the symbolic method to set permissions is the best method for all cases.

    b.   Using the symbolic method to set permissions is the best method to use in shell scripting.

    c.   Using the numeric method to set permissions is the best method to use in shell scripting.

    d.   It doesn't matter which method you use to set permissions.

8. Which of the following commands would set the SUID permission on a file that has read/write/execute permissions for the user and group, and read/execute permissions for others?

    a. `sudo chmod 2775 somefile`

    b. `sudo chown 2775 somefile`

    c. `sudo chmod 1775 somefile`

    d. `sudo chmod 4775 somefile`

9. Which of the following functions is served by setting the SUID permission on an executable file?

    a. It allows any user to use that file.

    b. It prevents accidental erasure of the file.

    c. It allows "others" to have the same privileges as the "user" of the file.

    d. It allows "others" to have the same privileges as the group that's associated with the file.

10. Why shouldn't users set the SUID or SGID permissions on their own regular files?

    a. It unnecessarily uses more hard drive space.

    b. It could prevent someone from deleting the files if needed.

    c. It could allow someone to alter the files.

    d. It could allow an intruder to compromise the system.

11. Which of the following `find` command options allows you to automatically perform a command on each file that `find` finds, without being prompted?

    a. `-exec`

    b. `-ok`

    c. `-xargs`

    d. `-do`

12. For the best security, always use the `600` permission setting for every `.conf` file on the system.

    a. True

    b. False

13. Which of the following is a true statement?

    a. Prevent users from setting SUID on files by mounting the / partition with the `nosuid` option.

    b. You must have the SUID permission set on certain system files for the operating system to function properly.

    c. Executable files must never have the SUID permission set.

    d. Executable files should always have the SUID permission set.

14. Which two of the following are security concerns for configuration files?

    a. With a default configuration, any normal user with command-line access can edit configuration files.

    b. Certain configuration files may contain sensitive information.

    c. With a default configuration, any normal user with command-line access can view configuration files.

    d. The configuration files on servers require more protection than the configuration files on IoT devices.

Further reading

- How to find files with SUID and SGID permissions in Linux: `https://www.tecmint.com/how-to-find-files-with-suid-and-sgid-permissions-in-linux/`
- Linux permissions: SUID, SGID, and sticky bit: `https://www.redhat.com/sysadmin/suid-sgid-sticky-bit`
- The Linux `find` command: `https://youtu.be/tCemsQ_ZjQ0`
- Linux and Unix file permissions: `https://youtu.be/K9FEz20Zhmc`
- Linux file permissions: `https://www.linux.com/tutorials/understanding-linux-file-permissions/`
- 25 simple examples of the Linux `find` command: `https://www.binarytides.com/linux-find-command-examples/`
- 35 practical examples of the Linux `find` command: `https://www.tecmint.com/35-practical-examples-of-linux-find-command/`

Answers

1. c
2. d
3. c
4. b
5. a
6. a
7. c
8. d
9. c
10. d
11. a
12. b
13. b
14. b and c

Join our book community

Join our community's Discord space for discussions with the author and other readers:

https://packt.link/CyberSec

9

Access Control Lists and Shared Directory Management

In the previous chapter, we reviewed the basics of **Discretionary Access Control (DAC)**. Normal Linux file and directory permissions settings aren't very granular. With an **access control list** (ACL), we can fine-tune things to get the exact set of permissions that we really want. We can also use this capability to control access to files in shared directories.

The topics in this chapter include the following:

- Creating an ACL for either a user or a group
- Creating an inherited ACL for a directory
- Removing a specific permission by using an ACL mask
- Using the `tar --acls` option to prevent loss of ACLs during a backup
- Creating a user group and adding members to it
- Creating a shared directory for a group
- Setting the SGID bit and the sticky bit on the shared directory
- Using ACLs to access files in the shared directory

Creating an ACL for either a user or a group

The normal Linux file and directory permissions settings are okay, but they're not very granular. With an ACL, we can allow only a certain person to access a file or directory, or we can allow multiple people to access a file or directory with different permissions for each person. If we have a file or a directory that's wide open for everyone, we can use an ACL to allow different levels of access for either a group or an individual. Toward the end of the chapter, we'll put what we've learned all together in order to manage a shared directory for a group.

You would use getfacl to view an ACL for a file or directory. (Note that you can't use it to view all files in a directory at once.) To begin, let's use getfacl to see if we have any ACLs already set on the acl_demo.txt file:

```
[donnie@localhost ~]$ touch acl_demo.txt

[donnie@localhost ~]$ getfacl acl_demo.txt
# file: acl_demo.txt
# owner: Donnie
# group: Donnie
user::rw-
group::rw-
other::r--

[donnie@localhost ~]$
```

All we see here are just the normal permissions settings, so there's no ACL.

The first step for setting an ACL is to remove all permissions from everyone except for the user of the file. That's because the default permissions settings allow members of the group to have read/write access, and others to have read access. So, setting an ACL without removing those permissions would be rather senseless:

```
[donnie@localhost ~]$ chmod 600 acl_demo.txt

[donnie@localhost ~]$ ls -l acl_demo.txt
-rw-------. 1 donnie donnie 0 Nov  9 14:37 acl_demo.txt
[donnie@localhost ~]$
```

When using setfacl to set an ACL, you can allow a user or a group to have any combination of read, write, or execute privileges. In our case, let's say that I want to let Maggie read the file and to prevent her from having write or execute privileges:

```
[donnie@localhost ~]$ setfacl -m u:maggie:r acl_demo.txt

[donnie@localhost ~]$ getfacl acl_demo.txt
# file: acl_demo.txt
# owner: Donnie
# group: Donnie
user::rw-
user:maggie:r--
group::---
mask::r--
other::---
```

```
[donnie@localhost ~]$ ls -l acl_demo.txt
-rw-r-----+ 1 donnie donnie 0 Nov  9 14:37 acl_demo.txt
[donnie@localhost ~]$
```

The -m option of setfacl means that we're about to modify the ACL. (Well, to *create* one in this case, but that's okay.) u: means that we're setting an ACL for a user. We then list the user's name, followed by another colon, and the list of permissions that we want to grant to this user. In this case, we're only allowing Maggie read access. We complete the command by listing the file to which we want to apply this ACL. The getfacl output shows that Maggie does indeed have read access. Finally, we see in the ls -l output that the group is listed as having read access, even though we've set the 600 permissions settings on this file. But, there's also a + sign, which tells us that the file has an ACL. When we set an ACL, the permissions for the ACL show up as group permissions in ls -l.

To take this a step further, let's say that I want Frank to have read/write access to this file:

```
[donnie@localhost ~]$ setfacl -m u:frank:rw acl_demo.txt

[donnie@localhost ~]$ getfacl acl_demo.txt
# file: acl_demo.txt
# owner: Donnie
# group: Donnie
user::rw-
user:maggie:r-
user:frank:rw-
group::---
mask::rw-
other::---

[donnie@localhost ~]$ ls -l acl_demo.txt
-rw-rw----+ 1 donnie donnie 0 Nov  9 14:37 acl_demo.txt
[donnie@localhost ~]$
```

So, we can have two or more different ACLs assigned to the same file. In the ls -l output, we see that we have rw permissions set for the group, which is really just a summary of permissions that we've set in the two ACLs.

We can set an ACL for group access by replacing u: with a g::

```
[donnie@localhost ~]$ getfacl new_file.txt
# file: new_file.txt
# owner: Donnie
# group: Donnie
user::rw-
group::rw-
other::r-
```

```
[donnie@localhost ~]$ chmod 600 new_file.txt

[donnie@localhost ~]$ setfacl -m g:accounting:r new_file.txt

[donnie@localhost ~]$ getfacl new_file.txt
# file: new_file.txt
# owner: Donnie
# group: Donnie
user::rw-
group::---
group:accounting:r—
mask::r—
other::---

[donnie@localhost ~]$ ls -l new_file.txt
-rw-r-----+ 1 donnie donnie 0 Nov  9 15:06 new_file.txt
[donnie@localhost ~]$
```

Members of the accounting group now have read access to this file.

Creating an inherited ACL for a directory

There may be times when you'll want all files that get created in a shared directory to have the same ACL. We can do that by applying an inherited ACL to the directory. Although, understand that even though this sounds like a cool idea, creating files in the normal way will cause files to have the read/write permissions set for the group, and the read permission set for others. So, if you're setting this up for a directory where users just create files normally, the best that you can hope to do is to create an ACL that adds either the write or execute permissions for someone. Either that or ensure that users set the 600 permissions settings on all files that they create, assuming that users really do need to restrict access to their files.

On the other hand, if you're creating a shell script that creates files in a specific directory, you can include chmod commands to ensure that the files get created with the restrictive permissions that are necessary to make your ACL work as intended.

To demo, let's create the new_perm_dir directory, and set the inherited ACL on it. I want to have read/write access for files that my shell script creates in this directory, and for Frank to only have read access. I don't want anyone else to be able to read any of these files:

```
[donnie@localhost ~]$ setfacl -m d:u:frank:r new_perm_dir

[donnie@localhost ~]$ ls -ld new_perm_dir
drwxrwxr-x+ 2 donnie donnie 26 Nov 12 13:16 new_perm_dir
[donnie@localhost ~]$ getfacl new_perm_dir
```

```
# file: new_perm_dir
# owner: Donnie
# group: Donnie
user::rwx
group::rwx
other::r-x
default:user::rwx
default:user:frank:r—
default:group::rwx
default:mask::rwx
default:other::r-x

[donnie@localhost ~]$
```

All I had to do to make this an inherited ACL was to add `d:` before `u:frank`. I left the default permissions settings on the directory, which allows everyone read access to the directory. Next, I'll create the `donnie_script.sh` shell script, which will create a file within that directory, and that will set read/write permissions for only the user of the new files:

```
#!/bin/bash
cd new_perm_dir
touch new_file.txt
chmod 600 new_file.txt
exit
```

After making the script executable, I'll run it and view the results:

```
[donnie@localhost ~]$ ./donnie_script.sh

[donnie@localhost ~]$ cd new_perm_dir

[donnie@localhost new_perm_dir]$ ls -l
total 0
-rw-------+ 1 donnie donnie 0 Nov 12 13:16 new_file.txt
[donnie@localhost new_perm_dir]$ getfacl new_file.txt
# file: new_file.txt
# owner: Donnie
# group: Donnie
user::rw-
user:frank:r-- #effective:---
group::rwx #effective:---
mask::---
other::---
```

```
[donnie@localhost new_perm_dir]$
```

So, `new_file.txt` got created with the correct permissions settings, and with an ACL that allows Frank to read it. (I know that this is a really simplified example, but you get the idea.)

Removing a specific permission by using an ACL mask

You can remove an ACL from a file or directory with the -x option. Let's go back to the `acl_demo.txt` file that I created earlier, and remove the ACL for Maggie:

```
[donnie@localhost ~]$ setfacl -x u:maggie acl_demo.txt

[donnie@localhost ~]$ getfacl acl_demo.txt
# file: acl_demo.txt
# owner: Donnie
# group: Donnie
user::rw-
user:frank:rw-
group::---
mask::rw-
other::---

[donnie@localhost ~]$
```

So, Maggie's ACL is gone. But, the -x option removes the entire ACL, even if that's not what you really want. If you have an ACL with multiple permissions set, you might just want to remove one permission, leaving the others. Here, we see that Frank still has his ACL that grants him read/write access. Let's now say that we want to remove the write permission, while still allowing him the read permission. For that, we'll need to apply a mask:

```
[donnie@localhost ~]$ setfacl -m m::r acl_demo.txt

[donnie@localhost ~]$ ls -l acl_demo.txt

-rw-r-----+ 1 donnie donnie 0 Nov  9 14:37 acl_demo.txt
[donnie@localhost ~]$ getfacl acl_demo.txt
# file: acl_demo.txt
# owner: Donnie
# group: Donnie
user::rw-
user:frank:rw-                 #effective:r-
group::---
```

```
    mask::r—
    other::---

[donnie@localhost ~]$
```

m::r sets a read-only mask on the ACL. Running getfacl shows that Frank still has a read/write ACL, but the comment to the side shows his effective permissions to be read-only. So, Frank's write permission for the file is now gone. And, if we had ACLs set for other users, this mask would affect them the same way.

Using the tar --acls option to prevent the loss of ACLs during a backup

The tar utility is a very handy tool for creating compressed archive files of your important directories. The only catch is that when you use it on files that have attached ACLs, you'll need to use the --acls option to prevent the loss of your ACLs. In this directory, you see that ACLs have been assigned to the bottom two files:

```
[donnie@localhost ~]$ cd perm_demo_dir
[donnie@localhost perm_demo_dir]$ ls -l
total 0
-rw-rw-r--. 1 donnie accounting 0 Nov  5 20:17 file1.txt
-rw-rw-r--. 1 donnie accounting 0 Nov  5 20:17 file2.txt
-rw-rw-r--. 1 donnie accounting 0 Nov  5 20:17 file3.txt
-rw-rw-r--. 1 donnie accounting 0 Nov  5 20:17 file4.txt
-rw-rw----+ 1 donnie donnie     0 Nov  9 15:19 frank_file.txt
-rw-rw----+ 1 donnie donnie     0 Nov 12 12:29 new_file.txt
[donnie@localhost perm_demo_dir]$
```

Now, I'll do the backup without --acls:

```
[donnie@localhost perm_demo_dir]$ cd
[donnie@localhost ~]$ tar cJvf perm_demo_dir_backup.tar.xz perm_demo_dir/
perm_demo_dir/
perm_demo_dir/file1.txt
perm_demo_dir/file2.txt
perm_demo_dir/file3.txt
perm_demo_dir/file4.txt
perm_demo_dir/frank_file.txt
perm_demo_dir/new_file.txt
[donnie@localhost ~]$
```

It looks good, right? Ah, but looks can be deceiving. Watch what happens when I delete the directory, and then restore it from the backup:

```
[donnie@localhost ~]$ rm -rf perm_demo_dir/

[donnie@localhost ~]$ tar xJvf perm_demo_dir_backup.tar.xz
perm_demo_dir/
. . .
[donnie@localhost ~]$ cd perm_demo_dir/
[donnie@localhost perm_demo_dir]$ ls -l
total 0
-rw-rw-r--. 1 donnie donnie 0 Nov 5 20:17 file1.txt
-rw-rw-r--. 1 donnie donnie 0 Nov 5 20:17 file2.txt
-rw-rw-r--. 1 donnie donnie 0 Nov 5 20:17 file3.txt
-rw-rw-r--. 1 donnie donnie 0 Nov 5 20:17 file4.txt
-rw-rw----. 1 donnie donnie 0 Nov 9 15:19 frank_file.txt
-rw-rw----. 1 donnie donnie 0 Nov 12 12:29 new_file.txt
[donnie@localhost perm_demo_dir]$
```

I don't even have to use getfacl to see that the ACLs are gone from the perm_demo_dir directory and all of its files, because the + signs are now gone. Now, let's see what happens when I include the --acls option. First, I'll show you that an ACL is set for this directory and its only file:

```
[donnie@localhost ~]$ ls -ld new_perm_dir
drwxrwxr-x+ 2 donnie donnie 26 Nov 13 14:01 new_perm_dir

[donnie@localhost ~]$ ls -l new_perm_dir
total 0
-rw-------+ 1 donnie donnie 0 Nov 13 14:01 new_file.txt
[donnie@localhost ~]$
```

Now, I'll use the tar command with the --acls option:

```
[donnie@localhost ~]$ tar cJvf new_perm_dir_backup.tar.xz new_perm_dir/ --acls
new_perm_dir/
new_perm_dir/new_file.txt
[donnie@localhost ~]$
```

I'll now delete the new_perm_dir directory and restore it from backup. As we did before, we'll use the --acls option:

```
[donnie@localhost ~]$ rm -rf new_perm_dir/

[donnie@localhost ~]$ tar xJvf new_perm_dir_backup.tar.xz —acls
new_perm_dir/
new_perm_dir/new_file.txt

[donnie@localhost ~]$ ls -ld new_perm_dir
drwxrwxr-x+ 2 donnie donnie 26 Nov 13 14:01 new_perm_dir

[donnie@localhost ~]$ ls -l new_perm_dir
total 0
-rw-------+ 1 donnie donnie 0 Nov 13 14:01 new_file.txt
[donnie@localhost ~]$
```

The presence of the + signs indicates that the ACLs did survive the backup-and-restore procedure. The one slightly tricky part about this is that you must use `--acls` for both the backup and the restoration. If you omit the option either time, you will lose your ACLs.

> You might be wondering if your preferred backup or archive tool needs any special options set in order to preserve ACLs. Well, I don't know, because it's impossible for me to investigate everything that's available. If you need to backup or archive files that have ACLs set, your best bet is to consult the documentation for your archive or backup software.

Next, let's talk at about user groups.

Creating a user group and adding members to it

So far, I've been doing all of the demos inside my own home directory, just for the sake of showing the basic concepts. But the eventual goal is to show you how to use this knowledge to do something more practical, such as controlling file access in shared directories.

Let's say that we want to create a marketing group for members of—you guessed it—the marketing department:

```
[donnie@localhost ~]$ sudo groupadd marketing
[sudo] password for donnie:
[donnie@localhost ~]$
```

Let's now add some members. We can do that in three different ways:

- Add members as we create their user accounts.
- Use usermod to add members that already have user accounts.
- Edit the /etc/group file.

Adding members as we create their user accounts

First, we can add members to the group as we create their user accounts, using the -G option of useradd. On Red Hat, AlmaLinux, or CentOS, the command would look like this:

```
[donnie@localhost ~]$ sudo useradd -G marketing cleopatra
[sudo] password for donnie:

[donnie@localhost ~]$ groups cleopatra
cleopatra : cleopatra marketing
[donnie@localhost ~]$
```

On Debian/Ubuntu, the command would look like this:

```
donnie@ubuntu3:~$ sudo useradd -m -d /home/cleopatra -s /bin/bash -G marketing
cleopatra

donnie@ubuntu3:~$ groups cleopatra
cleopatra : cleopatra marketing
donnie@ubuntu3:~$
```

And, of course, I'll need to assign Cleopatra a password in the normal manner:

```
[donnie@localhost ~]$ sudo passwd cleopatra
```

Using usermod to add an existing user to a group

The good news is that this works the same on either Red Hat/CentOS/AlmaLinux or Debian/Ubuntu:

```
[donnie@localhost ~]$ sudo usermod -a -G marketing maggie
[sudo] password for donnie:

[donnie@localhost ~]$ groups Maggie
maggie : maggie marketing
[donnie@localhost ~]$
```

In this case, the -a wasn't necessary, because Maggie wasn't a member of any other secondary group. But, if she had already belonged to another group, the -a would have been necessary to keep from overwriting any existing group information, thus removing her from the previous groups.

This method is especially handy for use on Ubuntu systems, where it is necessary to use adduser in order to create encrypted home directories. (As we saw in a previous chapter, adduser doesn't give you the chance to add a user to a group as you create the account.)

Adding users to a group by editing the /etc/group file

This final method is a good way to cheat to speed up the process of adding multiple existing users to a group. First, open the /etc/group file in your favorite text editor, and look for the line that defines the group to which you want to add members:

```
. . .
marketing:x:1005:cleopatra,Maggie
. . .
```

So, I've already added Cleopatra and Maggie to this group. Let's edit this to add a couple more members:

```
. . .
marketing:x:1005:cleopatra,maggie,vicky,Charlie
. . .
```

When you're done, save the file and exit the editor.

A groups command for each of them will show that our wee bit of cheating works just fine:

```
[donnie@localhost etc]$ sudo vim group
[donnie@localhost etc]$ groups vicky
vicky : vicky marketing

[donnie@localhost etc]$ groups charlie
charlie : charlie marketing
[donnie@localhost etc]$
```

This method is extremely handy for whenever you need to add lots of members to a group at the same time.

Creating a shared directory

The next act in our scenario involves creating a shared directory that all the members of our marketing department can use. Now, this is another one of those areas that engenders a bit of controversy. Some people like to put shared directories in the root level of the filesystem, while others like to put shared directories in the /home/ directory. Some people even have other preferences. But really, it's a matter of personal preference and/or company policy. Other than that, it really doesn't much matter where you put them. For our purposes, to make things simple, I'll just create the directory in the root level of the filesystem:

```
[donnie@localhost ~]$ cd /

[donnie@localhost /]$ sudo mkdir marketing
[sudo] password for donnie:

[donnie@localhost /]$ ls -ld marketing
drwxr-xr-x. 2 root root 6 Nov 13 15:32 marketing
[donnie@localhost /]$
```

The new directory belongs to the root user. It has a permissions setting of 755, which permits read and execute access to everybody, and write access only to the root user. What we really want is to only allow members of the marketing department to access this directory. We'll first change ownership and group association, and then we'll set the proper permissions:

```
[donnie@localhost /]$ sudo chown nobody:marketing marketing

[donnie@localhost /]$ sudo chmod 770 marketing

[donnie@localhost /]$ ls -ld marketing
drwxrwx---. 2 nobody marketing 6 Nov 13 15:32 marketing
[donnie@localhost /]$
```

In this case, we don't have any one particular user that we want to own the directory, and we don't really want the root user to own it. So, assigning ownership to the nobody pseudo-user account gives us a way to deal with that. I then assigned the 770 permissions value to the directory, which allows read/write/execute access to all marketing group members, while keeping everyone else out. Now, let's let one of our group members log in to see if she can create a file in this directory:

```
[donnie@localhost /]$ su - vicky
Password:

[vicky@localhost ~]$ cd /marketing

[vicky@localhost marketing]$ touch vicky_file.txt

[vicky@localhost marketing]$ ls -l
total 0
-rw-rw-r--. 1 vicky vicky 0 Nov 13 15:41 vicky_file.txt
[vicky@localhost marketing]$
```

Okay, it works, except for one minor problem. The file belongs to Vicky, as it should. But, it's also associated with Vicky's personal group. For the best access control of these shared files, we need them to be associated with the marketing group. Let's take care of that next.

Setting the SGID bit and the sticky bit on the shared directory

I've told you before that it's a bit of a security risk to set either the SUID or SGID permissions on files, especially on executable files. But it is both completely safe and very useful to set SGID on a shared directory.

SGID behavior on a directory is completely different from SGID behavior on a file. On a directory, SGID will cause any files that anybody creates to be associated with the same group with which the directory is associated.

So, bearing in mind that the SGID permission value is 2000, let's set SGID on our marketing directory:

```
[donnie@localhost /]$ sudo chmod 2770 marketing
[sudo] password for donnie:

[donnie@localhost /]$ ls -ld marketing
drwxrws---. 2 nobody marketing 28 Nov 13 15:41 marketing
[donnie@localhost /]$
```

The s in the executable position for the group indicates that the command was successful. Let's now let Vicky log back in to create another file:

```
[donnie@localhost /]$ su - Vicky
Password:
Last login: Mon Nov 13 15:41:19 EST 2017 on pts/0

[vicky@localhost ~]$ cd /marketing

[vicky@localhost marketing]$ touch vicky_file_2.txt

[vicky@localhost marketing]$ ls -l
total 0
-rw-rw-r--. 1 vicky marketing 0 Nov 13 15:57 vicky_file_2.txt
-rw-rw-r--. 1 vicky vicky     0 Nov 13 15:41 vicky_file.txt
[vicky@localhost marketing]$
```

Vicky's second file is associated with the marketing group, which is just what we want. Just for fun, let's let Charlie do the same:

```
[donnie@localhost /]$ su - Charlie
Password:

[charlie@localhost ~]$ cd /marketing

[charlie@localhost marketing]$ touch charlie_file.txt

[charlie@localhost marketing]$ ls -l
total 0
-rw-rw-r--. 1 charlie marketing 0 Nov 13 15:59 charlie_file.txt
-rw-rw-r--. 1 vicky   marketing 0 Nov 13 15:57 vicky_file_2.txt
-rw-rw-r--. 1 vicky   vicky     0 Nov 13 15:41 vicky_file.txt
[charlie@localhost marketing]$
```

Again, Charlie's file is associated with the `marketing` group. But, for some strange reason that nobody understands, Charlie really doesn't like Vicky and decides to delete her files, just out of pure spite:

```
[charlie@localhost marketing]$ rm vicky*
rm: remove write-protected regular empty file 'vicky_file.txt'? y

[charlie@localhost marketing]$ ls -l
total 0
-rw-rw-r--. 1 charlie marketing 0 Nov 13 15:59 charlie_file.txt
[charlie@localhost marketing]$
```

The system complains that Vicky's original file is write-protected since it's still associated with her personal group. But the system does still allow Charlie to delete it, even without `sudo` privileges. And, since Charlie has write access to the second file, due to its association with the `marketing` group, the system allows him to delete it without question.

Okay. So, Vicky complains about this and tries to get Charlie fired. But our intrepid administrator has a better idea. He'll just set the sticky bit in order to keep this from happening again. Since the SGID bit has a value of `2000` and the sticky bit has a value of `1000`, we can just add the two together to get a value of `3000`:

```
[donnie@localhost /]$ sudo chmod 3770 marketing
[sudo] password for donnie:

[donnie@localhost /]$ ls -ld marketing
drwxrws--T. 2 nobody marketing 30 Nov 13 16:03 marketing
[donnie@localhost /]$
```

The `T` in the executable position for others indicates that the sticky bit has been set. Since the `T` is uppercase, we know that the executable permission for others has not been set. Having the sticky bit set will prevent group members from deleting anybody else's files. Let's let Vicky show us what happens when she tries to retaliate against Charlie:

```
[donnie@localhost /]$ su - vicky
Password:
Last login: Mon Nov 13 15:57:41 EST 2017 on pts/0

[vicky@localhost ~]$ cd /marketing

[vicky@localhost marketing]$ ls -l
total 0
-rw-rw-r--. 1 charlie marketing 0 Nov 13 15:59 charlie_file.txt

[vicky@localhost marketing]$ rm charlie_file.txt
rm: cannot remove 'charlie_file.txt': Operation not permitted
```

```
[vicky@localhost marketing]$ rm -f charlie_file.txt
rm: cannot remove 'charlie_file.txt': Operation not permitted

[vicky@localhost marketing]$ ls -l
total 0
-rw-rw-r--. 1 charlie marketing 0 Nov 13 15:59 charlie_file.txt
[vicky@localhost marketing]$
```

Even with the -f option, Vicky still can't delete Charlie's file. Vicky doesn't have sudo privileges on this system, so it would be useless for her to try that.

Using ACLs to access files in the shared directory

As things currently stand, all members of the marketing group have read/write access to all other group members' files. Restricting access to a file to only specific group members is the same two-step process that we've already covered.

Setting the permissions and creating the ACL

First, Vicky sets the normal permissions to only allow herself to have read/write permissions on the file. Then, she'll create an ACL that will allow Cleopatra to read the file:

```
[vicky@localhost marketing]$ echo "This file is only for my good friend,
Cleopatra." > vicky_file.txt

[vicky@localhost marketing]$ chmod 600 vicky_file.txt

[vicky@localhost marketing]$ setfacl -m u:cleopatra:r vicky_file.txt

[vicky@localhost marketing]$ ls -l
total 4
-rw-rw-r--. 1 charlie marketing 0 Nov 13 15:59 charlie_file.txt
-rw-r-----+ 1 vicky marketing 49 Nov 13 16:24 vicky_file.txt

[vicky@localhost marketing]$ getfacl vicky_file.txt
# file: vicky_file.txt
# owner: vicky
# group: marketing
user::rw-
user:cleopatra:r--
group::---
mask::r--
other::---
```

```
[vicky@localhost marketing]$
```

There's nothing here that you haven't already seen. Vicky just removed all permissions from the group and from others and set an ACL that only allows Cleopatra to read the file. Let's see if Cleopatra actually can read it:

```
[donnie@localhost /]$ su - cleopatra
Password:


[cleopatra@localhost ~]$ cd /marketing


[cleopatra@localhost marketing]$ ls -l
total 4
-rw-rw-r--. 1 charlie marketing 0 Nov 13 15:59 charlie_file.txt
-rw-r-----+ 1 vicky marketing 49 Nov 13 16:24 vicky_file.txt


[cleopatra@localhost marketing]$ cat vicky_file.txt
This file is only for my good friend, Cleopatra.
[cleopatra@localhost marketing]$
```

So far, so good. But, can Cleopatra write to it? Let's take a look:

```
[cleopatra@localhost marketing]$ echo "You are my friend too, Vicky." >> vicky_
file.txt
-bash: vicky_file.txt: Permission denied
[cleopatra@localhost marketing]$
```

Cleopatra can't do that since Vicky only allowed her the read privilege in the ACL.

Now though, what about that sneaky Charlie, who wants to go snooping in other users' files? Let's see if Charlie can do it:

```
[donnie@localhost /]$ su - charlie
Password:
Last login: Mon Nov 13 15:58:56 EST 2017 on pts/0


[charlie@localhost ~]$ cd /marketing


[charlie@localhost marketing]$ cat vicky_file.txt
cat: vicky_file.txt: Permission denied
[charlie@localhost marketing]$
```

So yes, it's really true that only Cleopatra can access Vicky's file, and even then only for reading.

Hands-on lab — creating a shared group directory

For this lab, you'll just put together everything that you've learned in this chapter to create a shared directory for a group. You can do this on any of your virtual machines:

1. On any virtual machine, create the sales group:

```
sudo groupadd sales
```

2. Create the users mimi, mrgray, and mommy, adding them to the sales group as you create the accounts.

   On CentOS or AlamaLinux, do this:

```
sudo useradd -G sales mimi
sudo useradd -G sales mrgray
sudo useradd -G sales mommy
```

   On Ubuntu, do this:

```
sudo useradd -m -d /home/mimi -s /bin/bash -G sales mimi
sudo useradd -m -d /home/mrgray -s /bin/bash -G sales mrgray
sudo useradd -m -d /home/mommy -s /bin/bash -G sales mommy
```

3. Assign each user a password.

4. Create the sales directory in the root level of the filesystem. Set proper ownership and permissions, including the SGID and sticky bits:

```
sudo mkdir /sales
sudo chown nobody:sales /sales
sudo chmod 3770 /sales
ls -ld /sales
```

5. Log in as Mimi, and have her create a file:

```
su - mimi
cd /sales
echo "This file belongs to Mimi." > mimi_file.txt
ls -l
```

6. Have Mimi set an ACL on her file, allowing only Mr. Gray to read it. Then, have Mimi log back out:

```
chmod 600 mimi_file.txt
setfacl -m u:mrgray:r mimi_file.txt
getfacl mimi_file.txt
ls -l
exit
```

7. Have Mr. Gray log in to see what he can do with Mimi's file. Then, have Mr. Gray create his own file and log back out:

```
su - mrgray
cd /sales
cat mimi_file.txt
echo "I want to add something to this file." >> mimi_file.txt
echo "Mr. Gray will now create his own file." > mr_gray_file.txt

ls -l
exit
```

8. Mommy will now log in and try to wreak havoc by snooping in other users' files and by trying to delete them:

```
su - mommy
cat mimi_file.txt
cat mr_gray_file.txt
rm -f mimi_file.txt
rm -f mr_gray_file.txt
exit
```

9. End of lab.

Summary

In this chapter, we saw how to take DAC to the proverbial next level. We first saw how to create and manage ACLs to provide more fine-grained access control over files and directories. We then saw how to create a user group for a specific purpose, and how to add members to it. Then, we saw how we can use the SGID bit, the sticky bit, and ACLs to manage a shared group directory.

But sometimes, DAC might not be enough to do the job. For those times, we also have mandatory access control, which we'll cover in the next chapter. I'll see you there.

Questions

1. When creating an ACL for a file in a shared directory, what must you first do to make the ACL effective?

    a. Remove all normal permissions from the file for everyone except for the user.

    b. Ensure that the file has the permissions value of 644 set.

    c. Ensure that everyone in the group has read/write permissions for the file.

    d. Ensure that the SUID permission is set for the file.

2. What is the benefit of setting the SGID permission on a shared group directory?

    a. None. It's a security risk and should never be done.

    b. It prevents members of the group from deleting each others' files.

    c. It makes it so that each file that ges created within the directory will be associated with the group that's also associated with the directory.

    d. It gives anyone who accesses the directory the same privileges as the user of the directory.

3. Which of the following commands would set the proper permissions for the `marketing` shared group directory, with the SGID and sticky bit set?

    a. `sudo chmod 6770 marketing`

    b. `sudo chmod 3770 marketing`

    c. `sudo chmod 2770 marketing`

    d. `sudo chmod 1770 marketing`

4. Which of the following `setfacl` options would you use to remove just one specific permission from an ACL?

    a. `-xB. -r`

    b. `-w`

    c. `m: :`

    d. `-m`

    e. `x: :`

5. Which of the following statements is true?

    a. When using `tar`, you must use the `--acls` option for both archive creation and extraction in order to preserve the ACLs on the archived files.

    b. When using `tar`, you need to use the `--acls` option only for archive creation in order to preserve the ACLs on the archived files.

    c. When using `tar`, ACLs are automatically preserved on archived files.

    d. When using `tar`, it's not possible to preserve ACLs on archived files.

6. Which two of the following are *not* valid methods for adding the user Lionel to the `sales` group?

    a. `sudo useradd -g sales lionel`

    b. `sudo useradd -G sales lionel`

    c. `sudo usermod -g sales lionel`

    d. `sudo usermod -G sales lionel`

    e. By hand-editing the `/etc/group` file

7. What happens when you create an inherited ACL?

    a. Every file that gets created in the directory with that inherited ACL will be associated with the group that's associated with that directory.

    b. Every file that gets created in the directory with that inherited ACL will inherit that ACL.

    c. Every file that gets created in that directory with that inherited ACL will have the same permissions settings as the directory.

    d. Every file that gets created in that directory will have the sticky bit set.

8. Which of the following commands would you use to grant read-only privilege on a file to the user Frank?

    a. `chattr -m u:frank:r somefile.txt`

    b. `aclmod -m u:frank:r somefile.txt`

    c. `getfacl -m u:frank:r somefile.txt`

    d. `setfacl -m u:frank:r somefile.txt`

9. You've just done an `ls -l` command in a shared group directory. How can you tell from that whether an ACL has been set for any of the files?

    a. Files with an ACL set will have + at the beginning of the permissions settings.

    b. Files with an ACL set will have - at the beginning of the permissions settings.

    c. Files with an ACL set will have + at the end of the permissions settings.

    d. Files with an ACL set will have - at the end of the permissions settings.

    e. The `ls -l` command will show the ACL for that file.

10. Which of the following would you use to view the ACL on the `somefile.txt` file?

    a. `getfacl somefile.txt`

    b. `ls -l somefile.txt`

    c. `ls -a somefile.txt`

    d. `viewacl somefile.txt`

Further reading

- *How to create users and groups from the Linux command line*: `https://www.techrepublic.com/article/how-to-create-users-and-groups-in-linux-from-the-command-line/`
- Add a user to a group: `https://www.howtogeek.com/50787/add-a-user-to-a-group-or-second-group-on-linux/`
- SGID on directories: `https://www.toptip.ca/2010/03/linux-setgid-on-directory.html`
- What a sticky bit is and how to set it in Linux: `https://www.linuxnix.com/sticky-bit-set-linux/`

Answers

1. a
2. c
3. b
4. d
5. a
6. a and c
7. b
8. d
9. c
10. a

Join our book community

Join our community's Discord space for discussions with the author and other readers:

```
https://packt.link/CyberSec
```

Section 3

Advanced System Hardening Techniques

This section will teach you how to harden a Linux system with **Mandatory Access Control (MAC)**, *security profiles, and process isolation techniques. Audit a Linux system with* auditd *and logging services.*

The section contains the following chapters:

10

Implementing Mandatory Access Control with SELinux and AppArmor

As we saw in previous chapters, **Discretionary Access Control (DAC)** allows users to control who can access their own files and directories. But what if your company needs to have more administrative control over who accesses what? For this, we need some sort of **Mandatory Access Control (MAC)**.

The best way I know to explain the difference between DAC and MAC is to hearken back to my Navy days. I was riding submarines at the time, and I had to have a Top Secret clearance to do my job. With DAC, I had the physical ability to take one of my Top Secret books to the mess decks, and hand it to a cook who didn't have that level of clearance. With MAC, there were rules that prevented me from doing so. On operating systems, things work pretty much the same way.

There are several different MAC systems that are available for Linux. The two that we'll cover in this chapter are SELinux and AppArmor. We'll look at what both of them are, how to configure them, and how to troubleshoot them.

In this chapter, we'll cover the following topics:

- What SELinux is and how it can benefit a systems administrator
- How to set security contexts for files and directories
- How to use `setroubleshoot` to troubleshoot SELinux problems
- Looking at SELinux policies and how to create custom policies
- What AppArmor is and how it can benefit a systems administrator
- Looking at AppArmor policies
- Working with AppArmor command-line utilities
- Troubleshooting AppArmor problems
- Exploiting a system with an evil Docker container

Let's start out by looking at SELinux and how you can benefit from it.

How SELinux can benefit a systems administrator

SELinux is a free open source software project that was developed by the US National Security Agency. While it can theoretically be installed on any Linux distro, Red Hat-type distros are the only ones that come with it already set up and enabled. It uses code in Linux kernel modules, along with extended filesystem attributes, to help ensure that only authorized users and processes can access either sensitive files or system resources. There are three ways in which SELinux can be used:

- It can help prevent intruders from exploiting a system.
- It can be used to ensure that only users with the proper security clearance can access files that are labeled with a security classification. For example, it would prevent someone with only a *SECRET* clearance from accessing *TOP SECRET* documents. It would also prevent someone with a *TOP SECRET* clearance from storing *TOP SECRET* documents in an area where people with lower clearance levels could access them.
- In addition to MAC, SELinux can also be used as a type of role-based access control. An SELinux *role* would allow a person or a set of people to perform a certain assigned set of tasks, such as administering a specific type of server.

In this chapter, I'll only be covering the first of these three use cases because that is the most common way in which SELinux is used. (You'll likely never deal with the second and third use cases unless you're working for a government agency that has to safeguard classified documents.) There's also the fact that covering all three of these use cases would require writing a whole book, which I don't have space to do here.

> If you go through this introduction to SELinux and find that you still need more SELinux information, you'll find whole books and courses on just this subject on the Packt Publishing website.

So, how can SELinux benefit the busy systems administrator? Well, you might remember when, a few years ago, news about the Shellshock bug hit the world's headlines. Essentially, Shellshock was a bug in the Bash shell that allowed intruders to break into a system and to exploit it by gaining root privileges. For systems that were running SELinux, it was still possible for the bad guys to break in, but SELinux would have prevented them from successfully running their exploits.

SELinux is also yet another mechanism that can help protect data in users' home directories. If you have a machine that's set up as a Network File System server, a Samba server, or a web server, SELinux will prevent those daemons from accessing users' home directories, unless you explicitly configure SELinux to allow that behavior.

On web servers, you can use SELinux to prevent the execution of malicious CGI scripts or PHP scripts. If you don't need your server to run CGI or PHP scripts, you can disable them in SELinux.

With Docker and without SELinux, it's trivially easy for a normal user to break out of a Docker container and gain root-level access to the host machine. As we'll see at the end of this chapter, SELinux is a useful tool for hardening servers that run Docker containers.

So now, you're likely thinking that everyone would use such a great tool, right? Sadly, that's not the case. In its beginning, SELinux got a reputation for being difficult to work with, and many administrators would just disable it. In fact, a lot of tutorials you see on the web or on YouTube have disabling SELinux as the first step. In this section, I'd like to show you that things have improved and that SELinux no longer deserves its bad reputation.

Setting security contexts for files and directories

Think of SELinux as a glorified labeling system. It adds labels, known as security contexts, to files and directories through extended file attributes. It also adds the same type of label, known as domains, to system processes. To see these contexts and domains on your CentOS or AlmaLinux machines, use the -Z option with either ls or ps. For example, files and directories in my own home directory would look like the following:

```
[donnie@localhost ~]$ ls -Z
drwxrwxr-x. donnie donnie unconfined_u:object_r:user_home_t:s0 acl_demo_dir
-rw-rw-r--. donnie donnie unconfined_u:object_r:user_home_t:s0 yum_list.txt
[donnie@localhost ~]$
```

Processes on my system would look something like the following:

```
[donnie@localhost ~]$ ps -Z
LABEL                              PID TTY          TIME CMD
unconfined_u:unconfined_r:unconfined_t:s0-s0:c0.c1023 1322 pts/0 00:00:00 bash
unconfined_u:unconfined_r:unconfined_t:s0-s0:c0.c1023 3978 pts/0 00:00:00 ps
[donnie@localhost ~]$
```

Now, let's break this down. In the outputs of both the ls -Z and ps -Z commands, we have the following parts:

- *The SELinux user:* In both cases, the SELinux user is the generic unconfined_u.
- *The SELinux role:* In the ls -Z example, we see that the role is object_r, and in the ps -Z example, it's unconfined_r.
- *The type:* It's user_home_t in the ls -Z output and unconfined_t in the ps -Z output.
- *The sensitivity:* In the ls -Z output, it's s0. In the ps -Z output, it's s0-s0.
- *The category:* We don't see a category in the ls -Z output, but we do see c0.c1023 in the ps -Z output.

Out of all of the preceding security context and security domain components, the only one that interests us now is the **type**. For the purposes of this chapter, we're only interested in covering what a normal Linux administrator would need to know to keep intruders from exploiting the system, and the **type** is the only one of these components that we need to use for that. All of the other components come into play when we set up advanced, security classification-based access control and role-based access control.

Okay, the following is a somewhat oversimplified explanation of how this helps a Linux administrator maintain security. What we want is for system processes to only access objects that we allow them to access. (System processes include things such as the web server daemon, the FTP daemon, the Samba daemon, and the Secure Shell daemon. Objects include things such as files, directories, and network ports.) To achieve this, we'll assign a **type** to all of our processes and all of our objects. We'll then create policies that define which process types can access which object types.

Fortunately, whenever you install any Red Hat-type distro, pretty much all of the hard work has already been done for you. Red Hat-type distros all come with SELinux already enabled and set up with the **targeted** policy. Think of this targeted policy as a somewhat relaxed policy that allows a casual desktop user to sit down at the computer and actually conduct business without having to tweak any SELinux settings. But if you're a server administrator, you may find yourself having to tweak this policy in order to allow server daemons to do what you need them to do.

> The targeted policy, which comes installed by default, is what a normal Linux administrator will use in his or her day-to-day duties. If you look in the repositories of your CentOS or AlmaLinux virtual machines, you'll see that there are also several others, which we won't cover in this book.

Installing the SELinux tools

For some bizarre reason that I'll never understand, the tools that you need to administer SELinux don't get installed by default, even though SELinux itself does. So, the first thing you'll need to do on your CentOS or AlmaLinux virtual machine is to install them.

On CentOS 7, run this command:

```
sudo yum install setools policycoreutils policycoreutils-python
```

On AlmaLinux 8 and 9, run this command:

```
sudo dnf install setools policycoreutils policycoreutils-python-utils
```

Later on in this chapter, in the *Troubleshooting with setroubleshoot* section, we'll look at how to use setroubleshoot to help diagnose SELinux problems. In order to have some cool error messages to look at when we get there, go ahead and install setroubleshoot now, and activate it by restarting the auditd daemon. (There's no setroubleshoot daemon, because setroubleshoot is meant to be controlled by the auditd daemon.) Install setroubleshoot like so.

For CentOS 7, use these commands:

```
sudo yum install setroubleshoot
sudo service auditd restart
```

For AlmaLinux 8 and 9, use these commands:

```
sudo dnf install setroubleshoot
sudo service auditd restart
```

One of the little systemd quirks that we have to deal with on Red Hat-type systems is that you can't stop or restart the auditd daemon with the normal systemctl command. However, the old-fashioned service command works. For some reason that I don't understand, the Red Hat folk configured the auditd service file to disable the normal systemd way of doing things.

> Depending on the type of installation that you chose when installing CentOS or AlmaLinux, you might or might not already have setroubleshoot installed. To be sure, go ahead and run the command to install it. It won't hurt anything if setroubleshoot is already there.

You now have what you need to get started. Let's now look at what SELinux can do for a busy web server administrator.

Creating web content files with SELinux enabled

Now, let's look at what can happen if you have web content files that are set with the wrong SELinux type. First, we'll install, enable, and start the Apache web server on our CentOS virtual machines. (Note that including the --now option allows us to enable and start a daemon all in one single step.) Do the following on CentOS 7:

```
sudo yum install httpd
sudo systemctl enable --now httpd
```

On AlmaLinux, use the following command:

```
sudo dnf install httpd
sudo systemctl enable --now httpd
```

If you haven't done so already, configure the firewall to allow access to the web server:

```
[donnie@localhost ~]$ sudo firewall-cmd --permanent --add-service=http
success
[donnie@localhost ~]$ sudo firewall-cmd --reload
success
[donnie@localhost ~]$
```

When we look at the SELinux information for Apache processes, we'll see the following:

```
[donnie@localhost ~]$ ps ax -Z | grep httpd
system_u:system_r:httpd_t:s0       3689 ?         Ss      0:00 /usr/sbin/httpd
-DFOREGROUND
system_u:system_r:httpd_t:s0       3690 ?         S       0:00 /usr/sbin/httpd
-DFOREGROUND
system_u:system_r:httpd_t:s0       3691 ?         S       0:00 /usr/sbin/httpd
-DFOREGROUND
system_u:system_r:httpd_t:s0       3692 ?         S       0:00 /usr/sbin/httpd
-DFOREGROUND
system_u:system_r:httpd_t:s0       3693 ?         S       0:00 /usr/sbin/httpd
-DFOREGROUND
system_u:system_r:httpd_t:s0       3694 ?         S       0:00 /usr/sbin/httpd
-DFOREGROUND
unconfined_u:unconfined_r:unconfined_t:s0-s0:c0.c1023 3705 pts/0 R+   0:00 grep
--color=auto httpd
```

As I said before, we're not interested in the user or the role. However, we are interested in the type, which in this case is httpd_t.

On Red Hat-type systems, we would normally place web content files in the /var/www/html/ directory. Let's look at the SELinux context for that html directory:

```
[donnie@localhost www]$ pwd
/var/www
[donnie@localhost www]$ ls -Zd html/
drwxr-xr-x. root root system_u:object_r:httpd_sys_content_t:s0 html/
[donnie@localhost www]$
```

The type is httpd_sys_content, so it stands to reason that the httpd daemon should be able to access this directory. It's currently empty, so let's cd into it and create a simple index file:

```
[donnie@localhost www]$ cd html
[donnie@localhost html]$ pwd
/var/www/html
[donnie@localhost html]$ sudo vim index.html
```

Here's what I'll put into the file:

```
<html>
  <head>
    <title>
      Test of SELinux
    </title>
  </head>
```

```
    <body>
      Let's see if this SELinux stuff really works!
    </body>
  </html>
```

Okay, as I said, it's simple, since my HTML hand-coding skills aren't what they used to be. But still, it serves our present purposes.

Looking at the SELinux context, we see that the file has the same type as the html directory:

```
[donnie@localhost html]$ ls -Z
-rw-r--r--. root root unconfined_u:object_r:httpd_sys_content_t:s0 index.html
[donnie@localhost html]$
```

I can now navigate to this page from the web browser of my trusty openSUSE workstation:

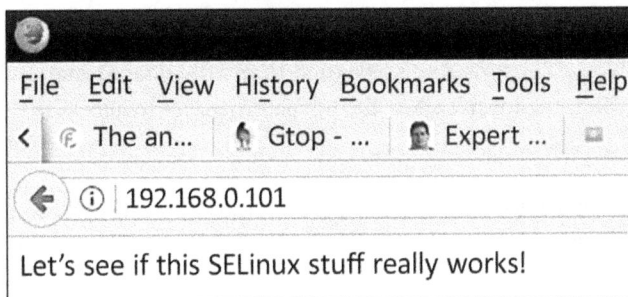

Figure 10.1: Testing SELinux

Now, though, let's see what happens if I decide to create content files in my own home directory and then move them to the html directory. First, let's see what the SELinux context is for my new file:

```
[donnie@localhost ~]$ pwd
/home/donnie
[donnie@localhost ~]$ ls -Z index.html
-rw-rw-r--. donnie donnie unconfined_u:object_r:user_home_t:s0 index.html
[donnie@localhost ~]$
```

The context type is now user_home_t, which is a surefire indicator that I created this in my home directory. I'll now move the file to the html directory, overwriting the old file:

```
[donnie@localhost ~]$ sudo mv index.html /var/www/html/
[sudo] password for donnie:

[donnie@localhost ~]$ cd /var/www/html

[donnie@localhost html]$ ls -Z
-rw-rw-r--. donnie donnie unconfined_u:object_r:user_home_t:s0 index.html
[donnie@localhost html]$
```

Even though I moved the file over to the `/var/www/html/` directory, the SELinux type is still associat-ed with users' home directories. Now, I'll go to the browser of my host machine to refresh the page:

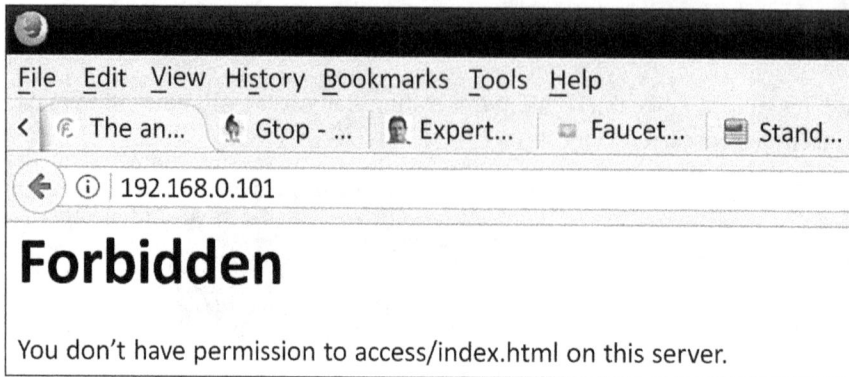

Figure 10.2: SELinux blocking access

So, I have a slight problem. The type that's assigned to my file doesn't match the type of the `httpd` daemon processes, so SELinux doesn't allow the `httpd` processes to access the file.

> Had I copied the file to the `html` directory instead of moving it, the SELinux context would have automatically changed to match that of the destination directory.

Fixing an incorrect SELinux context

Okay, so I have this web content file that nobody can access, and I really don't feel up to creating a new one. So, what do I do? Actually, we have three different utilities for fixing this:

* `chcon`
* `restorecon`
* `semanage`

Let's look at each of them.

Using chcon

There are two ways to use `chcon` to fix an incorrect SELinux type on a file or directory. The first is to just manually specify the proper type:

```
[donnie@localhost html]$ sudo chcon -t httpd_sys_content_t index.html
[sudo] password for donnie:

[donnie@localhost html]$ ls -Z
-rw-rw-r--. donnie donnie unconfined_u:object_r:httpd_sys_content_t:s0 index.
html
[donnie@localhost html]$
```

We can use chcon to change any part of the context, but as I keep saying we're only interested in the type, which gets changed with the -t option. You can see in the ls -Z output that the command was successful.

The other way to use chcon is to reference a file that has the proper context. For demo purposes, I changed the index.html file back to the home directory type and created a new file within the /var/www/html/ directory:

```
[donnie@localhost html]$ ls -Z
-rw-rw-r--. donnie donnie unconfined_u:object_r:user_home_t:s0 index.html
-rw-r--r--. root   root   unconfined_u:object_r:httpd_sys_content_t:s0 some_
file.html
[donnie@localhost html]$
```

As you can see, any files that I create within this directory will automatically have the proper SELinux context settings. Now, let's use that new file as a reference in order to set the proper context on the index.html file:

```
[donnie@localhost html]$ sudo chcon --reference some_file.html index.html
[sudo] password for donnie:

[donnie@localhost html]$ ls -Z
-rw-rw-r--. donnie donnie unconfined_u:object_r:httpd_sys_content_t:s0 index.
html
-rw-r--r--. root   root   unconfined_u:object_r:httpd_sys_content_t:s0 some_
file.html
[donnie@localhost html]$
```

So, I used the --reference option and specified the file that I wanted to use as a reference. The file that I wanted to change is listed at the end of the command. Now, that's all to the good, but I want to find an easier way that doesn't require quite as much typing. After all, I am an old man, and I don't want to overexert myself. So, let's take a look at the restorecon utility.

Using restorecon

Using restorecon is easy. Just type restorecon, followed by the name of the file that you need to change. Once again, I've changed the context of the index.html file back to the home directory type. This time, though, I'm using restorecon to set the correct type:

```
[donnie@localhost html]$ ls -Z
-rw-rw-r--. donnie donnie unconfined_u:object_r:user_home_t:s0 index.html

[donnie@localhost html]$ sudo restorecon index.html

[donnie@localhost html]$ ls -Z
-rw-rw-r--. donnie donnie unconfined_u:object_r:httpd_sys_content_t:s0 index.
html
[donnie@localhost html]$
```

And that's all there is to it.

> You can also use chcon and restorecon to change the context of an entire directory and its contents. For either one, just use the -R option. The following is an example:
>
> ```
> sudo chcon -R -t httpd_sys_content_t /var/www/html/
> sudo restorecon -R /var/www/html/
> ```
>
> (Remember: -R stands for recursive.)

There's still one last thing to take care of, even though it isn't really affecting our ability to access this file. That is, I need to change ownership of the file to the Apache user:

```
[donnie@localhost html]$ sudo chown apache: index.html
[sudo] password for donnie:

[donnie@localhost html]$ ls -l
total 4
-rw-rw-r--. 1 apache apache 125 Nov 22 16:14 index.html
[donnie@localhost html]$
```

Let's now look at the final utility, which is semanage.

Using semanage

In the scenario I've just presented, either chcon or restorecon will suit your needs just fine. The active SELinux policy mandates what security contexts in certain directories are supposed to look like. As long as you're using chcon or restorecon within directories that are defined in the active SELinux policy, you're good. But let's say that you've created a directory elsewhere that you want to use to serve out web content files. You would need to set the httpd_sys_content_t type on that directory and all of the files within it. However, if you use chcon or restorecon for that, the change won't survive a system reboot. To make the change permanent, you'll need to use semanage.

Let's say that, for some strange reason, I want to serve web content out of a directory that I've created in the /home/ directory:

```
[donnie@localhost home]$ pwd
/home

[donnie@localhost home]$ sudo mkdir webdir
[sudo] password for donnie:

[donnie@localhost home]$ ls -Zd webdir
drwxr-xr-x. root root unconfined_u:object_r:home_root_t:s0 webdir
[donnie@localhost home]$
```

Because I had to use my sudo powers to create the directory here, it's associated with the root user's home_root_t type, instead of the normal user_home_dir_t type. Any files that I create within this directory will have the same type:

```
[donnie@localhost webdir]$ ls -Z
-rw-r--r--. root root unconfined_u:object_r:home_root_t:s0 index.html
[donnie@localhost webdir]$
```

The next step is to use semanage to add a permanent mapping of this directory and the httpd_sys_content_t type to the active policy's context list:

```
[donnie@localhost home]$ sudo semanage fcontext -a -t httpd_sys_content_t "/home/webdir(/.*)?"

[donnie@localhost home]$ ls -Zd /home/webdir
drwxr-xr-x. root root unconfined_u:object_r:httpd_sys_content_t:s0 /home/webdir
[donnie@localhost home]$
```

Okay, here's the breakdown of the semanage command:

- fcontext: Because semanage has many purposes, we have to specify that we want to work with a file context.
- -a: This specifies that we're adding a new record to the context list for the active SELinux policy.
- -t: This specifies the type that we want to map to the new directory. In this case, we're creating a new mapping with the httpd_sys_content type.
- /home/webdir(/.*)?: This bit of gibberish is what's known as a **regular expression**. I can't go into the nitty-gritty details of regular expressions here, so suffice it to say that **Regular Expressions** is a language that we use to match text patterns. (And yes, I did mean to say *is* instead of *are*, since Regular Expressions is the name of the overall language.) In this case, I had to use this particular regular expression in order to make this semanage command recursive because semanage doesn't have the -R option switch. With this regular expression, I'm saying that I want anything that gets created in this directory to have the same SELinux type as the directory itself.

The final step is to do a restorecon -R on this directory to ensure that the proper labels have been set:

```
[donnie@localhost home]$ sudo restorecon -R webdir

[donnie@localhost home]$ ls -Zd /home/webdir
drwxr-xr-x. root root unconfined_u:object_r:httpd_sys_content_t:s0 /home/webdir
[donnie@localhost home]$
```

Yeah, I know. You're looking at this and saying, "But this ls -Zd output looks the same as it did after you did the semanage command." And you're right. After running the semanage command, the type seems to be set correctly. But the semanage-fcontext man page says to run restorecon anyway, so I did.

For more information on how to use semanage to manage security contexts, refer to the relevant man page by entering man `semanage-fcontext`.

Hands-on lab — SELinux type enforcement

In this lab, you'll install the Apache web server and the appropriate SELinux tools. You'll then view the effects of having the wrong SELinux type assigned to a web content file. If you're ready, let's go:

1. Install Apache, along with all the required SELinux tools on CentOS 7:

    ```
    sudo yum install httpd setroubleshoot setools policycoreutils
    policycoreutils-python
    ```

    On AlmaLinux 8 or 9, use the following command:

    ```
    sudo dnf install httpd setroubleshoot setools policycoreutils
    policycoreutils-python-utils
    ```

2. Activate setroubleshoot by restarting the auditd service:

    ```
    sudo service auditd restart
    ```

3. Enable and start the Apache service and open port 80 on the firewall:

    ```
    sudo systemctl enable --now httpd
    sudo firewall-cmd --permanent --add-service=http
    sudo firewall-cmd --reload
    ```

4. In the /var/www/html/ directory, create an index.html file with the following contents:

    ```
    <html>
      <head>
        <title>SELinux Test Page</title>
      </head>
      <body>
        This is a test of SELinux.
      </body>
    </html>
    ```

5. View the information about the index.html file:

    ```
    ls -Z index.html
    ```

6. In your host machine's web browser, navigate to the IP address of the CentOS virtual machine. You should be able to view the page.

7. Induce an SELinux violation by changing the type of the index.html file to something that's incorrect:

```
sudo chcon -t tmp_t index.html
ls -Z index.html
```

8. Go back to your host machine's web browser and reload the document. You should now see a Forbidden message.

9. Use restorecon to change the file back to its correct type:

```
sudo restorecon index.html
```

10. Reload the page in your host machine's web browser. You should now be able to view the page.

11. End of lab.

Now that we've seen how to use basic SELinux commands, let's look at a cool tool that makes troubleshooting much easier.

Troubleshooting with setroubleshoot

So, you're now scratching your head and saying, *When I can't access something that I should be able to, how do I know that it's an SELinux problem?* Ah, I'm glad you asked.

Viewing setroubleshoot messages

Whenever something happens that violates an SELinux rule, it gets logged in the /var/log/audit/audit.log file. Tools are available that can let you directly read that log, but to diagnose SELinux problems it's way better to use setroubleshoot. The beauty of setroubleshoot is that it takes cryptic, hard-to-interpret SELinux messages from the audit.log file and translates them into plain, natural language. The messages that it sends to the /var/log/messages file even contain suggestions about how to fix the problem. To show how this works, let's go back to our problem where a file in the /var/www/html/ directory has been assigned the wrong SELinux type. Of course, we knew right away what the problem was because there was only one file in that directory and a simple ls -Z showed what was wrong with it. However, let's ignore that for the moment and say that we didn't know what the problem was. By opening the /var/log/messages file in less and searching for sealert, we'll find this message:

```
Nov 26 21:30:21 localhost python: SELinux is preventing httpd from open access
on the file /var/www/html/index.html.#012#012*****  Plugin restorecon (92.2
confidence) suggests   ***********************#012#012If you want to fix
the label. #012/var/www/html/index.html default label should be httpd_sys_
content_t.#012Then you can run restorecon.#012Do#012# /sbin/restorecon -v /var/
www/html/index.html#012#012*****  Plugin catchall_boolean (7.83 confidence)
suggests   ******************#012#012If you want to allow httpd to read user
content#012Then you must tell SELinux about this by enabling the 'httpd_read_
user_content' boolean.#012#012Do#012setsebool -P httpd_read_user_content
1#012#012*****  Plugin catchall (1.41 confidence) suggests   ***************
**********#012#012If you believe that httpd should be allowed open access on
```

```
the index.html file by default.#012Then you should report this as a bug.#012You
can generate a local policy module to allow this access.#012Do#012allow this
access for now by executing:#012# ausearch -c 'httpd' --raw | audit2allow -M
my-httpd#012# semodule -i my-httpd.pp#012
```

The first line of this message tells us what the problem is. It's saying that SELinux is preventing us from accessing the `/var/www/html/index.html` file because it's set with the wrong type. It then gives us several suggestions on how to fix the problem, with the first one being to run the `restorecon` command, as I've already shown you how to do.

> 💡 A good rule of thumb to remember when reading these `setroubleshoot` messages is that the first suggestion in the message is normally the one that will fix the problem.

Using the graphical setroubleshoot utility

So far, I've only talked about using `setroubleshoot` on text mode servers. After all, it's very common to see Linux servers running in text-mode, so all of us Linux folk have to be text-mode warriors. But on desktop systems or on servers that have a desktop interface installed, there is a graphical utility that will automatically alert you when `setroubleshoot` detects a problem:

```
🅰 Applications   Places   Terminal                         Wed 14:51   🖧  🔊  ⏻

                                        donnie@cen   New SELinux security alert
                                                     AVC denial, click icon to view
File  Edit  View  Search  Terminal  Help
[donnie@centos7-class ~]$ ifconfig
enp0s3: flags=4163<UP,BROADCAST,RUNNING,MULTICAST>  mtu 1500
        inet 192.168.0.4  netmask 255.255.255.0  broadcast 192.168.0.255
        inet6 fe80::a00:27ff:fe19:64d6  prefixlen 64  scopeid 0x20<link>
        ether 08:00:27:19:64:d6  txqueuelen 1000  (Ethernet)
        RX packets 240  bytes 39933 (38.9 KiB)
        RX errors 0  dropped 0  overruns 0  frame 0
        TX packets 100  bytes 11227 (10.9 KiB)
        TX errors 0  dropped 0 overruns 0  carrier 0  collisions 0

lo: flags=73<UP,LOOPBACK,RUNNING>  mtu 65536
        inet 127.0.0.1  netmask 255.0.0.0
        inet6 ::1  prefixlen 128  scopeid 0x10<host>
        loop  txqueuelen 1  (Local Loopback)
        RX packets 64  bytes 5664 (5.5 KiB)
        RX errors 0  dropped 0  overruns 0  frame 0
        TX packets 64  bytes 5664 (5.5 KiB)
        TX errors 0  dropped 0 overruns 0  carrier 0  collisions 0

virbr0: flags=4099<UP,BROADCAST,MULTICAST>  mtu 1500
        inet 192.168.122.1  netmask 255.255.255.0  broadcast 192.168.122.255
        ether 52:54:00:8b:28:04  txqueuelen 1000  (Ethernet)
        RX packets 0  bytes 0 (0.0 B)
        RX errors 0  dropped 0  overruns 0  frame 0
        TX packets 0  bytes 0 (0.0 B)
        TX errors 0  dropped 0 overruns 0  carrier 0  collisions 0

[donnie@centos7-class ~]$ █

🖳 donnie@centos7-class:~                                              1 / 4
```

Figure 10.3: SELinux security alert

Click on that alert icon, and you'll see something like this:

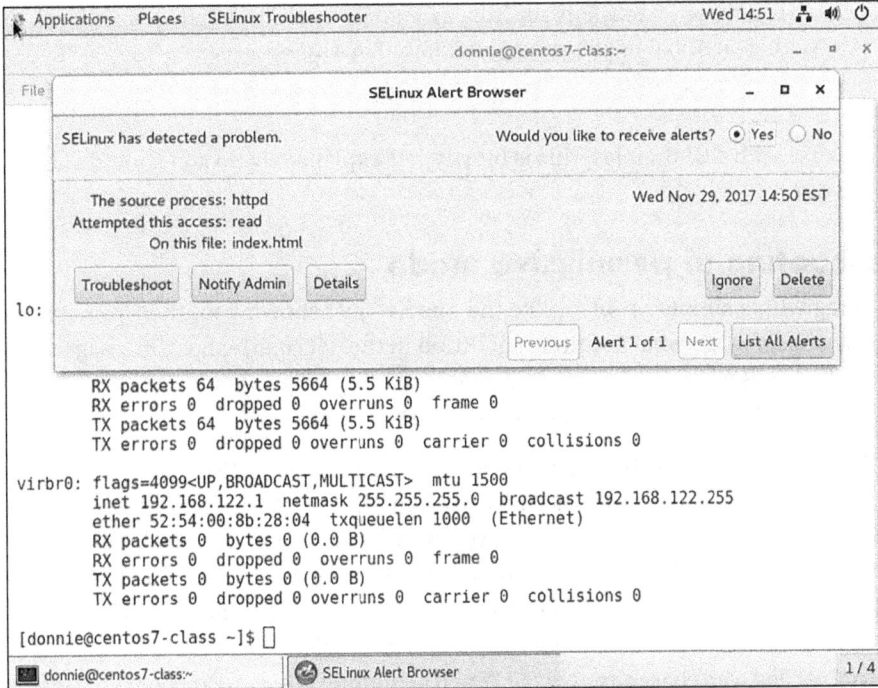

Figure 10.4: SELinux alert browser

Click the **Troubleshoot** button, and you'll see a list of suggestions on how to fix the problem:

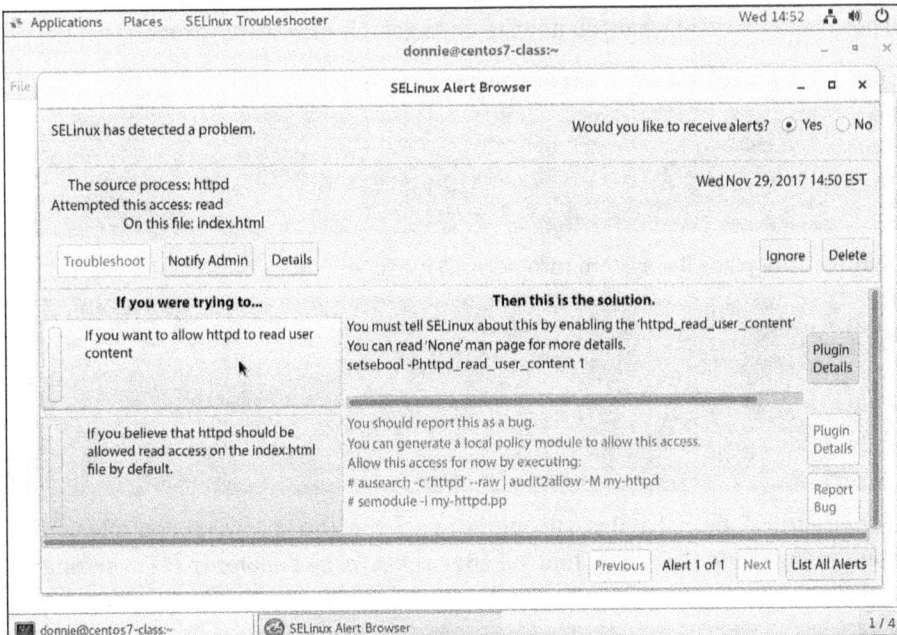

Figure 10.5: Fixing the problem

> Note that these screenshots are from a CentOS 7 machine, but they would look the same on either an AlmaLinux 8 or an AlmaLinux 9 machine.

As is often the case with GUI thingies, this is mostly self-explanatory, so you shouldn't have any problem figuring it out.

Troubleshooting in permissive mode

If you're dealing with a simple problem like the one I've just shown you, then you can probably assume that you can safely do what the first suggestion in the setroubleshoot message tells you to do. But there will be times when things get a bit more complex, where you might have more than one problem. For times like these, you need to use permissive mode.

When you first install your Red Hat, CentOS, or AlmaLinux system, SELinux is in enforcing mode, which is the default. This means that SELinux will actually stop actions that are in violation of the active SELinux policy. This also means that, if you have multiple SELinux problems when you try to perform a certain action, SELinux will stop the action from taking place after the first violation occurs. When it happens, SELinux won't even see the remaining problems, and they won't show up in the messages log file. If you try to troubleshoot these types of problem while in enforcing mode, you'll be like the proverbial dog who chases its own tail. You'll go round and round and will accomplish nothing.

In permissive mode, SELinux allows actions that violate policy to occur, but it will log them. By switching to permissive mode and doing something to induce the problem that you were seeing, the prohibited actions will take place but setroubleshoot will log all of them in the messages file. This way, you'll get a better view of what you need to do to get things working properly.

First, let's use getenforce to verify what our current mode is:

```
[donnie@localhost ~]$ sudo getenforce
Enforcing
[donnie@localhost ~]$
```

Now, let's temporarily place the system into permissive mode:

```
[donnie@localhost ~]$ sudo setenforce 0

[donnie@localhost ~]$ sudo getenforce
Permissive
[donnie@localhost ~]$
```

When I say *temporarily*, I mean that this will only last until you do a system reboot. After a reboot, you'll be back in enforcing mode. Also, note that a 0 after setenforce denotes that I'm setting permissive mode. To get back to enforcing mode after you're done with troubleshooting, replace the 0 with a 1:

```
[donnie@localhost ~]$ sudo setenforce 1
```

```
[donnie@localhost ~]$ sudo getenforce
Enforcing
[donnie@localhost ~]$
```

We're now back in enforcing mode.

At times, you may need to make permissive mode persist after a system reboot. An example of this would be if you ever have to deal with a system that has had SELinux disabled for a long period of time. In a case like that, you wouldn't want to just put SELinux into enforcing mode and reboot. If you try that, it will take forever for the system to properly create the file and directory labels that make SELinux work, and the system might lock up before it's done. By placing the system into permissive mode first, you'll avoid having the system lock up, although it will still take a long time for the relabeling process to complete.

To make permissive mode persistent across system reboots, you'll edit the selinux file in the /etc/sysconfig/ directory. Here's what it looks like by default:

```
# This file controls the state of SELinux on the system.
# SELINUX= can take one of these three values:
#     enforcing - SELinux security policy is enforced.
#     permissive - SELinux prints warnings instead of enforcing.
#     disabled - No SELinux policy is loaded.
SELINUX=enforcing
# SELINUXTYPE= can take one of three two values:
#     targeted - Targeted processes are protected,
#     minimum - Modification of targeted policy. Only selected processes are
protected.
#     mls - Multi Level Security protection.
SELINUXTYPE=targeted
```

The two important things you see here are that SELinux is in enforcing mode, and that it's using the targeted policy. To switch to permissive mode, just change the SELINUX= line, and save the file:

```
# This file controls the state of SELinux on the system.
# SELINUX= can take one of these three values:
#     enforcing - SELinux security policy is enforced.
#     permissive - SELinux prints warnings instead of enforcing.
#     disabled - No SELinux policy is loaded.
SELINUX=permissive
# SELINUXTYPE= can take one of three two values:
#     targeted - Targeted processes are protected,
#     minimum - Modification of targeted policy. Only selected processes are
protected.
#     mls - Multi Level Security protection.
SELINUXTYPE=targeted
```

The `sestatus` utility shows us lots of cool information about what's going on with SELinux:

```
[donnie@localhost ~]$ sudo sestatus
SELinux status:                 enabled
SELinuxfs mount:                /sys/fs/selinux
SELinux root directory:         /etc/selinux
Loaded policy name:             targeted
Current mode:                   enforcing
Mode from config file:          permissive
Policy MLS status:              enabled
Policy deny_unknown status:     allowed
Max kernel policy version:      28
[donnie@localhost ~]$
```

The two items that interest us here are the current mode and the mode from a configuration file. By changing the configuration file to permissive, we haven't changed the current running mode. So, we're still in enforcing mode. The switch to permissive won't happen until I either reboot this machine or until I manually switch by issuing a `sudo setenforce 0` command. And of course, you don't want to stay in permissive mode forever. As soon as you no longer need permissive mode, change the configuration file back to **enforcing** and do `sudo setenforce 1` to change the running mode.

Working with SELinux policies

So far, all we've looked at is what happens when we have an incorrect SELinux type set on a file and what to do to set the correct type. Another problem we may have would come about if we need to allow an action that is prohibited by the active SELinux policy.

Viewing Booleans

Booleans are part of what makes up an SELinux policy, and each Boolean represents a binary choice. In SELinux policies, a Boolean either allows something or it prohibits something. To see all Booleans on your system, run the `getsebool -a` command. (It's a long list, so I'll only show partial output here.):

```
[donnie@localhost ~]$ getsebool -a
abrt_anon_write --> off
abrt_handle_event --> off
abrt_upload_watch_anon_write --> on
antivirus_can_scan_system --> off
antivirus_use_jit --> off
auditadm_exec_content --> on
. . .

. . .
zarafa_setrlimit --> off
zebra_write_config --> off
```

```
zoneminder_anon_write --> off
zoneminder_run_sudo --> off
[donnie@localhost ~]$
```

To view more than one Boolean, the -a switch is mandatory. If you just happen to know the name of the Boolean that you want to see, leave the -a out and list it. In keeping with the Apache web server theme that we've had going, let's see whether we're allowing Apache to access files in users' home directories:

```
[donnie@localhost html]$ getsebool httpd_enable_homedirs
httpd_enable_homedirs --> off
[donnie@localhost html]$
```

The fact that this Boolean is off means that the Apache server daemon isn't allowed to access any content within the users' home directories. This is an important protection, and you really don't want to change it. Instead, just put web content files elsewhere so that you don't have to change this Boolean.

You'll rarely want to look at the entire list, and you likely won't know the name of the specific Boolean that you want to see. Rather, you'll probably want to filter the output through grep in order to look at just certain things. For example, to see all of the Booleans that affect a web server, do this:

```
[donnie@localhost html]$ getsebool -a | grep 'http'
httpd_anon_write --> off
httpd_builtin_scripting --> on
httpd_can_check_spam --> off
httpd_can_connect_ftp --> off
httpd_can_connect_ldap --> off
. . .
. . .
httpd_use_nfs --> off
httpd_use_openstack --> off
httpd_use_sasl --> off
httpd_verify_dns --> off
named_tcp_bind_http_port --> off
prosody_bind_http_port --> off
[donnie@localhost html]$
```

It's also a rather long list, but scroll down a little and you'll find the Boolean that you seek.

> I'm only able to show you a few different examples for using SELinux. But, you can get a more complete idea of what SELinux either can protect or is already protecting by perusing the output of the getsebool -a command.

Now, let's configure some Booleans.

Configuring the Booleans

Realistically, you'll likely never have reason to allow users to serve web content out of their home directories. It's much more probable that you'll set up something like a Samba server, which would allow users on Windows machines to use their graphical Windows Explorer to access their home directories on Linux servers. But if you set up a Samba server and don't do anything with SELinux, users will complain about how they don't see any of their files in their home directories of the Samba server. Because you're the proactive type and you want to avoid the pain of listening to complaining users, you'll surely just go ahead and configure SELinux to allow the Samba daemon to access users' home directories. You might not know the exact name of the Boolean, but you can find it easily enough, as follows:

```
[donnie@localhost html]$ getsebool -a | grep 'home'
git_cgi_enable_homedirs --> off
git_system_enable_homedirs --> off
httpd_enable_homedirs --> off
mock_enable_homedirs --> off
mpd_enable_homedirs --> off
openvpn_enable_homedirs --> on
samba_create_home_dirs --> off
samba_enable_home_dirs --> off
. . .
use_samba_home_dirs --> off
xdm_write_home --> off
[donnie@localhost html]$
```

Okay, you knew that the Boolean name probably had the word home in it, so you filtered for that word. About halfway down the list, you see `samba_enable_home_dirs --> off`. You'll need to change this to on to let users access their home directories from their Windows machines:

```
[donnie@localhost html]$ sudo setsebool samba_enable_home_dirs on

[sudo] password for donnie:
[donnie@localhost html]$ getsebool samba_enable_home_dirs
samba_enable_home_dirs --> on
[donnie@localhost html]$
```

Users can now access their home directories as they should be able to, but only until you do a system reboot. Without the -P option, any changes you make with setsebool will only be temporary. So, let's make the change permanent with -P:

```
[donnie@localhost html]$ sudo setsebool -P samba_enable_home_dirs on

[donnie@localhost html]$ getsebool samba_enable_home_dirs
samba_enable_home_dirs --> on
[donnie@localhost html]$
```

Congratulations, you've just made your first change to an SELinux policy.

Protecting your web server

Look at the output of the getsebool -a | grep 'http' command again, and you'll see that most httpd-related Booleans are turned off by default, with only a few turned on. There are two of them that you'll commonly need to turn on when setting up a web server.

If you ever need to set up a website with some sort of PHP-based content management system, such as Joomla or WordPress, you may have to turn on the httpd_unified Boolean. With this Boolean turned off, the Apache web server won't be able to interact properly with all of the components of the PHP engine:

```
[donnie@localhost ~]$ getsebool httpd_unified
httpd_unified --> off

[donnie@localhost ~]$ sudo setsebool -P httpd_unified on
[sudo] password for donnie:


[donnie@localhost ~]$ getsebool httpd_unified
httpd_unified --> on
[donnie@localhost ~]$
```

The other Boolean that you'll commonly need to turn on is the httpd_can_sendmail Boolean. If you ever need a website to send mail out through a form (or if you need to set up a mail server with a web-based frontend), you'll definitely need to set this to on:

```
[donnie@localhost ~]$ getsebool httpd_can_sendmail
httpd_can_sendmail --> off

[donnie@localhost ~]$ sudo setsebool -P httpd_can_sendmail on
[donnie@localhost ~]$ getsebool httpd_can_sendmail
httpd_can_sendmail --> on
[donnie@localhost ~]$
```

On the other hand, there are some Booleans that are turned on by default, and you might want to consider whether you really need them turned on. For example, allowing CGI scripts to run on a web server does represent a potential security risk. If an intruder were to somehow upload a malicious CGI script to the server and run it, much damage could occur as a result. Yet, for some bizarre reason, the default SELinux policy allows CGI scripts to run. If you're absolutely certain that nobody who hosts websites on your server will ever need to run CGI scripts, you might want to consider turning this Boolean off:

```
[donnie@localhost ~]$ getsebool httpd_enable_cgi
httpd_enable_cgi --> on
```

```
[donnie@localhost ~]$ sudo setsebool -P httpd_enable_cgi off

[donnie@localhost ~]$ getsebool httpd_enable_cgi
httpd_enable_cgi --> off
[donnie@localhost ~]$
```

Protecting network ports

Each network daemon that's running on your system has a specific network port or set of network ports assigned to it, on which it will listen. The /etc/services file contains a list of common daemons and their associated network ports, but it doesn't prevent someone from configuring a daemon to listen on some non-standard port. So, without some mechanism to prevent it, some sneaky intruder could potentially plant some sort of malware that would cause a daemon to listen on a non-standard port, possibly listening for commands from its master.

SELinux protects against this sort of malicious activity by only allowing daemons to listen on certain ports. Use semanage to look at the list of allowed ports:

```
[donnie@localhost ~]$ sudo semanage port -l
SELinux Port Type              Proto    Port Number

afs3_callback_port_t            tcp      7001
afs3_callback_port_t            udp      7001
afs_bos_port_t                  udp      7007
. . .

. . .
zented_port_t                   udp      1229
zookeeper_client_port_t         tcp      2181
zookeeper_election_port_t       tcp      3888
zookeeper_leader_port_t         tcp      2888
zope_port_t                     tcp      8021
[donnie@localhost ~]$
```

This is yet another of those very long lists, so I'm only showing partial output. However, let's narrow things down a bit. Let's say that I only want to look at a list of ports on which the Apache web server can listen. For this, I'll use my good friend grep:

```
[donnie@localhost ~]$ sudo semanage port -l | grep 'http'
[sudo] password for donnie:
http_cache_port_t               tcp      8080, 8118, 8123, 10001-10010
http_cache_port_t               udp      3130
http_port_t                     tcp      80, 81, 443, 488, 8008, 8009, 8443,
9000
pegasus_http_port_t             tcp      5988
```

```
pegasus_https_port_t                    tcp        5989
[donnie@localhost ~]$
```

Several `http` items come up, but I'm only interested in the `http_port_t` item because it's the one that affects normal web server operation. We see here that SELinux will allow Apache to listen on ports 80, 81, 443, 488, 8008, 8009, 8443, and 9000. Since the Apache server is one of the few daemons for which you'd ever have a legitimate reason for adding a non-standard port, let's demo with it.

First, let's go into the `/etc/httpd/conf/httpd.conf` file and look at the ports on which Apache is currently listening. Search for `Listen`, and you'll see the following line:

```
Listen 80
```

I don't have the SSL module installed on this machine, but if I did I would have an `ssl.conf` file in the `/etc/httpd/conf.d/` directory with this line:

```
Listen 443
```

So for normal, non-encrypted website connections, the default configuration only has Apache listening on port 80. For secure, encrypted website connections, Apache listens on port 443. Now, let's go into the `httpd.conf` file and change `Listen 80` to a port number that SELinux doesn't allow, for example, port 82:

```
Listen 82
```

After saving the file, I'll restart Apache to read in the new configuration:

```
[donnie@localhost ~]$ sudo systemctl restart httpd
Job for httpd.service failed because the control process exited with error
code. See "systemctl status httpd.service" and "journalctl -xe" for details.
[donnie@localhost ~]$
```

Yes, I have a problem. I'll look in the `/var/log/messages` file to see if `setroubleshoot` gives me a clue:

```
Nov 29 16:39:21 localhost python: SELinux is preventing /usr/sbin/httpd from
name_bind access on the tcp_socket port 82.#012#012***** Plugin bind_ports
(99.5 confidence) suggests ************************#012#012If you want to allow
/usr/sbin/httpd to bind to network port 82#012Then you need to modify the port
type.#012Do#012# semanage port -a -t PORT_TYPE -p tcp 82#012 where PORT_TYPE
is one of the following: http_cache_port_t, http_port_t, jboss_management_
port_t, jboss_messaging_port_t, ntop_port_t, puppet_port_t.#012#012***** Plugin
catchall (1.49 confidence) suggests ************************#012#012If you
believe that httpd should be allowed name_bind access on the port 82 tcp_socket
by default.#012Then you should report this as a bug.#012You can generate a
local policy module to allow this access.#012Do#012allow this access for now
by executing:#012# ausearch -c 'httpd' --raw | audit2allow -M my-httpd#012#
semodule -i my-httpd.pp#012
```

The first line of the message details how SELinux is preventing `httpd` from binding to port 82. The first suggestion we see for fixing this is to use `semanage` to add the port to the list of allowed ports. So, let's do that and then look at the list of Apache ports:

```
[donnie@localhost ~]$ sudo semanage port -a 82 -t http_port_t -p tcp

[donnie@localhost ~]$ sudo semanage port -l | grep 'http_port_t'
http_port_t                    tcp       82, 80, 81, 443, 488, 8008, 8009, 8443,
9000
pegasus_http_port_t            tcp       5988
[donnie@localhost ~]$
```

It's not clear in the `setroubleshoot` message, but you need to specify the port number that you want to add after `port -a`. The `-t http_port_t` part specifies the **type** for which you want to add the port, and `-p tcp` specifies that you want to use the TCP protocol.

Now for the moment of truth. Will the Apache daemon start this time? Let's see:

```
[donnie@localhost ~]$ sudo systemctl restart httpd
[sudo] password for donnie:
[donnie@localhost ~]$ sudo systemctl status httpd
  httpd.service - The Apache HTTP Server
   Loaded: loaded (/usr/lib/systemd/system/httpd.service; enabled; vendor
preset: disabled)
   Active: active (running) since Wed 2017-11-29 20:09:51 EST; 7s ago
     Docs: man:httpd(8)
. . .
. . .
```

It works, and we have achieved coolness. But now, I've decided that I no longer need this oddball port. Deleting it is just as easy as adding it:

```
[donnie@localhost ~]$ sudo semanage port -d 82 -t http_port_t -p tcp

[donnie@localhost ~]$ sudo semanage port -l | grep 'http_port_t'
http_port_t                    tcp       80, 81, 443, 488, 8008, 8009, 8443,
9000
pegasus_http_port_t            tcp       5988
[donnie@localhost ~]$
```

All I had to do was to replace `port -a` with `port -d`. And of course, I still need to go into the /etc/httpd/conf/httpd.conf file to change `Listen 82` back to `Listen 80`.

Creating custom policy modules

Sometimes, you'll run into a problem that you can't fix either by changing the type or by setting a Boolean. In times like these, you'll need to create a custom policy module, and you'll use the audit2allow utility to do that.

Here's a screenshot of a problem I had several years ago, when I was helping a client set up a Postfix mail server on CentOS 7:

```
SELinux is preventing /usr/libexec/dovecot/dict from read access on the file .

*****  Plugin catchall (100. confidence) suggests   ***************************

If you believe that dict should be allowed read access on the  file by default.
Then you should report this as a bug.
You can generate a local policy module to allow this access.
Do
allow this access for now by executing:
# grep dict /var/log/audit/audit.log | audit2allow -M mypol
# semodule -i mypol.pp
```

Figure 10.6: Using audit2allow

So, for some strange reason that I never understood, SELinux wouldn't allow Dovecot, the **Mail Delivery Agent (MDA)** component of the mail server, to read its own dict file. There's no Boolean to change and there wasn't a type problem, so setroubleshoot suggested that I create a custom policy module. It's easy enough to do, but you do need to be aware that this won't work with sudo on your normal user account. This is one of those rare times when you'll just have to go to the root user command prompt, and you'll also need to be in the root user's home directory:

```
sudo su -
```

Before you do it, be sure to put SELinux into permissive mode and then do something to induce the SELinux error. This way, you'll be sure that one problem isn't masking others.

When you run the command to create the new policy module, be sure to replace mypol with a custom policy name of your own choosing. In my case, I named the module dovecot_dict, and the command looked like this:

```
grep dict /var/log/audit/audit.log | audit2allow -M dovecot_dict
```

I'm using grep to search through the audit.log file for SELinux messages that contain the word dict. I then pipe the output of that into audit2allow and use the -M option to create a custom module with the name dovecot_dict.

After I created the new policy module, I inserted it into the SELinux policy like so:

```
semodule -i dovecot_dict.pp
```

There was also a second problem that required another custom module, but I just repeated this procedure to produce another module of a different name. After I got all that done, I reloaded the SELinux policy, in order to get my new modules to take effect:

```
semodule -R
```

With `semodule`, the `-R` switch stands for *reload*, rather than *recursive*, as it does with most Linux commands.

With all that done, I put SELinux back into enforcing mode and exited back to my own user account. And I tested the setup to make sure that I had fixed the problem.

Of course, you also want to bear in mind that you don't want to just modify SELinux policy or contexts every time you see an `sealert` message in the log files. For example, consider this snippet from the messages file of my Oracle Linux 7 machine, which I set up mainly to run Docker and Docker containers:

```
Jun  8 19:32:17 docker-1 setroubleshoot: SELinux is preventing /usr/bin/docker
from getattr access on the file /etc/exports. For complete SELinux messages.
run sealert -l b267929a-d3ad-45d5-806e-907449fc2739
Jun  8 19:32:17 docker-1 python: SELinux is preventing /usr/bin/docker from
getattr access on the file /etc/exports.#012#012*****  Plugin catchall (100.
confidence) suggests   **************************#012#012If you believe that
docker should be allowed getattr access on the exports file by default.#012Then
you should report this as a bug.#012You can generate a local policy module to
allow this access.#012Do#012allow this access for now by executing:#012# grep
docker /var/log/audit/audit.log | audit2allow -M mypol#012# semodule -i mypol.
pp#012
Jun  8 19:32:17 docker-1 setroubleshoot: SELinux is preventing /usr/bin/
docker from getattr access on the file /etc/shadow.rpmnew. For complete SELinux
messages. run sealert -l
. . .
```

These messages were caused by an early version of Docker trying to access resources on the host machine. As you can see, Docker is trying to access some rather sensitive files, and SELinux is preventing Docker from doing so. With Docker, and without some sort of MAC, it can be a trivial matter for a normal, unprivileged user to escape from the Docker container and have root user privileges on the host system. Naturally, when you see these sorts of messages, you don't want to automatically tell SELinux to allow the prohibited actions. It just may be that SELinux is preventing something truly bad from taking place.

> Be sure to get your copy of *The SELinux Coloring Book* from `https://opensource.com/business/13/11/selinux-policy-guide`

Hands-on lab — SELinux Booleans and ports

In this lab, you'll view the effects of having Apache try to listen on an unauthorized port:

1. View the ports that SELinux allows the Apache web server daemon to use:

```
sudo semanage port -l | grep 'http'
```

2. Open the /etc/httpd/conf/httpd.conf file in your favorite text editor. Find the line that says Listen 80 and change it to Listen 82. Restart Apache by entering the following:

```
sudo systemctl restart httpd
```

3. View the error message you receive by entering:

```
sudo tail -20 /var/log/messages
```

4. Add port 82 to the list of authorized ports and restart Apache:

```
sudo semanage port -a 82 -t http_port_t -p tcp
sudo semanage port -l
sudo systemctl restart httpd
```

5. Delete the port that you just added:

```
sudo semanage -d 82 -t http_port_t -p tcp
```

6. Go back into the /etc/httpd/conf/httpd.conf file and change Listen 82 back to Listen 80. Restart the Apache daemon to return to normal operation.

7. End of lab.

Okay, you've seen how SELinux can protect you against various bad things, and how to troubleshoot things that go wrong. Let's turn our attention to AppArmor.

How AppArmor can benefit a systems administrator

AppArmor is the MAC system that comes installed with the SUSE and the Ubuntu families of Linux. Although it's designed to do pretty much the same job as SELinux, its mode of operation is substantially different:

*   SELinux labels all system processes and all objects such as files, directories, or network ports. For files and directories, SELinux stores the labels in their respective inodes as extended attributes. (An inode is the basic filesystem component that contains all information about a file, except for the filename.)
*   AppArmor uses pathname enforcement, which means that you specify the path to the executable file that you want AppArmor to control. This way, there's no need to insert labels into the extended attributes of files or directories.
*   With SELinux, you have system-wide protection out of the box.
*   With AppArmor, you have a profile for each individual application.

- With either SELinux or AppArmor, you might occasionally find yourself having to create custom policy modules from scratch, especially if you're dealing with either third-party applications or homegrown software. With AppArmor, this is easier, because the syntax for writing AppArmor profiles is much easier than the syntax for writing SELinux policies. And AppArmor comes with utilities that can help you automate the process.

- Just as SELinux can, AppArmor can help prevent malicious actors from ruining your day and can help protect user data.

So, you see that there are advantages and disadvantages to both SELinux and AppArmor, and a lot of Linux administrators have strong feelings about which one they prefer. (To avoid being subjected to a flame war, I'll refrain from stating my own preference.) Also, note that even though we're working with an Ubuntu virtual machine, the information I present here, other than the Ubuntu-specific package installation commands, also works with the SUSE Linux distros.

Looking at AppArmor profiles

To begin, we'll install the lxc package so that we can have more to look at:

```
sudo apt install lxc
```

In the /etc/apparmor.d/ directory, you'll see the AppArmor profiles for your system. (SELinux folk say *policies*, but AppArmor folk say *profiles*.):

```
donnie@ubuntu3:/etc/apparmor.d$ ls -l
total 72
drwxr-xr-x 5 root root  4096 Oct 29 15:21 abstractions
drwxr-xr-x 2 root root  4096 Nov 15 09:34 cache
drwxr-xr-x 2 root root  4096 Oct 29 14:43 disable
. . .
. . .
-rw-r--r-- 1 root root   125 Jun 14 16:15 usr.bin.lxc-start
-rw-r--r-- 1 root root   281 May 23  2017 usr.lib.lxd.lxd-bridge-proxy
-rw-r--r-- 1 root root 17667 Oct 18 05:04 usr.lib.snapd.snap-confine.real
-rw-r--r-- 1 root root  1527 Jan  5  2016 usr.sbin.rsyslogd
-rw-r--r-- 1 root root  1469 Sep  8 15:27 usr.sbin.tcpdump
donnie@ubuntu3:/etc/apparmor.d$
```

All of the text files you see in this directory are AppArmor profiles. If you've installed the lxc package, you'll find a few other profiles in the lxc and lxc-containers subdirectories. Still, though, there's not a whole lot there in the way of application profiles.

> For some reason, a default installation of OpenSUSE comes with more installed profiles than Ubuntu Server does. To install more profiles on Ubuntu, just run this command:
>
> ```
> sudo apt install apparmor-profiles apparmor-profiles-extra
> ```

In the `abstractions` subdirectory, you'll find files that aren't complete profiles but that can be included in complete profiles. Any one of these abstraction files can be included in any number of profiles. This way, you don't have to write the same code over and over every time you create a profile. Just include an abstraction file instead.

> If you're familiar with programming concepts, just think of abstraction files as `include` files by another name.

Here's a partial listing of the abstraction files:

```
donnie@ubuntu3:/etc/apparmor.d/abstractions$ ls -l
total 320
-rw-r--r-- 1 root root  695 Mar 15  2017 apache2-common
drwxr-xr-x 2 root root 4096 Oct 29 15:21 apparmor_api
-rw-r--r-- 1 root root  308 Mar 15  2017 aspell
-rw-r--r-- 1 root root 1582 Mar 15  2017 audio
. . .

. . .
-rw-r--r-- 1 root root  705 Mar 15  2017 web-data
-rw-r--r-- 1 root root  739 Mar 15  2017 winbind
-rw-r--r-- 1 root root  585 Mar 15  2017 wutmp
-rw-r--r-- 1 root root 1819 Mar 15  2017 X
-rw-r--r-- 1 root root  883 Mar 15  2017 xad
-rw-r--r-- 1 root root  673 Mar 15  2017 xdg-desktop
donnie@ubuntu3:/etc/apparmor.d/abstractions$
```

To get a feel for how AppArmor rules work, let's peek inside the `web-data` abstraction file:

```
/srv/www/htdocs/ r,
/srv/www/htdocs/** r,
# virtual hosting
/srv/www/vhosts/ r,
/srv/www/vhosts/** r,
# mod_userdir
@{HOME}/public_html/ r,
@{HOME}/public_html/** r,

/srv/www/rails/*/public/ r,
/srv/www/rails/*/public/** r,

/var/www/html/ r,
/var/www/html/** r,
```

This file is just a list of directories from which the Apache daemon is allowed to read files. Let's break it down:

- Note that each rule ends with `r,` - this denotes that we want Apache to have read access to each listed directory. Also note that each rule has to end with a comma.
- `/srv/www/htdocs/ r,` : This means that the listed directory itself has read access for Apache.
- `/srv/www.htdocs/* * r,` : The `* *` wildcards make this rule recursive. In other words, Apache can read all files in all subdirectories of this specified directory.
- `# mod_userdir` : If installed, this Apache module allows Apache to read web content files from a subdirectory that's within a user's home directory. The next two lines go along with that.
- `@{HOME}/public_html/ r,` and `@{HOME}/public_html/ r,` : The `@{HOME}` variable allows this rule to work with any user's home directory. (You'll see this variable defined in the `/etc/apparmor.d/tunables/home` file.)
- Note that there's no specific rule that prohibits Apache from reading from other locations. It's just understood that anything that's not listed here is off-limits to the Apache web server daemon.

The `tunables` subdirectory contains files that have predefined variables. You can also use this directory to either define new variables or make profile tweaks:

```
donnie@ubuntu3:/etc/apparmor.d/tunables$ ls -l
total 56
-rw-r--r-- 1 root root  624 Mar 15  2017 alias
-rw-r--r-- 1 root root  376 Mar 15  2017 apparmorfs
-rw-r--r-- 1 root root  804 Mar 15  2017 dovecot
-rw-r--r-- 1 root root  694 Mar 15  2017 global
-rw-r--r-- 1 root root  983 Mar 15  2017 home
. . .

. . .
-rw-r--r-- 1 root root  440 Mar 15  2017 proc
-rw-r--r-- 1 root root  430 Mar 15  2017 securityfs
-rw-r--r-- 1 root root  368 Mar 15  2017 sys
-rw-r--r-- 1 root root  868 Mar 15  2017 xdg-user-dirs
drwxr-xr-x 2 root root 4096 Oct 29 15:02 xdg-user-dirs.d
donnie@ubuntu3:/etc/apparmor.d/tunables$
```

Space doesn't permit me to show you the details of how to write your own profiles from scratch. Thanks to the suite of utilities that we'll look at in the next section, you might never need to do that. Still, just to give you a better understanding about how AppArmor does what it does, the following is a chart of some example rules that you might find in any given profile:

Rule	Explanation
`/var/run/some_program.pid rw,`	The process will have read and write privileges for this process ID file.
`/etc/ld.so.cache r,`	The process will have read privileges for this file.

/tmp/some_program.* l,	The process will be able to create and delete links with the some_program name.
/bin/mount ux	The process has executable privileges for the mount utility, which will then run unconstrained. (*Unconstrained* means without an AppArmor profile.)

Now that you know about AppArmor profiles, let's look at some basic AppArmor utilities.

Working with AppArmor command-line utilities

Whether or not you have all the AppArmor utilities you need will depend on which Linux distro you have. On my OpenSUSE Leap workstation, the utilities were there out of the box. On my Ubuntu Server virtual machine, I had to install them myself:

```
sudo apt install apparmor-utils
```

First, let's look at the status of AppArmor on the Ubuntu machine. Since it's a rather long output, we'll look at it in sections. Here's the first section:

```
donnie@ubuntu2204-packt:~$ sudo aa-status
apparmor module is loaded.
61 profiles are loaded.
43 profiles are in enforce mode.
   /snap/snapd/17029/usr/lib/snapd/snap-confine
   /snap/snapd/17029/usr/lib/snapd/snap-confine//mount-namespace-capture-helper
   /snap/snapd/17336/usr/lib/snapd/snap-confine
   /snap/snapd/17336/usr/lib/snapd/snap-confine//mount-namespace-capture-helper
   /usr/bin/lxc-start
   /usr/bin/man
   /usr/bin/pidgin
   /usr/bin/pidgin//sanitized_helper
 . . .
 . . .
```

The first thing to note here is that AppArmor has an **enforce** mode and a **complain** mode. The enforce mode that's shown here does the same job as its enforcing mode counterpart in SELinux. It prevents system processes from doing things that the active policy doesn't allow, and it logs any violations.

Now, here's the second section:

```
 . . .
 . . .
0 processes are in enforce mode.
1 processes are in complain mode.
   /usr/sbin/dnsmasq (2485) dnsmasq
0 processes are unconfined but have a profile defined.
```

```
0 processes are in mixed mode.
0 processes are in kill mode.
donnie@ubuntu2204-packt:~$
```

Complain mode is the same as permissive mode in SELinux. It allows processes to perform actions that are prohibited by the active policy, but it records those actions in either the `/var/log/audit/audit.log` file, or the system log file, depending on whether you have `auditd` installed. (Unlike Red Hat-type distros, `auditd` doesn't come installed by default on Ubuntu.) You would use complain mode either to help with troubleshooting or to test new profiles.

Most enforce mode profiles we see here have to do with either network management or with `lxc` container management. Two exceptions we see are the two profiles for `snapd`, which is the daemon that makes the snap packaging technology work. The third exception is the `mysqld` profile.

> Snap packages are universal binary files that are designed to work on multiple distros. Snap technology is currently available for most major Linux distros.

Curiously, when you install a daemon package on Ubuntu, you'll sometimes get a predefined profile for that daemon and sometimes you won't. Even when a profile does come with the package that you've installed, it's sometimes already in enforce mode and sometimes isn't. For example, if you're setting up a **Domain Name Service (DNS)** server and you install the `bind9` package for it, you'll get an AppArmor profile that's already in enforce mode. If you're setting up a database server and install the `mysql-server` package, you'll also get a working profile that's already in enforce mode.

But, if you're setting up a database server and you prefer to install the `mariadb-server` instead of `mysql-server`, you'll get an AppArmor profile that's completely disabled and that can't be enabled. When you look in the `usr.sbin.mysqld` profile file that gets installed with the `mariadb-server` package, you'll see this:

```
# This file is intentionally empty to disable apparmor by default for newer
# versions of MariaDB, while providing seamless upgrade from older versions
# and from mysql, where apparmor is used.
#
# By default, we do not want to have any apparmor profile for the MariaDB
# server. It does not provide much useful functionality/security, and causes
# several problems for users who often are not even aware that apparmor
# exists and runs on their system.
#
# Users can modify and maintain their own profile, and in this case it will
# be used.
#
# When upgrading from previous version, users who modified the profile
# will be prompted to keep or discard it, while for default installs
# we will automatically disable the profile.
```

Okay, so apparently AppArmor isn't good for everything. (And whoever wrote this needs to take spelling lessons.)

And then there's Samba, which is a special case in more ways than one. When you install the samba package to set up a Samba server, you don't get any AppArmor profiles at all. For Samba and several other different applications as well, you'll need to install AppArmor profiles separately:

```
sudo apt install apparmor-profiles apparmor-profiles-extra
```

When you install these two profile packages, the profiles will all be in complain mode. That's okay, because we have a handy utility to put them into enforce mode. Since Samba has two different daemons that we need to protect, there are two different profiles that we'll need to place into enforce mode:

```
donnie@ubuntu5:/etc/apparmor.d$ ls *mbd
usr.sbin.nmbd   usr.sbin.smbd
donnie@ubuntu5:/etc/apparmor.d$
```

We'll use aa-enforce to activate enforce mode for both of these profiles:

```
donnie@ubuntu5:/etc/apparmor.d$ sudo aa-enforce /usr/sbin/nmbd usr.sbin.nmbd
Setting /usr/sbin/nmbd to enforce mode.
Setting /etc/apparmor.d/usr.sbin.nmbd to enforce mode.

donnie@ubuntu5:/etc/apparmor.d$ sudo aa-enforce /usr/sbin/smbd usr.sbin.smbd
Setting /usr/sbin/smbd to enforce mode.
Setting /etc/apparmor.d/usr.sbin.smbd to enforce mode.
donnie@ubuntu5:/etc/apparmor.d$
```

To use aa-enforce, you first need to specify the path to the executable file of the process that you want to protect. (Fortunately, you normally won't even have to look that up, since the path name is normally part of the profile filename.) The last part of the command is the name of the profile. Note that you'll need to restart the Samba daemon to get this AppArmor protection to take effect.

Placing a profile into other modes is just as easy. All you have to do is to replace the aa-enforce utility with the utility for the mode that you need to use. The following is a chart of utilities for the other modes:

Command	Explanation
aa-audit	Audit mode is the same as enforce mode, except that allowed actions get logged, as well as actions that have been blocked. (Enforce mode only logs actions that have been blocked.)
aa-disable	This completely disables a profile.
aa-complain	This places a profile into complain mode.

Okay, we're moving right along. You now know about basic AppArmor commands. Next up, we'll look at troubleshooting AppArmor problems.

Troubleshooting AppArmor problems

When I wrote the first edition of this book back in 2017, I sat here racking my brains for several days, trying to come up with a good troubleshooting scenario. It turns out that I didn't need to. The Ubuntu folk handed me a good scenario on a silver platter in the form of a buggy Samba profile. At the time, I was working with Ubuntu 16.04, which had the original version of the bug. The original bug got fixed for Ubuntu 18.04, but was replaced by two others. In Ubuntu 22.04, the profile is finally bug-free. I still want to show you how to troubleshoot AppArmor problems though, so I've left the 16.04 and 18.04 write-ups intact. (It's still possible to download and install Ubuntu 16.04 and 18.04, so you can create some virtual machines to follow along if you'd like. I'll leave that decision up to you.)

Troubleshooting an AppArmor profile – Ubuntu 16.04

As you've just seen, I used `aa-enforce` to put the two Samba-related profiles into **enforce** mode. But watch what happens now when I try to restart Samba in order to get the profiles to take effect:

```
donnie@ubuntu3:/etc/apparmor.d$ sudo systemctl restart smbd
Job for smbd.service failed because the control process exited with error code.
See "systemctl status smbd.service" and "journalctl -xe" for details.
donnie@ubuntu3:/etc/apparmor.d$
```

Okay, that's not good. Looking at the status for the `smbd` service, I see this:

```
donnie@ubuntu3:/etc/apparmor.d$ sudo systemctl status smbd
  smbd.service - LSB: start Samba SMB/CIFS daemon (smbd)
   Loaded: loaded (/etc/init.d/smbd; bad; vendor preset: enabled)
   Active: failed (Result: exit-code) since Tue 2017-12-05 14:56:35 EST; 13s
ago
     Docs: man:systemd-sysv-generator(8)
  Process: 31160 ExecStop=/etc/init.d/smbd stop (code=exited, status=0/SUCCESS)
  Process: 31171 ExecStart=/etc/init.d/smbd start (code=exited, status=1/
FAILURE)
Dec 05 14:56:35 ubuntu3 systemd[1]: Starting LSB: start Samba SMB/CIFS daemon
(smbd)...
Dec 05 14:56:35 ubuntu3 smbd[31171]:  * Starting SMB/CIFS daemon smbd
Dec 05 14:56:35 ubuntu3 smbd[31171]:    ...fail!
. . .
```

The important things to note here are all the places where some form of the word `fail` shows up.

The original error message said to use `journalctl -xe` to view the log message. You can do that if you like, or you can just use either `less` or `tail` to look in the `/var/log/syslog` log file:

```
Dec  5 20:09:10 ubuntu3 smbd[14599]:  * Starting SMB/CIFS daemon smbd
Dec  5 20:09:10 ubuntu3 kernel: [174226.392671] audit: type=1400
audit(1512522550.765:510): apparmor="DENIED" operation="mknod" profile="/usr/
sbin/smbd" name="/run/samba/msg.
lock/14612" pid=14612 comm="smbd" requested_mask="c" denied_mask="c" fsuid=0
ouid=0
Dec  5 20:09:10 ubuntu3 smbd[14599]:    ...fail!
Dec  5 20:09:10 ubuntu3 systemd[1]: smbd.service: Control process exited,
code=exited status=1
Dec  5 20:09:10 ubuntu3 systemd[1]: Failed to start LSB: start Samba SMB/CIFS
daemon (smbd).
Dec  5 20:09:10 ubuntu3 systemd[1]: smbd.service: Unit entered failed state.
Dec  5 20:09:10 ubuntu3 systemd[1]: smbd.service: Failed with result 'exit-
code'.
```

So, we see apparmor=DENIED. Obviously, Samba is trying to do something that the profile doesn't allow. Samba needs to write temporary files to the `/run/samba/msg.lock` directory, but it isn't allowed to. I'm guessing that the profile lacks a rule that allows that to happen.

But even if this log file entry gave me no clue at all, I could just cheat, using a troubleshooting technique that has served me well for many years. That is, I could just copy and paste the error message from the log file into my favorite search engine. Pretty much every time I've ever done that, I've found that other people before me have already had the same problem:

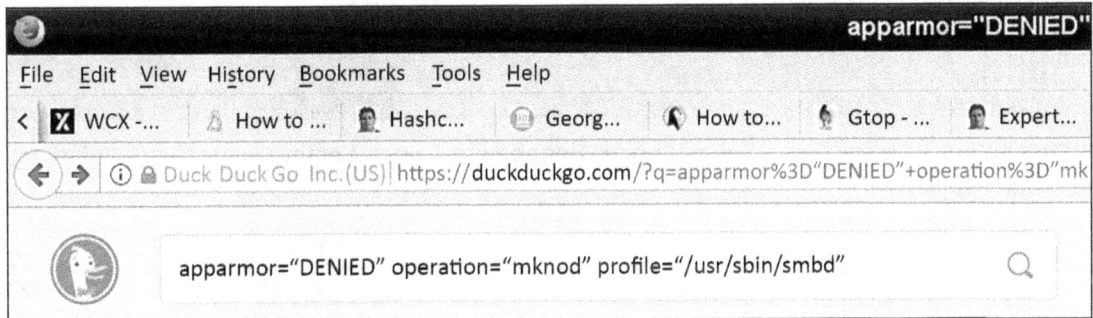

Figure 10.7: Looking up an AppArmor error message

Okay, I didn't paste in the entire error message, but I did paste in enough for DuckDuckGo to work with. And lo and behold, it worked:

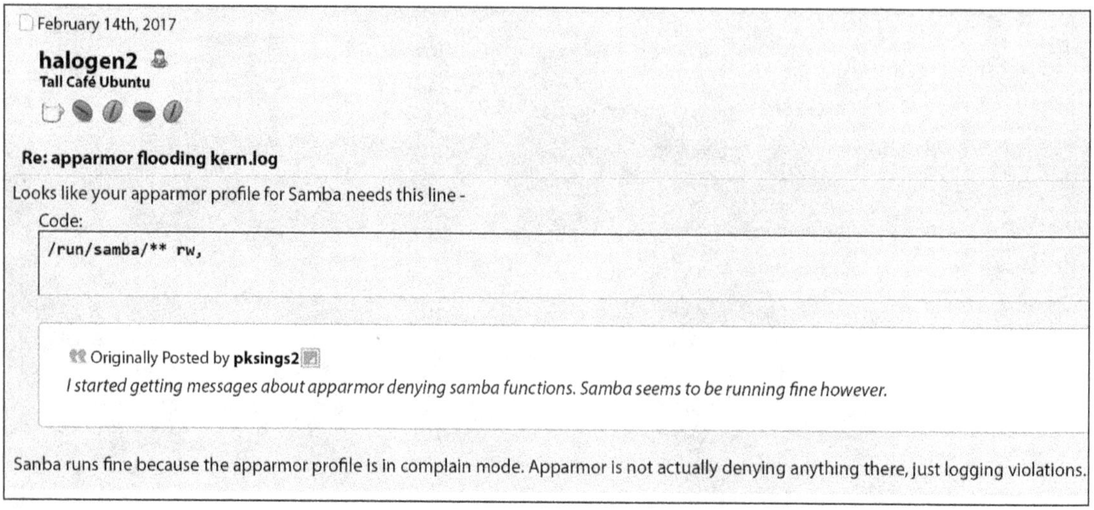
February 14th, 2017
halogen2
Tall Café Ubuntu
Re: apparmor flooding kern.log
Looks like your apparmor profile for Samba needs this line -
Code:
/run/samba/** rw,
Originally Posted by pksings2
I started getting messages about apparmor denying samba functions. Samba seems to be running fine however.
Samba runs fine because the apparmor profile is in complain mode. Apparmor is not actually denying anything there, just logging violations.

Figure 10.8: DuckDuckGo search results

Hmmm, it looks like my profile file might be missing an important line. So, I'll open the `usr.sbin.smbd` file and place this line at the end of the rule set:

```
/run/samba/** rw,
```

This line will allow read and write access to everything in the `/run/samba/` directory. After making the edit, I'll need to reload this profile because it's already been loaded with `aa-enforce`. For this, I'll use the `apparmor_parser` utility:

```
donnie@ubuntu3:/etc/apparmor.d$ sudo apparmor_parser -r usr.sbin.smbd
donnie@ubuntu3:/etc/apparmor.d$
```

All you need to do is use the `-r` option for reloading and list the name of the profile file. Now, let's try to restart Samba:

```
donnie@ubuntu3:/etc/apparmor.d$ sudo systemctl restart smbd

donnie@ubuntu3:/etc/apparmor.d$ sudo systemctl status smbd
  smbd.service - LSB: start Samba SMB/CIFS daemon (smbd)
   Loaded: loaded (/etc/init.d/smbd; bad; vendor preset: enabled)
   Active: active (running) since Wed 2017-12-06 13:31:32 EST; 3min 6s ago
     Docs: man:systemd-sysv-generator(8)
  Process: 17317 ExecStop=/etc/init.d/smbd stop (code=exited, status=0/SUCCESS)
  Process: 16474 ExecReload=/etc/init.d/smbd reload (code=exited, status=0/
SUCCESS)
  Process: 17326 ExecStart=/etc/init.d/smbd start (code=exited, status=0/
```

```
SUCCESS)
    Tasks: 3
   Memory: 9.3M
      CPU: 594ms
   CGroup: /system.slice/smbd.service
           ├─17342 /usr/sbin/smbd -D
           ├─17343 /usr/sbin/smbd -D
           └─17345 /usr/sbin/smbd -D


Dec 06 13:31:28 ubuntu3 systemd[1]: Stopped LSB: start Samba SMB/CIFS daemon
(smbd).
Dec 06 13:31:28 ubuntu3 systemd[1]: Starting LSB: start Samba SMB/CIFS daemon
(smbd)...
Dec 06 13:31:32 ubuntu3 smbd[17326]:  * Starting SMB/CIFS daemon smbd
Dec 06 13:31:32 ubuntu3 smbd[17326]:    ...done.
Dec 06 13:31:32 ubuntu3 systemd[1]: Started LSB: start Samba SMB/CIFS daemon
(smbd).
donnie@ubuntu3:/etc/apparmor.d$
```

And it works! The two Samba profiles are in enforce mode, and Samba finally starts up just fine.

The odd part about this is that I had this same problem with both Ubuntu 16.04 and Ubuntu 17.10. So, the bug has been there for a long time.

Troubleshooting an AppArmor profile – Ubuntu 18.04

As I said before, the bug in Ubuntu 16.04 got replaced by two others in Ubuntu 18.04. So, let's look at that.

I installed Samba and the additional AppArmor profiles on my Ubuntu 18.04 VM, and then set the two Samba profiles into enforce mode, the same way that I've already shown you for Ubuntu 16.04. When I tried to restart Samba, the restart failed. So, I looked in the /var/log/syslog file and found these two messages:

```
Oct 15 19:22:05 ubuntu-ufw kernel: [ 2297.955842] audit: type=1400
audit(1571181725.419:74): apparmor="DENIED" operation="capable" profile="/usr/
sbin/smbd" pid=15561 comm="smbd" capability=12  capname="net_admin"

Oct 15 19:22:05 ubuntu-ufw kernel: [ 2297.960193] audit: type=1400
audit(1571181725.427:75): apparmor="DENIED" operation="sendmsg" profile="/usr/
sbin/smbd" name="/run/systemd/notify" pid=15561 comm="smbd" requested_mask="w"
denied_mask="w" fsuid=0 ouid=0
```

Now that we know how to read the AppArmor error messages, this is easy to figure out. It looks like we need to allow the SMBD service to have net_admin capabilities so that it can properly access the network. And, it looks like we also need to add a rule to allow SMBD to write to the /run/systemd/notify socket file. So, let's edit the /etc/apparmor.d/usr.sbin.smbd file and add the two missing lines.

First, in the stanza with all of the `capability` lines, I'll add this line to the bottom:

```
capability net_admin,
```

Then, at the bottom of the rules list, just under the `/var/spool/samba/**  rw`, line, I'll add this line:

```
/run/systemd/notify rw,
```

It's now just a matter of reloading the policy and restarting the SMBD service, the same as we did for Ubuntu 16.04.

Hands-on lab – Troubleshooting an AppArmor profile

Perform this lab on an Ubuntu 18.04 VM. Carry out the following steps for troubleshooting:

1. Install the AppArmor utilities and the extra profiles:

   ```
   sudo apt install apparmor-utils apparmor-profiles apparmor-profiles-extra
   ```

2. Install Samba and verify that it's running:

   ```
   sudo apt install samba
   sudo systemctl status smbd
   sudo systemctl status nmbd
   ```

3. Set the two aforementioned Samba policies to enforce mode and try to restart Samba:

   ```
   cd /etc/apparmor.d
   sudo aa-enforce /usr/sbin/smbd usr.sbin.smbd
   sudo aa-enforce /usr/sbin/nmbd usr.sbin.nmbd
   sudo systemctl restart smbd
   ```

4. Note that Samba should fail to restart. (It will take quite a while before it finally errors out, so be patient.)

5. Look in the `/var/log/syslog` file to see if you can spot the problem.

6. Edit the `/etc/apparmor.d/usr.sbin.smbd` file. In the `capability` stanza, add this line:

   ```
   capability net_admin,
   ```

7. At the bottom of the rules sections, under the `/var/spool/samba/**  rw`, line, add this line:

   ```
   /run/systemd/notify rw,
   ```

8. Save the file and reload the policy:

   ```
   sudo apparmor_parser -r usr.sbin.smbd
   ```

9. As before, try to restart the Samba service, and verify that it started properly:

   ```
   sudo systemctl restart smbd
   sudo systemctl status smbd
   ```

10. End of lab.

Okay, you've just explored the basics of troubleshooting buggy AppArmor profiles. This is good knowledge to have, especially when your organization needs to deploy its own custom profiles that could end up being just as buggy.

Troubleshooting Samba problems in Ubuntu 22.04

I told you before that the buggy AppArmor profile for Samba has been fixed in Ubuntu 22.04. So, hallelujah for that, right? Well, not so fast. As I'm writing this in November, 2022, there's now a bug in certain versions of Samba that prevents Samba from starting if the AppArmor profile is enabled.

> This bug was also in SUSE 15.3 but has been fixed in SUSE 15.4. It has also been fixed in Ubuntu 22.10. By the time you read this, it might also have gotten fixed in Ubuntu 22.04.

First, install the samba, apparmor-profiles, apparmor-profiles-extra, and apparmor-util packages, as I described in the preceding sections. Doing a systemctl status smbd command should show that the Samba service is running normally. Next, we'll set the two Samba profiles to enforce mode:

```
cd /etc/apparmor.d
sudo aa-enforce /usr/sbin/smbd usr.sbin.smbd
sudo aa-enforce /usr/sbin/nmbd usr.sbin.nmbd
sudo systemctl restart smbd
```

This time, you won't see any error message until you do systemctl status smbd:

```
donnie@ubuntu2204-packt:~$ systemctl status smbd
× smbd.service - Samba SMB Daemon
     Loaded: loaded (/lib/systemd/system/smbd.service; enabled; vendor preset:
enabled)
     Active: failed (Result: exit-code) since Mon 2022-11-14 21:01:28 UTC; 7s
ago
       Docs: man:smbd(8)
             man:samba(7)
             man:smb.conf(5)
    Process: 1966 ExecStartPre=/usr/share/samba/update-apparmor-samba-profile
(code=exited, status=0/SUCCESS)
    Process: 1976 ExecStart=/usr/sbin/smbd --foreground --no-process-group
$SMBDOPTIONS (code=exited, status=1/FAILURE)
   Main PID: 1976 (code=exited, status=1/FAILURE)
     Status: "daemon failed to start: Samba failed to init printing subsystem"
      Error: 13 (Permission denied)
        CPU: 133ms
```

Unlike before, searching through the system log file won't tell you anything. If you search through the usr.sbin.smbd file, you'll see no problems at all. Instead, the problem this time is with the print service function of the Samba service. Fortunately, it's an easy fix, as long as you don't mind going without Samba print sharing. Just open the /etc/samba/smb.conf file in your text editor, and add the following line to the [global] section:

```
disable spoolss = yes
```

The Samba service should now start up without issues.

Now, I have to confess that I don't know what the exact impact of this directive will be. The smb.conf man page says that printing might be impacted for Windows NT/2000 systems, but it doesn't say anything about how it affects newer versions of Windows. At any rate, I'll leave this experimentation up to you if you really need Samba print server support.

All right, enough of this Samba business. Let's move on to something that's evil but also fun.

Exploiting a system with an evil Docker container

You might think that containers are somewhat like virtual machines, and you'd be partly correct. The difference is that a virtual machine runs an entire self-contained operating system, and a container doesn't. Instead, a container comes with the guests operating system's package management and libraries, but it uses the kernel resources of the host operating system. That makes containers much more lightweight. So, you can pack more containers on a server than you can virtual machines, which helps cut down on hardware and energy costs. Containers have been around for quite a few years, but they didn't become all that popular until Docker came on the scene.

But, the very thing that makes containers so lightweight – the fact that they use the host machine's kernel resources – can also make for some interesting security problems. Using some form of MAC is one thing you can do to help mitigate these problems.

One problem is that, to run Docker, a person needs either to have the proper sudo privileges, or be a member of the docker group. Either way, anyone who logs into a container will be at the root command prompt for that container. By creating a container that mounts the root filesystem of the host machine, a non-privileged user can take complete control of the host system.

Hands-on lab – Creating an evil Docker container

To demonstrate, I'll use a CentOS 7 VM in order to show how SELinux can help protect you. (I'm using CentOS 7 because the RHEL 8/9-type distros use podman instead of docker, which won't allow this exploit to happen.) Also, you'll need to do this from the local console of the VM because the root user will be locked out from logging in via SSH (you'll see what I mean in just a bit):

1. On your CentOS 7 VM, install Docker and enable the daemon:

```
sudo yum install docker
sudo systemctl enable --now docker
```

2. Create the docker group:

```
sudo groupadd docker
```

3. Create a user account for Katelyn, my teenage calico kitty, adding her to the docker group at the same time:

```
sudo useradd -G docker katelyn
sudo passwd katelyn
```

4. Log out of your own user account and log back in as Katelyn.

5. Have Katelyn create a Debian container that mounts the / partition of the host machine in the /homeroot mount point, and that opens a Bash shell session for the root user:

```
docker run -v /:/homeroot -it debian bash
```

> Note how Katelyn has done this without having to use any sudo privileges. Also note that there are no blank spaces in the /:/homeroot part.

6. The goal is for Katelyn to make herself the root user on the host machine. In order to do that, she'll need to edit the /etc/passwd file to change her own user ID to 0. To do that, she'll need to install a text editor. (Katelyn prefers Vim, but you can use nano if you really want to.) While still within the Debian container, run the following:

```
apt update
apt install vim
```

7. Have Katelyn cd into the host machine's /etc/ directory and attempt to open the passwd file in the text editor:

```
cd /homeroot/etc
vim passwd
```

8. She won't be able to do it, because SELinux prevents it.

9. Type exit to exit the container.

10. Log out from Katelyn's account and then log back into your own account.

11. Place SELinux into permissive mode:

```
sudo setenforce 0
```

12. Log out from your own account and log back in as Katelyn.

13. Repeat *steps 5* through *7*. This time, Katelyn will be able to open the /etc/passwd file in her text editor.

14. In the `passwd` file, have Katelyn find the line for her own user account. Have her change her user ID number to 0. The line should now look something like this:

```
katelyn:x:0:1002::/home/katelyn:/bin/bash
```

15. Save the file, and type `exit` to have Katelyn exit the container. Have Katelyn log out of the VM, and then log back in. This time, you'll see that she has successfully logged into the root user shell.

16. End of lab.

Okay, you've just seen one of Docker's security weaknesses and how SELinux can protect you from it. Since Katelyn doesn't have `sudo` privileges, she can't put SELinux into permissive mode, which prevents her from doing any Docker mischief. On the RHEL 8/9-type distros, things are even better. Even with SELinux in either permissive mode or completely disabled, you still won't be able to edit the `passwd` file from within a container on either of your AlmaLinux machines. That's because RHEL 8/9 and their offspring use `podman`, which is Red Hat's drop-in replacement for `docker`. `podman` has several advantages over Docker, mainly in the area of host machine security.

So now you're wondering if AppArmor on Ubuntu helps us with this. Well, not by default, because there's no pre-built profile for the Docker daemon. When you run Docker on an Ubuntu machine, it automatically creates a Docker profile for the container in the `/tmpfs/` directory, but it really doesn't do much. I tested this procedure on an Ubuntu 18.04 VM with AppArmor enabled, and Katelyn was able to do her evil deed just fine. (Note that `podman` is now also available for non-Red Hat Linux distros, including Ubuntu.)

Earlier in this chapter, I said that I would refrain from stating which of these two MAC systems I prefer. But, I lied. If you haven't figured it out by now, I'm definitely a big fan of SELinux, because it provides better out-of-the-box protection than AppArmor does. If you choose to use Ubuntu, then plan on writing a new AppArmor profile any time that your development team deploys a new application.

> If you'd rather not deal with the complexities of creating AppArmor profiles, you can instead place security directives in the `systemd` unit files for your services. You might find that this is a bit easier, and it can give you much of the same protection that AppArmor would. To read all about it, check out my other book, *Linux Service Management Made Easy with systemd*.

I do believe that this wraps things up for our discussion of MAC.

Summary

In this chapter, we looked at the basic principles of MAC and compared two different MAC systems. We saw what SELinux and AppArmor are and how they can help safeguard your systems against malicious actors. We then looked at the basics of how to use them and the basics of how to troubleshoot them. We also saw that, even though they're both meant to do the same job, they work in vastly different ways. We wrapped things up by showing you a practical example of how SELinux can protect you from evil Docker containers.

Whether you're working with AppArmor or with SELinux, you'll always want to thoroughly test a new system in either complain or permissive mode before you put it into production. Make sure that what you want to protect gets protected, while at the same time what you want to allow gets allowed. After you place the machine into production, don't just assume that you can automatically change a policy setting every time you see a policy violation occur. It could be that nothing is wrong with your MAC setup and that MAC is just doing its job, protecting you from the bad guys.

There's a lot more to both of these topics than we can cover here. Hopefully, though, I've given you enough to whet your appetite and help you out in your day-to-day duties.

In the next chapter, we'll look at more techniques for hardening the kernel and isolating processes. I'll see you there.

Questions

1. Which of the following would represent a MAC principle?

    a. You can set permissions on your own files and directories however you need to.

    b. You can allow any system process to access whatever you need it to access.

    c. System processes can only access whichever resources MAC policies allow them to access.

    d. MAC will allow access, even if DAC doesn't.

2. How does SELinux work?

    a. It places a label on each system object and allows or denies access according to what SELinux policies say about the labels.

    b. It simply consults a profile for each system process to see what the process is allowed to do.

    c. It uses extended attributes that an administrator would set with the `chattr` utility.

    d. It allows each user to set his or her own MACs.

3. Which of these utilities would you use to fix an incorrect SELinux security context?

    a. `Chattr`

    b. `Chcontext`

    c. `Restorecon`

    d. `setsebool`

4. For normal day-to-day administration of a Red Hat-type server, which of the following aspects of a security context would an administrator be most concerned about?

    a. User

    b. Role

    c. Type

    d. Sensitivity

5. You've set up a new directory that a particular daemon wouldn't normally access, and you want to permanently allow that daemon to access that directory. Which of the following utilities would you use to do that?

    a. chcon
    b. restorecon
    c. setseboo
    d. semanage

6. Which of the following constitutes one difference between SELinux and AppArmor?

    a. With SELinux, you have to install or create a policy profile for each system process that you need to control.
    b. With AppArmor, you have to install or create a policy profile for each system process that you need to control.
    c. AppArmor works by applying a label to each system object, while SELinux works by simply consulting a profile for each system object.
    d. It's much easier to write a policy profile for SELinux, because the language is easier to understand.

7. Which /etc/apparmor.d/ subdirectory contains files with pre-defined variables?

    a. tunables
    b. variables
    c. var
    d. functions

8. Which of the following utilities would you use to enable an AppArmor policy?

    a. aa-enforce
    b. aa-enable
    c. set-enforce
    d. set-enable

9. You've already enabled an AppArmor policy for a daemon, but you now need to change the policy. Which utility would you use to reload the modified policy?

    a. aa-reload
    b. apparmor_reload
    c. aa-restart
    d. apparmor_parser

10. You're testing a new AppArmor profile and you want to find any possible problems before you place the server into production. Which AppArmor mode would you use to test that profile?

    a. permissive
    b. enforce

     c. testing

     d. complain

Further reading

SELinux:

- Accessing SELinux policy documentation: `https://www.redhat.com/sysadmin/accessing-selinux-policy-documentation`

- Using SELinux: `https://access.redhat.com/documentation/en-us/red_hat_enterprise_linux/9/html/using_selinux/index`

- Four semanage commands to keep SELinux in enforcing mode: `https://www.redhat.com/sysadmin/semanage-keep-selinux-enforcing`

- SELinux System Administration – Third Edition: `https://www.packtpub.com/product/selinux-system-administration-third-edition/9781800201477`

- SELinux Policy for Pi-Hole: `https://unix.stackexchange.com/questions/451035/selinux-policy-for-pi-hole`

- SELinux Coloring Book: `https://opensource.com/business/13/11/selinux-policy-guide`

- Linux Service Management Made Easy with systemd: `https://www.packtpub.com/product/linux-service-management-made-easy-with-systemd/9781801811644?_ga=2.122984843.1038813545.1668463819-58585121.1668463819`

AppArmor:

- Ubuntu AppArmor wiki: `https://wiki.ubuntu.com/AppArmor`

- How to create an AppArmor profile: `https://tutorials.ubuntu.com/tutorial/beginning-apparmor-profile-development#0`

- The comprehensive guide to AppArmor: `https://medium.com/information-and-technology/so-what-is-apparmor-64d7ae211ed`

- Samba print server bug: `https://www.reddit.com/r/openSUSE/comments/q9cpcc/samba_share_doesnt_work_since_snapshot_20211012/`

Answers

1. c
2. a
3. c
4. c
5. d
6. b
7. a
8. a
9. d
10. d

Join our book community

Join our community's Discord space for discussions with the author and other readers:

`https://packt.link/CyberSec`

11

Kernel Hardening and Process Isolation

Although the Linux kernel is already fairly secure by design, there are still a few ways to lock it down even more. It's simple to do, once you know what to look for. Tweaking the kernel can help prevent certain network attacks and certain types of information leaks. (But fear not – you don't have to re-compile a whole new kernel to take advantage of this.)

With process isolation, our aim is to prevent malicious users from performing either a vertical or a horizontal privilege escalation. By isolating processes from each other, we can help prevent someone from taking control of either a root user process or a process that belongs to some other user. Either of these types of privilege escalation could help an attacker either take control of a system or access sensitive information.

In this chapter, we'll take a quick tour of the /proc filesystem and show you how to configure certain parameters within it to help beef up security. Then, we'll turn to the subject of process isolation and talk about various methods to ensure that processes remain isolated from each other.

In this chapter, we'll cover the following topics:

- Understanding the /proc filesystem
- Setting kernel parameters with sysctl
- Configuring the sysctl.conf file
- An overview of process isolation
- Control groups
- Namespace isolation
- Kernel capabilities
- SECCOMP and system calls
- Using process isolation with Docker containers
- Sandboxing with Firejail
- Sandboxing with Snappy

- Sandboxing with Flatpak

So, if you're ready and raring, we'll start by looking at the /proc filesystem.

Understanding the /proc filesystem

If you cd into the /proc/ directory of any Linux distro and take a look around, you'll be excused for thinking that there's nothing special about it. You'll see files and directories, so it looks like it could just be another directory. In reality, though, it's very special. It's one of several different **pseudo-filesystems** on the Linux system. (The definition of the word pseudo is *fake*, so you can also think of it as a fake filesystem.)

If you were to pull the primary operating system drive out of a Linux machine and mount it as the secondary drive on another machine, you'll see a /proc/ directory on that drive, but you won't see anything in it. That's because the contents of the /proc/ directory are created from scratch every time you boot a Linux machine, and then cleared out every time you shut down the machine. Within /proc/, you'll find two general classes of information:

- Information about user-mode processes
- Information about what's going on at the kernel-level of the operating system

We'll look at user-mode processes first.

Looking at user-mode processes

If you invoke the ls command within /proc/, you'll see a whole bunch of directories that have numbers as their names. Here's a partial listing from my CentOS VM:

```
[donnie@localhost proc]$ ls -l
total 0
dr-xr-xr-x. 9 root root 0 Oct 19 14:23 1
dr-xr-xr-x. 9 root root 0 Oct 19 14:23 10
dr-xr-xr-x. 9 root root 0 Oct 19 14:23 11
dr-xr-xr-x. 9 root root 0 Oct 19 14:23 12
dr-xr-xr-x. 9 root root 0 Oct 19 14:23 13
dr-xr-xr-x. 9 root root 0 Oct 19 14:24 1373
dr-xr-xr-x. 9 root root 0 Oct 19 14:24 145
dr-xr-xr-x. 9 root root 0 Oct 19 14:23 15
dr-xr-xr-x. 9 root root 0 Oct 19 14:23 16
dr-xr-xr-x. 9 root root 0 Oct 19 14:23 17
. . .
. . .
```

Each of these numbered directories corresponds to the **Process ID (PID)** number of a user-mode process. On any Linux system, PID 1 is always the init system process, which is the first user-mode process that starts when you boot a machine.

> On Debian/Ubuntu systems, the name of PID 1 is `init`. On RHEL/CentOS/AlmaLinux systems, it's called `systemd`. All of these distros run the `systemd` `init` system, but the Debian/Ubuntu folk have chosen to retain the old `init` name for PID 1.

Within each numbered directory, you'll see various files and subdirectories that contain information about a particular running process. For example, in the `1` directory, you'll see what pertains to the `init` process. Here's the partial listing:

```
[donnie@localhost 1]$ ls -l
ls: cannot read symbolic link 'cwd': Permission denied
ls: cannot read symbolic link 'root': Permission denied
ls: cannot read symbolic link 'exe': Permission denied
total 0
dr-xr-xr-x. 2 root root 0 Oct 19 14:23 attr
-rw-r--r--. 1 root root 0 Oct 19 15:08 autogroup
-r--------. 1 root root 0 Oct 19 15:08 auxv
-r--r--r--. 1 root root 0 Oct 19 14:23 cgroup
--w-------. 1 root root 0 Oct 19 15:08 clear_refs
-r--r--r--. 1 root root 0 Oct 19 14:23 cmdline
-rw-r--r--. 1 root root 0 Oct 19 14:23 comm
. . .
. . .
```

As you see, there are a few symbolic links that we can't access without root privileges. When we use `sudo`, we can see where the symbolic links point:

```
[donnie@localhost 1]$ sudo ls -l
total 0
dr-xr-xr-x. 2 root root 0 Oct 19 14:23 attr
-rw-r--r--. 1 root root 0 Oct 19 15:08 autogroup
-r--------. 1 root root 0 Oct 19 15:08 auxv
-r--r--r--. 1 root root 0 Oct 19 14:23 cgroup
--w-------. 1 root root 0 Oct 19 15:08 clear_refs
-r--r--r--. 1 root root 0 Oct 19 14:23 cmdline
-rw-r--r--. 1 root root 0 Oct 19 14:23 comm
-rw-r--r--. 1 root root 0 Oct 19 15:08 coredump_filter
-r--r--r--. 1 root root 0 Oct 19 15:08 cpuset
lrwxrwxrwx. 1 root root 0 Oct 19 15:08 cwd -> /
. . .
. . .
```

You can use the `cat` command to view the contents of some of these items, but not all of them. However, even when you can view the contents, you won't be able to make much sense of what's there, unless you're an operating system programmer. Rather than trying to view the information directly, you're better off using either top or ps, which pull their information from /proc/ and parse it so that humans can read it.

> I'm assuming that most of you are already familiar with top and ps. For those who aren't, here's the short explanation.
>
> ps provides a static display of what's going on with your machine's processes. There are loads of option switches that can show you different amounts of information. My favorite ps command is ps aux, which provides a fairly complete set of information about each process.
>
> top provides a dynamic, constantly changing display of the machine's processes. Some option switches are available, but just invoking top without any options is usually all you need.

Next, let's look at the kernel information.

Looking at kernel information

Within the top level of /proc/, the files and directories that have actual names contain information about what's going on with the Linux kernel. Here's a partial view:

```
[donnie@localhost proc]$ ls -l
total 0
. . .
dr-xr-xr-x. 2 root root 0 Oct 19 14:24 acpi
dr-xr-xr-x. 5 root root 0 Oct 19 14:24 asound
-r--r--r--. 1 root root 0 Oct 19 14:26 buddyinfo
dr-xr-xr-x. 4 root root 0 Oct 19 14:24 bus
-r--r--r--. 1 root root 0 Oct 19 14:23 cgroups
-r--r--r--. 1 root root 0 Oct 19 14:23 cmdline
-r--r--r--. 1 root root 0 Oct 19 14:26 consoles
-r--r--r--. 1 root root 0 Oct 19 14:24 cpuinfo
. . .
```

As with the user-mode stuff, you can use cat to look at some of the different files. For example, here's a partial output of the cpuinfo file:

```
[donnie@localhost proc]$ cat cpuinfo
processor    : 0
vendor_id    : AuthenticAMD
cpu family   : 16
model        : 4
```

```
model name      : Quad-Core AMD Opteron(tm) Processor 2380
stepping        : 2
microcode       : 0x1000086
cpu MHz          : 2500.038
cache size      : 512 KB
physical id     : 0
siblings        : 1
core id          : 0
cpu cores       : 1
. . .
```

Here, you can see the type and speed rating of my CPU, its cache size, and the fact that this CentOS VM is only running on one of the host machine's eight CPU cores. (Doing this on the Fedora host operating system would show information about all eight of the host machine's cores.)

> Yes, you did read that right. I wrote parts of the original version of this book on an antique, Opteron-equipped HP workstation from 2009. I got it from eBay for a very cheap price, and it runs beautifully with the LXDE spin of Fedora. And, the openSUSE machine that you'll see mentioned in other parts of this book is the exact same model and came from the same vendor. (So, now you know just how cheap I really am.) Sadly though, the RHEL 9-type distros won't run on the first generation of x86_64 CPUs, so I'm now using something newer to write this *Third Edition*.

However, for our present purposes, we don't need to go into the nitty-gritty details of everything that's in /proc/. What's more important to our present discussion is the different parameters that can be set from within /proc/. For example, within the /proc/sys/net/ipv4/ directory, we can see lots of different items that can be tweaked to change IPv4 network performance. Here's a partial listing:

```
[donnie@localhost ipv4]$ pwd
/proc/sys/net/ipv4
[donnie@localhost ipv4]$ ls -l
total 0
-rw-r--r--. 1 root root 0 Oct 19 16:11 cipso_cache_bucket_size
-rw-r--r--. 1 root root 0 Oct 19 16:11 cipso_cache_enable
-rw-r--r--. 1 root root 0 Oct 19 16:11 cipso_rbm_optfmt
-rw-r--r--. 1 root root 0 Oct 19 16:11 cipso_rbm_strictvalid
dr-xr-xr-x. 1 root root 0 Oct 19 14:23 conf
-rw-r--r--. 1 root root 0 Oct 19 16:11 fib_multipath_hash_policy
-rw-r--r--. 1 root root 0 Oct 19 16:11 fib_multipath_use_neigh
-rw-r--r--. 1 root root 0 Oct 19 16:11 fwmark_reflect
-rw-r--r--. 1 root root 0 Oct 19 16:11 icmp_echo_ignore_all
 . . .
 . . .
```

We can use the cat command to view each of these parameters, like so:

```
[donnie@localhost ipv4]$ cat icmp_echo_ignore_all
0
[donnie@localhost ipv4]$
```

So, the icmp_echo_ignore_all parameter is set to 0, which means that it's disabled. If I were to ping this machine from another machine, assuming that the firewall is configured to allow that, this machine would respond to the pings. Here are several ways to change that if need be:

- echo a new value into the parameter from the command line.
- Use the sysctl utility from the command line.
- Configure the /etc/sysctl.conf file.
- Add a new .conf file that contains the new configuration to the /etc/sysctl.d/ directory.
- Run a command from within a shell script.

Let's go ahead and look at these different methods in detail.

Setting kernel parameters with sysctl

The traditional method that you'll see in older Linux textbooks is to echo a value into a /proc/ parameter. This doesn't directly work with sudo, so you'll need to use the bash -c command to force the command to execute. Here, you can see me changing the value for the icmp_echo_ignore_all parameter:

```
[donnie@localhost ~]$ sudo bash -c "echo '1' > /proc/sys/net/ipv4/icmp_echo_
ignore_all"
[donnie@localhost ~]$ cat /proc/sys/net/ipv4/icmp_echo_ignore_all
1
[donnie@localhost ~]$
```

With the value set to 1, this machine will now ignore all ping packets, regardless of how the firewall is configured. Any value you set like this is temporary and will go back to its default setting when you reboot the machine.

Next in the list after this one is the icmp_echo_ignore_broadcasts setting, which looks like this:

```
[donnie@localhost ipv4]$ cat icmp_echo_ignore_broadcasts
1
[donnie@localhost ipv4]$
```

It's already enabled by default, so out of the box, Linux is already immune to **Denial-of-Service (DoS)** attacks that involve ICMP broadcast flooding.

Configuring /proc/ parameters with echo is old hat, and personally, I don't like to do it. It's better to use sysctl, which is the more modern way of doing business. It's easy to use, and you can read all about it in the sysctl man page.

To see a list of all the parameter settings, just do this:

```
[donnie@localhost ~]$ sudo sysctl -a
abi.vsyscall32 = 1
crypto.fips_enabled = 1
debug.exception-trace = 1
debug.kprobes-optimization = 1
dev.hpet.max-user-freq = 64
dev.mac_hid.mouse_button2_keycode = 97
dev.mac_hid.mouse_button3_keycode = 100
dev.mac_hid.mouse_button_emulation = 0
dev.raid.speed_limit_max = 200000
dev.raid.speed_limit_min = 1000
dev.scsi.logging_level = 0
fs.aio-max-nr = 65536

. . .

. . .
```

To set a parameter, use the -w option to write the new value. The trick to this is that the forward slashes in the directory path are replaced by dots, and you ignore the /proc/sys/ part of the path. So, to change the icmp_echo_ignore_all value back to 0, we'll do this:

```
[donnie@localhost ~]$ sudo sysctl -w net.ipv4.icmp_echo_ignore_all=0
net.ipv4.icmp_echo_ignore_all = 0
[donnie@localhost ~]$
```

In this case, the change is permanent because I'm just changing the parameter back to its default setting. Normally, though, any changes we make like this only last until we reboot the machine. Sometimes, that's okay. Other times, we might need to make the changes permanent.

Configuring the sysctl.conf file

There are some significant differences between the default configurations of Ubuntu and CentOS/AlmaLinux. They all use the /etc/sysctl.conf file, but on CentOS and AlmaLinux, that file doesn't have anything except for some explanatory comments. Ubuntu and CentOS/AlmaLinux all have files with default settings in the /usr/lib/sysctl.d/ directory, but there are more for CentOS and AlmaLinux than there are for Ubuntu. On Ubuntu, you'll find other files with default values in the /etc/sysctl.d/ directory. On CentOS and AlmaLinux, that directory only contains a symbolic link that points back to the /etc/sysctl.conf file. Also, you'll find that some things are hardcoded into the Linux kernel and aren't mentioned in any of the configuration files. In true Linux fashion, every distro has a different way of configuring all this, just to ensure that users remain thoroughly confused. One thing that's consistent is that on any of your virtual machines, you can use the systemd-analyze cat-config sysctl.d command to view a summary of the kernel settings that are defined in these files. (To see the complete list of kernel settings though, you'll still need to use the sysctl -a command.)

> In the `/usr/lib/sysctl.d/README` file on the AlmaLinux machine, you'll find additional information about how this works.

Now, with the introductory part out of the way, let's see if we can make sense of all this.

Configuring sysctl.conf — Ubuntu

In the `/etc/sysctl.conf` file on an Ubuntu machine, you'll see lots of comments and a few examples of things that you can tweak. The comments provide good explanations of what the various settings do. So, we'll start with it.

Much of this file contains settings that can help improve networking security. Toward the top of the file, we see this:

```
# Uncomment the next two lines to enable Spoof protection (reverse-path filter)
# Turn on Source Address Verification in all interfaces to
# prevent some spoofing attacks
#net.ipv4.conf.default.rp_filter=1
#net.ipv4.conf.all.rp_filter=1
```

A spoofing attack involves a bad actor who sends you network packets with spoofed IP addresses. Spoofing can be used for a few different things, such as DoS attacks, anonymous port scanning, or tricking access controls. These settings, when enabled, cause the operating system to verify if it can reach the source address that's in the packet header. If it can't, the packet is rejected. You may be wondering why this is disabled since it seems like such a good thing. However, this isn't the case. It is enabled in another file. If you look in the `/etc/sysctl.d/10-network-security.conf` file, you'll see it enabled there. So, there's no need to uncomment these two lines.

Next, we see this:

```
# Uncomment the next line to enable TCP/IP SYN cookies
# See http://lwn.net/Articles/277146/
# Note: This may impact IPv6 TCP sessions too
#net.ipv4.tcp_syncookies=1
```

One form of DoS attack involves sending massive amounts of SYN packets to a target machine, without completing the rest of the three-way handshake. This can cause the victim machine to have lots of half-open network connections, which would eventually exhaust the machine's ability to accept any more legitimate connections. Turning on SYN cookies can help prevent this type of attack. On Ubuntu 18.04, which is what I used to write the previous edition of this book, SYN cookies are already turned on in the `/etc/sysctl.d/10-network-security.conf` file. On Ubuntu 22.04, that setting is nowhere to be found in any of the `sysctl` configuration files, other than the disabled setting in the `sysctl.conf` file. However, a `sudo sysctl -a` command on the 22.04 machine will show us that SYN cookies are indeed enabled:

```
donnie@ubuntu-2204:~$ sudo sysctl -a | grep syncookie
net.ipv4.tcp_syncookies = 1
donnie@ubuntu-2204:~$
```

To find where this is set, we'll need to do a bit of clever detective work. In the /boot/ directory of the 22.04 machine, you'll see one config file for each installed kernel. When I used grep -i to perform a case-insensitive search for the syncookies text string in one of the config files, I couldn't find anything. So, I broadened the search for all syn text strings. Here's what that looks like:

```
donnie@ubuntu-2204:/boot$ grep -i 'syn' config-5.15.0-52-generic
. . .

. . .

CONFIG_SYN_COOKIES=y

. . .

. . .
```

So, we see that on Ubuntu 22.04, the developers chose to hard-code the SYN cookies setting into the kernel rather than to set it in a sysctl configuration file. So, as we saw before with the Ubuntu 18.04 machine, there's no need to uncomment the syncookies line in the sysctl.conf file.

Here's the next thing we see:

```
# Uncomment the next line to enable packet forwarding for IPv4
#net.ipv4.ip_forward=1
```

Uncommenting this line would allow network packets to flow from one network interface to another in machines that have multiple network interfaces. Unless you're setting up a router or a Virtual Private Network server, leave this setting as is.

We've been looking at nothing but IPv4 stuff so far. Here's one for IPv6:

```
# Uncomment the next line to enable packet forwarding for IPv6
#  Enabling this option disables Stateless Address Autoconfiguration
#  based on Router Advertisements for this host
#net.ipv6.conf.all.forwarding=1
```

In general, you'll also want to leave this one commented out, as it is now. Disabling **Stateless Address Autoconfiguration** on machines in an IPv6 environment would mean that you'd need to either set up a DHCPv6 server or set static IPv6 addresses on all hosts.

The next section controls ICMP redirects:

```
# Do not accept ICMP redirects (prevent MITM attacks)
#net.ipv4.conf.all.accept_redirects = 0
#net.ipv6.conf.all.accept_redirects = 0
# _or_
# Accept ICMP redirects only for gateways listed in our default
# gateway list (enabled by default)
```

```
# net.ipv4.conf.all.secure_redirects = 1
#
```

Allowing ICMP redirects can potentially allow a **Man-in-the-Middle (MITM)** attack to be successful. Uncommenting the two lines in the top section of this snippet would completely disable ICMP redirects. The bottom line in the bottom section allows redirects, but only if they come from a trusted gateway. This one is a bit deceiving, because even though this line is commented out, and even though there's nothing about this in any of the other configuration files, secure redirects are actually enabled by default. We can see this by filtering our sysctl -a output through grep:

```
donnie@ubuntu-2204:/etc$ sudo sysctl -a | grep 'secure_redirects'
net.ipv4.conf.all.secure_redirects = 1
net.ipv4.conf.default.secure_redirects = 1
net.ipv4.conf.enp0s3.secure_redirects = 1
net.ipv4.conf.lo.secure_redirects = 1
donnie@ubuntu-2204:/etc$
```

Here, we can see that secure redirects are enabled on all network interfaces. But if you're sure that your machine will never get used as a router, it's still best to completely disable ICMP redirects. (We'll do that in just a bit.)

The final networking item in this file involves Martian packets:

```
# Log Martian Packets
#net.ipv4.conf.all.log_martians = 1
#
```

Now, if you're as old as I am, you might remember a really silly television show from the '60s called *My Favorite Martian*. But, this setting has nothing to do with that. Martian packets have a source address that normally can't be accepted by a particular network interface. For example, if your Internet-facing server receives packets with a private IP address or a loopback device address, that's a Martian packet. Why are they called Martian packets? Well, it's because of someone's statement that these packets are not of this earth. Regardless, Martian packets can exhaust network resources, so it's good to know about them. You can enable logging for them either by uncommenting the line in the preceding snippet or by placing an override file in the /etc/sysctl.d/ directory. (We'll also do that in just a bit.)

The following snippet is a kernel parameter for the **Magic system request key**:

```
# Magic system request key
# 0=disable, 1=enable all
# Debian kernels have this set to 0 (disable the key)
# See https://www.kernel.org/doc/Documentation/sysrq.txt
# for what other values do
#kernel.sysrq=438
```

When this parameter is enabled, you can perform certain functions, such as shutting down or rebooting the system, sending signals to processes, dumping process debug information, and several other things, by pressing a sequence of **Magic Keys**. You would do this by pressing the *Alt + SysReq + command-key* sequence. (The *SysReq* key is the *PrtScr* key on some keyboards, while the command-key is the key that invokes some specific command.) A value of 0 for this would completely disable it, and a value of 1 would enable all Magic Key functions. A value greater than 1 would enable only specific functions. In this file, this option appears to be disabled. However, it's actually enabled in the /etc/sysctl.d/10-magic-sysrq.conf file. If you're dealing with a server that's locked away in a server room and that can't be remotely accessed from a serial console, this might not be a big deal. However, for a machine that's out in the open or that can be accessed from a serial console, you might want to disable this. (We'll do that in a bit as well.)

Under certain circumstances, bad guys could possibly create links to sensitive files so that they can easily access them. Link protection is turned on in the /etc/sysctl.d/10-link-restrictions.conf file on Ubuntu 18.04, and in the /usr/lib/sysctl.d/99-protect-links.conf file on Ubuntu 22.04. Here's what that looks like on 22.04:

```
# Protected links
#
# Protects against creating or following links under certain conditions
# Debian kernels have both set to 1 (restricted)
# See https://www.kernel.org/doc/Documentation/sysctl/fs.txt
fs.protected_fifos = 1
fs.protected_hardlinks = 1
fs.protected_regular = 2
fs.protected_symlinks = 1
```

That pretty much covers what we have in Ubuntu. Now, let's look at CentOS and AlmaLinux.

Configuring sysctl.conf — CentOS and AlmaLinux

On CentOS and AlmaLinux, the /etc/sysctl.conf file is empty, except for a few comments. These comments tell you to look elsewhere for the default configuration files and to make changes by creating new configuration files in the /etc/sysctl.d/ directory.

The default security settings for CentOS and AlmaLinux are pretty much the same as they are for Ubuntu, except they're configured in different places. For example, on CentOS and AlmaLinux, the spoof protection (rp_filter) parameters and the link protection parameters are in the /usr/lib/sysctl.d/50-default.conf file.

By piping a sysctl -a command into grep, you'll also see that SYN cookies are enabled:

```
[donnie@alma9 ~]$ sudo sysctl -a | grep 'syncookie'
net.ipv4.tcp_syncookies = 1
[donnie@alma9 ~]$
```

The same is true for `secure_redirects`:

```
[donnie@alma9 ~]$ sudo sysctl -a | grep 'secure_redirects'
net.ipv4.conf.all.secure_redirects = 1
net.ipv4.conf.default.secure_redirects = 1
net.ipv4.conf.enp0s3.secure_redirects = 1
net.ipv4.conf.lo.secure_redirects = 1
net.ipv4.conf.virbr0.secure_redirects = 1
net.ipv4.conf.virbr0-nic.secure_redirects = 1
[donnie@alma9 ~]$
```

As was the case with Ubuntu, the SYN cookies setting is hard-coded into the Linux kernel, as we see here:

```
[donnie@alma9 ~]$ cd /boot
[donnie@alma9 boot]$ grep -i cookies config-5.14.0-70.30.1.el9_0.x86_64
CONFIG_SYN_COOKIES=y
[donnie@alma9 boot]$
```

Okay, so far so good. Let's continue on.

Setting additional kernel-hardening parameters

What we've seen so far isn't too bad. Most of the parameters that we've looked at are already set to their most secure values. But is there room for improvement? Indeed there is. You wouldn't know it by looking at any of the configuration files, though. On Ubuntu, CentOS, and AlmaLinux, quite a few items have default values that aren't set in any of the normal configuration files. The best way to see this is to use a system scanner, such as **Lynis**.

Lynis is a security scanner that shows lots of information about a system. (We'll cover it in more detail in *Chapter 14, Vulnerability Scanning and Intrusion Detection*) For now, we'll just cover what it can tell us about hardening the Linux kernel.

After you run a scan, you'll see a `[+] Kernel Hardening` section in the screen output. It's fairly lengthy, so here's just part of it:

```
[+] Kernel Hardening
-----------------------------------
  - Comparing sysctl key pairs with scan profile
  - fs.protected_hardlinks (exp: 1) [ OK ]
  - fs.protected_symlinks (exp: 1) [ OK ]
  - fs.suid_dumpable (exp: 0) [ OK ]
  - kernel.core_uses_pid (exp: 1) [ OK ]
  - kernel.ctrl-alt-del (exp: 0) [ OK ]
  - kernel.dmesg_restrict (exp: 1) [ DIFFERENT ]
  - kernel.kptr_restrict (exp: 2) [ DIFFERENT ]
  - kernel.randomize_va_space (exp: 2) [ OK ]
  - kernel.sysrq (exp: 0) [ DIFFERENT ]
```

```
. . .
. . .
```

Everything that's marked as OK is as it should be for best security. What's marked as DIFFERENT should be changed to the suggested exp: value that's within the pair of parentheses. (**exp** stands for **expected**.) Let's do that now in a hands-on lab.

Hands-on lab — scanning kernel parameters with Lynis

Lynis is in the normal repositories for Ubuntu and in the EPEL repository for CentOS and AlmaLinux. It's always a few versions behind what you can get directly from the author's website, but for now, that's okay. When we get to *Chapter 14, Vulnerability Scanning and Intrusion Detection*, I'll show you how to get the newest version. Let's get started:

1. Install Lynis from the repository for Ubuntu, like this:

    ```
    sudo apt update
    sudo apt install lynis
    ```

    Do this for CentOS 07:

    ```
    sudo yum install lynis
    ```

    Do this for AlmaLinux 8 or 9:

    ```
    sudo dnf install lynis
    ```

2. Scan the system by using the following command:

    ```
    sudo lynis audit system
    ```

3. When the scan completes, scroll back up to the [+] Kernel Hardening section of the output. Copy and paste the sysctl key pairs into a text file. Save it as secure_values.conf in your own home directory. The contents of the file should look something like this:

    ```
    - fs.protected_hardlinks (exp: 1) [ OK ]
    - fs.protected_symlinks (exp: 1) [ OK ]
    - fs.suid_dumpable (exp: 0) [ OK ]
    - kernel.core_uses_pid (exp: 1) [ OK ]
    - kernel.ctrl-alt-del (exp: 0) [ OK ]
    - kernel.dmesg_restrict (exp: 1) [ DIFFERENT ]
    - kernel.kptr_restrict (exp: 2) [ DIFFERENT ]
    - kernel.randomize_va_space (exp: 2) [ OK ]
    - kernel.sysrq (exp: 0) [ DIFFERENT ]
    - kernel.yama.ptrace_scope (exp: 1 2 3) [ DIFFERENT ]
    - net.ipv4.conf.all.accept_redirects (exp: 0) [ DIFFERENT ]
    - net.ipv4.conf.all.accept_source_route (exp: 0) [ OK ]

    . . .

    . . .
    ```

4. Use grep to send all of the DIFFERENT lines to a new file. Name it 60-secure_values.conf:

```
grep 'DIFFERENT' secure_values.conf > 60-secure_values.conf
```

5. Edit the 60-secure_values.conf file to convert it into the sysctl configuration format. Set each parameter to the exp value that's currently within the pairs of parentheses. The finished product should look something like this:

```
kernel.dmesg_restrict = 1
kernel.kptr_restrict = 2
kernel.sysrq = 0
kernel.yama.ptrace_scope = 1 2 3
net.ipv4.conf.all.accept_redirects = 0
net.ipv4.conf.all.log_martians = 1
net.ipv4.conf.all.send_redirects = 0
net.ipv4.conf.default.accept_redirects = 0
net.ipv4.conf.default.log_martians = 1
net.ipv6.conf.all.accept_redirects = 0
net.ipv6.conf.default.accept_redirects = 0
```

6. Copy the file to the /etc/sysctl.d/ directory:

```
sudo cp 60-secure_values.conf /etc/sysctl.d/
```

7. Reboot the machine to read in the values from the new file:

```
sudo shutdown -r now
```

8. Repeat *step 2*. Most items should now show up with their most secure values. However, you might see a few DIFFERENT lines come up. That's okay; just move the lines for those parameters into the main /etc/sysctl.conf file and reboot the machine again.

That's the end of the lab—congratulations!

We've already talked about some of the items that we changed in this procedure. Here's a breakdown of the rest of them:

- kernel.dmesg_restrict = 1: By default, any non-privileged user can run the dmesg command, which allows the user to view different types of kernel information. Some of this information could be sensitive, so we want to set this parameter to 1 so that only someone with root privileges can use dmesg.

- kernel.kptr_restrict = 2: This setting prevents /proc from exposing kernel addresses in memory. Setting this to 0 completely disables it, while setting it to 1 prevents non-privileged users from seeing the address information. Setting it to 2, as we have here, prevents anyone from seeing address information, regardless of the person's privilege level. Note, though, that setting this to either 1 or 2 could prevent certain performance monitor programs, such as perf, from running. If you absolutely have to do performance monitoring, you might have to set this to 0. (That's not as bad as it might sound, because having the kernel.dmesg_restrict = 1 setting in place can help mitigate this issue.)

- `kernel.yama.ptrace_scope = 1 2 3`: This places restrictions on the `ptrace` utility, which is a debugging program that the bad guys can also use. 1 restricts `ptrace` to only debugging parent processes. 2 means that only someone with root privileges can use `ptrace`, while 3 prevents anyone from tracing processes with `ptrace`.

In this section, you learned how to configure various kernel parameters to help lock down your system. Next, we'll lock things down even more by restricting who can view process information.

Preventing users from seeing each others' processes

By default, users can use a utility such as `ps` or `top` to see everyone else's processes, as well as their own. To demonstrate this, let's look at the following partial output from a `ps aux` command:

```
[donnie@localhost ~]$ ps aux
USER         PID %CPU %MEM    VSZ    RSS TTY       STAT START    TIME COMMAND
root           1  0.0  0.7 179124 13752 ?          Ss   12:05    0:03 /usr/lib/
systemd/systemd --switched-root --system --deserialize 17
root           2  0.0  0.0      0      0 ?          S    12:05    0:00 [kthreadd]
root           3  0.0  0.0      0      0 ?          I<   12:05    0:00 [rcu_gp]
. . .
. . .
colord 2218 0.0 0.5 323948 10344 ? Ssl 12:06 0:00 /usr/libexec/colord
gdm 2237 0.0 0.2 206588 5612 tty1 Sl 12:06 0:00 /usr/libexec/ibus-engine-simple
root 2286 0.0 0.6 482928 11932 ? Sl 12:06 0:00 gdm-session-worker [pam/gdm-
password]
donnie 2293 0.0 0.5 93280 9696 ? Ss 12:06 0:00 /usr/lib/systemd/systemd --user
donnie 2301 0.0 0.2 251696 4976 ? S 12:06 0:00 (sd-pam)
donnie 2307 0.0 0.6 1248768 12656 ? S<sl 12:06 0:00 /usr/bin/pulseaudio
--daemonize=no
. . .
```

Even with just my normal user privileges, I can view processes that belong to the root user and various system users, as well as my own. (And if any of my cats were logged in, I'd also be able to view their processes.) This information can be quite useful to an administrator, but it can also help the bad guys. This information can help Joe or Jane Hacker plan an attack on your system, and it may also even reveal some sensitive information. The best way to deal with this is to mount the `/proc` filesystem with the `hidepid` option, as long as you're not working with some sort of RHEL 9-type distro.

This feature has been disabled for the RHEL 9-type distros. So, don't try this on any of your AlmaLinux 9 machines. Not only will it not work, it could break your machine.

On an Ubuntu, CentOS 7, or AlmaLinux 8 VM, you can do this by adding a line to the end of the /etc/ fstab file, like so:

```
proc    /proc    proc    hidepid=2    0    0
```

Then, remount /proc, like so:

```
sudo mount -o remount proc
```

Now, any user who doesn't have sudo privileges can only view his or her own processes. (Pretty slick, eh?)

> The three values for the hidepid option are as follows:
>
> 0: This is the default, which allows all users to see each others' processes.
>
> 1: This allows all users to see other users' process directories within /proc. However, users will only be able to cd into their own process directories. Also, they'll only be able to see their own process information with ps or top.
>
> 2: This hides all other users' process information, including the process directories within /proc.

Now that you've seen the inner workings of the /proc filesystem and how to configure it for best security, let's look at **process isolation**.

Understanding process isolation

A primary objective of any network intruder is to gain the privileges that are required to perform his or her dirty deeds. This normally involves logging in as a normal user and then performing some sort of **privilege escalation**. A **vertical escalation** involves obtaining root privileges, while a **horizontal escalation** involves gaining the privileges of some other normal user. If the other normal user has any sensitive documents in folders that he or she can access, then a horizontal escalation might be all that the intruder requires. Discretionary Access Control and Mandatory Access Control can help out, but we also want to isolate processes from each other and ensure that processes run with only the lowest possible privileges.

> When planning a defense against these types of attacks, consider that the attacks could come from either outsiders or insiders. So yes, you do need to guard against attacks from your organization's own employees.

In this section, we'll look at the various Linux kernel features that facilitate process isolation. Then, we'll look at some cool ways to use these features.

Understanding Control Groups (cgroups)

Control Groups, more commonly called **cgroups**, were introduced back in 2010 in Red Hat Enterprise Linux 6. Originally, they were just an add-on feature, and a user had to jump through some hoops to manually create them. Nowadays, with the advent of the systemd init system, cgroups are an integral part of the operating system, and each process runs in its own cgroup by default.

> When I wrote the first two editions of this book, all enterprise-grade systemd-based Linux distros were running **cgroups Version 1**. Now though, they've all switched to **cgroup Version 2**. (Yes, that really is cgroups for Version 1, and cgroup for Version 2. I have no idea why.) Although there's a substantial difference in the architecture of the two versions, there's not that much difference in how you would use them. The main difference is that Version 2 offers a few more features, and that the names of some of the parameters that you can set are different. If you want to read more about cgroups, check out my other book, *Linux Service Management Made Easy with systemd*.

With cgroups, processes run in their own kernel space and memory space. Should the need arise, an administrator can easily configure a cgroup to limit the resources that the process can use. This is not only good for security, but also for tuning system performance.

So, what is a cgroup? Well, it's really just a collection of processes that are grouped together for a particular purpose. Here's what you can do with cgroups:

- **Set resource limits:** For each cgroup, you can set resource limits for CPU usage, I/O usage, and memory usage.
- **Perform different accounting functions:** You can measure resource usage for each cgroup, which makes it easy to bill specific customers for the resources that they use.
- **Prioritize resources:** You can set limits on a user who's hogging resources like crazy.
- **Freezing, checkpointing, and restarting:** These functions are handy for troubleshooting. They allow you to stop a process, take a snapshot of the system state, and restore a system state from a backup.
- **Assign processes to specific CPU cores:** This is one of the cool features that come with Version 2.

There's not enough space to look at all of these functions, but that's okay. Right now, our primary interest is setting resource limits. With only some minor exceptions, things work the same on all systemd-based Linux distros. For now, let's look at it on an AlmaLinux 9 machine. To start, we'll install the Apache web server package, like this:

```
sudo dnf install httpd
sudo systemctl enable --now httpd
```

By default, each cgroup on the system has no defined resource limits. The first step in defining them is to enable accounting for CPU usage, memory usage, and I/O usage. We could do that by hand-editing the `systemd` service file for each service that we want to limit, but it's easier to just run a `systemctl` command, like so:

```
sudo systemctl set-property httpd.service MemoryAccounting=1 CPUAccounting=1
BlockIOAccounting=1
```

We've just turned on the accounting functions for the Apache web server on our AlmaLinux 9 machine. (The command would be the same on an Ubuntu machine, except that we would have `apache2.service` instead of `httpd.service`.) Now, when we look in the `/etc/systemd/system.control/` directory, we'll see that we've created an `httpd.service.d` directory. Within that directory are the files that turn on our accounting functions:

```
[donnie@localhost httpd.service.d]$ pwd
/etc/systemd/system.control/httpd.service.d
[donnie@localhost httpd.service.d]$ ls -l
total 12
-rw-r--r--. 1 root root 153 Oct 30 15:07 50-BlockIOAccounting.conf
-rw-r--r--. 1 root root 149 Oct 30 15:07 50-CPUAccounting.conf
-rw-r--r--. 1 root root 152 Oct 30 15:07 50-MemoryAccounting.conf
[donnie@localhost httpd.service.d]$
```

Inside each file, we can see two lines that modify the original `httpd.service` file in order to turn on accounting. For example, here's the one for `CPUAccounting`:

```
[donnie@localhost httpd.service.d]$ cat 50-CPUAccounting.conf
# This is a drop-in unit file extension, created via "systemctl set-property"
# or an equivalent operation. Do not edit.
[Service]
CPUAccounting=yes
[donnie@localhost httpd.service.d]$
```

Now that we've enabled accounting for the Apache service, we can place some resource limits on it. (By default, there are no limits.) Let's say that we want to limit Apache to only 40% of CPU usage and 500 MB of memory usage. We'll set both limits with the following command:

```
[donnie@localhost ~]$ sudo systemctl set-property httpd.service CPUQuota=40%
MemoryLimit=500M
[donnie@localhost ~]$
```

This command created two more files in the `/etc/systemd/system.control/httpd.service.d/` directory:

```
[donnie@localhost httpd.service.d]$ ls -l
total 20
-rw-r--r--. 1 root root 153 Oct 30 15:07 50-BlockIOAccounting.conf
```

```
-rw-r--r--. 1 root root 149 Oct 30 15:07 50-CPUAccounting.conf
-rw-r--r--. 1 root root 144 Oct 30 15:18 50-CPUQuota.conf
-rw-r--r--. 1 root root 152 Oct 30 15:07 50-MemoryAccounting.conf
-rw-r--r--. 1 root root 153 Oct 30 15:18 50-MemoryLimit.conf
[donnie@localhost httpd.service.d]$
```

Let's cat one of them, just to see the format of the files:

```
[donnie@localhost httpd.service.d]$ cat 50-CPUQuota.conf
# This is a drop-in unit file extension, created via "systemctl set-property"
# or an equivalent operation. Do not edit.
[Service]
CPUQuota=40%
[donnie@localhost httpd.service.d]$
```

We can allocate resources to other services in the same manner. For example, if this were a **Linux-Apache-MySQL/MariaDB-PHP (LAMP)** server, we could allocate a portion of the remaining CPU and memory resources to the PHP service, and the rest to the MySQL/MariaDB service.

> LAMP is the bedrock for many popular Content Management Systems, such as WordPress and Joomla.

We can also place resource limits on user accounts. For example, let's limit Katelyn to 20% of CPU usage and 500 MB of memory usage. First, we need to get Katelyn's User ID number. We'll do that with the id command:

```
[donnie@localhost ~]$ id katelyn
uid=1001(katelyn) gid=1001(katelyn) groups=1001(katelyn)
[donnie@localhost ~]$
```

So, her UID is 1001. Let's enable accounting for her and set her limits:

```
[donnie@localhost ~]$ sudo systemctl set-property user-1001.slice
MemoryAccounting=1 CPUAccounting=1 BlockIOAccounting=1

[donnie@localhost ~]$ sudo systemctl set-property user-1001.slice CPUQuota=20%
MemoryLimit=500M

[donnie@localhost ~]
```

If we look in the /etc/systemd/system.control/user-1001.slice.d/ directory, we'll see the same set of files that were created for the httpd service.

I've already mentioned the difference between doing this on CentOS/AlmaLinux and Ubuntu. That is, certain services have different names on each distro. In this case, the service is `httpd.service` on CentOS/AlmaLinux and `apache2.service` on Ubuntu. Other than that, things work the same for Ubuntu, CentOS 8, and AlmaLinux 8/9.

On CentOS 7, there's no `system.control` directory within the `/etc/systemd/` directory. Instead, the `httpd.service.d` directory is created within the `/etc/systemd/system/` directory. When I tried to set limits for Katelyn for the first time, again with UID 1001, CentOS 7 wouldn't allow me to do it until Katelyn logged in to activate her `slice`. Her files were created in the `/run/systemd/system/user-1001.slice.d/` directory, which only contains ephemeral runtime files. So, unlike with AlmaLinux 8/9, the files aren't persistent across reboots. This means that if you need to set user resource limits on CentOS 7, you need to be aware that they'll disappear once you reboot the machine.

There's a lot more to cgroups than what I have space to present here. But that's okay. In this section, we've looked at two ways cgroups can enhance security:

- They provide process isolation.
- Using them to limit resource usage can help prevent DoS attacks.

Next up, we'll take a brief look at the concepts of *namespaces* and *namespace isolation*.

Understanding namespace isolation

Namespaces are a kernel security feature that was introduced in Linux kernel version 2.4.19, all the way back in 2002. A namespace allows a process to have its own set of computer resources that other processes can't see. They're especially handy for times when you might have multiple customers sharing resources on the same server. The processes for each user will have their own namespaces. Currently, there are seven types of namespaces:

- **Mount (mnt):** This is the original namespace, which was introduced in Linux kernel 2.4.19. At the time, this was the only namespace. This allows each process to have its own root filesystem that no other processes can see, unless you choose to share it. This is a good way of preventing information leakage.
- **UTS:** The UTS namespace allows each process to have its own unique hostname and domain name.
- **PID:** Every running process can have its own set of PID numbers. PID namespaces can be nested so that a parent namespace can see the PIDs of child namespaces. (Note that child namespaces can't see into the parent namespaces.)
- **Network (net):** This allows you to create a whole virtual network for each process. Each virtual network can have its own subnets, virtual network interfaces, routing tables, and firewalls.
- **Interprocess Communication (ipc):** This also prevents data leakage by preventing two processes from sharing the same memory space. Each running process can access its own memory space, but other processes will be blocked.
- **Control group (cgroup):** This namespace hides the identity of the cgroup of which a process is a member.

- **User:** The User namespace allows a user to have different levels of privilege on different processes. For example, a user could have root-level privileges on one process, but only normal-user privileges on another process.

To see these namespaces, just go into any numbered directory within the /proc filesystem and view the contents of the ns directory. Here's an example from one of my machines:

```
[donnie@localhost ns]$ pwd
/proc/7669/ns
[donnie@localhost ns]$ sudo ls -l
total 0
lrwxrwxrwx. 1 donnie donnie 0 Oct 30 16:16 cgroup -> 'cgroup:[4026531835]'
lrwxrwxrwx. 1 donnie donnie 0 Oct 30 16:16 ipc -> 'ipc:[4026531839]'
lrwxrwxrwx. 1 donnie donnie 0 Oct 30 16:16 mnt -> 'mnt:[4026531840]'
lrwxrwxrwx. 1 donnie donnie 0 Oct 30 16:16 net -> 'net:[4026531992]'
lrwxrwxrwx. 1 donnie donnie 0 Oct 30 16:16 pid -> 'pid:[4026531836]'
lrwxrwxrwx. 1 donnie donnie 0 Oct 30 16:16 pid_for_children ->
'pid:[4026531836]'
lrwxrwxrwx. 1 donnie donnie 0 Oct 30 16:16 user -> 'user:[4026531837]'
lrwxrwxrwx. 1 donnie donnie 0 Oct 30 16:16 uts -> 'uts:[4026531838]'
[donnie@localhost ns]$
```

The sharp-eyed among you will see that there's an extra item in this directory that we haven't covered. The pid_for_children item tracks PIDs in child namespaces.

Although it's certainly possible for you to create your own namespaces, you likely never will, unless you're a software developer. Most likely, you'll just use products that have namespace technologies already built into them. Some modern web browsers use namespaces to create a sandbox for each open tab. You can use a product such as Firejail to run a normal program within its own security sandbox. (We'll look at this a bit later.) Then, there's Docker, which uses namespaces to help isolate Docker containers from each other and from the host operating system.

We've just had a high-level overview of what namespaces are all about. Next, let's look at kernel capabilities.

Understanding kernel capabilities

When you perform a ps aux command — or a sudo ps aux command if you've mounted /proc with the hidepid=1 or hidepid=2 option — you'll see many processes that are owned by the root user. This is because these processes have to access some sort of system resource that unprivileged users can't access. However, having services run with full root privileges can be a bit of a security problem. Fortunately, there are some ways to mitigate that.

For example, any web server service, such as Apache or NGINX, needs to start with root privileges in order to bind to ports 80 and 443, which are privileged ports. However, both Apache and Nginx mitigate this problem by either dropping root privileges once the service has started or by spawning child processes that belong to a non-privileged user. Here, we can see that the main Apache process spawns child processes that belong to the non-privileged apache user:

```
[donnie@centos7-tm1 ~]$ ps aux | grep http
root 1015 0.0 0.5 230420 5192 ? Ss 15:36 0:00 /usr/sbin/httpd -DFOREGROUND
apache 1066 0.0 0.2 230420 3000 ? S 15:36 0:00 /usr/sbin/httpd -DFOREGROUND
apache 1067 0.0 0.2 230420 3000 ? S 15:36 0:00 /usr/sbin/httpd -DFOREGROUND
apache 1068 0.0 0.2 230420 3000 ? S 15:36 0:00 /usr/sbin/httpd -DFOREGROUND
apache 1069 0.0 0.2 230420 3000 ? S 15:36 0:00 /usr/sbin/httpd -DFOREGROUND
apache 1070 0.0 0.2 230420 3000 ? S 15:36 0:00 /usr/sbin/httpd -DFOREGROUND
donnie 1323 0.0 0.0 112712 964 pts/0 R+ 15:38 0:00 grep --color=auto http
[donnie@centos7-tm1 ~]$
```

But not all software can do this. Some programs are designed to run with root privileges all the time. For some cases — not all, but some — you can fix that by applying a kernel capability to the program executable file.

Capabilities allow the Linux kernel to divide what the root user can do into distinct units. Let's say that you've just written a cool custom program that needs to access a privileged network port. Without capabilities, you'd either have to start that program with root privileges and let it run with root privileges, or jump through the hoops of programming it so that it can drop root privileges once it's been started. By applying the appropriate capability, a non-privileged user would be able to start it, and it would run with only the privileges of that user. (More about that later.)

There are too many capabilities to list here (there are about 40 in all), but you can see the full list with this command:

```
man capabilities
```

Returning to our previous example, let's say that we need to use Python to set up a very primitive web server that any non-privileged user can start. (We have to do this with Python 2, because it doesn't work with Python 3.) Let's do this on an AlmaLinux 8 machine, because Python 2 isn't available for either AlmaLinux 9 or Ubuntu 22.04.

The command for running a simple Python web server is:

```
python2 -m SimpleHTTPServer 80
```

However, this won't work because it needs to bind to port 80, which is the privileged port that's normally used by web servers. At the bottom of the output from this command, you'll see the problem:

```
socket.error: [Errno 13] Permission denied
```

Prefacing the command with sudo will fix the problem and allow the web server to run. However, we don't want that. We'd much rather allow non-privileged users to start it, and we'd much rather have it run without root user privileges. The first step in fixing this is to find the Python executable file, like so:

```
[donnie@localhost ~]$ which python2
/usr/bin/python2
[donnie@localhost ~]$
```

Most times, the python or python2 command is a symbolic link that points to another executable file. We'll verify that with a simple ls -l command:

```
[donnie@localhost ~]$ ls -l /usr/bin/python2
lrwxrwxrwx. 1 root root 9 Oct  8 17:08 /usr/bin/python2 -> python2.7
[donnie@localhost ~]$
```

So, the python2 link points to the python2.7 executable file. Now, let's see if there are any capabilities assigned to this file:

```
[donnie@localhost ~]$ getcap /usr/bin/python2.7
[donnie@localhost ~]$
```

No output means that there are none. When we consult the capabilities man page, we'll find that the CAP_NET_BIND_SERVICE capability seems to be what we need. The one-line description for it is: *bind a socket to Internet domain privileged ports (port numbers less than 1024)*. Okay, that sounds good to me. So, let's set that on the python2.7 executable file and see what happens. Since we used getcap to look at the file capabilities, you can probably guess that we'll use setcap to set a capability. (And, you'd be correct.) Let's do that now:

```
[donnie@localhost ~]$ sudo setcap 'CAP_NET_BIND_SERVICE+ep' /usr/bin/python2.7
[sudo] password for donnie:
[donnie@localhost ~]$ getcap /usr/bin/python2.7
/usr/bin/python2.7 = cap_net_bind_service+ep
[donnie@localhost ~]$
```

The +ep at the end of the capability name means that we're adding the capability as **effective** (activated) and **permitted**. Now, when I try to run this web server with just my own normal privileges, it will work just fine:

```
[donnie@localhost ~]$ python2 -m SimpleHTTPServer 80
Serving HTTP on 0.0.0.0 port 80 ...
```

When I use Firefox on my host machine to connect to this server, I will see a file and directory listing of everything that's in my home directory:

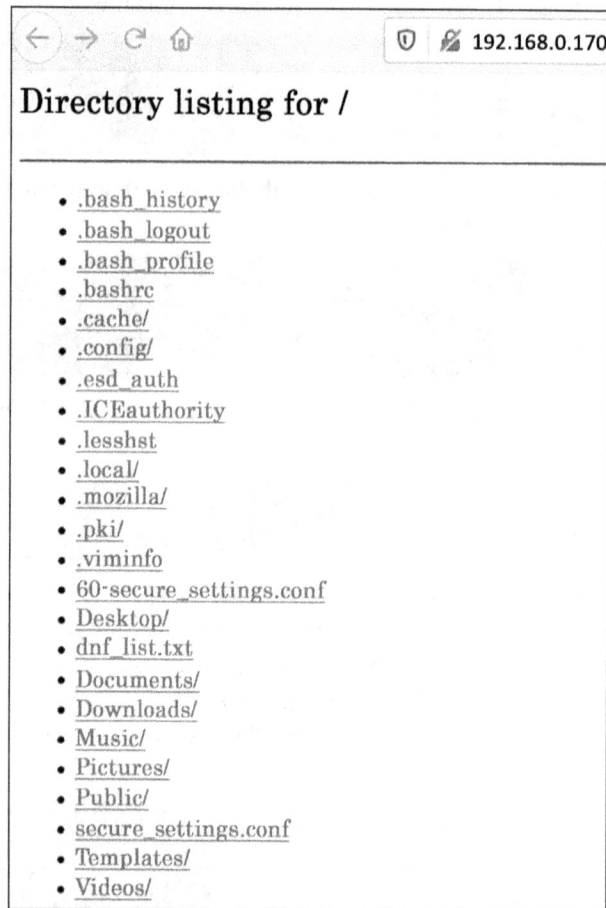

Directory listing for /

- .bash_history
- .bash_logout
- .bash_profile
- .bashrc
- .cache/
- .config/
- .esd_auth
- .ICEauthority
- .lesshst
- .local/
- .mozilla/
- .pki/
- .viminfo
- 60-secure_settings.conf
- Desktop/
- dnf_list.txt
- Documents/
- Downloads/
- Music/
- Pictures/
- Public/
- secure_settings.conf
- Templates/
- Videos/

Figure 11.1: Directory listing with SimpleHTTPServer

Linux capabilities can also be quite useful in other ways. On any Linux system, the ping utility needs root privileges in order to craft the network packets that it needs to do its job. However, everybody and his brother can use ping as just a normal user. If you look at the ping executable file on certain Linux distros, you'll see that two capabilities have been assigned to it by the Linux maintainers, as we see here on a CentOS 7 machine:

```
[donnie@localhost ~]$ getcap /usr/bin/ping
/usr/bin/ping = cap_net_admin,cap_net_raw+p
[donnie@localhost ~]$
```

Note that neither of these capabilities is set for either AlmaLinux 8 or 9, and only the cap_net_raw capability is set for Ubuntu 22.04.

As cool as all this seems, there are some downsides:

- Trying to figure out exactly which capabilities a program needs isn't always straightforward. In fact, it can require a good bit of experimentation before you can get things right.
- Setting capabilities isn't a cure-all. A lot of times, you'll see that setting a specific capability still won't allow the program to do what you need it to do. Indeed, there may not even be a capability that will allow the program to function without root privileges as you want it to.
- Performing a system update could replace executable files to which you've assigned capabilities. (With ping, we don't have to worry about this since the capabilities were set by the Linux maintainers.)

Okay, so there's a good chance that you might never actually have to set any capabilities. However, this is one of the tools that my IoT Security client uses to help lock down IoT devices, so this does have a practical use. And besides, capabilities are a building block for some of the technologies that we'll look at a bit later.

Hands-on lab – setting a kernel capability

For this lab, you'll allow a normal user to run a Python web server. You'll need to use Python 2 for this, which isn't in the newest Linux distros. (Python 3 won't work.) So for this one, use your AlmaLinux 8 VM. Let's get started:

1. If Apache is installed on your virtual machine, ensure that it's stopped:

```
sudo systemctl stop httpd
```

2. Install Python 2:

```
sudo dnf install python2
```

3. From within your own home directory, attempt to start the Python SimpleHTTPServer with just your normal user privileges, and note the error message:

```
python2 -m SimpleHTTPServer 80
```

4. See if any capabilities are set on the Python executable file:

```
getcap /usr/bin/python2.7
```

5. Set the CAP_NET_BIND_SERVICE capability on the Python executable file:

```
sudo setcap 'CAP_NET_BIND_SERVICE+ep' /usr/bin/python2.7
```

6. Repeat *steps 3* and *4*. This time, it should work.
7. Ensure that port 80 is open on the virtual machine firewall and use your host machine's web browser to access the server.
8. Shut down the web server using *Ctrl + C*.
9. View the capabilities that have been assigned to the ping executable:

```
getcap /usr/bin/ping
```

10. Review the capabilities of the man page, especially the part about the various capabilities that are there.

That's the end of the lab – congratulations!

So far, you've seen how to set file capabilities and what they can and can't do for you. Next, we'll look at how to control system calls.

Understanding SECCOMP and system calls

Multiple system calls, or **syscalls,** happen pretty much every time you run any command on a Linux machine. Each syscall takes a command from a human user and passes it to the Linux kernel. This tells the Linux kernel that it needs to perform some sort of privileged action. Opening or closing files, writing to files, or changing file permissions or ownership are just a few of the actions that require making some sort of a syscall. There are approximately 330 syscalls built into the Linux kernel. I can't say exactly how many, because new syscalls get added from time to time. Apart from this, syscalls differ between the various CPU architectures. So, an ARM CPU won't have exactly the same set of syscalls as an x86_64 CPU. The best way to see the list of syscalls that are available on your machine is to look at the man page, like this:

```
man syscalls
```

> Note that each individual syscall has its own man page.

To get an idea of how this works, here's the `strace` command, which shows the syscalls that get made by a simple `ls` command:

```
[donnie@localhost ~]$ strace -c -f -S name ls 2>&1 1>/dev/null | tail -n +3 |
head -n -2 | awk '{print $(NF)}'
access
arch_prctl
brk
close
execve
. . .
. . .
set_robust_list
set_tid_address
statfs
write
[donnie@localhost ~]$
```

In all, 22 syscalls are made from just doing 1s. (Due to formatting restrictions, I can't show all of them here.)

Secure Computing (SECCOMP), originally created for the Google Chrome web browser, allows you to either enable just a certain subset of syscalls that you want for a process to use or disable certain syscalls that you want to prevent a process from using. Unless you're a software developer or a Docker container developer, you probably won't be working with this directly all that much. However, this is yet another building block for the technologies that are used daily by normal humans.

Next, let's put all this cool stuff into perspective by looking at how it's used in real life.

Using process isolation with Docker containers

Container technology has been around for quite some time, but it took Docker to make containers popular. Unlike a virtual machine, a container doesn't contain an entire operating system. Rather, a container contains just enough of an operating system to run applications in their own private sandboxes. Containers lack their own operating system kernels, so they use the kernel of the host Linux machine. What makes containers so popular is that you can pack a lot more of them onto a physical server than you can with virtual machines. So, they're great for cutting the cost of running a data center.

Docker containers use the technologies that we've covered in this chapter. Kernel capabilities, cgroups, namespaces, and SECCOMP all help Docker containers remain isolated from both each other and from the host operating system, unless we choose otherwise. By default, Docker containers run with a reduced set of capabilities and syscalls, and Docker developers can reduce all that even more for the containers that they create.

> I can't go into the nitty-gritty details about how all this works in Docker because it would require explaining the development process for Docker containers. That's okay, though. In this section, you'll understand what to look out for if someone wants to deploy Docker containers in your data center.

But as good as all that sounds, Docker security is far from perfect. As I demonstrated in *Chapter 10, Implementing Mandatory Access Control with SELinux and AppArmor*, any non-privileged member of the docker group can mount the root filesystem of the host machine in a container of his or her own creation. The normally non-privileged member of the docker group has root privileges within the container, and those privileges extend to the mounted root filesystem of the host machine. In the demo, I showed you that only an effective Mandatory Access Control system, specifically SELinux, could stop Katelyn from taking control of the entire host machine.

To address this rather serious design flaw, the developers at Red Hat created their own Docker replacement. They call it podman, and it's available in the RHEL 8/9 and AlmaLinux 8/9 repositories. Security is much improved in podman, and the type of attack that I demonstrated for you doesn't work with it, even without SELinux. Personally, I wouldn't even consider anything other than Podman for running containers.

Podman used to only be available for RHEL and Fedora-type Linux distros. It's now also available for most other Linux distros.

Now that I've given you a high-level overview of how the process isolation technologies are used in Docker, let's look at how they're used in technologies that a mere mortal is more likely to use. We'll begin with Firejail.

Sandboxing with Firejail

Firejail uses namespaces, SECCOMP, and kernel capabilities to run untrusted applications in their own individual sandboxes. This can help prevent data leakage between applications, and it can help prevent malicious programs from damaging your system. It's in the normal repositories for Debian and its offspring, which include Raspbian for Raspberry Pi devices and probably every member of the Ubuntu family. On the Red Hat side, it's in the EPEL repository, so you'll need to install it first. Firejail is meant for use on single-user desktop systems, so we'll need to use a desktop version of Linux. So, go ahead and set up an AlmaLinux 9 VM with the Gnome desktop.

In the previous edition of this book, I demoed this with Lubuntu, which at the time was Ubuntu with the LXDE desktop. (Lubuntu has since switched to the LXQT desktop.) Unfortunately, the Ubuntu distros are now set up to install certain packages as Snap packages, which aren't compatible with Firejail. So, for this edition, I've switched to AlmaLinux 9 in order to make the demo work.

Before we get too far along, let's consider some of the use cases for Firejail:

- You want to make doubly sure that your web browser doesn't leak sensitive information when you access your bank's web portal.
- You need to run untrusted applications that you've downloaded from the Internet.

To install Firejail on your AlmaLinux 9 machine, use these commands:

```
sudo dnf install epel-release
sudo dnf install firejail
```

This installs Firejail, along with a whole bunch of profiles for different applications. When you invoke an application with Firejail, it will automatically load the correct profile for that application, if one exists. If you invoke an application that doesn't have a profile, Firejail will just load a generic one. To see the profiles, cd into /etc/firejail/ and take a look:

```
donnie@donnie-VirtualBox:/etc/firejail$ ls -l
total 4996
-rw-r--r-- 1 root root   894 Dec 21  2017 0ad.profile
-rw-r--r-- 1 root root   691 Dec 21  2017 2048-qt.profile
```

```
-rw-r--r-- 1 root root    399 Dec 21  2017 7z.profile
-rw-r--r-- 1 root root   1414 Dec 21  2017 abrowser.profile
-rw-r--r-- 1 root root   1079 Dec 21  2017 akregator.profile
-rw-r--r-- 1 root root    615 Dec 21  2017 amarok.profile
-rw-r--r-- 1 root root    722 Dec 21  2017 amule.profile
-rw-r--r-- 1 root root    837 Dec 21  2017 android-studio.profile
. . .
. . .
```

To easily count the number of profiles, just do this:

```
donnie@donnie-VirtualBox:/etc/firejail$ ls -l | wc -l
1231
donnie@donnie-VirtualBox:/etc/firejail$
```

Subtracting the `total 4996` line from the top of the output gives us a total of 1,230 profiles.

The simplest way to use Firejail is to preface the name of the application you want to run with `firejail`. Let's start with Firefox:

```
firejail firefox
```

The main problem with Firejail is that it doesn't work well consistently. A few years ago, a client had me do a writeup about Firejail, and I got it to mostly work on my Fedora workstation and on my Raspberry Pi with Raspbian. But even with the programs for which it did work, I lost some important functionality. For example, when running a web browser with Firejail on my Fedora machine, I wasn't able to watch videos on several different sites, including YouTube. Dropbox and Keepass didn't work at all under Firejail, even though there are specific profiles for both of them.

On a Lubuntu virtual machine, running Firefox under Firejail just gave me a blank browser page, regardless of where I tried to surf. So, I installed `chromium-browser` and tried it. It worked much better, and I could even watch YouTube videos with it. Then, I installed LibreOffice, which seemed to run fine with Firejail.

Among the many options that Firejail offers is the option to ensure that programs run either without any kernel capabilities enabled or with just the capabilities that you specify. Something that the man page recommends is to drop all capabilities for any programs that don't require root privileges. So, for Chromium, we'd do this:

```
firejail --caps.drop=all chromium-browser
```

So, what if you just want to start your applications from the **Start** menu, the way that you normally would, but still have Firejail protection? For that, you can do this:

```
sudo firecfg
```

This command creates symbolic links in the `/usr/local/bin/` directory for each program that has a Firejail profile. They look something like this:

```
donnie@donnie-VirtualBox:/usr/local/bin$ ls -l
total 0
lrwxrwxrwx 1 root root 17 Nov 14 18:14 audacious -> /usr/bin/firejail
lrwxrwxrwx 1 root root 17 Nov 14 18:14 chromium-browser -> /usr/bin/firejail
lrwxrwxrwx 1 root root 17 Nov 14 18:14 evince -> /usr/bin/firejail
lrwxrwxrwx 1 root root 17 Nov 14 18:14 file-roller -> /usr/bin/firejail
lrwxrwxrwx 1 root root 17 Nov 14 18:14 firefox -> /usr/bin/firejail
lrwxrwxrwx 1 root root 17 Nov 14 18:14 galculator -> /usr/bin/firejail
. . .
. . .
```

If you find that a program doesn't work under Firejail, just go into `/usr/local/bin/` and delete the link for it.

Now, you'll want to be aware of a very curious thing with the Firejail documentation. In both the Firejail man page and on the main page of the Firejail website, it says that you can use Firejail to sandbox desktop applications, server applications, and user login sessions. However, if you click on the **Documentation** tab of the Firejail website, it says that Firejail is only meant for single-user desktop systems. That's because, in order to do its job, the Firejail executable has to have the SUID permission bit set. The Firejail developers consider it a security risk to allow multiple users to access a machine with this SUID program.

All right, that's enough talk. Let's get some practice in.

Hands-on lab — using Firejail

For this lab, you'll use an AlmaLinux 9 virtual machine with the Gnome desktop. Let's get started:

1. Create an AlmaLinux virtual machine with the Gnome desktop option.
2. Install the EPEL repository and update the VM with these commands:

```
sudo dnf install epel-release
sudo dnf upgrade
```

   Then, reboot the machine.

3. Install Firejail, LibreOffice, and Chromium:

```
sudo dnf install firejail libreoffice-x11 chromium
```

4. In one terminal window, start Chromium without any kernel capabilities:

```
firejail --caps.drop=all chromium-browser
```

5. Surf to various websites to see if everything works as it should.

6. In another terminal window, start LibreOffice, also without any capabilities:

```
firejail --caps.drop=all libreoffice
```

7. Create the various types of LibreOffice documents and try out various LibreOffice functions to see how much still works properly.

8. Shut down both Chromium and LibreOffice.

9. Configure Firejail so that it automatically sandboxes every application you start, even if you do this from the normal **Start** menu:

```
sudo firecfg
```

10. Look at the symbolic links that were created:

```
ls -l /usr/local/bin
```

11. Try to open Firefox from the normal menu and verify whether or not it works. Then, shut down Firefox.

12. To be able to run Firefox without Firejail, just delete its symbolic link from the /user/local/bin/ directory, like so:

```
sudo rm /usr/local/bin/firefox
```

13. Try to run Firefox again. You should see that it starts normally.

You've completed this lab – congratulations!

There are a lot more Firejail options than what I can show you here. For more information, see the Firejail man page and the documentation on the Firejail website.

So far, you've seen both the good and the bad of using Firejail. Next up, we'll look at a couple of universal packaging systems for Linux.

Sandboxing with Snappy

In the Windows world and the Mac world, operating systems and the applications that they can run are sold independently of each other. So, you buy a computer that runs either Windows or macOS, and then you buy the applications separately. When it comes to doing updates, you have to update the operating system, and then update each application separately.

In the Linux world, most applications that you'll ever need are in the repositories of your Linux distro. To install an application, you just use your distro's package management utility – apt, yum, dnf, or whatever else – to install it. However, this has turned out to be both a blessing and a curse. It does make it easier to keep track of your applications and to keep the latest bug fix and security updates installed. But unless you're running a rolling release distro such as Arch, the application packages will become out of date before your Linux distro's end of life. That's because distro maintainers use application versions that are current when the distro version is released, and they don't upgrade to new application versions until the next version of the distro is released.

This also makes things hard for application developers, because each family of Linux distros uses its own packaging format. So, wouldn't it be nice to have a universal packaging format that works across all Linux distros, and that can be kept up to date with ease?

Universal packaging began several years ago with AppImage packages. However, they never really caught on that well, and they don't provide any sandboxing features. So, this is all I'll say about them.

Next came Ubuntu's Snappy system, which allows developers to create snap packages that are supposed to run on any system on which the Snappy system can be installed. Each snap application runs in its own isolated sandbox, which helps protect the system from malicious programs. Each snap package is a self-contained unit, which means you don't have to worry about installing dependencies. You can even create snap packages for servers that contain multiple services. The snapd daemon constantly runs in the background, automatically updating both itself and any installed snap applications.

As good as this all sounds, there are a couple of things about Snappy that make it a bit controversial. First, the Ubuntu folk refuse to release the source code for the Snappy application server. So, it's not possible to look at the source code, and it's not possible to set up your own local Snappy server. If you develop snap packages and want to deploy them, even if this is just on your own local network, you have no choice but to use the central snap package portal that's run by Canonical, Ubuntu's parent company. This does fly in the face of software freedom, which the whole GNU/Linux ecosystem is supposed to represent. However, the Canonical folk do it this way to verify the security of snap packages that get served out.

Secondly, even though snap packages are sandboxed in order to protect the system, other weird things can happen. Soon after the Snappy system came online, a package developer got caught sneaking some Monero mining software into one of his packages. Although he just wanted to monetize his efforts and meant no harm, it's still not good to sneak that sort of thing into your packages without telling your potential customers. After that, the Canonical folk stepped up their efforts to scan packages that get uploaded to the portal, in order to prevent that sort of thing from happening again.

And then, there's the matter of user control. A user can delay snap updates for up to 60 days, but can't turn them off altogether. At some point, the snapd daemon will update your installed packages, whether or not you really want it to.

And lastly, the practice of making each snap package a self-contained unit and storing the three previous versions of every snap increases disk space usage. Each package contains all the linked libraries that its application uses, which means that you might have multiple packages that all use the same libraries. This isn't necessarily that big of a deal with today's modern, large capacity hard drives, but it could be a problem if you're low on disk space.

If you're running any recent version of Ubuntu, you'll have the Snappy service running already. At some point (I forget when), the Ubuntu folk started including Snappy in a default installation of Ubuntu Server. It's now also installed by default in the desktop versions of Ubuntu. In fact, Ubuntu now automatically uses Snappy to install certain packages, such as Firefox and Chromium, even if you use a normal sudo apt install command to install them.

Snappy is also available in the repositories of many non-Ubuntu distros. It's in the normal repositories for Fedora, and in the EPEL repositories for Red Hat and all of its offspring. (Note though that I gave up on using snaps on my Fedora systems, because it was causing too many weird problems with SELinux.)

So, how can Snappy be useful to a busy administrator? Well, let's say that your pointy-haired boss has just told you to set up a Nextcloud server so that employees can have a central place to store their documents. However, you're in a time crunch, and you don't want to jump through the hoops of setting up all the individual components of a LAMP system. No problem – just install a snap. First, let's see what's available for our Ubuntu server:

```
donnie@ubuntu2204:~$ snap search nextcloud
Name Version Publisher Notes Summary
nextcloud 16.0.5snap3 nextcloud√ - Nextcloud Server - A safe home for all your
data
spreedme 0.29.5snap1 nextcloud√ - Spreed.ME audio/video calls and conferences
feature for the Nextcloud Snap
onlyoffice-desktopeditors 5.4.1 onlyoffice√ - A comprehensive office suite for
editing documents, spreadsheets and presentations
qownnotes 19.11.13 pbek - Plain-text file markdown note taking with Nextcloud /
ownCloud integration
nextcloud-port8080 1.01 arcticslyfox - Nextcloud Server

. . .
. . .
```

There are quite a few choices. We can use the `info` option to narrow things down a bit:

```
donnie@ubuntu2204:~$ snap info nextcloud
name: nextcloud
summary: Nextcloud Server - A safe home for all your data
publisher: Nextcloud√
contact: https://github.com/nextcloud/nextcloud-snap
license: AGPL-3.0+
description: |
 Where are your photos and documents? With Nextcloud you pick a server of your
choice, at home, in
 a data center or at a provider. And that is where your files will be.
Nextcloud runs on that
 server, protecting your data and giving you access from your desktop or mobile
devices. Through
 Nextcloud you also access, sync and share your existing data on that FTP drive
at school, a
 Dropbox or a NAS you have at home.

. . .
. . .
```

It looks like this is what I need. So, let's install it:

```
donnie@ubuntu2204:~$ snap install nextcloud
```

We're not worried about using sudo here, because snap will prompt you for a password for this particular operation. Note that for other snap operations, this doesn't work, so you'll need to use sudo.

To start it, just do this:

```
donnie@ubuntu2204:~$ sudo snap start nextcloud
Started.
donnie@ubuntu2204:~$
```

Finally, from a desktop machine, navigate to the IP address of the Nextcloud server and create an admin account. Once you've filled in all the details, click **Finish Setup**:

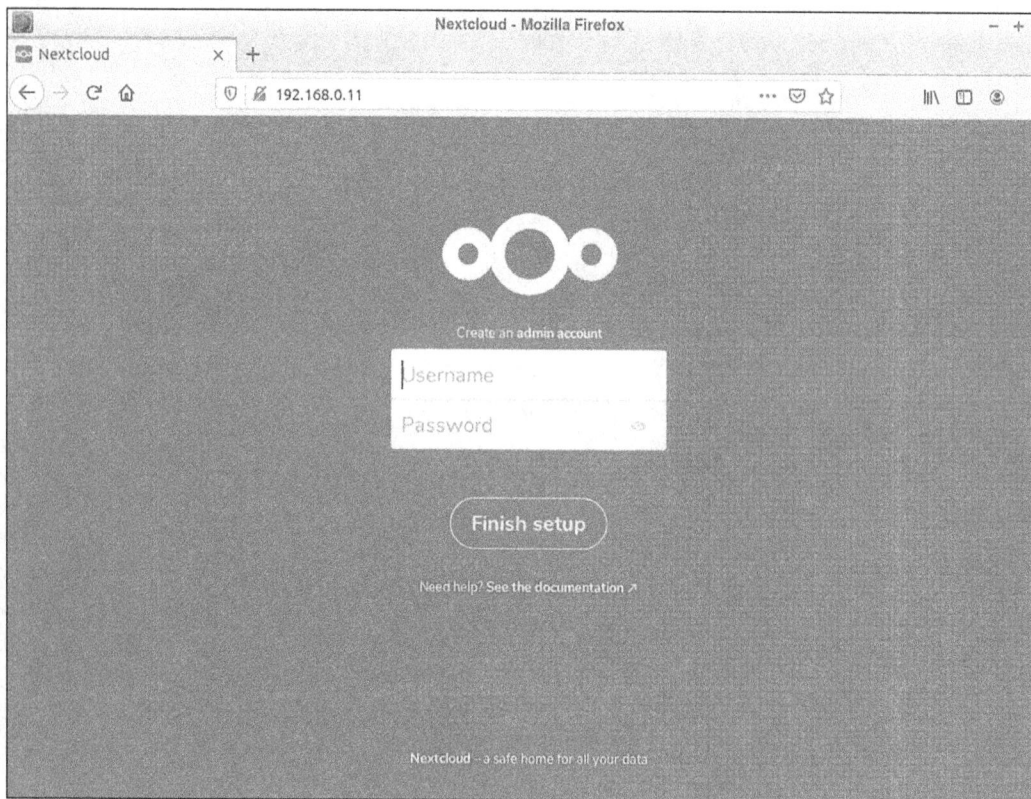

Figure 11.2: Nextcloud

Simple, right? Imagine how long that would have taken doing it the old-fashioned way. The only slight catch is that it's running on an unencrypted HTTP connection, so you definitely don't want to expose this to the Internet. (There is a way to reconfigure this to use an encrypted connection, but that's beyond the scope of this topic.)

The Snapcraft store is Canonical's official repository for snap packages. Anyone who wants to can create an account and upload his or her own snaps. There are plenty of applications there for desktop/workstations, servers, and IoT devices. Several different machine architectures, including x86_64, ARM, and PowerPC, are supported. (So yes, this can even be useful for your Raspberry Pi device.) This can be seen in the following screenshot:

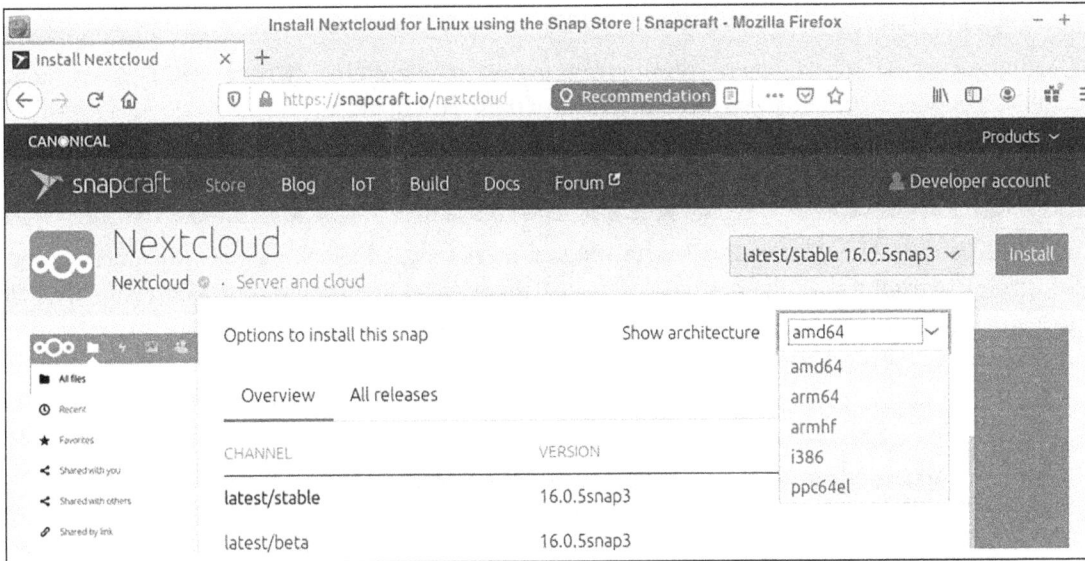

Figure 11.3: The Snapcraft store

That's pretty much all there is to it. Despite the controversies, it's still a pretty cool concept.

> If you have to deploy IoT devices, you might want to look into Ubuntu Core. It's a stripped-down version of Ubuntu that consists wholly of snap packages. Space doesn't permit me to cover it in detail here, but you can read all about it at `https://ubuntu.com/core`.

Now that you've seen how to work with Ubuntu's Snappy system, we'll look at Fedora's Flatpak system.

Sandboxing with Flatpak

The Flatpak system, which was created by the Fedora Linux team, works toward the same goal as Ubuntu's Snappy system, but there are significant differences in their implementation. You can have one or both systems running on any given Linux machine. With either system, you can create a universal package that runs on any machine that has Snappy or Flatpak installed. And, both systems run each of their applications in their own security sandbox.

However, as I mentioned previously, there are differences:

- Instead of having each application package entirely self-contained, Flatpak installs shared runtime libraries that the application can access. This helps cut down on disk space usage.

- The Fedora folk operate a central repository that they call Flathub. However, they also made the server code available for anyone who wants to set up his or her own Flatpak repository.
- Flatpak requires just a tiny bit more effort to set up because after you install it, you have to configure it to use the desired repository.
- The Snapcraft store has packages for server, desktop, and IoT use. Flathub mainly has desktop applications.

Depending on which distro you're running, you may or may not already have the Flatpak system installed. On Debian/Ubuntu systems, install it with these commands:

```
sudo apt update
sudo apt install flatpak
```

On RHEL, CentOS, AlmaLinux, and Fedora systems, there's a good chance that it's already installed. If it isn't, just install it with the normal yum or dnf commands. After you've installed Flatpak, go to the Flatpak **Quick Setup** page to see how to configure it. Click on the icon for the distro that you're running and follow the directions.

> You'll find the **Quick Setup** page here: https://flatpak.org/setup/.

After installing the repository, restart the machine. After the machine has rebooted, you'll be ready to install some applications. To pick one, go to the Flathub website and browse until you find something you want.

> You'll find Flathub here: https://flathub.org/home.

Let's say that you've browsed through the Productivity apps and found the Bookworm e-book reader. Click on the link to go to the Bookworm app page. You'll see an **Install** button at the top of it. If you click on that button, you'll download the install file for Bookworm. To install it, you'll still need to type a command at the command line. Your best bet is to scroll down to the bottom of the page, where you'll see the command that will both download and install the app at the same time:

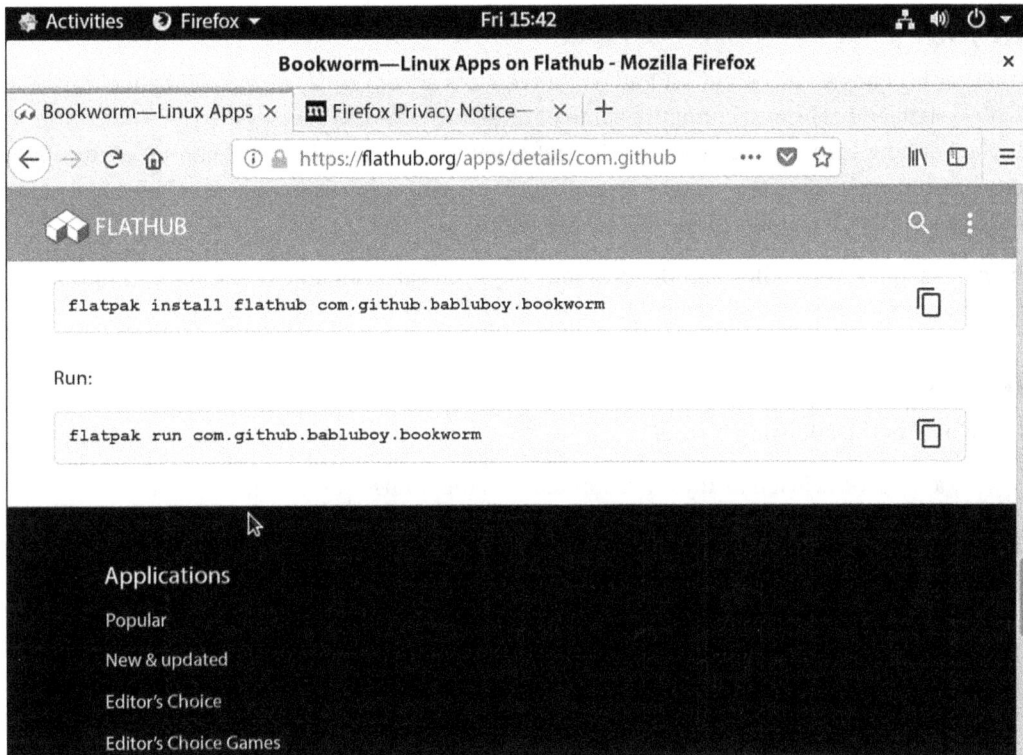

Figure 11.4: The Flathub repository

There's also the command to run the app, but you might not need it. Depending on which distro you're running, you might or might not have an icon created for you in your **Start** menu.

> Flatpak sometimes requires admin privileges, and sometimes it doesn't. Whenever it does, it will prompt you for a password, so there's no need to preface your `flatpak` commands with `sudo`.

Unlike Snappy, Flatpak doesn't automatically update its apps. You'll have to do that yourself by periodically implementing this command:

```
flatpak update
```

In this section, you looked at the basics of using the Snappy and Flatpak universal packaging systems. With each one, developers can package their applications just once, instead of doing it multiple times with multiple types of packages. End users can use them so that their applications are always up to date, instead of having to stick with the more outdated versions that are in their distro repositories. And, in keeping with the overall context of this book, understand that by running applications in their own isolated sandboxes, both of these systems provide an extra measure of application security.

Summary

So, another big chapter is behind us, and we've seen lots of cool stuff. We started by looking at the /proc filesystem and at how to configure some of its settings for the best security possible. After that, we looked at how cgroups, namespaces, kernel capabilities, and SECCOMP can be used to isolate processes from each other. We wrapped this chapter up with some examples of utilities and package management systems that use these cool technologies.

In the next chapter, we'll talk about the different ways you can scan, audit, and harden your systems. I'll see you there.

Questions

1. Which of the following is true?

    a. /proc is just like any other directory in the Linux filesystem.

    b. /proc is the only pseudo-filesystem in Linux.

    c. /proc is one of several pseudo-filesystems in Linux.

    d. You can set values for /proc parameters with the systemctl command.

2. Which of the following commands would you use to set a value for a /proc parameter?

    a. sudo systemctl -w

    b. sudo sysctl -w

    c. sudo procctl -w

    d. sudo sysctl -o

    e. sudo systemctl -o

3. You need a program executable to run with one specific root privilege, without having to grant any root privileges to the person who will be running it. What would you do?

    a. Add a namespace.

    b. Create a SECCOMP profile.

    c. Add the SUID permission.

    d. Add a kernel capability.

4. Where would you find information about user processes?

    a. In the numbered subdirectories of the /proc filesystem.

    b. In the alphabetically named subdirectories of the /proc filesystem.

    c. In the /dev directory.

    d. In each user's home directory.

5. What is a syscall?

    a. It tells the Linux kernel to perform a privileged action on behalf of a user.

    b. It calls new system information into the kernel.

c. It keeps track of everything that the system kernel is doing.

d. It isolates calls to system resources from each other.

6. On non-RHEL 9-type Linux distros, what is the best way to allow users to only see information about their own processes?

a. Add the `hidepid=2` option to the kernel startup parameters in the GRUB configuration.

b. Add the `nopid=1` option to the kernel startup parameters in the GRUB configuration.

c. Add the `nopid=1` option to the `/etc/fstab` file.

d. Add the `hidepid=1` option to the `/etc/fstab` file.

7. Which of the following commands would you use to see which kernel parameters need to be changed for the best security?

a. `sudo audit system`

b. `sudo lynis audit system`

c. `sudo system audit`

d. `sudo lynis system audit`

8. Which of the following commands would allow a non-privileged user to start a Python web server on `Port 80` without using root privileges?

a. `sudo setcap 'CAP_NET_SERVICE+ep' /usr/bin/python2.7`

b. `sudo setcap 'CAP_NET_BIND_SERVICE+ep' /usr/bin/python2.7`

c. `sudo getcap 'CAP_NET_BIND_SERVICE+ep' /usr/bin/python2.7`

d. `sudo setcap 'CAP_NET_SERVICE+ep' /usr/bin/python2.7`

9. What is a major difference between the Snappy and Flatpak systems?

a. There are none.

b. Flatpak packages are completely self-contained, but Snappy packages have you install separate runtime packages.

c. Snappy packages are completely self-contained, but Flatpak packages have you install separate runtime packages.

d. Flatpak packages run in their own sandbox, but Snappy packages don't.

e. Snappy packages run in their own sandbox, but Flatpak packages don't.

10. You need to limit the number of syscalls that your Docker container can make. How would you do that?

a. Create the container in its own cgroup and configure the syscall limits for that cgroup.

b. Create the container in its own namespace and configure the syscall limits for that namespace.

c. Run the container under Firejail.

d. Create the container with a SECCOMP profile.

Further reading

- Exploring the /proc filesystem: `https://www.tecmint.com/exploring-proc-file-system-in-linux/`

- Linux kernel security subsystem wiki: `https://kernsec.org/wiki/index.php/Main_Page`

- Linux Magic System Request Key Hacks: `https://www.kernel.org/doc/html/latest/admin-guide/sysrq.html`

- Linux to get kernel "lockdown" feature: `https://www.zdnet.com/article/linux-to-get-kernel-lockdown-feature/`

- Protect hard and symbolic links in RHEL/CentOS: `https://www.tecmint.com/protect-hard-and-symbolic-links-in-centos-rhel/`

- Log suspicious Martian packets: `https://www.cyberciti.biz/faq/linux-log-suspicious-martian-packets-un-routable-source-addresses/`

- Protect against the usage of ptrace: `https://linux-audit.com/protect-ptrace-processes-kernel-yama-ptrace_scope/`

- Introduction to Linux Control Groups (cgroups) Version 1: `https://access.redhat.com/documentation/en-us/red_hat_enterprise_linux/7/html/resource_management_guide/chap-introduction_to_control_groups`

- RHEL 7: How to get started with cgroups Version 1: `https://www.certdepot.net/rhel7-get-started-cgroups/`

- Introduction to cgroup Version 2: `https://access.redhat.com/documentation/en-us/red_hat_enterprise_linux/9/html/monitoring_and_managing_system_status_and_performance/setting-limits-for-applications_monitoring-and-managing-system-status-and-performance`

- Limit CPU Usage on Ubuntu 19.10 with systemd cgroups: `https://youtu.be/_AODvcO5Q_8`

- Control Groups versus Namespaces: `https://youtu.be/dTOT9QKZ2Lw`

- How to manage Linux file capabilities: `https://www.howtoforge.com/how-to-manage-linux-file-capabilities/`

- getcap, setcap, and file capabilities: `https://www.insecure.ws/linux/getcap_setcap.html`

- Docker security features – SECCOMP profiles: `https://blog.aquasec.com/new-docker-security-features-and-what-they-mean-seccomp-profiles`

- Docker documentation – Docker Security: `https://docs.docker.com/engine/security/security/`

- Firejail website: `https://firejail.wordpress.com/`

- Firejail documentation: `https://firejail.wordpress.com/documentation-2/`

- Introduction to App Packages on Linux: `https://fosspost.org/education/app-packages-linux-snap-flatpak-appimage`

- The Ubuntu snap Usage Tutorial: `https://tutorials.ubuntu.com/tutorial/basic-snap-usage#0`
- How to manage snap updates: `https://snapcraft.io/blog/how-to-manage-snap-updates`
- The Official Canonical Snapcraft Store: `https://snapcraft.io/`
- The future of Linux desktop application delivery is Flatpak and Snap: `https://www.zdnet.com/article/the-future-of-linux-desktop-application-delivery-is-flatpak-and-snap/`
- Flathub: `https://flathub.org/home`
- Three approaches to secrets management for Flatpak applications: `https://opensource.com/article/19/11/secrets-management-flatpak-applications`

Answers

1. c
2. b
3. d
4. a
5. a
6. d
7. b
8. b
9. c
10. d

Join our book community

Join our community's Discord space for discussions with the author and other readers:

`https://packt.link/CyberSec`

12

Scanning, Auditing, and Hardening

A common misconception is that Linux users never need to worry about malware. Yes, it's true that Linux is much more resistant to viruses than Windows is. But viruses are only one type of malware, and other types of malware can be planted on Linux machines. And, if you're running a server that will share files with Windows users, you'll want to make sure that you don't share any virus-infected files with them.

While Linux system log files are nice, they don't always give a good picture of who does what or who accesses what. It could be that either intruders or insiders are trying to access data that they're not authorized to access. What we really want is a good auditing system to alert us when people do things that they're not supposed to do.

And then there's the issue of regulatory compliance. Your organization may have to deal with one or more regulatory bodies that dictate how you harden your servers against attacks. If you're not in compliance, you could be fined or put out of business.

Fortunately, we have ways to deal with all of these issues, and they aren't all that complicated.

In this chapter, we'll cover the following topics:

- Installing and updating ClamAV and maldet
- Scanning with ClamAV and maldet
- SELinux considerations
- Scanning for rootkits with Rootkit Hunter
- Performing quick malware analysis with strings and VirusTotal
- Controlling the `auditd` daemon
- Creating audit rules
- Using the `ausearch` and `aureport` utilities to search the audit logs for problems
- Using `inotifywait` for quick and easy auditing

- `oscap`, the command-line utility for managing and applying OpenSCAP policies
- OpenSCAP Workbench, the GUI utility for managing and applying OpenSCAP policies
- OpenSCAP policy files and the compliance standards that each of them is designed to meet
- Applying a policy during operating system installation

If you're ready, let's begin by looking at a Linux-based virus scanning solution.

Installing and updating ClamAV and maldet

Although we don't have to worry much about viruses infecting our Linux machines, we do need to worry about sharing infected files with Windows users. ClamAV is a **Free Open Source Software (FOSS)** antivirus solution that is available for Linux, Windows, and macOS. The included `freshclam` utility allows you to update virus signatures.

Linux Malware Detect, which you'll often see abbreviated as either **LMD** or **maldet**, is another FOSS antivirus program that can work alongside ClamAV. (To save typing, I'll just refer to it as either LMD or maldet from now on.) As far as I know, it's not available in the repositories of any Linux distro, but it's still simple enough to install and configure. One of its features is that it automatically generates malware detection signatures when it sees malware on the network's edge intrusion detection systems. End users can also submit their own malware samples. When you install it, you'll get a `systemd` service that's already enabled and a `cron` job that will periodically update both the malware signatures and the program itself. It works with the Linux kernel's `inotify` capability to automatically monitor directories for files that have changed.

> You can get all the nitty-gritty details about LMD at `https://www.rfxn.com/projects/linux-malware-detect/`.

The reason that we're installing ClamAV and LMD together is that, as the LMD folk freely admit, the ClamAV scan engine gives much better performance when scanning large file sets. Also, by having them both together, ClamAV can use the LMD malware signatures as well as its own malware signatures.

> Just to be clear...
>
> Viruses are a real problem for computers that run the Windows operating system. But, as far as anyone has been able to tell, there's no such thing as a virus that can harm a Linux-based operating system. So, the only real reason to run an antivirus solution on a Linux machine is to prevent infecting any Windows machines on your network. This means that you don't need to worry about installing an antivirus product on your Linux-based DNS servers, DHCP servers, and so forth. But, if you have a Linux-based email server, Samba server, download server, or any other Linux-based machine that shares files with Windows computers, then installing an antivirus solution is a good idea.

All right, so much for the theory. Let's get our hands dirty, shall we?

Hands-on lab — installing ClamAV and maldet

We'll begin by installing ClamAV. (It's in the normal repository for Ubuntu, but not for CentOS or AlmaLinux. For CentOS and AlmaLinux, you'll need to install the EPEL repository, as I showed you in *Chapter 1, Running Linux in a Virtual Environment*.) We'll also install wget, which we'll use to download LMD. For this lab, you can use Ubuntu, CentOS 7, or either version of AlmaLinux. Let's get started:

1. The following command will install ClamAV, inotify-tools and wget on Ubuntu:

    ```
    donnie@ubuntu3:~$ sudo apt install clamav wget inotify-tools
    ```

    The following command will install ClamAV, inotify-tools, and wget on CentOS 7:

    ```
    [donnie@localhost ~]$ sudo yum install clamav clamav-update wget inotify-
    tools
    ```

    For AlmaLinux 8 or AlmaLinux 9, do this:

    ```
    [donnie@localhost ~]$ sudo dnf install clamav clamav-update wget inotify-
    tools
    [donnie@localhost ~]$ sudo systemctl enable --now clamav-freshclam
    ```

    > Note that if you chose the **Minimal** installation option when creating a CentOS or an AlmaLinux **virtual machine** (**VM**), you may also have to install the perl and the tar packages.

    For Ubuntu, the clamav package contains everything you need. For CentOS or AlmaLinux, you'll need to also install clamav-update in order to obtain virus updates.

    The rest of the steps will be the same for either VM.

2. Next, you'll download and install LMD.

    Here, you'll want to do something that I rarely tell people to do. That is, you'll want to log in to the root user shell. The reason is that, although the LMD installer works fine with sudo, you'll end up with the program files being owned by the user who performed the installation, instead of by the root user. Performing the installation from the root user's shell saves us the trouble of tracking down those files and changing the ownership. So, download the file as follows:

    ```
    sudo su -
    wget http://www.rfxn.com/downloads/maldetect-current.tar.gz
    ```

    Now, you'll have the file in the root user's home directory.

3. Extract the archive and enter the resultant directory:

    ```
    tar xzvf maldetect-current.tar.gz
    cd maldetect-1.6.4/
    ```

4. Run the installer. Once the installer finishes, copy the README file to your own home directory so that you can have it for ready reference. (This README file is the documentation for LMD.) Then, exit from the root user's shell back to your own shell:

```
root@ubuntu3:~/maldetect-1.6.4# ./install.sh
Created symlink from /etc/systemd/system/multi-user.target.wants/maldet.
service to /usr/lib/systemd/system/maldet.service.
update-rc.d: error: initscript does not exist: /etc/init.d/maldet
. . .

. . .
maldet(22138): {sigup} signature set update completed
maldet(22138): {sigup} 15218 signatures (12485 MD5 | 1954 HEX | 779 YARA
| 0 USER)

root@ubuntu3:~/maldetect-1.6.4# cp README /home/donnie

root@ubuntu3:~/maldetect-1.6.4# exit
logout
donnie@ubuntu3:~$
```

As you see, the installer automatically creates the symbolic link that enables the maldet service, and it also automatically downloads and installs the newest malware signatures.

5. For CentOS or AlmaLinux, the maldet.service file that the installer copied to the /lib/systemd/system/ directory has the wrong SELinux context, which will prevent maldet from starting. Correct the SELinux context like this:

```
sudo restorecon /lib/systemd/system/maldet.service
```

6. You've reached the end of the lab – congratulations!

Hands-on lab — configuring maldet

In previous versions, maldet was configured by default to automatically monitor and scan users' home directories. In its current version, the default is for it to only monitor the /dev/shm/, /var/tmp/, and /tmp/ directories. We're going to reconfigure it so that we can add some directories. Let's get started:

1. Open the /usr/local/maldetect/conf.maldet file for editing. Find these two lines:

```
default_monitor_mode="users"
# default_monitor_mode="/usr/local/maldetect/monitor_paths"
```

2. Change them to look like this:

```
# default_monitor_mode="users"
default_monitor_mode="/usr/local/maldetect/monitor_paths"
```

3. At the top of the file, enable email alerts and set your username as the email address. The two lines should now look something like this:

```
email_alert="1"
email_addr="donnie"
```

4. LMD isn't already configured to move suspicious files to the quarantine folder, and we want to make it do that. Further down in the conf.maldet file, look for the line that says:

```
quarantine_hits="0"
```

5. Change it to this:

```
quarantine_hits="1"
```

> You'll see a few other quarantine actions that you can configure, but, for now, this is all we need.

6. Save the conf.maldet file, because that's all the changes that we need to make to it.

7. Open the /usr/local/maldetect/monitor_paths file for editing. Add the directories that you want to monitor, like this:

```
/var/tmp
/tmp
/home
/root
```

> Since viruses affect Windows and not Linux, just monitor the directories with files that will be shared with Windows machines.

8. After you save the file, start the maldet daemon:

```
sudo systemctl start maldet
```

> You can add more directories to the monitor_paths file at any time, but remember to restart the maldet daemon any time that you do, in order to read in the new additions.

You've reached the end of the lab – congratulations!

Now, let's talk about keeping ClamAV and maldet updated.

Updating ClamAV and maldet

The good news for busy admins is that you don't have to do anything to keep either of these updated. To verify that they are getting updated, we can look in the system log file:

```
Dec 8 20:02:09 localhost freshclam[22326]: ClamAV update process started at Fri
Dec 8 20:02:09 2017
Dec 8 20:02:29 localhost freshclam[22326]: Can't query current.cvd.clamav.net
Dec 8 20:02:29 localhost freshclam[22326]: Invalid DNS reply. Falling back to
HTTP mode.
Dec 8 20:02:29 localhost freshclam[22326]: Reading CVD header (main.cvd):
Dec 8 20:02:35 localhost freshclam[22326]: OK
Dec 8 20:02:47 localhost freshclam[22326]: Downloading main-58.cdiff [100%]
Dec 8 20:03:19 localhost freshclam[22326]: main.cld updated (version: 58, sigs:
4566249, f-level: 60, builder: sigmgr)
. . .

. . .

Dec 8 20:04:45 localhost freshclam[22326]: Downloading daily.cvd [100%]
. . .

. . .
```

You'll see these same entries in either the Ubuntu logs, the CentOS logs, or the AlmaLinux logs. However, there is a difference between how the updates get run automatically.

Look in the `/lib/systemd/system/` directory of your Ubuntu or AlmaLinux VMs, and you'll see the `clamav-freshclam.service` file:

```
[donnie@localhost ~]$ cd /lib/systemd/system
[donnie@localhost system]$ ls -l clamav-freshclam.service
-rw-r--r--. 1 root root 389 Nov  7 06:51 clamav-freshclam.service
[donnie@localhost system]$
```

This service is automatically enabled and started on Ubuntu, but you'll need to enable and start it yourself on AlmaLinux, like so:

```
[donnie@localhost ~]$ sudo systemctl enable --now clamav-freshclam
Created symlink /etc/systemd/system/multi-user.target.wants/clamav-freshclam.
service → /usr/lib/systemd/system/clamav-freshclam.service.
[donnie@localhost ~]$
```

Without a `freshclam.conf` configuration file, AlmaLinux just runs the update service every two hours. Ubuntu, on the other hand, uses the `/etc/clamav/freshclam.conf` file to change the update interval to every hour, as you see at the bottom of the file:

```
# Check for new database 24 times a day
Checks 24
DatabaseMirror db.local.clamav.net
DatabaseMirror database.clamav.net
```

If you have the crypto policy set to FUTURE mode on your AlmaLinux 8/9 machine, the ClamAV database update won't work. That's because the ClamAV site uses a security certificate that's not compatible with FUTURE mode. So, if you want to run ClamAV on any type of RHEL 8 or 9 machine, you'll just have to leave the crypto policy set to DEFAULT mode.

On your CentOS 7 machine, you'll see a `clamav-update` cron job in the /etc/cron.d/ directory that looks like this:

```
## Adjust this line...
MAILTO=root

## It is ok to execute it as root; freshclam drops privileges and becomes
## user 'clamupdate' as soon as possible
0  */3 * * * root /usr/share/clamav/freshclam-sleep
```

The */3 in the second column from the left indicates that ClamAV will check for updates every three hours. You can change that if you like, but you'll also need to change the setting in the /etc/sysconfig/freshclam file.

Let's say that you want CentOS 7 to also check for ClamAV updates every hour. In the cron job file, change */3 to *. (You don't need to do */1 because the asterisk by itself in that position already indicates that the job will run every hour.) Then, in the /etc/sysconfig/freshclam file, look for this line:

```
# FRESHCLAM_MOD=
```

Uncomment that line and add the number of minutes that you want between updates. To set it to 1 hour, so that it matches the cron job, it will look like this:

```
FRESHCLAM_MOD=60
```

A disabled `clamav-freshclam.service` file also gets installed on CentOS 7. If you'd rather use the service instead of the cron job, just delete the /etc/cron.d/clamav-update file, and then enable the `clamav-freshclam` service.

To prove that `maldet` is being updated, you can look in its own log files in the /usr/local/maldetect/logs/ directory. In the event_log file, you'll see these messages:

```
Dec 06 22:06:14 localhost maldet(3728): {sigup} performing signature update
check...
Dec 06 22:06:14 localhost maldet(3728): {sigup} local signature set is version
2017070716978
Dec 06 22:07:13 localhost maldet(3728): {sigup} downloaded https://cdn.rfxn.
com/downloads/maldet.sigs.ver
Dec 06 22:07:13 localhost maldet(3728): {sigup} new signature set
(201708255569) available
```

```
Dec 06 22:07:13 localhost maldet(3728): {sigup} downloading https://cdn.rfxn.
com/downloads/maldet-sigpack.tgz

. . .

. . .

Dec 06 22:07:43 localhost maldet(3728): {sigup} unpacked and installed maldet-
clean.tgz
Dec 06 22:07:43 localhost maldet(3728): {sigup} signature set update completed
Dec 06 22:07:43 localhost maldet(3728): {sigup} 15218 signatures (12485 MD5 |
1954 HEX | 779 YARA | 0 USER)
Dec 06 22:14:55 localhost maldet(4070): {scan} signatures loaded: 15218 (12485
MD5 | 1954 HEX | 779 YARA | 0 USER)
```

In the /usr/local/maldetect/conf.maldet file, you'll see these two lines, but with some comments in between them:

```
autoupdate_signatures="1"

autoupdate_version="1"
```

Not only will LMD automatically update its malware signatures but it will also ensure that you have the latest version of LMD itself.

Scanning with ClamAV and maldet

LMD's maldet daemon constantly monitors the directories that you specify in the /usr/local/ maldetect/monitor_paths file. When it finds a suspicious file, it will perform the action that you specified in the conf.maldet file.

You can test your setup by downloading a simulated virus file from the **European Institute for Computer Antivirus Research (EICAR)** site.

> There are four different simulated virus files that you can download from https://www. eicar.org/download-anti-malware-testfile/. Note that if you're running a Windows host machine, these files could get flagged by the Windows antivirus. So, your best bet is to download the files directly to your Linux virtual machines.

Just download one or all of the EICAR test files and transfer them to your home directory on the virtual machines. Your best bet is to download the files directly to your virtual machines, with these four commands:

```
wget https://secure.eicar.org/eicar.com
wget https://secure.eicar.org/eicar.com.txt
wget https://secure.eicar.org/eicar_com.zip
wget https://secure.eicar.org/eicarcom2.zip
```

Wait just a few moments, and you should see the files disappear. Then, look in the `/usr/local/` `maldetect/logs/event_log` file to verify that the LMD moved the files to quarantine:

```
Dec 01 15:18:31 localhost maldet(6388): {hit} malware hit {HEX}EICAR.TEST.3
found for /home/donnie/eicar.com.txt
Dec 01 15:18:31 localhost maldet(6388): {quar} malware quarantined from '/
home/donnie/eicar.com.txt' to '/usr/local/maldetect/quarantine/eicar.com.
txt.113345162'
Dec 01 15:18:31 localhost maldet(6388): {mon} scanned 5 new/changed files with
clamav engine
Dec 01 15:20:32 localhost maldet(6388): {mon} warning clamd service not
running; force-set monitor mode file scanning to every 120s
. . .
. . .
Dec 01 15:20:56 localhost maldet(6388): {quar} malware quarantined from '/
home/donnie/eicar_com.zip' to '/usr/local/maldetect/quarantine/eicar_com.
zip.216978719'
```

Ignore the `warning clamd service not running` messages, because we don't need to use that service.

There's still a bit more to LMD than what I can show you here. However, you can read all about it in the `README` file that comes with it.

SELinux considerations

It used to be that doing an antivirus scan on a Red Hat-type system would trigger an SELinux alert. But, in the course of proofing this chapter, the scans all worked as they should, and SELinux never bothered me once.

If you ever do generate any SELinux alerts with your virus scans, all you need to do to fix it is to change one Boolean:

```
[donnie@localhost ~]$ getsebool -a | grep 'virus'
antivirus_can_scan_system --> off
antivirus_use_jit --> off
[donnie@localhost ~]$
```

What interests us here is the `antivirus_can_scan_system` Boolean, which is off by default. To turn it on to enable virus scans, just do this:

```
[donnie@localhost ~]$ sudo setsebool -P antivirus_can_scan_system on
[sudo] password for donnie:
```

```
[donnie@localhost ~]$ getsebool antivirus_can_scan_system
antivirus_can_scan_system --> on
[donnie@localhost ~]$
```

That should fix any SELinux-related scan problems that you may have. But, as things stand now, you probably won't need to worry about it.

Scanning for rootkits with Rootkit Hunter

Rootkits are exceedingly nasty pieces of malware that can definitely ruin your day. They can listen for commands from their masters, steal sensitive data and send it to their masters, or provide an easy-access back door for their masters. They're designed to be stealthy, with the ability to hide themselves from plain view. Sometimes, they'll replace utilities such as ls or ps with their own trojaned versions that will show all files or processes on the system except for the ones that are associated with the rootkit. Rootkits can infect any operating system, even our beloved Linux.

In order to plant a rootkit, an attacker has to have already gained administrative privileges on a system. This is one of the many reasons why I always cringe when I see people doing all of their work from the root user's shell and why I'm a firm advocate of using sudo whenever possible. I mean, really, why should we make it easy for the bad guys?

Several years ago, back in the dark days of Windows XP, Sony Music got into a bit of trouble when someone discovered that they had planted a rootkit on their music CDs. They didn't mean to do anything malicious, but only wanted to stop people from using their computers to make illegal copies. Of course, most people ran Windows XP with an administrator account, which made it really easy for the rootkit to infect their computers. Windows users still mostly run with administrator accounts, but they at least now have User Access Control to help mitigate these types of problems.

There are a couple of different programs that scan for rootkits, and both are used pretty much the same way. One is called **Rootkit Hunter**, and the other is called **chkrootkit**. Now, understand that I'm showing you these programs because as a Linux administrator, you'll be expected to know about them. In reality, they're not very useful, because there are a whole lot of rootkits that neither of them will detect. If you really want to prove that, just go to GitHub and do a keyword search for *rootkit*. Find a rootkit that will run on Linux, download the source code to a virtual machine, and then follow the included directions for how to compile and install it. Once it's installed, do a scan with either one of the rootkit scan programs. Most likely, the rootkit won't get detected. Also, don't expect AppArmor or SELinux to prevent someone from installing a rootkit, because they won't.

Not every rootkit on Github will compile correctly for you, so finding ones that work will involve a bit of trial-and-error. One that I did get to compile and install correctly is the Reptile rootkit, which you can download from here: https://github.com/f0rb1dd3n/Reptile

Okay, let's move on to the lab.

Hands-on lab – installing and updating Rootkit Hunter

For Ubuntu, Rootkit Hunter is in the normal repository. For CentOS or AlmaLinux, you'll need to install the EPEL repository, as I showed you how to do in *Chapter 1, Running Linux in a Virtual Environment*. For all of these Linux distros, the package name is rkhunter. Let's get started:

1. Use one of the following commands to install Rootkit Hunter, as appropriate. For Ubuntu, do this:

```
sudo apt install rkhunter
```

For CentOS 7, do the following:

```
sudo yum install rkhunter
```

For AlmaLinux 8 or AlmaLinux 9, do this:

```
sudo dnf install rkhunter
```

2. After it's been installed, you can look at its options with this command:

```
man rkhunter
```

3. Next, update the rootkit signatures using the --update option:

```
[donnie@localhost ~]$ sudo rkhunter --update
[ Rootkit Hunter version 1.4.4 ]
Checking rkhunter data files...
  Checking file mirrors.dat [ Updated ]
  Checking file programs_bad.dat [ Updated ]
  Checking file backdoorports.dat [ No update ]
  Checking file suspscan.dat [ Updated ]
  Checking file i18n/cn [ No update ]
  Checking file i18n/de [ Updated ]
  Checking file i18n/en [ Updated ]
  Checking file i18n/tr [ Updated ]
  Checking file i18n/tr.utf8 [ Updated ]
  Checking file i18n/zh [ Updated ]
  Checking file i18n/zh.utf8 [ Updated ]
  Checking file i18n/ja [ Updated ]
```

4. Now, we're ready to scan.
5. You've reached the end of the lab – congratulations!

Scanning for rootkits

To run your scan, use the -c option. (That's -c for *check*.) Be patient, because it will take a while:

```
sudo rkhunter -c
```

When you run the scan in this manner, Rootkit Hunter will periodically stop and ask you to hit the *Enter* key to continue. When the scan completes, you'll find a rkhunter.log file in the /var/log/ directory.

To have Rootkit Hunter automatically run as a cron job, use the --cronjob option, which will cause the program to run all the way through without prompting you to keep hitting the *Enter* key. You might also want to use the --rwo option, which will cause the program to only report warnings, instead of also reporting on everything that's good. From the command line, the command would look like this:

```
sudo rkhunter -c --cronjob --rwo
```

To create a cron job that will automatically run Rootkit Hunter on a nightly basis, open the crontab editor for the root user:

```
sudo crontab -e -u root
```

Let's say that you want to run Rootkit Hunter every night at 20 minutes past 10. Enter this into the crontab editor:

```
20 22 * * * /usr/bin/rkhunter -c --cronjob --rwo
```

Since cron only works with 24-hour clock time, you'll have to express 10:00 P.M. as 22. (Just add 12 to the normal P.M. clock times that you're used to using.) The three asterisks mean that the job will run every day of the month, every month of the year, and every day of the week, respectively. You'll need to list the entire path for the command. Otherwise, cron won't be able to find it.

You'll find more options that might interest you in the rkhunter man page, but this should be enough to get you going with it.

> A few moments ago, I told you that these rootkit scanner programs aren't very effective, because there are many rootkits that they won't detect. That's why the best way to deal with rootkits is to prevent them from getting installed in the first place. So, be sure to keep your systems locked down to prevent malicious actors from gaining root privileges.

Next, let's look at a couple of quick techniques for analyzing malware.

Performing a quick malware analysis with strings and VirusTotal

Malware analysis is one of those advanced topics that I can't cover in detail here. However, I can show you a couple of quick ways to analyze a suspicious file.

Analyze a file with strings

Executable files often have strings of text embedded in them. You can use the `strings` utility to look at those strings. (Yeah, that makes sense, right?) Depending on your distro, `strings` might or might not already be installed. It's already on CentOS and AlmaLinux, but to get it on Ubuntu, you'll need to install the `binutils` package, like so:

```
sudo apt install binutils
```

As an example, let's look at a `Your File Is Ready To Download_2285169994.exe` file that was automatically downloaded from a cryptocoin faucet site. To examine the file, I'll do this:

```
strings "Your File Is Ready To Download_2285169994.exe" > output.txt
vim output.txt
```

I saved the output to a text file that I can open in `vim` so that I can view the line numbers. To see the line numbers, I entered `:set number` at the bottom of the `vim` screen. (In `vim` parlance, we're using the last line mode.)

It's hard to say exactly what to search for, so you'll just need to browse through until you see something interesting. In this case, look at what I've found starting at line 386:

```
386 The Setup program accepts optional command line parameters.
387 /HELP, /?
388 Shows this information.
389 /SP-
390 Disables the This will install... Do you wish to continue? prompt at the
beginning of Setup.
391 /SILENT, /VERYSILENT
392 Instructs Setup to be silent or very silent.
393 /SUPPRESSMSGBOXES
394 Instructs Setup to suppress message boxes.
. . .
399 /NOCANCEL
400 Prevents the user from cancelling during the installation process.
. . .
```

It's saying that the installation process of this program can be made to run in SILENT mode, without popping up any dialog boxes. It can also be made to run in such a way that the user can't cancel the installation. Of course, the line at the top says that these are `optional command line parameters`. But, are they really optional, or are they hard coded in as the default? It's not clear, but in my mind, any installer that can be made to run in SILENT mode and that can't be canceled looks a bit suspicious, even if we're talking about `optional` parameters.

Okay, so you're probably wondering, *What is a cryptocoin faucet?* Well, it's a website where you can go to claim a small amount of cryptocoin, such as Bitcoin, Ethereum, or Monero, in exchange for viewing the advertising and solving some sort of CAPTCHA puzzle. Most faucet operators are honest, but the advertising they allow on their sites often isn't and is often laden with malware, scams, and Not-Safe-For-Work images.

Now, this little trick works fine sometimes, but not always. More sophisticated malware might not contain any text strings that can give you any type of a clue. So, let's look at another little quick trick for malware analysis.

Scanning the malware with VirusTotal

VirusTotal is a website where you can upload suspicious files for analysis. It uses a multitude of various virus scanners, so if one scanner misses something, another is likely to find it. Here are the results of scanning the `Your File Is Ready To Download_2285169994.exe` file:

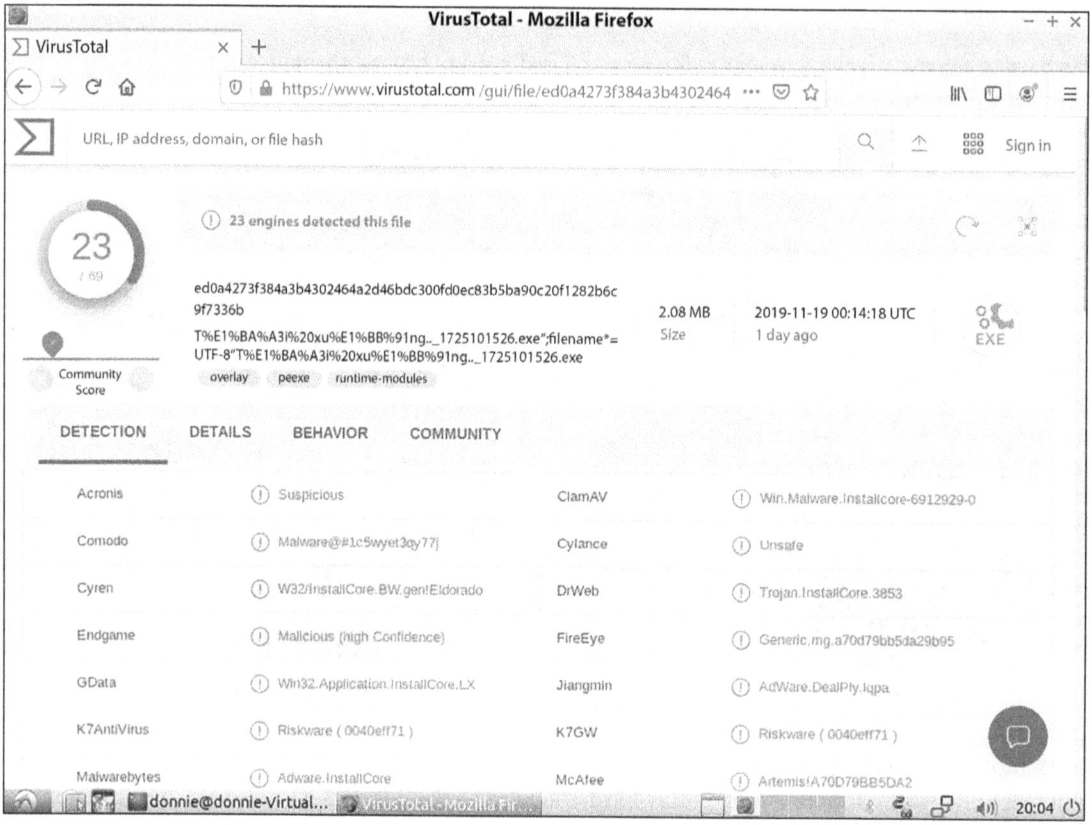

Figure 12.1: The VirusTotal scanner

Here, we see that different virus scanners classify this file in different ways. But whether it's classified as `Win.Malware.Installcore`, `Trojan.InstallCore`, or whatever else, it's still bad.

As good as VirusTotal is, you'll want to use it with caution. Don't upload any files that contain sensitive or confidential information, because it will get shared with other people.

So, what is this particular piece of malware all about? Well, it's actually a fake Adobe Flash installer. Of course, you don't want to test that by installing it on a production Windows machine. But, if you have a Windows VM handy, you can test the malware on it. (Either make a snapshot of the VM before you begin or be prepared to trash the VM afterward.)

As I said at the beginning, malware analysis is quite an in-depth topic and there are lots of more sophisticated programs to use for it. However, if you have suspicions about something and need to just do a quick check, these two techniques might be all you need.

Next, let's look at how to automatically audit the system for different events.

Understanding the auditd daemon

So, you have a directory full of super-secret files that only a very few people need to see, and you want to know when unauthorized people try to see them. Or, maybe you want to see when a certain file gets changed, or you want to see when people log into the system and what they're doing once they do log in. For all this and more, you have the auditd system. It's a really cool system, and I think that you'll like it.

One of the beauties of auditd is that it works at the Linux kernel level, rather than at the user-mode level. This makes it much harder for attackers to subvert.

On Red Hat-type systems, auditd comes installed and enabled by default. So, you'll find it already there on your CentOS and AlmaLinux machines. On Ubuntu, it won't be installed, so you'll have to do it yourself:

```
sudo apt install auditd
```

On Ubuntu, you can control the auditd daemon with the normal systemctl commands. So, if you need to restart auditd to read in a new configuration, you can do that with:

```
sudo systemctl restart auditd
```

On RHEL-type machines, auditd is configured to not work with the normal systemctl commands. (For all other daemons, they do.) So, on your CentOS and AlmaLinux machines, you'll restart the auditd daemon with the old-fashioned service command, like so:

```
sudo service auditd restart
```

Other than this minor difference, everything I tell you about auditd from here on will apply to all of your virtual machines.

Creating audit rules

Okay, let's start with something simple and work our way up to something awesome. First, let's check to see whether any audit rules are in effect:

```
[donnie@localhost ~]$ sudo auditctl -l
[sudo] password for donnie:
No rules
[donnie@localhost ~]$
```

As you see, the `auditctl` command is what we use to manage audit rules. The `-l` option lists the rules.

Auditing a file for changes

Now, let's say that we want to see when someone changes the `/etc/passwd` file. (The command that we'll use will look a bit daunting, but I promise that it will make sense once we break it down.) Here goes:

```
[donnie@localhost ~]$ sudo auditctl -w /etc/passwd -p wa -k passwd_changes
[sudo] password for donnie:

[donnie@localhost ~]$ sudo auditctl -l
-w /etc/passwd -p wa -k passwd_changes
[donnie@localhost ~]$
```

Here's the breakdown:

- `-w`: This stands for where, and it points to the object that we want to monitor. In this case, it's `/etc/passwd`.
- `-p`: This indicates the object's permissions that we want to monitor. In this case, we're monitoring to see when anyone either tries to (w)rite to the file or tries to make (a)ttribute changes. (The other two permissions that we can audit are (r)ead and e(x)ecute.)
- `-k`: The k stands for key, which is just `auditd`'s way of assigning a name to a rule. So, `passwd_changes` is the key, or the name, of the rule that we're creating.

The `auditctl -l` command shows us that the rule is indeed there.

Now, the slight problem with this is that the rule is only temporary and will disappear when we reboot the machine. To make it permanent, we need to create a custom `rules` file in the `/etc/audit/rules.d/` directory. Then, when you restart the `auditd` daemon, the custom rules will be inserted into the `/etc/audit/audit.rules` file. Because the `/etc/audit/` directory can only be accessed by someone with root privileges, I'll just open the file by listing the entire path to the file, rather than trying to enter the directory:

```
sudo less /etc/audit/audit.rules
```

There's not a whole lot in this default file:

```
## This file is automatically generated from /etc/audit/rules.d
-D
-b 8192
-f 1
```

Here's the breakdown for this file:

- `-D`: This will cause all rules and watches that are currently in effect to be deleted so that we can start from a clean slate. So, if I were to restart the `auditd` daemon right now, it would read this `audit.rules` file, which would delete the rule that I just created.
- `-b 8192`: This sets the number of outstanding audit buffers that we can have going at one time. If all of the buffers get full, the system can't generate any more audit messages.
- `-f 1`: This sets the failure mode for critical errors, and the value can be either 0, 1, or 2. `-f 0` would set the mode to silent, meaning that `auditd` wouldn't do anything about critical errors. `-f 1`, as we see here, tells `auditd` to only report the critical errors, while `-f 2` would cause the Linux kernel to go into panic mode. According to the `auditctl` man page, anyone in a high-security environment would likely want to change this to `-f 2`. For our purposes, though, `-f 1` works.

You could use your text editor to create a new `rules` file in the `/etc/audit/rules.d/` directory. Alternatively, you could just redirect the `auditctl -l` output into a new file, like this:

```
[donnie@localhost ~]$ sudo sh -c "auditctl -l > /etc/audit/rules.d/custom.
rules"
[donnie@localhost ~]$ sudo service auditd restart
```

On Ubuntu:

```
sudo systemctl restart auditd
```

Since the Bash shell doesn't allow me to directly redirect information into a file in the `/etc/` directory, even with `sudo`, I have to use the `sudo sh -c` command in order to execute the `auditctl` command. After restarting the `auditd` daemon, our `audit.rules` file now looks like this:

```
## This file is automatically generated from /etc/audit/rules.d
-D
-b 8192
-f 1


-w /etc/passwd -p wa -k passwd_changes
```

Now, the rule will take effect every time the machine is rebooted, and every time that you manually restart the `auditd` daemon.

Auditing a directory

Vicky and Cleopatra, my solid gray kitty and my gray-and-white tabby kitty, have some super sensitive secrets that they need to safeguard. So, I created the `secretcats` group and added them to it. Then, I created the `secretcats` shared directory and set the access controls on it, as I showed you how to do in *Chapter 9, Access Control Lists and Shared Directory Management*:

```
[donnie@localhost ~]$ sudo groupadd secretcats
[sudo] password for donnie:

[donnie@localhost ~]$ sudo usermod -a -G secretcats vicky
[donnie@localhost ~]$ sudo usermod -a -G secretcats cleopatra

[donnie@localhost ~]$ sudo mkdir /secretcats
[donnie@localhost ~]$ sudo chown nobody:secretcats /secretcats/
[donnie@localhost ~]$ sudo chmod 3770 /secretcats/

[donnie@localhost ~]$ ls -ld /secretcats/
drwxrws--T. 2 nobody secretcats 6 Dec 11 14:47 /secretcats/
[donnie@localhost ~]$
```

Vicky and Cleopatra want to be absolutely sure that nobody gets into their stuff, so they requested that I set up an auditing rule for their directory:

```
[donnie@localhost ~]$ sudo auditctl -w /secretcats/ -k secretcats_watch
[sudo] password for donnie:

[donnie@localhost ~]$ sudo auditctl -l
-w /etc/passwd -p wa -k passwd_changes
-w /secretcats -p rwxa -k secretcats_watch
[donnie@localhost ~]$
```

As before, the `-w` option denotes what we want to monitor, while the `-k` option denotes the name of the audit rule. This time, I left out the `-p` option because I want to monitor for every type of access. In other words, I want to monitor for any read, write, attribute change, or execute actions. (Because this is a directory, the execute action happens when somebody tries to `cd` into the directory.) You can see in the `auditctl -l` output that by leaving out the `-p` option, we will now monitor for everything. However, let's say that I only want to monitor for when someone tries to `cd` into this directory. I could have made the rule look like this:

```
sudo auditctl -w /secretcats/ -p x -k secretcats_watch
```

Easy enough so far, right?

> Plan carefully when you create your own custom audit rules. Auditing more files and directories than you need to can have a bit of a performance impact and could drown you in excessive information. Just audit what you really need to audit, as called for by either the scenario or what any applicable governing bodies require.

Now, let's look at something a bit more complex.

Auditing system calls

Creating rules to monitor when someone performs a certain action isn't hard, but the command syntax is a bit trickier than what we've seen so far. With this rule, we're going to be alerted every time Charlie either tries to open a file or tries to create a file:

```
[donnie@localhost ~]$ sudo auditctl -a always,exit -F arch=b64 -S openat -F
auid=1006
[sudo] password for donnie:

[donnie@localhost ~]$ sudo auditctl -l
-w /etc/passwd -p wa -k passwd_changes
-w /secretcats -p rwxa -k secretcats_watch
-a always,exit -F arch=b64 -S openat -F auid=1006
[donnie@localhost ~]$
```

Here's the breakdown:

- `-a always,exit`: Here, we have the action and the list. The `exit` part means that this rule will be added to the system call `exit` list. Whenever the operating system exits from a system call, the `exit` list will be used to determine if an audit event needs to be generated. The `always` part is the action, which means that an audit record for this rule will always be created on exit from the specified system call. Note that the action and list parameters have to be separated by a comma.
- `-F arch=b64`: The `-F` option is used to build a rule field, and we can see two rule fields in this command. This first rule field specifies the machine's CPU architecture. `b64` means that the computer is running with an x86_64 CPU. (Whether it's Intel or AMD doesn't matter.) Considering that 32-bit machines are dying off and that Sun SPARC and PowerPC machines aren't all that common, `b64` is what you'll now mostly see.
- `-S openat`: The `-S` option specifies the system call that we want to monitor. `openat` is the system call that either opens or creates a file.
- `-F auid=1006`: This second audit field specifies the user ID number of the user that we want to monitor. (Charlie's user ID number is `1006`.)

> A complete explanation of system calls, or syscalls, is a bit too esoteric for our present purpose. For now, suffice it to say that a syscall happens whenever a user issues a command that requests that the Linux kernel provide a service. If you're so inclined, you can read more about syscalls at https://blog.packagecloud.io/eng/2016/04/05/the-definitive-guide-to-linux-system-calls/.

What I've presented here are just a few of the many things that you can do with auditing rules. To see more examples, check out the auditctl man page:

```
man auditctl
```

So, now you're wondering, *Now that I have these rules, how do I know when someone tries to violate them?* As always, I'm glad that you asked.

Using ausearch and aureport

The auditd daemon logs events to the /var/log/audit/audit.log file. Although you could directly read the file with something such as less, you really don't want to. The ausearch and aureport utilities will help you translate the file into a language that makes some sort of sense.

Searching for file change alerts

Let's start by looking at the rule that we created that will alert us whenever a change is made to the /etc/passwd file:

```
sudo auditctl -w /etc/passwd -p wa -k passwd_changes
```

Now, let's make a change to the file and look for the alert message. Rather than add another user, since I'm running out of cats whose names I can use, I'll just use the chfn utility to add contact information to the comment field for Cleopatra's entry:

```
[donnie@localhost etc]$ sudo chfn cleopatra
Changing finger information for cleopatra.
Name []: Cleopatra Tabby Cat
Office []: Donnie's back yard
Office Phone []: 555-5555
Home Phone []: 555-5556

Finger information changed.
[donnie@localhost etc]
```

Now, I'll use ausearch to look for any audit messages that this event may have generated:

```
[donnie@localhost ~]$ sudo ausearch -i -k passwd_changes
----
type=CONFIG_CHANGE msg=audit(12/11/2017 13:06:20.665:11393) : auid=donnie
```

```
ses=842 subj=unconfined_u:unconfined_r:unconfined_t:s0-s0:c0.c1023 op=add_rule
key=passwd_changes li
st=exit res=yes
----
type=CONFIG_CHANGE msg=audit(12/11/2017 13:49:15.262:11511) : auid=donnie
ses=842 op=updated_rules path=/etc/passwd key=passwd_changes list=exit res=yes
[donnie@localhost ~]$
```

Here's the breakdown:

- -i: This takes any numeric data and, whenever possible, converts it into text. In this case, it takes user ID numbers and converts them into the actual username, which shows up here as auid=donnie. If I were to leave the -i out, the user information would show up as auid=1000, which is my user ID number.
- -k passwd_changes: This specifies the key, or the name, of the audit rule for which we want to see the audit messages.

Here, you see that there are two parts to this output. The first part just shows when I created the audit rule, so we're not interested in that. In the second part, you can see when I triggered the rule, but it doesn't show how I triggered it. So, let's use aureport to see whether it will give us a bit more detail:

```
[donnie@localhost ~]$ sudo aureport -i -k | grep 'passwd_changes'
1. 12/11/2017 13:06:20 passwd_changes yes ? donnie 11393
2. 12/11/2017 13:49:15 passwd_changes yes ? donnie 11511
3. 12/11/2017 13:49:15 passwd_changes yes /usr/bin/chfn donnie 11512
4. 12/11/2017 14:54:11 passwd_changes yes /usr/sbin/usermod donnie 11728
5. 12/11/2017 14:54:25 passwd_changes yes /usr/sbin/usermod donnie 11736
[donnie@localhost ~]$
```

What's curious is that with ausearch, you have to specify the name, or key, of the audit rule that interests you after the -k option. With aureport, the -k option means that you want to look at all log entries that have to do with all audit rule keys. To see log entries for a specific key, just pipe the output into grep. The -i option does the same thing that it does for ausearch.

As you see, aureport parses the cryptic language of the audit.log file into plain language that's easier to understand. I wasn't sure about what I had done to generate events 1 and 2, so I looked in the /var/log/secure file to see whether I could find out. I saw these two entries for those times:

```
Dec 11 13:06:20 localhost sudo: donnie : TTY=pts/1 ; PWD=/home/donnie ;
USER=root ; COMMAND=/sbin/auditctl -w /etc/passwd -p wa -k passwd_changes
. . .
. . .
Dec 11 13:49:24 localhost sudo: donnie : TTY=pts/1 ; PWD=/home/donnie ;
USER=root ; COMMAND=/sbin/ausearch -i -k passwd_changes
```

So, event 1 was from when I initially created the audit rule, and event 2 happened when I did an ausearch operation.

I must confess that the events in lines *4* and *5* are a bit of a mystery. Both were created when I invoked the usermod command, and both of them correlate to the secure log entries where I added Vicky and Cleopatra to the secretcats group:

```
Dec 11 14:54:11 localhost sudo:  donnie : TTY=pts/1 ; PWD=/home/donnie ;
USER=root ; COMMAND=/sbin/usermod -a -G secretcats vicky
Dec 11 14:54:11 localhost usermod[14865]: add 'vicky' to group 'secretcats'
Dec 11 14:54:11 localhost usermod[14865]: add 'vicky' to shadow group
'secretcats'
Dec 11 14:54:25 localhost sudo:  donnie : TTY=pts/1 ; PWD=/home/donnie ;
USER=root ; COMMAND=/sbin/usermod -a -G secretcats cleopatra
Dec 11 14:54:25 localhost usermod[14871]: add 'cleopatra' to group 'secretcats'
Dec 11 14:54:25 localhost usermod[14871]: add 'cleopatra' to shadow group
'secretcats'
```

The strange part about this is that adding a user to a secondary group doesn't modify the passwd file. So, I really don't know why the rule was triggered to create the events in lines *4* and *5*.

This leaves us with the event in line *3*, which is where I used chfn to actually modify the passwd file. Here's the secure log entry for that:

```
Dec 11 13:48:49 localhost sudo:  donnie : TTY=pts/1 ; PWD=/etc ; USER=root ;
COMMAND=/bin/chfn cleopatra
```

So, out of all of these events, the one in line *3* is the only one where the /etc/passwd file was actually modified.

> The /var/log/secure file that I keep mentioning here is on Red Hat-type operating systems, such as CentOS and AlmaLinux. On your Ubuntu machine, you'll see the /var/log/auth.log file instead.

Searching for directory access rule violations

For our next scenario, we'll create a shared directory for Vicky and Cleopatra and then create an audit rule for it that looks like this:

```
sudo auditctl -w /secretcats/ -k secretcats_watch
```

So, all access or attempted access to this directory should trigger an alert. First, let's have Vicky enter the /secretcats/ directory and run an ls -l command:

```
[vicky@localhost ~]$ cd /secretcats
[vicky@localhost secretcats]$ ls -l
total 4
```

```
-rw-rw-r--. 1 cleopatra secretcats 31 Dec 12 11:49 cleopatrafile.txt
[vicky@localhost secretcats]$
```

Here, we see that Cleopatra has already been there and has created a file. (We'll get back to that in a moment.) When an event triggers an auditd rule, it often creates multiple records in the /var/log/audit/audit.log file. If you look through each record for an event, you'll see that each one covers a different aspect of that event. When I do an ausearch command, I see a total of five records just from that one ls -l operation. For the sake of saving space, I'll just put the first one here:

```
sudo ausearch -i -k secretcats_watch | less


type=PROCTITLE msg=audit(12/12/2017 12:15:35.447:14077) : proctitle=ls
--color=auto -l
type=PATH msg=audit(12/12/2017 12:15:35.447:14077) : item=0 name=.
inode=33583041 dev=fd:01 mode=dir,sgid,sticky,770 ouid=nobody ogid=secretcats
rdev=00:00 obj=unconfined_u:object_r:default_t:s0 objtype=NORMAL
type=CWD msg=audit(12/12/2017 12:15:35.447:14077) : cwd=/secretcats
type=SYSCALL msg=audit(12/12/2017 12:15:35.447:14077) : arch=x86_64
syscall=openat success=yes exit=3 a0=0xffffffffffffff9c a1=0x2300330 a2=O_
RDONLY|O_NONBLOCK|O_DIRECTORY|O_CLOEXEC a3=0x0 items=1 ppid=10805 pid=10952
auid=vicky uid=vicky gid=vicky euid=vicky suid=vicky fsuid=vicky egid=vicky
sgid=vicky fsgid=vicky tty=pts0 ses=1789 comm=ls exe=/usr/bin/ls subj=unconfine
d_u:unconfined_r:unconfined_t:s0-s0:c0.c1023 key=secretcats_watch
```

I'll put the last one here:

```
type=PROCTITLE msg=audit(12/12/2017 12:15:35.447:14081) : proctitle=ls
--color=auto -l
type=PATH msg=audit(12/12/2017 12:15:35.447:14081) : item=0 name=cleopatrafile.
txt inode=33583071 dev=fd:01 mode=file,664 ouid=cleopatra ogid=secretcats
rdev=00:00 obj=unconfined_u:object_r:default_t:s0 objtype=NORMAL
type=CWD msg=audit(12/12/2017 12:15:35.447:14081) : cwd=/secretcats
type=SYSCALL msg=audit(12/12/2017 12:15:35.447:14081) : arch=x86_64
syscall=getxattr success=no exit=ENODATA(No data available) a0=0x7fff7c266e60
a1=0x7f0a61cb9db0 a2=0x0 a3=0x0 items=1 ppid=10805 pid=10952 auid=vicky
uid=vicky gid=vicky euid=vicky suid=vicky fsuid=vicky egid=vicky sgid=vicky
fsgid=vicky tty=pts0 ses=1789 comm=ls exe=/usr/bin/ls subj=unconfined_u:unconfi
ned_r:unconfined_t:s0-s0:c0.c1023 key=secretcats_watch
```

In both records, you see the action that was taken (ls -l) and information about the person – or cat, in this case – that took the action. Since this is a RHEL-type machine, you also see SELinux context information. In the second record, you can also see the name of the file that Vicky saw when she did the ls command.

Next, let's say that that sneaky Charlie guy logs in and tries to get into the /secretcats/ directory:

```
[charlie@localhost ~]$ cd /secretcats
-bash: cd: /secretcats: Permission denied
[charlie@localhost ~]$ ls -l /secretcats
ls: cannot open directory /secretcats: Permission denied
[charlie@localhost ~]$
```

Charlie isn't a member of the secretcats group and doesn't have permission to go into the secretcats directory. So, he should trigger an alert message. Well, he actually triggered one that consists of four records, and I'll again just list the first one and the last one. Here's the first one:

```
sudo ausearch -i -k secretcats_watch | less

type=PROCTITLE msg=audit(12/12/2017 12:32:04.341:14152) : proctitle=ls
--color=auto -l /secretcats
type=PATH msg=audit(12/12/2017 12:32:04.341:14152) : item=0 name=/secretcats
inode=33583041 dev=fd:01 mode=dir,sgid,sticky,770 ouid=nobody ogid=secretcats
rdev=00:00 obj=unconfined_u:object_r:default_t:s0 objtype=NORMAL
type=CWD msg=audit(12/12/2017 12:32:04.341:14152) :  cwd=/home/charlie
type=SYSCALL msg=audit(12/12/2017 12:32:04.341:14152) : arch=x86_64
syscall=lgetxattr success=yes exit=35 a0=0x7ffd8d18f7dd a1=0x7f2496858f8a
a2=0x12bca30 a3=0xff items=1 ppid=11637 pid=11663 auid=charlie uid=charlie
gid=charlie euid=charlie suid=charlie fsuid=charlie egid=charlie sgid=charlie
fsgid=charlie tty=pts0 ses=1794 comm=ls exe=/usr/bin/ls subj=unconfined_u:uncon
fined_r:unconfined_t:s0-s0:c0.c1023 key=secretcats_watch
```

Here's the last one:

```
type=PROCTITLE msg=audit(12/12/2017 12:32:04.341:14155) : proctitle=ls
--color=auto -l /secretcats
type=PATH msg=audit(12/12/2017 12:32:04.341:14155) : item=0 name=/secretcats
inode=33583041 dev=fd:01 mode=dir,sgid,sticky,770 ouid=nobody ogid=secretcats
rdev=00:00 obj=unconfined_u:object_r:default_t:s0 objtype=NORMAL
type=CWD msg=audit(12/12/2017 12:32:04.341:14155) :  cwd=/home/charlie
type=SYSCALL msg=audit(12/12/2017 12:32:04.341:14155) : arch=x86_64
syscall=openat success=no exit=EACCES(Permission denied) a0=0xffffffffffffff9c
a1=0x12be300 a2=O_RDONLY|O_NONBLOCK|O_DIRECTORY|O_CLOEXEC a3=0x0 items=1
ppid=11637 pid=11663 auid=charlie uid=charlie gid=charlie euid=charlie
suid=charlie fsuid=charlie egid=charlie sgid=charlie fsgid=charlie tty=pts0
ses=1794 comm=ls exe=/usr/bin/ls subj=unconfined_u:unconfined_r:unconfined_t
:s0-s0:c0.c1023 key=secretcats_watch
```

There are two things to note here. First, just attempting to cd into the directory doesn't trigger an alert. However, using ls to try to read the contents of the directory does. Secondly, note the Permission denied message that shows up in the second record.

The last set of alerts that we'll look at were created when Cleopatra created her `cleopatrafile.txt` file. This event triggered an alert that consists of 30 records. I'll just show you two of them, with the first one here:

```
type=PROCTITLE msg=audit(12/12/2017 11:49:37.536:13856) : proctitle=vim
cleopatrafile.txt
type=PATH msg=audit(12/12/2017 11:49:37.536:13856) : item=0 name=.
inode=33583041 dev=fd:01 mode=dir,sgid,sticky,770 ouid=nobody ogid=secretcats
rdev=00:00 obj=unconfined_u:o
bject_r:default_t:s0 objtype=NORMAL
type=CWD msg=audit(12/12/2017 11:49:37.536:13856) :  cwd=/secretcats
type=SYSCALL msg=audit(12/12/2017 11:49:37.536:13856) : arch=x86_64
syscall=open success=yes exit=4 a0=0x5ab983 a1=O_RDONLY a2=0x0 a3=0x63 items=1
ppid=9572 pid=9593 auid=cle
opatra uid=cleopatra gid=cleopatra euid=cleopatra suid=cleopatra
fsuid=cleopatra egid=cleopatra sgid=cleopatra fsgid=cleopatra tty=pts0 ses=1779
comm=vim exe=/usr/bin/vim sub
j=unconfined_u:unconfined_r:unconfined_t:s0-s0:c0.c1023 key=secretcats_watch
```

Here's the second one:

```
type=PROCTITLE msg=audit(12/12/2017 11:49:56.001:13858) : proctitle=vim
cleopatrafile.txt
type=PATH msg=audit(12/12/2017 11:49:56.001:13858) : item=1 name=/secretcats/.
cleopatrafile.txt.swp inode=33583065 dev=fd:01 mode=file,600 ouid=cleopatra
ogid=secretcats rdev
=00:00 obj=unconfined_u:object_r:default_t:s0 objtype=DELETE
type=PATH msg=audit(12/12/2017 11:49:56.001:13858) : item=0 name=/secretcats/
inode=33583041 dev=fd:01 mode=dir,sgid,sticky,770 ouid=nobody ogid=secretcats
rdev=00:00 obj=unc
onfined_u:object_r:default_t:s0 objtype=PARENT
type=CWD msg=audit(12/12/2017 11:49:56.001:13858) :  cwd=/secretcats
type=SYSCALL msg=audit(12/12/2017 11:49:56.001:13858) : arch=x86_64
syscall=unlink success=yes exit=0 a0=0x15ee7a0 a1=0x1 a2=0x1 a3=0x7ffc2c82e6b0
items=2 ppid=9572 pid=9593
auid=cleopatra uid=cleopatra gid=cleopatra euid=cleopatra suid=cleopatra
fsuid=cleopatra egid=cleopatra sgid=cleopatra fsgid=cleopatra tty=pts0 ses=1779
comm=vim exe=/usr/bin
/vim subj=unconfined_u:unconfined_r:unconfined_t:s0-s0:c0.c1023 key=secretcats_
watch
```

You can tell that the first of these two messages happened when Cleopatra saved the file and exited vim because the second message shows `objtype=DELETE`, where her temporary vim swap file was deleted.

Okay, this is all good, but what if this is too much information? What if you just want a quick and sparse list of all of the security events that got triggered by this rule? For that, we'll use aureport. We'll use it just like we did previously.

First, let's pipe the aureport output into less instead of into grep so that we can see the column headers:

```
[donnie@localhost ~]$ sudo aureport -i -k | less

Key Report
===============================================
# date time key success exe auid event
===============================================
1. 12/11/2017 13:06:20 passwd_changes yes ? donnie 11393
2. 12/11/2017 13:49:15 passwd_changes yes ? donnie 11511
3. 12/11/2017 13:49:15 passwd_changes yes /usr/bin/chfn donnie 11512
4. 12/11/2017 14:54:11 passwd_changes yes /usr/sbin/usermod donnie 11728
5. 12/11/2017 14:54:25 passwd_changes yes /usr/sbin/usermod donnie 11736
. . .

. . .
```

The status in the success column will be either yes or no, depending upon whether the user was able to successfully perform an action that violated a rule. Or, it could be a question mark if the event isn't the result of the rule being triggered.

For Charlie, we see a yes event in line *48*, with the events in lines *49* through *51* all having a no status. We can also see that all of these entries were triggered by Charlie's use of the ls command:

```
[donnie@localhost ~]$ sudo aureport -i -k | grep 'secretcats_watch'
6. 12/11/2017 15:01:25 secretcats_watch yes ? donnie 11772
8. 12/12/2017 11:49:29 secretcats_watch yes /usr/bin/ls cleopatra 13828
9. 12/12/2017 11:49:37 secretcats_watch yes /usr/bin/vim cleopatra 13830
10. 12/12/2017 11:49:37 secretcats_watch yes /usr/bin/vim cleopatra 13829
. . .

. . .

48. 12/12/2017 12:32:04 secretcats_watch yes /usr/bin/ls charlie 14152
49. 12/12/2017 12:32:04 secretcats_watch no /usr/bin/ls charlie 14153
50. 12/12/2017 12:32:04 secretcats_watch no /usr/bin/ls charlie 14154
51. 12/12/2017 12:32:04 secretcats_watch no /usr/bin/ls charlie 14155
[donnie@localhost ~]$
```

You'd be tempted to think that the yes event in line *48* indicates that Charlie was successful in reading the contents of the secretcats directory. To analyze this further, let's look at the event numbers at the end of each line and correlate them to the output of our previous ausearch command. You'll see that event numbers 14152 through 14155 belong to records that all have the same timestamp. We can see this in the first line of each record:

```
[donnie@localhost ~]$ sudo ausearch -i -k secretcats_watch | less

type=PROCTITLE msg=audit(12/12/2017 12:32:04.341:14152) : proctitle=ls
--color=auto -l /secretcats

type=PROCTITLE msg=audit(12/12/2017 12:32:04.341:14153) : proctitle=ls
--color=auto -l /secretcats

type=PROCTITLE msg=audit(12/12/2017 12:32:04.341:14154) : proctitle=ls
--color=auto -l /secretcats

type=PROCTITLE msg=audit(12/12/2017 12:32:04.341:14155) : proctitle=ls
--color=auto -l /secretcats
```

As we noted previously, the last record of this series shows `Permission denied` for Charlie, and that's what really counts.

> Space doesn't permit me to give a full explanation of each individual item in an audit log record. However, you can read about it here, in the official Red Hat documentation: https://access.redhat.com/documentation/en-us/red_hat_enterprise_linux/9/html/security_hardening/auditing-the-system_security-hardening#understanding-audit-log-files_auditing-the-system.

Searching for system call rule violations

The third rule that we created was to monitor that sneaky Charlie. This rule will alert us whenever Charlie tries to open or create a file. (As we noted previously, `1006` is Charlie's user ID number.):

```
sudo auditctl -a always,exit -F arch=b64 -S openat -F auid=1006
```

Even though Charlie hasn't done that much on this system, this rule gives us a lot more log entries than what we bargained for. We'll look at just a couple of entries:

```
time->Tue Dec 12 11:49:29 2017
type=PROCTITLE msg=audit(1513097369.952:13828):
proctitle=6C73002D2D636F6C6F723D6175746F
type=PATH msg=audit(1513097369.952:13828): item=0 name="."
inode=33583041 dev=fd:01 mode=043770 ouid=99 ogid=1009 rdev=00:00
obj=unconfined_u:object_r:default_t:s0 objtype=NO
RMAL
type=CWD msg=audit(1513097369.952:13828):  cwd="/secretcats"
type=SYSCALL msg=audit(1513097369.952:13828): arch=c000003e syscall=257
success=yes exit=3 a0=ffffffffffffff9c a1=10d1560 a2=90800 a3=0 items=1
ppid=9572 pid=9592 auid=1004 u
id=1004 gid=1006 euid=1004 suid=1004 fsuid=1004 egid=1006
```

```
sgid=1006 fsgid=1006 tty=pts0 ses=1779 comm="ls" exe="/usr/bin/ls"
subj=unconfined_u:unconfined_r:unconfined_t:s0-s0
:c0.c1023 key="secretcats_watch"
```

This record was generated when Charlie tried to access the /secretcats/ directory. So, we can expect to see this one. But, what we didn't expect to see was the exceedingly long list of records of files that Charlie indirectly accessed when he logged into the system through **Secure Shell** (**SSH**). Here's one:

```
time->Tue Dec 12 11:50:28 2017
type=PROCTITLE msg=audit(1513097428.662:13898):
proctitle=737368643A20636861726C6965407074732F30
type=PATH msg=audit(1513097428.662:13898): item=0 name="/proc/9726/
fd" inode=1308504 dev=00:03 mode=040500 ouid=0 ogid=0 rdev=00:00
obj=unconfined_u:unconfined_r:unconfined_t
:s0-s0:c0.c1023 objtype=NORMAL
type=CWD msg=audit(1513097428.662:13898):  cwd="/home/charlie"
type=SYSCALL msg=audit(1513097428.662:13898): arch=c000003e syscall=257
success=yes exit=3 a0=ffffffffffffff9c a1=7ffc7ca1d840 a2=90800 a3=0 items=1
ppid=9725 pid=9726 auid=1
006 uid=1006 gid=1008 euid=1006 suid=1006 fsuid=1006 egid=1008
sgid=1008 fsgid=1008 tty=pts0 ses=1781 comm="sshd" exe="/usr/sbin/sshd"
subj=unconfined_u:unconfined_r:unconfin
ed_t:s0-s0:c0.c1023 key=(null)
```

Here's another one:

```
time->Tue Dec 12 11:50:28 2017
type=PROCTITLE msg=audit(1513097428.713:13900):
proctitle=737368643A20636861726C6965407074732F30
type=PATH msg=audit(1513097428.713:13900): item=0 name="/etc/
profile.d/" inode=33593031 dev=fd:01 mode=040755 ouid=0 ogid=0 rdev=00:00
obj=system_u:object_r:bin_t:s0 objtype=
NORMAL
type=CWD msg=audit(1513097428.713:13900):  cwd="/home/charlie"
type=SYSCALL msg=audit(1513097428.713:13900): arch=c000003e syscall=257
success=yes exit=3 a0=ffffffffffffff9c a1=1b27930 a2=90800 a3=0 items=1
ppid=9725 pid=9726 auid=1006 u
id=1006 gid=1008 euid=1006 suid=1006 fsuid=1006 egid=1008 sgid=1008
fsgid=1008 tty=pts0 ses=1781 comm="bash" exe="/usr/bin/bash"
subj=unconfined_u:unconfined_r:unconfined_t:s
0-s0:c0.c1023 key=(null)
```

In the first record, we see that Charlie accessed the /usr/sbin/sshd file. In the second, we see that he accessed the /usr/bin/bash file. It's not that Charlie chose to access those files. The operating system accessed those files for him in the course of just a normal login event. So as you see, when you create audit rules, you have to be careful what you wish for because there's a definite danger that the wish might be granted. If you really need to monitor someone, you'll want to create a rule that won't give you quite this much information.

While we're at it, we might as well see what the aureport output for this looks like:

```
[donnie@localhost ~]$ sudo aureport -s -i | grep 'openat'
1068. 12/12/2017 11:49:29 openat 9592 ls cleopatra 13828
1099. 12/12/2017 11:50:28 openat 9665 sshd charlie 13887
1100. 12/12/2017 11:50:28 openat 9665 sshd charlie 13889
1101. 12/12/2017 11:50:28 openat 9665 sshd charlie 13890
1102. 12/12/2017 11:50:28 openat 9726 sshd charlie 13898
1103. 12/12/2017 11:50:28 openat 9726 bash charlie 13900
1104. 12/12/2017 11:50:28 openat 9736 grep charlie 13901
1105. 12/12/2017 11:50:28 openat 9742 grep charlie 13902
1108. 12/12/2017 11:50:51 openat 9766 ls charlie 13906
1110. 12/12/2017 12:15:35 openat 10952 ls vicky 14077
1115. 12/12/2017 12:30:54 openat 11632 sshd charlie 14129
. . .
. . .
```

In addition to what Charlie did, we also see what Vicky and Cleopatra did. That's because the rule that we set for the /secretcats/ directory generated openat events when Vicky and Cleopatra accessed, viewed, or created files in that directory.

Generating authentication reports

You can generate user authentication reports without having to define any audit rules. Just use aureport with the -au option switch. (Remember au, the first two letters of *authentication*.):

```
[donnie@localhost ~]$ sudo aureport -au
[sudo] password for donnie:
Authentication Report
============================================
# date time acct host term exe success event
============================================
1. 10/28/2017 13:38:52 donnie localhost.localdomain tty1 /usr/bin/login yes 94
2. 10/28/2017 13:39:03 donnie localhost.localdomain /dev/tty1 /usr/bin/sudo yes
102
3. 10/28/2017 14:04:51 donnie localhost.localdomain /dev/tty1 /usr/bin/sudo yes
147
. . .
```

```
. . .
239. 12/12/2017 11:50:20 charlie 192.168.0.222 ssh /usr/sbin/sshd no 13880
244. 12/12/2017 12:10:06 cleopatra 192.168.0.222 ssh /usr/sbin/sshd no 13992
. . .
```

For login events, this tells us whether the user logged in at the local terminal or remotely through SSH. To see the details of any event, use ausearch with the -a option, followed by the event number that you see at the end of a line. (Strangely, the -a option stands for an *event*.)

Let's look at event number **14122** for Charlie:

```
[donnie@localhost ~]$ sudo ausearch -a 14122
----
time->Tue Dec 12 12:30:49 2017
type=USER_AUTH msg=audit(1513099849.322:14122): pid=11632 uid=0 auid=4294967295
ses=4294967295 subj=system_u:system_r:sshd_t:s0-s0:c0.c1023 msg='op=pubkey
acct="charlie" exe="/usr/sbin/sshd" hostname=? addr=192.168.0.222 terminal=ssh
res=failed'
```

The problem with this is that it really doesn't make any sense. I'm the one who did the logins for Charlie, and I know for a fact that Charlie never had any failed logins. In fact, we can correlate this with the matching entry from the /var/log/secure file:

```
Dec 12 12:30:53 localhost sshd[11632]: Accepted password for charlie from
192.168.0.222 port 34980 ssh2
Dec 12 12:30:54 localhost sshd[11632]: pam_unix(sshd:session): session opened
for user charlie by (uid=0)
```

The timestamps for these two entries are a few seconds later than the timestamp for the ausearch output, but that's okay. There's nothing in this log file to suggest that Charlie ever had a failed login, and these two entries clearly show that Charlie's login really was successful. The lesson here is that when you see something strange in either the ausearch or aureport output, be sure to correlate it with the matching entry in the proper authentication log file to get a better idea of what's going on. (By authentication log file, I mean /var/log/secure for Red Hat-type systems and /var/log/auth.log for Ubuntu systems. The names may vary for other Linux distros.)

Using pre-defined rulesets

In the /usr/share/doc/audit-version_number/rules/ directory of your CentOS 7 machine and the /usr/share/audit/sample-rules/ directory of your AlmaLinux machines, you'll see some pre-made rulesets for different scenarios. Once you install auditd on Ubuntu, you'll have audit rules in the /usr/share/doc/auditd/examples/rules/ directory. In any case, some of the rulesets are common among all three of these distros. Let's look at the AlmaLinux 9 machine to see what we have there:

```
[donnie@localhost ~]$ cd /usr/share/audit/sample-rules/
[donnie@localhost sample-rules]$ ls -l
total 160
. . .
-rw-r--r--. 1 root root 4943 Oct 27 07:15 30-nispom.rules
. . .
-rw-r--r--. 1 root root 6179 Oct 27 07:15 30-pci-dss-v31.rules
-rw-r--r--. 1 root root 6624 Oct 27 07:15 30-stig.rules
-rw-r--r--. 1 root root 1458 Oct 27 07:15 31-privileged.rules
-rw-r--r--. 1 root root  213 Oct 27 07:15 32-power-abuse.rules
. . .
[donnie@localhost sample-rules]$
```

The three files I want to focus on are the nispom, pci-dss, and stig files. Each of these three rulesets is designed to meet the auditing standards of a particular certifying agency. In order, these rulesets are:

- **nispom**: The National Industrial Security Program – you'll see this ruleset used at either the US Department of Defense or its contractors.
- **pci-dss**: Payment Card Industry Data Security Standard – if you work in the banking or financial industries, or even if you're just running an online business that accepts credit cards, you'll likely become very familiar with this.
- **stig**: Security Technical Implementation Guides – if you work for the US government, or possibly other governments, you'll be dealing with this one.

To use one of these rules sets, just copy the appropriate files over to the /etc/audit/rules.d/ directory:

```
[donnie@localhost rules]$ sudo cp 30-pci-dss-v31.rules /etc/audit/rules.d
[donnie@localhost rules]$
```

After you've copied the rule file over, restart the auditd daemon to read in the new rules.

For Red Hat, CentOS, or AlmaLinux, do this:

```
sudo service auditd restart
```

For Ubuntu, do this:

```
sudo systemctl restart auditd
```

Of course, there's always the chance that a particular rule in one of these sets might not work for you or that you might need to enable a rule that's currently disabled. If so, just open the appropriate rules file in your text editor and comment out what doesn't work or uncomment what you need to enable.

Even though auditd is very cool, bear in mind that it only alerts you about potential security breaches. It doesn't do anything to harden the system against them.

Hands-on lab – using auditd

In this lab, you'll practice using the features of `auditd`. Let's get started:

1. For Ubuntu only, install `auditd`:

    ```
    sudo apt update
    sudo apt install auditd
    ```

2. View the rules that are currently in effect:

    ```
    sudo auditctl -l
    ```

3. From the command line, create a temporary rule that audits the `/etc/passwd` file for changes. Verify that the rule is in effect:

    ```
    sudo auditctl -w /etc/passwd -p wa -k passwd_changes
    sudo auditctl -l
    ```

4. Create a user account for Lionel. On Ubuntu, do this:

    ```
    sudo adduser lionel
    ```

    On CentOS or AlmaLinux, do this:

    ```
    sudo useradd lionel
    sudo passwd lionel
    ```

5. Search for audit messages regarding any changes to the `passwd` file:

    ```
    sudo ausearch -i -k passwd_changes
    sudo aureport -i -k | grep 'passwd_changes'
    ```

6. Log out of your own account and log in as Lionel. Then, log out of Lionel's account and back in to your own.

7. Do an authentication report:

    ```
    sudo aureport -au
    ```

8. Create the `/secrets` directory and set the permissions so that only the root user can access it:

    ```
    sudo mkdir /secrets
    sudo chmod 700 /secrets
    ```

9. Create a rule that monitors the `/secrets` directory:

    ```
    sudo auditctl -w /secrets -k secrets_watch
    sudo auditctl -l
    ```

10. Log out of your account, and log in as Lionel. Have him try to view what's in the /secrets directory:

```
ls -l /secrets
```

11. Log out of Lionel's account and log in to your own. View the alerts that Lionel created:

```
sudo ausearch -i -k secrets_watch | less
```

12. You now have two temporary rules that will disappear when you reboot the machine. Make them permanent by creating a custom.rules file:

```
sudo sh -c "auditctl -l > /etc/audit/rules.d/custom.rules"
```

13. Reboot the machine and verify that the rules are still in effect:

```
sudo auditctl -l
```

You've reached the end of the lab – congratulations!

Hands-on lab —Using pre-configured rules with auditd

In this lab, we'll simulate that the US government is our client, and that we need to set up a server that will meet their **Security Technical Implementation Guides (STIG)** auditing standards. To do that, we'll use several pre-configured rulesets that get installed when you install auditd. Note that this lab will work on any of your virtual machines:

Delete the custom.rules file that you created in the previous lab, and then restart the auditd service.

Copy the 10-base-config.rules, 30-stig.rules, 31-privileged.rules, and 99-finalize.rules files to the /etc/audit/rules.d/ directory. (These rules files are in the /usr/share/doc/auditd/examples/ rules/ directory on Ubuntu, and in the /usr/share/audit/sample-rules/ directory on AlmaLinx.):

```
[donnie@almalinux9 sample-rules]$ pwd
/usr/share/audit/sample-rules
[donnie@almalinux9 sample-rules]$ sudo cp 10-base-config.rules 30-stig.rules
31-privileged.rules 99-finalize.rules /etc/audit/rules.d
[donnie@almalinux9 sample-rules]$
```

Restart the auditd service, and then use sudo auditctl -l to view the new active ruleset.

End of lab.

> You've just seen that we can sometimes use several different pre-configured rulesets at once *if* they complement each other. Understand though that you'll never use *all* of the pre-configured rulesets at once.

In this section, you looked at some examples of how to work with auditd. Next, let's look at a simpler method of auditing files and directories.

Auditing files and directories with inotifywait

There might be times when you'll just want a quick and easy way to monitor a file or a directory in real time. Instead of having audit messages sent to the audit.log file, you can use inotifywait to have a message pop up in your terminal as soon as someone accesses a designated file or directory. This tool is part of the inotify-tools package on both Ubuntu and AlmaLinux. It's not installed by default, so go ahead and install it if it isn't already.

To monitor a single file, just do:

```
donnie@donnie-ca:~$ sudo inotifywait -m /secrets/donnie_file.txt
[sudo] password for donnie:
Setting up watches.
Watches established.
/secrets/donnie_file.txt OPEN
/secrets/donnie_file.txt CLOSE_NOWRITE,CLOSE
```

The /secrets/ directory is set so that only someone with root privileges can access it, so I have to use sudo to make this work. The -m option causes inotifywait to perform continuous monitoring, instead of exiting as soon as something happens. The OPEN message came up when I opened the file with less, and the CLOSE_NOWRITE, CLOSE message came up when I exited less. Now, let's close this down and monitor the whole directory. All we have to do is to add the -r option and leave out the file name, like this:

```
donnie@donnie-ca:~$ sudo inotifywait -m -r /secrets/
Setting up watches.  Beware: since -r was given, this may take a while!
Watches established.
/secrets/ OPEN donnie_file.txt
/secrets/ CREATE .donnie_file.txt.swp
/secrets/ OPEN .donnie_file.txt.swp
/secrets/ CREATE .donnie_file.txt.swx
. . .
. . .
/secrets/ CLOSE_NOWRITE,CLOSE donnie_file.txt
/secrets/ OPEN donnie_file.txt
/secrets/ CLOSE_NOWRITE,CLOSE donnie_file.txt
/secrets/ MODIFY .donnie_file.txt.swp
/secrets/ MODIFY .donnie_file.txt.swp
```

This time, I opened the donnie_file.txt file in vim, which caused a whole bunch of messages to come up. That's because when you open a file in vim, it creates some temporary files that will get cleared out when you exit vim. (Note that I haven't actually edited the file yet, and that more messages will get created when I do.)

As good as `inotifywait` seems to be, there is one downside. It's just that to use it, you'll need to stayed glued to your workstation, keep the terminal window from which you're running `inotifywait` open, and watch for messages to pop up. There's no logging mechanism, and no daemon mode. But, if you need to monitor something in real-time, this could be useful.

That's all there is to it for `inotifywait`. Next, we'll look at OpenSCAP, which can actually remediate a less-than-secure system.

Applying OpenSCAP policies with oscap

The **Security Content Automation Protocol (SCAP)** was created by the US **National Institute of Standards and Technology (NIST)**. It consists of hardening guides, hardening templates, and baseline configuration guides for setting up secure systems. OpenSCAP is a set of FOSS tools that can be used to implement SCAP. It consists of the following:

- Security profiles that you can apply to a system. There are different profiles for meeting the requirements of several different certifying agencies.
- Security guides to help with the initial setup of your system.
- The `oscap` command-line utility to apply security templates.
- On systems that have a desktop interface, you have SCAP Workbench, a GUI-type utility.

You can install OpenSCAP on either the Red Hat or the Ubuntu distros, but it's much better implemented on the Red Hat distros. For one thing, when you install a Red Hat-type operating system, you can choose to apply a SCAP profile during installation. You can't do that with Ubuntu. All of the Red Hat-type distros come with a fairly complete set of ready-to-use profiles. Ubuntu 22.04 comes with outdated profiles for Fedora 14 and RHEL 6, and none for Ubuntu 22.04, which I think is totally bizarre. Not to worry though, because I'll show you how to get some good Ubuntu profiles in just a bit.

When doing initial system builds, it's desirable to start with a security checklist that's appropriate for your scenario, because there are certain things the OpenSCAP can't automate for you. Then, use OpenSCAP to do the rest. I'll tell you more about security checklists at the end of *Chapter 16, Security Tips and Tricks for the Busy Bee*.

All right, let's learn how to install OpenSCAP and how to use the command-line utility that's common to all of our distros.

Installing OpenSCAP

On your CentOS 7 machine, assuming that you didn't install OpenSCAP during the operating system installation, do this:

```
sudo yum install openscap-scanner scap-security-guide
```

Do the following for either AlmaLinux 8 or AlmaLinux 9:

```
sudo dnf install openscap-scanner scap-security-guide
```

Do the following on an Ubuntu 22.04 machine:

```
sudo apt install python-openscap
```

Viewing the profile files

On the CentOS 7 machine and the AlmaLinux machines, you'll see the profile files in the /usr/share/xml/scap/ssg/content/ directory.

As I already mentioned, Ubuntu only gives us some outdated Fedora 14 and RHEL 6 profiles in the /usr/share/openscap/ directory, and none at all for any flavor of Ubuntu. (Why that is, I have no clue.) The profile files are in .xml format, and each one contains one or more profiles that you can apply to the system. For example, here are some from the CentOS 7 machine:

```
[donnie@localhost content]$ pwd
/usr/share/xml/scap/ssg/content
[donnie@localhost content]$ ls -l
total 50596
-rw-r--r--. 1 root root  6734643 Oct 19 19:40 ssg-centos6-ds.xml
-rw-r--r--. 1 root root  1596043 Oct 19 19:40 ssg-centos6-xccdf.xml
-rw-r--r--. 1 root root 11839886 Oct 19 19:41 ssg-centos7-ds.xml
-rw-r--r--. 1 root root  2636971 Oct 19 19:40 ssg-centos7-xccdf.xml
-rw-r--r--. 1 root root      642 Oct 19 19:40 ssg-firefox-cpe-dictionary.xml
. . .
-rw-r--r--. 1 root root 11961196 Oct 19 19:41 ssg-rhel7-ds.xml
-rw-r--r--. 1 root root   851069 Oct 19 19:40 ssg-rhel7-ocil.xml
-rw-r--r--. 1 root root  2096046 Oct 19 19:40 ssg-rhel7-oval.xml
-rw-r--r--. 1 root root  2863621 Oct 19 19:40 ssg-rhel7-xccdf.xml
[donnie@localhost content]$
```

You'll see a somewhat similar list on your AlmaLinux 8 machine, except that they'll be specific to AlmaLinux 8. On AlmaLinux 9, things are a bit different. At the time of this writing, all we have is just one profile file. That's because the RHEL 9 distros are quite new, so the development of SCAP profiles for them isn't yet complete. Anyway, here's AlmaLinux 9 file:

```
[donnie@almalinux9 content]$ pwd
/usr/share/xml/scap/ssg/content
[donnie@almalinux9 content]$ ls -l
total 21524
-rw-r--r--. 1 root root 22040119 Oct 27 08:37 ssg-almalinux9-ds.xml
[donnie@almalinux9 content]$
```

The command-line utility for working with OpenSCAP is oscap. On our AlmaLinux 9 machine, let's use this with the info switch to view information about any of the profile files. Let's look at the ssg-almalinux9-ds.xml file:

```
[donnie@almalinux9 content]$ pwd
/usr/share/xml/scap/ssg/content
[donnie@almalinux9 content]$ sudo oscap info ssg-almalinux9-ds.xml
. . .

. . .
    Profiles:
        Title: ANSSI-BP-028 (enhanced)
        Id: xccdf_org.ssgproject.content_profile_anssi_bp28_enhanced
        Title: ANSSI-BP-028 (high)
        Id: xccdf_org.ssgproject.content_profile_anssi_bp28_high
        Title: ANSSI-BP-028 (intermediary)
        Id: xccdf_org.ssgproject.content_profile_anssi_bp28_intermediary
        Title: ANSSI-BP-028 (minimal)
        Id: xccdf_org.ssgproject.content_profile_anssi_bp28_minimal
        . . .
```

Due to formatting constraints, I can't show you the entire list of profiles. So, do this for yourself and scroll down the list. You'll see profiles for **STIG** and **PCI-DSS**, just as we had for the auditing rules. There's also a **HIPAA** profile for medical facilities here in the US, several benchmark profiles from the **Center for Internet Security, (CIS)**, and several that are specific for certain non-US countries, among others.

Getting the missing profiles for Ubuntu

We've seen that there aren't any SCAP profiles for Ubuntu in the Ubuntu repositories. So, is all hope lost for Ubuntu users? Absolutely not. Fortunately, the scap-security-guide package that you can install on a Fedora Server virtual machine comes with SCAP profiles for a variety of other Linux distros, including the newest versions of Ubuntu. So, your best bet for setting up OpenSCAP on Ubuntu is to create a Fedora Server VM, install the scap-security-guide package in the same manner that you just did for AlmaLinux, and then copy the appropriate profile file from Fedora's /usr/share/xml/scap/ssg/content/ directory to your Ubuntu machine. After that, you're golden.

Scanning the system

In this section, we'll work with our AlmaLinux 9 VM.

> This procedure works the same for most all Linux distros, except that the names of the profiles will differ.

Now, let's say that we need to ensure that our systems are compliant with **Payment Card Industry** standards. First, we'll scan the AlmaLinux 9 machine to see what needs remediation. (Note that the following command is very long and wraps around on the printed page.):

```
sudo oscap xccdf eval --profile xccdf_org.ssgproject.content_profile_pci-
dss --fetch-remote --results scan-xccdf-results.xml /usr/share/xml/scap/ssg/
content/ssg-almalinux9-ds.xml
```

As we always like to do, let's break this down:

- xccdf eval: The **Extensible Configuration Checklist Description Format** is one of the languages that we can use to write security profile rules. We're going to use a profile that was written in this language to perform an evaluation of the system.
- --profile xccdf_org.ssgproject.content_profile_pci-dss: Here, I specified that I want to use the Payment Card Industry-Data Security Standard profile to evaluate the system. (Profile names come from the Id lines in the profile file.)
- --fetch-remote: Use this option to fetch additional rules. (Note that this option won't work if you have the system crypto policy set to FUTURE mode.)
- --results scan-xccdf-results.xml: I'm going to save the scan results to this .xml format file. When the scan has finished, I'll create a report from this file.
- /usr/share/xml/scap/ssg/content/ssg-almalinux9-ds.xml: This is the profile file that contains the xccdf_org.ssgproject.content_profile_pci-dss profile.

As the scan progresses, the output will be sent to the screen, as well as to the designated output file. It's a long list of items, so I'll only show you a few of them. Here are a couple of items that look okay:

```
Title    Ensure Software Patches Installed
Rule     xccdf_org.ssgproject.content_rule_security_patches_up_to_date
OVAL Definition ID oval:org.almalinux.alsa:def:20227967
OVAL Definition Title      ALSA-2022:7967: qemu-kvm security, bug fix, and
enhancement update (Moderate)
Result   pass


Title    Ensure Software Patches Installed
Rule     xccdf_org.ssgproject.content_rule_security_patches_up_to_date
OVAL Definition ID oval:org.almalinux.alsa:def:20227959
OVAL Definition Title      ALSA-2022:7959: guestfs-tools security, bug fix, and
enhancement update (Low)
Result   pass
```

Here are a couple of items that need to be fixed:

```
Title    Ensure PAM Displays Last Logon/Access Notification
Rule     xccdf_org.ssgproject.content_rule_display_login_attempts
Result   fail
```

```
Title    Limit Password Reuse
Rule     xccdf_org.ssgproject.content_rule_accounts_password_pam_unix_remember
Result   fail


Title    Lock Accounts After Failed Password Attempts
Rule     xccdf_org.ssgproject.content_rule_accounts_passwords_pam_faillock_deny
Result   fail


Title    Set Lockout Time for Failed Password Attempts
Rule     xccdf_org.ssgproject.content_rule_accounts_passwords_pam_faillock_
unlock_time
Result   fail
```

So, we have patches for certain security vulnerabilities installed, which is good. However, it seems that we have some problems with our password policies.

Now that I've run the scan and created an output file with the results, I can build my report:

```
sudo oscap xccdf generate report scan-xccdf-results.xml > scan-xccdf-results.
html
```

This extracts information from the .xml format file that isn't meant to be read by humans and transfers it to a .html file that you can open in your web browser. (For the record, the report says that there are 49 problems that need to be fixed.)

Remediating the system

So, we have 49 problems that we need to fix before our system can be considered compliant with Payment Card Industry standards. Let's see how many of them oscap can fix for us:

```
sudo oscap xccdf eval --remediate --profile xccdf_org.ssgproject.content_
profile_pci-dss --fetch-remote --results scan-xccdf-results.xml /usr/share/xml/
scap/ssg/content/ssg-almalinux9-ds.xml
```

This is the same command that I used to perform the initial scan, except that I added the --remediate option and I'm saving the results to a different file. You'll want to have a bit of patience when you run this command because fixing some problems involves downloading and installing software packages. In fact, even as I type this, oscap is busy downloading and installing the missing AIDE intrusion detection system package.

Okay, here are some of the things that were fixed:

```
Title    Verify and Correct File Permissions with RPM
Rule     xccdf_org.ssgproject.content_rule_rpm_verify_permissions
Result   fixed
```

```
Title    Install AIDE
Rule     xccdf_org.ssgproject.content_rule_package_aide_installed
Result   fixed


Title    Build and Test AIDE Database
Rule     xccdf_org.ssgproject.content_rule_aide_build_database
Result   fixed


Title    Configure Periodic Execution of AIDE
Rule     xccdf_org.ssgproject.content_rule_aide_periodic_cron_checking
Result   fixed
```

There are a couple of errors because of things that oscap couldn't fix, but that's normal. At least you know about them so that you can try to fix them yourself.

Now, check this out. Do you remember how in *Chapter 3, Securing User Accounts*, I made you jump through hoops to ensure that users had strong passwords that expire on a regular basis? Well, by applying this OpenSCAP profile, you get all that fixed for you automatically. Here are a few of the items that were fixed:

```
Title    Lock Accounts After Failed Password Attempts
Rule     xccdf_org.ssgproject.content_rule_accounts_passwords_pam_faillock_deny
Result   fixed


Title    Set Lockout Time for Failed Password Attempts
Rule     xccdf_org.ssgproject.content_rule_accounts_passwords_pam_faillock_
unlock_time
Result   fixed


Title    Ensure PAM Enforces Password Requirements - Minimum Digit Characters
Rule     xccdf_org.ssgproject.content_rule_accounts_password_pam_dcredit
Result   fixed


Title    Ensure PAM Enforces Password Requirements - Minimum Lowercase
Characters
Rule     xccdf_org.ssgproject.content_rule_accounts_password_pam_lcredit
Result   fixed
```

So, yeah, OpenSCAP is pretty cool, and even the command-line tools aren't hard to use. However, if you have to use a GUI, we have a tool for that, which we'll look at next.

Using SCAP Workbench

For machines with a desktop environment installed, we have SCAP Workbench. However, if you've ever worked with early versions of the tool, you were likely quite disappointed. Indeed, the early versions of Workbench were so bad that they weren't even usable. Thankfully, things have since improved. Now, Workbench is quite a nice little tool.

To get SCAP Workbench, just use the appropriate installation command. On CentOS 7, do this:

```
sudo yum install scap-workbench
```

On AlmaLinux 8 or AlmaLinux 9, do this:

```
sudo dnf install scap-workbench
```

On Ubuntu, do the following:

```
sudo apt install scap-workbench
```

Yeah, the package name is just scap-workbench instead of openscap-workbench. I don't know why, but I do know that you'll never find it if you're searching for openscap packages.

Once you've installed it, you'll see its menu item on the **Show Applications** portion of the **Activities** page:

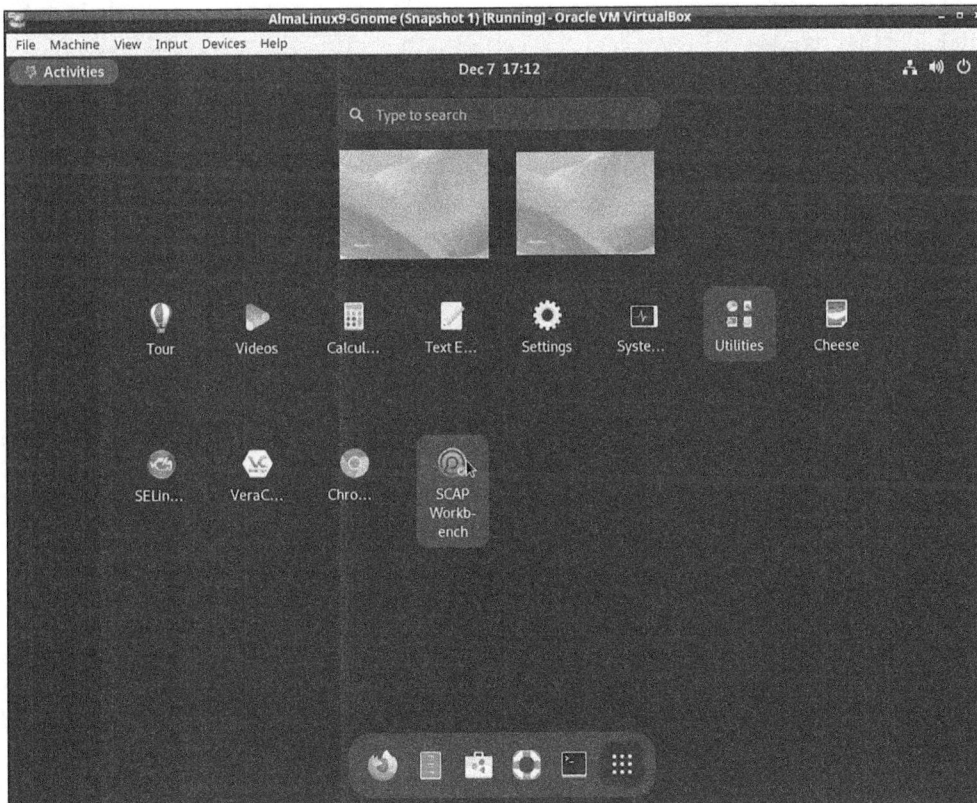

Figure 12.2: SCAP Workbench on the Gnome 3 desktop

When you first open the program, you would think that the system would ask you for a root or sudo password. But, it doesn't. We'll see if that affects us in a moment.

The first thing you'll see on the opening screen is a drop-down list for you to select the type of content that you want to load. I'll select **AlmaLinux9** and then click on the **Load Content** button:

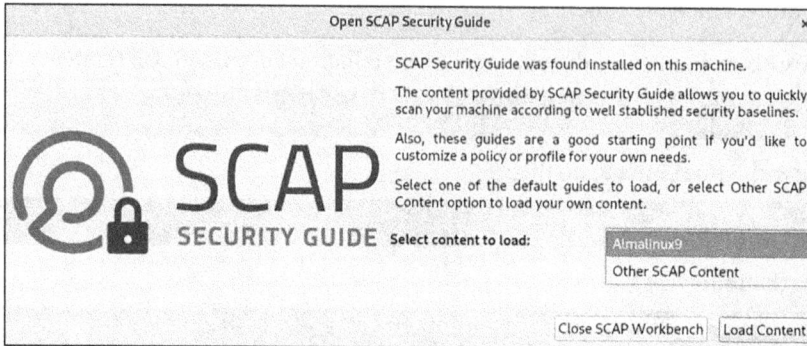

Figure 12.3: Select content to load

Next, you'll see the top panel, where you can select the desired profile. You can also choose to customize the profile, and whether you want to run the scan on the local machine or on a remote machine. In the bottom pane, you'll see a list of rules for that profile. You can expand each rule item to get a description of that rule:

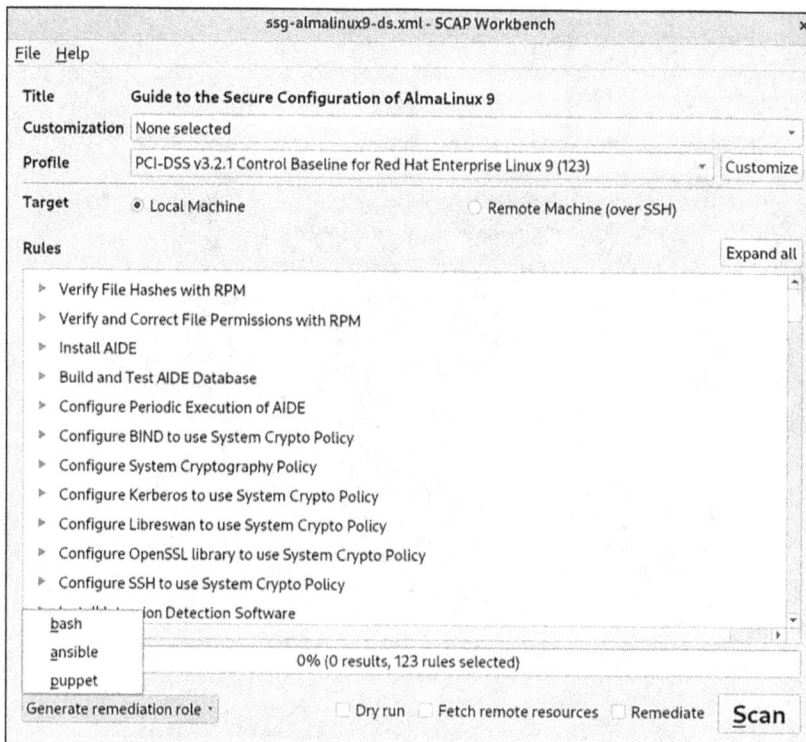

Figure 12.4: Viewing the rules, and generating a remediation role

At the bottom of this screen, you see some cool options. Click on the **Generate remediation role** button, and you can choose to create a Puppet manifest, an Ansible playbook, or a Bash shell script that you can distribute and apply to other AlmaLinux 9 machines on your network. You can also choose to **Fetch remote resources** and to **Remediate**.

Now, let's click that **Scan** button to see what happens:

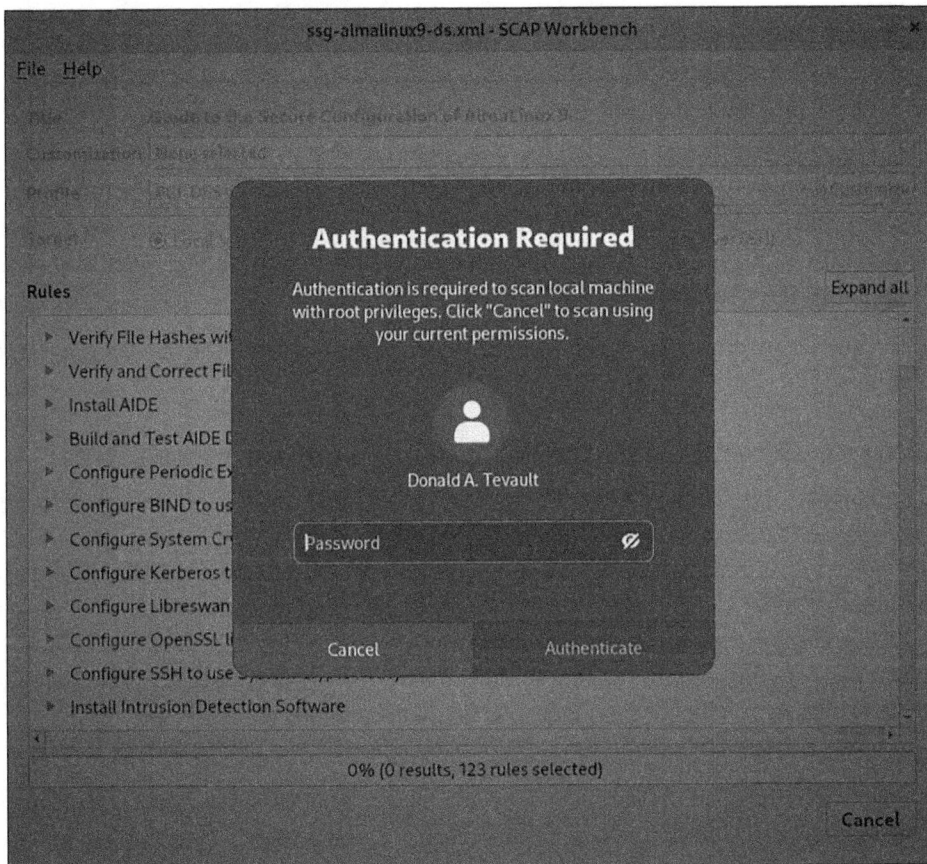

Figure 12.5: Enter your password

Cool! As I had hoped, it prompts you for your sudo password. Beyond that, I'll leave you to play with it. It's just another one of those GUI-thingies, so the rest of it should be fairly easy to figure out.

Next, we'll take a look at how to choose an appropriate OpenSCAP profile.

Choosing an OpenSCAP profile

So, now, you're saying, *Okay, this is all good, but how do I find out what's in these profiles and which one I need?* Well, there are several ways.

The first way, which I've just shown you, is to install SCAP Workbench on a machine with a desktop interface and read through the descriptions of all the rules for each profile.

The second way, which might be a bit easier, is to go to the OpenSCAP website and look through the documentation that they have there.

You'll find information about the available OpenSCAP profiles at `https://www.open-scap.org/security-policies/choosing-policy/`.

As far as knowing which profile to choose, there are a few things to consider:

- If you work in the financial sector or in a business that does online financial transactions, then go with the `pci-dss` profile.
- If you work for a government agency, especially if it's the US government, then go with either the `stig` profile or the `nispom` profile, as dictated by the particular agency.
- If neither of these two considerations applies to your situation, then you'll just want to do some research and planning in order to figure out what really needs to be locked down. Look through the rules in each profile and read through the documentation on the OpenSCAP website to help you decide what you need.

With Red Hat and its offspring, you can even apply a policy as you install the operating system. We'll look at that next.

Applying an OpenSCAP profile during system installation

One of the things that I love about the Red Hat folk is that they totally get this whole security thing. Yeah, we can lock down other distros and make them more secure, as we've already seen. But with Red Hat distros, it's a bit easier. For a lot of things, the maintainers of the Red Hat-type distros have set secure default options that aren't securely set by default on other distros. (For example, prior to the release of Ubuntu 22.04, Red Hat distros had been the only ones that come with users' home directories locked down by default.) For other things, the Red Hat-type distros come with tools and installation options that help make life easier for a busy, security-conscious administrator.

When you install a Red Hat-type distro, you'll be given the chance to apply an OpenSCAP profile during the operating system installation. Here, on this AlmaLinux 9 installer screen, you'll see the option to choose a security profile in the bottom right-hand corner of the screen:

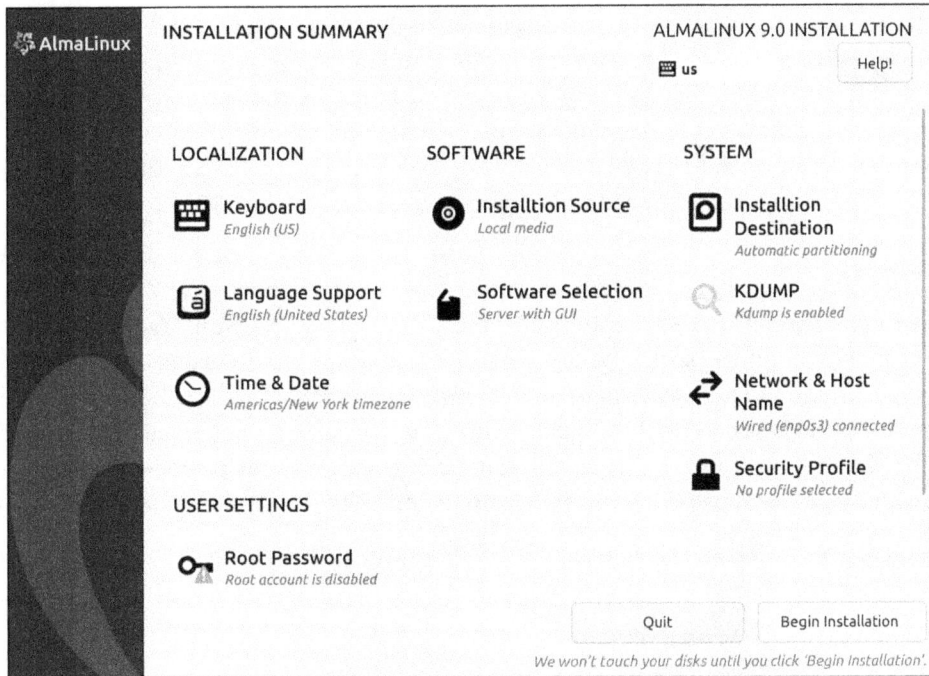

Figure 12.6: Select a SCAP profile during installation

All you have to do is click on that and then choose your profile:

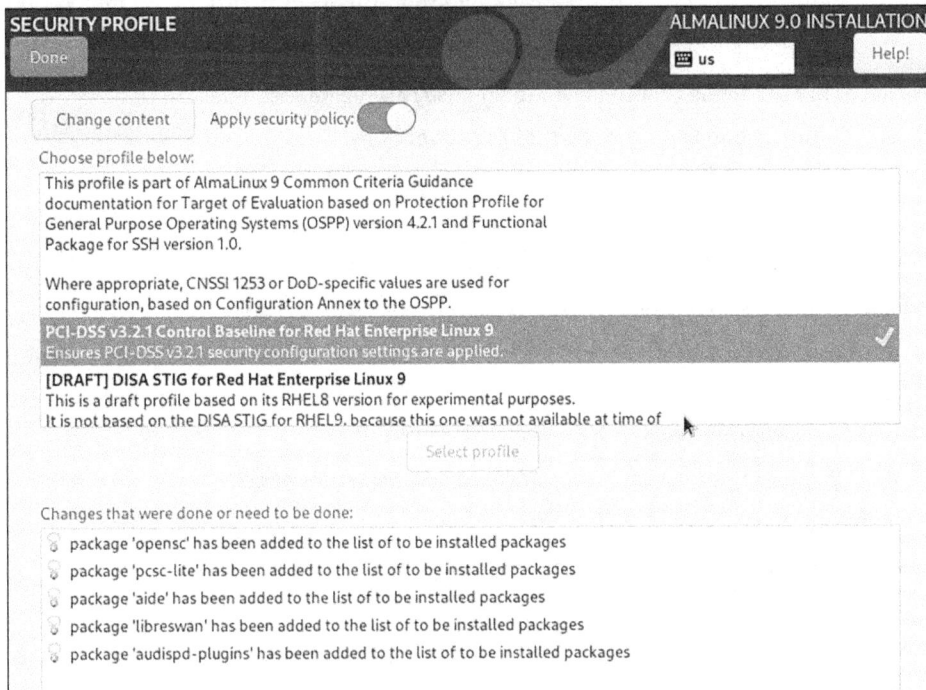

Figure: 12.7: Selecting the PCI-DSS profile

Okay, that pretty much wraps it up for our discussion of OpenSCAP. The only thing left to add is that, as great as OpenSCAP is, it won't do everything. For example, some security standards require that you have certain directories, such as /home/ or /var/, on their own separate partitions. An OpenSCAP scan will alert you if that's not the case, but it can't change your existing partitioning scheme. So, for things like that, you'll need to get a checklist from the governing body that dictates your security requirements and do a bit of advanced work before you even touch OpenSCAP.

Summary

We covered a lot of ground in this chapter, and we saw some really cool stuff. We began by looking at a couple of antivirus scanners so that we can prevent infecting any Windows machines that access our Linux servers. In the *Scanning for rootkits with Rootkit Hunter* section, we saw how to scan for those nasty rootkits. We also saw a couple of quick techniques to examine a potentially malicious file. It's important to know how to audit systems, especially in high-security environments, and we saw how to do that. Finally, we wrapped things up with a discussion of hardening our systems with OpenSCAP.

In the next chapter, we'll look at logging and log file security. I'll see you there.

Questions

1. Which of the following is true about rootkits?

    a. They only infect Windows operating systems.

    b. The purpose of planting a rootkit is to gain root privileges to a system.

    c. An intruder must have already gained root privileges in order to plant a rootkit.

    d. A rootkit isn't very harmful.

2. Which of the following methods would you use to keep `maldet` updated?

    a. Manually create a `cron` job that runs every day.

    b. Do nothing, because `maldet` automatically updates itself.

    c. Once a day, run the normal update command for your operating system.

    d. Run the `maldet update` utility from the command line.

3. Which of the following is true about the `auditd` service?

    a. On an Ubuntu system, you'll need to stop or restart it with the `service` command.

    b. On a Red Hat-type system, you'll need to stop or restart it with the `service` command.

    c. On an Ubuntu system, it comes already installed.

    d. On a Red Hat-type system, you'll need to install it yourself.

4. You need to create an auditing rule that will alert you every time a particular person reads or creates a file. Which of the following syscalls would you use in that rule?

    a. `openfile`

    b. `fileread`

    c. `openat`

    d. `fileopen`

5. Which file does the `auditd` service use to log auditing events?

   a. `/var/log/messages`

   b. `/var/log/syslog`

   c. `/var/log/auditd/audit`

   d. `/var/log/audit/audit.log`

6. You need to create custom auditing rules for `auditd`. Where would you place the new rules?

   a. `/usr/share/audit-version_number/`

   b. `/etc/audit/`

   c. `/etc/audit.d/rules/`

   d. `/etc/audit/rules.d/`

7. You're setting up a web server for a bank's customer portal. Which of the following SCAP profiles might you apply?

   a. STIG

   b. NISPOM

   c. PCI-DSS

   d. Sarbanes-Oxley

8. Which of the following is true about OpenSCAP?

   a. It can't remediate everything, so you'll need to do advance planning with a checklist before setting up a server.

   b. It can automatically remediate every problem on your system.

   c. It's only available for Red Hat-type distros.

   d. Ubuntu comes with a better selection of SCAP profiles.

9. Which of the following commands would you use to generate a user authentication report?

   a. `sudo ausearch -au`

   b. `sudo aureport -au`

   c. Define an audit rule, then do `sudo ausearch -au`.

   d. Define an audit rule, then do `sudo aureport -au`.

10. Which set of Rootkit Hunter options would you use to have a rootkit scan automatically run every night?

    a. `-c`

    b. `-c --rwo`

    c. `--rwo`

    d. `-c --cronjob --rwo`

Further reading

- How to install and configure maldet: `https://www.servernoobs.com/how-to-install-and-configure-maldet-linux-malware-detect-lmd/`
- Symbiote: Evasive Linux rootkit malware: `https://www.theregister.com/2022/06/10/symbiote_linux_malware/`
- Configuring and auditing Linux systems with `auditd` daemon: `https://linux-audit.com/configuring-and-auditing-linux-systems-with-audit-daemon/`
- Monitor changes in directories with `inotifywatch`: `https://distrowatch.com/weekly.php?issue=20220905`
- The OpenSCAP portal: `https://www.open-scap.org/`
- Practical OpenSCAP: `https://www.redhat.com/files/summit/session-assets/2016/SL45190-practical-openscap_security-standard-compliance-and-reporting.pdf`
- Center for Internet Security (CIS) benchmarks: `https://www.cisecurity.org/cis-benchmarks/`
- Auditing the System documentation for RHEL 9: `https://access.redhat.com/documentation/en-us/red_hat_enterprise_linux/9/html/security_hardening/auditing-the-system_security-hardening#doc-wrapper`

Answers

1. c
2. b
3. b
4. c
5. d
6. d
7. c
8. a
9. b
10. d

Join our book community

Join our community's Discord space for discussions with the author and other readers:

`https://packt.link/CyberSec`

13

Logging and Log Security

System logs are an important part of every IT administrator's life. They can tell you how well your system is performing, how to troubleshoot problems, and what the users—both authorized and unauthorized—are doing on the system.

In this chapter, I'll give you a brief tour of the Linux logging systems, and then show you a cool trick to help make your log reviews easier. Then, I'll show you how to set up a remote logging server, complete with Transport Layer Security (TLS)-encrypted connections to the clients.

The topics that we will be covering are:

- Understanding the Linux system log files
- Understanding rsyslog
- Understanding journald
- Making things easier with Logwatch
- Setting up a remote log server
- Maintaining Logs in Large Enterprises

The focus of this chapter is on logging tools that are either already built into your Linux distro or that are available in your distro repositories. Other Packt Publishing books, such as the *Linux Administration Cookbook*, by Adam K. Dean, show you some of the fancier, more advanced third-party log aggregation and analysis tools.

So, if you're ready and raring to go, let's look at those Linux log files.

Understanding the Linux system log files

You'll find the Linux log files in the /var/log/ directory. The structure of Linux log files is pretty much the same across all Linux distros. But, in the Linux tradition of trying to keep us all confused, the main log files have different names on different distros. On Red Hat-type systems, the main log file is the messages file, and the log for authentication-related events is the secure file. On Debian/Ubuntu-type systems, the main log file is the syslog file, and the authentication log is the auth.log file. Other log files you'll see include the following:

- `/var/log/kern.log`: On Debian/Ubuntu-type systems, this log contains messages about what's going on with the Linux kernel. As we saw in *Chapter 4, Securing Your Server with a Firewall – Part 1*, and *Chapter 5, Securing Your Server with a Firewall – Part 2*, this includes messages about what's going on with the Linux firewall. So, if you want to see whether any suspicious network packets have been blocked, this is the place to look. Red Hat-type systems don't have this file. Instead, Red Hat systems send their kernel messages to the `messages` file.

- `/var/log/wtmp` and `/var/run/utmp`: The two files do essentially the same thing. They both record information about users who are logged in to the system. The main difference is that `wtmp` holds historical data from `utmp`. Unlike most Linux log files, these are in binary format, rather than normal text-mode format. The `utmp` file is the only file we'll look at that isn't in the `/var/log/` directory.

- `/var/log/btmp`: This binary file holds information about failed login attempts. The `pam_tally2` module that we looked at in *Chapter 3, Securing Normal User Accounts*, uses the information that's in this file.

- `/var/log/lastlog`: This binary file holds information about the last time that users logged in to the system.

- `/var/log/audit/audit.log`: This text-mode file records information from the auditd daemon. We already discussed it in *Chapter 12, Scanning, Hardening, and Auditing*, so I won't discuss it here.

There are quite a few other log files that contain information about applications and system boot-ups. But the log files that I've listed here are the main ones we're concerned about when looking at system security.

Now that we've looked at what log files we have, let's look at them in more detail.

The system log and the authentication log

It doesn't matter whether you're talking about the `syslog` and `auth.log` files on Debian/Ubuntu or the `messages` and `secure` files on RHEL/CentOS/AlmaLinux. On any of these systems, the files are the same, just with different names. The system log files and the authentication log files have the same basic structure and are all plaintext files. This makes it easy to search for specific information with tools that are already built into Linux. It doesn't really matter which virtual machine we use for this, other than to keep the names of the files straight.

To begin, let's look at a simple message from the system log:

```
Jul  1 18:16:12 localhost systemd[1]: Started Postfix Mail Transport Agent.
```

Here's the breakdown:

- `Jul 1 18:16:12`: This is the date and time that the message was generated.
- `localhost`: This is the hostname of the machine that generated the message. This is important because one Linux machine can serve as the central log repository for other Linux machines. By default, messages from other machines will just get dumped into the same log file that the local machine uses. So, we need this field to let us know what's happening on each machine.

- systemd[1]: This is the service that generated the message. In this case, it was the systemd daemon.
- The rest of the line is the specific message.

There are several ways to extract information from the text-mode log files. For now, we'll just open the files in less, as in this example:

```
sudo less syslog
```

Then, to search for a specific text string, hit the / key, type in the string that you want to find, and hit *Enter*.

So, what kind of security-related information can we expect to find in these files? To start, let's look at the permissions on the server's private SSH keys:

```
donnie@orangepione:/etc/ssh$ ls -l
total 580
. . .
-rw-------+ 1 root root   1679 Feb 10  2019 ssh_host_rsa_key
-rw-r--r-- 1 root root    398 Feb 10  2019 ssh_host_rsa_key.pub
donnie@orangepione:/etc/ssh$
```

This private key, the ssh_host_rsa_key file, has to have permissions set for only the root user. But, the + sign at the end of the permissions settings denotes that someone has set an **access-control list** (**ACL**) on that file. getfacl will show us exactly what's going on:

```
donnie@orangepione:/etc/ssh$ getfacl ssh_host_rsa_key
# file: ssh_host_rsa_key
# owner: root
# group: root
user::rw-
user:sshdnoroot:r--
group::---
mask::r--
other::---
donnie@orangepione:/etc/ssh$
```

So, someone has created the sshdnoroot user and assigned it the read permission for the server's private SSH keys. Now, if I try to restart the OpenSSH daemon, it will fail. A peek into the system log—the syslog file, in this case—will tell me why:

```
Mar 13 12:47:46 localhost sshd[1952]: @@@@@@@@@@@@@@@@@@@@@@@@@@@@@@@@@@@@@@@
Mar 13 12:47:46 localhost sshd[1952]: @ WARNING: UNPROTECTED PRIVATE KEY FILE!
@
Mar 13 12:47:46 localhost sshd[1952]: @@@@@@@@@@@@@@@@@@@@@@@@@@@@@@@@@@@@@@@
Mar 13 12:47:46 localhost sshd[1952]: Permissions 0640 for '/etc/ssh/ssh_host_
```

```
rsa_key' are too open.
Mar 13 12:47:46 localhost sshd[1952]: It is required that your private key
files are NOT accessible by others.
Mar 13 12:47:46 localhost sshd[1952]: This private key will be ignored.
Mar 13 12:47:46 localhost sshd[1952]: key_load_private: bad permissions
Mar 13 12:47:46 localhost sshd[1952]: Could not load host key: /etc/ssh/ssh_
host_rsa_key
```

So, the SSH daemon won't start if someone other than the root user has any access permissions for the server's private keys. But how did this happen? Let's search through the authentication file—auth.log, in this case—to see if there's a clue:

```
Mar 13 12:42:54 localhost sudo:    donnie : TTY=tty1 ; PWD=/etc/ssh ; USER=root
; COMMAND=/usr/bin/setfacl -m u:sshdnoroot:r ssh_host_ecdsa_key ssh_host_
ed25519_key ssh_host_rsa_key
```

Ah, so that donnie character did this. Why, this is an outrage! Fire that guy immediately! Oh wait, that's me. On second thought, let's not fire him. But seriously, this shows the value of forcing users to use sudo instead of allowing them to do everything from the root shell. If I had done this from the root shell, the authentication log would have shown where I logged in as the root user, but it wouldn't have shown anything I did as the root user. With sudo, every root-level action gets logged, along with who did it.

There are several ways to obtain specific information from the log files. These include:

- Using the search feature of the less utility, as I mentioned earlier
- Using grep to search for text strings through either one file or multiple files at once
- Writing scripts in languages such as bash, Python, or awk

Here's an example of using grep:

```
sudo grep 'fail' syslog
```

In this case, I'm searching through the syslog file for all lines that contain the text string fail. By default, grep is case-sensitive, so this command won't find any instances of fail with uppercase letters. Also, by default, grep finds text strings that are embedded within other text strings. So, in addition to just finding fail, this command will also find failed, failure, or any other text string that contains the text string fail.

To make the search case-insensitive, add the -i option, like so:

```
sudo grep -i 'fail' syslog
```

This will find all forms of fail in either uppercase or lowercase letters. To only search for the fail text string, and to exclude where it's embedded in other text strings, use the -w option, like so:

```
sudo grep -w 'fail' syslog
```

You can combine the two options like this:

```
sudo grep -iw 'fail' syslog
```

In general, if you don't know exactly what you're looking for, start off with a more generic search that will probably show you too much. Then, narrow things down until you find what you want.

Now, this is all good when you just want to search through the log files for specific information. But it's rather tedious when you need to do your daily log review. Later on, I'll show you a tool that will make that much easier. For now, let's look at the binary log files.

The utmp, wtmp, btmp, and lastlog files

Unlike the system log files and the authentication log files, all of these files are binary files. So, we can't use our normal text tools, such as less or grep, to read them or extract information from them. Instead, we'll use some special tools that can read these binary files.

The w and who commands pull information about who's logged in and what they're doing from the /var/run/utmp file. Both commands have their own option switches, but you likely won't ever need them. If you just want to see the list of users who are currently logged in, use who like so:

```
donnie@orangepione:/var/log$ who
donnie    tty7          2019-08-02 18:18 (:0)
donnie    pts/1         2019-11-21 16:21 (192.168.0.251)
donnie    pts/2         2019-11-21 17:01 (192.168.0.251)
katelyn   pts/3         2019-11-21 18:15 (192.168.0.11)
lionel    pts/4         2019-11-21 18:21 (192.168.0.15)
donnie@orangepione:/var/log$
```

It shows me with three different logins. The tty7 line is my local terminal session, and the pts/1 and pts/2 lines are my two remote SSH sessions from the 192.168.0.251 machine. Katelyn and Lionel are remotely logged in from two other machines.

The w command shows you not only who's logged in, but also what they're doing:

```
donnie@orangepione:/var/log$ w
 18:29:42 up 2:09, 5 users, load average: 0.00, 0.00, 0.00
USER TTY FROM LOGIN@ IDLE JCPU PCPU WHAT
donnie tty7 :0 02Aug19 111days 6.28s 0.05s /bin/sh /etc/xdg/xfce4/xinitrc -- /
etc/X11/xinit/xserverrc
donnie pts/1 192.168.0.251 16:21 4.00s 2.88s 0.05s w
donnie pts/2 192.168.0.251 17:01 7:10 0.81s 0.81s -bash
katelyn pts/3 192.168.0.11 18:15 7:41 0.64s 0.30s vim somefile.txt
lionel pts/4 192.168.0.15 18:21 8:06 0.76s 0.30s sshd: lionel [priv]
donnie@orangepione:/var/log$
```

This shows five users, but there are really only three since it counts each of my login sessions as a separate user. The :0 under the FROM column for my first login means that this login is at the machine's local console. The /bin/sh part shows that I have a terminal window open, and the /etc/xdg/xfce4/xinitrc -- /etc/X11/xinit/xserverrc stuff means that the machine is in graphical mode, with the XFCE desktop. The pts/1 line shows that I've run the w command in that window, and the pts/2 line shows that I'm not doing anything in that window, other than just having the Bash shell open.

Next, we see that Katelyn is editing a file. So, I think that she's all good. But look at Lionel. The [priv] in his line indicates that he's doing some sort of privileged action. To see what that action is, we'll peek into the authentication file, where we see this:

```
Nov 21 18:21:42 localhost sudo:    lionel : TTY=pts/4 ; PWD=/home/lionel ;
USER=root ; COMMAND=/usr/sbin/visudo
```

Oh, come now. What fool gave Lionel the privileges to use visudo? I mean, we know that Lionel isn't supposed to have that privilege. Well, we can investigate. Further up in the authentication file, we see this:

```
Nov 21 18:17:53 localhost sudo:    donnie : TTY=pts/2 ; PWD=/home/donnie ;
USER=root ; COMMAND=/usr/sbin/visudo
```

This shows that that donnie character opened visudo, but it doesn't show what edits he made to it. But since this line comes soon after the line where donnie created Lionel's account, and no other users have used visudo, it's a safe bet that donnie is the one who gave Lionel that visudo privilege. So, we can surmise that that donnie character is a real loser who deserves to be fired. Oh, wait. That was me again, wasn't it? Okay, never mind.

In normal usage, the last command pulls information from the /var/log/wtmp file, which archives historical data from the /var/run/utmp file. Without any option switches, last shows when each user has logged in or out, and when the machine has been booted:

```
donnie@orangepione:/var/log$ last
lionel    pts/4        192.168.0.15     Thu Nov 21 18:21   still logged in
lionel    pts/4        192.168.0.15     Thu Nov 21 18:17 - 18:17  (00:00)
katelyn   pts/3        192.168.0.11     Thu Nov 21 18:15   still logged in
katelyn   pts/3        192.168.0.251    Thu Nov 21 18:02 - 18:15  (00:12)
donnie    pts/2        192.168.0.251    Thu Nov 21 17:01   still logged in
donnie    pts/1        192.168.0.251    Thu Nov 21 16:21   still logged in
donnie    tty7         :0               Fri Aug  2 18:18   gone - no logout
reboot    system boot  4.19.57-sunxi    Wed Dec 31 19:00   still running
. . .
wtmp begins Wed Dec 31 19:00:03 1969
donnie@orangepione:/var/log$
```

To show a list of failed login attempts, use the -f option to read the /var/log/btmp file. The catch is that this requires sudo privileges because we generally want to keep information about failed logins confidential:

```
donnie@orangepione:/var/log$ sudo last -f /var/log/btmp
[sudo] password for donnie:
katelyn ssh:notty 192.168.0.251 Thu Nov 21 17:57 gone - no logout
katelyn ssh:notty 192.168.0.251 Thu Nov 21 17:57 - 17:57 (00:00)
katelyn ssh:notty 192.168.0.251 Thu Nov 21 17:57 - 17:57 (00:00)
```

```
btmp begins Thu Nov 21 17:57:35 2019
donnie@orangepione:/var/log$
```

Of course, we could see about Katelyn's three failed logins in the auth.log or secure file, but it's handier and quicker to see about them here.

Finally, there's the lastlog command, which pulls information from—you guessed it—the /var/log/lastlog file. This shows a record of all users on the machine, even system users, and when they logged in last:

```
donnie@orangepione:/var/log$ lastlog
Username         Port     From              Latest
root             tty1                       Tue Mar 12 15:29:09 -0400 2019
. . .
messagebus                                 **Never logged in**
sshd                                       **Never logged in**
donnie           pts/2    192.168.0.251     Thu Nov 21 17:01:03 -0500 2019
sshdnoroot                                 **Never logged in**
. . .
katelyn          pts/3    192.168.0.11      Thu Nov 21 18:15:44 -0500 2019
lionel           pts/4    192.168.0.15      Thu Nov 21 18:21:33 -0500 2019
donnie@orangepione:/var/log$
```

There are a lot more logs in the /var/log/ directory, but I've just given you the quick tour of the logs that pertain to system security. Next, we'll look at the two major logging systems that are built into most Linux distros, starting with the rsyslog system.

Understanding rsyslog

The old syslog logging system was created back in the 1980s for use on Unix and other Unix-like systems. It finally saw its last days in the Linux world only a few years ago. Nowadays, we use rsyslog, which is a bit more robust and has a few more features. It works mainly the same on both Debian/Ubuntu-based and Red Hat-based distros, with only some differences in how the configuration files are set up. But, before we look at the differences, let's look at what's the same.

Understanding rsyslog logging rules

Logging rules define where to record messages for each particular system service:

- On Red Hat/CentOS/AlmaLinux systems, the rules are stored in the /etc/rsyslog.conf file. Just scroll down until you see the #### RULES #### section.
- On Debian/Ubuntu systems, the rules are in separate files in the /etc/rsyslog.d/ directory. The main file that we care about for now is the 50-default.conf file, which contains the main logging rules.

To explain the structure of an `rsyslog` rule, let's look at this example from an AlmaLinux machine:

```
authpriv.*              /var/log/secure
```

Here's the breakdown:

- `authpriv`: This is the facility, which defines the type of message.
- `.`: The dot separates the facility from the level, which is the next field.
- `*`: This is the level, which indicates the importance of the message. In this case, we just have a wildcard, which means that all levels of the `authpriv` facility get logged.
- `/var/log/secure`: This is the action, which is really the destination of this message. (I have no idea why someone decided to call this an action.)

When we put this all together, we see that `authpriv` messages of all levels will get sent to the `/var/log/secure` file.

Here's a handy list of the predefined `rsyslog` facilities:

- `auth`: Messages generated by the authorization system (`login`, `su`, `sudo`, and so forth)
- `authpriv`: Messages generated by the authorization system but which are only readable by selected users
- `cron`: Messages generated by the `cron` daemon
- `daemon`: Messages generated by all system daemons (for example, `sshd`, `ftpd`, and so forth)
- `ftp`: Messages for `ftp`
- `kern`: Messages generated by the Linux kernel
- `lpr`: Messages generated by the line printer spooling
- `mail`: Messages generated by the mail system
- `mark`: Periodic timestamp message in the system log
- `news`: Messages generated by network news system
- `rsyslog`: Messages generated internally by `rsyslog`
- `user`: Messages generated by users
- `local0-7`: Custom messages for writing your own scripts

Here's a list of the different levels:

- `none`: Disables logging for a facility
- `debug`: Debug only
- `info`: Information
- `notice`: Issues to review
- `warning`: Warning messages
- `err`: Error conditions
- `crit`: Critical conditions
- `alert`: Urgent messages
- `emerg`: Emergency

Except for the debug level, whatever level you set for a facility will cause messages of that level up through emerg to get logged. For example, when you set the info level, all messages of the info levels through emerg get logged. With that in mind, let's look at a more complex example of a logging rule, also from an AlmaLinux machine:

```
*.info;mail.none;authpriv.none;cron.none      /var/log/messages
```

Here's the breakdown:

- `*.info`: This refers to messages from all facilities of the info level and higher.
- `;`: This is a compound rule. The semicolons separate the different components of this rule from each other.
- `mail.none;authpriv.none;cron.none`: These are the three exceptions to this rule. Messages from the mail, authpriv, and cron facilities will not get sent to the /var/log/messages file. These three facilities have their own rules for their own log files. (The authpriv rule that we just looked at earlier is one of them.)

The rules on an Ubuntu machine aren't exactly the same as the ones on an AlmaLinux machine. But, if you understand these examples, you won't have any trouble figuring out the Ubuntu rules.

If you ever make changes to the rsyslog.conf file or add any rules files to the /etc/rsyslog.d/ directory, you'll need to restart the rsyslog daemon to read in the new configuration. Do that like this:

```
[donnie@localhost ~]$ sudo systemctl restart rsyslog
[sudo] password for donnie:
[donnie@localhost ~]$
```

Now that you have a basic understanding of rsyslog, let's look at journald, which is the new kid in town.

Understanding journald

You'll find the journald logging system on any Linux distro that uses the systemd ecosystem. Instead of sending its messages to text files, journald sends messages to binary files. Instead of using normal Linux text file utilities to extract information, you have to use the journalctl utility. At the time of writing, I don't know of any Linux distro that has made the complete transition to journald. Current Linux distros that use systemd run journald and rsyslog side by side. Currently, the default on RHEL-type systems is for journald log files to be temporary files that get erased every time you reboot the machine. (You can configure journald to make its log files persistent, but there's probably not much point as long as we still need to keep the old rsyslog files.) On Ubuntu, the default is for both journald and rsyslogd to maintain persistent log files.

On RHEL 8/9-type distros, journald, instead of rsyslog, is now what actually collects log messages from the rest of the operating system. But rsyslog is still there, collecting the messages from journald and sending them to the old-fashioned rsyslog text files. So, the way you do log file management hasn't really changed.

It will likely take a few more years to completely transition away from `rsyslog`. One reason is that third-party log aggregation and analysis utilities, such as LogStash, Splunk, and Nagios Log Server, are still set up to read text files instead of binary files. Another reason is that, at this point, using `journald` as a remote, central log server is still in a proof-of-concept stage that isn't ready for production use. So, for now, `journald` isn't a suitable substitute for `rsyslog`.

> Several years ago, the Fedora team released a version of Fedora that only used `journald`, and that left out `rsyslog`. Too many people complained about that, so they had to bring back `rsyslog` for the next version of Fedora.

To view the `journald` log file in its entirety, use the `journalctl` command. With Ubuntu, the person who installed the operating system has been added to the `adm` group, which allows that person to use `journalctl` without `sudo` or root privileges. Any users who are added later would only be able to see their own messages. In fact, here's what happened for Frank:

```
frank@ubuntu4:~$ journalctl
Hint: You are currently not seeing messages from other users and the system.
      Users in groups 'adm', 'systemd-journal' can see all messages.
      Pass -q to turn off this notice.
-- Logs begin at Tue 2019-11-26 17:43:28 UTC, end at Tue 2019-11-26 17:43:28
UTC. --
Nov 26 17:43:28 ubuntu4 systemd[10306]: Listening on GnuPG cryptographic agent
and passphrase cache.
Nov 26 17:43:28 ubuntu4 systemd[10306]: Reached target Timers.
Nov 26 17:43:28 ubuntu4 systemd[10306]: Listening on GnuPG cryptographic agent
and passphrase cache (restricted).
. . .
. . .
Nov 26 17:43:28 ubuntu4 systemd[10306]: Reached target Basic System.
Nov 26 17:43:28 ubuntu4 systemd[10306]: Reached target Default.
Nov 26 17:43:28 ubuntu4 systemd[10306]: Startup finished in 143ms.
frank@ubuntu4:~$
```

To see messages from either the system or from other users, these new users would have to be added to either the `adm` or the `systemd-journal` group, or granted the proper sudo privileges. With RHEL/CentOS/AlmaLinux, no users are automatically added to either the `adm` or `systemd-journal` group. So, initially, only users who have sudo privileges can view the `journald` logs.

Doing either `journalctl` or `sudo journalctl`, as appropriate, automatically opens the log in the `less` pager. What you'll see looks pretty much the same as what you'd see in the normal `rsyslog` log files, with the following exceptions:

- Long lines run past the right-hand edge of the screen. To see the rest of the lines, use the right cursor key.

- You'll also see color-coding and highlighting to make different types of messages stand out. Messages of ERROR level and higher are in red, while messages from NOTICE level up to ERROR level are highlighted with bold characters.

There are lots of options that can display different types of information in various formats. For example, to only see messages about the SSH service on CentOS or AlmaLinux, use the --unit option, like so:

```
[donnie@localhost ~]$ sudo journalctl --unit=sshd
-- Logs begin at Tue 2019-11-26 12:00:13 EST, end at Tue 2019-11-26 15:55:19
EST. --
Nov 26 12:00:41 localhost.localdomain systemd[1]: Starting OpenSSH server
daemon...
Nov 26 12:00:42 localhost.localdomain sshd[825]: Server listening on 0.0.0.0
port 22.
Nov 26 12:00:42 localhost.localdomain sshd[825]: Server listening on :: port
22.
Nov 26 12:00:42 localhost.localdomain systemd[1]: Started OpenSSH server
daemon.
Nov 26 12:22:08 localhost.localdomain sshd[3018]: Accepted password for donnie
from 192.168.0.251 port 50797 ssh2
Nov 26 12:22:08 localhost.localdomain sshd[3018]: pam_unix(sshd:session):
session opened for user donnie by (uid=0)
Nov 26 13:03:33 localhost.localdomain sshd[4253]: Accepted password for goldie
from 192.168.0.251 port 50912 ssh2
Nov 26 13:03:34 localhost.localdomain sshd[4253]: pam_unix(sshd:session):
session opened for user goldie by (uid=0)
[donnie@localhost ~]$
```

You can't use the grep utility with these binary logs, but you can search for a string with the -g option. By default, it's case-insensitive and finds your desired text string even when it's embedded in another text string. Here, we see it finding the text string, fail:

```
[donnie@localhost ~]$ sudo journalctl -g fail
[sudo] password for donnie:
Feb 03 15:14:06 localhost kernel: acpi PNP0A03:00: fail to add MMCONFIG
information, can't access extended PCI configuration space under this bridge.
Feb 03 15:14:06 localhost systemd[1]: dracut ask for additional cmdline
parameters was skipped because all trigger condition checks failed.
Feb 03 15:14:06 localhost systemd[1]: dracut pre-trigger hook was skipped
because all trigger condition checks failed.
Feb 03 15:14:06 localhost systemd[1]: nm-initrd.service was skipped because
of a failed condition check (ConditionPathExists=/run/NetworkManager/initrd/
neednet).
Feb 03 15:14:06 localhost systemd[1]: nm-wait-online-initrd.service was skipped
because of a failed condition check (ConditionPathExists=/run/NetworkManager/
```

```
initrd/neednet).
. . .
```

There are lots more options besides just these. To see them, just do:

```
man journalctl
```

Now that you've seen the basics of using both `rsyslog` and `journald`, let's look at a cool utility that can help to ease the pain of doing log reviews.

Making things easier with Logwatch

You know how important it is to do a daily log review. But you also know how much of a drag it is, and that you'd rather take a severe beating. Fortunately, there are various utilities that can make the job easier. Of the various choices in the normal Linux distro repositories, Logwatch is my favorite.

Logwatch doesn't have the fancy bells and whistles that the third-party log aggregators have, but it's still quite good. Every morning, you'll find a summary of the previous day's logs delivered to your mail account. Depending on how your mail system is configured, you can have the summaries delivered to your user account on the local machine or to an email account that you can access from anywhere. It's as easy as can be to set up, so let's demonstrate with a hands-on lab.

Hands-on lab – installing Logwatch

To deliver its messages, Logwatch requires that the machine also has a running mail server daemon. Depending on the options you chose when installing the operating system, you might or might not already have the Postfix mail server installed. When Postfix is set up as a local server, it will deliver system messages to the root user's local account.

To view the Logwatch summaries on the local machine, you'll also need to install a text-mode mail reader, such as `mutt`.

For this lab, you can use any of your VMs:

1. Install Logwatch, mutt, and Postfix. (On Ubuntu, choose the `local` option when installing Postfix. With CentOS or AlmaLinux, the `local` option is already the default.) For Ubuntu, do this:

```
sudo apt install postfix mutt logwatch
```

For CentOS 7, do this:

```
sudo yum install postfix mutt logwatch
```

For AlmaLinux, do this:

```
sudo dnf install postfix mutt logwatch
```

2. On Ubuntu only, create a mail spool file for your user account:

```
sudo touch /var/mail/your_user_name
```

3. Open the /etc/aliases file in your favorite text editor. Configure it to forward the root user's mail to your own normal account by adding the following line at the bottom of the file:

```
root:       your_user_name
```

4. Save the file, and then copy the information from it to a binary file that the system can read. Do that with this:

```
sudo newaliases
```

5. At this point, you have a fully operational implementation of Logwatch that will deliver daily log summaries with a *low level* of detail. To see the default configuration, look at the default configuration file:

```
less /usr/share/logwatch/default.conf/logwatch.conf
```

6. To change the configuration, edit the /etc/logwatch/conf/logwatch.conf file on CentOS and AlmaLinux, or create the file on Ubuntu. Change to a medium level of logging detail by adding this line:

```
Detail = Med
```

> Logwatch is a Python script that runs every night on a scheduled basis. So, there's no daemon that you have to restart to make configuration changes take effect.

7. Perform some actions that will generate some log entries. You can do that by performing a system update, installing some software packages, and using sudo fdisk -l to view the partition configuration.

8. If possible, allow your VM to run overnight. In the morning, view your log summary by doing this:

```
mutt
```

9. When prompted to create a Mail directory in your home directory, hit the *Y* key.

10. End of lab.

Now that you've seen the easy way of doing a log review, let's move on to the final topic of this chapter, which is how to set up a central log server.

Setting up a remote log server

So far, we've just been dealing with log files on a local machine. But instead of having to log into each individual machine to review log files, wouldn't it be nice to just have all of the log files from every machine on just one server? Well, you can do that. The best part is that it's easy.

But convenience isn't the only reason to collect log files on one central server. There's also the matter of log file security. If we leave all log files on each individual host, it's easier for network intruders to find the files and modify them to delete any messages about their nefarious activities. (That's easy to do since most log files are just plaintext files that can be edited in a normal text editor.)

Hands-on lab – setting up a basic log server

Setting up the server is identical on Ubuntu, CentOS, and AlmaLinux. There's only one minor difference in setting up the clients. For best results, ensure that the server VM and the client VM each have a different hostname:

1. On the log-collecting server VM, open the `/etc/rsyslog.conf` file in your favorite text editor and look for these lines, which are near the top of the file:

    ```
    # Provides TCP syslog reception
    #module(load="imtcp") # needs to be done just once
    #input(type="imtcp" port="514")
    ```

2. Uncomment the bottom two lines and save the file. The stanza should now look like this:

    ```
    # Provides TCP syslog reception
    module(load="imtcp") # needs to be done just once
    input(type="imtcp" port="514")
    ```

3. Restart the `rsyslog` daemon:

    ```
    sudo systemctl restart rsyslog
    ```

4. If the machine has an active firewall, open port 514/`tcp`.

5. Next, configure the client machines. For Ubuntu, add the following line to the bottom of the `/etc/rsyslog.conf` file, substituting the IP address of your own server VM:

    ```
    @@192.168.0.161:514
    ```

6. For CentOS and AlmaLinux, look for this stanza at the bottom of the `/etc/rsyslog.conf` file:

    ```
    # ### sample forwarding rule ###
    #action(type="omfwd"
    # An on-disk queue is created for this action. If the remote host is
    # down, messages are spooled to disk and sent when it is up again.
    #queue.filename="fwdRule1"       # unique name prefix for spool files
    #queue.maxdiskspace="1g"         # 1gb space limit (use as much as
    possible)
    #queue.saveonshutdown="on"       # save messages to disk on shutdown
    #queue.type="LinkedList"         # run asynchronously
    #action.resumeRetryCount="-1"    # infinite retries if host is down
    # Remote Logging (we use TCP for reliable delivery)
    ```

```
# remote_host is: name/ip, e.g. 192.168.0.1, port optional e.g. 10514
#Target="remote_host" Port="XXX" Protocol="tcp"
```

Remove the comment symbols from each line that isn't obviously a real comment. Add the IP address and port number for the log server VM. The finished product should look like this:

```
# ### sample forwarding rule ###
action(type="omfwd"
# An on-disk queue is created for this action. If the remote host is
# down, messages are spooled to disk and sent when it is up again.
queue.filename="fwdRule1"          # unique name prefix for spool files
queue.maxdiskspace="1g"            # 1gb space limit (use as much as
possible)
queue.saveonshutdown="on"          # save messages to disk on shutdown
queue.type="LinkedList"            # run asynchronously
action.resumeRetryCount="-1"       # infinite retries if host is down
# Remote Logging (we use TCP for reliable delivery)
# remote_host is: name/ip, e.g. 192.168.0.1, port optional e.g. 10514
Target="192.168.0.161" Port="514" Protocol="tcp")
```

7. Save the file and then restart the rsyslog daemon.
8. On the server VM, verify that messages from both the server VM and the client VM are getting sent to the log files. (You can tell by the different hostnames for different messages.)
9. This is the end of the lab.

As cool as this is, there are still a couple of flaws with the setup. One is that we're using a non-encrypted, plaintext connection to send the log files to the server. Let's fix that.

Creating an encrypted connection to the log server

We'll use the stunnel package to create our encrypted connection. It's easy, except that the procedures for Ubuntu and AlmaLinux are different. These differences are:

- With AlmaLinux 8/9, FIPS modules are available free of charge, as I showed you in *Chapter 6, Encryption Technologies*. They're not available for CentOS 7, and they're only available for Ubuntu if you're willing to purchase a support contract. So, for now, the only way we can take advantage of FIPS mode in stunnel is to set it up on either AlmaLinux 8/9 or some other RHEL 8/9 clone.
- On AlmaLinux, stunnel runs as a systemd service. On Ubuntu, for some bizarre reason, it's still set up to run with an old-fashioned init script. So, we have to deal with two different methods of controlling the stunnel daemon.

Let's begin with the AlmaLinux procedure.

Creating a stunnel connection on AlmaLinux 9 – server side

For this lab, we're using an AlmaLinux 9 VM that's been set to run in FIPS-compliant mode (see the steps for that in *Chapter 6, Encryption Technologies*):

1. On an AlmaLinux VM, install `stunnel`:

```
sudo dnf install stunnel
```

2. On the server, within the `/etc/stunnel/` directory, create a new `stunnel.conf` file with the following contents:

```
cert=/etc/stunnel/stunnel.pem
fips=yes

[hear from client]
accept=30000
connect=127.0.0.1:6514
```

3. On the server, while still within the `/etc/stunnel/` directory, create the `stunnel.pem` certificate file:

```
sudo openssl req -new -x509 -days 3650 -nodes -out stunnel.pem -keyout
stunnel.pem
```

4. On the server, open port `30000` on the firewall, and close port 514:

```
sudo firewall-cmd --permanent --add-port=30000/tcp
sudo firewall-cmd --permanent --remove-port=514/tcp
sudo firewall-cmd --reload
```

> Port **6514**, which you see in the `stunnel.conf` file, is strictly for internal communication between `rsyslog` and `stunnel`. So, for that, we don't need to open a firewall port. We're configuring `stunnel` to listen on port **30000** on behalf of `rsyslog`, so we no longer need to have port **514** open on the firewall.

5. Enable and start the `stunnel` daemon by doing this:

```
sudo systemctl enable --now stunnel
```

6. In the `/etc/rsyslog.conf` file, look for this line at the top of the file:

```
input(type="imtcp" port="514")
```

Change it to this:

```
input(type="imtcp" port="6514")
```

7. After saving the file, restart `rsyslog`:

```
sudo systemctl restart rsyslog
```

The server is now ready to receive log files from remote clients via an encrypted connection.

Next, we'll configure an AlmaLinux VM to send its logs to this server.

Creating a stunnel connection on AlmaLinux — client side

In this procedure, we'll configure an AlmaLinux machine to send its logs to the log server (it doesn't matter whether the log server is running on CentOS, AlmaLinux, or Ubuntu):

1. Install stunnel:

```
sudo dnf install stunnel
```

2. In the /etc/stunnel/ directory, create the stunnel.conf file with the following contents:

```
client=yes
fips=yes

[speak to server]
accept=127.0.0.1:6514
connect=192.168.0.161:30000
```

> In the connect line, substitute the IP address of your own log server for the one you see here.

3. Enable and start the stunnel daemon:

```
sudo systemctl enable --now stunnel
```

4. At the bottom of the /etc/rsyslog.conf file, look for this line:

```
Target="192.168.0.161" Port="514" Protocol="tcp")
```

Change it to this:

```
Target="127.0.0.1" Port="6514" Protocol="tcp")
```

5. After saving the file, restart the rsyslog daemon:

```
sudo systemctl restart rsyslog
```

6. On the client, use logger to send a message to the log file:

```
logger "This is a test of the stunnel setup."
```

7. On the server, verify that the message got added to the /var/log/messages file.
8. This is the end of the lab.

Let's now turn our attention to Ubuntu.

Creating a stunnel connection on Ubuntu — server side

For this, we'll use an Ubuntu 22.04 VM. I don't understand why, but Ubuntu still uses an old-style init script for stunnel, instead of a systemd service. So, the commands that you'll use for this will be different than what you're used to using:

1. Install stunnel:

    ```
    sudo apt install stunnel
    ```

2. In the /etc/stunnel/ directory, create the stunnel.conf file with the following contents:

    ```
    cert=/etc/stunnel/stunnel.pem
    fips=no

    [hear from client]
    accept=30000
    connect=6514
    ```

3. While still in the /etc/stunnel/ directory, create the stunnel.pem certificate:

    ```
    sudo openssl req -new -x509 -days 3650 -nodes -out stunnel.pem -keyout
    stunnel.pem
    ```

4. Start the stunnel daemon:

    ```
    sudo service stunnel4 start
    ```

5. To make it automatically start when you reboot the system, create a cron job for the root user. First, open the crontab editor, like this:

    ```
    sudo crontab -e -u root
    ```

    Add this line to the end of the file:

    ```
    @reboot service stunnel4 start
    ```

6. In the /etc/rsyslog.conf file, look for this line at the top:

    ```
    input(type="imtcp" port="514")
    ```

    Change it to this:

    ```
    input(type="imtcp" port="6514")
    ```

7. After saving the file, restart the rsyslog daemon:

    ```
    sudo systemctl restart rsyslog
    ```

8. Using the appropriate iptables, ufw, or nftables command, open port 30000/tcp on the firewall, and close port 514.

9. This is the end of the lab.

Next, we'll configure the client.

Creating a stunnel connection on Ubuntu — client side

Using this procedure on an Ubuntu client will allow it to send its files to either an AlmaLinux or an Ubuntu log server:

1. Install stunnel:

```
sudo apt install stunnel
```

2. In the /etc/stunnel/ directory, create the stunnel.conf file with the following contents:

```
client=yes
fips=no

[speak to server]
accept = 127.0.0.1:6514
connect=192.168.0.161:30000
```

> Note that even though we can't use FIPS mode on the Ubuntu clients, we can still have them send log files to an AlmaLinux log server that is configured to use FIPS mode. (So, yes, we can mix and match.)

3. Start the stunnel daemon:

```
sudo service stunnel4 start
```

4. To make it automatically start when you reboot the system, create a cron job. Open the crontab editor by doing:

```
sudo crontab -e -u root
```

Add this line to the end of the file:

```
@reboot service stunnel4 start
```

5. At the bottom of the /etc/rsyslog.conf file, look for the line that has the IP address of the log server. Change it to this:

```
@@127.0.0.1:6514
```

6. After saving the file, restart the rsyslog daemon:

```
sudo systemctl restart rsyslog
```

7. Use logger to send a message to the log server:

```
logger "This is a test of the stunnel connection."
```

8. On the server, verify that the message is in the `/var/log/messages` or `/var/log/syslog` file, as appropriate.

9. End of lab.

Okay, we now have a secure connection, which is a good thing. But the messages from all of the clients still get jumbled up in the server's own log files. Let's fix that.

Separating client messages into their own files

This is something else that's easy-peasy. We'll just make a couple of simple edits to the `rsyslog` rules on the log server and restart the `rsyslog` daemon. For our demo, I'll use the AlmaLinux 9 VM.

> You won't be able to use Logwatch if you implement this trick. Well, you actually can, except that Logwatch will just take all of the events from all of the client files and jumble them up into one big summary. So, you won't be able to see which client machines generate the events.

In the RULES section of the `/etc/rsyslog.conf` file, look for this line:

```
*.info;mail.none;authpriv.none;cron.none    /var/log/messages
```

Change it to this:

```
*.info;mail.none;authpriv.none;cron.none ?Rmessages
```

Above that line, insert this line:

```
$template Rmessages,"/var/log/%HOSTNAME%/messages"
```

Do likewise for the `auth` messages:

```
# authpriv.* /var/log/secure
$template Rauth,"/var/log/%HOSTNAME%/sec
auth.*,authpriv.* ?Rauth
```

Finally, restart `rsyslog`:

```
sudo systemctl restart rsyslog
```

Look in the `/var/log/` directory, and you'll see directories for each of the clients that are sending logs to this server. Pretty slick, eh?

> The trick here is to always have a `$template` line *precede* the affected rule.

Next, let's take a brief look at how things might be a bit different in large enterprises.

Maintaining Logs in Large Enterprises

Any large enterprise will have a diverse mix of network end-points. In addition to Linux servers, there will also be various brands of switches and routers, firewalls, Windows servers, Windows or Linux workstations, network-connected printers, and various forms of network-attached storage devices. Most of these devices generate system logs, and administrators need a convenient way to review logs for the gear that they administer. Sadly, using only the logging systems that come with these devices is anything but convenient for a large enterprise.

Collecting log files from such a diverse collection of end-points isn't the real challenge. The real challenge is twofold:

- To transform the log files from the various end-points, which all have their own unique log file formats, into a common format that can be read and parsed by a centralized logging program.

- To parse and display log data in a way that allows administrators to quickly spot potential problems.

I've already mentioned Splunk and Nagios Log Server, which are two commercial solutions. In *Chapter 14*, *Vulnerability Scanning and Intrusion Detection*, I'll show you Security Onion, which includes a free open source log aggregation solution.

The Elastic Stack, formerly known as **The ELK Stack**, is another Free Open Source Software solution that's extremely flexible and very well-suited for enterprise use. It's free to download and use, and it can be installed on Linux, macOS, or Windows servers. Fee-based support is available for anyone who needs it.

> You can find out more about The Elastic Stack here:
>
> https://www.elastic.co/elastic-stack/

And that wraps it up for another chapter. You now know about what to look for in log files, how to make log reviews easier, and how to set up a secure remote log server. We also took a brief look at logging solutions for the enterprise.

Summary

In this chapter, we looked at the different types of log files, with an emphasis on files that contain security-related information. Then, we looked at the basic operation of the rsyslog and journald logging systems. To make log reviews a bit easier, we introduced Logwatch, which automatically creates a summary of the preceding day's log files. We wrapped things up by setting up a central, remote log server that collects log files from other network hosts.

In the next chapter, we'll look at how to do vulnerability scanning and intrusion detection. I'll see you there.

Questions

1. Which two of the following are log files that record authentication-related events?

    a. syslog

    b. authentication.log

    c. auth.log

    d. secure.log

    e. secure

2. Which log file contains the current record about who is logged into the system and what they're doing?

    a. /var/log/syslog

    b. /var/log/utmp

    c. /var/log/btmp

    d. /var/run/utmp

3. Which of the following is the main logging system that runs on pretty much every modern Linux distro?

    a. syslog

    b. rsyslog

    c. journald

    d. syslog-ng

4. Which of the following is peculiar to RHEL 8/9 and their offspring, such as AlmaLinux 8/9?

    a. On RHEL 8/9 systems, journald collects log data from the rest of the system and sends them to rsyslog.

    b. On RHEL 8/9 systems, journald has completely replaced rsyslog.

    c. On RHEL 8/9 systems, rsyslog collects data from the rest of the system and sends them to journald.

    d. RHEL 8/9 systems use syslog-ng.

5. Which of the following is a consideration when setting up stunnel?

    a. On AlmaLinux systems, FIPS mode is not available.

    b. On Ubuntu systems, FIPS mode is not available.

    c. On Ubuntu systems, FIPS mode is available, but only if you purchase a support contract.

    d. On AlmaLinux 8/9, FIPS mode is available, but only if you purchase a support contract.

6. Which of the following two statements are true about stunnel?

    a. On RHEL systems, stunnel runs as a normal systemd service.

    b. On RHEL systems, stunnel still runs under an old-fashioned init script.

      c.   On Ubuntu systems, `stunnel` runs as a normal `systemd` service.

      d.   On Ubuntu systems, `stunnel` runs under an old-fashioned `init` script.

7.   Which file must you edit to have the root user's messages forwarded to your own user account?

8.   After you edit the file that's referenced in *Question 7*, which command must you run to transfer the information to a binary file that the system can read?

9.   To create a `stunnel` setup for your remote log server, you must create a security certificate for both the server and for each client.

      a.   True

      b.   False

10. Which of the following commands would you use to find the `fail` text string in `journald` log files?

      a.   `sudo grep fail /var/log/journal/messages`

      b.   `sudo journalctl -g fail`

      c.   `sudo journalctl -f fail`

      d.   `sudo less /var/log/journal/messages`

Further reading

- Five open source log management programs: `https://fosspost.org/lists/open-source-log-management`
- *What is a SIEM?*: `https://www.tripwire.com/state-of-security/incident-detection/log-management-siem/what-is-a-siem/`
- *12 Critical Linux Log Files You Must be Monitoring*: `https://www.eurovps.com/blog/important-linux-log-files-you-must-be-monitoring/`
- *Analyzing Linux Logs*: `https://www.loggly.com/ultimate-guide/analyzing-linux-logs/`
- Linux log files with examples: `https://www.poftut.com/linux-log-files-varlog/`
- The `rsyslog` home page: `https://www.rsyslog.com/`
- *Why journald?*: `https://www.loggly.com/blog/why-journald/`
- Journalctl cheat sheet: `https://www.golinuxcloud.com/view-logs-using-journalctl-filter-journald/`
- *Linux Administration Cookbook*, by Adam K. Dean: `https://www.packtpub.com/virtualization-and-cloud/linux-administration-cookbook`
- The Logwatch project page: `https://sourceforge.net/projects/logwatch/`
- The `stunnel` home page: `https://www.stunnel.org/`
- *Linux Service Management Made Easy with systemd*, by Donald A. Tevault: `https://www.packtpub.com/product/linux-service-management-made-easy-with-systemd/`

Answers

1. c, e
2. d
3. b
4. a
5. c
6. a, d
7. `/etc/aliases`
8. `sudo newaliases`
9. b
10. c

Join our book community

Join our community's Discord space for discussions with the author and other readers:

`https://packt.link/CyberSec`

14

Vulnerability Scanning and Intrusion Detection

There are lots of threats out there, and some of them might even penetrate your network. You'll want to know when that happens, so you'll want to have a good Network Intrusion Detection System (NIDS) or Network Intrusion Prevention System (NIPS) in place. In this chapter, we'll look at Snort, which is probably the most famous one. Then, I'll show you a way to cheat so that you can have a good NIDS/NIPS up and running in no time at all. I'll also show you a quick and easy way to set up an edge firewall appliance, complete with a built-in NIPS.

We've already learned how to scan a machine for viruses and rootkits by installing scanning tools on the machines that we want to scan. However, there are a lot more vulnerabilities for which we can scan, and I'll show you some cool tools that you can use for that.

The following topics will be covered in this chapter:

- Introduction to Snort and Security Onion
- IPFire and its built-in **Intrusion Prevention System (IPS)**
- Scanning and hardening with Lynis
- Finding vulnerabilities with the Greenbone Security Assistant
- Web server scanning with Nikto

So, if you're ready, let's begin by digging into the Snort Network Intrusion Detection System.

Introduction to Snort and Security Onion

Snort is a **Network Intrusion Detection System (NIDS)**, which is offered as a free open source software product. The program itself is free of charge, but you'll need to pay if you want to have a complete, up-to-date set of threat detection rules. Snort started out as a one-man project, but it's now owned by Cisco. Understand, though, this isn't something that you install on the machine that you want to protect. Rather, you'll have at least one dedicated Snort machine someplace on the network, just monitoring all network traffic, watching for anomalies.

When it sees traffic that shouldn't be there – something that indicates the presence of a bot, for example – it can either just send an alert message to an administrator or it can even block the anomalous traffic, depending on how the rules have been configured. For a small network, you can have just one Snort machine that acts as both a control console and a sensor. For large networks, you could have one Snort machine set up as a control console and have it receive reports from other Snort machines that are set up as sensors.

Snort isn't too hard to deal with, but setting up a complete Snort solution from scratch can be a bit tedious. After we look at the basics of Snort usage, I'll show you how to vastly simplify things by setting up a pre-built NIPS appliance.

> Space doesn't permit me to present a comprehensive tutorial about Snort. Instead, I'll present a high-level overview and then present you with other resources if you want to learn about Snort in detail.
>
> Also, you might be wondering how a NIDS and a NIPS are different. Well, a NIDS is supposed to do nothing but alert network administrators about the suspicious network traffic that it detects. A NIPS will not only alert the administrator, but will also automatically block the suspicious traffic. However, the lines between the two types of systems are somewhat blurred, because some systems that are marketed as a NIDS can be configured to function as a NIPS.

First, let's download and install Snort.

Obtaining and installing Snort

Snort 3, the newest version of Snort, isn't in the official repository of any Linux distro. So, you'll need to get it from the Snort website. It used to be available as installer packages for either Windows or Linux, but that's no longer the case. Now, with the introduction of Snort 3, it's available either as source code that you'll need to compile yourself or as a pre-built Docker container. Oddly, there's no mention of the container option on the Snort home page, and I only found it after doing a DuckDuckGo search.

> You can get Snort and Snort training from the official Snort website: https://www.snort.org.

Hands-on lab – installing Snort via a Docker container

You'll definitely want to go with the container option instead of the source code option. That's because the directions for setting up the source code option aren't as clear as they should be, and one particular library package doesn't always compile properly. Instead of using the official Docker software, I'll be showing you how to use Podman, which is Red Hat's drop-in replacement for Docker. Podman's security is better than that of Docker, and it's available for pretty much every Linux distro. Podman is already installed on your AlmaLinux 8 and 9 virtual machines, but you'll need to install it yourself on Ubuntu.

1. On Ubuntu only, install the `podman` package:

```
sudo apt update
sudo apt install podman
```

2. On Ubuntu only, open the `/etc/containers/registries.conf` file in your text editor. Find this line:

```
# unqualified-search-registries = ["example.com"]
```

3. Change it to this:

```
unqualified-search-registries = ["docker.io"]
```

4. Download and start the container:

```
podman run --name snort3 -h snort3 -u snorty -w /home/snorty -d -it
ciscotalos/snort3 bash
```

5. Next, enter the container so that you can interact with the Snort commands:

```
podman exec -it snort3 bash
```

6. If this command executes successfully, you'll find yourself at the `snorty@snort3` command prompt.

7. Validate the Snort configuration with this single-word command:

```
snort
```

8. Snort requires a set of rules that define the potential problems that it should analyze. Paying customers will receive up-to-date rulesets, while non-paying users can download rulesets that are about one month behind. An old ruleset from 2018 comes with the Docker container, so you'll want something that's a bit more recent. You won't be able to download the rulesets directly to your container, so you'll need to download them to either your virtual machine or to your host machine, and then transfer them to the container. On either your host machine or in another terminal that's connected to the virtual machine, download the latest community ruleset, like this:

```
wget https://www.snort.org/downloads/community/snort3-community-rules.
tar.gz
```

9. You can't use `scp` or `sftp` to connect to the container from the virtual machine or your host machine, but you can use them to connect to the virtual machine or host machine from the container. So, from within the container, use `sftp` to transfer in the new ruleset file. Your commands should look something like this:

```
sftp donnie@192.168.0.20
get snort3-community-rules.tar.gz
bye
```

10. While still within the container, unarchive the ruleset file and transfer the new ruleset to its proper location:

```
snort3-community-rules.tar.gz
cd snort3-community-rules
cp snort3-community.rules ~/snort3/etc/rules/
```

11. Test things out by examining a `.pcap` file that's included with the example files:

```
snort -q --talos --rule-path snort3/etc/rules/ -r examples/intro/lab2/
eternalblue.pcap
```

12. Take a look at the tutorial videos at the Snort website. You can see them here: `https://www.snort.org/resources`

13. When you're done, type `exit` to get out of the container. To shutdown the container, do this:

```
podman kill snort3
```

14. End of lab.

Here are some of the significant differences between the new Snort 3 and the older Snort 2 that I covered in previous editions of this book:

- There were several cool graphical front-ends that you could install for Snort 2, but there aren't any for Snort 3. So, the new Snort 3 is strictly a command-line mode program.
- Snort 3 can save its output files in `.json` format, which makes it easy for centralized log aggregators to read and parse them.
- The configuration files and rules files for Snort 3 are in `.yaml` format.
- The Snort 3 rules syntax has been somewhat streamlined, making rules easier to write.

Next, let's look at a cool appliance that has another Intrusion Detection System built into it.

Using Security Onion

Security Onion consists of a set of **Free Open Source Software** (**FOSS**) tools that you can install on your own local Linux machine. It's also offered as a pre-built Linux distro image, which is really the preferred method of installation. In the previous editions of this book, I showed you the original version of Security Onion, which was built on Xubuntu Linux. This version had a graphical desktop interface, used Snort 2 as the IDS, and included several graphical front-ends for Snort. The new Security Onion 2 is a completely different animal. It's now built on a text-mode installation of CentOS 7, and offers way more functionality over the original version. In addition to using it as an IDS/IPS, you can now use it as a forensics analyzer, a log file aggregator, and a log file analyzer. For log file collection and analysis, it includes the ELK stack.

> ELK stands for **Elastic Search, Logstash,** and **Kibana.** Logstash, used with the appropriate collection agents on the end-points that you want to monitor, collects log files from the network end-points. Elastic Search stores the log messages in a searchable database. Kibana is the web-based graphical component that displays the collected log messages.

Instead of Snort, Security Onion 2 now uses Suricata, which is a Snort alternative. In place of the graphical front-ends for Snort, Security Onion 2 now uses the **Security Onion Console**, which is a web-based front-end.

For a couple of reasons, I'm not going to provide a hands-on lab for this. In the first place, there's no real point, because you'll find detailed tutorials on Security Onion's YouTube channel. Also, there's a good chance that any hands-on lab that I were to provide here would be outdated by the time you read this. That's because the next version of Security Onion, which will be released sometime in 2023, will be based on Rocky Linux 9 instead of CentOS 7. So, I'm sure that the installation and usage procedures will be somewhat different from what they are now.

> You can download Security Onion 2 from here: `https://securityonionsolutions.com/`
>
> You can find the Security Onion YouTube channel here: `https://www.youtube.com/@security-onion`
>
> Fee-based support options, training options, and physical appliances with Security Onion pre-installed are also available.

In lieu of a lab, allow me to leave you with a screenshot of the Security Onion Console:

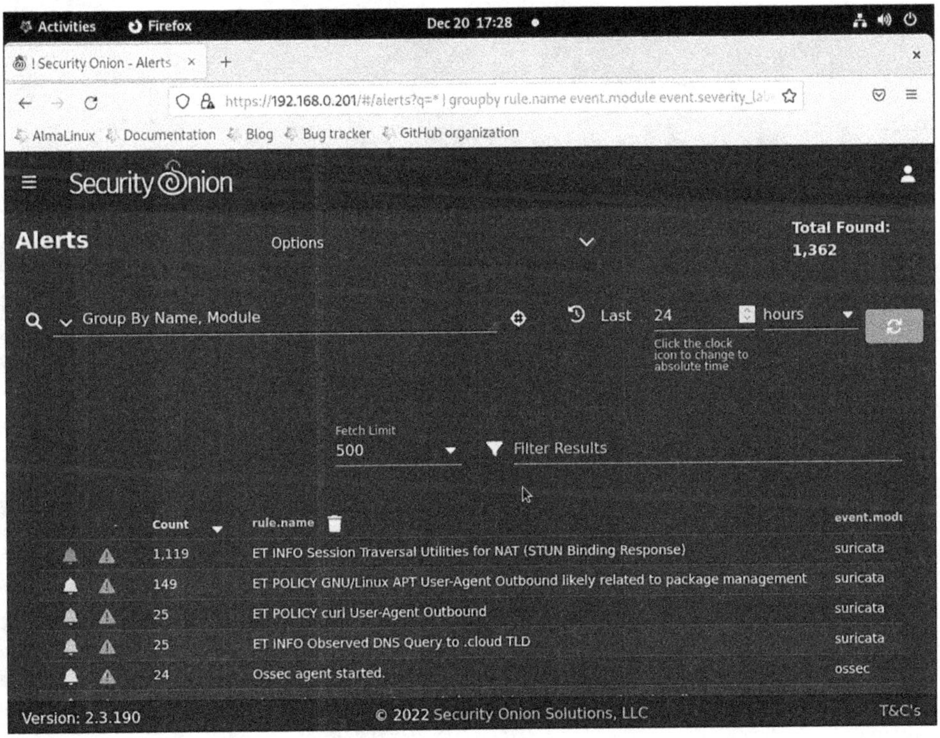

Figure 14.1: The Security Onion Console

Now, let's turn our attention to a cool pre-built firewall appliance that also has its own Intrusion Prevention System.

IPFire and its built-in Intrusion Prevention System (IPS)

When I wrote the original edition of this book, I included a discussion of IPFire in the Snort section. At that time, IPFire had Snort built into it. It was a neat idea because you had an edge firewall and an **Intrusion Detection System (IDS)** all in one handy package. But, in the summer of 2019, the IPFire folk replaced Snort with their own IPS. So, I've moved IPFire down here into its own section.

> The difference between an IDS and an IPS is that an IDS informs you of problems, but doesn't block them. An IPS also blocks them.

If you think back to our discussion of firewalls in *Chapter 4, Securing Your Server with a Firewall – Part 1* and *Chapter 5, Securing Your Server with a Firewall – Part 2,* I completely glossed over any discussion of creating the **Network Address Translation (NAT)** rules that you would need in order to set up an edge or gateway type of firewall. That's because there are several Linux distros and BSD distros that have been created specifically for this purpose. One such distro is **IPFire**.

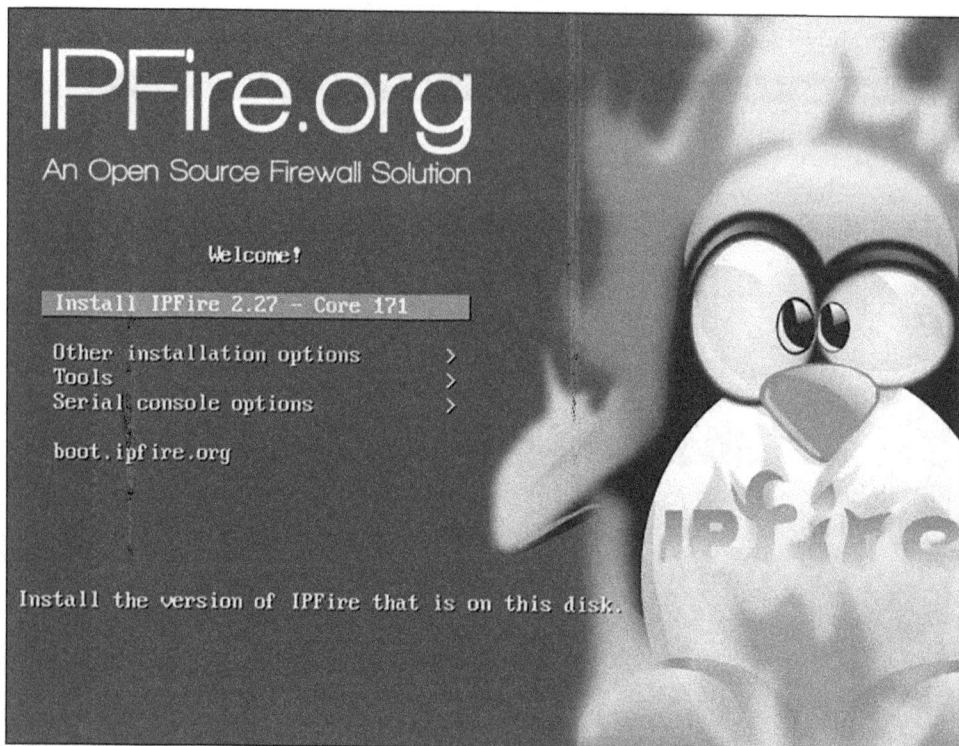

Figure 14.2: IPFire installer

IPFire is completely free of charge, and it only takes a few minutes to set up. You install it on a machine with at least two network interface adapters and configure it to match your network configuration. It's a proxy type of firewall, which means that in addition to doing normal firewall-type packet inspection, it also includes caching, content filtering, and NAT capabilities. You can set up IPFire in a number of different configurations:

- On a computer with two network interface adapters, you can have one connected to the Internet and the other connected to the internal LAN.
- With three network adapters, you can have one connection to the Internet, one to the internal LAN, and one to the **Demilitarized Zone (DMZ)**, where you have your Internet-facing servers.
- With a fourth network adapter, you can have all of what we just mentioned, plus protection for a wireless network.

With all that said, let's give it a try.

Hands-on lab — Creating an IPFire virtual machine

You won't normally run IPFire in a virtual machine. Instead, you'll install it on a physical machine that has at least two network interfaces. But, just for the sake of letting you see what it looks like, setting it up in a virtual machine will do for now. Let's get started:

> You can download IPFire from their website: https://www.ipfire.org/

1. Create a virtual machine with two network interfaces. Set one to **Bridged** mode and leave the other in **NAT** mode. Install IPFire into this virtual machine. During the setup portion, select the **Bridged** adapter as the Green interface and select the **NAT** adapter as the Red interface.
2. After you install IPFire, you'll need to use the web browser of your normal workstation to navigate to the IPFire dashboard. Do this with this URL: https://192.168.0.190:444

   (Of course, substitute your own IP address for your Green interface.)

3. Under the **Firewall** menu, you'll see an entry for **Intrusion Prevention**. Click on that to get to this screen, where you can enable Intrusion Prevention. The first step for that is to click on the **Add provider** button that's under the **Ruleset Settings** section.

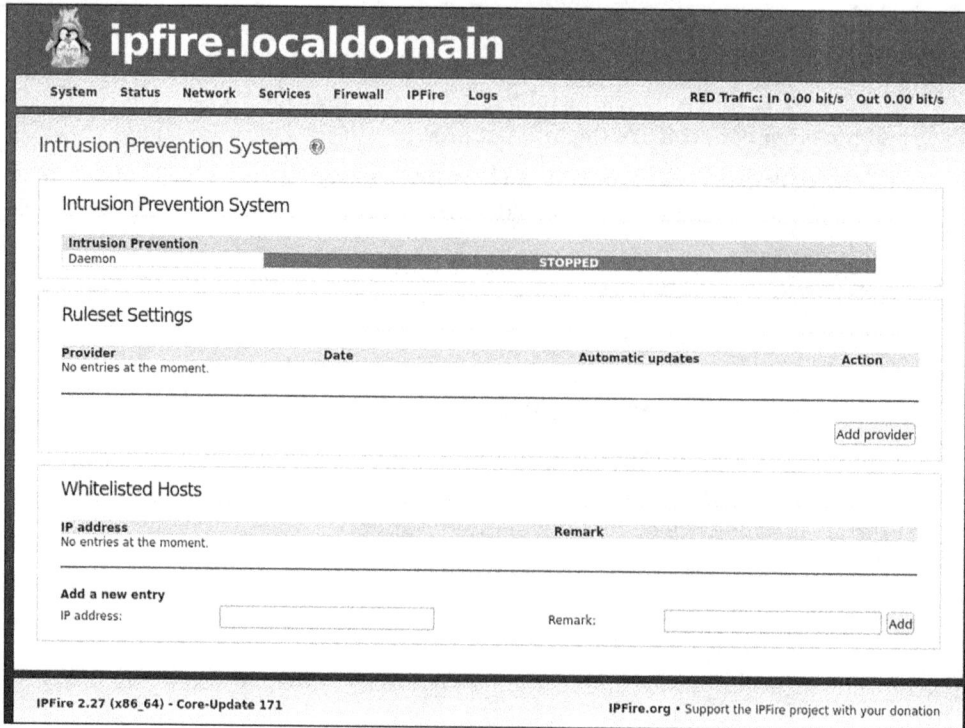

Figure 14.3: Click the Add provider button

4. On the next page, select the ruleset that you want to use. Leave the **Enable automatic updates** checkbox enabled. Then, hit the **Add** button:

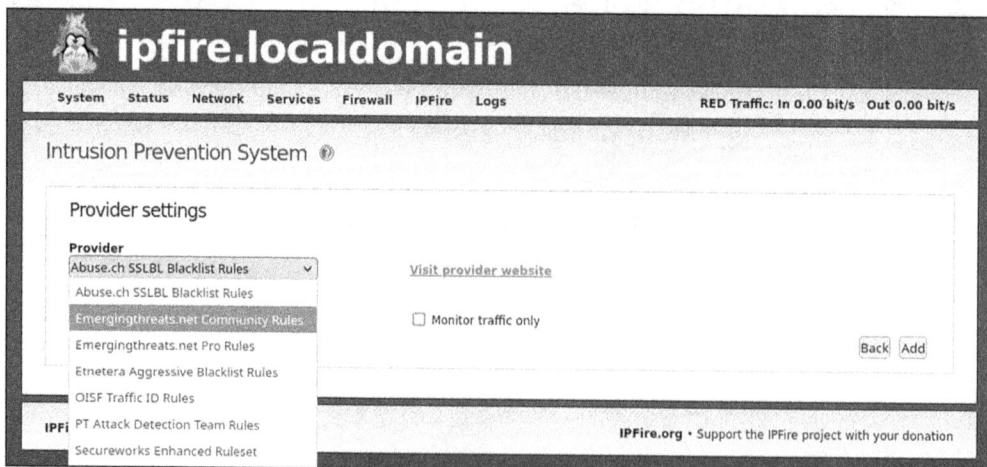

Figure 14.4: Select the ruleset

5. You will then see this screen, where you'll select the interfaces for which you want to enable intrusion prevention. (Select both interfaces.) Then, select the **Enable Intrusion Prevention System** checkbox and click on **Save**:

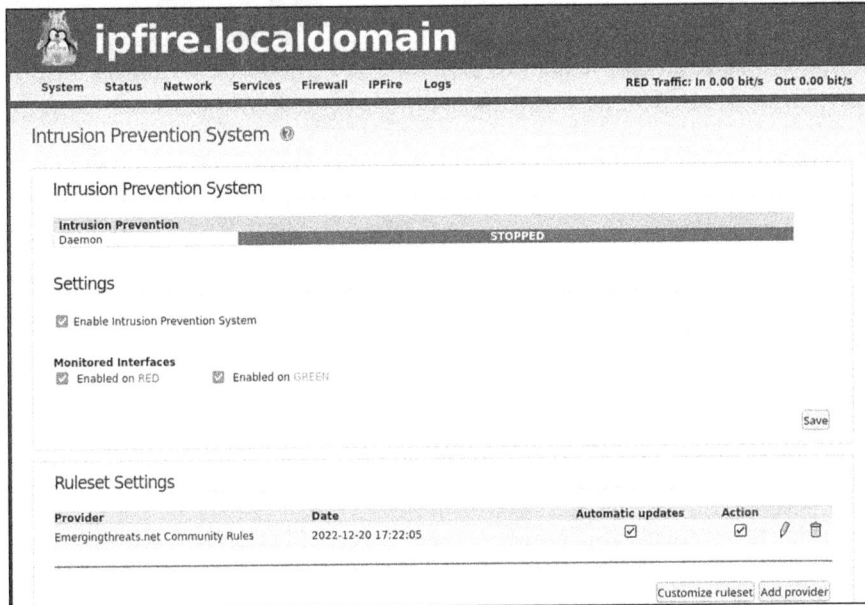

Figure 14.5: Enable the IPS

If all goes well, you'll see the following output:

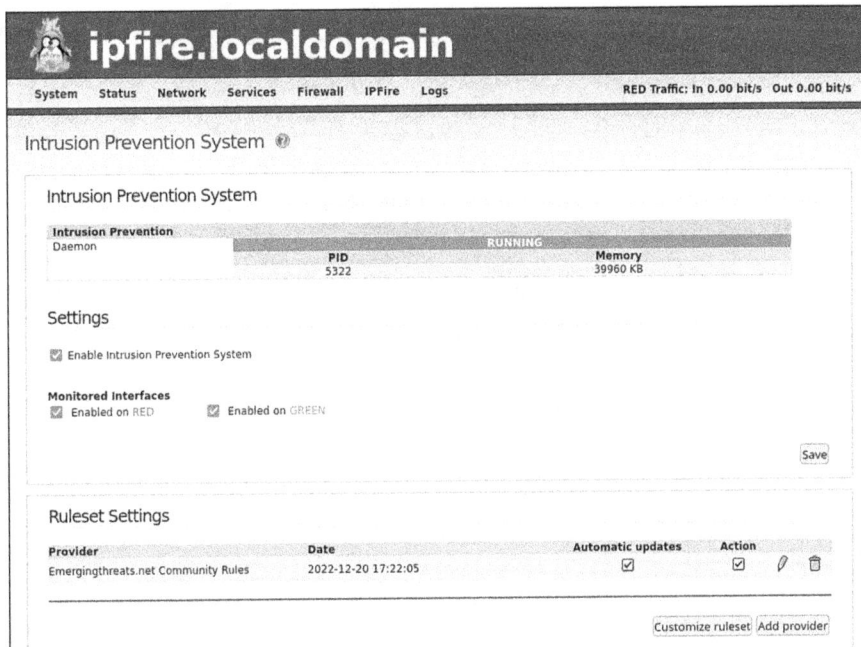

Figure 14.6: With the IPS enabled

6. In the **Ruleset Settings** section, click the **Customize ruleset** button. On the next page, click on the rules that you want to enable. Then, at the bottom of the screen, click the **Apply** button:

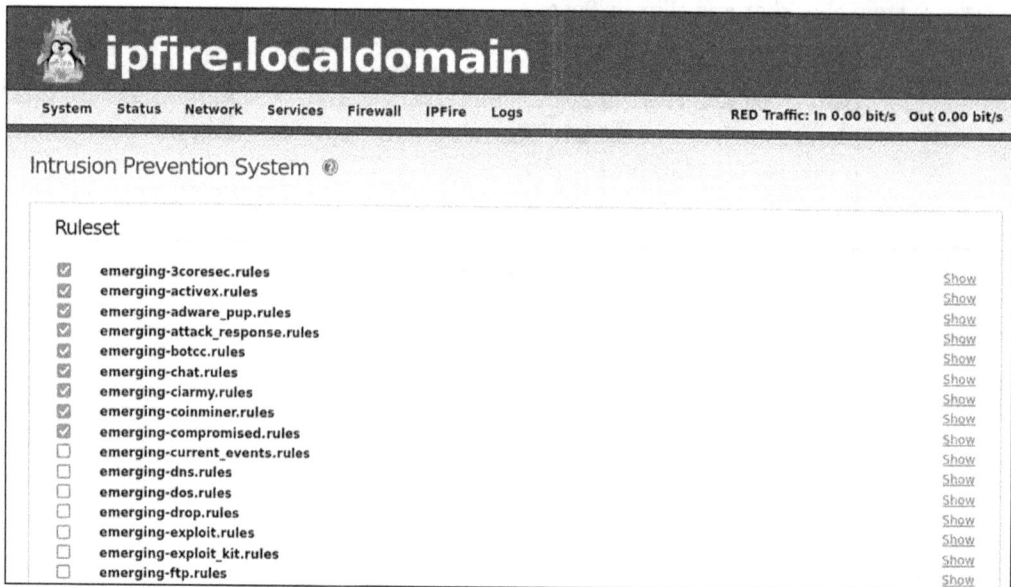

Figure 14.7: Select the desired rules

7. View what's going on with the IPS by selecting **Log/IPS Logs**. (Note that what you see will depend upon which rules that you've chosen to enable. Even then, it might take a while for any entries to show up.)

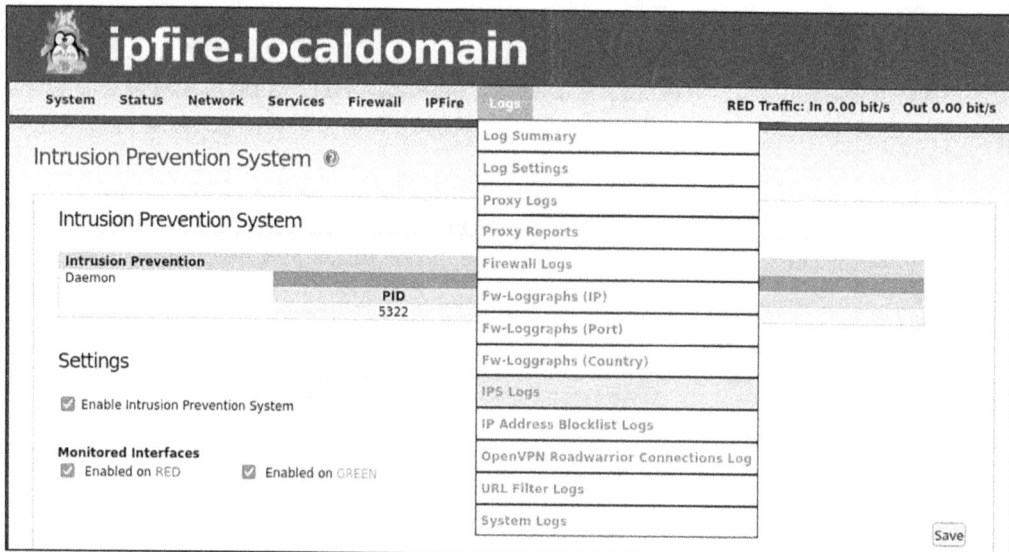

Figure 14.8: Look at the IPS logs

8. Click on the other menu items to view IPFire's other features.

You have completed this lab – congratulations!

You've just seen the easy way to set up an edge firewall with its own network IPS. Now, let's look at some scanning tools.

Scanning and hardening with Lynis

Lynis is yet another FOSS tool that you can use to scan your systems for vulnerabilities and bad security configurations. It comes as a portable shell script that you can use not only on Linux, but also on a variety of different Unix and Unix-like systems. It's a multipurpose tool that you can use for compliance auditing, vulnerability scanning, or hardening. Unlike most vulnerability scanners, you install and run Lynis on the system that you want to scan. According to the creator of Lynis, this allows for more in-depth scanning.

The Lynis scanning tool is available as a free-of-charge version, but its scanning capabilities are somewhat limited. If you need all that Lynis has to offer, you'll need to purchase an enterprise license.

Installing Lynis on Red Hat/CentOS

Red Hat, CentOS 7, and AlmaLinux 8/9 users will find an up-to-date version of Lynis in the EPEL repository. So, if you have EPEL installed, as I showed you in *Chapter 1, Running Linux in a Virtual Environment*, installation is just a simple matter of doing:

```
sudo yum install lynis
```

Installing Lynis on Ubuntu

Ubuntu has Lynis in its own repository, but it's just a little bit behind what's current. If you're okay with using an older version, the command to install it is:

```
sudo apt install lynis
```

> If you want the newest version for Ubuntu or if you want to use Lynis on operating systems that don't have it in their repositories, you can download Lynis from https://cisofy.com/downloads/lynis/

The cool thing about this is that once you download it, you can use it on any Linux, Unix, or Unix-like operating system. (This even includes macOS, which I confirmed by running it on my old Mac Pro that was running with macOS High Sierra.)

Since the executable file is nothing but a common shell script, there's no need to perform an actual installation. All you need to do is extract the archive file, cd into the resultant directory, and run Lynis from there:

```
tar xzvf lynis-3.0.8.tar.gz
cd lynis
sudo ./lynis -h
```

The lynis -h command shows you the help screen, along with all of the Lynis commands that you need to know about.

Scanning with Lynis

Lynis commands work the same regardless of which operating system that you want to scan. The only difference is that if you're running it from the archive file that you downloaded from the website, you would cd into the lynis directory and precede the lynis commands with a ./. (That's because, for security reasons, your own home directory isn't in the path setting that allows the shell to automatically find executable files.)

To scan your system that has Lynis installed, execute this command:

```
sudo lynis audit system
```

To scan a system that you just downloaded the archive file on, execute these commands:

```
cd lynis
sudo ./lynis audit system
```

Running Lynis from the shell script in your home directory presents you with this message:

```
donnie@ubuntu:~/lynis$ sudo ./lynis audit system

. . .
[X] Security check failed

    Why do I see this error?
    --------------------------------
    This is a protection mechanism to prevent the root user from executing
user created files. The files may be altered, or including malicious pieces of
script.


    . . .


[ Press ENTER to continue, or CTRL+C to cancel ]
```

This isn't hurting anything, so you can just hit *Enter* to continue. Or, if seeing this message really bothers you, you can change ownership of the Lynis files to the root user, as the message tells you. For now, I'll just press *Enter*.

Running a Lynis scan in this manner is similar to running an OpenSCAP scan against a generic security profile. The major difference is that OpenSCAP has an automatic remediation feature, while Lynis doesn't. Lynis tells you what it finds and suggests how to fix what it perceives to be a problem, but it doesn't fix anything for you.

Space doesn't permit me to show the entire scan output, but I can show you a couple of example snippets:

```
[+] Boot and services
-------------------------------------
  - Service Manager                                    [ systemd ]
  - Checking UEFI boot                                 [ DISABLED ]
  - Checking presence GRUB                             [ OK ]
  - Checking presence GRUB2                            [ FOUND ]
    - Checking for password protection                 [ WARNING ]
  - Check running services (systemctl)                 [ DONE ]
        Result: found 21 running services
  - Check enabled services at boot (systemctl)         [ DONE ]
        Result: found 28 enabled services
  - Check startup files (permissions)                  [ OK ]
```

This warning message shows that I don't have password protection for my GRUB2 bootloader. That may or may not be a big deal because the only way someone can exploit it is to gain physical access to the machine. If it's a server that's locked away in a room that only a few trusted individuals can access, then I'm not going to worry about it, unless rules from an applicable regulatory agency dictate that I do. If it's a desktop machine that's out in an open cubicle, then I would definitely fix that. (We'll look at GRUB password protection in *Chapter 16, Security Tips and Tricks for the Busy Bee*).

In the **File systems** section, we can see some items with the **SUGGESTION** flag next to them:

```
[+] File systems
-------------------------------------
  - Checking mount points
    - Checking /home mount point                       [ SUGGESTION ]
    - Checking /tmp mount point                        [ SUGGESTION ]
    - Checking /var mount point                        [ SUGGESTION ]
  - Query swap partitions (fstab)                      [ OK ]
  - Testing swap partitions                            [ OK ]
  - Testing /proc mount (hidepid)                      [ SUGGESTION ]
  - Checking for old files in /tmp                     [ OK ]
  - Checking /tmp sticky bit                           [ OK ]
  - ACL support root file system                       [ ENABLED ]
  - Mount options of /                                 [ NON DEFAULT ]
```

Exactly what Lynis suggests comes near the end of the output:

```
  . . .
  . . .

  * To decrease the impact of a full /home file system, place /home on a
separated partition [FILE-6310]
      https://cisofy.com/controls/FILE-6310/
```

```
    * To decrease the impact of a full /tmp file system, place /tmp on a
  separated partition [FILE-6310]
        https://cisofy.com/controls/FILE-6310/


    * To decrease the impact of a full /var file system, place /var on a
  separated partition [FILE-6310]
        https://cisofy.com/controls/FILE-6310/
  . . .
  . . .
```

The last thing we'll look at is the scan details section at the end of the output:

```
  Lynis security scan details:
  Hardening index : 67 [#############        ]
  Tests performed : 218
  Plugins enabled : 0
  Components:
  - Firewall              [V]
  - Malware scanner       [X]
  Lynis Modules:
  - Compliance Status     [?]
  - Security Audit        [V]
  - Vulnerability Scan    [V]
  Files:
  - Test and debug information       : /var/log/lynis.log
  - Report data                      : /var/log/lynis-report.dat
```

For **Components**, there's a red **X** by **Malware Scanner**. That's because I don't have ClamAV or maldet installed on this machine, so Lynis couldn't do a virus scan.

For **Lynis Modules**, we see a question mark by **Compliance Status**. That's because this feature is reserved for the Enterprise version of Lynis, which requires a paid subscription. As we saw in the previous chapter, you have OpenSCAP profiles to make a system compliant with several different security standards, and it doesn't cost you anything. With Lynis, you have to pay for the compliance profiles, but you have a wider range to choose from. For example, Lynis Enterprise can scan for Sarbanes-Oxley compliance issues, while OpenSCAP can't.

The last thing I want to say about Lynis is in regard to the Enterprise version. In the following screenshot, which is from their website, you can see the current pricing and the differences between the different subscription plans:

Figure 14.9: Pricing for Lynis Enterprise

As you see, you have choices.

> You'll find information about pricing on the Cisofy website: `https://cisofy.com/pricing/`

That pretty much wraps things up as regards our discussion of Lynis. Next, we'll look at an external vulnerability scanner.

Finding vulnerabilities with the Greenbone Security Assistant

In the previous versions of this book, I told you about OpenVAS, which stands for Open Vulnerability Assessment Scanner. It's still with us, but its publisher has changed the name to **Greenbone Security Assistant (GSA)**. Although it's a commercial product, Greenbone also offers a Free Open Source Community Edition that's free-of-charge.

The Greenbone Security Assistant is something that you would use to perform remote vulnerability scans. You can use it to scan a variety of network devices.

The big three security distros are Kali Linux, Parrot Linux, and BlackArch. They're aimed at security researchers and penetration testers, but they contain tools that would also be good for just a normal security administrator of either the Linux or Windows variety. GSA is one such tool. All three of these security distros have their unique advantages and disadvantages. Since Kali is the most popular, we'll go with it for the demos.

> You can download Kali Linux from `https://www.kali.org/get-kali/`.

When you go to the Kali download page, you'll see lots of choices. You can download a normal installer image for x86, x86_64, and Apple Silicon. Other options include:

- Images for ARM devices, such as the Raspberry Pi
- The Cloud
- Pre-built virtual machine images for VMWare, VirtualBox, and QEMU
- Pre-built Docker containers
- Images for mobile devices
- Windows Subsystem for Linux

Kali is built from Debian Linux, so installing it and keeping it updated is pretty much the same as installing and updating Debian.

> Greenbone Security Assistant is a rather memory-hungry program, so if you're installing Kali in a virtual machine, be sure to allocate at least 3 GB of memory.

The first thing you'll want to do after installing Kali is to update it, which is done in the same way that you'd update any Debian/Ubuntu-type of distro. Then, install GSA, like this:

```
sudo apt update
sudo apt dist-upgrade
sudo apt install openvas
```

Note that the openvas package is a **transitional package** that will automatically install all of the proper Greenbone packages.

After the GSA installation completes, you'll need to run a script that will create the security certificates and download the vulnerability database:

```
sudo gvm-setup
```

This will take a long time, so you might as well go grab a sandwich and a coffee while it's running. When it's finally done, you'll be presented with the password that you'll use to log in to GSA. Write it down and keep it in a safe place:

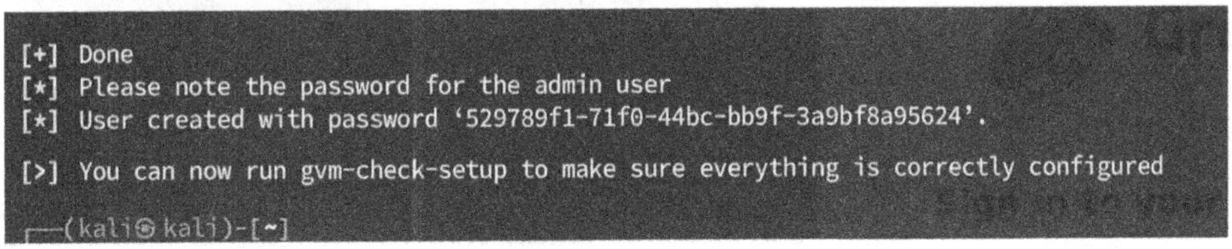

```
[+]  Done
[*]  Please note the password for the admin user
[*]  User created with password '529789f1-71f0-44bc-bb9f-3a9bf8a95624'.

[>]  You can now run gvm-check-setup to make sure everything is correctly configured

┌──(kali㉿kali)-[~]
```

Figure 14.10: Copy the password

Next, start the Greenbone services by doing:

```
sudo gvm-check-setup
```

To ensure that everything works properly, you'll need to manually sync the data feeds, and then restart the GVA services:

```
sudo greenbone-feed-sync --type GVMD_DATA
sudo greenbone-feed-sync --type SCAP
sudo greenbone-feed-sync --type CERT
sudo gvm-stop
```

Wait for 30 seconds, and then restart the services:

```
sudo gvm-start
```

Once the service startup has completed, open Firefox and navigate to https://localhost:9392. You'll get a security alert because GVA uses a self-signed security certificate, but that's okay. Just click on the **Advanced** button, and then click on **Add Exception**.

On the login page, enter admin as the user and then enter the password that was generated by the gvm-setup script.

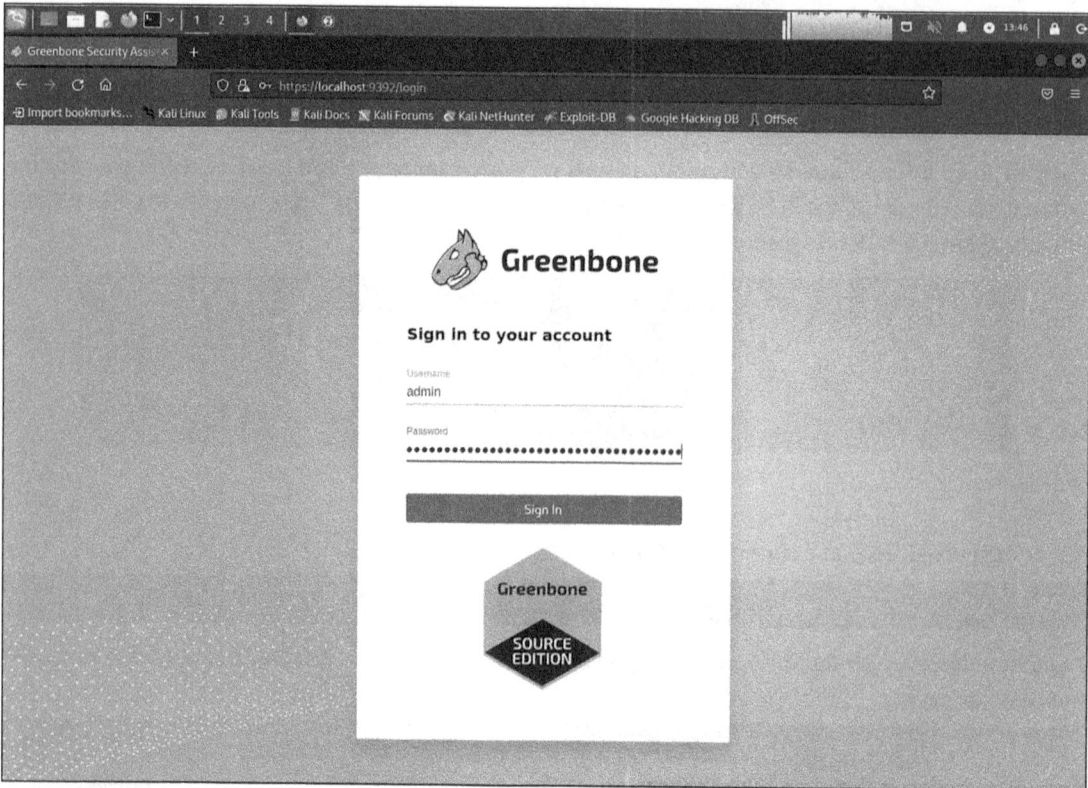

Figure 14.11: The GVA login screen

There's all kinds of fancy stuff that you can do with GVA, but for now, we'll just look at how to do a basic vulnerability scan. To begin, select **Tasks** from the **Scans** menu on the GVA dashboard:

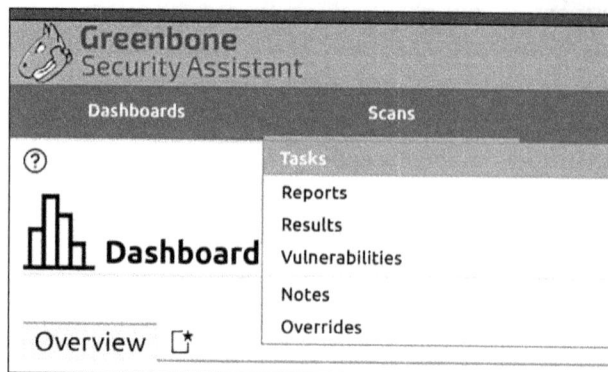

Figure 14.12: Select Tasks

When the Tasks page comes up, look for the little magic wand at the upper left-hand corner. Roll your mouse cursor over this wand, and you'll see the various choices for the Task Wizard:

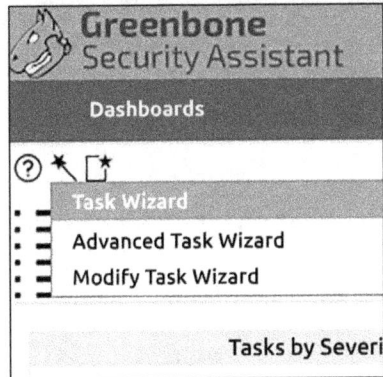

Figure 14.13: Task Wizard choices

For now, we'll just select the **Task Wizard** option, which will choose all of the default scan settings for us. The only thing you need to do here is enter the IP address of the machine that you want to scan, and then start the scan:

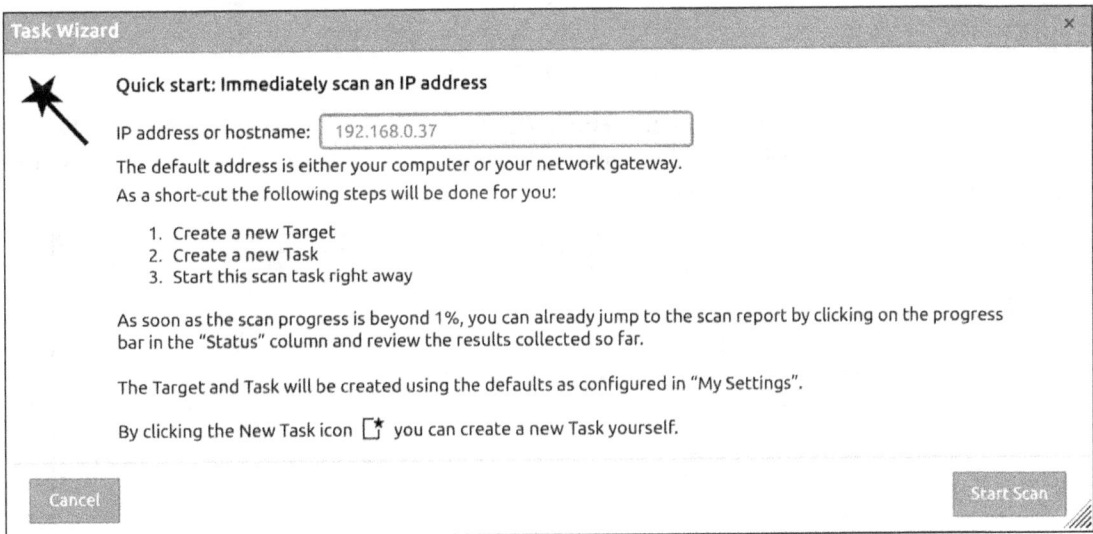

Figure 14.14: Start a basic scan

The scan will take some time, so you might as well go grab a drink:

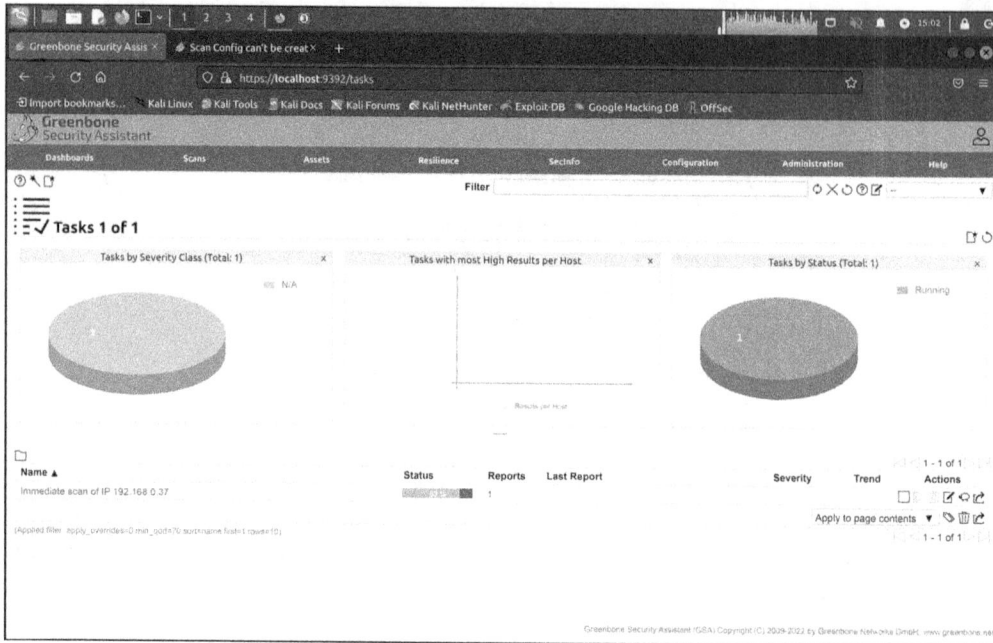

Figure 14.15: Performing a basic scan

The type of scan that you're doing is named **Full and Fast**, which is the most comprehensive type of scan that's now offered. To select another type of scan and to configure other scan options, use the **Advanced Task Wizard**, as shown here:

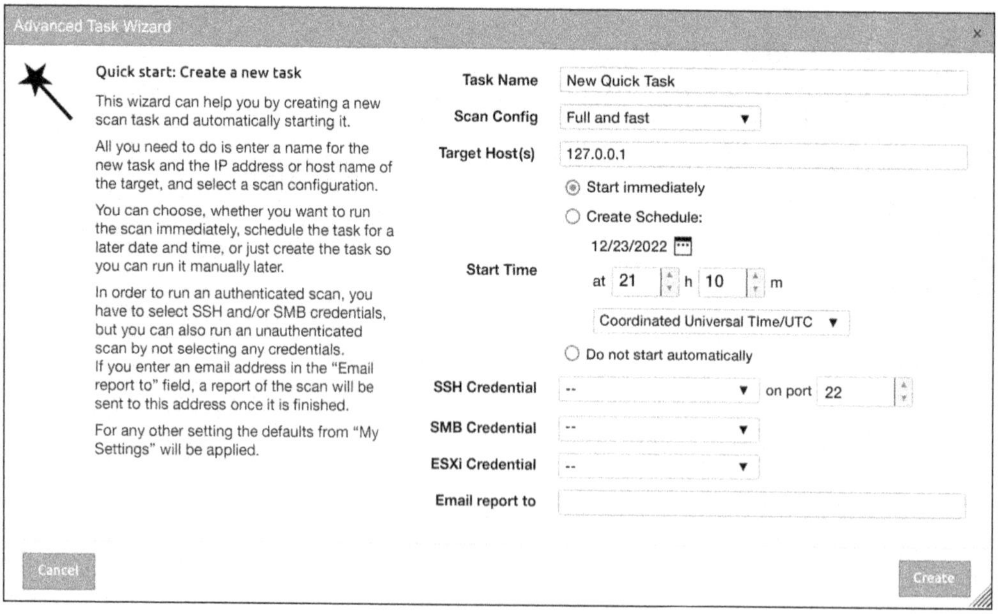

Figure 14.16: Selecting the scan options

When the scan has completed, click on the **Scans/Results** menu item:

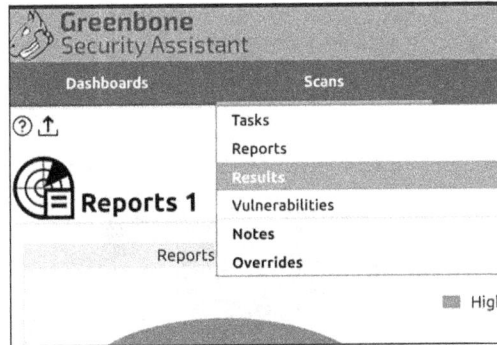

Figure 14.17: View the results

For the sake of showing you some interesting stuff, I purposely chose a target machine that's nearly 20 years old, with an outdated operating system and lots of vulnerabilities. Here, you see that the machine is using weak encryption algorithms for Secure Shell, which is classified as medium severity. Even worse is that it supports SSH version 1, which is classified as a high severity problem. Yikes!

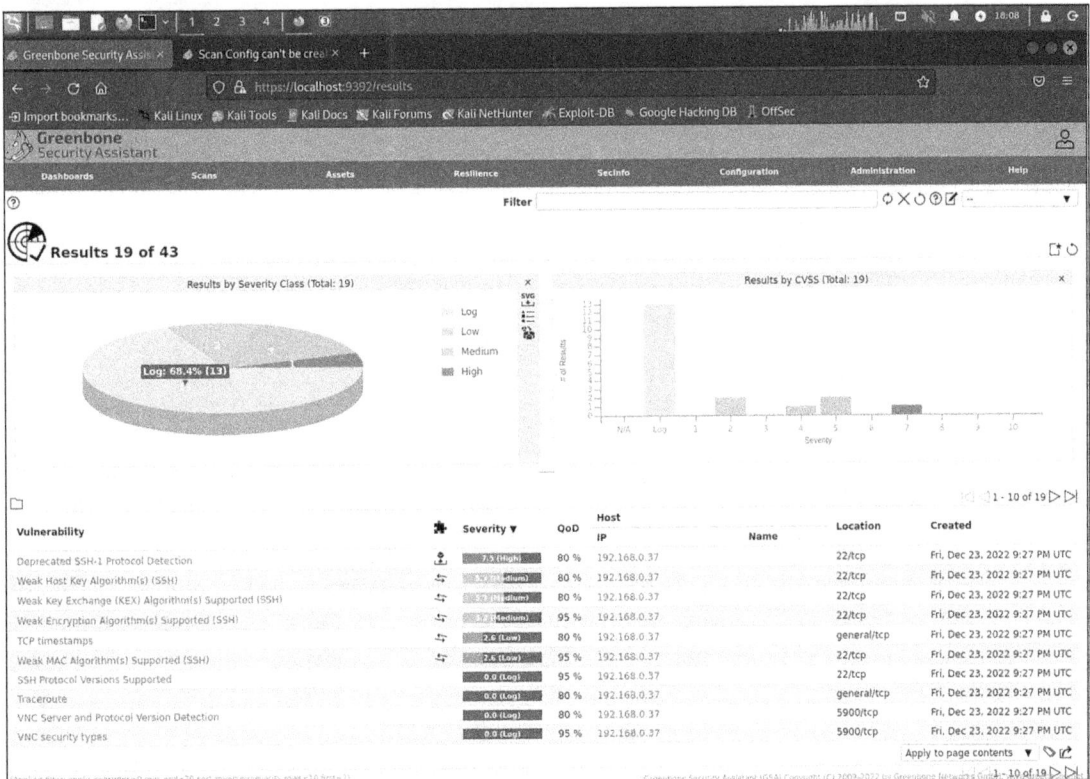

Figure 14.18: Scan results

You also want to pay attention to the items that aren't flagged as vulnerabilities. For example, the **VNC security types** item shows that port 5900 is open. This means that the **Virtual Network Computing** (VNC) daemon is running, which allows users to remotely log in to this machine's desktop. If this machine were an Internet-facing machine, that would be a real problem because there's no real security with VNC like there is with Secure Shell.

By clicking on a vulnerability item, I can see an explanation of the vulnerability:

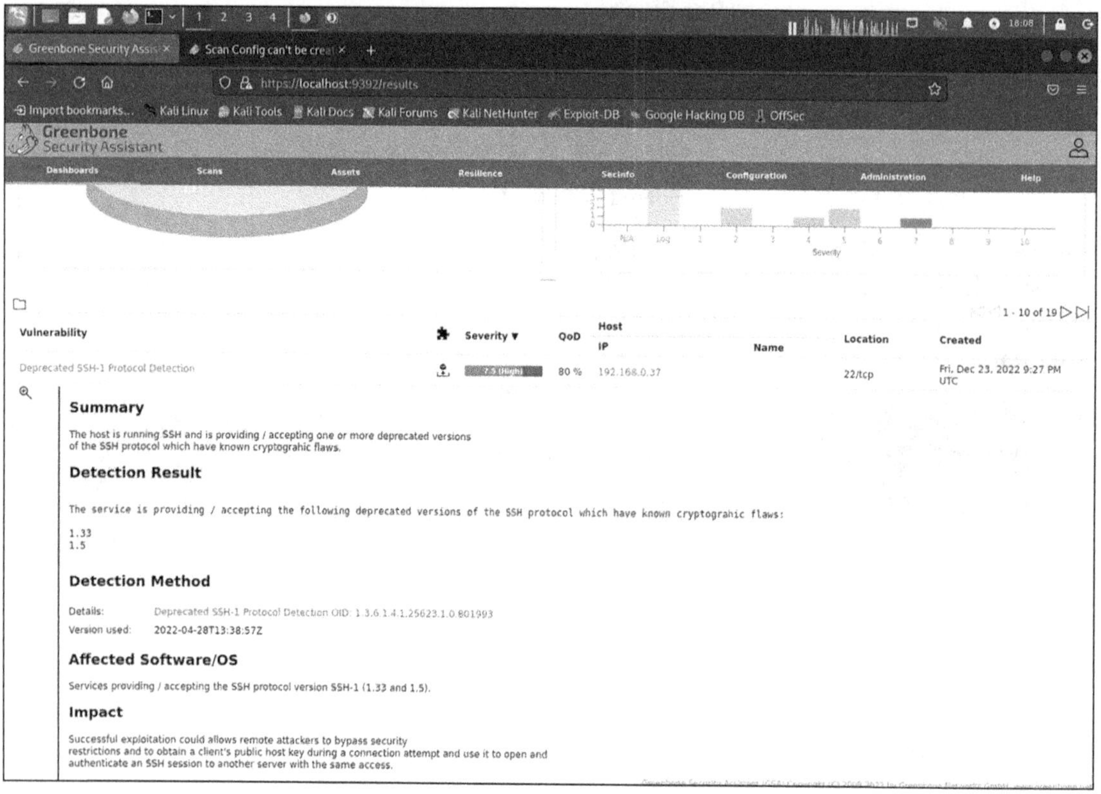

Figure 14.19: An explanation of a vulnerability

Keep in mind that the target machine, in this case, is a desktop machine. If it were a server, there's a good chance that we'd see even more problems.

And that pretty much wraps things up for the Greenbone Security Assistant. As I mentioned previously, there's a lot of awesome stuff that you can do with it. However, what I've shown you here should be enough to get you started. Play around with it and try out the different scan options to see the difference in results.

> If you want to find out more about Kali Linux, you'll find a great selection of books about it on the Packt Publishing website.

Okay, you now know how to do a vulnerability scan with GSA. Now, let's look at a scanner that's specifically designed for web servers.

Web server scanning with Nikto

The Greenbone Security Assistant, which we just looked at, is a general-purpose vulnerability scanner. It can find vulnerabilities for most any kind of operating system or for most any server daemon. However, as we've just seen, a GSA scan can take a while to run, and it might be more than what you need.

Nikto is a special-purpose tool with only one purpose. That is, it's meant to scan web servers, and only web servers. It's easy to install, easy to use, and capable of doing a comprehensive scan of a web server fairly quickly.

Nikto in Kali Linux

If you have Kali Linux, you'll find that Nikto is already installed under the **Vulnerability Analysis** menu:

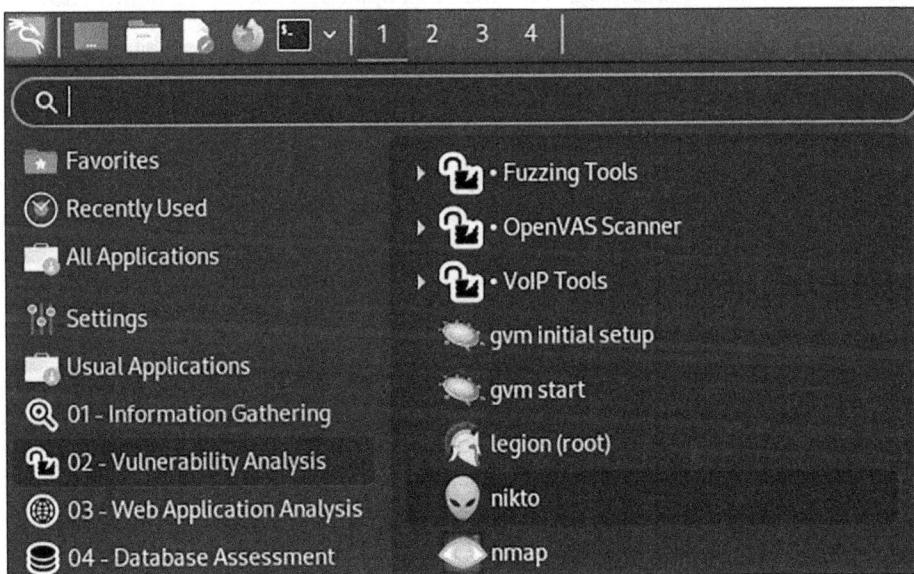

Figure 14.20: Nikto on the Kali Linux menu

However, your best bet is to ignore it, and instead use the more up-to-date version that you'll download directly from Github. That's because the Nikto signature database that's installed on Kali hasn't been updated since 2019, as you see here:

```
┌──(kali㉿kali)-[~]
└─$ cd /var/lib/nikto/databases


┌──(kali㉿kali)-[/var/lib/nikto/databases]
└─$ ls -l
total 1652
```

```
-rw-r--r-- 1 root root     2093 Mar  9  2019 db_404_strings
-rw-r--r-- 1 root root     3147 Mar  9  2019 db_content_search
-rw-r--r-- 1 root root    15218 Mar  9  2019 db_dictionary
. . .

. . .

-rw-r--r-- 1 root root     4868 Mar  9  2019 db_variables



┌──(kali㉿kali)-[/var/lib/nikto/databases]
└─$
```

You used to be able to update the database with the `sudo nikto -update` command, but that no longer works because the author has deprecated the -update option. (I had hoped that doing a normal `sudo apt dist-upgrade` command would bring in some updates, but no such luck.) Now, the author recommends using the `git` commands to download and update Nikto. So, let's look at how to do that.

Hands-on lab—Installing Nikto from Github

To make things easy, we'll do this on Kali, because it already has all of the `perl` modules that Nikto needs to operate. If you do this on Debian or Ubuntu, it should work, but you'll need to chase down the `perl` modules that it needs yourself. And, forget about doing this on AlmaLinux, because the necessary `perl` modules aren't even in any of the AlmaLinux or EPEL repositories. (There's an alternate way to install them, but that's beyond the scope of this book.)

1. In your normal user home directory, clone the Nikto repository. Then, `cd` into the `nikto` directory, and check out the current branch:

    ```
    git clone https://github.com/sullo/nikto.git
    cd nikto
    git checkout nikto-2.5.0
    ```

2. To run Nikto, `cd` into the program subdirectory, and invoke Nikto from there. For example, to see the Nikto help screen, do this:

    ```
    cd program
    ./nikto -help
    ```

3. Periodically, you'll want to update the Nikto signature databases. Just `cd` into the `nikto` directory and do:

    ```
    git pull
    ```

4. End of lab.

Next, let's do something useful with Nikto.

Scanning a web server with Nikto

To do a simple scan, use the -h option to specify the target host, like this:

```
cd nikto/program
./nikto -h 192.168.0.9
./nikto -h www.example.com
```

Let's look at some sample output. Here's the top part:

```
+ Allowed HTTP Methods: POST, OPTIONS, GET, HEAD
+ OSVDB-396: /_vti_bin/shtml.exe: Attackers may be able to crash FrontPage by
requesting a DOS device, like shtml.exe/aux.htm -- a DoS was not attempted.
+ /cgi-bin/guestbook.pl: May allow attackers to execute commands as the web
daemon.
+ /cgi-bin/wwwadmin.pl: Administration CGI?
+ /cgi-bin/Count.cgi: This may allow attackers to execute arbitrary commands on
the server
```

At the top, we can see that there's an shtml.exe file present, which is supposedly for the FrontPage web authoring program. I have no idea why it's there, considering that this is a Linux server and that that's a Windows executable. Nikto is telling me that by having that file there, someone could possibly do a **Denial of Service (DOS)** attack against this site.

Next, we can see that there are various scripts in the /cgi-bin/ directory. You can see from the explanatory messages that that's not a good thing because it could allow attackers to execute commands on my server.

Let's look at the second part:

```
+ OSVDB-28260: /_vti_bin/shtml.exe/_vti_
rpc?method=server+version%3a4%2e0%2e2%2e2611: Gives info about server settings.
+ OSVDB-3092: /_vti_bin/_vti_aut/author.
exe?method=list+documents%3a3%2e0%2e2%2e1706&service%5fname=&listHiddenDocs=true&
listExplorerDocs=true&listRecurse=false&listFiles=true&listFolders=true&listLink
Info=true&listIncludeParent=true&listDerivedT=false&listBorders=fals: We seem
to have authoring access to the FrontPage web.
```

Here, we can see that there's an author.exe file in the vti_bin directory, which could theoretically allow someone to have authoring privileges.

And now, the final part:

```
+ OSVDB-250: /wwwboard/passwd.txt: The wwwboard password file is browsable.
Change wwwboard to store this file elsewhere, or upgrade to the latest version.
+ OSVDB-3092: /stats/: This might be interesting...
+ OSVDB-3092: /test.html: This might be interesting...
+ OSVDB-3092: /webstats/: This might be interesting...
```

```
+ OSVDB-3092: /cgi-bin/wwwboard.pl: This might be interesting...
+ OSVDB-3233: /_vti_bin/shtml.exe/_vti_rpc: FrontPage may be installed.
+ 6545 items checked: 0 error(s) and 15 item(s) reported on remote host
+ End Time:          2017-12-24 10:54:21 (GMT-5) (678 seconds)
```

The final item of interest is the `passwd.txt` file that's in the `wwwboard` directory. Apparently, this password file is browsable, which is definitely not a good thing.

Now, before you accuse me of making these problems up, I will reveal that this is a scan of a real production website on a real hosting service. (And yes, I do have permission to scan it.) So, these problems are real and need to be fixed.

Here are a couple of other sample messages that I got from scanning a web server that's running WordPress:

```
HTTP TRACK method is active, suggesting the host is vulnerable to XST
Cookie wordpress_test_cookie created without the httponly flag
```

To cut a long story short, both of these two problems could potentially allow an attacker to steal user credentials. The fix, in this case, would be to see whether the WordPress folk have issued any updates that would fix the problem.

So, how can we protect a web server against these kinds of vulnerabilities? Let's see:

- As we saw in the first example, you want to ensure that you don't have any risky executable files on your web server. In this case, we found two `.exe` files that might not hurt anything on our Linux server, since Windows executable files don't run on Linux. On the other hand, it could be a Linux executable that's disguised as a Windows executable. We also found some `perl` scripts that definitely would run on Linux and that could pose a problem.

- In the event that someone were to plant some malicious script on your web server, you'll want to have some form of mandatory access control, such as SELinux or AppArmor, that would keep the malicious scripts from accessing things that they shouldn't access. (See *Chapter 10*, *Implementing Mandatory Access Control with SELinux and AppArmor*, for details of that.)

- You may also consider installing a web application firewall, such as ModSecurity. Space doesn't permit me to cover the details of ModSecurity, but you'll find a book that covers it on the Packt Publishing website.

- Keep your systems updated, especially if you're running a PHP-based content management system such as WordPress. If you keep up with the IT security news, you'll see stories about WordPress vulnerabilities more often than you'd like to.

I can't reveal the URL of the site that I scanned here, but you can download a vulnerable virtual machine from `https://www.vulnhub.com/`

Choose a virtual machine to download, and then import it into VirtualBox. To do that, choose **Import Appliance** under the **File** menu.

There are other scan options that you can see by just typing `./nikto` at the command line. For now though, this is enough to get you started with basic web server scanning.

Summary

We've reached yet another milestone in our journey, and we saw some cool stuff. We started with a discussion about the basics of setting up Snort as a NIDS. Then, I showed you how to seriously cheat by deploying a specialty Linux distro that already has a NIDS set up and ready to go. As a bonus, I showed you a quick and easy edge firewall appliance that comes with a built-in NIPS.

Next, I introduced you to Lynis and how you can use it to scan your system for various vulnerabilities and compliance issues. Finally, we wrapped things up with working demos of the Greenbone Security Assistant and Nikto.

In the next chapter, we'll look at how to block certain applications from running. I'll see you there.

Questions

1. Which of the following best describes IPFire?

    a. A host-based firewall appliance with a built-in NIDS

    b. An edge firewall appliance with a built-in NIDS

2. Which of the following utilities is best for scanning Sarbanes-Oxley compliance issues?

    a. Lynis

    b. Lynis Enterprise

    c. Greenbone Security Assistant

    d. OpenSCAP

3. Which of the following best represents what Snort is?

    a. HIDS

    b. GIDS

    c. NIDS

    d. FIDS

4. Which of the following would you use as a general-purpose, external vulnerability scanner?

    a. Greenbone Security Assistant

    b. Nikto

    c. OpenSCAP

    d. Lynis

5. Which of these problems would you be most likely to find with a Nikto scan?

    a. That the Samba service is running, although it shouldn't be

    b. That the root user account is exposed to the Internet via SSH

    c. That potentially malicious scripts reside in a CGI directory

    d. That the root user account is configured with a weak password

6. What is a unique characteristic about Lynis?

    a. It's a proprietary, closed-source vulnerability scanner.

    b. It's a shell script that can be used to scan any Linux, Unix, or Unix-like operating system for vulnerabilities.

    c. It's an external vulnerability scanner.

    d. It can only be installed on a specialty security distro, such as Kali Linux.

7. Which of these problems would you most likely find with Snort?

    a. A root user account with a weak password

    b. Servers without active firewalls

    c. Cryptocoin mining malware active on the network

    d. Root user accounts exposed to the Internet via SSH

Further reading

- Lynis home page: `https://cisofy.com/lynis/`
- How Lynis and auditd are different: `https://linux-audit.com/how-are-auditd-and-lynis-different/`
- Greenbone home page: `https://securityonionsolutions.com/`
- Snort home page: `https://www.snort.org/`
- Nikto home page: `https://cirt.net/nikto2`
- Security Onion home page: `https://securityonionsolutions.com/`
- Tutorial for installing Greenbone Security Manager: `https://youtu.be/OUiRTv4Q80c`

Answers

1. b
2. b
3. c
4. a
5. c
6. b
7. c

Join our book community

Join our community's Discord space for discussions with the author and other readers:

`https://packt.link/CyberSec`

15

Prevent Unwanted Programs from Running

Once upon a time, we didn't have to worry much about Linux malware. While it's still true that Linux users don't have to worry about viruses, there are other types of malware that can definitely ruin a Linux user's day. Cryptomining programs planted on your server can eat up memory and CPU cycles, causing your server to work much harder and use more power than it should. Ransomware, which can encrypt either important files or a system's bootloader, can make these important files or even the whole system inaccessible. Even paying the demanded ransom isn't always a guarantee that your system will be returned to proper order. One way to prevent these programs from doing their damage is to only allow authorized programs to run, and to block everything else. We have two ways of doing that, which are the topics of this chapter:

- Mount partitions with the no options
- Use fapolicyd on Red Hat-type systems

So, if you're ready, let's get going.

Mount Partitions with the no options

In *Chapter 12, Scanning, Auditing, and Hardening,* I showed you how OpenSCAP can automatically bring your Linux systems into compliance with the security standards of certain regulatory bodies. I also told you the inconvenient truth that there are certain things that OpenSCAP can't do, and that you'll have to do for yourself. One thing that it can't do is to partition your system drives as some of these regulatory bodies require. For example, the **Security Technical Implementation Guides (STIGs)** that the US Government uses require the following Linux system and data directories to be mounted on their own partitions:

- /var
- /var/log/
- /var/tmp/

- `/var/log/audit/`
- `/tmp/`
- `/home/`
- `/boot/`
- `/boot/efi/` (You'll only have this one if your machine is set up in EFI mode.)

The reason for this is twofold:

- If the root (/) partition of a Linux operating system becomes too full, it can cause the operating system to completely lock up. Mounting these directories in their own partitions can help prevent the / partition from filling up.
- The STIGs, and possibly other security regulations, require that these partitions be mounted with options that prevent executable programs from running on them, SGID and SUID file permissions from being effective, and device files to be created on them.

As I mentioned, OpenSCAP won't automatically set up this partitioning scheme for you. So, you'll need to set it up as you install the operating system. This requires careful planning in order to get the partitions sized correctly. I mean, you don't want to waste space by making certain partitions too large, and you don't want to run out of space on partitions that really need the extra space.

> RHEL 9.1 and all of its clones were released a few weeks before I began writing this chapter. You might already have noticed that there's a bug in the 9.1 installer that wasn't in the 9.0 installer. That is, the option to create a normal user account isn't visible on the installer screen. I mean, it's there, but you can't see it and can't scroll down to it. To bring it up, just keep hitting the *Tab* key until you've highlighted the option to create the root user password. Then, hit the *Tab* key once more, and then hit the *Enter* key. (Of course, there's always the chance that the problem will get fixed by the time you read this.)

To get this set up, you'll need to select the installer option to create a custom partitioning scheme. To make this somewhat realistic, set the size of your virtual machine's virtual drive to about 1 TB. (Don't worry if you don't have that much space on your host machine's drive. VirtualBox will create a dynamically-sized drive that won't use 1 TB worth of space on the host drive unless you put 1 TB worth of files on it.) Let's see what this looks like on AlmaLinux 9:

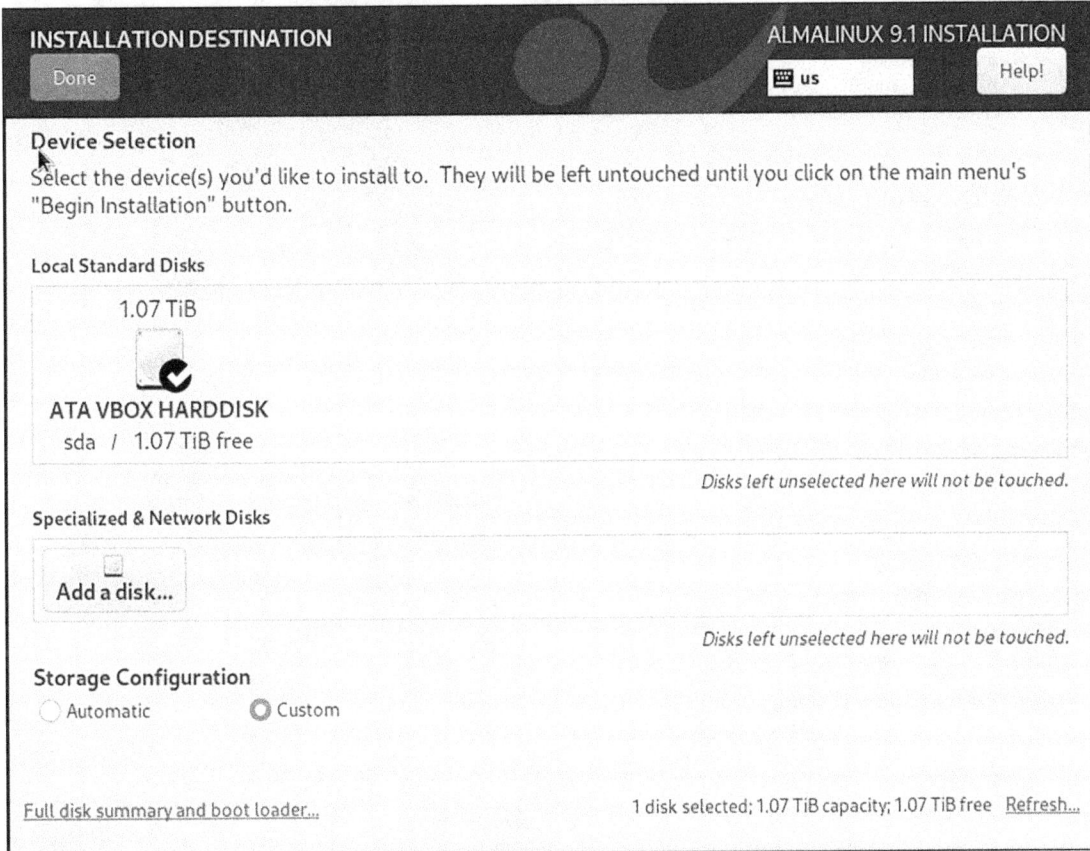

Figure 15.1: Choose to create a custom partitioning scheme

After selecting the **Custom** option, hit the **Done** button at the top of the screen. On the next screen, click the + box to create a mount point. Note that you can create a standard partition, a logical volume, or a thin-provisioned logical volume. (I'm going to go with standard partitions.)

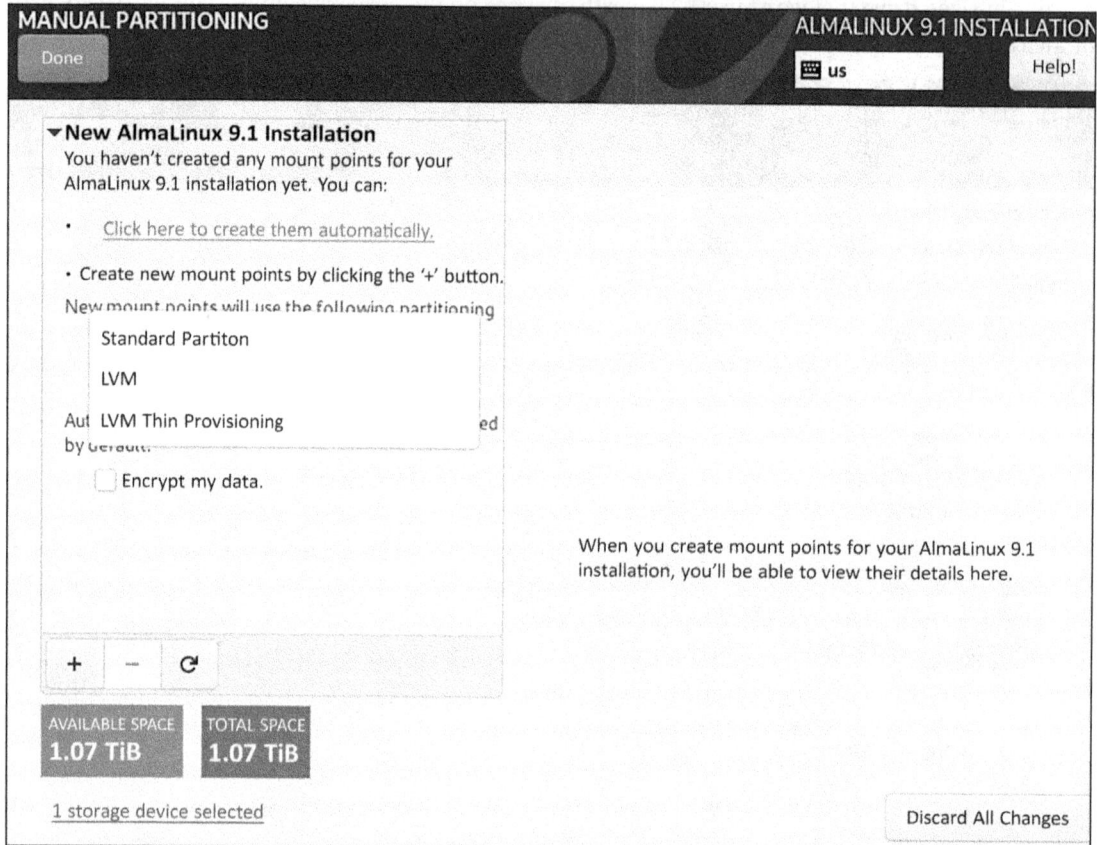

MANUAL PARTITIONING   ALMALINUX 9.1 INSTALLATION

Done   ⌨ us   Help!

▼ **New AlmaLinux 9.1 Installation**
You haven't created any mount points for your
AlmaLinux 9.1 installation yet. You can:

•   Click here to create them automatically.

• Create new mount points by clicking the '+' button.
New mount points will use the following partitioning

Standard Partiton

LVM

Aut   LVM Thin Provisioning   ed
by ᴜᴇʀᴀᴜᴛᴛ.

☐ Encrypt my data.

                                    When you create mount points for your AlmaLinux 9.1
                                    installation, you'll be able to view their details here.

+   —   ↻

AVAILABLE SPACE   TOTAL SPACE
1.07 TiB   **1.07 TiB**

1 storage device selected   Discard All Changes

Figure 15.2: Create a mount point

Let's start by creating the /boot/ mount point:

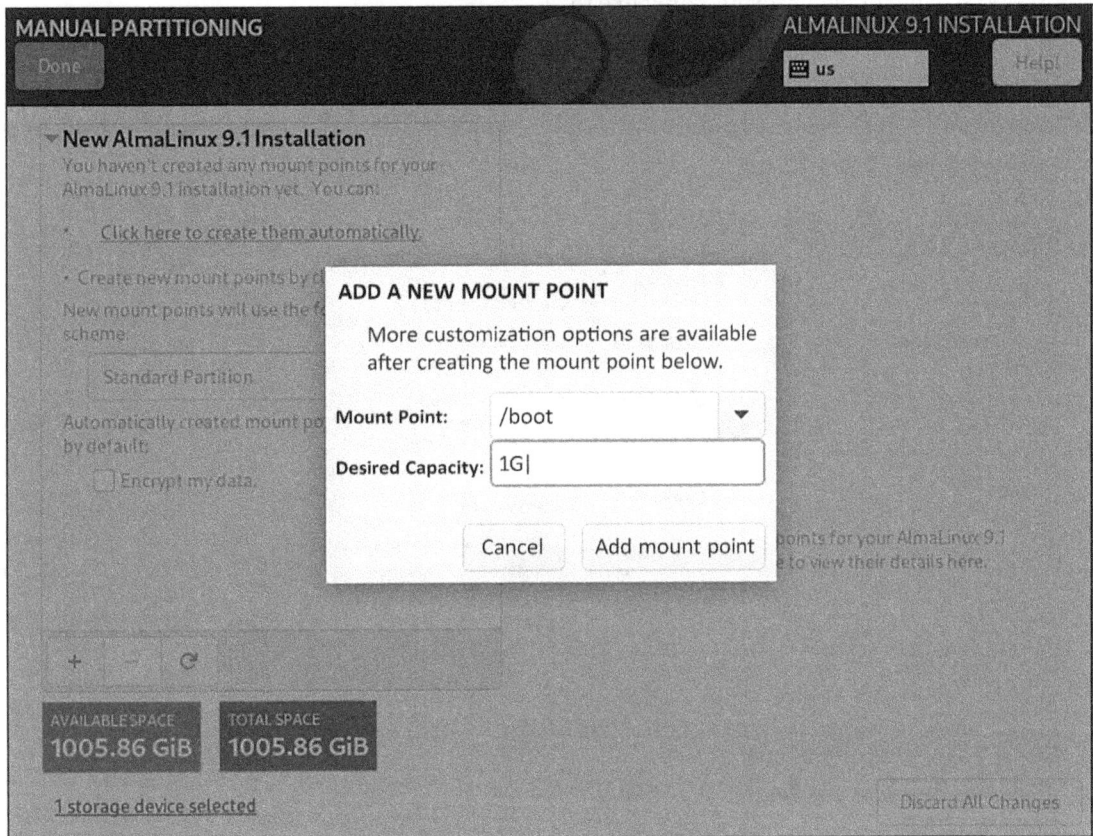

MANUAL PARTITIONING   ALMALINUX 9.1 INSTALLATION

Done   ⌨ us   Help!

▼ New AlmaLinux 9.1 Installation
You haven't created any mount points for your
AlmaLinux 9.1 installation yet. You can:

• Click here to create them automatically.

• Create new mount points by
New mount points will use the f
scheme:

Standard Partition

Automatically created mount po
by default:

☐ Encrypt my data.

ADD A NEW MOUNT POINT

More customization options are available
after creating the mount point below.

Mount Point: /boot   ▼

Desired Capacity: 1G|

Cancel   Add mount point   points for your AlmaLinux 9.1
                                                to view their details here.

\+   −   ↻

AVAILABLE SPACE   TOTAL SPACE
1005.86 GiB   **1005.86 GiB**

1 storage device selected   Discard All Changes

Figure 15.3: Creating the first mount point

Create the rest of the required mount points for the partitions that I mentioned in the above list. Your completed scheme might look something like this:

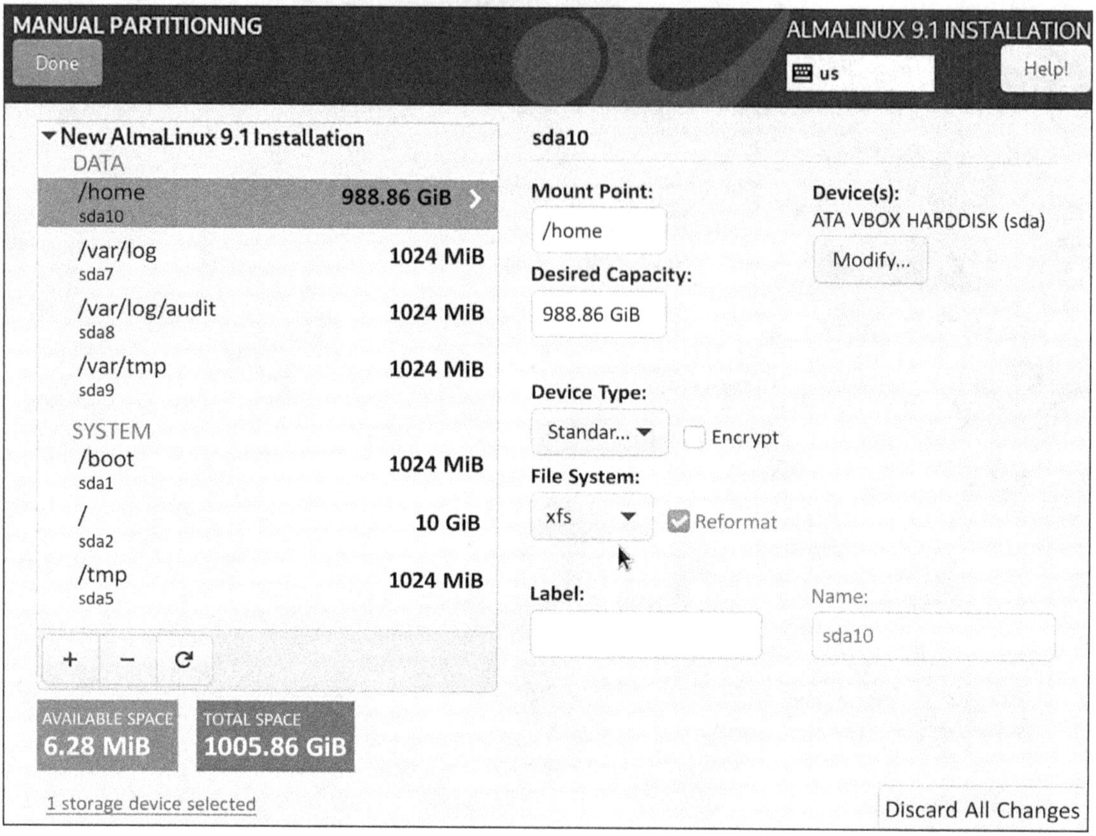

Figure 15.4: Create the rest of the mount points

Of course, your own use case will dictate how large you make each of these partitions. Here, you see that the /home/ directory is the largest, which suggests that I want to use this machine as a Samba file server. If I were to use this machine for some other purpose, such as a database server, I would resize these partitions as required.

> There's a long-standing upstream bug in the RHEL installer that also affects the RHEL clones. That is, regardless of how much or how little space you need for each partition, you'll have to make each one at least 1 GB in size. Otherwise, the installation will fail with an error in POSTTRANS scriptlet in rpm package kernel-core message. This has been a known problem for a long time, but it still hasn't been fixed. (Yes, it does waste some disk space, but there's nothing we can do about it.)

Now, here's where we're going to cheat a bit. We're going to pretend that we're dealing with the US government, which requires us to meet the STIG specifications. So, on the installer screen, we'll click on the option to apply a security profile. On the next screen, we'll scroll down to where we see the STIG profile, and select it. At the bottom, you'll see that this profile adds the noexec, nodev, and nosuid options to the partitions, as applicable. (The /var/ partition only requires the nodev option, and the /boot/ partition only requires the nodev and nosuid options.)

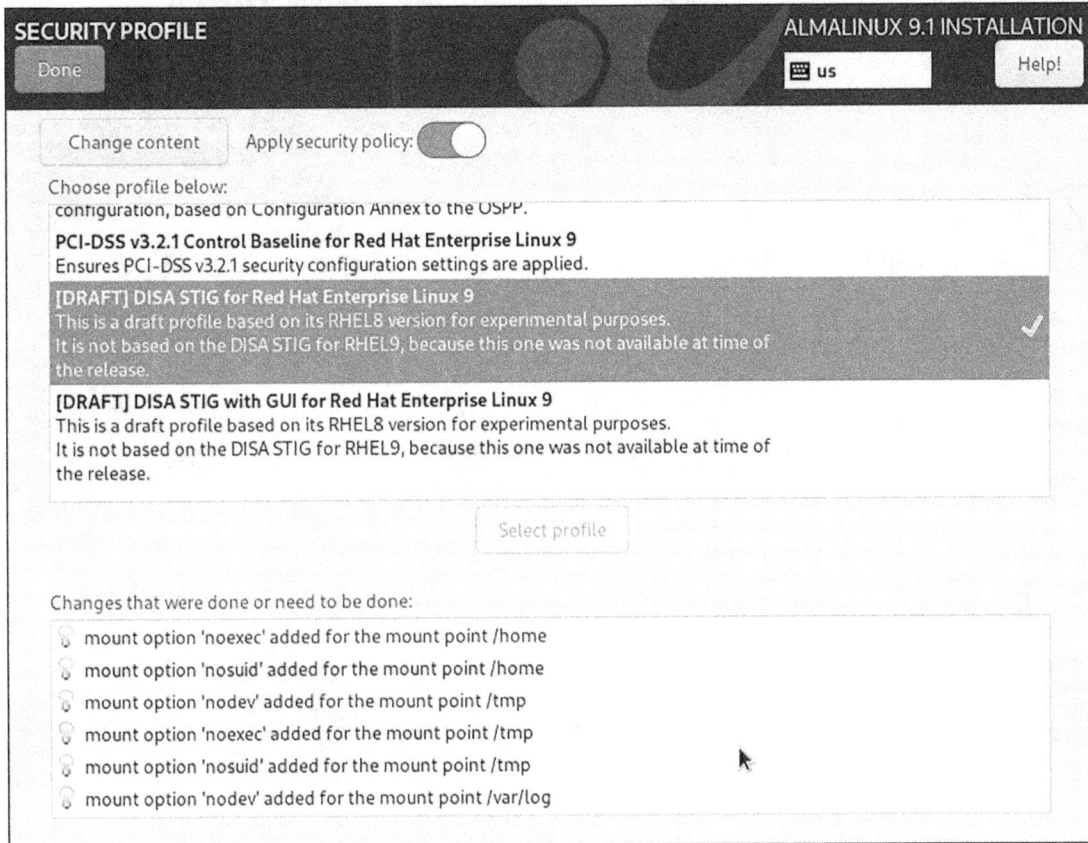

Figure 15.5: Applying the STIG profile

Here's what these three mount options do for us:

- noexec: Executable files cannot run from any partition that's mounted with this option. (This includes executable shell scripts, unless you invoke the script with sh. I'll show you more about this in just a bit.)
- nodev: Users can't create any device files on partitions that are mounted with this option.
- nosuid: On partitions that are mounted with this option, adding either the SUID or SGID permission to files will have no effect.

When the installation completes, our /etc/fstab file will look something like this:

```
UUID=72d0a3b3-cd07-45c0-938e-4e3377750adb /              xfs       defaults
0 0
UUID=7bf3315e-525e-4940-b562-7e0b634d65de /boot          xfs
defaults,nosuid,nodev 0 0
UUID=4df2f723-e875-4194-9ccd-b4a2733fd617 /home          xfs
defaults,noexec,nosuid,nodev 0 0
UUID=d89b01b1-c3ee-48b6-bb40-0311fdd2838a /tmp           xfs
defaults,nodev,noexec,nosuid 0 0
UUID=d79889b0-1635-47d5-950d-8dbca088c464 /var           xfs       defaults,nodev
0 0
UUID=be9a3d41-0e07-4466-8eb7-57fb850df2d4 /var/log       xfs
defaults,nodev,noexec,nosuid 0 0
UUID=ed001588-333b-4027-bef1-754fcc5e868d /var/log/audit     xfs
defaults,nodev,noexec,nosuid 0 0
UUID=05c1b1e9-7f32-4791-9d41-492fce6f5166 /var/tmp       xfs
defaults,nodev,noexec,nosuid 0 0
UUID=c4fdabb8-7e45-4717-b7f5-1cad5f8e7720 none              swap      defaults
0 0
tmpfs /dev/shm tmpfs defaults,relatime,inode64,nodev,noexec,nosuid 0 0
```

(Note that some of these lines might wrap around on the printed page.)

Now, let's see if we can run an executable script from any of these directories. In my own home directory, I created a shell script that looks like this:

```
#!/bin/bash
echo "This is a test of the noexec option."
exit
```

After adding the executable permission for myself, I tried to run it. Then, I copied it to the /tmp/ directory and tried to run it again. Here's what I got:

```
[donnie@localhost ~]$ chmod u+x donnie_script.sh
[donnie@localhost ~]$ ./donnie_script.sh
-bash: ./donnie_script.sh: Permission denied
[donnie@localhost ~]$ cp donnie_script.sh /tmp
[donnie@localhost ~]$ cd /tmp
[donnie@localhost tmp]$ ./donnie_script.sh
-bash: ./donnie_script.sh: Permission denied
[donnie@localhost tmp]$
```

So, I can't run it, at least not as a normal user. But, what if I were to try it with sudo? Let's see:

```
[donnie@localhost tmp]$ sudo ./donnie_script.sh
[sudo] password for donnie:
sudo: unable to execute ./donnie_script.sh: Permission denied
[donnie@localhost tmp]$
```

Cool, the noexec option actually works. Well, for this it does. What would happen if we were to invoke the script with sh? Let's see:

```
[donnie@localhost ~]$ sh ./donnie_script.sh
This is a test of the noexec option.
[donnie@localhost ~]$ cd /tmp
[donnie@localhost tmp]$ sh ./donnie_script.sh
This is a test of the noexec option.
[donnie@localhost tmp]$
```

So, with shell scripts, the blocking isn't perfect. Let's see what happens with a compiled executable file. Start by downloading the command-line wallet/mining program for the DERO cryptocurrency project from here: https://dero.io/download.html#linux

Transfer the file to your virtual machine and untar it:

```
[donnie@localhost ~]$ tar xzvf dero_linux_amd64.tar.gz
./dero_linux_amd64/
./dero_linux_amd64/Start.md
./dero_linux_amd64/explorer-linux-amd64
./dero_linux_amd64/simulator-linux-amd64
./dero_linux_amd64/dero-miner-linux-amd64
./dero_linux_amd64/derod-linux-amd64
./dero_linux_amd64/dero-wallet-cli-linux-amd64
[donnie@localhost ~]$
```

Note that the executable permission is already set for all of the executable files, so you won't have to add it.

Now, for the moment of truth. Enter the dero_linux_amd64 directory and attempt to run the derod-linux-amd64 program:

```
[donnie@localhost ~]$ cd dero_linux_amd64/
[donnie@localhost dero_linux_amd64]$ ./derod-linux-amd64
-bash: ./derod-linux-amd64: Permission denied
[donnie@localhost dero_linux_amd64]$
```

Since this is a compiled executable instead of a shell script, prefacing the command with sh won't do anything for us in any case. Anyway, keep this DERO stuff handy, because we'll use it again in the next section.

If you're wondering what DERO is, think of it as a private version of Ethereum. You can build other tokens on it and create smart contract applications on it, just like you can do with Ethereum. The difference is that DERO protects your privacy, and Ethereum doesn't.

In *Chapter 12*, *Scanning, Auditing, and Hardening*, I showed you that only the RHEL-type distros give us the option of applying a SCAP profile as we install the operating system. On non-RHEL distros, you'll need to apply the SCAP profile after the installation has completed, assuming that an appropriate profile is available for your distro. In any case, if you don't need to apply a whole SCAP profile but still want to add these security options to your partitions, or if no SCAP profile is available for your distro, just hand-edit the /etc/fstab file to add them in.

Next, we'll look at another control mechanism that, so far at least, is exclusive to the world of Red Hat.

Understanding fapolicyd

The **File Access Policy Daemon** (**fapolicyd**) is a fairly new addition to Red Hat Enterprise Linux and its various clones. It's free-as-in-speech software so that anyone can use it, but so far neither Ubuntu nor SUSE have made it available for their distros. To get a quick feel for how it works, go back to the virtual machine that you've just been using. First, move the entire derod-linux-amd64 directory over to the top level of the / partition:

```
[donnie@localhost ~]$ sudo mv dero_linux_amd64/ /
[sudo] password for donnie:
[donnie@localhost ~]$
```

By moving the directory instead of copying it, your ownership of the directory and its files will be preserved:

```
[donnie@localhost /]$ ls -ld dero_linux_amd64/
drwx------. 3 donnie donnie 4096 Jan  2 15:42 dero_linux_amd64/
[donnie@localhost /]$
```

Now, copy the script that you created over to /usr/local/bin/:

```
[donnie@localhost dero_linux_amd64]$ cd
[donnie@localhost ~]$ sudo cp donnie_script.sh /usr/local/bin
[sudo] password for donnie:
[donnie@localhost ~]$
```

When you look at the permissions settings on this script file, you'll see something very unusual:

```
[donnie@localhost ~]$ cd /usr/local/bin
[donnie@localhost bin]$ ls -l
total 16364
-rwx------. 1 root root        61 Dec 31 16:01 donnie_script.sh
[donnie@localhost bin]$
```

You see that doing a `cp` operation automatically changes the ownership of this file to the owner of the target directory, which in this case is the root user. That's just normal operation, so there's nothing to see there. What's so unusual is that we have a permissions setting of `700` on this file. That's because of something else that our STIG profile has done. That is, the STIG profile has set a **UMASK** of `077` on this system, as we see here:

```
[donnie@localhost ~]$ umask
0077
[donnie@localhost ~]$
```

This means that any normal files that you create will have read and write permissions for only the user, and any directories that you create will have read, write, and execute permissions for only the user. To make this demo work we'll need to change the permissions settings to a value of 755, like so:

```
[donnie@localhost bin]$ sudo chmod 755 donnie_script.sh
[sudo] password for donnie:
[donnie@localhost bin]$ ls -l
total 16364
-rwxr-xr-x. 1 root root        61 Dec 31 16:01 donnie_script.sh
[donnie@localhost bin]$
```

Cool. We can now make the demo work. We'll start by entering the `/dero-linux-amd64/` directory and trying to invoke the `derod-linux-amd64` executable:

```
[donnie@localhost ~]$ cd /dero_linux_amd64/
[donnie@localhost dero_linux_amd64]$ derod-linux-amd64
-bash: /dero_linux_amd64/derod-linux-amd64: Operation not permitted
[donnie@localhost dero_linux_amd64]$
```

Even though you're now invoking this program from a partition that isn't mounted with the `noexec` option, you're still not allowed to run it. That's because it's now being blocked by `fapolicyd`. That is, you can't run it with your normal user privileges, even though both the directory and the executable file belong to you.

> There's an idiosyncrasy with `fapolicyd` that I haven't seen documented anywhere, and that I only found out by accident. That is, it will only block untrusted programs when a normal, unprivileged user tries to run them. But, you can run them just fine with the proper `sudo` privileges. (This is all the more reason to grant only limited `sudo` privileges to all but your most trusted administrators.)

Next, let's see what we can do with the shell script:

```
[donnie@localhost bin]$ donnie_script.sh
This is a test of the noexec option.
[donnie@localhost bin]$
```

So, why can I invoke this script here, but not in my home directory? It's because in my home directory, the noexec mount option is blocking the script. But here in the /usr/local/bin/ directory, we don't have that mount option. Instead, all we have is just fapolicyd. We can use the fapolicyd-cli -list command to view the rules that are in effect, which might explain why I was able to run this script. (Note that formatting constraints don't allow me to show the entire output):

```
[donnie@localhost ~]$ sudo fapolicyd-cli -list
[sudo] password for donnie:
. . .

. . .
11. deny_audit perm=any all : ftype=%languages
12. allow perm=any all : ftype=text/x-shellscript
13. deny_audit perm=execute all : all
14. allow perm=open all : all
[donnie@localhost ~]$
```

Look at rule number 12. This rule allows shell scripts to run on all partitions that don't have the noexec mount option, even by unprivileged users. That makes sense, considering that even unprivileged users make extensive use of shell scripts in order to automate repetitive tasks. But, if you're absolutely certain that no unprivileged user will ever have cause to run shell scripts on a system, you can always disable that rule. And, in any case, you'd still be able to run shell scripts if you have the proper sudo privileges.

And, speaking of rules, let's look at them next.

Understanding the fapolicyd rules

The fapolicyd framework uses rules in the /etc/fapolicyd/rules.d/ directory to create a list of programs that are either allowed or denied to execute on the system. When you install fapolicyd, you'll get a set of default rules that are already set up and ready to go. If you need to allow more than what the default rules allow, you can create your own custom rules or add your desired program to the list of trusted applications.

In the /etc/fapolicyd/rules.d/ directory, there are 11 rules files. Each one serves a different purpose:

```
[donnie@localhost ~]$ sudo ls -l /etc/fapolicyd/rules.d
[sudo] password for donnie:
total 44
-rw-r--r--. 1 root fapolicyd 456 Dec 29 14:42 10-languages.rules
-rw-r--r--. 1 root fapolicyd 131 Dec 29 14:42 20-dracut.rules
-rw-r--r--. 1 root fapolicyd 192 Dec 29 14:42 21-updaters.rules
-rw-r--r--. 1 root fapolicyd 225 Dec 29 14:42 30-patterns.rules
-rw-r--r--. 1 root fapolicyd 101 Dec 29 14:42 40-bad-elf.rules
-rw-r--r--. 1 root fapolicyd 248 Dec 29 14:42 41-shared-obj.rules
```

```
-rw-r--r--. 1 root fapolicyd  71 Dec 29 14:42 42-trusted-elf.rules
-rw-r--r--. 1 root fapolicyd 143 Dec 29 14:42 70-trusted-lang.rules
-rw-r--r--. 1 root fapolicyd  96 Dec 29 14:42 72-shell.rules
-rw-r--r--. 1 root fapolicyd  76 Dec 29 14:42 90-deny-execute.rules
-rw-r--r--. 1 root fapolicyd  69 Dec 29 14:42 95-allow-open.rules
[donnie@localhost ~]$
```

The numbers at the beginning of the filenames indicate the order in which these rules files will be processed, because the order in which the rules get processed really does matter. Rather than try to explain what these different classes of rules do for us, I'll just let you open each file and read the contents. They're all very short and include a comment to explain what each file does.

Although you can create custom rules for your own custom applications, that's not the recommended method. For performance and safety reasons, it's better to just add your application to the trusted list, like so:

```
[donnie@localhost ~]$ sudo fapolicyd-cli --file add /dero_linux_amd64/derod-
linux-amd64
[sudo] password for donnie:
[donnie@localhost ~]$
```

I mentioned *safety* reasons because when you write your own custom rules, it's easy to make a mistake that will lock up the entire system. You don't have to worry about that so much if you're just adding files to the trusted list.

This command adds the desired file, along with its associated SHA256 hash value, to the /etc/fapolicyd/fapolicyd.trust file, as we see here:

```
[donnie@localhost ~]$ sudo cat /etc/fapolicyd/fapolicyd.trust
[sudo] password for donnie:
# AUTOGENERATED FILE VERSION 2
# This file contains a list of trusted files
#
#  FULL PATH       SIZE                        SHA256
# /home/user/my-ls 157984
61a9960bf7d255a85811f4afcac51067b8f2e4c75e21cf4f2af95319d4ed1b87

/dero_linux_amd64/derod-linux-amd64 16750936
847ea80b83a1df887d245085db60a9b0626aacb6cd4f0f192eb2e982643c5529
[donnie@localhost ~]$
```

To make this change take effect, we need to update the database and restart the `fapolicyd` service, like so:

```
[donnie@localhost ~]$ sudo fapolicyd-cli --update
[sudo] password for donnie:
Fapolicyd was notified
[donnie@localhost ~]$ sudo systemctl restart fapolicyd
[sudo] password for donnie:
[donnie@localhost ~]$
```

Now, when I invoke this application with my normal user privileges, it will run just fine:

```
[donnie@localhost ~]$ cd /dero_linux_amd64/
[donnie@localhost dero_linux_amd64]$ ./derod-linux-amd64
02/01 16:13:31  INFO    derod    DERO HE daemon :  It is an alpha version, use
it for testing/evaluations purpose only.
02/01 16:13:31  INFO    derod    Copyright 2017-2021 DERO Project. All rights
reserved.
02/01 16:13:31  INFO    derod            {"OS": "linux", "ARCH": "amd64",
"GOMAXPROCS": 1}
02/01 16:13:31  INFO    derod            {"Version": "3.5.2-114.DEROHE.
STARGATE+01102022"}
. . .
. . .
```

So now, you're likely wondering if you have to manually add each new application that you would install to the trusted list. Well, that depends upon how you install it. If you just download a compiled program as we did in the previous example, or compile one yourself, then yeah, you will have to manually add it to the trusted list. But, by default, every program that gets installed by the system package manager is automatically trusted. That means that if you use either `dnf` to install a package from the repository, or `rpm` to install an `rpm` package that you either downloaded or created, then the associated application is automatically trusted.

So far, we've looked at how the three *no* mount options and `fapolicyd` work together and complement each other. In this case, the mount options and `fapolicyd` all got set up automatically because we applied the STIG OpenSCAP profile as we installed the operating system. We can also install `fapolicyd` without the STIG profile, which is what we'll look at next.

Installing fapolicyd

Normally, `fapolicyd` isn't automatically installed on AlmaLinux. In this case it was, because the STIG profile that we applied requires it as well as the restrictive mounting options for our partitions. To install `fapolicyd` on a system on which it hasn't already been installed, just do:

```
[donnie@localhost ~]$ sudo dnf install fapolicyd
. . .
```

```
. . .
[donnie@localhost ~]$ sudo systemctl enable --now fapolicyd
Created symlink /etc/systemd/system/multi-user.target.wants/fapolicyd.service →
/usr/lib/systemd/system/fapolicyd.service.
[donnie@localhost ~]$
```

There's still a bit more about `fapolicyd` that I haven't shown you, but I think you've seen enough to get the gist of it. To get more details about it and to see how to also use it as a file-integrity checker, be sure to visit the official Red Hat documentation for it. (The link is below in the *Further reading* section.)

Adding the `noexec`, `nosuid`, and `nodev` mount options to your partitions works well, except that you can't add them to all of your partitions. Obviously, you can't add them to any partitions that are supposed to have executable files in them, or else your system would never work. The `fapolicyd` framework gives you a way to prevent rogue programs from running on those partitions, as long as the malicious intruder hasn't already gained root privileges.

All right, let's wrap this baby up.

Summary

In this chapter, we looked at two ways to prevent untrusted programs from running on your systems. The first method, which can be used on any Linux distro, is to separate the various system and data directories into their own separate partitions, and then to mount each of these partitions with the appropriate combination of the `noexec`, `nosuid`, and `nodev` options. The second method, which so far is only available on Red Hat and its clones, is to use the `fapolicyd` framework. We saw how to automatically enable both of these methods by applying the STIG OpenSCAP profile as we install the operating system. Finally, we saw how to install `fapolicyd` separately, without having to apply the STIG profile.

In the next chapter, we'll be wrapping things up with a quick look at various topics that didn't neatly fit into any of the preceding chapters. I'll see you there.

Further reading

1. The bug in the RHEL installer: `https://forums.rockylinux.org/t/kernel-core-error-at-install/3683`
2. The STIG for Red Hat 8: `https://www.stigviewer.com/stig/red_hat_enterprise_linux_8/`
3. Linux Ransomware: `https://phoenixnap.com/blog/linux-ransomware`
4. Linux File Access Policy Daemon (`fapolicyd`) video: `https://youtu.be/txThobi7oqc`
5. Official `fapolicyd` documentation at Red hat: `https://access.redhat.com/documentation/en-us/red_hat_enterprise_linux/9/html/security_hardening/assembly_blocking-and-allowing-applications-using-fapolicyd_security-hardening`

Questions

1. Which of the following statements is true?

    a. You can use the noexec, nosuid, and nodev mount options on any Linux distro.

    b. You can use fapolicyd on any Linux distro.

    c. You can prevent rogue programs from running by using the noexec mounting option on the / partition.

    d. To use the noexec, nosuid, and nodev mount options, you can edit the /etc/mtab file.

2. You need to run a program that fapolicyd normally won't allow. What is the best way to deal with this?

    a. Add it by hand-editing the /etc/fapolicyd/fapolicyd.trust file.

    b. Add it by creating a custom rule.

    c. Add it by running the sudo fapolicyd-cli --file add command.

    d. Add it by hand-editing the /etc/fapolicyd/fapolicyd.conf file.

3. When you apply the STIG OpenSCAP profile, what permissions settings will files and directories have when you create them?

    a. 644 for files, 755 for directories.

    b. 600 for files, 700 for directories.

    c. 640 for files, 750 for directories.

    d. 755 for files, 755 for directories.

4. Which of the following is true about applying the STIG OpenSCAP profile?

    a. You can apply the profile to any Linux operating system during the installation process.

    b. Applying the STIG profile to the operating system during the installation process does everything for you.

    c. Before you apply the STIG profile, you'll need to set up a custom partition scheme to separate certain directories onto their own partitions.

    d. On Red Hat-type systems, you can only apply the STIG profile after you've installed the system.

5. What type of hash value does fapolicyd use in its fapolicyd.trust file?

    a. SHA1

    b. Blowfish

    c. MD5

    d. SHA256

Answers

1. a
2. c
3. b
4. c
5. d

Join our book community

Join our community's Discord space for discussions with the author and other readers:

`https://packt.link/CyberSec`

16

Security Tips and Tricks for the Busy Bee

In this final chapter, I'd like to do a roundup of some quick tips and tricks that don't necessarily fit in with the previous chapters. Think of these tips as time savers for the busy administrator. First, you will learn about some quick ways to see which system services are running, in order to ensure that nothing that isn't needed is running. Then, we'll look at how to password-protect the GRUB 2 bootloader, how to securely configure BIOS/UEFI to help prevent attacks on a physically accessible machine, and how to use a checklist to perform a secure initial system setup.

In this chapter, we will cover the following topics:

- Auditing system services
- Password-protecting the GRUB2 configuration
- Securely configuring and then password-protecting UEFI/BIOS
- Using a security checklist when setting up your system

If you're ready, let's get going.

Technical requirements

The code files for this chapter are available here: `https://github.com/PacktPublishing/Mastering-Linux-Security-and-Hardening-3E`.

Auditing system services

A basic tenet of server administration, regardless of which operating system we're talking about, is to never have anything that you don't absolutely need installed on a server. You especially don't want any unnecessary network services running because that would give the bad guys extra ways to get into your system. And, there's always a chance that some evil hacker might have planted something that acts as a network service, and you'd definitely want to know about that. In this section, we'll look at a few different ways to audit your system to ensure that no unnecessary network services are running on it.

Auditing system services with systemctl

On Linux systems that come with `systemd`, the `systemctl` command is pretty much a universal command that does many things for you. In addition to controlling your system's services, it can also show you the status of those services, like so:

```
donnie@linux-0ro8:~> sudo systemctl -t service --state=active
```

Here's the breakdown of the preceding command:

- `-t service`: We want to view information about the services – or, what used to be called daemons – on the system.
- `--state=active`: This specifies that we want to view information about all the system services that are actually running.

A partial output of this command looks something like this:

```
UNIT                                              LOAD    ACTIVE SUB
DESCRIPTION
accounts-daemon.service                           loaded active running
Accounts Service
after-local.service                               loaded active exited  /
etc/init.d/after.local Compatibility
alsa-restore.service                              loaded active exited
Save/Restore Sound Card State
apparmor.service                                  loaded active exited
Load AppArmor profiles
auditd.service                                    loaded active running
Security Auditing Service
avahi-daemon.service                              loaded active running
Avahi mDNS/DNS-SD Stack
cron.service                                      loaded active running
Command Scheduler
. . .
. . .
```

Generally, you won't want to see quite this much information, although you might at times. This command shows the status of every service that's running on your system. What really interests us now is the network services that can allow someone to connect to your system. So, let's look at how to narrow things down a bit.

Auditing network services with netstat

Here are two reasons why you would want to keep track of what network services are running on your system:

- To ensure that no legitimate network services that you don't need are running

- To ensure that you don't have any malware that's listening for network connections from its master

The netstat command is both handy and easy to use. First, let's say that you want to see a list of network services that are listening, waiting for someone to connect to them. (Due to formatting restrictions, I can only show part of the output here. We'll look at some lines that I can't show here in just a moment. Also, you can download the text file with the full output from the Packt Publishing website.):

```
donnie@linux-0ro8:~> netstat -lp -A inet
(Not all processes could be identified, non-owned process info
 will not be shown, you would have to be root to see it all.)
Active Internet connections (only servers)
Proto Recv-Q Send-Q Local Address Foreign Address State PID/Program name
tcp 0 0 *:ideafarm-door *:* LISTEN -
tcp 0 0 localhost:40432 *:* LISTEN 3296/SpiderOakONE
tcp 0 0 *:ssh *:* LISTEN -
tcp 0 0 localhost:ipp *:* LISTEN -
tcp 0 0 localhost:smtp *:* LISTEN -
tcp 0 0 *:db-lsp *:* LISTEN 3246/dropbox
tcp 0 0 *:37468 *:* LISTEN 3296/SpiderOakONE
tcp 0 0 localhost:17600 *:* LISTEN 3246/dropbox
. . .
. . .
```

Here's the breakdown:

- -lp: The l means that we want to see which network ports are listening. In other words, we want to see which network ports are waiting for someone to connect to them. The p means that we want to see the name and process ID number of the program or service that is listening on each port.
- -A inet: This means that we only want to see information about the network protocols that are members of the inet family. In other words, we want to see information about the raw, tcp, and udp network sockets, but we don't want to see anything about the Unix sockets that only deal with interprocess communications within the operating system.

Since this output is from the openSUSE workstation that I used to write the original version of this chapter, you won't see any of the usual server-type services here. However, you will see a few things that you likely won't want to see on your servers. For example, let's look at the very first item:

```
Proto Recv-Q Send-Q Local Address    Foreign Address       State     PID/
Program name
tcp         0        0 *:ideafarm-door    *:*                   LISTEN    -
```

The Local Address column specifies the local address and port of this listening socket. The asterisk means that this socket is on the local network, while ideafarm-door is the name of the network port that is listening. (By default, netstat will show you the names of ports whenever possible by pulling the port information out of the /etc/services file.)

Now, because I didn't know what the `ideafarm-door` service is, I used my favorite search engine to find out. By plugging the term `ideafarm-door` into DuckDuckGo, I found the answer:

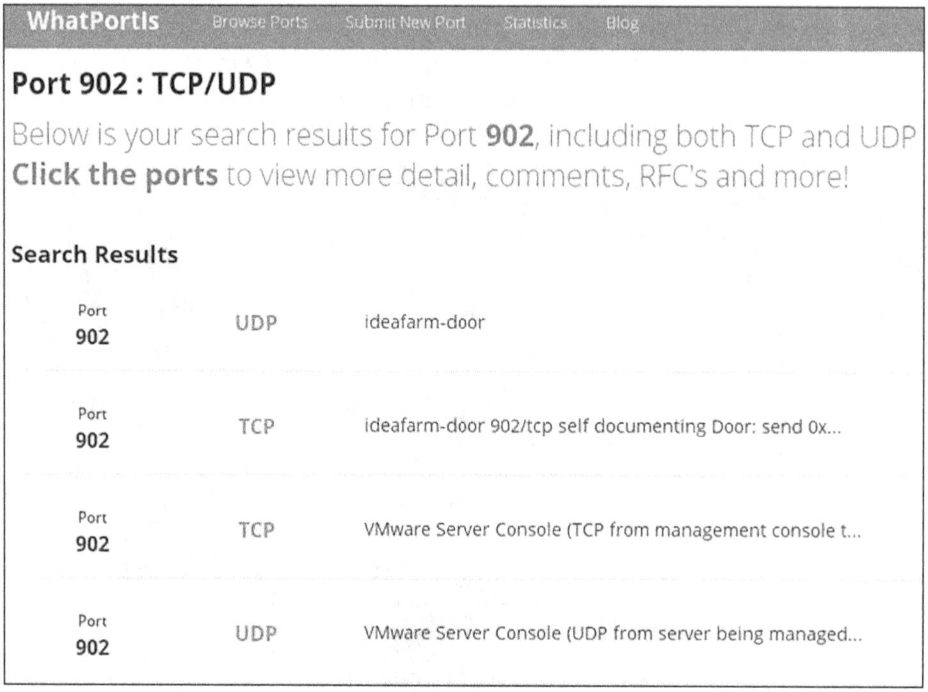

| WhatPortIs | Browse Ports | Submit New Port | Statistics | Blog |

Port 902 : TCP/UDP

Below is your search results for Port **902**, including both TCP and UDP
Click the ports to view more detail, comments, RFC's and more!

Search Results

Port 902	UDP	ideafarm-door
Port 902	TCP	ideafarm-door 902/tcp self documenting Door: send 0x...
Port 902	TCP	VMware Server Console (TCP from management console t...
Port 902	UDP	VMware Server Console (UDP from server being managed...

Figure 16.1: WhatPortIs

The top search result took me to a site named **WhatPortIs**. According to this, `ideafarm-door` is, in reality, port `902`, which belongs to the VMware Server Console. Okay, that makes sense because I do have VMware Player installed on this machine. So, that's all good.

You can check out the WhatPortIs site here: `http://whatportis.com/`.

Here's the next item on the list:

```
tcp        0        0 localhost:40432      *:*         LISTEN        3296/SpiderOakONE
```

This item shows the local address as `localhost` and that the listening port is port `40432`. This time, the `PID/Program Name` column actually tells us what this is. `SpiderOak ONE` is a cloud-based backup service that you might or might not want to see running on your server.

Now, let's look at a few more items:

```
tcp 0        0 *:db-lsp             *:*         LISTEN        3246/dropbox
tcp 0        0 *:37468              *:*         LISTEN        3296/SpiderOakONE
```

```
tcp 0       0 localhost:17600          *:*        LISTEN    3246/dropbox
tcp 0       0 localhost:17603          *:*        LISTEN    3246/dropbox
```

Here, we can see that dropbox and SpiderOakONE are both listed with the asterisk for the local address. So, they're both using the local network address. The name of the port for dropbox is db-lsp, which stands for **Dropbox LAN Sync Protocol**. The SpiderOakONE port doesn't have an official name, so it's just listed as port 37468. The bottom two lines show that dropbox also uses the local machine's address, on ports 17600 and 17603.

So far, we've looked at nothing but TCP network sockets. Let's see how they differ from UDP sockets:

```
udp     0      0 192.168.204.1:ntp       *:*
-
udp     0      0 172.16.249.1:ntp        *:*
-
udp     0      0 linux-0ro8:ntp          *:*
-
```

The first thing to note is that there's nothing under the State column. That's because, with UDP, there are no states. They are actually listening for data packets to come in, and they're ready to send data packets out. But since that's about all that UDP sockets can do, there was really no sense in defining different states for them.

In the first two lines, we see some strange local addresses. That's because I have both VMware Player and VirtualBox installed on this workstation. The local addresses of these two sockets are for the VMware and VirtualBox virtual network adapters. The last line shows the hostname of my OpenSUSE workstation as the local address. In all three cases, the port is the **Network Time Protocol** port, for time synchronization.

Now, let's look at one last set of UDP items:

```
udp     0      0 *:58102           *:*                          5598/
chromium --pas
udp     0      0 *:db-lsp-disc     *:*                          3246/
dropbox
udp     0      0 *:43782           *:*                          5598/
chromium --pas
udp     0      0 *:36764           *:*

udp     0      0 *:21327           *:*                          3296/
SpiderOakONE
udp     0      0 *:mdns            *:*                          5598/
chromium --pas
```

Here, we see that my Chromium web browser is ready to accept network packets on a few different ports. We also see that Dropbox uses UDP to accept discovery requests from other local machines that have Dropbox installed. I assume that port 21327 performs the same function for SpiderOak ONE.

Of course, since this machine is one of my workhorse workstations, Dropbox and SpiderOak ONE are almost indispensable to me. I installed them myself, so I've always known that they were there. However, if you see anything like this on a server, you'll want to investigate to see if the server admins know that these programs are installed, and then find out why they're installed. It could be that they're performing a legitimate function, and it could be that they're not.

> A difference between Dropbox and SpiderOak ONE is that with Dropbox, your files don't get encrypted until they've been uploaded to the Dropbox servers. So, the Dropbox folk have the encryption keys to your files. On the other hand, SpiderOak ONE encrypts your files on your local machine, and the encryption keys never leave your possession. So, if you really do need a cloud-based backup service and you're dealing with sensitive files, something such as SpiderOak ONE would definitely be better than Dropbox. (And no, the SpiderOak ONE folk aren't paying me to say that.)

If you want to see port numbers and IP addresses instead of network names, add the n option. As before, here's the partial output:

```
donnie@linux-0ro8:~> netstat -lpn -A inet
(Not all processes could be identified, non-owned process info
 will not be shown, you would have to be root to see it all.)
Active Internet connections (only servers)
Proto Recv-Q Send-Q Local Address       Foreign Address       State      PID/
Program name
tcp        0      0 0.0.0.0:902         0.0.0.0:*             LISTEN     -
tcp        0      0 127.0.0.1:40432     0.0.0.0:*             LISTEN     3296/
SpiderOakONE
tcp        0      0 0.0.0.0:22          0.0.0.0:*             LISTEN     -
tcp        0      0 127.0.0.1:631       0.0.0.0:*             LISTEN     -
tcp        0      0 127.0.0.1:25        0.0.0.0:*             LISTEN     -
tcp        0      0 0.0.0.0:17500       0.0.0.0:*             LISTEN     3246/
dropbox
tcp        0      0 0.0.0.0:37468       0.0.0.0:*             LISTEN     3296/
SpiderOakONE
tcp        0      0 127.0.0.1:17600     0.0.0.0:*             LISTEN     3246/
dropbox
. . .
. . .
```

All you have to do to view the established TCP connections is to leave out the l option. On my workstation, this makes for a very long list, so I'll only show a few items:

```
donnie@linux-0ro8:~> netstat -p -A inet
(Not all processes could be identified, non-owned process info
 will not be shown, you would have to be root to see it all.)
```

```
Active Internet connections (w/o servers)
Proto Recv-Q Send-Q Local Address       Foreign Address        State       PID/
Program name
tcp       1      0 linux-0ro8:41670    ec2-54-88-208-223:https CLOSE_WAIT
3246/dropbox
tcp       0      0 linux-0ro8:59810    74-126-144-106.wa:https ESTABLISHED
3296/SpiderOakONE
tcp       0      0 linux-0ro8:58712    74-126-144-105.wa:https ESTABLISHED
3296/SpiderOakONE
tcp       0      0 linux-0ro8:caerpc   atl14s78-in-f2.1e:https ESTABLISHED
10098/firefox
. . .
. . .
```

The Foreign Address column shows the address and port number of the machine at the remote end of the connection. The first item shows that the connection with a Dropbox server is in a CLOSE_WAIT state. This means that the Dropbox server has closed the connection, and we're now waiting on the local machine to close the socket.

Because the names of those foreign addresses don't make much sense, let's add the n option to see the IP addresses instead:

```
donnie@linux-0ro8:~> netstat -np -A inet
(Not all processes could be identified, non-owned process info
 will not be shown, you would have to be root to see it all.)
Active Internet connections (w/o servers)
Proto Recv-Q Send-Q Local Address       Foreign Address      State
PID/Program name
tcp       0      1 192.168.0.222:59594  37.187.24.170:443    SYN_SENT
10098/firefox
tcp       0      0 192.168.0.222:59810  74.126.144.106:443   ESTABLISHED
3296/SpiderOakONE
tcp       0      0 192.168.0.222:58712  74.126.144.105:443   ESTABLISHED
3296/SpiderOakONE
tcp       0      0 192.168.0.222:38606  34.240.121.144:443   ESTABLISHED
10098/firefox
. . .
. . .
```

This time, we see something new. The first item shows a SYN_SENT state for the Firefox connection. This means that the local machine is trying to establish a connection to the foreign IP address. Also, under Local Address, we can see the static IP address for my OpenSUSE workstation.

If I had space to display the entire netstat output here, you'd see nothing but tcp under the Proto column. That's because the UDP protocol doesn't establish connections in the same way that the TCP protocol does.

Something to keep in mind is that rootkits can replace legitimate Linux utilities with their own trojaned versions. For example, a rootkit could have its own trojaned version of `netstat` that would show all network processes except for those that are associated with the rootkit. That's why you want to do everything you can to prevent unauthorized users from gaining root privileges, to prevent them from being able to install rootkits.

If you need more information about `netstat`, see the `netstat` man page.

Hands-on lab – viewing network services with netstat

In this lab, you'll practice what you've just learned about `netstat`. Do this on a virtual machine that has a desktop interface so that you can use Firefox to visit websites. Follow these steps:

1. View the list of network services that are listening for a connection:

```
netstat -lp -A inet
netstat -lpn -A inet
```

2. View the list of established connections:

```
netstat -p -A inet
netstat -pn -A inet
```

3. Open Firefox and navigate to any website. Then, repeat *step 2*.

4. Repeat *step 2* again, but preface each command with `sudo`. Note how the output is different from that of *step 2*.

5. From your host machine, log into the virtual machine via SSH. Then, repeat *step 2*.

You've reached the end of the lab – congratulations!

You've just seen how to audit network services with `netstat`. Now, let's learn how to do this with Nmap.

Auditing network services with Nmap

The `netstat` tool is very good, and it can give you lots of good information about what's going on with your network services. The slight downside is that you have to log in to every individual host on your network in order to use it.

If you'd like to remotely audit your network to see what services are running on each computer without having to log in to each and every one, then you need a tool such as Nmap. It's available for all the major operating systems, so even if you're stuck having to use Windows on your workstation, you're in luck. An up-to-date version is already installed on Kali Linux, if that's what you're using. It's also in the repositories of every major Linux distro, so installing it is quite simple. If you're running Windows or macOS, you can download a version for either of them directly from the Nmap website.

You can download Nmap for all of the major operating systems from `https://nmap.org/download.html`.

In all cases, you'll also find instructions for installation.

You'll use Nmap the same way on all operating systems, with only one exception. On Linux and macOS machines, you'll preface certain Nmap commands with sudo, while on Windows machines, you won't. (Although, on Windows 10/11, you might have to open the command.exe terminal as an administrator.) Since I just happen to be working on my trusty OpenSUSE workstation, I'll show you how it works on Linux. Let's start by doing a SYN packet scan:

```
donnie@linux-0ro8:~> sudo nmap -sS 192.168.0.37

Starting Nmap 6.47 ( http://nmap.org ) at 2017-12-24 19:32 EST
Nmap scan report for 192.168.0.37
Host is up (0.00016s latency).
Not shown: 996 closed ports
PORT STATE SERVICE
22/tcp open ssh
515/tcp open printer
631/tcp open ipp
5900/tcp open vnc
MAC Address: 00:0A:95:8B:E0:C0 (Apple)

Nmap done: 1 IP address (1 host up) scanned in 57.41 seconds
donnie@linux-0ro8:~>
```

Here's the breakdown:

- -sS: The lowercase s denotes the type of scan that we want to perform. The uppercase S denotes that we're doing a SYN packet scan. (More on that in a moment.)
- 192.168.0.37: In this case, I'm only scanning a single machine. However, I could also scan either a group of machines or an entire network.
- Not shown: 996 closed ports: The fact that it's showing all of these closed ports instead of filtered ports tells me that there's no firewall on this machine. (Again, more on that in a moment.)

Next, we see a list of ports that are open. (More on that in a moment.)

The MAC address of this machine indicates that it's an Apple product of some sort. In a moment, I'll show you how to get more details about what kind of Apple product that it might be.

Now, let's look at this more in detail.

Port states

An Nmap scan will show the target machine's ports in one of three **port states**:

- filtered: This means that the port is blocked by a firewall.
- open: This means that the port is not blocked by a firewall and that the service that's associated with that port is running.

- `closed`: This means that the port is not blocked by a firewall, and that the service that's associated with that port is not running.

So, in our scan of the Apple machine, we see that the Secure Shell service is ready to accept connections on port 22, that the print service is ready to accept connections on ports 515 and 631, and that the **Virtual Network Computing** (VNC) service is ready to accept connections on port 5900. All of these ports would be of interest to a security-minded administrator. If Secure Shell is running, it would be interesting to know if it's configured securely. The fact that the print service is running means that this is set up to use the **Internet Printing Protocol** (IPP). It would be interesting to know why we're using IPP instead of just regular network printing, and it would also be interesting to know if there are any security concerns with this version of IPP. And of course, we already know that VNC isn't a secure protocol, so we would want to know why it's even running at all. We also saw that no ports are listed as `filtered`, so we would also want to know why there's no firewall on this machine.

One little secret that I'll finally reveal is that this machine is the same one that I used for the Greenbone Security Assistant scan demos. So, we already have some of the needed information. The Greenbone scan told us that Secure Shell on this machine uses weak encryption algorithms and that there's a security vulnerability with the print service. In just a bit, I'll show you how to get some of that information with Nmap.

Scan types

There are lots of different scanning options, each with its own purpose. The SYN packet scan that we're using here is considered a stealthy type of scan because it generates less network traffic and fewer system log entries than certain other types of scans. With this type of scan, Nmap sends a SYN packet to a port on the target machine, as if it were trying to create a TCP connection to that machine. If the target machine responds with a SYN/ACK packet, it means that the port is in an open state and is ready to create the TCP connection. If the target machine responds with an RST packet, it means that the port is in a `closed` state. If there's no response at all, it means that the port is `filtered`, blocked by a firewall. As a normal Linux administrator, this is one of the types of scans that you would do most of the time.

The `-sS` scan shows you the state of TCP ports, but it doesn't show you the state of UDP ports. To see the UDP ports, use the `-sU` option:

```
donnie@linux-0ro8:~> sudo nmap -sU 192.168.0.37

Starting Nmap 6.47 ( http://nmap.org ) at 2017-12-28 12:41 EST
Nmap scan report for 192.168.0.37
Host is up (0.00018s latency).
Not shown: 996 closed ports
PORT      STATE          SERVICE
123/udp   open           ntp
631/udp   open|filtered  ipp
3283/udp  open|filtered  netassistant
5353/udp  open           zeroconf
```

```
MAC Address: 00:0A:95:8B:E0:C0 (Apple)

Nmap done: 1 IP address (1 host up) scanned in 119.91 seconds
donnie@linux-0ro8:~>
```

Here, you see something a bit different: two ports are listed as open|filtered. That's because, due to the way that UDP ports respond to Nmap scans, Nmap can't always tell whether a UDP port is open or filtered. In this case, we know that these two ports are probably open because we've already seen that their corresponding TCP ports are open.

ACK packet scans can also be useful, but not to see the state of the target machine's network services. Rather, it's a good option for when you need to see if there might be a firewall blocking the way between you and the target machine. An ACK scan command looks like this:

```
sudo nmap -sA 192.168.0.37
```

You're not limited to scanning just a single machine at a time. You can scan either a group of machines or an entire subnet at once:

```
sudo nmap -sS 192.168.0.1-128
sudo nmap -sS 192.168.0.0/24
```

The first command scans only the first 128 hosts on this network segment. The second command scans all 254 hosts on a subnet that's using a 24-bit netmask.

A discovery scan is useful for when you need to just see what devices are on the network:

```
sudo nmap -sn 192.168.0.0/24
```

With the -sn option, Nmap will detect whether you're scanning the local subnet or a remote subnet. If the subnet is local, Nmap will send out an **Address Resolution Protocol** (ARP) broadcast that requests the IPv4 addresses of every device on the subnet. That's a reliable way of discovering devices because ARP isn't something that will ever be blocked by a device's firewall. (I mean, without ARP, the network would cease to function.) However, ARP broadcasts can't go across a router, which means that you can't use ARP to discover hosts on a remote subnet. So, if Nmap detects that you're doing a discovery scan on a remote subnet, it will send out ping packets instead of ARP broadcasts. Using ping packets for discovery isn't as reliable as using ARP because some network devices can be configured to ignore ping packets. Anyway, here's an example from my own home network:

```
donnie@linux-0ro8:~> sudo nmap -sn 192.168.0.0/24

Starting Nmap 6.47 ( http://nmap.org ) at 2017-12-25 14:48 EST
Nmap scan report for 192.168.0.1
Host is up (0.00043s latency).
MAC Address: 00:18:01:02:3A:57 (Actiontec Electronics)
Nmap scan report for 192.168.0.3
Host is up (0.0044s latency).
```

```
MAC Address: 44:E4:D9:34:34:80 (Cisco Systems)
Nmap scan report for 192.168.0.5
Host is up (0.00026s latency).
MAC Address: 1C:1B:0D:0A:2A:76 (Unknown)
. . .

. . .
```

We see three hosts in this snippet, and there are three lines of output for each host. The first line shows the IP address, the second shows whether the host is up, and the third shows the MAC address of the host's network adapter. The first three pairs of characters in each MAC address denote the manufacturer of that network adapter. (For the record, that unknown network adapter is on a recent model Gigabyte motherboard. I have no idea why it's not in the Nmap database.)

The final scan that we'll look at does four things for us:

- It identifies open, closed, and filtered TCP ports.
- It identifies the versions of the running services.
- It runs a set of vulnerability scanning scripts that come with Nmap.
- It attempts to identify the operating system of the target host.

The scan command that does all of these things looks like this:

```
sudo nmap -A 192.168.0.37
```

I guess that you could think of the -A option as the *all* option since it really does do it all. (Well, almost all, since it doesn't scan UDP ports.) First, here's the command that I ran to do the scan:

```
donnie@linux-0ro8:~> sudo nmap -A 192.168.0.37
```

Here are the results, broken down into sections for formatting purposes:

```
Starting Nmap 6.47 ( http://nmap.org ) at 2017-12-24 19:33 EST
Nmap scan report for 192.168.0.37
Host is up (0.00016s latency).
Not shown: 996 closed ports
```

Right away, we see that there's no active firewall on this machine because no ports are in the filtered state. By default, Nmap scans only the 1,000 most popular ports. Since 996 ports are in the closed state, we obviously only have four active network services that would listen on any of these 1,000 ports:

```
PORT STATE SERVICE VERSION
22/tcp open ssh OpenSSH 5.1 (protocol 1.99)
|_ssh-hostkey: ERROR: Script execution failed (use -d to debug)
|_sshv1: Server supports SSHv1
515/tcp open printer?
```

Port 22 is open for Secure Shell access, which we would normally expect. However, look at the SSH version. Version 5.1 is a really old version of OpenSSH. (At the time of writing, the current version is version 9.1.) What's worse is that this OpenSSH server supports version 1 of the Secure Shell protocol. Version 1 is seriously flawed and is easily exploitable, so you never want to see this on your network.

Next, we have amplifying information on the print service vulnerability that we found with the Greenbone Security Assistant scan:

```
631/tcp open ipp CUPS 1.1
| http-methods: Potentially risky methods: PUT
|_See http://nmap.org/nsedoc/scripts/http-methods.html
| http-robots.txt: 1 disallowed entry
|_/
|_http-title: Common UNIX Printing System
```

In the 631/tcp line, we see that the associated service is ipp. This protocol is based on the same HTTP that we use to look at web pages. The two methods that HTTP uses to send data from a client to a server are POST and PUT. What we really want is for every HTTP server to use the POST method because the PUT method makes it very easy for someone to compromise a server by manipulating a URL. So, if you scan a server and find that it allows using the PUT method for any kind of HTTP communications, you have a potential problem. In this case, the solution would be to update the operating system and hope that the updates fix the problem. If this were a web server, you'd want to have a chat with the web server administrators to let them know what you found.

Next, we see that the VNC service is running on this machine:

```
5900/tcp open vnc Apple remote desktop vnc
| vnc-info:
| Protocol version: 3.889
| Security types:
|_ Mac OS X security type (30)
1 service unrecognized despite returning data. If you know the service/version,
please submit the following fingerprint at http://www.insecure.org/cgi-bin/
servicefp-submit.cgi :
SF-Port515-TCP:V=6.47%I=7%D=12/24%Time=5A40479E%P=x86_64-suse-linux-gnu%r(
SF:GetRequest,1,"\x01");
MAC Address: 00:0A:95:8B:E0:C0 (Apple)
Device type: general purpose
```

VNC can be handy at times. It's like Microsoft's Remote Desktop service for Windows, except that it's free, open source software. But it's also a security problem because it's an unencrypted protocol. So, all your information goes across the network in plain text. If you must use VNC, run it through an SSH tunnel.

Next, let's see what Nmap found out about the operating system of our target machine:

```
Running: Apple Mac OS X 10.4.X
OS CPE: cpe:/o:apple:mac_os_x:10.4.10
OS details: Apple Mac OS X 10.4.10 - 10.4.11 (Tiger) (Darwin 8.10.0 - 8.11.1)
Network Distance: 1 hop
Service Info: OS: Mac OS X; CPE: cpe:/o:apple:mac_os_x
```

Wait, what? Mac OS X 10.4? Isn't that really, really ancient? Well, yeah, it is. The secret that I've been guarding for the past couple of chapters is that the target machine for my Greenbone Security Assistant and Nmap scan demos has been my ancient, collectible Apple eMac from the year 2003. I figured that scanning it would give us some interesting results to look at, and it would appear that I was right. (And yes, that is *eMac*, not *iMac*.)

The final thing we see is the TRACEROUTE information. It's not very interesting, though, because the target machine was sitting right next to me, with only one Cisco switch between us:

```
TRACEROUTE
HOP RTT ADDRESS
1 0.16 ms 192.168.0.37

OS and Service detection performed. Please report any incorrect results at
http://nmap.org/submit/ .
Nmap done: 1 IP address (1 host up) scanned in 213.92 seconds
donnie@linux-0ro8:~>
```

> Let's say that the target machine has had its SSH service changed to some alternate port, instead of having it run on the default port, 22. If you scan the machine with a normal -sS or -sT scan, Nmap won't correctly identify the SSH service on that alternate port. However, a -A scan will correctly identify the SSH service, regardless of which port it's using.

Okay, let's do a lab.

Hands-on lab — scanning with Nmap

In this lab, you'll see the results of scanning a machine with various services either enabled or disabled. You'll start with a virtual machine that has its firewall disabled. Let's get started:

1. Briefly peruse the Nmap help screen by using the following command:

```
nmap
```

2. From either your host machine or from another virtual machine, perform these scans against a virtual machine that has its firewall disabled (substitute your own IP address for the one I'm using here):

```
sudo nmap -sS 192.168.0.252
sudo nmap -sT 192.168.0.252
sudo nmap -SU 192.168.0.252
sudo nmap -A 192.168.0.252
sudo nmap -sA 192.168.0.252
```

3. Stop the SSH service on the target machine on Ubuntu:

```
sudo systemctl stop ssh
```

4. On either CentOS or AlmaLinux, use this command:

```
sudo systemctl stop sshd
```

5. Repeat *step 2*.

You've reached the end of this lab – congratulations!

Now that you've seen how to scan a system, let's look at the GRUB2 bootloader.

Password-protecting the GRUB2 bootloader

People sometimes forget passwords, even if they're administrators. And sometimes, people buy used computers but forget to ask the seller what the password is. (Yes, I've done that.) That's okay, though, because all of the major operating systems have ways to let you either reset or recover a lost administrator password. That's handy, except that it does kind of make the whole idea of having login passwords a rather moot point when someone has physical access to the machine. Let's say that your laptop has just been stolen. If you haven't encrypted the hard drive, it would only take a few minutes for the thief to reset the password and steal your data. If you have encrypted the drive, the level of protection would depend on which operating system you're running. With standard Windows folder encryption, the thief would be able to access the encrypted folders just by resetting the password. With LUKS whole-disk encryption on a Linux machine, the thief wouldn't be able to get past the point of having to enter the encryption passphrase.

With Linux, we have a way to safeguard against unauthorized password resets, even if we're not using whole-disk encryption. All we have to do is to password-protect the **Grand Unified Bootloader** (GRUB), which would prevent a thief from booting into emergency mode to do the password reset.

Whether or not you need the advice in this section depends upon your organization's physical security setup. That's because booting a Linux machine into emergency mode requires physical access to the machine. It's not something that you can do remotely. In an organization with proper physical security, servers – especially ones that hold sensitive data – are locked away in a room that's locked within another room. Only a very few trusted personnel are allowed to enter, and they have to present their credentials at both access points. So, setting a password on the bootloader of those servers would be rather pointless, unless you're dealing with a regulatory agency that dictates otherwise.

On the other hand, password-protecting the bootloaders of workstations and laptops that are out in the open could be quite useful. However, that alone won't protect your data. Someone could still boot the machine from a live disk or a USB memory stick, mount the machine's hard drive, and obtain the sensitive data. That's why you also want to encrypt your sensitive data, as I showed you in *Chapter 6, Encryption Technologies*.

To reset a password, all you have to do is interrupt the boot process when the boot menu comes up and either change a couple of kernel parameters, or select the **recovery mode** option if it's available. Either way, the machine will boot into emergency mode without asking for a password. However, resetting passwords isn't the only thing you can do from emergency mode. Once you've booted into emergency mode, you have full root user control over the whole system.

Now, just so you'll know what I'm talking about when I say that you can edit kernel parameters from the GRUB 2 boot menu, let me show you how to perform a password reset on a Red Hat-type system.

Hands-on lab – resetting the password for Red Hat/CentOS/AlmaLinux

With only one very minor exception, this procedure works exactly the same on CentOS 7, AlmaLinux 8, and AlmaLinux 9. Let's get started:

1. Boot the virtual machine. When the boot menu comes up, interrupt the boot process by hitting the *down* arrow key once. Then, hit the *up* arrow key once to select the default boot option:

```
CentOS Linux (3.10.0-693.11.1.el7.x86_64) 7 (Core)
CentOS Linux (3.10.0-693.5.2.el7.x86_64) 7 (Core)
CentOS Linux (3.10.0-693.el7.x86_64) 7 (Core)
CentOS Linux (0-rescue-2eda73dbd53444c5b4f8d6e607d581d5) 7 (Core)




      Use the ↑ and ↓ keys to change the selection.
      Press 'e' to edit the selected item, or 'c' for a command prompt.
```

Figure 16.2: Selecting the boot option

2. Hit the *e* key to edit the kernel parameters. When the GRUB 2 configuration comes up, cursor down until you see this line:

```
        linux16 /vmlinuz-3.10.0-693.11.1.el7.x86_64 root=/dev/mapper/centos-ro\
ot ro crashkernel=auto rd.lvm.lv=centos/root rd.luks.uuid=luks-2d7f02c7-864f-4\
2ce-b362-50dd830d9772 rd.lvm.lv=centos/swap rhgb quiet LANG=en_US.UTF-8
```

Figure 16.3: Edit the kernel options

> Note that on CentOS 7, the line begins with linux16, as shown here. On AlmaLinux 8/9, the line begins with linux.

3. Delete the words rhgb quiet from this line and then add rd.break enforcing=0 to the end of the line. Here's what these two new options do for you:

    *   rd.break: This will cause the machine to boot into emergency mode, which gives you root user privileges without you having to enter a root user password. Even if the root user password hasn't been set, this still works.
    *   enforcing=0: When you do a password reset on an SELinux-enabled system, the security context for the /etc/shadow file will change to the wrong type. If the system is in enforcing mode when you do this, SELinux will prevent you from logging in until the shadow file is relabeled. However, relabeling during the boot process can take a very long time, especially with a large drive. By setting SELinux to permissive mode, you can wait until after you've rebooted to restore the proper security context on just the shadow file.

4. When you've finished editing the kernel parameters, hit *Ctrl + X* to continue the boot process. This will take you to emergency mode with the switch_root command prompt:

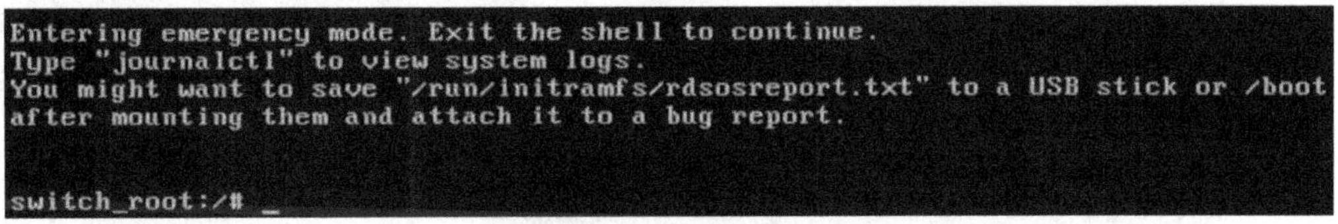

```
Entering emergency mode. Exit the shell to continue.
Type "journalctl" to view system logs.
You might want to save "/run/initramfs/rdsosreport.txt" to a USB stick or /boot
after mounting them and attach it to a bug report.

switch_root:/#
```

Figure 16.4: In emergency mode

5. In emergency mode, the filesystem is mounted as read-only. You'll need to remount it as read-write and enter chroot mode before you can reset the password, using these two commands:

```
mount -o remount,rw /sysroot
chroot /sysroot
```

After you enter these two commands, the command prompt will change to that of a normal Bash shell:

```
switch_root:/# mount -o remount,rw /sysroot
switch_root:/# chroot /sysroot
sh-4.2# _
```

Figure 16.5: Entering chroot mode

Now that you've reached this stage, you're finally ready to reset the password.

6. If you want to reset the root user password, or even if you want to create a root password where none previously existed, just enter:

```
passwd
```

Then, enter the new desired password.

7. If the system has never had a root user password and you still don't want it to have one, you can reset the password for an account that has full sudo privileges. For example, on my system, the command would look like this:

```
passwd donnie
```

8. Next, remount the filesystem as read-only. Then, enter exit twice to resume rebooting:

```
mount -o remount,ro /
exit
exit
```

9. The first thing you need to do after rebooting is to restore the proper SELinux security context on the /etc/shadow file. Then, put SELinux back into enforcing mode:

```
sudo restorecon /etc/shadow
sudo setenforce 1
```

Here's a before and after screenshot of the context settings for my shadow file:

```
[donnie@localhost ~]$ cd /etc
[donnie@localhost etc]$ ls -Z shadow
----------. root root system_u:object_r:unlabeled_t:s0 shadow
[donnie@localhost etc]$ sudo restorecon shadow
[sudo] password for donnie:
[donnie@localhost etc]$ ls -Z shadow
----------. root root system_u:object_r:shadow_t:s0     shadow
[donnie@localhost etc]$ _
```

Figure 16.6: SELinux context settings for the shadow file

Here, you see that resetting the password changed the type of the file to `unlabeled_t`. Running the `restorecon` command changed the type back to `shadow_t`.

You've reached the end of this lab – congratulations!

Now, we'll look at the same procedure for Ubuntu.

Hands-on lab — resetting the password for Ubuntu

The procedure for resetting a password on an Ubuntu system is quite a bit different and quite a bit simpler. However, there is one slight difference between doing this on Ubuntu 16.04 and Ubuntu 18.04 or newer. That is, to see the boot menu on Ubuntu 16.04, you don't have to do anything. On Ubuntu 18.04, you have to press either the *Shift* key (on BIOS-based systems) or the *Esc* key (on UEFI-based systems) in order to see the boot menu. On the current Ubuntu 22.04, you'll press the *Esc* key for either BIOS-based or UEFI-based systems. Other than that, the procedure is identical for everything from Ubuntu 16.04 through the current Ubuntu 22.04. So now, let's get started:

1. Boot the virtual machine. Press the *Esc* key to bring up the boot menu.
2. Press the *down* arrow key to highlight the **Advanced Options for Ubuntu** menu item, and press the *Enter* key:

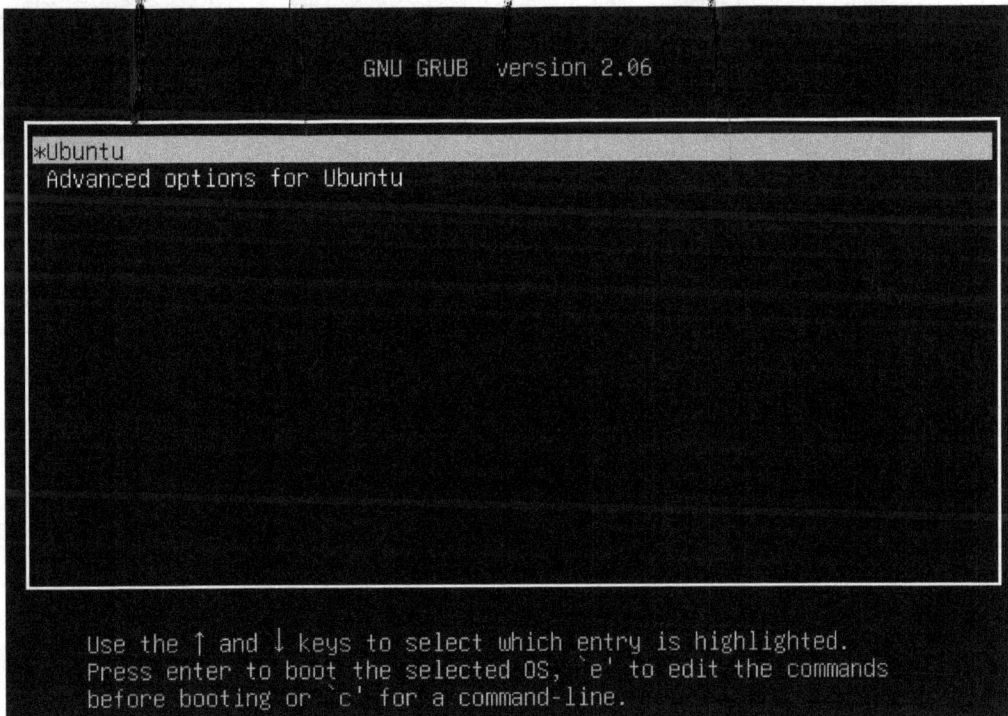

```
                        GNU GRUB  version 2.06

 *Ubuntu
  Advanced options for Ubuntu








     Use the ↑ and ↓ keys to select which entry is highlighted.
     Press enter to boot the selected OS, `e' to edit the commands
     before booting or `c' for a command-line.
```

Figure 16.7: Ubuntu Advanced Options submenu

3. From the **Advanced Options for Ubuntu** submenu, select the **recovery mode** option, and press *Enter*:

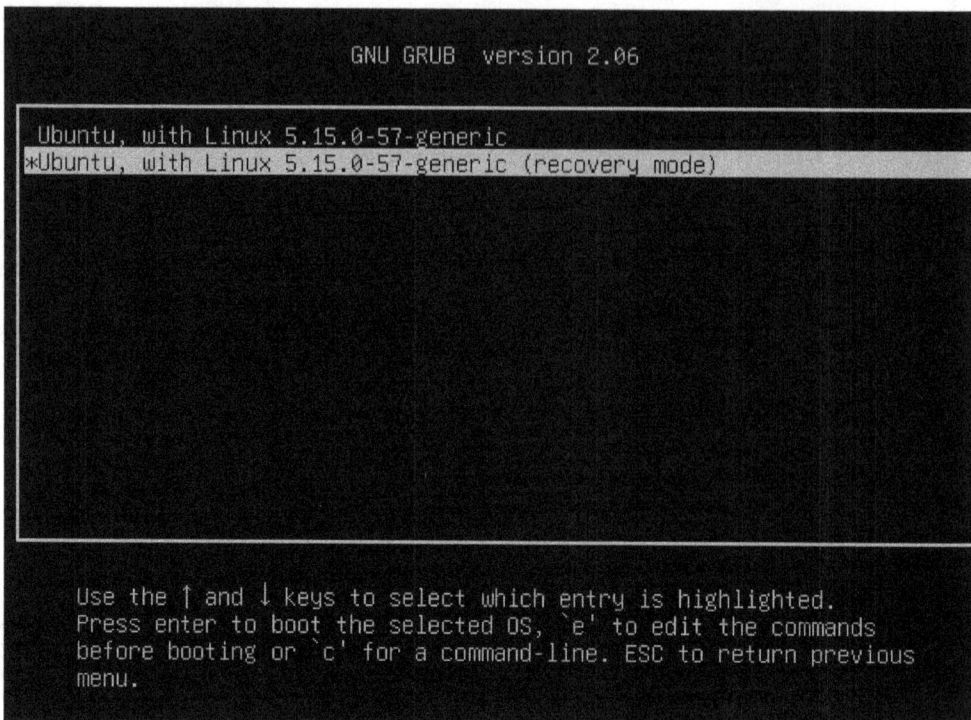

```
                    GNU GRUB  version 2.06


 Ubuntu, with Linux 5.15.0-57-generic
*Ubuntu, with Linux 5.15.0-57-generic (recovery mode)









   Use the ↑ and ↓ keys to select which entry is highlighted.
   Press enter to boot the selected OS, `e' to edit the commands
   before booting or `c' for a command-line. ESC to return previous
   menu.
```

Figure 16.8: Select the recovery mode option

4. When the **Recovery Menu** comes up, select the **root** option, and press the *Enter* key:

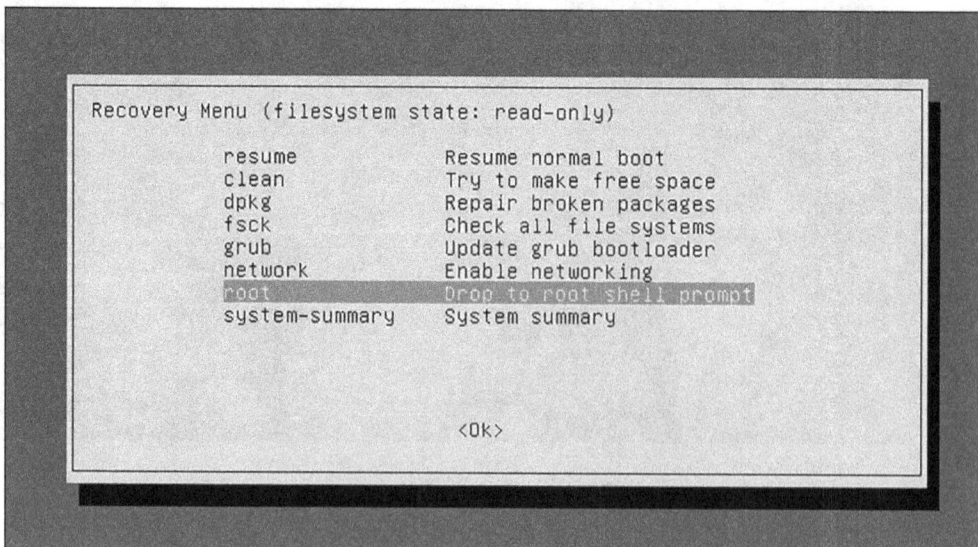

```
 Recovery Menu (filesystem state: read-only)

          resume            Resume normal boot
          clean             Try to make free space
          dpkg              Repair broken packages
          fsck              Check all file systems
          grub              Update grub bootloader
          network           Enable networking
          root              Drop to root shell prompt
          system-summary    System summary



                          <Ok>
```

Figure 16.9: Select the root option

5. Press the *Enter* key again. This will take you to a root shell:

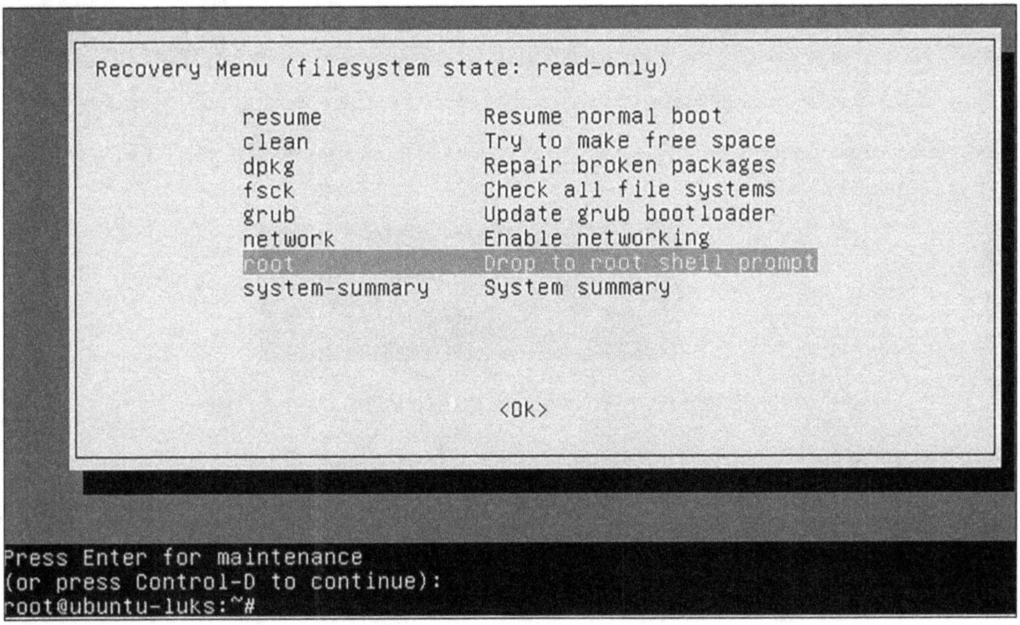

```
Recovery Menu (filesystem state: read-only)
            resume          Resume normal boot
            clean           Try to make free space
            dpkg            Repair broken packages
            fsck            Check all file systems
            grub            Update grub bootloader
            network         Enable networking
            root            Drop to root shell prompt
            system-summary  System summary


                            <Ok>



Press Enter for maintenance
(or press Control-D to continue):
root@ubuntu-luks:~#
```

Figure 16.10: In recovery mode

6. Since Ubuntu doesn't normally have a password assigned to the root user, you would most likely just reset the password of whoever had full sudo privileges, like so:

```
passwd donnie
```

7. When you've finished, reboot as you normally would:

```
shutdown -r now
```

The machine will now boot up for normal operation.

You've reached the end of this lab – congratulations!

Of course, we don't want everybody and his or her brother to be able to edit kernel parameters or enter **recovery mode** when booting a machine. So, let's fix that.

Preventing kernel parameter edits on Red Hat/CentOS/ AlmaLinux

Ever since the introduction of Red Hat/CentOS 7.2, setting a GRUB 2 password to prevent kernel parameter edits is easy. Fortunately, this trick still works on the newest iterations of Red Hat and AlmaLinux. All you have to do is to run one command and choose a password:

```
[donnie@localhost ~]$ sudo grub2-setpassword

[sudo] password for donnie:
```

```
Enter password:
Confirm password:
[donnie@localhost ~]$
```

That's all there is to it. The password hash will be stored in the /boot/grub2/user.cfg file.

Now, when you reboot the machine and try to do a kernel parameter edit, you'll be prompted to enter a username and password:

```
Enter username:
root
Enter password:
_
```

Figure 16.11: Password-protection for RHEL 7.2 and newer

Note that you'll enter root as the username, even if the root user's password hasn't been set on the system. The root user, in this case, is just the superuser for GRUB 2.

When you boot your Red Hat, CentOS, or AlmaLinux machine, you'll see a **0-rescue** option come up at the bottom of the boot menu. (You can see it above in Figure 16.2.) If you select it, you'll find that it does nothing but take you to a normal login prompt that will require you to enter your username and password. (Red Hat-type distros really do have a Rescue mode, but you have to boot the machine from the installation media to get to it.)

Preventing kernel parameter edits or recovery mode access on Ubuntu

Ubuntu doesn't have that cool utility that Red Hat, CentOS, and AlmaLinux have, so you'll have to set a GRUB 2 password by hand-editing a configuration file.

In the /etc/grub.d/ directory, you'll see the files that make up the GRUB 2 configuration:

```
donnie@ubuntu3:/etc/grub.d$ ls -l
total 76
-rwxr-xr-x 1 root root  9791 Oct 12 16:48 00_header
-rwxr-xr-x 1 root root  6258 Mar 15  2016 05_debian_theme
-rwxr-xr-x 1 root root 12512 Oct 12 16:48 10_linux
-rwxr-xr-x 1 root root 11082 Oct 12 16:48 20_linux_xen
-rwxr-xr-x 1 root root 11692 Oct 12 16:48 30_os-prober
-rwxr-xr-x 1 root root  1418 Oct 12 16:48 30_uefi-firmware
-rwxr-xr-x 1 root root   214 Oct 12 16:48 40_custom
-rwxr-xr-x 1 root root   216 Oct 12 16:48 41_custom
-rw-r--r-- 1 root root   483 Oct 12 16:48 README
donnie@ubuntu3:/etc/grub.d$
```

The file you want to edit is the 40_custom file. However, before you edit the file, you'll need to create the password hash. Do that with the grub-mkpasswd-pbkdf2 utility:

```
donnie@ubuntu3:/etc/grub.d$ grub-mkpasswd-pbkdf2
Enter password:
Reenter password:
PBKDF2 hash of your password is grub.pbkdf2.sha512.10000.
F1BA16B2799CBF6A6DFBA53
7D43222A0D5006124ECFEB29F5C81C9769C6C3A66BF53C2B3AB71BEA7
84D4386E86C991F7B5D33CB6C29EB6AA12C8D11E0FFA0D40.371648A84CC4131C3CFFB53604ECCBA4
6DA75AF196E970C98483385B0BE026590C63A1BAC23691517BC4A5D3EDF89D026B599A0D3C49F2FB66
6F9C12B56DB35D
donnie@ubuntu3:/etc/grub.d$
```

Open the 40_custom file in your favorite text editor and add a line that defines who the superuser(s) will be. Add another line for the password hash. In my case, the file now looks like this:

```
#!/bin/sh
exec tail -n +3 $0
# This file provides an easy way to add custom menu entries. Simply type the
# menu entries you want to add after this comment. Be careful not to change
# the 'exec tail' line above.

set superusers="donnie"

password_pbkdf2 donnie grub.pbkdf2.sha512.10000.F1BA16B2799CBF6A6DFBA537D43222A
0D5006124ECFEB29F5C81C9769C6C3A66BF53C2B3AB71BEA7
84D4386E86C991F7B5D33CB6C29EB6AA12C8D11E0FFA0D40.371648A84CC4131C3CFFB53604ECC
BA46DA75AF196E970C98483385B0BE026590C63A1BAC23691517BC4A5D3EDF89D026B599A0D3C4
9F2FB666F9C12B56DB35D
```

> The string of text that begins with password_pbkdf2 is all one line that wraps around on the printed page.

After you save the file, the last step is to generate a new grub.cfg file:

```
donnie@ubuntu3:/etc/grub.d$ sudo update-grub

Generating grub configuration file ...
Found linux image: /boot/vmlinuz-4.4.0-104-generic
Found initrd image: /boot/initrd.img-4.4.0-104-generic
Found linux image: /boot/vmlinuz-4.4.0-101-generic
```

```
Found initrd image: /boot/initrd.img-4.4.0-101-generic
Found linux image: /boot/vmlinuz-4.4.0-98-generic
Found initrd image: /boot/initrd.img-4.4.0-98-generic
done
donnie@ubuntu3:/etc/grub.d$
```

Now, when I reboot this machine, I have to enter my password before I can either edit kernel parameters or access the **Advanced Options for Ubuntu** submenu:

```
Enter username:
donnie
Enter password:
_
```

Figure 16.12: Password-protection for Ubuntu

There's only one problem with this. Not only does this prevent anyone except the superuser from editing the kernel parameters, but it also prevents anyone except for the superuser from booting normally. Yes, that's right. Even for normal booting, Ubuntu will now require you to enter the username and password of the authorized superuser. Fortunately, this is an easy fix.

The fix requires inserting a single word into the /boot/grub/grub.cfg file. Easy enough, right? However, it's not an elegant solution because you're not really supposed to hand-edit the grub.cfg file. At the top of the file, we see this:

```
# DO NOT EDIT THIS FILE
#
# It is automatically generated by grub-mkconfig using templates
# from /etc/grub.d and settings from /etc/default/grub
#
```

This means that every time we do something that will update the grub.cfg file, any hand-edits that we've made to the file will be lost. This includes when we do a system update that installs a new kernel, or when we do a sudo apt autoremove that removes any old kernels that we no longer need. The supreme irony though is that the official GRUB 2 documentation tells us to hand-edit the grub.cfg file to deal with these sorts of problems. A much better way is to modify the shell script that the update-grub utility uses to build the grub.cfg file. This will prevent you from accidentally overwriting any changes that you need to preserve.

In the /etc/grub.d/ directory, you'll see several scripts that are used to build grub.cfg. The one we want is in the 10_linux file. Open it in your text editor, and navigate down to the vicinity of line number 197. Look for these two lines:

```
echo "menuentry '$(echo "$title" | grub_quote)' ${CLASS} \$menuentry_id_option
'gnulinux-$version-$type-$boot_device_id' {" | sed "s/^/$submenu_indentation/"

. . .

. . .

echo "menuentry '$(echo "$os" | grub_quote)' ${CLASS} \$menuentry_id_option
'gnulinux-simple-$boot_device_id' {" | sed "s/^/$submenu_indentation/"
```

(Note that each of these is one line that wraps around on the printed page.)

In each line, add --unrestricted after {CLASS}, so that the lines now look like this:

```
echo "menuentry '$(echo "$title" | grub_quote)' ${CLASS} --unrestricted
\$menuentry_id_option 'gnulinux-$version-$type-$boot_device_id' {" | sed
"s/^/$submenu_indentation/"

. . .

. . .

echo "menuentry '$(echo "$os" | grub_quote)' ${CLASS} --unrestricted
\$menuentry_id_option 'gnulinux-simple-$boot_device_id' {" | sed "s/^/$submenu_
indentation/"
```

Finally, run the sudo update-grub command, and you'll be able to boot the machine normally on the default option. But, it's a different story if you want to enter the **Advanced Options for Ubuntu** submenu. With a superuser password set, you'll always need to enter the superuser password in order to enter the **Advanced Options for Ubuntu** submenu. This is true even with the --unrestricted option that you added to 10_linux script. Effectively, this prevents anyone without the password from accessing the **Recovery** option.

Disabling the submenu for Ubuntu

On Ubuntu systems, you can easily disable the Ubuntu submenu so that you'll see all boot options by default, which will look something like this:

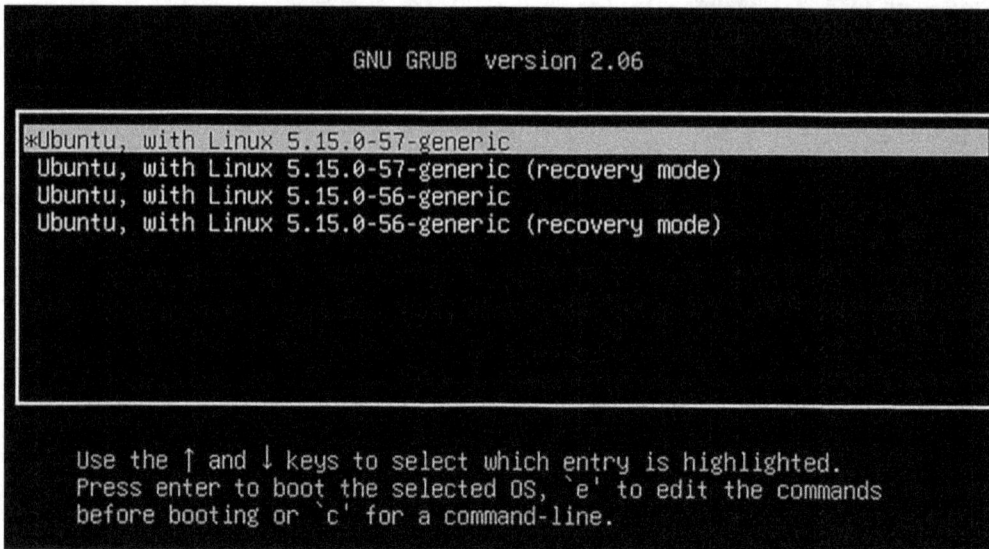

```
                        GNU GRUB   version 2.06

*Ubuntu, with Linux 5.15.0-57-generic
 Ubuntu, with Linux 5.15.0-57-generic (recovery mode)
 Ubuntu, with Linux 5.15.0-56-generic
 Ubuntu, with Linux 5.15.0-56-generic (recovery mode)




     Use the ↑ and ↓ keys to select which entry is highlighted.
     Press enter to boot the selected OS, `e' to edit the commands
     before booting or `c' for a command-line.
```

Figure 16.13: The Ubuntu boot menu without the submenu

If desired, you can also make it so that you don't have to press the *Shift* or *Esc* key in order to see the boot menu.

First, open the /etc/default/grub file in your text editor. Disable the submenu by adding the GRUB_DISABLE_SUBMENU=y line. To make the boot menu visible by default, look for these two lines:

```
GRUB_TIMEOUT_STYLE=hidden
GRUB_TIMEOUT=0
```

Comment out the first line, and change the value for the second line to a non-zero number. The lines should now look something like this:

```
# GRUB_TIMEOUT_STYLE=hidden
GRUB_TIMEOUT=10
```

Finally, run the sudo update-grub command. Now, when you reboot the machine, you'll see the boot menu come up by itself, and you'll see the whole list of boot options instead of just the default boot option and a submenu option. After a ten-second timeout, the system will automatically boot on the default option.

The major flaw with disabling the Ubuntu submenu is that if you've configured GRUB with the --unrestricted option as I've just shown you, users will be able to boot into **recovery mode** without entering a password. So, it's now just as if you never password-protected GRUB in the first place. If you do disable the Ubuntu submenu, remember to also disable the **recovery mode** option. Open the /etc/default/grub file in your editor, and look for this line:

```
# GRUB_DISABLE_RECOVERY="true"
```

Remove the # sign from in front of the line so that it now looks like this:

```
GRUB_DISABLE_RECOVERY="true"
```

Update the GRUB configuration as you've done before:

```
sudo update-grub
```

Finally, reboot the machine and verify that the **recovery mode** option is gone. If you disable the **Recovery** boot menu option and still need to boot into **recovery mode,** you can still do that by editing the kernel parameters at the beginning of the boot process. The procedure is somewhat different from what you've just seen with AlmaLinux, since you don't have to worry about SELinux on Ubuntu. Rather than duplicate the procedure here, I'll leave a link to a tutorial for it in the *Further reading* section. (The linked article is for Ubuntu 18.04, but the procedure still works for the current Ubuntu 22.04.)

So, you're now asking, *why would I ever need to disable the Ubuntu submenu?* Well, you'll never actually *need* to. For me, it's just a matter of preference. Unlike the Red Hat distros, Ubuntu doesn't automatically delete old Linux kernels if a new one gets installed during an update operation. If you don't remember to do a sudo apt autoremove command after you update in order to get rid of them, you could fill up your /boot/ partition, which could prevent future updates from installing a new kernel. By disabling the submenu and making the boot menu visible by default, I can see how many Linux kernels are installed as soon as I boot the machine. (But hey, that's just me, and I'm kind of weird. Just ask anyone who knows me.) On a production machine, it would make more sense to leave both the submenu and the **Recovery** option enabled, and set a GRUB 2 password.

> You'll find the security section of the official GRUB 2 documentation at http://www.gnu.org/software/grub/manual/grub/grub.html#Security.

Securely configuring BIOS/UEFI

This topic is different from anything we've looked at thus far because it has nothing to do with the operating system. Rather, we're now going to talk about the computer hardware.

Every computer motherboard has either a BIOS or a UEFI chip, which stores both the hardware configuration for the computer and the bootstrap instructions that are needed to start the boot process after the power is turned on. UEFI has replaced the old-style BIOS on newer motherboards, and it has more security features than the old BIOS had.

I can't give you any specific information about BIOS/UEFI setup because every model motherboard has a different way of doing things. What I can give you is some more generalized information.

When you think about BIOS/UEFI security, you might be thinking about disabling the ability to boot from anything other than the normal system drive. In the following screenshot, you see that I've disabled all SATA drive ports except for the one to which the system drive is connected:

Figure 16.14: Disabling drive ports on my Hewlett-Packard Envy

When computers are out in the open where the general public can have easy physical access to them, this might be a consideration. For servers that are locked away in their own secure room with limited access, there's no real reason to worry about this, unless the security requirements of some regulatory body dictate otherwise. For machines that are out in the open, having the whole disk encrypted would prevent someone from stealing data after booting from either an optical disk or a USB device. However, you may still have other reasons to prevent anyone from booting the machine from these alternate boot devices.

Another consideration might be if you work in a secure environment where super-sensitive data are handled. If you're worried about unauthorized exfiltration of sensitive data, you might consider disabling the ability to write to USB devices. This will also prevent people from booting the machine from USB devices:

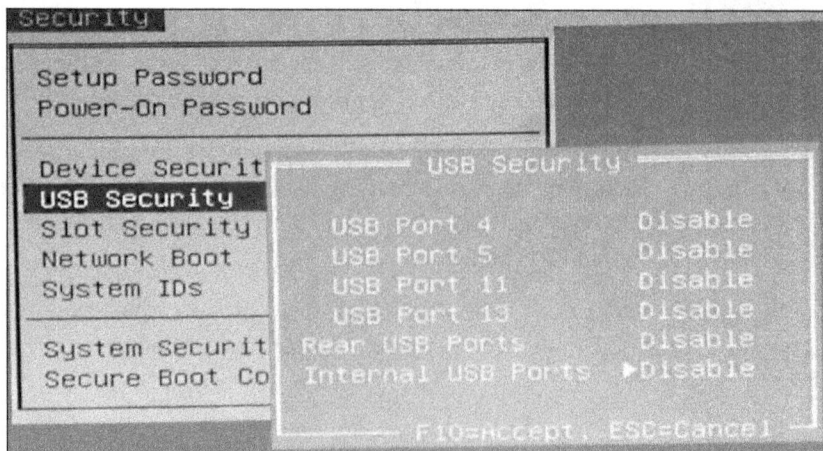

Figure 16.15: Disabling USB devices

At times, you might not want to completely disable a machine's USB ports. Instead, you can leave them enabled and use USBGuard to allow only certain USB devices to be connected. Rather than do my own write-up about it, I'll refer you to this excellently-written tutorial that I found:

`https://www.cyberciti.biz/security/how-to-protect-linux-against-rogue-usb-devices-using-usbguard/`

The main catch with USBGuard is that it still won't prevent someone from booting from a USB device.

However, there's more than just this to BIOS/UEFI security. Today's modern server CPUs come with a variety of security features to help prevent data breaches. For example, let's look at a list of security features that are implemented in Intel Xeon CPUs:

- Identity-protection technology
- Advanced Encryption Standard New Instructions
- Trusted Execution Technology
- Hardware-assisted virtualization technology

AMD, that plucky underdog in the CPU market, have their own new security features in their line of EPYC server CPUs. These features include:

- Secure Memory Encryption
- Secure Encrypted Virtualization

In any case, you would configure these CPU security options in your server's UEFI setup utility.

You can read about Intel Xeon security features at `https://www.intel.com/content/www/us/en/newsroom/news/xeon-scalable-platform-built-sensitive-workloads.html`.

You can read about AMD EPYC security features at `https://semiaccurate.com/2017/06/22/amds-epyc-major-advance-security/` and at `https://www.servethehome.com/amd-psb-vendor-locks-epyc-cpus-for-enhanced-security-at-a-cost/`.

And of course, for any machines that are out in the open, it's a good idea to password-protect the BIOS or UEFI:

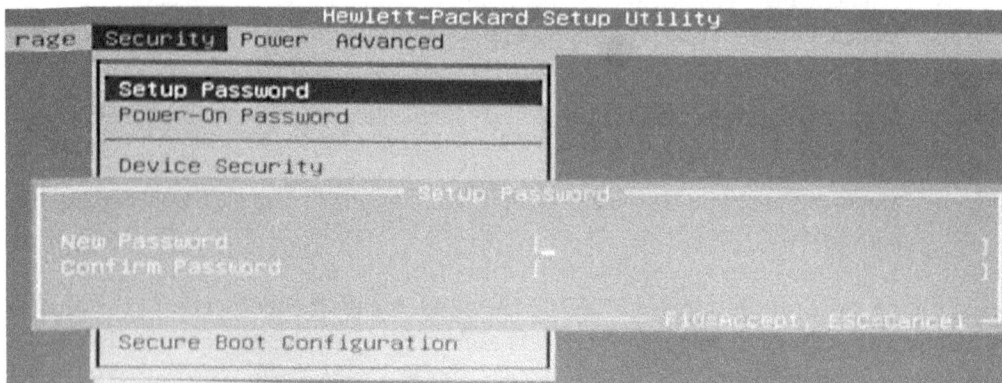

Figure 16.16: Password-protect the BIOS/UEFI

If for no other reason, do it to keep people from monkeying around with your settings.

Now that you know a bit about locking down BIOS/UEFI, let's talk about security checklists.

Using a security checklist for system setup

Previously, I told you about OpenSCAP, which is a really useful tool for locking down your system with just a minimal amount of effort. OpenSCAP comes with various profiles that you can apply to help bring your systems into compliance with the standards of different regulatory agencies. However, there are certain things that OpenSCAP can't do for you. For example, certain regulatory agencies require that your server's hard drive be partitioned in a certain way, with certain directories separated out into their own partitions. If you've already set up your server with everything under one big partition, you can't fix that just by doing a remediation procedure with OpenSCAP. The process of locking down your server to ensure that it's compliant with any applicable security regulations has to begin before you even install the operating system. For this, you need the appropriate checklist.

There are a few different places where you can obtain a generic security checklist if that's all you need. The University of Texas at Austin published a generic checklist for Red Hat Enterprise Linux 7, which you can adjust if you need to use it with CentOS 7, Oracle Linux 7, or Scientific Linux 7. (Sadly, they don't offer anything that's more up-to-date.)

You might find that some checklist items don't apply to your situation, and you can adjust them as required:

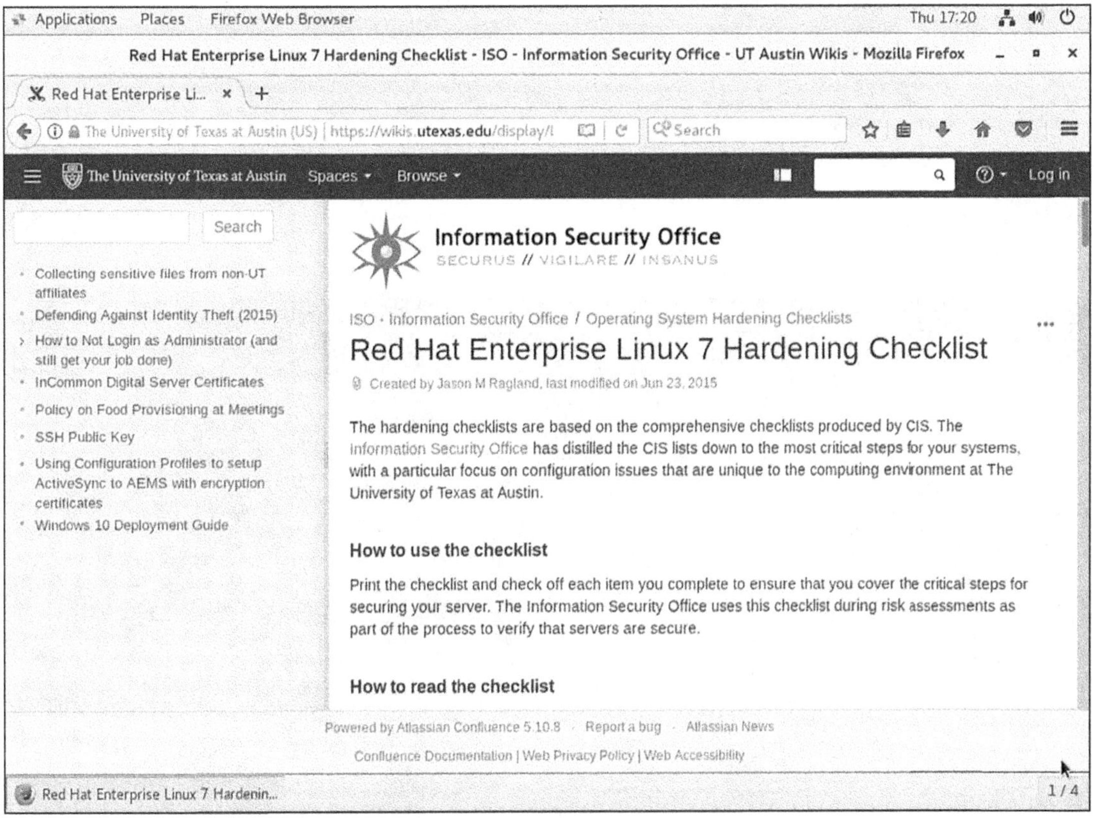

Figure 16.17: University of Texas checklist

For specific business fields, you'll need to get a checklist from the applicable regulatory body. If you work in the financial sector or with a business that accepts credit card payments, you'll need a checklist from the Payment Card Industry Security Standards Council:

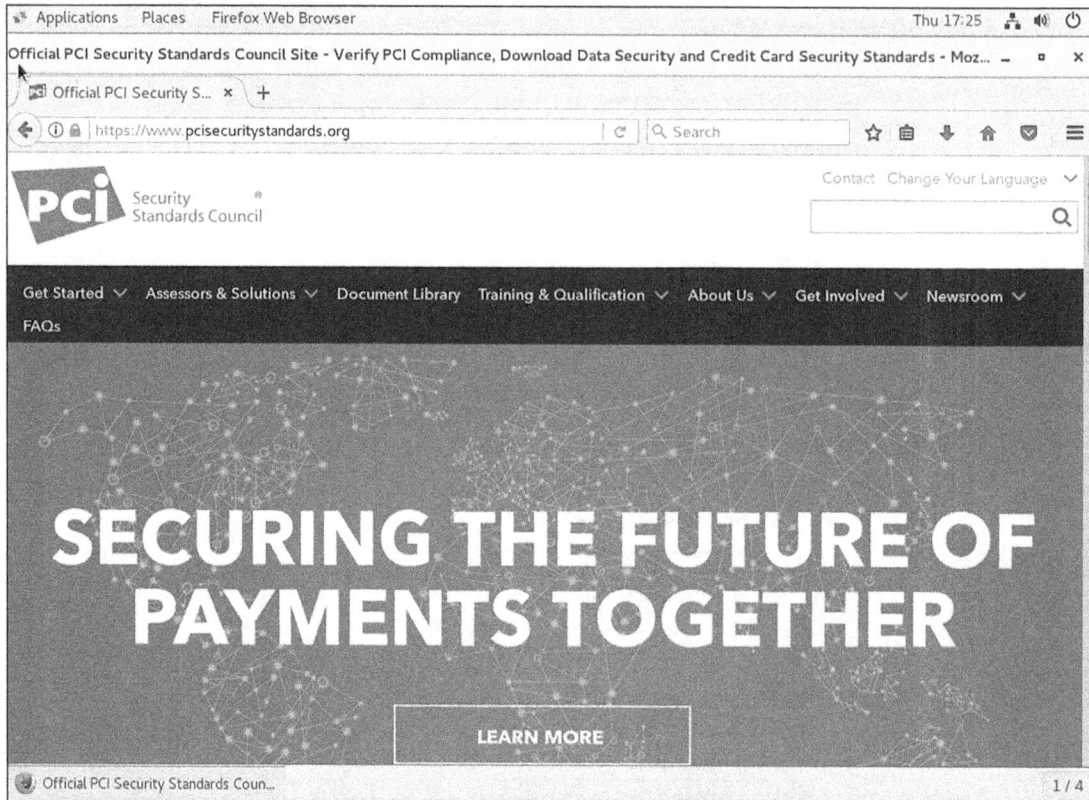

Figure 16.18: The PCI-DSS website

For healthcare organizations here in the US, there's HIPAA with its requirements. For publicly-traded companies here in the US, there's Sarbanes-Oxley with its requirements.

> You can get the University of Texas checklist at `https://wikis.utexas.edu/display/ISO/Operating+System+Hardening+Checklists`.
>
> You can get a PCI-DSS checklist at `https://www.pcisecuritystandards.org/`.
>
> You can get a HIPAA checklist at `https://www.hhs.gov/hipaa/for-professionals/security/guidance/cybersecurity/index.html`.
>
> You can get a Sarbanes-Oxley checklist at `https://www.sarbanes-oxley-101.com/sarbanes-oxley-checklist.htm`.

Other regulatory bodies may also have their own checklists. If you know that you have to deal with any of them, be sure to get the appropriate checklist.

Summary

Once again, we've come to the conclusion of another chapter, and we covered a lot of cool topics. We started by looking at various ways to audit which services are running on your systems, and we saw some examples of what you probably don't want to see. We then saw how to use the password-protection features of GRUB 2, and we saw the little quirks that we have to deal with when using those features. Next, we had a change of pace by looking at how to further lock down a system by properly setting up a system's BIOS/UEFI. Finally, we looked at why we need to begin preparations to set up a hardened system by obtaining and following the proper checklist.

Not only does this conclude another chapter, but it also concludes this book. However, this doesn't conclude your journey into the land of *Mastering Linux Security and Hardening*. Oh, no. As you continue this journey, you'll find that there's still more to learn, and still more that won't fit into the confines of just one book. Where you go from here mainly depends on the particular area of IT administration in which you work. Different types of Linux servers, whether they be web servers, DNS servers, or whatever else, have their own special security requirements, and you'll want to follow the learning path that best fits your needs.

I've enjoyed the part of the journey on which I've been able to accompany you. I hope that you've enjoyed it just as much as I have.

Questions

1. You need to see a list of network services that are listening for incoming connections. Which of the following commands would you use?

    a. `sudo systemctl -t service --state=active`

    b. `netstat -i`

    c. `netstat -lp -A inet`

    d. `sudo systemctl -t service --state=listening`

2. Which of the following commands would you use to see only a list of established TCP connections?

    a. `netstat -p -A inet`

    b. `netstat -lp -A inet`

    c. `sudo systemctl -t service --state=connected`

    d. `sudo systemctl -t service --state=active`

3. When Nmap tells you that a port is in an open state, what does that mean?

    a. That the port is open on the firewall.

    b. That the port is open on the firewall and that the service that's associated with that port is running.

    c. That the port is accessible via the Internet.

    d. That the port's Access Control List is set to open.

4. Which of these Nmap scan options would you most likely use to scan for open TCP ports?

    a. `-sn`

    b. `-sU`

    c. `-sS`

    d. `-sA`

5. What do you want to do when resetting the root user password on a Red Hat/CentOS/AlmaLinux machine?

    a. Ensure that AppArmor is in enforcing mode.

    b. Ensure that SELinux is in enforcing mode.

    c. Ensure that AppArmor is in complain mode.

    d. Ensure that SELinux is in permissive mode.

6. How does discovery mode work in Nmap?

    a. It discovers network devices by sending ping packets to the network's broadcast address.

    b. It discovers network devices by sending SYN packets to the network's broadcast address.

    c. It sends out ARP packets for a local network and ping packets for a remote network.

    d. It sends out ping packets for a local network and ARP packets for a remote network.

7. You want to use Nmap to perform a UDP port scan of an entire subnet. Which of the following commands would you use?

    a. `sudo nmap -sU 192.168.0.0`

    b. `sudo nmap -U 192.168.0.0`

    c. `sudo nmap -U 192.168.0.0/24`

    d. `sudo nmap -sU 192.168.0.0/24`

8. How would you begin the process of hardening a new computer system?

    a. Apply an OpenSCAP profile when installing the operating system.

    b. Begin the initial setup by following a checklist.

    c. Install the operating system, then apply an OpenSCAP profile.

    d. Install the operating system, then follow a hardening checklist.

9. On a Red Hat/CentOS/AlmaLinux server, what would you most likely do to force users to enter a password before editing kernel parameters during bootup?

    a. Enter the `sudo grub2-password` command.

    b. Hand-edit the grub configuration file.

    c. Enter the `sudo grub2-setpassword` command.

    d. Enter the `sudo grub-setpassword` command.

    e. Enter the `sudo grub-password` command.

Further reading

- *netstat – The easy tutorial*: https://openmaniak.com/netstat.php
- *4 ways to find which process is listening on a specific port*: https://www.putorius.net/process-listening-on-port.html
- *netstat versus ss Usagte Guide*: https://computingforgeeks.com/netstat-vs-ss-usage-guide-linux/
- The official Nmap website: https://nmap.org/
- The GNU GRUB manual: https://www.gnu.org/software/grub/manual/grub/grub.html
- *How to boot Ubuntu 18.04 into emergency and rescue mode* (An alternate method that still works on Ubuntu 22.04.): https://linuxconfig.org/how-to-boot-ubuntu-18-04-into-emergency-and-rescue-mode
- How to see the GRUB boot menu on Ubuntu 18.04: https://askubuntu.com/questions/16042/how-to-get-to-the-grub-menu-at-boot-time

Answers

1. c
2. a
3. b
4. c
5. d
6. c
7. d
8. b
9. c

Join our book community

Join our community's Discord space for discussions with the author and other readers:

https://packt.link/CyberSec

‹packt›

packt.com

Subscribe to our online digital library for full access to over 7,000 books and videos, as well as industry leading tools to help you plan your personal development and advance your career. For more information, please visit our website.

Why subscribe?

- Spend less time learning and more time coding with practical eBooks and Videos from over 4,000 industry professionals
- Improve your learning with Skill Plans built especially for you
- Get a free eBook or video every month
- Fully searchable for easy access to vital information
- Copy and paste, print, and bookmark content

At www.packt.com, you can also read a collection of free technical articles, sign up for a range of free newsletters, and receive exclusive discounts and offers on Packt books and eBooks.

Other Books You May Enjoy

If you enjoyed this book, you may be interested in these other books by Packt:

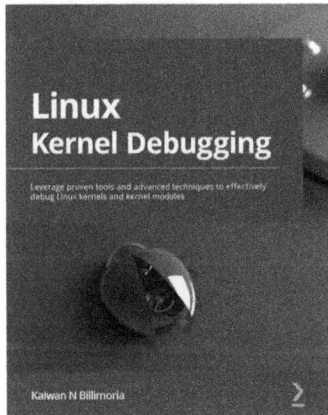

Linux Kernel Debugging

Kaiwan Billimoria

ISBN: 9781801075039

- Explore instrumentation-based printk along with the powerful dynamic debug framework
- Use static and dynamic Kprobes to trap into kernel/module functions
- Catch kernel memory defects with KASAN, UBSAN, SLUB debug, and kmemleak
- Interpret an Oops in depth and precisely identify it's source location
- Understand data races and use KCSAN to catch evasive concurrency defects
- Leverage Ftrace and trace-cmd to trace the kernel flow in great detail
- Write a custom kernel panic handler and detect kernel lockups and hangs
- Use KGDB to single-step and debug kernel/module source code

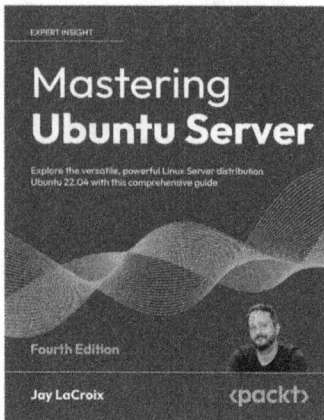

Mastering Ubuntu Server – 4E

Jay LaCroix

ISBN: 9781803234243

- Install Ubuntu Server on physical servers and on the Raspberry Pi
- Deploy Ubuntu Server in the cloud and host websites on your own server
- Deploy your applications to their own containers and scale your infrastructure
- Set up popular applications such as Nextcloud
- Automate deployments and configuration with Ansible to save time
- Containerize applications via LXD to maximize efficiency
- Discover best practices and troubleshooting techniques

Packt is searching for authors like you

If you're interested in becoming an author for Packt, please visit `authors.packtpub.com` and apply today. We have worked with thousands of developers and tech professionals, just like you, to help them share their insight with the global tech community. You can make a general application, apply for a specific hot topic that we are recruiting an author for, or submit your own idea.

Share your thoughts

Now you've finished *Mastering Linux Security and Hardening, Third Edition*, we'd love to hear your thoughts! Scan the QR code below to go straight to the Amazon review page for this book and share your feedback or leave a review on the site that you purchased it from.

`https://packt.link/r/1837630518`

Your review is important to us and the tech community and will help us make sure we're delivering excellent quality content.

Index

Download a free PDF copy of this book

Thanks for purchasing this book!

Do you like to read on the go but are unable to carry your print books everywhere?

Is your eBook purchase not compatible with the device of your choice?

Don't worry, now with every Packt book you get a DRM-free PDF version of that book at no cost.

Read anywhere, any place, on any device. Search, copy, and paste code from your favorite technical books directly into your application.

The perks don't stop there, you can get exclusive access to discounts, newsletters, and great free content in your inbox daily

Follow these simple steps to get the benefits:

1.   Scan the QR code or visit the link below

https://packt.link/free-ebook/9781837630516

2.   Submit your proof of purchase
3.   That's it! We'll send your free PDF and other benefits to your email directly

www.ingramcontent.com/pod-product-compliance
Lightning Source LLC
Chambersburg PA
CBHW081457190326
41458CB00015B/5272